Taxation
of
Employments

Eleventh Edition

by

Robert W Maas FCA FTII FIIT TEP

of Blackstone Franks LLP

Tottel Publishing
Maxwelton House
41-43 Boltro Road
Haywards Heath
West Sussex
RH16 1BJ

A CIP Catalogue record for this book is available from the British Library.

ISBN 1 84592 014 7

Typeset by Phoenix Photosetting, Chatham, Kent
Printed and bound in Great Britain by Antony Rowe Ltd, Chippenham, Wiltshire

Preface

I hope that this year the Chancellor has given up trying to compete with himself as the author of the largest Finance Act ever and that in future no Chancellor will get anywhere near his 634 pages. As always these contain a number of changes to the legislation on the Taxation of Employments. Indeed, half of the Finance Act relates to the new pension scheme rules that he proposed to introduce from 1996/97. Unfortunately these leave a lot to be dealt with by statutory instrument and, I suspect, more primary legislation next year. There are also yet more changes to the legislation on employee share schemes and corrections of errors in the Income Tax (Earnings and Pensions) Act 2003.

The Act also contains substantial new rules on childcare and company vans in addition to less significant changes in other benefit in kind areas.

As always the courts have been as prolific as the Chancellor. Indeed, there seems to me to have been a lot more important cases last year than for several years.

With such a vast volume of new material to consider I would not be surprised if there are areas where I have not explained things in sufficient detail for readers to understand or where my initial interpretation of the law may turn out to be incorrect. I hope that readers who identify such areas will let me know so that I can seek to eliminate the shortcomings in the next edition.

A preface is an author's opportunity to acknowledge the help of others involved in the production of a book. In particular, I would like to thank Pat Miller for typing the original manuscript and Jill and Sophie Holland for the updating of this issue. I also acknowledge the help of my partners and colleagues at Blackstone Franks, particularly Subhash Thakrar, for his help on points of interpretation.

The law referred to in this book in general reflects the position at 1 July 2004.

London EC1, July 2004   **Robert W Maas**

Contents

Contents

Contents

Contents

Contents

Contents

Abbreviations and References

ABBREVIATIONS

CA	=	Contributions Agency
CGT	=	Capital Gains Tax
CGTA	=	Capital Gains Tax Act 1979
CIR	=	Commissioners of Inland Revenue
DSS	=	Department of Social Security
ESC	=	Extra Statutory Concession
ESOT	=	Employee Share Option Trust
FA	=	Finance Act
FURBS	=	Funded Unapproved Retirement Benefits Scheme
ICAEW	=	Institute of Chartered Accountants in England and Wales
ICTA 1988	=	Income and Corporation Taxes Act 1988
ITEPA	=	Income Tax (Earnings and Pensions) Act 2003
IRPR	=	Inland Revenue Press Release
Para	=	Paragraph
PAYE	=	Pay As You Earn
PEP	=	Personal Equity Plan
PRP	=	Profit-related pay
PSO	=	Pension Schemes Office
Reg	=	Regulation
s	=	Section
SCD	=	Simon's Special Commissioners' Decisions
Sch	=	Schedule
SI	–	Statutory Instrument
SMP	=	Statutory Maternity Pay
SP	=	Statement of Practice
SpC	=	Special Commissioners' decision
SSP	=	Statutory Sick Pay
TCGA 1992	=	Taxation of Chargeable Gains Act 1992
TMA 1970	=	Taxes Management Act 1970
VAT	=	Value Added Tax

REFERENCES

AC	=	Law Reports, Appeal Cases (Incorporated Council of Law Reporting for England and Wales, 3 Stone Buildings, Lincoln's Inn, London WC2A 3XN)
All E R	=	All England Law Reports (Butterworth & Co (Publishers) Ltd, Halsbury House, 35 Chancery Lane, London WC2A 1EL
BTC	=	British Tax Cases, (CCH Editions Ltd, Telford Road, Bicester, Oxon OX6 0XD)

Ch	=	Law Reports, Chancery Division
CLR	=	Criminal Law Reports
DLR	=	Dominion Law Reports (Canada)
ICR	=	Law Reports, Industrial Cases Reports
IR	=	Irish Reports (Law Reporting Council, Law Library, Four Courts, Dublin)
ITC	=	Irish Tax Cases (Government Publications, 1 & 3 GPO Arcade, Dublin 1)
KB	=	Law Reports, King's Bench Division
QB	=	Law Reports, Queen's Bench Division
STC(SCD)	=	Simon's Special Commissioners' Decisions (Butterworth & Co (Publishers) Ltd, as above)
STC	=	Simon's Tax Cases (Butterworth & Co (Publishers) Ltd, as above)
TC	=	Official Reports of Tax Cases (HMSO, PO Box 276, London SW8 5DT)
TLR	=	Times Law Reports
WLR	=	Weekly Law Reports (Incorporated Council of Law Reporting, as above)

Table of Cases

Table of Statutes

Chapter 1

Introduction

Introduction of Income Tax

1.1   Income tax was first introduced in the UK in 1799. It was a temporary tax to help finance the Napoleonic wars and was abolished in 1802 when the treaty of Amiens was signed. It was, however, reimposed a year later when England again declared war on France and continued until the final defeat of Napoleon in 1815, when the tax was again abolished. It was reintroduced as a temporary measure in 1842, but unfortunately over 150 years later the needs that prompted its reintroduction are still with us and Parliament has thought fit to reimpose the tax every year since then.

Schedular system

1.2   From its inception in its modern form in 1842 the tax has been assessed on a Schedular system. In other words, tax is charged 'in respect of all property, profits or gains respectively described or comprised in the Schedules marked A, B, C, D and E, contained in the First Schedule to this Act and in accordance with the Rules respectively applicable to those Schedules'. The words up to the last comma in the above quotation are those in *section 1(1)* of the *Income and Corporation Taxes Act 1988* with the exception that Schedule B was abolished by the *Finance Act 1988* and Schedule C by the *Finance Act 1996* and Schedule F has been added. The quotation is in fact from *section 1* of the *Income Tax Act 1918*, but the five Schedules actually derive from the *Income Tax Act 1842*.

1.3   Under a Schedular system it is necessary to determine into which Schedule a particular source of income falls before the tax on it can be calculated, as the rules of each Schedule can differ quite radically. If the source of an item of income cannot be brought within the scope of the rules of any of the Schedules it will be outside the scope of the tax. The Schedular system seems likely to disappear under the Tax Law Rewrite Project. The rewrite Act in relation to Schedule E income, the *Income Tax (Earnings and Pensions) Act 2003 (ITEPA 2003)* has dropped the expression, 'Schedule E', albeit that it has retained the computational rules.

The Schedule E charge

1.4   This Act now charges income tax on employment income, pension income and social security income. [*ITEPA 2003, s 1(1)*]. In 1842

Schedule (E) charged tax 'upon every public Office or Employment of Profit, and upon every Annuity, Pension or Stipend payable by Her Majesty out of the Public Revenue of the United Kingdom, except Annuities before charged to the Duties in Schedule (C)'. [*ITA 1842, s 1*]. In other words it was limited to public offices and employments. This did not mean that the salary from a non-public employment escaped tax; Schedule (D) imposed tax 'upon the annual Profits or gains arising or accruing to any Person residing in Great Britain from any Profession, Trade, Employment or Vocation'. *Section 146* of the *Income Tax Act 1842* contained ten rules for calculating the taxable income under Schedule E.

Pay As You Earn

1.5   Over the years the shape of Schedule E obviously changed significantly but most of the basic principles laid down in 1842 remain relatively unscathed. The first major change was introduced by *section 18* of the *Finance Act 1922* which provided that 'such profits or gains arising or accruing to any person from an office, employment or pension as are, under the *Income Tax Act 1918* chargeable to tax under Schedule D . . . shall cease to be chargeable under that Schedule and shall be chargeable to tax under Schedule E'. The next significant change was the enactment of the *Income Tax (Employments) Act 1943* which introduced for 1944/45 onwards the deduction of tax at source under the PAYE rules. Deduction of tax from earnings had actually been introduced a few years earlier, by *section 11* of the *Finance (No 2) Act 1940*, but the PAYE system represented a great simplification.

Expenses and benefits

1.6   The next major change was the introduction in *sections 38–46* of the *Finance Act 1948* of rules for the taxation of expenses and benefits in kind in respect of directors and employees earning £2,000 or more. These special rules were in general designed to ensure that tax was charged on the cost of providing benefits to such people not merely on the realisable value, if any, of such benefits. The rules were substantially recast in the mid-1970s, starting with the *Finance (No 2) Act 1975*, and continuing in the *Finance Act 1976* (which recast much of the previous year's legislation) and the 1977 and 1978 *Acts* (which supplemented the 1976 rules).

1.7   The last major change took place in 1996/97. This was the introduction of voluntary self-assessment.

1.8   The major changes have been supplemented along the way with other less drastic ones, such as the granting of relief for expenses (by *FA 1853, s 51*), for pension contributions [*FA 1921, s 32*], and retirement annuities [*FA 1956, s 22*], and the introduction of special rules on share options in 1966, employee shareholdings in 1972, approved profit sharing schemes in 1968, approved share options in 1971 and again in 1984, the short-lived profit-related pay in 1987, employee share ownership trusts in

1989 and employee share ownership plans (since renamed share incentive plans) and enterprise management incentives in 2000.

1.9 The overall result is a complex set of rules which interrelate with one another and reflect changes in government policy from time to time rather than a coherent attempt to formulate a sensible system of taxing income from employment. In particular, many of the changes in recent years seem to have been prompted more by a desire to minimise the Inland Revenue's workload than to produce a fair and comprehensible system of taxation. ITEPA 2003 is akin to a consolidation act. It has not changed the scope of the legislation but has reproduced it in more modern and readily understandable language.

1.10 Furthermore, the legislation cannot be looked at in isolation. It is supplemented by a large number of court decisions, which interpret areas of difficulty in the legislation (*Tolley's Tax Cases 2004* covers no less than 260 cases on employment and pension income and a further 37 on PAYE), and by Inland Revenue concessions and statements of practice, which alleviate some of the areas where the legislation can cause unfairness or anomalies.

1.11 Most taxpayers' major source of income is from an employment. Accordingly, the tax law in relation to employments has an impact on the vast majority of taxpayers. Because of the system of deduction of tax at source most salary and wage-earners give little thought to whether anything might be done to minimise their tax burden—or indeed whether the calculation for those within the scope of self-assessment submitting returns before the 30 September deadline that has been done by the Inland Revenue is correct.

Wages or salaries

1.12 It may be appropriate to mention here that at least as far as the Inland Revenue are concerned there is no distinction between wages and salaries—if indeed there is any real difference between the two terms. This was well expressed over 70 years ago by Lord Sumner in one of the landmark cases on Schedule E, *Great Western Rly Co v Bater (8 TC 231)*. 'It is, however, a purely arbitrary distinction and so indefinite as to be really accidental. For economic purposes it is convenient to treat wage-earners as a class, and for political purposes the receipt of a salary is often supposed to involve a different point of view from that which attaches to the earning of wages, but the first term really refers more to the nature and condition of manual work done than to the remuneration paid for it, and the second denotes social aspirations rather than any Revenue Category. Fashions change fast in this matter and many a man or woman, who took wages without objection thirty years ago, receives a salary now of no greater amount than the service would command under the old name.' This is, of course, as true today as it was in 1922.

1.13 This book is not intended to enable the average salary or wage-earner to check his tax bill as such. Nor does it cover in depth the operation of the PAYE system. It would be hard to rival the Revenue's own booklets in this area, CWG2 (2004) (*Employer's Further Guide to PAYE and NICs*) and 480 (2004) (*Expenses and Benefits: A Tax Guide*), which are issued free to employers.

1.14 The intention is to explain the legislation in depth, to point to tax planning opportunities, and to illuminate anomalies and danger areas in the legislation.

Self-assessment

1.15 Self-assessment applies to employees like anyone else. There is an obligation to notify chargeability of untaxed income and capital gains within six months after the end of the tax year and an obligation to complete a tax return if the Inland Revenue request an employee to do so. There is no obligation to complete a tax return if the Revenue decide not to issue one. Their practice is to issue tax returns to all company directors and to employees in receipt of significant amounts of untaxed income but not to issue returns generally where a person's income can be wholly dealt with through PAYE—including where small amounts of untaxed income can be taxed by an adjustment in the employee's PAYE coding notice. The Revenue also occasionally issue returns to other employees to check that there are no sources of untaxed income which have not been notified to them.

1.16 Prior to the introduction of self-assessment, benefits in kind and any taxable element of expenses were generally calculated by the Inland Revenue based on information provided by employers via the form P11D. For 1996/97 onwards the form P11D has been redesigned and employers are required to calculate the taxable benefits for their employees. The employee is entitled to a copy of his form P11D so that he can put the appropriate figures on his tax return if he is required to complete one. Those who are employed at 5 April in a tax year are entitled to the copy P11D information automatically by 6 July following or within 30 days whichever is later (*Reg 94*); those who left during the year must be given it on request within 30 days of the request if that is later than 6 July. The employer is entitled to calculate the benefits on the basis of the information he has, which may well be incomplete. The employee is nevertheless required to put the correct benefit figure on his return— which means he will need to recalculate it if he disagrees with his employer's figure as can happen in respect of interest free loans where the employer may not know that the money was spent for a qualifying purpose. In such circumstances he should obviously put a note on his return to explain why he has not adopted the P11D figure. He is still not entitled to a detailed breakdown of the figures on his P11D, so unless the employer volunteers this he will, in practice, be forced to rely on many of the employer's figures. Although the employer has to calculate the taxable benefits, the expenses figures that go on the form are still total expenses. It is then up to the employee to formulate a claim for relief for bona fide business expenses.

1.17   Self-assessment is voluntary. However, as a taxpayer is required to calculate and return each item of his income and capital gains, the only thing that those who choose not to self-assess escape is the need to add up the figures on their returns and calculate the tax thereon. As the price for avoiding these chores is a need to submit the tax return four months earlier—by 30 September following the end of the tax year— many people choose to self-assess.

1.18   Self-assessment does not merely shift the burden of assessing from the Inland Revenue to the taxpayer. It is a radical reform of the entire system of personal tax. From 1996/97 an individual has had to file his tax return by 31 January after the end of the tax year, the return for the year to 5 April 2003 being due on 31 January 2004. The return must be complete. Previously it was common to show against the space for earnings, 'per PAYE' (or sometimes for directors, 'per accounts') and against expenses and benefits, 'per P11D'. The Revenue now reject such returns as incomplete and ask the taxpayer to complete the form with the possibility of missing the 31 January deadline, thereby incurring interest and penalties.

1.19   At the same time as he submits his 2003/04 return a taxpayer must also send a cheque for the balance of the tax payable for that year. In the case of employees this will be primarily the tax on benefits in kind. He may also need to send a cheque for his first instalment of tax for 2004/05. This is because income tax (but not capital gains tax) is payable in three instalments, the first interim payment on 31 January in the year of assessment, i.e. 31 January 2005 for 2004/05; the second interim payment on the following 31 July, i.e. 31 July 2005 for 2004/05; and the third and final with the tax return on the following 31 January, i.e. 31 January 2006 for 2004/05. The first two instalments are based on the tax payable (not the taxable income) for the previous year, i.e. on the 2003/04 tax liability for 2004/05. There is a right to reduce the tax if the taxpayer thinks his liability for the current year is less, but penalties will be imposed for making such a reduction without good reason. The interim payments do not have to be made if at least 80 per cent of the income of the previous year was received under deduction of tax. Accordingly, most employees do not need to make interim payments as the PAYE deduction should satisfy this test unless benefits in kind are very high or the employee has other sources of untaxed income.

1.20   Under self-assessment, although the Revenue review all returns, they do not look at them in detail unless a return contains something that raises questions. This does not mean there is no check. The Revenue have been given extensive powers to obtain information including a right to randomly enquire into returns.

Format of this book

1.21   The format adopted has been to consider first the basic rules of assessment to give the reader an understanding of the scope of the taxation of income from employments and pensions. As mentioned above, tax is chargeable on the emoluments from an office or employment. Accordingly, Chapters 3 and 4 expand on the basic principles by considering the meaning of emoluments and of employment, and attempting to distinguish employment from self-employment. The special rules on expenses and benefits are then dealt with in Chapters 5 to 9.

1.22   The basic rules having been covered, the book then looks at ancillary matters; Chapter 10 dealing with pensions and Chapter 11 with termination payments, signing-on fees and similar lump sum payments. Rather than scatter throughout the book the variants to the basic rules that relate to people who are resident or not domiciled in the UK, those are collected together in Chapter 12. The following chapter deals with the special rules applying to UK residents working overseas.

1.23   Chapters 14–18 deal with the special provisions in relation to employee shareholdings and similar incentives for employees. A brief mention is made of national insurance. Although not nominally part of the tax system, an appreciation of the taxation of income from employment is incomplete without at least a brief survey of this impost. Finally, a chapter is included on the VAT implications of certain benefit payments.

Chapter 2

The Basic Rules

Meaning of 'employee'

2.1   ITEPA 2003 imposes tax on income from offices and employments. For simplicity reference will normally be made below to 'employees' as meaning persons taxable on employment income. It must be borne in mind however that, unless the context indicates otherwise, this expression also includes an office-holder, such as the director of a company.

2.2   The basic rules were recast in the *Finance Act 1989*, when the then Chancellor indicated that his changes would 'greatly simplify' the tax affairs of those taxpayers who regularly receive pay some time after the year for which it is earned.

Basis of assessment

2.3   Prior to the change it was necessary to ascertain the period to which remuneration related, determine its taxability by reference to the taxpayer's position at that time, and tax it as income of the period to which it related. Now it is necessary 'simply' to ascertain the period to which remuneration relates, determine its taxability by reference to the taxpayer's position at that time, and tax it as income of the year of assessment in which it is paid, unless it is a pension, in which case it is taxed as income of the year of assessment for which it was earned, i.e. a one-stage process has been 'simplified' into a two-stage one. Under the new system statutory rules are obviously needed to determine when remuneration is paid, which was relatively unimportant under the pre-1989 rules, as in family companies in particular, remuneration may well not be physically paid over as such.

2.4   It is important to realise that there is a two-stage process. Whether remuneration is assessable must be determined by reference to the time it is earned. When it is assessable depends on the date it is paid (a concept that has a technical meaning—see 2.44).

The charging provisions

2.5   For most people the ITEPA 2003 charges tax on 'general earnings' plus 'specific employment income' for the tax year. [*ITEPA 2003, s 9(2)(4)*]. General earnings is defined as earnings within Chapter 1, Part 3 of that Act. [*ITEPA 2003, s 7(3)*]. This in turn defined as any salary, wages or fees, any gratuity or other profit or incidental benefit of any kind obtained by the employee if it is money or money's worth, or anything else that constitutes an emolument of the employment. [*ITEPA 2003, s 62(2)*]. Specific employment income is defined as any amount which counts as employment income by virtue of Part 6 of that Act (income which is not earnings or share related – mainly receipts from pension schemes and payments on termination of employment) or Part 7 (share related income) or any other enactment. [*ITEPA 2003, s 7(4)(6)*].

2.6   Special rules apply to employees who are resident, ordinarily resident or domiciled outside the UK. [*ITEPA 2003, s 20*]. 'Overseas earnings' of a person who is resident and ordinarily resident in the UK but not domiciled here are taxed only when and to the extent that they are brought into the UK. [*ITEPA 2003, s 23*]. Earnings are overseas earnings if the employment is with a foreign employer and the duties of the employment are performed wholly outside the UK. [*ITEPA 2003, s 23(2)*].

2.7   Where an employee is resident but not ordinarily resident in the UK general earnings other than in respect of duties performed in the UK (and earnings from overseas Crown employment subject of UK tax) are also taxable only when, and to the extent that, they are remitted to the UK. [*ITEPA 2003, s 26(2)*].

2.8   If an employee is not resident in the UK for a tax year he is taxable here only in relation to earnings for duties performed in the UK (and earnings from an overseas Crown appointment), and only to the extent that such earnings are remitted to the UK. [*ITEPA 2003, s 27*].

2.9   Prior to 2003/04 the rules were the same but the tax charge was under one of three Cases of Schedule E. Case I applied to any emoluments for a year of assessment in which the employee was both resident and ordinarily resident in the UK, but subject to an exception for foreign emoluments (which had the same meaning as overseas earnings), which were taxed under Case III. Case II applied to emoluments in respect of duties performed in the UK for a year of assessment in which the employee was either not resident in the UK or, if resident, not ordinarily resident in the UK. Case III applied to emoluments for a year of assessment in which the employee was resident in the UK (irrespective of whether he was also ordinarily resident here). It was the provision that taxed remittances to the UK of foreign emoluments and of other earnings taxed here on a remittance basis. [*ICTA 1988, s 19*].

2.10   A person who is taxable on overseas earnings whether they are remitted or not, e.g. someone who is resident, ordinarily resident and domiciled in the UK or someone who is non-resident and works partly in the UK but is paid wholly overseas, can be taxable on money that he is unable to bring into the UK to pay the tax because of foreign currency controls. Such a person will nevertheless have to raise the money to pay the tax from other sources. There is no relief for delayed remittances corresponding to that which applies to the remittance basis (see 12.25).

2.11   If a person who is not UK resident, or is resident but not ordinarily resident in the UK, has an employment where some of the duties are performed in the UK (including those performed in Eire) and some are performed elsewhere, the remuneration has to be apportioned to ascertain the amount applicable to the UK duties. The part attributable to non-UK duties will be taxable if the employee is UK resident, and outside the scope of UK tax if he is not. It is in fact most unusual for a person to be ordinarily resident in the UK but not resident there. The converse is far more common. If the duties of the employment of such a person are carried on wholly outside the UK, Case II cannot apply to them as it only taxes remuneration for UK work. Where the remuneration from an employment is taxable partly on an earnings basis and partly on a remittance basis the apportionment between the two is essentially a question of fact. However, the Revenue will accept time apportionment based on the number of working days in and outside the UK. Where the remuneration is wholly paid abroad the Revenue will regard remittances to the UK as representing the emoluments taxed on an earnings basis rather than those taxed only on a remittance basis. Where part is paid in the UK, and part abroad the Revenue regard overseas earnings as having been remitted only if the aggregate of the emoluments paid in the UK, benefits enjoyed in the UK, and remittances to the UK, exceed the taxable UK earnings for the year of assessment (*SP 5/84*). Strictly speaking, the apportionment should probably be based on the total number of days in the UK (including non-working days) as, unless the contract provides otherwise, the law treats salary as accruing on a daily basis. It is worth considering if such an apportionment may be more beneficial to the employee.

Meaning of 'residence'

2.12   In order to ascertain whether remuneration is taxable in the UK it is obviously necessary to know what is meant by residence, ordinary residence and domicile. Unfortunately these terms are not defined in the tax legislation. Furthermore, the cases that have come before the courts, whilst helpful, have not sought to formulate definitions but have been determined very much on their own facts. Based on these cases the Inland Revenue have evolved a set of rules for deciding whether or not a person is resident in the UK. Although these are generally accepted they are amenable to challenge in the courts.

2.13   These rules are as follows:

(*a*)   A person is resident in the UK if he is present in the UK for 183 days or more during a year of assessment. The Revenue say that there are no exceptions to this rule. Strictly speaking the 183-day period should probably be arrived at by aggregating hours and minutes where a person is in the UK for parts of days (*Wilkie v IRC 32 TC 495*). In practice the Revenue ignore parts of days and count a day as a day of presence in the UK only if the person is present there throughout that entire day. It does not matter why the 183-day limit is breached. If a person intends to leave after 182 days but is prevented from doing so by illness or by a transport strike he will be resident in the UK for the year of assessment even though he had no intention of remaining in the UK for over 182 days.

(*b*)   A person is also resident in the UK for a year of assessment if he is present there on average for more than 90 days a year. This is normally looked at over a four-year period including the relevant year. It could well be that a person who regularly visits the UK for 88 or 89 days would be held to be UK resident, so this test should be approached with caution.

For this purpose (but not for (*a*) above), any days which are spent in the UK because of exceptional circumstances beyond an individual's control, such as illness, will be excluded from the calculation (*SP 2/91*). Although *SP 2/91* states that such days 'will' be excluded, it goes on to say that 'each case where this relaxation of the normal rules may be appropriate will be considered in the light of its own facts.' This suggests that this practice is very much at the discretion of the Revenue and cannot be relied upon. As the 90-day figure is not statutory in any event, *SP 2/91* does not seem much of a concession.

(*c*)   For years prior to 1993/94 a person was also resident in the UK in a year of assessment if he had accommodation available for his use in the UK and visited the UK at all—even in the Revenue's view for as little as a day—in that year of assessment. He did not have to own the accommodation or even have a right to reside there. Nor did it matter whether or not he actually stayed there when visiting the UK, although in practice the Revenue were sometimes prepared to ignore the point if the visit was to a different part of the country. The test was whether the person knew that he could in practice stay in the accommodation (other than as a mere guest of the occupier) whenever he visited the UK. This test did not in any event apply where a person worked full-time in an office or employment all of the duties of which were performed outside the UK. [*Section 335*]. UK duties which were 'merely incidental' to the performance of overseas duties were ignored. Merely incidental does not mean minimal in amount, it means subsidiary to overseas duties. In particular attendance at board meetings in the UK by a director of a UK company was not regarded as incidental to his full-time executive responsibilities overseas.

(*d*)   Although the above reflects the Revenue's long-standing position, they have recently begun to contend that mobile workers, such as long distance lorry drivers and salesmen who make frequent trips abroad, and who are present in the UK for less than 90 days a year on average but whose home is in the UK are resident in the UK. This accords with the decisions in some very old cases relating to master mariners, such as the 1875 decision in *In Re Young 1 TC 57* and the 1879 case of *Lloyd v Sulley 2 TC 37* (*Tax Bulletin 52, April 2001*).

Ordinary residence

2.14   Ordinary residence implies a slightly greater degree of permanence than residence. The Revenue regard someone as being ordinarily resident in the UK once he has been there for three consecutive fiscal years (and often earlier where it appears probable that he will stay for over three years). It is probably possible for a person to be ordinarily resident in the UK without being physically present there at all during a year of assessment, but as it would be impossible for him to perform UK duties in such circumstances so as to bring Case II into operation this is not relevant for Schedule E purposes. The 'available accommodation' rule (see 2.13(*c*)) may still be relevant for the purpose of ordinary residence. The Revenue's initial Press Release of 16 March 1993 suggested that its abolition affected only temporary visitors to the UK—which does not seem apt to cover emigrants—but the 1996 and subsequent editions of their booklet *IR20, Residents and non-residents*, indicates that the rule has been completely abolished.

Domicile

2.15   Domicile is a very difficult concept. As a very rough rule of thumb, a person who was born in the UK (or rather in either England and Wales, Scotland or Northern Ireland as each has their own legal system) is likely to be domiciled here and a person who was born overseas will normally not be domiciled here, unless he has come to the UK with the intention of staying here either for the rest of his life or indefinitely. A person is domiciled in the country that he regards as his home. A person starts life with a domicile of origin, which is the father's domicile at the time of the child's birth. That domicile can be replaced by a domicile of choice by going to another country with the intention of living there permanently or indefinitely. If a domicile of choice is lost, the original domicile of origin automatically revives. A person born overseas to a non-UK domiciled father who comes to England to work and intends to return to his home country when his working life is over is most unlikely to acquire a new English domicile of choice.

2.16   A full consideration of the meaning of these expressions is outside the scope of this book. It is hoped that the above will suffice to enable one to determine under which of the three cases of Schedule E a person is assessable. Any dispute regarding whether a person is or has been domiciled or ordinary resident in the UK is to be decided by the

Board of Inland Revenue, subject to a right of appeal to the Special Commissioners. Notice of appeal must be given within three months of the date on which the taxpayer is given notice of the Board's decision, not the normal 30 days. [*ITEPA 2003, ss 42–43*].

Year of payment

2.17   To decide whether or not emoluments fall within the charging provisions it is necessary to determine the year to which they relate. This is normally relatively simple as remuneration is generally paid for a specific week, month or year. However, it is possible for remuneration or other emoluments not to be specifically related to any period. For example, a company may decide to pay a loyalty bonus to all employees who have been with it for at least five years. In such circumstances the bonus will be regarded as being in respect of the year in which it is paid. This can give rise to problems if the employment does not exist in the year of payment. In *Bray v Best [1989] STC 159* the assets of an employee trust were distributed to ex-employees in 1979/80, the employment having ceased in 1978/79 following a takeover and the transfer of the staff to another group company. It was held that, although the funds distributed were emoluments of the employment, as they were not referable to a specific period they could only be emoluments of 1979/80, and thus escaped tax as the employees did not hold the employments at any time in 1979/80 (and thus the emoluments did not fall within the Schedule E charging provisions).

2.18   To prevent this state of affairs recurring, it is now provided that from 1989/90 where emoluments would otherwise be for a year of assessment in which the recipient does not hold the employment:

(*a*)   they must be treated as emoluments for the first year of assessment in which the employment is held, if they are paid in respect of a prospective employment; and

(*b*)   they must be treated as emoluments for the year of assessment in which the employment ceased if they relate to a past employment.

[*ITEPA 2003, ss 17, 30*].

2.19   In *Griffin v Standish [1995] STC 825* a taxpayer was awarded a bonus for 1987 payable on 14 April 1988. The taxpayer contended that following *Bray v Best* it was assessable for 1988/89. It was held that although the bonus was not paid for a specific tax year it was clearly in respect of the calendar year 1987 and so should be apportioned between 1986/87 and 1987/88.

2.20   The residence status of the taxpayer at the time he receives the emoluments appears irrelevant. It is only necessary to ascertain whether or not the receipt constitutes emoluments from the employment, not whether they would have been assessable on him had the employment existed at the time of receipt.

Place of performance of duties

2.21   If a person ordinarily performs all or part of the duties of his employment in the UK, the emoluments for any period of absence from the office or employment must be treated as being for duties performed in the UK (unless it can be shown that, but for that absence, they would have been for duties performed outside the UK). [*ITEPA 2003, s 38(2)*]. For example, suppose that an employee of a UK company is given by his employer a sabbatical (spanning a complete tax year) which he spends wholly overseas. He cannot claim that the salary for that year relates to non-UK work and is therefore not taxable. The position might be different if the employer asked the employee to work for a period in, say, the firm's Japanese branch and gave him a sabbatical prior to his actually taking up the position in Japan. In *Leonard v Blanchard [1993] STC 259* Nourse LJ indicated that the provision has a fairly narrow application. To come within it the taxpayer would need to show that if he had turned up for duty he would have performed the duties outside the UK.

2.22   If the duties of an employment in a chargeable period are mainly performed outside the UK, any duties performed in the UK which are merely incidental to the performance of those overseas duties are also taken to be performed outside the UK. [*ITEPA 2003, s 39(2)*]. This presumption does not deem the employee to be present in the UK for the purpose of determining whether there is a 365-day qualifying period when he is actually abroad carrying out such duties, nor does it prevent the employment from being one the duties of which are performed partly outside the UK for the purpose of *section 193(1)* (see paragraph 13.15 below). [*ITEPA 2003, s 39(3)*].

2.23   It was held in *Robson v Dixon (48 TC 527)* that duties are not merely incidental to other duties if, although they may be small in terms of time, they are an essential ingredient of the duties. In that case it was held that a few flights to UK airports by an airline pilot based in Amsterdam and normally flying internationally were not merely incidental to his employment in Holland.

2.24   The following duties must be treated as performed in the UK irrespective of where they are actually performed:

(*a*)   the duties of an office or employment under the Crown which is of a public nature and the emoluments of which are payable out of the public revenue of the UK or of Northern Ireland [*ITEPA 2003, ss 25(1), 27(1), 28*]; and

(*b*)   any duties which a person performs on a ship or other vessel engaged on a voyage between two ports both of which are in the UK, or which a UK resident performs on a vessel or aircraft engaged on a journey beginning or ending in the UK (or on a part beginning or ending in the UK of a longer voyage or journey). [*ITEPA 2003, s 40*].

Head (*a*) above does not apply to employees engaged locally (i.e. not based in the UK) if the maximum pay for their grade is less than that of an executive officer in the UK Civil Service working in Inner London (*ESC A25*).

Directors' fees

2.25   Where fees are received in respect of directorships held by members of a professional partnership the Revenue are prepared to treat the fees as partnership trading income provided that the directorship is a normal incidence of the profession (and the practice), the fees are small in relation to the practice's profits, and the fees are pooled for division among the partners (*ESC A37*). Also, the director will not be assessed on the reimbursed travelling expenses provided that either the partnership recognises them as income and claims a deduction or it does not claim a deduction under Schedule D and the expenses are reasonable in amount (*ESC A4*). Similarly where a company appoints a director to the board of another company and requires the director to pay over the fees, the nominating company can opt to treat the fees as its own trading income (*ESC A37*).

Pensions

2.26   Tax in respect of an annuity (other than one taxable under Schedule C, which applies to interest, etc.), pension or stipend payable by the Crown or out of the public revenue of the UK or Northern Ireland is taxable under *ITEPA 2003, s 566*. This includes the social security retirement pension, widow's pension, and industrial death benefit pensions [*ITEPA 2003, s 77*] but not war widow's pension. [*ITEPA 2003, s 639*]. So is any other pension paid by a person in the UK unless it is paid on behalf of a non-UK resident. [*ITEPA 2003, s 569*]. In some cases so is a lump sum paid under an unapproved pension scheme. [*ITEPA 2003, s 394*]. The detailed rules are considered at 10.57–10.63.

Sickness benefits

2.27   Sickness or disability benefits paid to an employee on a weekly or monthly basis (as opposed to a lump sum, which would not normally constitute income) and which are financed by the employer, e.g. through insurance premiums, are regarded as emoluments from the employment. Prior to 1982 the Revenue did not, in practice, tax such receipts unless the benefit had been received for at least twelve months prior to the start of the year of assessment concerned. However, this concession now applies only where the employee himself pays the insurance premiums and even in such circumstances it is limited to the first twelve months' benefit (*ESC A26* superseded by *ESC A83*).

2.28   Where an ex-employee receives a pension awarded on retirement through disability caused by injury on duty, by a work-related illness (e.g. pneumoconiosis) or by war wounds, and this exceeds the pension he would have received had he retired on the grounds of ordinary ill health, the excess is not treated as income. [*ITEPA 2003, s 644* enacting *ESC A62*].

Voluntary pensions

2.29   A pension arising from a past employment of the pensioner (or of the spouse, parent or a relative or dependant of the pensioner) and which is paid by the ex-employer or his successor, is taxable under Schedule E even if it is voluntary and even though it is capable of being discontinued. [*ITEPA 2003, s 633*]. If the pension is paid by or on behalf of a non-UK resident it may still be taxable in the UK, but the taxable amount is limited to the amount on which tax would have been chargeable if the pension were taxable under Case V of Schedule D. [*ITEPA 2003, s 635*]. This not only applies the remittance basis to such a pension but also may take it outside the scope of UK tax completely, as if the pension is truly voluntary it is probably not a foreign 'possession'.

Other pensions

2.30   Any other government pension receivable by a UK resident is also taxable under Schedule E if it is payable in the UK by (or through) any public department, officer or agent of:

(*a*)   a country forming part of Her Majesty's dominions;

(*b*)   any other country for the time being mentioned in *Schedule 3* to the *British Nationality Act 1981*; and

(*c*)   any other territory under Her Majesty's protection,

and is payable either to:

(i)   a person who has been employed in the service of the Crown (or service under the government of one of the above territories) outside the UK; or

(ii)   a widow, child, relative or dependant of any such person, and is in respect of that service.

[*ITEPA 2003, s 615*].

2.31   Only 90 per cent of such a pension is taxable however—or, to be precise, one-tenth of it may be deducted in charging the pension to tax. [*ITEPA 2003, s 617*]. This does not apply if the pension is payable by the UK Government as such pensions are regarded as UK, not foreign pensions.

2.32   The residence and domicile status of the recipient is irrelevant in relation to pensions, except, of course, to the extent that his tax treatment may be affected by one of the UK's double taxation agreements with other countries. The OECD model double tax agreement, which the UK normally follows, provides that pensions are taxable only in the country in which the recipient is resident, with the exception of government (or local authority, etc.) pensions. These are taxable only by the paying country unless the recipient is both a national and a resident of the other country, in which case they are instead taxed in that country. For example a pension paid by a UK company to a US resident will be exempt from UK tax (and taxed in the USA). One paid by the UK government or a local authority is taxable in the UK (and exempted in the USA) unless the recipient is a US national in which case it is taxed in the US instead. The State social security retirement pension is not regarded as a government pension for this purpose.

2.33   A pension not falling within any of the above categories, such as one paid by a non-UK and non-government employer in respect of services performed overseas, is not taxable under Schedule E but under Case V of Schedule D.

2.34   Certain pensions payable by the German and Austrian governments to victims of Nazi persecution are exempt from tax. (*ITEPA 2003, s 642*). The main ones are those payable under the following:

(*a*)   the Law for Compensation to Members of the Public Service (BWGoD);

(*b*)   the Equalisation of Burdens Law (LAG);

(*c*)   the Law to Compensate Austrian Public Servants;

(*d*)   the Law Concerning Compensation for National Socialist Injustice in Social Insurance (WGSVG);

(*e*)   pensions paid to victims of National Socialist Persecution whose social security contributions were paid in the German Reich outside the Federal Republic or in Danzig and to certain others whose entitlement derives from contributions in the territories annexed by Germany in 1938 and 1939 (under *s 99, Employers Insurance Law* (AVG), *s 1320, Reich Insurance Code* (RVO) or *s 9, Refugees and Foreign Pensions Law* (FAG), *s 108, Miners Pension Law* (RGK) or *ss 18* and *19* of the law to regulate compensation for National Socialist injustice in social insurance (WGSVG).

(Inspector's Manual, para 1584).

Other assessable items

Sick pay

2.35   In certain trades, such as the building industry, where it is common for a person to work for short periods in a succession of employments, employers contribute to a central industry-wide fund during the period they employ a person, so that if he is off sick the cost of sick pay is effectively spread amongst all the employers and is not a burden on the one for whom the individual happens to be working at a particular point in time. Without such an arrangement few employers would be prepared to pay sick pay, or holiday pay, where they engage a worker for only a few weeks. With such centralised schemes the sick pay is not paid by the employer but by the central fund. Furthermore, it would not be attributable to any one of the employments, and in the absence of special provisions might escape tax as there would be no source from which it derives.

2.36 It is accordingly provided that if a person holding an employment is absent from work by reason of sickness or disability, any sick pay or similar payment to the employee (or to his order, or for his benefit or that of a member of his family or household, i.e. his spouse, his children and their spouses, his parents and his dependants) is taxable as earnings of the employment if it arises as a result of any arrangements entered into by his employer. [*ITEPA 2003, s 221*]. If the fund for making such payments is contributed to partly by the employee and partly by employers, only a proportion of the payment is taxable, namely the part that it is just and reasonable to attribute to the employer's contributions. [*ITEPA 2003, s 221(4)*].

2.37 This ensures that where sick pay is paid not by the employer but, for example, by a trade association, the amount constitutes taxable income.

Other taxable payments

2.38 It is specifically provided that the following statutory payments under social security and other legislation are income taxable under Schedule E. [*ITEPA 2003, s 660*].

(*a*) Allowances under the *Job Release Act 1977* payable for periods more than twelve months before the recipient reached pensionable age. That *Act* allowed schemes to be set up to encourage people to retire earlier than normal in exchange for periodic payments until they reach normal pensionable age. [*Section 150*]. Allowances paid in the twelve months prior to reaching pensionable age are not taxable. [*ICTA 1988, s 191*]. The *Act* expired on 29.9.1988.

(*b*) Maternity pay within *section 33* of the *Employment Protection (Consolidation) Act 1978* (or the corresponding Northern Ireland legislation), whether or not paid during the subsistence of a contract of employment. Such payments ceased in August 1996.

(*c*) Statutory sick pay under *section 1* of the *Social Security and Housing Benefits Act 1982* (or the corresponding Northern Ireland legislation).

(*d*) Statutory maternity pay under the *Social Security Act 1986* (or the corresponding Northern Ireland enactment).

(*e*) Statutory paternity pay and statutory adoption pay under *Parts 12ZA* or *12ZB* of the *Social Security Contributions and Benefits Act 1992*.

(*f*) Income support under the Social Security Act 1986 which is paid in respect of a period during which the claimant is:

    (i) is one of a married or unmarried couple (as defined in the Social Security Act 1986) and although he is engaged in a trade dispute the other person is not. [*ITEPA 2003, s 665*].

If the income support paid for a week (or part of a week) exceeds the 'taxable maximum' for that period the excess is not taxable. [*ITEPA 2003, s 667*]. The taxable maximum is 50 per cent of the 'applicable amount' under the *Social Security Act 1986*, [*ITEPA 2003, s 668*]. Where a single person or both of a couple are on strike no income support is due except in respect of any addition for dependants, so there is nothing to tax.

(g) Jobseeker's allowance under the *Jobseekers Act 1995*. If it exceeds the taxable maximum the excess is not taxable. Where an income-based jobseeker's allowance is paid to one of a married or unmarried couple the taxable maximum is the portion of the applicable amount (as defined in the Regulations under that Act) included therein. Where such an allowance is paid to anyone else it is the age-related amount that would be applicable if a contribution-based allowance had been paid. Where a contribution-based jobseeker's allowance is paid to one of a couple it is the portion of the applicable amount that would have applied had an income-based jobseeker's allowance been paid. For other contribution-based job-seeker's allowance recipients it is the age related amount applicable to him. If an income-based jobseeker's allowance is paid to one of a couple the other of which is barred from allowance because of a trade dispute the taxable maximum is half of the applicable amount. [*ITEPA 2003, ss 670–676*].

(h) Unemployment benefit (up to 6 October 1996) and supplementary benefit under the *Social Security Act 1975*, the *Social Security Pensions Act 1975* (both now consolidated into the *Social Security Contributions and Benefits Act 1992*) and the corresponding Northern Ireland legislation. Also invalid care allowance and widowed mother's allowance, in each case apart from any dependent child addition. [*Hansard 7 June 1993, col 49*].

(i) Incapacity benefit under the *Social Security (Incapacity for Work) Act 1994* other than benefit for a period for which short-term incapacity benefit is payable otherwise than at the higher rate (i.e. other than under *Social Security Contributions and Benefits Act 1992, ss 30B(5), 40(8) or 41(7)*) and any increase in benefit in respect of a child, and the continuing benefit where the period of incapacity began before 13 April 1995. [*ITEPA 2003, ss 663, 664*].

2.39   The following social security benefits are not taxable: attendance allowance, back to work bonus, bereavement payment, child benefit, child's special allowance, child tax credit, council tax benefit, disability living allowance, guardian's allowance, housing benefit, industrial injuries benefit (other than death benefit), pensioner's Christmas bonus, payments out of the Social Fund, severe disablement allowance, state maternity allowance, state pension credit, working tax credit and payments to reduce under occupation by housing benefit claimants [*ITEPA 2003, s 677*]. Short term incapacity benefit, disability living allowance, invalidity benefit, compensation payments where child support is reduced due to a change in legislation, child maintenance bonus and increases in other benefits attributable to a child, all of which are no longer payable, were also not taxed. [*ITEPA 2003, s 677*]. A Parliamentary written answer (*Hansard 7 June 1993, col 49*) also indicated that one-parent benefit is not taxable. By concession the Revenue do not tax payments made under the Department of Education and Training's Jobmatch programme under which long-term unemployed people are entitled to a £50 a week allowance for six months when they take a part-time job of between 16 and 30 hours a week. They also do not tax the training vouchers of up to £300 given to participants made under the scheme (*ESC A97*). Employment Retention and Advancement Scheme payments and Return to Work Credit Scheme payments under those government pilot schemes are also exempt from tax [*Taxation of Benefits under Government Pilot Schemes (Return to Work Credit and Employment Retention and Advancement Schemes) Order 2003 (SI 2003 No 2339)*].

2.40   There is a special appeals procedure for taxable unemployment benefit or income support. Under this a Department of Social Security benefits officer notifies the recipient of the amount on which he is taxable. Such notice must state the date of issue and contain a statement that the recipient is entitled to object to the notice within 60 days. [*Section 152(1)*]. The benefits officer has power to extend this 60-day period if he is satisfied that there was a reasonable excuse for an objection not having been made in time. [*Section 152(5)*]. If no objection is made (or one is made but subsequently withdrawn) the taxable amount cannot subsequently be challenged on an appeal against the assessment. [*Section 152(2)*]. If an objection is made and an amended figure is subsequently agreed (and confirmed in writing by the benefits officer) there is again no further right of appeal, although the recipient can repudiate or resile from the agreement within 60 days of its having been made. [*Section 152(3)(4)*]. If, having issued a notice, the benefits officer changes his mind as to the amount, he can issue a notice of alteration which will supersede the original notice—but that notice will not give a fresh right of appeal. [*Section 152(6)*]. Presumably if the original figure was acceptable but the new one is not, the issue of the amended notice would be a reasonable ground for not having appealed within the 60-day limit.

2.41   Curiously, there appears to be no procedure for the General or Special Commissioners to hear an appeal against such a notice. The objection simply preserves the taxpayer's right to challenge the amount on an appeal against the assessment when it is eventually raised. There is a right of appeal against a benefits officer's refusal to accept a late objection [*Section 152(5)*], but again it appears that the Commissioners can merely determine whether or not there is a reasonable excuse for it not having been submitted on time, and cannot consider what the true amount should be unless at the same time they hear an appeal against the assessment.

2.42   Payments made by foreign governments which correspond to UK social security benefits which are exempt from tax, or to child benefit, are also not taxed. [*ITEPA 2003, s 681*].

2.43   It should also be mentioned at this stage that some other statutory provisions deem certain receipts to be income taxable as earnings. [*ITEPA 2003, s 7(5)*]. Such a provision can operate independently. It may not be necessary to bring the circumstances within the three Cases of Schedule E to trigger the tax charge. (*Nichols v Gibson* [*1996*] *STC 1008*—see 11.35).

The receipts basis of assessment

2.44   Having ascertained that emoluments fall within the charging provisions, it is next necessary to discover the year in which they are to be assessed. Tax on employment income is normally charged on the amount of the earnings from the employment received in a year of assessment (subject to a possible 100 per cent reduction for overseas employments of seafarers extending for over twelve months—see Chapter 12 below). [*ITEPA 2003, s 15*]. If the employee is resident and ordinarily resident but not domiciled in the UK tax on overseas earnings (see 2.6) is chargeable on the amount received in (or remitted to) the UK in the year of assessment. [*ITEPA 2003, s 23*]. If he is resident but not ordinarily resident in the UK his chargeable earnings are again the amount received in the UK in the tax year, except to the extent that they derive from duties performed in the UK where the taxable amount is the amount received (whether in the UK or elsewhere) in the tax year. [*ITEPA 2003, s 26*]. A non-resident individual is taxable only on earnings which both relate to duties performed in the UK and are received in the UK during the tax year. [*ITEPA 2003, s 27*].

2.45   It does not matter whether the emoluments relate to the year of assessment in which they are received or to some other year nor, indeed, whether the employment is held in the year of receipt (or the year of remittance). They will be assessable in the year of receipt even if this is before the employment starts or after it has ceased provided that the remuneration relates to a year of assessment for which the charging provisions impose a tax charge, or is deemed to relate to such a year under *sections 17* or *30* [*ITEPA 2003, ss 15(3), 21(3), 26(3), 27(3)*]. It does not even matter that the money may be received after the employee's death (or, as the case may be, may be remitted to the UK by his executors or administrators). In such circumstances the charge under Schedule E is made on the estate of the deceased employee. [*ITEPA 2003, s 13(4)*]. The receipt basis does not apply to pension income, social security income or employment income arising before 1989/90. Where such income is received more than six years after the year to which it relates it can nevertheless be assessed to tax at any time during the six tax years following that in which it was received. [*TMA 1970, s 35*].

Determining date of receipt

2.46   For the purpose of establishing the appropriate tax year for remuneration taxable the following rules apply to determine when an amount is received. If more than one of them applies, the earliest date fixed by any of them must be adopted. [*ITEPA 2003, s 18*].

(*a*)   The time when payment is made of, or on account of, the emoluments. Although on this wording a payment on account appears to trigger tax on the entire emoluments the intention is obviously that it should trigger tax only on the payment on account itself, and that is how the Inland Revenue interpret it.

(*b*)   The time when a person becomes entitled to payment of or on account of the earnings. For example, if a person is entitled under his contract of employment to receive his March 2004 salary on 31 March 2004 but because of a shortage of funds his employer does not actually pay it until after 6 April 2004 it will nevertheless be assessable for 2003/04. The employer must deduct tax under PAYE and account for it to the Inland Revenue as if the remuneration had been paid on 31 March 2004. It is possible to structure a contract of employment so that a person becomes entitled to a bonus on the termination of the employment or such earlier time as he may request. In such circumstances he would not become entitled to payment of the emoluments until he makes such a request. If a person is entitled to commission on sales that he makes during March 2004 but his contract provides that this will be paid with his April salary he will not become entitled *to payment of* the commission until April, even though legally he may well be entitled to the commission immediately on making the sales.

(*c*)   The time when sums on account of the earnings are credited in the company's accounts or records. This only applies if the recipient is a company director and the earnings are from an office or employment with the company. The most obvious example is where an amount is credited to a director's current account. However, this head is wider than that. It would also apply, for example, if the amount is simply included as a general creditor in the company's accounts—provided, of course, that the amount is identifiable as being in respect of emoluments for a particular individual.

For this purpose any restriction on the right to withdraw the money must be disregarded. [*ITEPA 2003, s 18(2)*]. Suppose, for example, remuneration is credited to a director's current account but he has agreed with the company's bankers that he will not withdraw the money until the company's overdraft falls below a specified sum. The remuneration is nevertheless to be treated as paid when it is credited. Remuneration being credited subject to a restriction must be distinguished from sums conditionally credited, which will not trigger a tax charge. Thus, if the remuneration was voted conditional on the overdraft falling below the specified level, and provisionally credited to the account it would not be regarded as paid at the time of crediting as it is not 'earnings' until such time as the condition is satisfied.

(*d*)   If the amount of the earnings is determined during the course of a company's accounting year (or other period in respect of which the emoluments are paid) it is deemed to be paid at the end of that year or period. Again this only applies if the recipient is a company director and the earnings are from an office or employment with the company.

(*e*)   If the amount of the emoluments for a period is not known until it is determined after the end of that period, then the emoluments are deemed to be paid at the time the amount is determined. This test also applies only where the recipient is a company director and the earnings are from an office or employment with the company. The obvious example is the common situation under *Table A* of the *Companies Act 1948* where a director is not entitled to any remuneration until it is determined by the company in general meeting, which is usually done at the time the accounts are approved.

2.47   Heads (*c*), (*d*) and (*e*) in 2.46 above, apply irrespective of whether the remuneration relates to the office of director. [*ITEPA 2003, s 18(1)*]. For example, if a person is a director of a company, for which he is paid director's fees, and in addition is employed by the company as a sales executive these heads will apply to his salary as sales executive by reason of the fact that he is a director of the company. Furthermore, these three heads apply if the person is a director of the company at any time in the year of assessment in which the remuneration falls. [*ITEPA 2003, s 18(2)*]. For example, suppose a person is an employee until 31 March 2004 and is appointed a director on 1 April 2004. Suppose also that a bonus for the year to 31 March 2004 is credited for him to an account in the company's books during March 2004, and that this sum is paid over to him in May 2004. Because he became a director during 2004/05 the remuneration will be deemed to be paid in March 2004 even though at that time he was not a director. The converse also seems to apply. If a person was a director at 31 March 2004 but then resigns and a bonus for him is credited to the company's books in December 2004 and paid over to him in May 2005 it will be remuneration of 2005/06 (under head (*a*) of 2.46 above) as he was not a director at any time during 2004/05 when the remuneration was credited and determined, so heads (*c*) and (*e*) would not apply to it.

Meaning of 'director'

2.48   For the purpose of heads (*c*), (*d*) and (*e*) of 2.46 above, a 'director' means:

(*a*)   in relation to a company whose affairs are managed by a board of directors or similar body, a member of that board or body;

(*b*)   in relation to a company whose affairs are managed by a single director or similar person, that person; and

(*c*)   in relation to a company whose affairs are managed by the members themselves, a member of the company.

[*ITEPA 2003, s 18(3)*].

2.49   The word 'director' also includes any person in accordance with whose directions or instructions the company's directors are accustomed to act. However, a person cannot be deemed to be a director under this test by reason only that the directors act on advice given by him in a professional capacity. [*ITEPA 2003, s 18(3)(4)*]. This is the same definition as that of a 'shadow director' under the *Companies Act 1985*. This provision does not exclude all outside advisers, however. The person concerned must be carrying on a profession. In *Currie v* and *Durant v IRC* (both *12 TC 245*) it was held that an income tax repayment agent was not carrying on a profession and neither was an insurance broker. There are also a number of VAT tribunal decisions on what is a profession, but these are not concerned with the types of people that might be expected to act as outside advisers to a company.

Special provisions

2.50   Some legislative provisions deem certain types of emoluments to be paid at specific dates. Such provisions obviously override the five basic rules set out above.

2.51   The sections of *ITEPA 2003* concerned are:

s 87(1)	non-cash vouchers (see 6.20 below)
s 94	credit tokens (see 6.29 below)
s 81	cash voucher (see 6.16 below)
s 327	living accommodation (see 8.3 below)
s 401	compensation for loss of office, etc. (see 11.14 below)
s 72	benefits in kind (see 6.41 below)
s 114	cars available for private use (see 7.2 below)
s 150	car fuel (see 7.46 below)
s 175	beneficial loans (see 9.1 below)
s 188	release of beneficial loans (see 9.28 below)
s 446u	disposal of shares acquired at an undervalue (see 14.83 below)
s 223	director's tax paid by employer (see 9.30 below)
s 222	payment by employer where tax deduction not possible (see 2.113 below).

[*ITEPA 2003, ss 19(2), 32(2)*].

2.52   If emoluments take the form of a benefit not consisting of money (and not within one of the above statutory provisions) the five rules set out in 2.46 above do not apply. Instead, the emoluments are treated as received at the time the benefit is provided. [*ITEPA 2003, ss 19(1), 32(1)*].

Pensions

2.53   Pensions are not affected by the adoption of the receipts basis of taxation. They are taxed as income of the year in which they accrue, irrespective of whether or not they are paid in that year. This applies to pensions chargeable under *ITEPA 2003, s 566* (see 2.26 above); voluntary pensions taxable under *ITEPA 2003, s 633* (see 2.29 above); income support under the *Social Security Act 1986* assessable under *ITEPA 2003, s 665* (see 2.38 above); pensions paid under retirement benefit schemes which are taxable under *ITEPA 2003, s 580* (see 10.21) and the national insurance state pension which is taxable under *ITEPA 2003, s 577* (see 2.26 above). Pensions payable under personal pension and retirement annuity schemes take the form of annuities and as such are taxable under Case III of Schedule D, but as earned income [*ICTA 1988, ss 643(3), 619(1)(b)*]. They are, nevertheless, subject to PAYE (see 2.118). In the case of retirement annuities if the whole of the premiums did not qualify for relief only the proportion attributable to the part that did is earnings. The personal pension rules require any premium not qualifying for relief to be repaid, so that situation cannot arise. If income withdrawals are taken from a personal pension scheme (see 10.28) they are assessable under Schedule E and subject to PAYE (*ITEPA 2003, s 598*). Income withdrawals cannot be taken from retirement annuities.

PAYE

2.54   Income tax on salaries and other remuneration taxable under Schedule E is normally collected by deduction at source under the Pay As You Earn (PAYE) system. This requires the employer to withhold income tax by reference to tax tables published by the Inland Revenue and account for it to the Inland Revenue. Interest is chargeable from 14 days after the end of the tax year on the amount unpaid at that time. [*Regulation 82*]. There is still no interest on late payment of the monthly amounts due during the tax year though.

2.55   For 2004/05 onwards a large employer (one who pays PAYE income to 250 or more employees) must account for PAYE electronically if required to do so by the Revenue. All such employers of whom the Revenue are aware will be so required. Both large and medium-sized employers must file forms P35 and P14 electronically. There are heavy penalties for failure to do so. [*FA 2002, s 135; FA 2003, s 204; Regs 189–216*]. Small employers who voluntarily file such forms electronically will receive a small incentive payment up to 2008/09. [*Income Tax (Incentive Payments for Voluntary Electronic Communications of PAYE Returns) Regulations 2003 (SI 2003 No. 2495)*]. From 2009/10 onwards all employers will be required to file such returns electronically.

Requirements for employers

2.56   The legislation requires an employer to deduct income tax (in accordance with *regulations*) on the making of any payment of, or on account of, any income assessable to tax as earnings. [*ITEPA 2003, s 684*]. Payment for this purpose (and for the purpose of the *PAYE Regulations*) has the same meaning as under the taxation of employment income rules, i.e. the five rules set out in 2.46 above apply (with the substitution of 'paid' for 'received') to determine the date on which PAYE needs to be deducted, or in the case of a 'net payment', accounted for. [*ITEPA 2003, s 686*]. It does not matter if the income is assessable in the year of receipt or some other year (e.g. because *ITEPA 2003, ss 17* or *30* applies, see 2.18 above). Nor does it matter that no assessment may have been made in respect of the tax. Obviously, in most cases no assessment will have been made as the information needed to raise an assessment will not become available until after the end of the tax year.

Payments by intermediaries

2.57   Where a payment of assessable income is made after 3 May 1994 by an intermediary, the employer (not the intermediary) is treated as making the payment, and thus becomes liable to deduct PAYE from it, unless the intermediary has himself applied PAYE. [*ITEPA 2003, s 687*]. An intermediary for this purpose is a person acting on the employer's behalf and at his expense (or at the expense of a person connected with him) or a trustee holding property for persons (or a class of persons) including the employer.

2.58   *Section 203B* was considered by the high court in *DTE Financial Services Ltd v Wilson* [*1999*] *STC 1061*. The decision in favour of the Revenue in that case was upheld by the Court of Appeal; [*2001*] *ECWA Civ 455* [*2001*] *STC 777*) on the basis of the *Ramsay* principle. It accordingly held that the analysis involving *section 203B* did not arise. As the Court of Appeal did not consider the correctness or otherwise of Hart J's analysis it is still good law. In that case the company entered into a marketed national insurance avoidance scheme which involved the following steps:

(*a*)   the company decided that a director, Mr McDonald, should be paid a £40,000 bonus;

(*b*)   an unconnected Manx company, GV, set up a discretionary trust with £40,300;

(*c*)   three days later the trustees appointed the whole capital of the trust to GV contingent on its remaining in existence for a further four days;

(*d*)   the next day DTE Financial paid GV £40,600 in consideration of its assigning to Mr McDonald its interest in the settlement; and finally

(*e*)   the interest in the settlement duly fell in and the £40,000 trust capital was paid to Mr McDonald.

The Revenue contended that the trustees had made a payment of assessable income to Mr McDonald within *section 203B*. Hart J quickly dismissed this claim. The emolument received by Mr McDonald was the contingent interest; the £40,000 was not the emolument, it was a fruit of that emolument. However it was also held that if the principle enunciated by the House of Lords in *W T Ramsay Ltd v IRC* [*1981*] *STC 174* applied (which enables steps inserted into a composite transaction solely for tax avoidance purposes to be excised to identify the real transaction) the payment of £40,000 made by the trustees would clearly have fallen within *section 203B* (as the real transaction would have been a decision by the company to pay a bonus of £40,000 to Mr McDonald combined with the payment to him of £40,000 by the trustees). The *Ramsay* principle was held to apply so PAYE should have been accounted for under *section 203B*.

2.59   If an employee works for someone other than his employer and the *PAYE Regulations* do not apply to the employer (or other person who pays his salary), for example, because he is a non-UK resident, the person for whom the employee works is deemed to have paid the salary for PAYE purposes. [*ITEPA 2003, s 689*]. This appears to bring within the scope of PAYE employees of overseas companies who are seconded to their UK subsidiaries, although the Minister has assured Parliament that it 'creates no new liabilities to tax' but merely 'will remove doubt' about the validity of the *PAYE Regulations* (*Hansard 19 April 1994, cols 748 & 749*).

2.60   If at a time after 5 April 1998 the employer is treated as making a payment of any amount to the employee under any of *ITEPA 2003, ss 696–702* (see 2.88–2.103) he is also deemed to have made an actual payment of that amount so as to trigger an obligation on the person for whom the employee works to account for PAYE. The transitional rule in 2.107 below applies where the notional payment was made before 31 July 1998. [*ICTA 1988, s 203C(3A)* and *FA 1998, s 69(6)*].

2.61   Where an employee who is not both resident and ordinarily resident in the UK works partly in the UK and partly overseas he is taxable only on the proportion of his salary that relates to UK duties (see 2.7). From 3 May 1994 the whole of the salary payable to such a person is brought within the scope of PAYE—with the employee having a right to reclaim through a Schedule E assessment the tax overdeducted. However, the employer (or a person designated by him for the purpose of the section) can apply to the Revenue for authority to deduct tax on only a proportion of the salary, i.e. the proportion that is estimated to be applicable to UK duties. The application must obviously give all available information relevant to the calculation of the relevant proportion. [*ITEPA 2003, s 690*]. Curiously, prior to 2003/04 it appeared that the Revenue could not grant such a request unless the proportion of the salary applicable to UK duties was not ascertainable at the time the application was made. If it could be ascertained PAYE had to be applied to the entire payment, including the part applicable to non-UK duties! [*ICTA 1988, s 203D(2)(b),(8)*]. It is difficult to believe that this was intended. The rewrite Act has corrected this anomaly.

2.62   From 3 May 1994 if a person ('the relevant person') enters into an agreement that employees of another person ('the contractor') shall work for the relevant person and 'it is likely that' the contractor will not apply PAYE, the Revenue can direct the relevant person to apply PAYE to payments that he makes to the contractor in respect of work done by the employees. The direction must specify the name of the relevant person and the contractor, must be given by notice (which means that it must be in writing—see *Hansard 19 April 1994, col 754*) and a copy must be given to the relevant person (unless the Revenue cannot find him). The relevant person must apply PAYE to the entire payment, i.e. including the contractor's profit loading, as if it were remuneration of the employee. [*ITEPA 2003, s 691*]. It is not clear how he is to apportion the payment if it is in respect of work done by more than one employee. The Minister has said that 'it is not part of our purpose to provide as a normal state of affairs that a farmer should be required to provide for PAYE for labour employed by a gang master' (*Hansard 19 April 1994, col 753*). The purpose is obviously to ensure that the Revenue can collect the tax where they believe that the contractor will disappear before they can collect the PAYE from him. It is not clear that either the relevant person or the contractor can challenge the Revenue's belief that it is likely that the contractor will not account for PAYE. Although the side-heading to the *section* is 'mobile UK workforce' there is nothing in the *section* itself to so limit its application. There seems no reason why the Revenue should not give a direction under it simply because the contractor is tardy with accounting for PAYE or the Revenue fear that he could become insolvent. There are two slight protections against this. First, it is the belief of the Board, not an officer of the Board, that is required before a notice can be given. Secondly, an assurance was given by the then Minister that 'it is not our intention to create in the new clause an obligation which does not already exist within the piece of secondary legislation to which I referred in my opening remarks' (*Hansard 19 April 1994, col 753*). He did not specify what that piece of legislation is. It was probably *regulation 4* of the *PAYE Regulations* which was revoked by *FA 1994, s 133*.

2.63   Prior to the enactment of the above rules where a person worked under the general control and management of a person who was not his immediate employer, that person ('the principal employer') was deemed by *regulation 4* of the *1993 PAYE Regulations* (which was repealed by *section 133* of the *Finance Act 1994* as it is replaced by the above provisions) to be the employer for PAYE purposes. *Regulation 4* provided that if the emoluments were actually paid by the immediate employer, the principal employer had to notify him of the tax to be deducted and to himself deduct the tax out of the payment that he made to the immediate employer. This effectively treated the immediate employer as a mere agent of the principal employer. It was accepted in *Andrews v King* [*1991*] *STC 481* (see 2.71 and 4.50 below) that *regulation 4* overrode *regulation 2* so that the immediate employer ceased to be an employer altogether for the purpose of the *PAYE Regulations*. *Regulation 4* seemed apt to cover, for example, a site foreman who was given the aggregate net wages of each of the employees at that site and paid the money over to the individual employees. As none of the above provisions seem to cover such a case it is not readily apparent why the *regulation* has been repealed.

The PAYE Regulations

2.64   The Board of Inland Revenue have power to make *regulations* with respect to the assessment, charge, collection and recovery of income tax. Such *regulations* can include provisions:

(*a*)   requiring any person who makes a payment of (or on account of) remuneration to deduct tax (either at the basic rate or other rates in such cases or classes as the *regulation* may provide) by reference to tax tables prepared by the Board, and making such persons liable to account for such tax to the Inland Revenue;

(*b*)   for the production to persons authorised by the Board of wages sheets and other documents and records for their inspection to satisfy themselves that income tax is being deducted in accordance with the *regulations*;

(*c*)   for the collection and recovery of income tax in respect of remuneration which has not been deducted during the year;

(*d*)   requiring the payment of interest on tax due to the Board which is not paid by the due date, for determining the date from which interest is to be calculated (provided that it is not earlier than 14 days after the end of the year of assessment) and for enabling the repayment or remission of such interest;

(*e*)   requiring the payment of interest on repayments due from the Board and for determining the date from which such interest is to be calculated (which cannot be earlier than one year after the end of the year of assessment);

(*f*)   for the assessment and charge of income tax by the Inspector in relation to income subject to PAYE; and

(*g*)   for appeals in relation to matters arising under the *regulations* where there would not otherwise be a right of appeal.

[*ITEPA 2003, s 684*].

2.65   Interest under head (*d*) of 2.64 above, must be paid without deduction of income tax and is not to be taken into account in computing income, profits or losses for any tax purpose. [*ITEPA 2003, s 684(6)*].

2.66   The Board must construct the tax tables with a view to securing that, as far as possible:

(*a*)   the total income tax payable in respect of any income assessable under Schedule E for any year of assessment is deducted from such income payable during the year—it can be assumed for the purpose of estimating the total income tax payable that the income will continue to accrue for the rest of the year at the same rate as has been earned from 6 April to the date of making the payment from which the deduction falls to be made; and

(*b*)   the income tax deductible (or repayable) on the occasion of any payment of income is such that the total net income tax deducted from the beginning of the year of assessment bears the same proportion to the total income tax payable for the year that the part of the year which ends with the date of the payment bears to the whole year. [*ITEPA 2003, s 685*].

It is doubtful if the tax tables in fact complied with this requirement until 6 April 1993 as where benefits in kind exceeded an employee's personal allowances, the tables assumed nil allowances and left tax on the excess benefits to be collected by assessment. From that date K codes, negative code numbers, were introduced to rectify this problem.

2.67   The total income tax payable for the year means, for the purpose of heads (*a*) and (*b*) of 2.64 above, the total income tax estimated to be payable in respect of the income from the employment subject to a provisional deduction for allowances and reliefs, and subject also (if necessary) to an adjustment for amounts overpaid or underpaid in respect of previous years. [*ITEPA 2003, s 685(2)*].

2.68   An interesting point arose in *Blackburn v Keeling* [2003] EWHC 754 (Ch), [*2003*] *STC 1162*. Mr Keeling incurred a loss as a Lloyds underwriter. Under special rules that apply to underwriters this was a 2003/04 loss but the figure was provisional and would not be finalised until May 2003. In February 2002 Mr Keeling elected to carry back the loss to 2002/03 under *ICTA 1988, s 380* and asked the Revenue to amend his 2003/03 PAYE coding to reflect the loss. The Revenue refused on the grounds that the loss had not by then been 'established' and would not be established until after the end of 2002/03. The Commissioners and the judge both disagreed. Peter Smith J thought that the Inspector, (and, on appeal, the Commissioners), was entitled to 'take into account all matters known to him at the time he prepares the code to arrive at the fairest and most realistic code that is likely to be the nearest to the true position of the taxpayer when the taxpayer's affairs for that tax year are finally worked out'. Unfortunately, the Court of Appeal disagreed. Although, it felt it arguably contrary to the spirit of the PAYE system that tax should be deducted in 2002/3 when everyone knew that Mr Keeling would in due course be entitled to claim loss relief for that year it felt the wording of *regulation 7(2)(a)* ('the release from income tax to which the employee is entitled for the year … so far as his title to those reliefs has been established at the time of the determination') that the appeal had to be rejected.

2.69   The *regulations* may provide that no repayment of tax is to be made to any person if at the time:

(*a*)   he has claimed jobseeker's allowance in respect of a period including that time;

(*b*)   he is disqualified from receiving jobseeker's allowance because he is on strike (or would be so disqualified if he satisfied the other qualifying conditions); or

(*c*)   prior to 2003/04 he has claimed income support under the *Social Security Act 1986* (now consolidated into the *Social Security Contributions and Benefits Act 1992*) in respect of a period including that time and his right to income support is conditional on his being available for employment.

[*ITEPA 2003, s 708*].

2.70   The Board have made *regulations* covering all of these matters. They are now the *Income Tax (Pay As You Earn) Regulations 2003 (SI 2003 No 2682)*. It is not proposed to consider all of these *regulations* in detail but there are a number of them that are of particular importance.

2.71   *Regulation 2*, 'Interpretation' adopts the definition of employment in *ITEPA 2003, ss 4 and 5* (see 4.1 and 4.12) and specifies that employer has a corresponding meaning. However this is subject to *Regulations 10 to 12* which provide respectively that agencies, pension payers and 'other payers' are to be treated as employers (except for specified purposes). An agency is deemed to cease to employ the worker (so must issue form P45) if it makes no relevant payments to the worker for a period of three months (*Reg 10(2)*). *Prima facie Regulation 12* seems to impose the responsibility of applying the *PAYE Regulations* on many people who are not employers in the normal sense of the word at all. For example, if A collects B's wage packet for him because B is sick on payday, A may become B's employer because he is paying the emoluments to B. The wages clerk of a company may become an employer if wages are paid in cash as he is the person making the payment. Fortunately, in *Andrews v King [1991] STC 481*, where the Revenue put forward a similar claim, it was held that *regulation 4* (see 2.63 above) overrides the definition of employer in *regulation 2*. It was held in *R v Walton General Commrs, ex p Wilson (1983 STC 464)* that the reference in the *1993 PAYE Regulations* to emoluments was wide enough to cover benefits-in-kind. The *2003 Regulations* no longer refer to emoluments but to PAYE income (*regulation 2*). This is defined in *ITEPA 2003, s 683* as any PAYE employment income for the year, any PAYE pension income for the year and any PAYE social security income for the year. PAYE employment income is in turn defined as income which consists of any taxable earnings from an employment in the year and any taxable specific income from an employment for the year (i.e. the full amount of any specific income which by virtue of any enactment counts as employment income for that year in respect of the employment), which is probably as broad as the previous concept of emoluments [*ITEPA 2003, ss 10(3), 683(2)*]. PAYE does not in general apply to benefits as there is an obligation to deduct tax only 'on making a relevant payment' (*Regulation 21(1)*) and a relevant payment is a payment 'of, or on account of PAYE income' (*Reg 4(1)*). The provision of a benefit is not the making of a payment. The December 1998 Special Commissioners' decision in *Paul Dunstall Organisation Ltd v Hedges, [1999] STC SCD 26* casts some doubt on the position in relation to benefits. The company negotiated a sale of a piece of land for £1.5m. It was advised that if it transferred the land to its director prior to exchange of contract it would avoid national insurance. It did not wish to give the whole value to the director. It accordingly voted him a bonus of £800,000 to be paid in the form of a proportion of the land. It contracted to sell the remainder of the land to the director for £680,000. The director then entered into the sale contract and sold the site for £1.5m, making a £20,000 property dealing profit (a capital gain in the eyes of the Commissioners). The Revenue contended that PAYE should have been applied to the payment of emoluments of £800,000 and the Special Commissioners upheld this.

2.72   The basis of their decision was that 'payment' is a word that takes its meaning from its context. As the *1993 PAYE Regulations* referred to 'any payment of emoluments' and it is well established that emoluments can take the form of perquisites, they inferred that payment did not mean 'payment in money'. The director received a perquisite that could be turned into money. They accepted that if a deduction was to be made from perquisites there had to be machinery enabling this to be done. They also accepted that there could be difficulties in valuing benefits in kind that could not be turned into money. They concluded that where something was capable of valuation PAYE fell to be deducted from the amount for which the perquisite could be sold when received and that the machinery for deduction was through the coding notice. The transactions took place in 1998.

2.73   In some ways this is an understandable decision. The accepted wisdom now has long been that if a person is voted a bonus of a specified amount to be satisfied by the transfer of an asset to him there is a risk that the amount is pay for PAYE purposes. Nowadays most 'advisers' would have suggested a bonus of the piece of land without placing a figure on it. It is unclear whether the Special Commissioners would have arrived at the same conclusion if that had been done. Worryingly, their reasoning suggests that they would have. This is somewhat frightening. In most cases the Revenue have been content to assess the director. It appears that they could now go back and raise a *regulation 72* assessment on the company—and collect from it interest on overdue tax—and repay the director's Schedule E assessment. They are not constrained by the 'general view of the law' principle, as they have always contended that there was a Schedule E liability even though they have generally not enforced it. Some companies have voluntarily paid the tax 'on behalf of' the employees on the PAYE due date. Even such companies may not be safe.

2.74   In other ways the decision is extraordinary. The concept that the coding notice provides a machinery for deduction is far-fetched. In most cases the bonus would exceed a year's basic salary, so the deduction is impracticable. It would almost certainly be *ultra vires* for the *PAYE Regulations* to require an employer to account to the Revenue for an amount that it is in practice impossible for him to deduct. Parliament provided in 1994 a procedure for applying PAYE to tradeable assets. In

1998 it extended this to readily convertible assets (see 2.96). It would hardly have done so if it had all along 'intended' that the PAYE system should apply to such assets. Yet in applying the law the courts seek to reflect the intention of Parliament.

2.75   The Special Commissioners relied heavily on *Garforth v Newsmith Stainless Ltd [1979] STC 129* (see 2.58), where an amount credited to a director's current account was held to have been paid 'when money is placed unreservedly at the disposal of directors'. Although Walton J there referred to 'money', the Special Commissioners took his wording as authority for the view that 'payment' has no settled meaning, which somewhat stretches what was actually said. There was a problem with *IRC v Herd* (see 2.78), where the court held that PAYE could not be applied where only part of a payment was assessable, but the Commissioners resolved that by holding that that was a narrow point which did not greatly assist them! They also got round the small problem that the £800,000 bonus voted at 11.00 am on 22 June 1998 differed from the £820,000 sale price achieved at 12.50 pm on the next day by ascribing this to 'the volatility of the market', even though the value of the balance of the land did not apparently move during that 26-hour period.

2.76   Subject to the above case and to the statutory exceptions described below, the provision of a benefit will not make the provider an employer under the *regulations* and he will not be a person 'paying' emoluments. On the other hand, in *Booth v Mirror Group Newspapers plc [1992] STC 615* where Mirror Group Newspapers made a payment to an employee of a subsidiary, Pergamon Media Trust plc, to induce him to enter into employment with Pergamon it was held that Mirror Group Newspapers was liable to deduct tax (by reference to an emergency coding) because by making the payment it was itself deemed to be an employer of Mr Booth by virtue of *regulation 2*. As a result, everyone who tips a waiter or an employed taxi driver without deducting PAYE should be aware that he is committing an offence under the *PAYE Regulations*!

2.77   *Regulation 49* deals with new employees (other than those producing a form P45 (which will show the employee's code number) or who are former full-time students). It imposes an obligation on the employer to complete a form P46 and send it to the Revenue when he makes the first relevant payment. The *1993 Regulations* only required this to be done where the person was being paid at an annual rate which exceeded the personal allowance (or at a rate of more than £1 a week or £4 a month if the employee had other employment). The employer must also of course deduct tax on the cumulative basis using the emergency code (which grants the personal allowance) if the employee was formerly a full-time student or using the basic rate code if he was not. This is another change. Under the *1993 Regulations* the basic rate code was used only if the employee had other employment.

2.78   If the employer fails to deduct tax from a payment of emoluments, *regulation 72(1)(3)* empowers the Revenue to recover the tax that should have been deducted under PAYE from the employee concerned, if they are satisfied that the employer took reasonable care to comply with the *PAYE Regulations* and the under-deduction was due to an error made in good faith. They have a similar power to require the employee to pay the tax if they believe that he knew that the employer 'has wilfully failed to deduct' PAYE. [*Regulation 72(1)(4)*]. If they direct that the employee should pay the tax under either provision the employer ceases to have any liability to pay it. Notice of a direction under *regulation 72* must be given both to the employer and the employee (unless the Revenue are not aware of the employee's address). The employer is entitled to request a direction under *regulation 72(3)*. The employer has a right of appeal against the refusal of such a request and the employee has a right of appeal against the direction. The employee also has a right of appeal against a direction under *regulation 72(4)*. [*Regulations 72A–72D* inserted by the *Income Tax (PAYE) (Amendment) Regulations 2004 (SI 2004 No 851)*]. Prior to 2004/05 there was no right for either employer or employee to make representations before the direction was made and no specific right of appeal for either. However, it appears that the Revenue needed to make an assessment on the employee, which carried with it the normal right of appeal. If the employee succeeded in his appeal it appears that the tax was wholly irrecoverable as there was no longer a right of recovery against the employer. In *IRC v Herd [1993] STC 436* it was held that unless a direction has been made under *regulation 42* the Revenue have no power to recover the tax from the employee, i.e. they cannot assess him direct under Schedule E for tax which ought to have been deducted under PAYE. However, Lord Mackay felt that neither *ITEPA 2003, s 684* nor the *regulations* were wide enough to impose an obligation to apply PAYE to a payment only part of which was assessable under PAYE. In that case the payment was the purchase price of shares, the gain on which was assessable under Schedule E but the element of the price that reflected their original cost was not. Accordingly, PAYE could not apply. Logically, the same principle should apply to other mixed payments, such as compensation for loss of office where the first £30,000 is exempt from tax, if anyone is brave enough to take the point. A problem can arise in a family business where directors' drawings are voted as net salary at the end of the year. This appears to have been what happened in *R v IRC ex p McVeigh [1996] STC 91*. May J held that including the tax liability in creditors in the accounts and the amount net of deductions in the loan account would no doubt constitute a deduction of tax if the tax were paid over to the Revenue. However, he felt it would 'be a misuse of language to say that the bookkeeping and accounting alone, without actual payment and without any of the procedures which the Regulations require, constituted a deduction of tax from the gross payment'. Accordingly, the Revenue were entitled to assess Mr McVeigh as he knew that the company had failed to 'deduct' PAYE.

2.79 The harshness of the principle is well illustrated by the Special Commissioners decision in *Black v Inspector of Taxes [2000] STC (SCD) 540*. Black, Brown, Green and White were directors of a subsidiary company. Jones, the chairman and chief executive, promised them each bonuses of a specified sum. At a board meeting of the parent company it was resolved to pay these bonuses by way of transfer of units in a unit trust. The Revenue assessed Black and his colleagues on the value of the units as benefits in kind. Black and his colleagues appealed, contending that the company ought to have deducted tax under PAYE before providing the units to them. It was agreed that for PAYE purposes 'payment' was the transfer of money or money's worth where quantified in money (e.g. cheque or credit card). Accordingly if there was a legal entitlement to payment of money prior to the transfer of the units the satisfaction of that entitlement constituted payment; if there was no legal entitlement the transfer could not amount to payment but would be a benefit in kind (it would now of course be subject to PAYE under the readily convertible asset rules—see 2.88—but these did not exist at the time). If there is such a general principle it is curious that it was not annunciated in the *Paul Dunstall* case (see 2.71). Nevertheless, the parties were content to adopt it. It was held that Mr Jones had power to bind the company and his agreement to pay the bonuses created a legal entitlement to the appropriate sum of money. Accordingly PAYE should have been deducted. The Commissioner considered that the agreement was not to pay a net amount; the directors were entitled to bonuses of £250,000 and if the company had deducted tax when paying the bonus they would have no complaint. Nevertheless she held that PAYE should have been deducted from the whole sum. It is not wholly clear why. If the legal entitlement was to receive £250,000 less tax—say £150,000—and the taxpayer received value of £250,000 it is hard to see how the additional £100,000 can be in satisfaction of the legal entitlement. On the face of it that £100,000 ought to be a benefit in kind.

2.80   *Regulation 73* deals with the submission of the end of year return, form P35. *Regulation 73* requires the return to be rendered within 44 days after the end of the tax year, i.e. by 19 May. Failure to do so renders the employer liable to a heavy penalty, namely £1,200 for each 50 employees plus a further penalty of £100 a month per 50 employees for each month the failure continues after a penalty has been imposed (up to the end of the year after that to which the P35 relates only), plus, if the failure continues for more than a year, 100 per cent of the PAYE for the year. If the number of employees is not a multiple of 50 the £100 figure applies to the excess number (or the lesser number if the total is under 50). If a return is made, but it is incorrect because it was made fraudulently or negligently, the penalty is an amount equal to the tax omitted from the return. These penalties are maxima; they are fully mitigable.The penalty for the first twelve months is a fixed non-mitigable amount of £100 a month per 50 employees for each month the failure continues. Such penalties were initially imposed by the appeal Commissioners but since 20 May 1995 have been imposed virtually automatically by the Inland Revenue. [*TMA 1970, s 98A*].

2.81   *Regulation 90* requires an employer to make a quarterly return of cars provided to employees and available for their private use. This must be done within 28 days of the end of each income tax quarter (i.e. 5 April, 5 July, 5 October, 5 January). The return must show for each car that becomes available to an employee (or ceases to be available to him) in that quarter the employee's name and national insurance number, the car and its original list price, any capital contribution by the employee, any amount the employee is required to pay during the tax year as a condition of the car being available for his private use, and whether fuel is provided for private use.

2.82   The tax is normally payable to the Revenue 14 days after the end of each income tax month. [*Regulation 69*]. If no payment is made within that period, *regulation 77* gives the Collector of Taxes power to require the company to make a return of emoluments paid in that month and of the tax payable thereon. Alternatively, *regulation 78* gives the Collector power to estimate the tax that he thinks is likely to be due, demand it from the employer and, unless the employer pays the tax actually due within seven days or convinces the Collector that nothing is due, enforce payment of that estimated sum. If the total of PAYE, national insurance and construction industry subcontractors' deductions is likely to be below £1,500 per month on average for a tax year, *regulation 70* allows the employer to account quarterly (the first payment falling due on 5 July) instead of monthly. The £1,500 figure relates to the aggregate of PAYE, national insurance, student loan deductions and building industry sub-contractors' deductions less tax credits payable (Working Families Tax Credit (WFTC) or Disabled Persons Tax Credit (DPTC)—see 20.42).

2.83   *Regulation 80*, 'Determination of unpaid tax', is increasingly being used by the Revenue. Where it appears to the Revenue that there may be tax due under PAYE that has not been paid to the Collector, they can 'determine the amount of the tax that to the best of judgement' and serve notice of that determination on the employer. Subject to the normal right of appeal, the amount of the determination is recoverable as if the determination were an assessment and the amount of tax determined were tax payable by the company. An Inspector will frequently make a *regulation 80* determination on the directors' remuneration shown in accounts submitted to him or on amounts of untaxed emoluments found as a result of a PAYE inspection. There are a number of points to note.

(*a*)   The Revenue consider that it is not open to the employer to appeal against a determination on the grounds that the code number used by the Inspector does not fully reflect the allowances due to the employee, as the obligation on the employer under the *regulations* is to deduct tax in accordance with the code number that has been issued to him. As no time limit within which an appeal against a coding notice must be made is specified this is of dubious validity.

(*b*)   As the tax payable on a *regulation 80* determination is a liability of the employer, he has no right to recover it from the employee and the employee is not entitled to any credit for it in his Schedule E assessment. In practice the employee is normally given credit for it, but is not allowed a repayment of any excess unless he can show that he has reimbursed the tax to the employer.

2.84   A more serious consequence of a *regulation 80* determination is that it carries interest. This interest runs not from the date of the determination but from 19 April following the year of assessment to which it relates. [*Regulation 82*].

2.85   If a regulation 80 assessment is not paid within 30 days from the date on which the determination becomes final the Revenue can recover the tax from the employee if either they consider that the employee received the income knowing that the employer had wilfully failed to deduct the tax or the tax is tax on a notional payment [Regulation 81]. For 2004/05 onwards (but not for earlier years) the employee has a right of appeal against such a direction [*Regulation 81A inserted by the Income Tax (PAYE) (Amendment) Regulations 2004, SI 2004 No. 851*].

2.86   It has been held that an employer is liable to operate PAYE even if non-UK resident provided that it has 'a trading presence in the UK' (*Clark v Oceanic Contractors 56 TC 183*). In that case an overseas company was engaged, through a Belgian branch, in installing pipelines in the UK sector of the North Sea. It had a permanent establishment in the UK but paid the employees direct from Belgium in US dollars. The House of Lords held that the critical factor in implying a territorial limitation into a section establishing a method of tax collection is whether, in the circumstances, it could be made effective. As Oceanic had a permanent establishment in the UK to which a *regulation 80* determination could be issued, this was a sufficient tax presence to bring it within the scope of PAYE.

Organised arrangements for sharing tips (Troncs)

2.87   In some industries, such as hotels and catering, tips and gratuities are shared out not by the employer but by a third party, such as the head waiter. In such circumstances the employer cannot apply PAYE to the tips as he does not know what has been paid to each employee. Instead the person responsible for sharing out the money (called the troncmaster) is required to apply PAYE when making payments to individual employees. There must be 'an organised arrangement' for gratuities or service charges' to be shared (*Regulation 100*). There is no corresponding provision for National Insurance. Accordingly tips, gratuities and service charges paid to employees via a tronc escape both employer's and employees' NIC. Although it is the responsibility of the troncmaster to account for PAYE the employer must notify the Revenue of the existence of the tronc, and, if he knows it, the name of the troncmaster immediately he becomes aware that a tronc is being operated [Regulation 100(2)]. There was no such obligation prior to 6 April 2004. The Revenue have power to require the employer to operate PAYE if they believe that the troncmaster has failed to carry out his obligations (*Reg 100(5)*). They cannot make such a direction retrospectively though. If a director of an employer company acts as troncmaster it is important to document that he does so personally, not on behalf of the employer (as if the company is troncmaster the normal PAYE rules apply). That is what happened in *Figael v Fox (64 TC 441)*. The Court of Appeal said that the General Commissioners were entitled to infer that the director was acting in his capacity as director so that the company was liable for the PAYE. For NIC purposes NICO differentiate between a voluntary service charge and a mandatory one. Their view is that if the service charge is mandatory and is paid to the employer NICs are due even if the money is passed to the troncmaster for division between the staff. They also take the view that if the employer influences how the money is shared out, including if he guarantees a minimum level of tips, NIC is payable. Both of these views are questionable.

Readily convertible assets

2.88   If assessable income of an employee is paid after 3 May 1994 in the form of a tradeable asset, or after 6 April 1998 in the form of a readily convertible asset, the employer is treated as making a payment to which he must apply PAYE of the amount which, on the best estimate that can reasonably be made, is the amount of income likely to be taxable under Schedule E in respect of the provision of the asset. [*ITEPA 2003, s 696*]. This appears to apply irrespective of whether the asset is provided by the employer, an intermediary, or a third party. A readily convertible asset is:

(*a*)   any asset capable of being sold or realised on a recognised investment exchange (within the meaning of the *Financial Services Act 1986*) or the London Bullion Market;

(*b*)   any asset capable of being sold or otherwise realised on the New York Stock Exchange or on a market for the time being specified in PAYE regulations;

(*c*)   the rights of an assignee (or any other rights) in respect of a money debt that is or may become due to the employer or any other person (e.g. a trade debt which is assigned to the employee);

(*d*)   any property (or right in such property) that is subject to a 'warehousing regime';

(*e*)   an asset consisting of anything that is likely (without anything being done by the employee) to give rise to (or to become) a right enabling a person to obtain an amount of money which is likely to be similar to the expense of providing the asset;

(*f*)   an asset for which 'trading arrangements' are in existence; or

(*g*)   an asset for which trading arrangements are likely to come into existence in accordance with any arrangements of another description existing when the asset is provided (or in accordance with any understanding existing at the time).

(*h*)   from 1 January 2003 shares or securities which do not fall within the above heads must be treated as readily convertible assets unless they are shares which are corporation tax deductible (see 2.98).

[*ITEPA 2003, s 702(1)*].

2.89   A warehousing regime for this purpose means that the item is held within a Customs warehouse within *VATA 1994, s 18*, a fiscal warehouse within *VATA 1994, s 18A* or any corresponding regime in another EEA (European Economic Area) State. [*ITEPA 2003, s 702(6)*]. There are trading arrangements for an asset if any arrangement exists, the effect of which is to enable the employee, or a member of his family or household (as defined in *ICTA 1988, s 168(4)*—see 6.43), to obtain an amount of money that is (or is likely to be) similar to the expense incurred in the provision of the asset. [*ITEPA 2003, s 702(2)*].

2.90   The reference in 2.88(*e*) and 2.89 to obtaining an amount of money means enabling an amount to be obtained by any means at all, including in particular:

(*a*)   by using the asset or other property as security for a loan or advance; or

(*b*)   by using any rights comprised in or attached to the asset or other property to obtain any asset for which trading arrangements exist.

The term includes references to cases where the employee (or some other person) is enabled to obtain an amount as a member of a class or description of persons as well as where he is enabled to obtain it in his own right. [*ITEPA 2003, s 702(4)*].

2.91   An amount is similar to the expense incurred in the provision of an asset if it is equal to or exceeds such expense or is not substantially less than it. [*ITEPA 2003, s 702(5)*].

2.92   An asset for this purpose includes any property (particularly any right or interest falling within *Part 3* of the *Financial Services and Markets Act 2000 (Regulated Activities) Order 2001 (SI 2001 No 544)*), other than a non-cash voucher, credit token or cash voucher (see 6.20, 6.29 and 2.105 respectively), a payment subject to PAYE, or certain shares issued under approved share schemes. There is also power for the PAYE Regulations to lay down further exclusions. [*ITEPA 2003, s 701*]. The excluded shares are shares acquired by the employee under an approved SAYE scheme (see 16.5), an approved profit sharing scheme (see 16.35), an approved CSOP scheme (see 16.8) (provided that the option was exercised between 3 and 10 years of its grant or from 18 June 2004 was exercised in accordance with the relevant rules – see

16.11(*b*)(ii)) or on the exercise of a pre-27 November 1996 option. The shares must be ordinary share capital of a company which is the employer company, one which controls that company, or a company which is a member of a consortium which owns the employer company or a company which controls it (or which controls a member of such a consortium). Prior to 18 June 2004 the exclusion also applied to interests in or rights over shares acquired under an approved scheme. From that date the exclusion for pre-27 November 1996 options apply only where the avoidance of tax or NIC is not the main purpose (or one of the main purposes) of any arrangements under which the option was obtained or exercised. Also from that date the exclusion of such shares applies only to their acquisition. It does not apply to anything that changes their value subsequent to the acquisition. [*ITEPA 2003, s 701(2)(c),(3)–(5)* enacting the *Income Tax (Employments) (Notional Payments) Regulations 1994 (SI 1994 No 1212)* as amended by *FA 2004, s 88(9)(10)*].

Prior to 27 November 1996 the exemption was wider, covering shares acquired under a share option on the exercise of which the employee was taxable under *section 135* (see 14.109), and other shares, or rights over shares, in the employer company or its parent (or any of its 'parents' in the case of a consortium company).

2.93 Shares will of course normally be readily convertible assets only if they are quoted or trading arrangements are in place in respect of them at the time they are transferred to the employee. From 4 August 1998 the reference to shares was extended to shares whose value has been enhanced as mentioned in *ITEPA 2003, s 696,* formerly *ICTA 1988, s 203FA* (see 2.100) and the exemption also applies to *ITEPA 2003, ss 696–700*.

2.94 This provision was considered in *DTE Financial Services Ltd v Wilson [2001] STC 777; [2001] EWCA Civ 455*. The scheme adopted there is set out at 2.56. The Revenue contended that the appointment of the contingent interest to Mr McDonald constituted an arrangement, the purpose of which was to enable him to obtain an amount similar to the expense incurred in the provision of the asset within *ICTA 1988, s 203K(2)(a)* (see 2.108). Whilst Hart J thought this a possible interpretation the Court of Appeal disagreed. It felt that *ICTA 1988, s 203F* contemplates trading arrangements which are extraneous to the asset itself. It is not possible to find trading arrangements relating to an asset by analysing the incidents of the asset itself.

2.95 From 10 July 2003 an asset consisting of shares or securities which is not a readily convertible asset must be treated as one unless it is shares that are corporation tax deductible, i.e. for which the company is entitled to relief under *FA 2003, Sch 23*. A scrip or rights issue on such shares (or any other shares acquired by virtue of holding such shares) is treated as corporation tax deductible. So are shares received on a share exchange for such shares provided that it constitutes a new holding for capital gains tax purposes. [*ITEPA 2003, s 702(5A)–(5D)* inserted by *FA 2003, 22 Sch 15*].

2.96   Prior to 2 July 1997 the provision only applied to tradeable assets, which were assets within 2.88(*a*), (*b*) and (*f*) above. Between that date and 5 April 1998 it also applied to assets within 2.88(*c*) but only if the debt was a trade debt due (or which would become due) to the employer. [*ICTA 1988, s 203F*]. However, the obligation to deduct tax in respect of such para 2.88(*c*) payments made before 18 March 1998 was to deduct it only from cash salary payments made between 24 March and 5 April 1998. To the extent that the tax exceeded such payments the employee had to account for the balance on 19 April 1998 in accordance with *section 203J* (see 2.106). [*FA 1998, s 64(6)*]. Similarly, the employer did not have to account for tax on payments made between 6 April and 31 July 1998 until 19 August 1998. [*FA 1998, s 65(7)* and *Income Tax (Employments) (Notional Payments) Regulations 1994 (SI 1994 No 1212) Regulation 8A*].

2.97   This provision is designed to prevent the avoidance of PAYE— and thus the deferral of payment of the tax until it can be collected in a Schedule E assessment—by the payment of bonuses in gold bars and similar assets. Such payments became popular in the late 1980s primarily to avoid national insurance but the PAYE benefit was a useful bonus. Curiously, such devices seem to have attracted the ire of the Inland Revenue more than that of the Contributions Agency (the predecessor of the Revenue's National Insurance Contributions Office). The former regularly attacked such schemes whereas the Contributions Agency tolerated them until the loss of revenue became sufficiently serious to seek a change in the law.

2.98   From 1 January 2003 shares or securities which do not fall within 2.88(*a*)–(*g*) must nevertheless be treated as readily convertible assets unless they are shares which are corporation tax deductible. Shares are corporation tax deductible for this purpose if they are acquired by a person by reason of his (or another person's) employment with a company (or pursuant to an option so acquired) and the company is entitled to corporation tax relief in respect of the shares under *FA 2003, 23 Schedule* [*ITEPA 2003, s 702(5A)(5B)* inserted by *FA 2003, 22 Schedule 15)*]. Shares are treated as corporation tax deductible during an accounting period which begun before 1 January 2003 if they would have been corporation tax deductible had the accounting period began on or after that date. [*FA 2003, 22 Schedule 15(4)*]. If a person acquires additional shares by virtue of holding shares that are corporation tax deductible they are also treated as corporation tax deductible. [*ITEPA 2003, s 702(5C)*]. If a person ceases to be beneficially entitled to shares that are corporation tax deductible and acquires other shares that constitute a new holding within *TCGA 1992,* *ss 127–130* (company reorganisations and share exchanges) the new holding is treated as if it were corporation tax deductible. [*ITEPA 2003, s 702(5D)*].

2.99 If assessable income is provided after 5 April 1998 by enhancing the value of an asset in which the employee or a member of his family or household already has an interest and the asset as enhanced is a readily convertible asset, *section 696* is to apply as if the employee had been provided with the enhanced asset. [*ITEPA 2003, s 697(1)*]. Such deeming merely triggers the operation of the section. The amount on which PAYE is payable is the best estimate that can reasonably be made of the amount assessable in respect of the enhancement—which will, of course, normally be the cost of making the enhancement. [*ITEPA 2003, ss 696, 697(2)*].

2.100 An asset is enhanced for this purpose if either:

(*a*)   the asset, or any right or interest in it, is improved or otherwise made more valuable by the provision of any service (e.g. improvements are made to the employee's house); or

(*b*)   property is added to the asset which improves it or otherwise increases its value (e.g. an additional premium is paid to an existing insurance policy); or

(*c*)   money or other property is applied to the improvement of the asset in question, or to securing an increase in its value or in the value of any right or interest in it.

The exclusions set out at 2.92 also apply for this purpose, the exclusion, of course, being of the improved shares. [*ITEPA 2003, ss 697(3)* and *710(2)(a)*, and *regulation 3* and *3B* of the *Income Tax (Employments) (Notional Payments) Regulations 1994 (SI 1994 No 1212)*]. So does the transitional relief mentioned in 2.96 where the enhancement took place between 6 April and 31 July 1998. [*FA 1998, s 64(6)*].

2.101 The obligation to deduct PAYE under *section 696* applies also to gains from share options assessable on an employee under *ITEPA 2003, ss 473* (see 14.91), *476* and *477* (see 14.94) and *4.77* (see 14.97) and their predecessors (see 14.118, 14.190 and 14.201) (unless the trigger event (normally the exercise of the option) took place before 6 April 1998. Where the option is exercised, the employee is treated as if he were provided at that time with assessable income in the form of such shares and as if that income were being provided in respect of the employment by reason of which he was granted the option. The amount to which PAYE has to be applied is the amount on which tax is likely to be chargeable under the relevant provision. [*ITEPA 2003, s 700(4)*]. A similar obligation arises under *ITEPA 2003, ss 698, 699* (as substituted by *FA 2003, 22 Schedule 12, 13*) in relation to the tax charges on employment related securities under *ITEPA 2003, ss 426–484* (see 14.22–14.105).

2.102   If the trigger event is the assignment or release of the option (or of any other right to acquire shares), PAYE must be applied on the amount of any payment for the assignment or release or, if less, the amount assessable under *section 476*. If the consideration consists not of cash but of the provision of an asset which is either a readily convertible asset under *section 702* or a non-cash voucher, credit token or cash voucher, the employee is treated as receiving assessable income from the employment in respect of which the right was granted in the form of that asset and PAYE must be applied to the amount on which tax is likely to be chargeable under the trigger provisions. If the trigger event under *sections 426–447* PAYE is applicable as if the employee were provided with PAYE income in the form of the employment-related securities, cash received or other consideration received at the relevant date under those provisions. [*ITEPA 2003, s 699*]. Under the prior legislation if it was the shares ceasing to be wholly conditional under *section 422* (old) PAYE was applied as if the employee had been provided at that time with a further interest in the shares which was not wholly conditional. [*ITEPA 2000, s 698* (old)]. If the trigger was the conversion of shares PAYE was applied as if the original provision of the convertible shares included the ones into which they are converted (i.e. as if the converted shares were received by reason of the employment for which the employee was granted the convertible shares). The amount on which PAYE is applied is the amount likely to be chargeable by virtue of *section 140D*. If there are a series of conversions, the amount is, of course, related back to the issue of the initial holding of convertible shares. [*ITEPA 2003, s 700(4)*]. Where the employee agrees to pay the employer's NIC (see 14.49, 14.58 and 14.102) the amount on which PAYE is due is the amount after deducting that NIC. [*ITEPA 2003, s 698(2A), 700(4A) inserted by FA 1994, 16 Schedule 4*].

2.103   The exclusions for shares received under an approved share scheme described at 2.92 also applies to amounts within *section 700*. So does the transitional relief described at 2.96 where the trigger event occurred between 6 April and 31 July 1998. [*FA 1998, s 67(3)*].

Vouchers and credit tokens

2.104   PAYE must also be applied by the employer where a 'cash voucher' is received by an employee. [*ITEPA 2003, s 693(1)*]. Again it appears irrelevant whether the voucher is provided by the employer, an intermediary or a third party. PAYE does not apply to either the provision of the voucher or its use if it is used to meet expenses and the expenses would not have been taxable as earnings had they been paid direct by the employee. The *PAYE Regulations* can provide for further exclusions [*ITEPA 2003, s 693(2)–(4)*]. A cash voucher provided after 5 April 1998 is deemed to be provided to an employee for this purpose when it is appropriated to him (whether by attaching it to a card held for him or in any other way). [*ITEPA 2003, s 693(5)*].

2.105   A cash voucher is any voucher, stamp or similar document capable of being exchanged (either on its own or together with other vouchers, stamps or documents) for a sum of money equal to (or greater than, or not substantially less than) the expense incurred in providing it. It includes a voucher exchangeable only after a time and also a voucher that is capable of being exchanged either for cash or for goods or services. [*ITEPA 2003, s 75*]. The taxable amount is of course the amount for which the voucher can be exchanged. [*ITEPA 2003, s 81*]. As tax cannot physically be deducted from a voucher it must of course be deducted from the cash element of the employee's salary. [*ITEPA 2003, s 710(1)*]. Any money, goods or services obtained in exchange for the voucher is obviously not also taxable as a benefit under the basic definition of emoluments. [*ITEPA 2003, s 95*].

2.106   PAYE must also be applied by the employer when an employee receives a non-cash voucher—again, apparently, irrespective of whom he receives it from—if at the time the voucher is provided either:

(*a*)   it is capable of being exchanged for anything which, if it had been provided to the employee at the time the voucher was received, would have been a readily convertible asset for the purpose of *ITEPA 2003, s 696* (see 2.88); or

(*b*)   but for *ITEPA 2003, s 701(2)* (which excludes non-cash vouchers from being readily convertible assets), the voucher would itself have fallen to be regarded as a readily convertible asset.

There is power for vouchers to be excluded from these provisions under the *PAYE Regulations* but no such exclusions have so far been made. The voucher is deemed to have been provided to the employee at the time that it is appropriated to him (whether by attaching it to a card held by him or in some other way). [*ITEPA 2003, s 694(7)*].

2.107   Prior to 6 April 1998 the rules were different. It was the time the voucher was received by the employee or, in the case of a cheque voucher, the time it was spent by him. The scope of this provision was also more limited. It applied only if at the time the voucher was provided either:

(*a*)   it was capable of being sold or otherwise realised on an exchange or market within *section 203F(2)(a)* or *(b)*, i.e. the London Bullion Market or a recognised investment exchange, or of being exchanged for goods which could be so sold or realised; or

(*b*)   trading arrangements existed either for the voucher or for goods for which it could be exchanged. [*ICTA 1988, s 203G*].

2.108   The meaning of a non-cash voucher is dealt with at 6.19–6.27. The taxable amount is that described at 6.20. [*ICTA 1988, s 203G(1)*]. Trading arrangements were any arrangements for the purpose of enabling the person to whom the voucher was provided to obtain an amount similar to the expense incurred in the provision of the goods, if the voucher was exchangeable for goods, or in the provision of the voucher if it was not. [*ICTA 1988, s 203K(2)(a)–(c)*]. An amount was similar to the expense incurred if it was greater than, equal to, or not substantially less than, that expense. [*ICTA 1988, s 203K(3)(b)*]. An amount was enabled to be obtained if it could be obtained by any means—in particular by using the asset or goods as security for a loan. [*ICTA 1988, s 203K(3)(a)*]. From 6 April 1998, *section 203K* has been replaced by the more extensive provisions in respect of readily convertible assets outlined above (see 2.88).

2.109   *Section 203K* appears to have been ineffective where the voucher was exchangeable for goods as the person providing them would not normally be providing the voucher and, as he would wish to make a profit, his expense incurred in the provision of the goods would normally be less than the face value of the voucher. As the Government of the day refused, by the use of a guillotine motion, to allow any parliamentary debate in standing committee on these PAYE clauses, they can hardly complain if people exploit their deficiencies. Another obvious problem is that the rules did not apply at all to vouchers exchangeable for services.

2.110   The employer must also be treated as making a payment subject to PAYE on each occasion on which an employee uses a credit token provided to him (by anyone) by reason of his employment. [*ITEPA 2003, s 695*]. This is something which would fall to be regarded as a readily convertible asset within *section 702*. Prior to 6 April 1998 PAYE fell to be applied only if the credit token was used to obtain money or goods which were capable of being sold or otherwise realised on an exchange or market falling within *section 203F(2)(a)* or *(b)*, or goods for which trading arrangements existed. [*ICTA 1988, s 203H*]. The meaning of a credit token and the ascertainment of the assessable amount are considered at 6.28–6.33. It is not clear how an employer is expected to know that the credit token has been exchanged, particularly where it is provided by a third party. PAYE need not be deducted from a credit token which is used to obtain money to defray expenses and would not have been taxable as earnings if the money had been paid direct to the employee and he had incurred the expense. The *PAYE Regulations* can provide for further exclusions [*ITEPA 2003, s 695(2)(3)*].

The mechanics of the deduction

2.111   Where PAYE is payable by virtue of any of paragraphs 2.59–2.63 or 2.88–2.103 above, the obligation to deduct PAYE arises at such time as may be prescribed by the *PAYE Regulations* and is an obligation to deduct it from any payment or payments that the employer actually makes of 'PAYE income' of that employee. [*ITEPA 2003, s 710(1)(2)*]. It is not possible to make a real deduction from notional income. It is obviously intended to mean other income assessable under Schedule E which is paid in cash. The Revenue are empowered to prescribe the time at which this deduction is to be made. [*ITEPA 2003, s 710(5)*]. They have prescribed the occasion of any salary payment made in the same income tax month as the notional payment and falling on or after the time of that payment. If the employer accounts quarterly for PAYE it is any salary payment in the same quarters. [*Regulation 62*]. It will be apparent that in many, if not most, cases, salary payments in that period will be insufficient to enable the deduction to be made. Accordingly, the Revenue have turned these rules into an '*in terrorem*' provision, i.e. they are not to collect tax but to dissuade employers from making such payments.

2.112   If because of an insufficiency of salary payments in the same tax month the employer is unable to deduct the full amount of tax on the notional payment, he must nevertheless account to the Revenue for the PAYE on it 14 days after the end of the month in the normal way. [*ITEPA 2003, s 710(3)(4)*].

2.113   If the employee does not reimburse such tax within 90 days from the date on which the notional payment was deemed to be made (30 days for payments made before 9 April 2003), the tax is itself deemed to be emoluments of the employment (which arise on the date of the notional payment) assessable on him under Schedule E. [*ITEPA 2003, s 222*]. Prior to 2002/03 the amount was deemed to be income of the employee. The reason for the change to deem it emoluments is apparently to ensure that the amount is brought into account to determine whether the employee is in higher paid employment (see 6.4). It also appears to subject the amount to National Insurance. It should be noted that the 30-day period runs from the date of the notional payment and, as the tax is payable 14 days after the end of the tax month in which that payment is deemed to have been made, the right of recovery will often have expired before the tax is paid over to the Revenue and the right to reimbursement arises. In such circumstances the right to reimbursement is illusory; the notional payment needs to be grossed up for Schedule E purposes although not for PAYE; the tax on the PAYE does not itself appear to be collectible under the PAYE system! It is not clear what can amount to reimbursement—'make good' is actually the statutory wording. An agreement by the employee that the tax should be debited to an account of his with the employer on which there is a credit balance is almost certainly making good; but debiting to an already overdrawn account, or the employer making a loan to the employee to satisfy the obligation, may well not be.

2.114   This question was in issue before the Special Commissioners in *Ferguson v IRC [2001] STC (SCD) 1*. The taxpayers were awarded a bonus in the form of rhodium metal. This was sold on 26 September 1995 and the proceeds credited to the company's bank account and posted to the directors' current accounts. Mr Ferguson had been erroneously advised that the tax was payable on 16 April 1996 (instead of 19 October 1995). The Revenue contended that Mr Ferguson had not made the requisite payment to the company that he was required to make before 25 October 1995. The Special Commissioner had no hesitation in finding that he had done so. While, in theory, he could have withdrawn the tax money erroneously credited to the current account it was clear from the evidence that this would and could not have happened.

2.115   Where a notional payment takes the form of a non-cash voucher which is a cheque voucher the payment is treated as made when the cheque is handed over in exchange for money, goods or services – or the time it is posted if sent by post. In the case of any other non-cash voucher it is the later of the time when the chargeable expense is incurred or the voucher is received by the employee. [*ITEPA 2003, s 694(5)(6)*].

Definitions

2.116   For the purpose of applying *ITEPA 2003, ss 687–692* to events after 6 April 1998 an 'employee' means a person who holds or has held an office or employment under or with another person and 'employer' means a person under or with whom that employee holds or has held the office or employment. In relation to any assessable income of an employee, his employer means the person who is the employer in relation to the office or employment in respect of which that income is provided or by reference to which it falls to be regarded as assessable. [*ITEPA 2003, s 712(1)*].

2.117   If the remuneration receivable by an individual is treated as emoluments under the agency rules in *section 44* (see 19.1), *ITEPA 2003, ss 687–692* (but not *691*), *ss 693–702* and *s 710* apply as if that individual held an employment with the agency. However, if in such a case a payment of (or on account of) assessable income of that individual is made by a person acting on behalf of the client (and at the expense of the client or a person connected with him), *ITEPA 2003, ss 687* and *710* apply in relation to that payment as if the client, not the agency, were the employer for the purposes of those provisions. [*ITEPA 2003, s 688(1)(2)*]. The transitional rules set out at 2.96 applied also for this purpose. [*FA 1998, s 69(6)*].

Pensions

2.118   PAYE is also applicable to certain pensions. It has always applied to pensions paid direct by the employer. Where, however, the pension was paid by an insurance company or other pension provider it was previously generally treated as an annuity and tax deducted at the basic rate only. The insurance company must apply PAYE to such pensions paid under a company pension scheme. [*ITEPA 2003, s 683(3)*, formerly *ICTA 1988, s 597(3)*]. The same applies to pensions paid under personal pension schemes (but not retirement annuities); apparently irrespective of whether the recipient was formerly an employee or self-employed. [*ITEPA 2003, s 683(3)*].

Collection from the employee

2.119   As indicated in 2.78 above it was held in *IRC v Herd* [*1993*] *STC 436* that where an item is within the scope of PAYE the Revenue's recourse is normally only against the employer. There is no right of recovery from the employee unless either he was aware that tax had not been deducted or the Collector absolves the employer from liability.

2.120 Tax on items such as benefits in kind, any taxable element of expenses that are outside the PAYE scheme, and deemed employment income under the share incentive rules, etc. is collectable from the employee either under the self-assessment procedure or by direct collection.

2.121 The due date of payment for tax on directly collected earnings is 14 days after the date on which the Collector first makes an application for payment of the tax. [*Regulation 147*]. Interest on overdue tax runs from that date irrespective of whether an appeal is made. [*TMA 1970, s 86(1)(3)*].

2.122 Where an assessment relates to income which has been taken into account for PAYE and was received at least twelve months before the start of the year of assessment in which it was made, it must be made in accordance with the practice generally prevailing at the end of the year following the year of assessment to which it relates if it is raised after that time. [*ITEPA 2003, s 709*]. The meaning of this provision was considered by the Court of Appeal in *Walters v Tickner* [*1993*] *STC 624*. In that case an assessment for 1983/84 was made on 22 August 1988, more than twelve months after 1983/84. The taxpayer contended that *section 206* merely required the Revenue to raise the assessment in accordance with the generally prevailing practice and did not affect the taxpayer's right of appeal.

2.123 Nolan LJ was reluctant to hold that the taxpayer's right to challenge a generally prevailing practice should depend on whether or not the Revenue chose to make the assessment within twelve months rather than whether the taxpayer asked them to do so. Finding the wording to be 'ambiguous and obscure' he resorted to the *Pepper v Hart* [*1992*] *STC 898* principle and referred to the *1991 Hansard* where he found 'If a taxpayer has been formally assessed and the assessment is regarded as settled, he cannot reopen the assessment. If however he has not been assessed, he can, at any time within five years, demand an assessment. Therefore, there is liable to be the anomalous position . . . in which there is a change in practice which follows from a decision of one of the superior Courts. The taxpayer who has not been formally assessed can then demand an assessment . . . while somebody else in an exactly comparable position will be precluded if he has been formally assessed to tax. *Subsection (1)* removes that anomaly and ensures that the rule of practice shall be that which obtained at the expiration of the period of twelve months immediately following the year of assessment.'

2.124 This inclined him towards the Revenue's interpretation but as the case dealt with scholarship income he was able to hold that the specific exemption for such income overrode *ICTA 1988, s 206* so he did not have to decide what *section 206* means. He added a plea to Parliament to amend the wording.

2.125   The Revenue do not need to issue a Schedule E assessment for a tax year if the tax deducted in accordance with the PAYE tables is the same as it would have been if all the relevant circumstances had been known to all parties throughout the year, i.e. a formal assessment is not necessary if the correct amount of tax has been deducted under PAYE. In practice they do not normally issue an assessment if the tax deducted is correct to within about £30. The taxpayer can, however, ask to be issued with a tax return—which will trigger the normal self-assessment procedures. The time limit for such a request is five years after 31 October following the year of assessment. [*ITEPA 2003, s 711*].

Chapter 3

The Meaning of 'Earnings'

Money and money's worth

3.1   Prior to 2003/04 there was no exhaustive statutory definition of emoluments, although the word was expressed to include all salaries, fees, wages, perquisites and profits whatsoever. [*ICTA 1988, s 13(1)*]. For 2003/04 onwards there is a definition of earnings from an employment. This means any salary, wages or fee, any gratuity or other profit or incidental benefit of any kind obtained by the employee if it is money or money's worth, and anything else that constitutes an emolument of the employment. [*ITEPA 2003, s 62(2)*]. Unfortunately, this reverts to the use of the word 'emolument' as a sweep-up term and, like its predecessor, does not attempt to define it. Indeed, it does not use the word anywhere else in the Act, having chosen to replace it by general earnings – a term which it then defines by reference to *section 62(2)*! It is, however, clear that not every benefit received by an employee falls within the scope of earnings. In *Tennant v Smith 3 TC 158* Lord Halsbury states 'Your Lordships are to ascertain not whether Mr Tennant has got advantages which enable him to spend more of his income than if he did not possess them, but whether he has got that which any words in the Statute point out as the subject on which it imposes taxation.' He went on to say 'I came to the conclusion that the Act refers to money payments made to the person who receives them, though, of course, I do not deny that if substantial things of money value were capable of being turned into money they might for that purpose represent money's worth and be therefore taxable.'

3.2   Lord Halsbury was influenced to some extent by the fact that the wording of the legislation in 1890 when this case was heard provided that tax should be charged under Schedule E on all 'salaries, fees, wages, perquisites or profits' and perquisites was defined as 'fees or other emoluments' payable either by the Crown or the subject. The word 'payable' does not appear in the current legislation. Nevertheless the concept that what is taxable is money or money's worth, and not anything else, is so well established that it is unlikely to be challenged. This is in any event a relatively unimportant limitation as most benefits in kind are now specifically brought within the tax net and the taxpayer is normally indifferent as to whether he is taxed on them because they are emoluments or because they are benefits.

Employer discharging liability

3.3 In *Hartland v Diggines 10 TC 247* Mr Hartland was paid a bonus, and in addition his employer paid to the Revenue the tax thereon. Mr Hartland contended—it is not wholly clear why—that only the net sum was income of his; the tax was a voluntary payment by his employer which was nothing to do with him. Lord Pollock analysed the position as follows. 'Mr Hartland is responsible to the Revenue to pay the tax in respect of his emoluments and salary and perquisites which he receives; and in effect . . . he has received a certain amount of money into his hands, and he has received an indemnity against any liability to pay any part of it to the Revenue. In effect, there-fore, what he has received is the money paid into his hands, plus that immunity; and . . . one has to look at the substance of the matter . . . The substance of the matter is that the salary paid to Mr Hartland is not all he has received. He has received money's worth to the extent of the sum which has been paid in respect of that salary to the Revenue.'

3.4 Although this was a case heard in 1924, long before the intro-duction of PAYE, the concept that relieving a person of a liability is an emolument was reaffirmed in *Richardson v Worrall 58 TC 642*. That case was concerned with purchases through credit cards. Mr Worrall paid for petrol with a credit card in his employer's name. He contended that this was an expense incurred by his employer and as such was cov-ered by the round sum car use benefit (see 7.2 below—the fuel benefit (see 7.46 below) did not exist at the time). It was held that at the moment he put petrol into his car he had incurred a liability to pay for the petrol. As he had not specifically told the garage attendant that he was filling up the car on behalf of his employer before taking the petrol, this liability was a personal liability (even if he was acting as agent for an undisclosed principal he incurred a joint personal liability). Accordingly, when he paid for the petrol with the company credit card the company was discharging a pre-existing liability of Mr Worrall and the payment was taxable on him as emoluments—so that the benefits in kind provisions, which Mr Worrall was challenging, were not relevant to the taxability.

3.5 In *Perrons v Spackman 55 TC 403* it was held that a mileage allowance paid to an employee when he used his own car on his employer's business was part of his emoluments. The taxpayer claimed that it was a reimbursement of travelling expenses, not an emolument. Not surprisingly this contention was dismissed as it was a cash payment clearly arising from the employment. The real issue was whether an equivalent sum was deductible under what is now *section 336* (see 5.2 below) as an expense. The taxpayer had based his claim on the House of Lords judgment in *Pook v Owen 45 TC 571* but Vinelott J felt that that case had proceeded on the basis that the car allowance in *Pook v Owen* was a reimbursement of actual expenses. In Mr Perrons' case there was no evidence that the mileage allowance was a mere reimbursement of expenses actually incurred by Mr Perrons in making journeys in the course of his duties. It included a significant contribution to the overhead costs of putting his car on the road and maintaining it for his own private use as well as for business use. Accordingly the allowance had to be treated as emoluments with Mr Perrons then making a claim for a deduction against it under *section 336*. Unfortunately, the claim failed because the whole expense of maintaining the car could not be said to be an expense that he was necessarily obliged to incur as part of the expense of travelling in the performance of his duties.

3.6 The breadth of the word 'emoluments' is well illustrated by *Weight v Salmon 19 TC 174*. The managing director of a listed company was entitled to a fixed salary but in addition each year the board of directors by resolution gave him the privilege of applying at par for a specified number of shares in the company. The shares acquired were worth substantially more than par and the Revenue assessed him on the difference between the two figures. The House of Lords had no difficulty in holding that the advantage of being able to acquire the shares at an undervalue came within 'or profits whatsoever'.

3.7 Money does not have to come from the employer for it to be taxable. In *Hunter v Dewhurst 16 TC 605*, which was concerned with compensation for loss of office, Lord Atkin stated that the question was whether the payment was received 'from' the office. He thought that the wording 'appears to me to indicate emoluments either received from the employer or from some third party (such as tips, permitted commission and the like) as a reward for services rendered in the course of the employment'. In the light of this it is not surprising that in *Calvert v Wainwright 27 TC 475* it was held that tips received by an employed taxi driver formed part of his emoluments. Indeed, as early as 1878 it was held that a pecuniary gift received at Christmas by a clergyman from his congregation as a token of their regard for him, although voluntarily paid, accrued to him by reason of his holding his office under the Church of Scotland and in respect of the discharge of his duties of that office. It was accordingly an emolument (*In Re Strong, 1 TC 207*). In *Herbert v McQuade 4 TC 489* and *Cooper v Blakiston 5 TC 347* payments to clergymen by third parties were again held to be part of their emoluments.

3.8 There is no reason why a non-cash reward from a third party should be excluded provided of course that it is capable of conversion into money (so that it is money's worth) and is paid as a result of the individual holding the employment. The amount of the emoluments in such a case is of course the price that could be obtained from a disposal of the item or right in accordance with *Wilkins v Rogerson 39 TC 344* (see 6.68). By concession the Revenue do not, however, tax gifts from a third party if that gift consists of goods (or a voucher or token only capable of being used to obtain goods), the donor is not connected with the employer, the gift is not made in recognition of the performance of particular services in the course of the employment (or in anticipation of such services), it has not been directly or indirectly procured by the employer, and the total cost of all gifts made by the donor to the employee in the tax year does not exceed

£150 (£100 before 1995/96) *(ESC A70)*. There is also a statutory exclusion from the benefit in kind·rules for the higher paid (see 6.36) for the provision of entertaining (including hospitality of any kind) provided for staff of others provided it is not in recognition of particular services and not procured directly or indirectly by their employer. [*ITEPA 2003, s 265*]. This is intended to cover such things as invitations to social events, football matches, etc.

3.9   More recently the meaning of emoluments fell to be considered by the Special Commissioners in *Sports Club plc v Inspector of Taxes* [*2000*] *STC (SCD) 443*. Evelyn and Jocelyn, two international footballers, each entered into service agreements with Sports Club plc. They also entered into promotional agreements with companies unconnected with Sports Club plc. Sports Club plc then made substantial advance payments to the promotional companies for the right to exploit the 'image rights', (ie the right to exploit and use the player's name, image, signature and voice) of Evelyn and Jocelyn respectively. Sports Club plc also entered into a further agreement with Evelyn's company (owned by his manager) under which that company would provide consultancy advice to Sports Club plc. The Revenue contended that the payments for the image rights and the consultancy advice were in reality additional remuneration of Evelyn and Jocelyn. The Special Commissioners asked themselves four questions: Did the promotional agreements have independent value? Did the consultancy agreement have an independent value? Were the promotional agreements a smokescreen for additional remuneration? And were the payments under the agreement emoluments 'from' the employment? They answered the first two in the affirmative based on the evidence. They also held that on the facts the promotional and consultancy agreements were not a smokescreen but gave the Club valuable rights that they intended to exploit (albeit that for various reasons they had not in fact derived significant income from them). It was a short step from that to find that the payments under those agreements were made in return for promotional rights and consultancy services respectively, and not in reference to the playing of football which was the service rendered by the players under their service agreement. Accordingly, the payments were not emoluments from the employments of Evelyn or Jocelyn.

3.10   When this decision was first published some people felt that it created a significant tax avoidance opportunity. This is probably not the case. Many sportspeople and entertainers have the ability to generate 'merchandising' income in addition to their performance income. Image rights are simply a form of merchandising. Many sportsmen have substantial promotional contracts with commercial companies such as Nike or Adidas to exploit specific image rights. Indeed, Jocelyn already had contracts with Mizuna (a clothing manufacture) and McDonald's for exploitation of his image when the image rights contract with Sports Club plc was entered into. The Revenue have never sought to treat such contracts as derived from the player's performance. It is hard to see why the Revenue thought that it should make any difference that in the case of Evelyn and Jocelyn the promotional contracts were with the Club rather than with a third party.

Furthermore, it is hard to see on what basis they hoped to recharacterise payments to a third party as emoluments of the players.

3.11   The Revenue put forward an alternative contention that the payments were benefits in kind. The Commissioners accepted that the words 'by reason of the employment' in *ITEPA 2003, s 70* (see 6.41) are wider than the definition of employment income in *ITEPA 2003, s 7* (formerly 'emoluments from the employment' in *ICTA 1988, s 19*). However, they had already held that the payments under the agreements were not made 'by reason of the employment' of Evelyn or Jocelyn; they were paid by reason of the separate commercial contracts to provide promotional and consultancy services. They also felt that the expression 'benefit' in *ITEPA 2003, s 201* 'must exclude anything provided in return for good consideration under a separate commercial contract'. Finally, they did not see how they could lift the corporate veil and consider the ultimate destination of the payments to the companies—and even if they could do so the ultimate destination of the consultancy payments was not Evelyn but his manager.

Payment or present?

3.12   The deciding principle is whether the payment is a voluntary payment for services or a mere present. In *Calvert v Wainwright*, Atkinson J gave the illustration of a person who takes the same taxi every day and, in addition to the ordinary tip he gives, says to the driver at Christmas 'you have been very attentive to me, here is a £10 note'. That £10 would be a present and not assessable 'because it had been given to the man because of his qualities, his faithfulness, and the way he has stuck to the passenger', whereas a tip given in the ordinary way is given as remuneration for services rendered.

3.13   This distinction between a reward for services and a personal testimonial was developed in the Court of Appeal in *Bridges v Bearsley 37 TC 289*. Mr Bearsley was the managing director of a company that he had greatly helped to build. The founder of the company, Frank Hornby, owned the major part of the company. Mr Bearsley and two other directors had from time to time pressed him to allow them to have fairly substantial holdings of shares in the company. From time to time Frank Hornby had transferred to them small numbers of shares. Mr Hornby had promised to 'look after' Mr Bearsley but did not make any significant transfer of shares to him. Mr Bearsley had gained the impression that Mr Hornby would leave him a reasonable number of shares in his will. Unfortunately he did not do so. Mr Bearsley and his fellow directors decided to approach Mr Hornby's sons to express their unhappiness. Mr Donald Hornby thought that his father had been remiss in not leaving them shares in his will. He agreed with the three directors that they ought to have a further 20,000 shares between them. These shares could, however, only come out of his father's estate after the death of his mother, the life tenant. In these circumstances the three directors felt they ought to have a written agreement to this effect. In the mistaken belief that a deed needed consideration the solicitor expressed the gift of shares to be 'in consideration of the Covenantee continuing his present engagement with Meccano Limited until the expiry of four years from the date hereof'. In spite of this the Court of Appeal held that the value of the shares transferred was a personal testimonial, not an emolument of Mr Bearsley's office as a director. Schedule E charges tax 'in respect of any office or employment on emoluments therefrom'. 'The word "therefrom" must be construed in its context . . . The reference is to what is received by the holder of an office or employment in that capacity: to the holder of the office or employment as such' (Morris LJ). Mr Bearsley would not have received the shares but for what he had done in the past, i.e. all the years before 1945 when the deed was entered into and the four years after 1945. 'In one sense he received the shares by reason of his office. Had he not held the office he would not have had them. But that merely shows that he would not have had the shares, either as remuneration or as a gift, if he had not given many years' service to the company . . . the Hornby brothers made it a condition of their promise that Mr Bearsley would go on serving the company for four years. They did not exact from him a promise that he would continue to serve the company . . . the Hornby brothers in effect said "Because of your good work in the past we will at some uncertain future date transfer to you some shares that will come to us provided that you go on serving the company for four years". It does not seem to me that the promise they made has the attributes of remuneration or that it lacks the features of a personal gift.'

3.14   The vital distinction as to whether a payment is made by virtue of the employment, and is thus an emolument of it, or by virtue of something extraneous to the employment, and thus is not an emolument, was considered by the House of Lords in *Hochstrasser v Mayes 38 TC 673*. Mr Mayes was an employee of Imperial Chemical Industries Ltd (ICI). ICI operated a housing agreement under which if an employee was transferred to another part of the country, ICI would either buy his existing house at cost or make good to the employee any loss on sale. Mr Mayes sold his house at a loss of £350 which ICI paid to him. The amount payable to an employee under the housing agreement was completely independent of his salary. The agreement was to facilitate ICI transferring staff between its different sites. Lord Cohen cited with approval the remarks of Morris LJ in *Bridges v Bearsley* with the proviso that 'I am prepared to accept that statement of the law, but it is, I think, clear from the final conclusion of Morris LJ . . . that it is not enough for the Crown to establish that the employee would not have received the sum on which tax is claimed had he not been an employee. The Court must be satisfied that the service agreement was the *causa causans* and not merely the *causa sine qua non* of the receipt of the profit'. Viscount Simmonds made the same point but added a word of warning: 'If in such cases as these the issue turns, as I think it does, upon whether the fact of employment is the *causa causans* or only the *sine qua non* of the benefit, which perhaps is only to give the natural meaning to the word "therefrom" in the statute, it must often be difficult to draw the line and say on which side of it a particular case falls . . . It is for the Crown, seeking to tax the subject, to prove that the tax is exigible, not for the subject to prove that his case falls within exceptions which are not expressed in the Statute but arbitrarily inferred from it'. The distinction between the expressions *causa causans*, the reason for the payment, and *causa sine qua non*, the event without which the payment would not have come about, was brought out clearly by Jenkins LJ in the High Court: 'I think it may well be said here that, while the employee's employment with ICI was a *causa sine qua non* of his entering into the housing agreement . . . the *causa causans* was the distinct contractual relationship subsisting between ICI and the employee under the housing agreement'. In other words, the employment merely enabled Mr Mayes to enter into the housing agreement. The payment of £350 arose because he had entered into that agreement. Lord Denning 'tried by the touchstone of common sense—which is perhaps rather a rash test to take in a revenue matter', unlike his colleagues, regarded the case as plain: 'No one coming fresh to it, untrammelled by cases, could regard this £350 as a profit from the employment . . . It was not a remuneration or reward or return for his services in any sense of the word'.

3.15 The distinction drawn in *Hochstrasser v Mayes* has been blurred somewhat by the Court of Appeal decision in *Hamblett v Godfrey 59 TC 694*. Miss Hamblett was a civil servant employed at GCHQ, Cheltenham. The Government decided that for security reasons, it was necessary to restrict the staff's right to have recourse to industrial tribunals or to be a member of a trade union. They paid Miss Hamblett an ex gratia sum of £1,000 in recognition of her agreeing to give up such rights. She, not unnaturally, contended that whilst her employment was the *causa sine qua non* of her entering into the agreement with the Government the *causa causans* of the payment of £1,000 was her giving up her statutory rights under that agreement. In a unanimous decision the Court of Appeal dismissed this approach. 'The rights, the loss of which was being recognised were rights under the employment protection legislation and the right to join a union . . . Both those rights . . . are directly connected with the facts of the taxpayer's employment. If the employment did not exist, there would be no need for the rights in the particular context in which the taxpayer found herself.' (Purchas LJ). Accordingly, as the rights were not severable from the employment it followed in the judge's view that the £1,000 arose from the employment and was thus part of the emoluments of the employment. Quoting both Lord Radcliffe, 'it is assessable if it has been paid to him in return for acting as or being an employee', and Viscount Simmonds, 'the test of taxability is whether from the standpoint of the person who receives it the profit accrues to him by virtue of his office', in *Hochstrasser v Mayes*, Neill LJ thought the cases 'demonstrate to my mind that emoluments from employment are not restricted to payments made in return for the performance of services'. The facts in the *Hamblett* case pointed to the conclusion that 'the source of the payment was the employment. It was paid because of the employment and because of the conditions of employment and for no other reason'.

3.16   Accordingly, the current state of the law is that whilst the principle formulated in *Hochstrasser v Mayes* still holds good if the payment can be shown to be not directly related to the employment, if it arises directly from the employment it will be emoluments. Mr Mayes' £350 arose from the decision of ICI to move him to a different job. It is difficult to know in what circumstances the *Hochstrasser* principle still applies. *Hochstrasser* was a House of Lords decision whereas *Hamblett* stopped at the Court of Appeal, so the *Hamblett* case cannot have overruled the *Hochstrasser* principle entirely.

3.17   Indeed, *Wilcock v Eve* [*1995*] *STC 18*, emphasises that the *Hochstrasser v Mayes* principle still lives. Mr Eve was a director of a company, LBUA, which was a wholly owned subsidiary of Hill Samuel Group plc. In May 1986 there was a management buyout of LBUA. As a result Mr Eve was unable to exercise his rights under the Hill Samuel approved share option scheme. In April 1987 Hill Samuel became concerned about its reputation for fairness and decided to make ex-gratia payment to people in Mr Eve's position to compensate them for the loss of the option rights. The first Mr Eve knew of this was when Hill Samuel sent him a cheque for £10,000 in September 1987. It was held that although Mr Eve remained an employee of LBUA, the payment by Hill Samuel did not derive from that employment and was not an emolument from it. It was also held not to be a benefit within *ICTA 1988, s 154* (now *ITEPA 2003, s 201*). The payment was not 'by reason' of Mr Eve's employment with LBUA.

3.18   Mr McBride was not so lucky. He was a Lloyds name and following the substantial losses suffered in the early 1990s became involved in the committees of two action groups. Following the settlement these action groups decided to make ex gratia payments to various members of their committees, including Mr McBride, to recognise the substantial amount of work they had done on behalf of the action group. The constitution of both groups provided that members of the committee were not entitled to any remuneration. The Special Commissioners held that the payments were emoluments of an office (*McBride v Blackburn,* [*2003*] *STC (SCD) 139*).

3.19   Another interesting case on whether income is received by virtue of the employment is *O'Leary v McKinlay* [*1991*] *STC 42*. David O'Leary was resident in England and domiciled in Ireland. His employer, Arsenal FC Ltd, entered into an arrangement designed to pay him an additional £28,985 per annum. To achieve this a third party set up a Jersey trust with a nominal £10. Arsenal lent the trustees £266,000 interest-free and repayable on demand. The trustees invested this to produce £28,985. This money was paid to O'Leary but not remitted by him to the UK. He contended that this income was income from a foreign possession taxable under Case V of Schedule D on a remittance basis. It was held, however, that it was an emolument of his employment and thus assessable under Schedule E on an arising basis. The test posed by Vinelott J was 'how would an ordinary member of the public have perceived the money?'. He would have said without hesitation that it was an emolument of the taxpayer's employment by Arsenal. The judge was very much influenced by the fact that there was an overall scheme. If an employer lent money to an employee interest-free and the employee was free to exploit the money in any manner he chose, his employment could not be said to be the source of the income it generated. However, in O'Leary's case he never had the free use of the £266,000. The purpose of the arrangement was to provide him with the income of £28,985. The trustees could not have invested it in any other manner without O'Leary's consent (and undoubtedly Arsenal's too).

3.20   Although the actual decision has in most cases been superseded by legislation *Abbott v Philbin 39 TC 82* sheds an interesting light on what is meant by money's worth, following on from *Tennant v Smith 3 TC 158*, in which it was held that a non-cash benefit can be emoluments only if it is capable of being turned into money. In 1954 Mr Abbott was granted an option to acquire shares at the market price on the date the option was offered. The option was non-assignable. It was exercised in 1956. The Revenue claimed that the option was not money's worth, but on its exercise in 1956 the acquisition of the shares would be. The taxpayer contended that the option was money's worth but that having paid tax on the value in 1954 the difference between the price paid for the shares in 1956 and their value at that time was not taxable. It was common ground that if the tax charge arose on the grant of the option a further charge could not arise at a later date. It was held that the option was money's worth and its value assessable in 1954. The fact that it was non-assignable affected the value but did not mean that it could not be turned to pecuniary account. Indeed, Viscount Simmonds thought that 'if it had no ascertainable value then it was a perquisite of no value'. Lord Denning, whilst agreeing that the charge arose on the grant of the option, added that if no payment had been made for the option, he would have arrived at a different conclusion. The option would then have been unenforceable at law and the taxpayer would only have an expectation, which he could not turn into account, rather than a right, which he could. This demonstrates the importance of getting the documentation right!

3.21   The Revenue also consider that if an employee acquires an asset from an employer at a price exceeding its market value that excess constitutes emoluments (*IR Press Release 27 April 1994*).

3.22   The Revenue's Statement of Practice on commissions, etc. (*SP 4/97*) states that it is a question of fact whether something is received in the capacity of employee/office-holder or in some other capacity such as the purchaser of an insurance policy, goods or services. It goes on to express the view that if an employee is entitled to commission in respect of goods or services sold to third parties he is assessable on the full amount of that commission even if it is passed to the customer or, indeed, paid direct to the customer. In such circumstances he may be able to claim a deduction for the payment to the customer if he can show that he is 'obliged' to make the payment wholly, exclusively and necessarily in performing the duties of his employment, e.g. it is a contractual term of the sale to the customer. If the purchaser pays a discounted price there is no income tax liability on the employee unless the purchaser is a member of his family or household of the employee or a member of his household receives something (money or benefits) in consequence of the discounted payment. If the purchaser is a member of the employee's family there is unlikely to be an income tax charge if the price paid covers the cost to the employer of providing the goods or services. Where a commission or discount is available to an employee on the same basis as it is available to the general public, it will not arise from the employment. Subject to that a commission on the employee's own purchase constitutes taxable emoluments. Even if his contractual right is not to a commission but to make a reduced payment the Revenue consider that the reduction is an emolument of the employment if it derives from the employer, although not necessarily if it derives from a third party.

Statutory payments

3.23   An interesting area is statutory payments. In *Mairs v Haughey [1993] STC 569* (see 11.59) the House of Lords held that in law a redundancy payment is not an emolument. The redundancy legislation reflects an appreciation that an employee has a stake in his/her employment which justifies them receiving compensation if they lose that stake. It is not a payment from being or becoming an employee. In *Hamblett v Godfrey 59 TC 694* (see 3.15) in contrast, a payment to restrict an employee's right to have recourse to industrial tribunals or to be a member of a trade union, was held by the Court of Appeal to be taxable as the source of the payment was the employment. *Mintec Ltd v CIR [2001] STC (SCD) 101* was concerned with compensation in respect of the employer's failure to comply with its statutory duty to consult with employee representatives regarding proposed redundancies. By agreement with the trade unions it agreed to pay all affected employees 'a payment of £2,500 in recognition of any entitlement under the consultation process including pay in lieu of notice, etc'. In a very brief decision the Special Commissioner (Stephen Oliver QC) held that the payments were not taxable under *section 19*. The *Trade Union and Labour Relations (Consolidation) Act 1992* provides for protective awards to employees. Had such awards been made they would not have been emoluments as the source of the awards would have been the 1992 Act. Following *Mairs v Haughey* as a payment in lieu of such an award, the £2,500 should not be treated in any different way from the protective award itself. A word of warning. It is difficult to square this decision with the dicta in *Drummond v Austin Brown 58 TC 67*, a capital gains tax case, which differentiated the receipt of compensation from a payment to head off the litigation which would give rise to that compensation.

Apprenticeship schemes at universities and technical colleges

3.24   Payments made by employers to employees for periods at attendance on a full-time educational course, including a 'sandwich' course, are regarded as covered by the general exemption for scholarship income under *ICTA 1988, s 331* provided the following conditions are met:

(*a*)   the employee is enrolled at a university, technical college or similar external establishment for at least one academic year;

(*b*)   he actually attends that establishment for an aggregate period of at least 20 weeks a year; and

(*c*)   the rate of payment (including lodging, subsistence and travel expenses, but excluding any course fees paid by the employee) does not exceed £7,000 p.a. (£5,500 prior to 6 April 1992) (*SP 4/86* as amended by *IR Press Release 1 November 1992*).

If the payments exceed £7,000 p.a. the whole amount, not merely the excess, is taxable. If it can be shown that a public grant awarding body, such as a research council, would have paid a higher grant to an individual in similar personal circumstances the exemption is increased to that higher amount. The relief does not apply to payments to the employee for periods actually spent working for the employer—whether during vacations or term time. Nor does it apply to education at an employer's own training centre or one run by an employer's association.

Chapter 4

Employed or Self-employed

4.1   Tax is charged on employment income in relation to offices and employments. Neither of these terms is defined for tax purposes, although an office is expressed to include in particular any position which has an existence independent of the person who holds it and may be filled by successive holders. [*ITEPA 2003, s 5*]. A good dictionary definition of an office is 'the task or service attaching to a particular post or station'. An office generally continues its existence independent of the persons who from time to time occupy it.

Meaning of 'office'

4.2   The best legal definition is attributed to Rowlatt J in 1920 in *Great Western Rly Co v Bater 8 TC 231*: 'what those who use the language of the *Act* of 1842 meant . . . was an office or employment which was a subsisting, permanent, substantive position, which had an existence independent from the person who filled it, which went on and was filled in succession by successive holders' (*8 TC* at p. 235). In fact this definition was put forward by Counsel and although Rowlatt approved it he felt constrained by earlier authorities not to decide that that was the meaning of the word. This definition was however endorsed by Lord Atkinson when the case reached the House of Lords. It has also been endorsed in subsequent cases, in particular by Lord Atkin in *McMillan v Guest 24 TC 190* where it was held that a director of a company holds an office.

Public office

4.3   The *Great Western Rly* case was actually concerned with the interpretation of the phrase 'public offices and employments of profit' and, whilst Rowlatt J treated this as a single phrase, Lord Atkinson thought that it embraced two distinct things, public offices and public employments. At the time only income from public offices and employments was assessed under Schedule E (the old rule for taxing employment income). Income from other employments was assessed under Schedule D. Furthermore, the assessment was on an annual basis, the person assessed having a right of recovery against his predecessor in the office. In the case of a railway company the assessment was on the company, leaving it to recover the tax from the office-holder from time to time. Accordingly the concept of permanence was perhaps implicit in the legislation of the time rather than in the natural meaning of the word 'office'.

Obscurity of legislation

4.4   The problem of definition was compounded by the obscurity of the legislation—a complaint that may, unfortunately, still frequently be made against modern legislation. Thus the Master of the Rolls complained, 'in fact it comes back to be a question of fact. It is an unsatisfactory conclusion at which to arrive, because I should wish, if I could, to be able to lay down some rule which would be a guide in the division of this staff into taxable and non-taxable people under Schedule E, but I do not see my way to do it; I do not think it possible.' (*8 TC* at p. 239). Lord Wrenbury was far more scathing: 'if any useful purpose could be served by censuring the Legislatures of 1842 or 1853, no censure could be too strong, I think, for having expressed an Act, and that a taxing Act, in language so involved, so slovenly and so unintelligible as is the language of the Acts of 1842 and 1853. But there it is. A Court cannot say it means nothing and cannot be construed at all ... If parliament had the time, which it has not, the law of Income Tax, which now so vitally affects the subjects of the Realm, ought as speedily as possible to be expressed in a new Statute which should bear and express an intelligible meaning.' (*8 TC* at p. 255).

4.5   As an aside, another dictum from that case, which is unfortunately still true some 70 years later, is that of Lord Sumner in relation to tax litigation: 'Where a decision which limits the right of the Crown has long been unquestioned, far more practical weight attaches to this consideration of lapse of time than would have been the case had the decision been the other way. In these contests the subject is always at a great disadvantage. Decisions in favour of the Crown may often go unchallenged not because their correctness is generally recognised, but because no private person can face the cost of disputing them. Decisions to the contrary effect stand in a different position. The Crown is always very ably advised, in Revenue as in other matters, and for an appeal against the doubtful ruling affecting Income Tax the funds can always be found.' (*8 TC* at p. 253).

Edwards v Clinch

4.6   The meaning of an office fell to be considered again more recently by the House of Lords in the 1981 case of *Edwards v Clinch 56 TC 367*. Mr Clinch, a distinguished civil engineer, was engaged from time to time by the Government to hold public local enquiries. He held the enquiry entirely as he thought fit. He received no salary but rendered a fee account after completion of each enquiry. Each enquiry was of indeterminate duration. It could last several days, or weeks, or months. The Revenue accepted that Mr Clinch was not employed by the

Secretary of State or by anyone else. They contended, however, that his appointment to hold an enquiry was an office and that accordingly his fees could not be included as part of his Schedule D profits as a civil engineer but had to be assessed separately as employment income. The courts accordingly had to consider whether or not continuity was an essential attribute of an office. If it was not, Mr Clinch would be taxable on it as employment income. It was held by a three-to-two majority that Mr Clinch did not hold a series of offices and was properly assessable under Schedule D.

4.7   Ackner LJ thought each enquiry 'was a temporary, *ad hoc*, appointment confined to the taxpayer. He was not appointed to a position which had an existence of its own. It had no quality of permanency about it . . . It was . . . a transient, indeterminate, once-only, execution of a task for which the taxpayer was peculiarly qualified.' Lord Salmon quoted these words approvingly and added: 'I cannot agree that the dictionary meaning of the word "office" can or was intended to be of any real help in construing the word "office" in Schedule E.' (*56 TC* at p. 415). Lord Lowry thought that 'the mere appointment to perform a function (in this case the statutory function of holding a public local enquiry) does not by itself mean that the person appointed holds an office within the meaning of Schedule E. To say that the alleged office has no name, since the word "inspector" is merely a convenient description, may put the matter too simply, but it is the base from which I set out . . . I consider that the ordinary meaning of "office" in this context involves the notion of a specific post to which a person can be appointed, which he can hold and which he can vacate. I concede that this is not the only sense in which the word can be understood, but I feel satisfied that it is the primary sense . . . There is a subtler but perhaps more cogent argument in the [taxpayer's] favour than the mere absence of a name. The "office" comes into being with the act of appointment and automatically ceases to exist when the person appointed concludes his task. I think that to regard this as the holding of an office by the appointed person confuses his function with his so-called office. The [taxpayer] here was in one sense "in an official position", but not, in my opinion, in an official post (or office). A genuine office does not lapse because the holder dies, retires or completes his assignment. To be in a position of authority is not necessarily to hold an office, and when you appoint somebody to *do* something you do not thereby appoint him to *be* something (in other words to hold an office) unless the Act or other relevant instrument says so.' (*56 TC* at pp. 418–19).

4.8   Lord Lowry felt that his decision was a logical development from the test formulated by Rowlatt J. 'If I may indulge in a metaphor from the occupation of gold mining, I would say (without any disrespect, I hope) that the *Bater* test is the crude ore which has now by a series of processes . . . been refined into something of superior quality . . . *Bater* was followed by a series of cases which satisfied the *Bater* test, and therefore further refinement was unlikely in the meantime, but, like my noble and learned friend, Lord Bridge, I do not forget the words of

Harman LJ in *Mitchell and Edon v Ross 40 TC 11*: "An office is a position or post which goes on without regard to the identity of the holder of
it from time to time" . . . Thus, when the present case came to be
decided, some refining had already been done. The emphasis on permanence and continuity had lessened and the possibility of a once-only
appointment had been recognised. But the concept of an office which
exists independently of its holder still held sway . . . I think I can fairly
summarise the Court of Appeal's attitude by saying that all the Judges
recognised the changes since *Bater* and accepted the principle in *Farrell
v Alexander [1976] 2 All ER 721* but still considered that a degree of permanence and continuity was essential and were unwilling to disregard a
clear thread of supporting opinion which ran through a long line of cases.
The characteristic of permanence need only amount to the independent
existence of an office, as opposed to its incidental creation and automatic
demise with the beginning and end respectively of the appointment of an
individual to perform a task. And the continuity required need have no
magic beyond the existence of the post (subject always to its abolition *ab
extra*) after the holder has left it, with the *possibility* of successor's being
appointed . . . The contrast now, however, is not between public and private occupations but between trade, profession or vocation on the one
hand, and office or employment on the other. We might therefore look for
logical links between office and employment and should not be too ready
to equate an independent contractor with an office holder, since the latter
has a deemed employer and his holding of an office has much in common with employment . . . a person does *not* hold a so-called office if it
comes into being only as the inevitable accompaniment of the fact of the
alleged holder's appointment to perform a task . . . I respectfully agree
that it would be unsound to deny the existence of an office or employment in every case where a post did not exhibit all the *indicia* postulated
by Rowlatt J . . . Following the example of Lord Wrenbury in *Bater's*
case and respectfully sharing his view of the difficulties of the tax legis
lation, I consider that my only safe course is to decide the individual case
before us without showing too much concern for supposed analogies and
contradictions, but remembering that the case, if decided in favour of the
Crown, would provide the first example of innominate office under
Schedule E.' (*56 TC* at pp. 421, 423–24, 426–27).

4.9   Lord Bridge of Harwich, in contrast, in a dissenting judgment
felt that *Bater* is no longer good law. 'At first blush, it seems to me
that the appointed person holding a public local enquiry . . . occupies an
"office" . . . Under the *Act* of 1842 tax was charged under Schedule D on
"the annual profits or gains arising or accruing . . . from any profession,
trade, *employment* or vocation"; it was charged under Schedule E on
"every *public* office or employment of profit" . . . These charging
words and the distinction they drew between the two Schedules survived
unaltered in the consolidating *Income Tax Act 1918*. The *Finance Act
1922* made the important change of transferring from Schedule D to
Schedule E . . . the charge to tax on the profits of "any office or employment". Hence the public element in Schedule E ceased to be of importance . . . all the relevant authorities hark back to *Bater's* case . . . I

hope I can say without any disrespect that the endorsement of the opinion of Rowlatt J and Lord Atkinson in all the cases following *Bater's* case, has been quite uncritical, since there has been, so far as I can discover ... no occasion before the instant case when any Court ... has been invited ... to re-examine the foundation on which it rests to see if it is still valid as applied to the phrase "office or employment" in Schedule E in the form it assumed in 1956, which reappears in the consolidating *Act* of 1970. It is precisely such a re-examination that your Lordships now have to undertake. It leads, in my opinion, inevitably to the conclusion that the opinion is no longer good law. The rule on which Rowlatt J and Lord Atkinson based their interpretation has gone. Moreover, now that Schedule E embraces all employments, it would surely be absurd to suggest that "employment" under the Schedule can be limited to "a subsisting, permanent, substantive position which has an existence independent of the person who fills it". If that construction no longer applies to "employment" in Schedule E, I can see no logic whatever in continuing to apply it to "office". So far as authority is concerned, therefore, your Lordships are, in my opinion, wholly unconstrained and free to give to the word "office" its ordinary dictionary meaning.' (*56 TC* at pp. 429–30, 433).

4.10   It is nonetheless likely that there is still some distinction between an office and an employment for tax purposes. A company directorship is an office. So are the positions of company secretary, auditor and, probably, registrar. So are most public appointments such as a judge, or an MP.

4.11   Indeed the question came before the courts again in June 1991 in *McMenamin v Diggles [1991] STC 419.* Mr Diggles was the senior clerk in a set of barristers' chambers and had served under a contract of employment until 7 October 1985. From that date new contractual arrangements were entered into under which, in return for a specified percentage of the gross income of each member of chambers, Mr Diggles agreed to provide at his own cost and expense a full clerking service for each member. Under the agreement he could either act as head clerk himself or provide some other suitably qualified person to act. In practice he filled the role himself. The Revenue contended that Mr Diggles held an office on the basis that the code of conduct of the Bar Council required every practising barrister 'to have the services of the clerk of chambers'. It was accepted by both parties that it was possible to have an office without an instrument creating it, to have an office which had no public element, and to which there was no formality of appointment. It was held that the Commissioners had, on weighing up all the facts, correctly concluded that Mr Diggles did not hold an office within the meaning of the statute and their decision was not vulnerable to attack under the principle in *Edwards v Bairstow 36 TC 207.* An interesting feature of this case is that the work Mr Diggles actually did after 7 October 1985 does not appear to have been any different to what he previously did as an employee. This reinforces the importance attaching to the agreement where the nature of the work does not clearly point to either employment or self-employment (see also *Massey v Crown Life Assurance Co* at 4.26–4.28 below).

Meaning of 'employment'

4.12   An employment is easier to define but less easy to recognise. Again it is not exhaustively defined in the legislation but is expressed to include in particular any employment under a contract of service, any employment under a contract of apprenticeship and any employment in the service of the Crown, and 'employed' 'employee' and 'employer' are to have corresponding meanings. [*ITEPA 2003, s 4*]. The problem normally is to distinguish it from a trade, profession or vocation. An employment is the relationship that exists between master and servant, but in the modern world the distinction between a servant and an independent contractor is often blurred. The dictionary defines a servant as 'a person employed by another person or body of persons to work under direction for wages'. In the past the emphasis has been on 'under direction'; if a person is subject to control by another he is his servant. However, in recent years the courts have made it clear that control is just one of a number of tests that need to be looked at. This is sensible. Every relationship under which someone performs a task for another involves an element of control. If someone wants his house painted he will control the colour the painter uses, will exert a degree of control over the time he does the work, etc. However, this will not make the painter an employee of the customer.

Distinguished from self-employment

4.13   The distinction between an employee and a person who is self-employed is one of the most difficult to draw, yet for tax purposes it is vital to do so as employments are taxed under under the rules relating to employment income and the self-employed under Cases I and II of Schedule D. The question to be asked is whether the person is engaged under a contract 'of service' or a contract 'for services'. In other words, is the person undertaking to enter the service of another, in which case he is an employee, or is he undertaking to provide a service of some sort to that other person, in which case he will not be? To put it another way, is the person undertaking merely to provide his labour or is he undertaking to provide some service which another person requires, albeit that his labour is a major component of that service? In *Market Investigations Ltd v Minister of Social Security [1968] 3 All ER 732* Cooke J formulated the test as to whether the person is 'in business on his own account'. This was a national insurance case, as are the majority of the cases on this question. The test is the same for both income tax and national insurance. In recent years the Government have made clear that once a person's status has been established with one of these authorities the other will accept their decision. Indeed, the two have issued a joint leaflet setting out their combined views, although the fact that they could not even agree how to identify it—the Inland Revenue calling it IR56 and the Contributions Agency NI39—did not inspire confidence in their ability to work together. The Revenue do not however consider themselves bound by decisions of the Secretary of State under the national insurance rules. They say these are not lawful precedents, relate to the named contributor only and depend on their individual facts, so cannot be applied even to workers in similar circumstances (*Tax Bulletin 48, August 2000*).

4.14   The leaflet concludes 'If you are not sure whether you are employed or self-employed, please get in touch with your local Tax Enquiry Centre, Tax Office or Contributions Agency Office of the DSS for advice. If you can't agree with their decision you can appeal against it'. The author would be interested to hear from any reader who has followed this advice and been told that the Revenue think he is self-employed. The author has on a number of occasions approached them on behalf of clients seeking confirmation that they agree with his view that an individual is self-employed, and can think of only one instance where he has had a positive response— the request has normally initiated an argument.

Case law

4.15   Before considering the Revenue's guidance it may be helpful to look at some of the cases from which their tests are drawn. The distinction between employment and self-employment has been before the Courts on a number of occasions and the approaches taken by the judges are far more helpful in determining the tests to be applied than the brief distillation that the Revenue have developed from them.

4.16   The best starting point is probably three national insurance cases decided in the late 1960s; *Ready Mixed Concrete (South East) Ltd v Minister of Pensions & National Insurance [1968] 1 All ER 433*, *Argent v Minister of Social Security [1968] 3 All ER 208*, and *Market Investigations Ltd v Ministry of Social Security [1968] 3 All ER 732*.

Test for contract of service

4.17   The issue in the *Ready Mixed Concrete* case was whether a person who owned his own lorry and was engaged by the company to deliver concrete to its customers was an employee. MacKenna J formulated the test as to whether or not a contract of service existed, and then sought to identify what such a contract involves. 'A contract of service exists if the following three conditions are fulfilled:

(*a*)   The servant agrees that in consideration of a wage or other remuneration he will provide his own work and skill in the performance of some service for his master;

(*b*)   He agrees, expressly or impliedly, that in the performance of that service he will be subject to the other's control in a sufficient degree to make that other master; and (*c*)   The other provisions of the contract are consistent with its being a contract of service.'

4.18   He felt that (*a*) did not call for comment other than to make clear that an employment required remuneration, but helpfully expanded upon the other two tests. 'As to (*b*). Control includes the power of deciding the thing to be done, the way in which it shall be done, the means to be employed in doing it, the time when, and the place where it shall be done. All these aspects of control must be considered in deciding whether the right exists in a sufficient degree to make one party the master and the other his servant. The right need not be unrestricted . . . If the contract does not expressly provide which party shall have the right, the question must be answered in the ordinary way by implication.'

4.19   He went on to say: 'The third and negative condition is for my purpose the important one, and I shall try with the help of five examples to explain what I mean by provisions inconsistent with the nature of a contract of service.

(*a*)   A contract obliges one party to build for the other, providing at his own expense the necessary plant and materials. This is not a contract of service, even though the builder may be obliged to use his own labour only and to accept a high degree of control: it is a building contract. It is not a contract to serve another for a wage, but a contract to produce a thing (or a result) for a price.

(*b*)   A contract obliges one party to carry another's goods, providing at his own expense everything needed for performance. This is not a contract of service . . . it is a contract of carriage.

(*c*)   A contract obliges a labourer to work for a builder, providing some simple tools, and to accept the builder's control. Notwithstanding the obligation to provide the tools, the contract is one of service. That obligation is not inconsistent with the nature of a contract of service. It is not a sufficiently important matter to affect the substance of the contract.

(*d*)   A contract obliges one party to work for the other, accepting his control, and to provide his own transport. This is still a contract of service . . . Transport in this example is incidental to the main purpose of the contract . . .

(*e*)   The same instrument provides that one party shall work for the other subject to the other's control, and also that he shall sell him his land. The first part of the instrument is no less a contract of service because the second part imposes obligations of a different kind.'

4.20   In other words 'an obligation to do work subject to the other party's control is a necessary, though not always a sufficient, condition of a contract of service. If the provisions of the contract as a whole are inconsistent with its being a contract of service, it will be some other kind of contract . . .'. MacKenna J also adopted the tests applied in two earlier cases. The first, on the meaning of control, from *Zuijus v Wirth Bros Pty Ltd (1955) 93 CLR 561*. 'What matters is lawful authority to command, so far as there is scope for it. And there must always be some room for it, if only in incidental or collateral matters.' The second from Denning LJ in *Bank voor Handel en Scheepvaart NV v Slatford* [*1952*] *2 All E R 956*: 'I would observe the test of being a servant does not rest nowadays on submission to orders. It depends on whether the person is part and parcel of the organisation' (*[1968] 1 All ER* at pp. 440–441).

Part-time employment

4.21   The question in the *Argent* case was whether a part-time teacher at a drama school was an employee. Unlike most cases in this area, Mr Argent claimed to be an employee whereas both the school and the Ministry contended that he was not. Roskill J's approach was to look at the reality of the engagement: 'One has a picture of an actor of some experience sometimes going off and doing whole-time or near whole-time acting . . . but at other times teaching . . . being paid hourly rates or by fixed fees for the work he was doing. It is also relevant to point out that . . . the appellant had no administrative or disciplinary duties at the school except to mark a register . . . In those circumstances is he a man who can properly be said to have been employed . . . under a contract of service, or is the true position . . . that he was really working under a services contract doing part-time work . . .?' (*[1968] 3 All ER* at p. 215). He concluded that Mr Argent was self-employed.

Test for self-employment

4.22   The *Market Investigations* case was concerned with part-time interviewers for a market research organisation. Cooke J considered a number of previous authorities including that of Denning LJ in the *Bank voor Handel* case mentioned above, Lord Wright in a Canadian case, *Montreal Locomotive Works Ltd v Montreal* [*1947*] *1 DLR 161*, and various US cases from which he concluded: 'The observations of Lord Wright, of Denning LJ and of the judges of the Supreme Court in the USA suggest that the fundamental test to be applied is this: "Is the person who has engaged himself to perform these services performing them as a person in business on his own account?". If the answer to that question is "Yes", then the contract is a contract for services. If the answer is "No" then the contract is a contract of service. No exhaustive list has been compiled and perhaps no exhaustive list can be compiled of considerations which are relevant in determining that question, nor can strict rules be laid down as to the relative weight which the various considerations should carry in particular cases. The most that can be said is that control will no doubt have to be considered, although it can no longer be regarded as the sole determining factor; and that factors, which may be of importance, are such matters as whether the man performing the services provides his own equipment, whether he hires his own helpers, what degree of financial risk he takes, what degree of responsibility for investment and management he has, and whether and how far he has an opportunity of profiting from sound management in the performance of his task.' (*[1968] 3 All ER* at pp. 737–738).

4.23   This is how the test is nowadays usually phrased. It is, of course, the same test, although in an expanded form, as that adopted in *Argent*. In *Hall v Lorimer* (see 4.63) Nolan J cast doubt on whether this test was necessarily the right approach so it needs to be treated with a degree of caution. Where the person already has a business organisation the test is relatively easy to apply. If he does not, particularly if the services to be supplied do not require anything other than the person's labour, it is more difficult. However, Cooke J made it clear that the absence of such an organisation is not fatal: 'A person who engages himself to perform services for another may well be an independent contractor even though he has not entered into the contract in the course of an existing business carried on by him.'

4.24   On the facts, however, he found that the interviewer was an employee: 'It is apparent that the control which the company had the right to exercise in this case was very extensive indeed. It was in my view so extensive as to be entirely consistent with Mrs Irving being employed under a contract of service. The fact that Mrs Irving had a limited discretion when she should do the work was not in my view inconsistent with the existence of a contract of service . . . Nor is there anything inconsistent . . . in the fact that Mrs Irving was free to work for others during the relevant period.' (*[1968] 3 All ER* at p. 739). It will be apparent from this that the 'overall reality' test is merely a different approach to MacKenna J's three principles set out at 4.17 above.

Other case law

4.25   The decision in the *Argent* case reflects the reality that Mr Argent was a full-time actor who taught drama during such periods as his acting engagements permitted. In a later income tax case, *Sidey v Phillips 59 TC 458*, a part-time lecturer was held to be an employee, as was the taxpayer in a 1956 case, *Fuge v McClelland 36 TC 571*. The status of a teacher was also at issue in *Walls v Sinnett 60 TC 150*. Mr Walls, a professional singer, was appointed to the post of lecturer of music at a technical college. He was required to attend the college four days a week during term time but was permitted—indeed, encouraged—to undertake outside work. Vinelott J felt that, 'What is striking about this case is that the engagement, to use a neutral word, is full-time . . . Mr Walls says that, although full-time, he was able to carry on a great deal of other work, but that is neither one way nor the other; it was an engagement . . . of employment as a very senior teacher or lecturer, and such teachers frequently have a relatively light teaching load and are encouraged to engage in other activities which can add to their experience ... The other point that is very much stressed by the taxpayer is the degree of control ... In some contexts the degree of control exercised over a man may be very important in deciding whether he is an employee or servant or not, but in the case of a senior lecturer at a college of further education, more particularly one who like Mr Walls came into teaching from active work as a singer, it is not surprising to find he was given a very wide degree of latitude in the organisation of his work and time.' (*60 TC* at p. 165). This emphasises the importance of looking at the overall picture. The fact that an employer does not seek to dictate to an expert how he should utilise his expertise is not inconsistent with a contract being one of service. Nor is the fact that if the duties of an employment do not utilise a person's full time he is free to undertake other work which is consistent with his being available to fulfil his obligations under his employment contract.

4.26   Lord Denning, in his normal robust way, thought that the decision is largely a matter of common sense. In *Massey v Crown Life Assurance Co [1978] 2 All ER 576* he simply stated: 'I will not today attempt to formulate the distinction except to repeat what I said in *Stevenson Jordan & Harrison Ltd v McDonald and Evans [1952] 1 TLR 101*. "It is often easy to recognise a contract of service when you see it but difficult to say where the difference lies. A ship's master, a chauffeur and a reporter on the staff of a newspaper are all employed under a contract of service; but a ship's pilot, a taxi-man and a newspaper contributor are employed under a contract for services." '

4.27   It is well established that the label that the parties to a relationship choose to put on it is not conclusive as to what that relationship is. The *Massey* case concerned a branch manager of an insurance company. He originally had a contract of employment. On the advice of his accountant he persuaded his employer to engage him instead as a self-employed contractor. The employer signed a new form of contract engaging him to provide services to the company.

4.28   Mr Massey was subsequently dismissed and sought to claim unfair dismissal as an employee. Lord Denning would have none of it. 'The law as I see it, is this: If the true relationship of the parties is that of master and servant under a contract of service, the parties cannot alter the truth of that relationship by putting a different label on it. If they should put a different label on it, and use it as a dishonest device to deceive the Inland Revenue, I should have thought it was illegal and could not be enforced by either party and they could not get any advantage out of it, or at any rate not in any case where they had to rely on it as the basis of a claim ... On the other hand if their relationship is ambiguous and is capable of being one or the other, then the parties can remove that ambiguity by the very agreement itself which they make with one another. The agreement itself then becomes the best material from which to gather the true legal relationship between them.'

Agreement between parties

4.29   The importance of the wording of the agreement between the parties was emphasised in the Privy Council case of *Narich Pty Ltd v Comr Pay-Roll Tax [1984] ICR 286* where Lord Brandon stated: 'The first principle is that, subject to one exception, where there is a written contract between the parties whose relationship is in issue, a court is confined, in determining the nature of that relationship, to a consideration of the terms, express or implied, of that contract in the light of the circumstances surrounding the making of it; and it is not entitled to consider also the manner in which the parties subsequently acted in pursuance of such contract. The one exception to that rule is that, where the subsequent conduct of the parties can be shown to have amounted to an agreed addition to, or modification of, the original written contract, such conduct may be considered and taken into account by the court.' In other words, if all the terms are contained in a written agreement the Courts will look only at that agreement, not what happened in practice, to determine whether or not the relationship was an employment, unless the facts suggest that what happened in practice indicates that the contract was orally varied in some way. Obviously the agreement will also be ignored if the Revenue can demonstrate that it is a sham.

4.30   It should be borne in mind that the inclusion of some things in an agreement may have the opposite effect to that intended. For example if there is doubt whether a person is really self-employed there is a temptation to include a clause stating that the contractor is responsible for his own tax and national insurance. However, this would be a very strange clause to find in a genuine arm's length contract with an independent contractor who is providing a service in the course of his business. A businessman would never think that there was the remotest possibility that he could be liable for the tax of his solicitor, accountant, valuer, or other adviser and would not dream of seeking to provide for such an eventuality when engaging the adviser. Accordingly, the inclusion of such a clause in an agreement with his self-employed bookkeeper, salesman, etc. is likely to be taken as an indication—at the least—that in the eyes of the parties the status of the relationship is open to doubt. PAYE Audit division are likely to regard the inclusion of such a provision as an indication that the relationship needs to be scrutinised carefully as it could well be one of master and servant.

4.31   Whether a person is an employee or an independent contractor is a question of law. However, the answer will depend very much on the facts. In *O'Kelly v Trusthouse Forte plc [1983] 3 All ER 456* Sir John Donaldson MR expressed the distinction thus: 'The test to be applied in identifying whether a contract is one of employment or for services is a pure question of law and so is its application to the facts. But it is for the tribunal of fact not only to find those facts but to assess them qualitatively and within limits, which are indefinable in the abstract, those findings and that assessment will dictate the correct legal answer. In the familiar phrase, it is all a question of fact and degree. It is only if the weight given to a particular factor shows a self-misdirection in law that an appellate court with a limited jurisdiction can interfere. It is difficult to demonstrate such a misdirection and, to the extent that it is not done, the issue is one of fact.' (*[1983] 3 All ER* at p. 478). In that case casual employees taken on by a hotel for functions as and when required (regular casuals) were held by a tribunal to be self-employed. The Court of Appeal upheld this decision on the *Edwards v Bairstow 36 TC 207* principle, i.e. that it was not a decision that a reasonable tribunal properly instructed in the law could not have reached and that therefore the courts were not entitled to overturn it.

4.32   Although decisions of the Special Commissioners were not reported prior to 1995, the case of *Specialeyes (Optical Services) Ltd* (see *Taxation 4 July 1991*) is interesting. The company, which traded as optical retailers through a nationwide chain of shops, engaged a large number of self-employed opticians to carry out eye examinations. Most of these had only one client, the appellant, which is in the business of providing sight tests to the public. An optician received a fixed fee for each eye test performed, out of which he paid the company a facility fee to cover the use of its premises and equipment. The opticians were at liberty to stipulate the hours during which they were prepared to attend the branch. They were responsible for their own professional indemnity insurance. The Commissioners upheld the company's contention that the opticians were not employees. The rationale seems largely to have been based on the fact that the company's degree of control is limited to deciding at which branch and on which day the optician will be given the opportunity to carry out sight tests—and even that was obtained only by agreement and sometimes after considerable negotiation. The Commissioners were also influenced by the fact that the opticians were not 'part and parcel' of the company's organisation and by the terms of the contract between the parties. The Revenue have opted not to take this decision to appeal. The Revenue cited only three cases, *Market Investigations* (see 4.22 above), *Global Plant Ltd v Secretary of State for Health and Social Security [1971] 3 All ER 385* and a Privy Council appeal in a Hong Kong case, *Lee Ting Sang v Chung Chi-Keung [1990] 2 AC 374*. The Commissioners felt that the facts in the latter two cases were far removed from the case under consideration. It is intriguing that the Revenue seem increasingly to rely on Hong Kong decisions: this suggests that they are unable to draw much comfort from the large number of UK cases considered above.

4.33   The *Lee Ting Sang* case was an industrial injuries case. Mr Sang was a stonemason working for a subcontractor. His tools were provided by the subcontractor. He had worked on the site for 20 days prior to the accident; he was normally paid in accordance with the amount of concrete chiselled as measured by the subcontractor (or sometimes a wage of HK$220 a day); if he finished his work before 5pm he would assist the subcontractor to sharpen chisels—for which he would be paid on an hourly basis; he would give the subcontractor priority if others wanted him; and he gave evidence that he believed he would be sacked if he disappeared from the site. His work was not supervised but was inspected periodically by the main contractor's foreman.

4.34 The Revenue probably like the case because the decision reversed that of the Court of Appeal of Hong Kong, as 'the facts . . . point out so clearly to the existence of a contract of service that the finding that the applicant was working as an independent contractor was . . . a view of the facts which could not reasonably be entertained and is to be regarded as an error of law'.

4.35 The case is important because it is based on English law. Lord Griffiths, giving the judgment of the Privy Council, said, 'The question is to be answered by applying English common law standards to determine whether the workman was working as an employee or as an independent contractor. What then is the standard to apply? This has proved to be a most elusive question and despite a plethora of authorities the courts have not been able to devise a single test that will conclusively point to the distinction in all cases. Their Lordships agree with the Court of Appeal [of Hong Kong] when they said that the matter had never been put better than by Cooke J in *Market Investigations Ltd v Minister of Social Security*.' He then quoted the passage set out at 4.22 above.

4.36 Lord Griffiths placed no weight on the fact that Mr Sang worked from 8 am to 5 pm each day: 'This accords with the common sense of the matter for if the applicant was free to come and go at will it is difficult to see how the first respondent could carry out timeous performance of his subcontract'; or on the lack of supervision: 'It is true that he was not supervised in his work, but this is not surprising, he was a skilled man and he had been told the beams upon which he was to work and the depth to which they were to be cut and his work was measured to see that he achieved that result. There was no question of him being called upon to exercise any skill or judgement as to which beams required chipping or as to the depth that they were to be cut. He was simply told what to do and left to get on with it.'

4.37 His overall impression of the facts was that, 'The picture emerges of a skilled artisan, earning his living by working for more than one employer as an employee and not as a small businessman venturing into business on his own as an independent contractor with all its attendant risks. The applicant ran no risk whatever save that of being unable to find employment which is, of course, a risk faced by casual employees who move from one job to another. . . . It must now be taken to be firmly established that the question of whether or not the work was performed in the capacity of an employee or as an independent contractor is to be regarded by the appellate court as a question of fact to be determined by the trial court. At first sight it seems rather strange that this should be so, for whether or not a certain set of facts should be classified under one legal head rather than another would appear to be a question of law. However . . . it was held in a series of decisions in the Court of Appeal and in the House of Lords under the English *Workmen's Compensation Acts 1906 and 1925* that a finding by a county court judge that a workman was, or was not, employed under a contract of service was a question of fact.'

4.38   He played down the weight to be given to *Stevenson Jordan & Harrison Ltd v McDonald & Evans* (see 4.26) and *Bank voor Handel en Scheepvaart NV v Slatford* (see 4.20), although it appears solely on the basis of the wording of the Hong Kong legislation, not because what Lord Denning said in those cases was wrong in principle. 'In arriving at his conclusion the district judge relied upon two dicta of Denning J which, whilst no doubt of value in the determination of the cases in which they were spoken, would appear to have little relevance to the facts of the present case and if misapplied may have led to an erroneous conclusion . . . To apply the test of whether a person is "part and parcel of the organisation" is likely to be misleading in the context of a statute which expressly contemplates that casual workers and workers working for two or more employers concurrently may be employed under a contract of service.'

Mutuality of obligations

4.39   Another important factor not brought out in the above cases is mutuality of obligations, i.e. that whilst an employee has duties to their employer the employer also has duties to the employee in particular to offer them work to do. The absence of such mutuality is a strong pointer to self-employment. Indeed many people feel that it is of itself conclusive that there is not an employment. In *R (on the application of Professional Contractors Group Ltd) v IRC [2001] EWHC Admin 236 [2001] STC 629* the judge was fairly scathing of the Revenue guidance, particularly that on this area. The case itself was a challenge to the validity of the 'IR 35' legislation (see 19.33) but in the course of his judgment Burton J said, 'It is essential to any consideration of the common law test as to whether an individual is trading as an employee or as an independent contractor, that consideration should be given as to whether he is in business on his own account.' He later says, 'It cannot be right for the Revenue simply to conclude, as it does in another such guidance document, *ESM 0514*, that "mutuality of obligation" is not a relevant issue: "Do not consider this factor when reviewing a work status unless the engager or worker raises it". It has now recently been emphasised by the House of Lords in *Carmichael v National Power plc [1999] 1 WLR 2042*, that the test adopted in *Nethermere (St Neots) Ltd v Gardner [1984] ICR 612, CA* by Stephenson LJ of an "irreducible minimum of mutual obligation" is another central piece of guidance in the analysis of whether there is employment or self-employment.'

4.40   *Carmichael v National Power plc* involved two part-time guides at Blyth Power Station. They claimed to have a continuing employment with National Power, not a series of individual employments covering only the times when they were actually working as guides. The industrial tribunal held that their case foundered on the rock of absence of mutuality and the House of Lords held that was a correct analysis.

4.41 The reference in the *Professional Contractors Group* case to *ESM 0514* is to the Revenue's *Employment Status Manual*. That paragraph in fact starts, 'This aspect is rarely of practical use from a tax or NIC's point of view and can confuse the issue.'

The Inland Revenue's approach

4.42 The Inland Revenue in their leaflet IR56 say that the distinction between employment and self-employment 'is something to be decided in a commonsense way'. Unfortunately this is not always how they seem to approach the question in practice. They frequently seem to start with the concept that anyone who works on his own in an occupation where his own labour is a major component of the service that he provides is an employee unless there is strong evidence to suggest otherwise. They will normally start from the old, discredited test of control—seizing on the slightest degree of control to reinforce their initial presumption.

Nevertheless, although they do not in practice seem to place much weight on some of the tests, the Revenue have formulated some helpful guidelines.

Revenue guidelines

4.43 Factors that 'usually' indicate that a person may be self-employed are as follows.

(*a*) Whether he has the final say in how the business is run. The difficulty with this test is that when dealing with the provision of personal services there is often not a great deal of running to do. There is also the problem of identifying the business. A person who has a skill that he sells to A on Monday, to B on Tuesday and C on Wednesday and to D on Friday, having decided to take Thursday off to play golf, clearly has the final say on how his business is run as he is the only one involved in the entire business. However, the Revenue may well take the view that the business is not the aggregation of what the person does during the week but that he works during the course of the week for four businesses, A's, B's, C's and D's, and in looking at how the 'business' is run one needs to look separately at his activities in each of such businesses.

(*b*) Whether he risks his own money in the business. Unfortunately, a business which consists of selling a particular skill of the proprietor often needs no money to be risked. The proprietor risks his time and may be in severe financial difficulties should he not be paid for it, but the Revenue are not normally prepared to regard this as a recognisable risk.

(c)   Whether he is responsible for meeting losses as well as enjoying profits. Again, a business that requires little finance is unlikely to incur losses and losses of time tend to be ignored.

(d)   Whether he provides the major items of equipment that he needs. The Revenue consider that the provision of 'small tools' is not indicative of self-employment. The author has known them to regard equipment costing hundreds of pounds as small for this purpose.

(e)   Whether the person is free to hire other people on terms of his choice to do the work he has undertaken to perform, and, if so, whether he pays that person out of his own pocket. In practice, of course, a customer will frequently contract with a business because they want a particular expertise which they believe that business to have, and would regard it as a breach of contract if the business were to sub-contract the task to someone else. Accordingly, it seems doubtful whether in modern conditions the absence of a right to delegate is indicative that a person is not self-employed.

(f)   Whether the person has to correct unsatisfactory work in his own time and at his own expense. This is a rather odd test. Many employees would regard themselves as morally obliged to correct unsatisfactory work in their own time.

4.44   If a positive answer can be given to all of the above questions a person has a strong claim to self-employed status. If such an answer cannot be given, albeit because most of these questions are not relevant to his circumstances, he can expect the Revenue to regard him as an employee. Two further factors the Revenue consider relevant are set out at 4.68.

4.45   Factors that indicate to the Revenue that a person is 'probably' an employee are as follows.

(a)   Whether the person has to do the work personally rather than hire someone else to do it for him. It seems doubtful whether it is actually indicative of anything in modern conditions. A person is frequently engaged to perform a task because he possesses a particular skill. There is an implied condition in such circumstances that the person will do the work personally, but this could not of itself make him an employee.

(b)   Whether someone can tell the person at any time what to do or when and how to do it. Most jobs give the worker a large degree of discretion as to what he does at any time, and if he has a particular skill it would be foolish for anyone to seek to dictate how he performs his task. Of course an employer can tell an employee to do a particular task at a particular time—but a contractor can likewise instruct his subcontractor—as in today's complex society it is necessary for all of the people engaged on a project to work together, albeit that they are all independent contractors, to enable the project to be completed promptly and efficiently.

(*c*) Whether the person is paid by the hour, the week or the month, and if he gets overtime pay. The author, like most professional advisers, is paid by his clients by the hour, so this is not really indicative of anything. The contrast the Revenue are seeking to make is, of course, that they would expect an independent contractor to perform a task for a fixed fee irrespective of how long it took. While some businesses work in this manner, many do not. Lest anyone assumes that if he is not paid an hourly rate or weekly or monthly wage he is unlikely to be an employee, the Revenue add, 'even if you are paid by commission or on a piecework basis you may still be an employee'.

(*d*) Whether the person works set hours or a given number of hours per week or month. Again this is probably a neutral factor. A doctor who agrees to attend at a company's premises every Thursday afternoon to be available for consultation by staff is unlikely to be an employee of the company even though he provides his services at set hours and the number of hours for which he will work has been agreed in advance.

(*e*) Whether the person works at the premises of the person he is working for, or at a place or places that they decide. This is not always a helpful test. The nature of the services to be provided will often determine where they are performed. If one wants a painter to decorate one's house the painter has to carry out the work at that house. The requirement does not, of course, make him an employee. Nor would the fact that he agrees with the householder when he will do the job or how many coats of paint he will apply or even all of these things.

4.46 Whilst it is easy to denigrate the tests that the Revenue have formulated, they do cover the main factors to be taken into consideration and in some cases their application will point clearly to the right answer. The Revenue's *Employment Status Manual* is also helpful in defining the principles involved although the strictures of Burton J in *R v CIR ex parte Professional Contractors Group Ltd and others (2001) STC 629* (see 4.39) emphasise that it does not necessarily present an unbiased view. It must also be appreciated that the nature of the relationship between the parties can only be discerned by weighing up *all* the relevant factors. In an attempt to demonstrate that a subcontractor is not an employee people sometimes include as standard a clause in consultancy contracts which states that a person is entitled to use a substitute. If the contractor is relying on the specific expertise of a subcontractor such a clause is clearly artificial and is likely to do more harm than good as it raises the question as to why it should have been inserted, unless the parties had a genuine doubt as to whether the subcontractor was self-employed. A provision that the subcontractor will be responsible for his own tax and national insurance is another provision that would not normally be found in a contract for services and thus highlights a doubt as to the status of the arrangement.

4.47   The freedom to refuse to undertake a particular task is normally likely to be inconsistent with a contract of employment. In the *O'Kelly* case (see 4.31 above) Ackner LJ pointed out that the casuals there were free to choose whether or not to work for a particular function and that 'however irritating it might have been to the company if faced with refusal, it would have been quite unreal to conclude that either party would have thought it was a breach of contract'.

4.48   In *Horner v Hasted [1995] STC 766* an employee of a firm of chartered accountants had the status within the firm equivalent to that of a partner. He was not a chartered accountant and was prevented by the then rules of the ICAEW from being a partner. He contended that he was not, in fact, an employee. It was held that he plainly was. The duties he undertook were very unusual incidents of a contract of employment, but it was a very unusual contract arising in very unusual circumstances. The circumstances were not incompatible with a contract of employment. Such a contract is well able to subsist in a one-off situation. The lack of 'control' or the relationship of boss and underling, or master and servant was not of the significance today it once might have been. It is not a universal litmus test and the importance and relevance depended on the role to be played by the 'employee' in the employer's business. A contrary decision was reached by the General Commissioners in the case of a journalist, Margaret Leslie who was held to be self-employed in relation to her shifts on a national newspaper, largely because she had no guarantee for future work beyond the immediate eight-hour shift and was not subject to grievance or disciplinary procedures (*Taxline, January 1995, item 19*). This decision appears questionable in the light of the above case.

4.49   Lord Sumner in *Great Western Rly Co v Bater*, while holding that Mr Hall was not within Schedule E ('nor does he hold any office at all; he merely sits in one') added 'I regret this decision, for it will, I fear, lead to persons escaping tax which they ought to pay, because they cannot be traced by the Revenue officials, or can be got at only at a disproportionate expense'. In recent years the Inland Revenue appear to have launched a campaign to bring within the Schedule E net everyone who offers his services for hire and whose business consists primarily in the exploitation of his own talents. It is probable that this is prompted by the same consideration, i.e. that the Revenue do not trust the self-employed to account for tax on their earnings: a conclusion undoubtedly based on experience. If, however, a person is an employee, the Revenue can collect the tax from his employer, with a right of recourse to the employee in many cases, if the employer does not pay.

4.50   In *Andrews v King [1991] STC 481*, Mr Andrews was engaged by a potato merchant company on various days over a two-year period.

The company would contact Mr Andrews and tell him how many men were required on a particular day (it would be six, including Mr Andrews, for potato picking or four for grading). Mr Andrews would put together a team of the appropriate size. He drove them to the site in his own van, all six (or four) sharing the cost of the petrol. The company provided all necessary machinery and equipment. The price for the work was agreed by the company from time to time jointly with Mr Andrews and the rest of the team. Mr Andrews was treated no more favourably than the other members of the team. At the end of a day the company would pay Mr Andrews the agreed consideration in cash, he would deduct from this each member's petrol contribution and divide the balance equally between the other workers and himself. He did not keep any records of what payments he made to the other workers.

4.51   The Revenue contended that Mr Andrews was a self-employed gangmaster and that the other workers were employees of his. This seems a very harsh claim in the circumstances. Fortunately, Sir Nicholas Browne-Williamson had no hesitation in dismissing their claim. He held that Mr Andrews was not a self-employed gangmaster. He exerted no control over the other workers, who were subject to the supervision of the company. The only equipment that he provided was his van, but this was not used in the work, only in getting to and from it and the cost of doing so was shared by all the workers. Although Mr Andrews selected the workers it could not be said that he hired them. He did not pay them himself and present their services to the company in return for a fee. All of the workers together negotiated their fee with the company. Mr Andrews took no financial risk and had no opportunity to benefit by sound management. In these circumstances the court could not identify any business carried on by the taxpayer on his own account. The Commissioners, in holding that he did, had reached a conclusion that was not possible as a matter of law. An interesting facet of this case is that the court looked at the status of the supposed 'employer' not that of the employee. This emphasises that in a status dispute it is worth considering the position of both parties to determine the nature of the contract.

4.52   The Revenue contended as an alternative that, even if Mr Andrews was not in fact the employer of the other workers, he could be deemed to be the employer under the *PAYE Regulations. Regulation 2* of the *1993 Regulations* defined an 'employer' as 'any person paying emoluments' (*Regulation 12* of the *2003 Regulations* has the same effect). However, *regulation 4* (which has since been repealed and replaced by *ITEPA 2003, ss 687–702*) provided that 'where an employee works under the general control and management of a person who is not his immediate employer, that person . . . shall be deemed to be the employer'. The judge held that *regulation 4* overrode *regulation 2* and that, as Mr Andrews worked alongside the other workers, there was nothing to indicate that he had any control over them. He could not therefore be their employer as they worked under the general control and management of the company.

Casual employees

4.53   A particular problem arises with casual employees. Many people assume that an employment implies a degree of continuity. This is not the case. A person who is engaged to work for someone for a few hours only can nevertheless be an employee if the relationship meets MacKenna J's three conditions (see 4.17 above). The Inland Revenue's booklet CWG2 (2004), page 62, the *Employer's Further Guide to PAYE and NICs,* sets out a procedure for dealing with casuals.

(*a*)   If the person will work for the employer for a week or less and the remuneration is less than the PAYE and national insurance thresholds, the employer need only keep a record of the person's name and address and the amount paid.

(*b*)   If the pay exceeds the PAYE limit, tax must be deducted on an emergency code basis (unless the employer knows that the worker has other employment, when it must be deducted at basic rate).

(*c*)   If the person will work for more than a week (or he actually works for more than a week—or there is an agreement with him that he will work for the employer again) or the employee produces a form P45, the normal PAYE procedures will apply. This involves deduction of tax under the emergency code if the employee declares on a form P46 that he has no other employment, or at basic rate if he does not.

4.54   The Revenue's approach is that anyone who does not follow this procedure cannot complain if the Revenue subsequently seek to recover from him tax and national insurance in relation to casual employees. In practice, of course, at that stage the employer is not in a position to recover the tax from the worker as he is normally no longer in contact with him.

One-man companies

4.55   Whether a person is an employee of another is largely a question of fact. Many potential customers who are reluctant to engage a self-employed person to provide his skills for them for several weeks or months on a virtually full-time basis for fear that he will be regarded by the Revenue as an employee, are happy to engage a company that is wholly owned by that person and has no activities other than to exploit his skills, to perform the same task. It is doubtful whether, legally, this makes any difference. From a practical point of view, however, the Revenue generally seem to be content that the person is taxable under PAYE, albeit only on his salary from his one-man company (or personal services company, or loan-out company, or service company as such companies are alternatively called) and do not normally seek to show that he is really an employee of the person who engages the company to provide the service. Indeed, it can be inferred from the fact that the government felt it necessary to introduce anti-avoidance rules on the provision of services through intermediaries (see 19.33) that the Revenue believed that they could not tackle the perceived problem by attacking the existence of the personal services company or other intermediary.

4.56   There were indications a few years ago that the Revenue intended to mount an attack on the film industry, and require the film production company to deduct tax under PAYE from the payments it was contracted to make to the one-man company as if the fee was remuneration due to the worker himself. The Revenue appear to have backed away from a confrontation. They have not conceded this point though. Their Schedule E manual states, 'To avoid PAYE many film and video workers in Schedule E grades have set up limited companies. Normally the worker is the major shareholder and a director. It is alleged that the service company supplies the services of the individual to a film or video production company. An examination of many such cases has shown that such arrangements often fail. The worker remains an employee of the production company' (para 7324). Paragraph 7329 contains an identical comment in relation to television and radio workers. Whilst experience suggests that 'often' may be an exaggeration, this obviously emphasises the importance of getting the documentation right. The position is likely to depend on the real agreement between the parties and on the nature of the task to be performed. If the nature of the task is that the worker will function as a servant of the ultimate customer, the real terms of the agreement may be that the worker undertakes to be a servant of the customer in consideration of the customer making payments to the one-man company. Such an agreement would be an employment agreement.

4.57   On the other hand, if the one-man company has substance, e.g. a proper board of directors that regularly meets and makes decisions, it should be perfectly feasible to draw up a contract under which the one-man company agrees to provide the customer with the skills of the worker for a fee, with the worker remaining under the control of the one-man company but the one-man company acting in accordance with the directions of the customer. Such an agreement is unlikely to constitute an employment of the worker by the customer. It needs to be remembered that there are two contracts involved in such a case; one between the worker and his company and the other between the company and the person who wants to use its services. Each needs to be approached with great care from a tax point of view even though the first may seem unimportant from a commercial one.

4.58   One interesting case where the interposition of a one-man company proved successful was *Cooke v Blacklaws (1984) 58 TC 255*. The taxpayer in that case, a New Zealander, was not concerned to avoid the ultimate customer, the National Health Service, treating him as an employee, as his activities were clearly Schedule D activities. His purpose was to pursue the tax advantages that could be obtained by an employee of an overseas company but were not available to a self-employed person. Mr Blacklaws entered into an oral contract with a Panamanian company at a fixed salary and the company orally agreed to make his services available to a UK dental practice for a fee based on a proportion of the NHS fees that Mr Blacklaws generated. The Inland Revenue sought to set aside the company and assess Mr Blacklaws on its income under Schedule D. In spite of the lack of documentation, the Special Commissioners found that he had carried out dental work for the practice as an employee of the Panamanian company. This decision was upheld in the High Court on the *Edwards v Bairstow* principle (see 4.31 above). This case should not be taken as an indication that a written contract does not matter. The contract provides an opportunity to set out the factual arrangement between the parties. As stated at 4.29, where there is a written contract the Courts will normally limit themselves to construing that contract. If there is no written agreement the Court will need to ascertain the facts, or at least those facts that can be proved, and then try to discern the contractual arrangement from such facts.

4.59   On which side of the Revenue's line a particular arrangement falls will depend very much on the facts. Some other questions that might be relevant are: can the customer dismiss the worker or must it cancel the contract and require the one-man company to remove its employee from the customer's premises? Does the customer have to pay the one-man company when the worker is sick or on holiday? If so what is the commercial justification? Can the customer tell the worker what to do or does it request him (as director of his one-man company) to arrange for himself (as the company's employee) to do the particular task?

Employment income taxed as receipts of Schedule D trades, etc.

4.60   A difficult area, in which there would appear to be little consistency of treatment, is what happens where, in the course of a trade or profession, a person enters into engagements that looked at on their own contractually constitute the acceptance of an employment or office.

Davies v Braithwaite

4.61   In *Davies v Braithwaite 18 TC 198* an actress entered into a contract to perform in the USA. At the time earnings of a UK resident from an employment carried on wholly overseas were assessable on a remittance basis. Miss Braithwaite contended that her contract with the US theatre was an employment contract and that as she had not remitted the earnings they were not taxable. The Inland Revenue contended that the agreement, albeit in the form of an employment agreement, was merely an incidence of her profession as an actress and that the earnings fell to be treated as part of her Schedule D income.

4.62   Upholding the Revenue's claim, Rowlatt J said 'it seems to me that where one finds a method of earning a livelihood which does not contemplate the obtaining of a post and staying in it, but essentially contemplates a series of engagements and moving from one to the other—and in the case of an actor's or actress's life it certainly involves going from one to the other and not going on playing one part for the rest of his or her life, but in obtaining first one engagement and then another, and a whole series of them—then each of the engagements could not be considered an employment, but is a mere engagement in the course of exercising a profession . . .' (*18 TC* at p. 204).

Fall v Hitchen

4.63   In a later case, *Fall v Hitchen 49 TC 433* a ballet dancer was engaged under a standard British Actor's Equity Association form of contract to perform at a theatre in England and following *Davies v Braithwaite*, sought to treat the earnings as part of his Schedule D activities. It was held that the case was distinguishable from the Braithwaite case and that the earnings should be assessed as employment income. It is not clear on what basis the judge saw a distinction. The most likely is that the contract in Braithwaite was of a few weeks duration only whereas that in Hitchen lasted for approximately six months.

4.64   Although *Fall v Hitchen* was decided in 1972 the Revenue was content for a long time to leave all such earnings within a performer's Schedule D accounts. However, in 1990, 18 years later, they adopted the stance that not only should they apply the decision in *Fall v Hitchen* rigidly but also, despite the fact that the judge specifically accepted that *Davies v Braithwaite* was still good law, they should regard the decision as applicable to all engagements under Equity contracts, however short in duration. In effect they seemed to be contending that the *Hitchen* case in reality overrode *Braithwaite* and that the latter was wrongly decided. They however exercised their 'care and management' powers (that the Revenue have discretion to do what they think necessary for the efficient care and management of the tax system) so as to allow established artists to treat their earnings from Equity contracts as part of their Schedule D activities. The cynical might feel that if the Revenue choose to ignore those Court decisions which they find inconvenient it is a clever ploy to exclude from the effect of such a decision those who can afford to challenge such a stance through the Courts! The Revenue's change of approach generated some protest in Parliament and, as a slight concession, the Government permitted entertainers to claim tax relief for agent's fees, although the relief in *FA 1990, s 77*, although extended slightly by *FA 1991, s 69*, is tightly circumscribed.

4.65   In 1993 Equity backed two 'test cases' before the Special Commissioners. These related to Alec McCowan, a long-established actor, and Sam West, a relative newcomer to the profession. The Commissioner held that the *Braithwaite* and *Fall v Hitchen* cases were not contradictory but dealt with different situations, and that both Mr McCowan and Mr West were self-employed.

Unfortunately, Equity having thought it had agreed that these were test cases, the Revenue subsequently decided not to appeal and stated that they do not consider the decision of general application within the acting profession.

This left the theatrical profession in a state of complete confusion. Following the decision in *Fall v Hitchen* the Revenue themselves had suggested to Equity that they should take a test case. This not having happened, they decided to give general effect to the decision—or rather partial effect to it—from 6 April 1990. By administrative edict they created a new class of taxpayer, those with 'reserved Schedule status'. These were performers who either:

(*a*)   had been taxed as such under Schedule D for 1986/87, 1987/88 and 1988/89 and had submitted accounts forming the basis of assessment of at least one of those years before 31 May 1989; or

(*b*)   had been taxed as such under Schedule D for at least three tax years from 1979/80 to 1988/89, had a satisfactory history of Schedule D treatment, had submitted accounts and tax returns for all years up to 1986/87 by 31 May 1989, and were taxable under Schedule D on their last theatrical engagement starting prior to 6 April 1990.

A person with reserved Schedule D status remained taxable under Schedule D—but only so long as he continued to meet his tax obligations satisfactorily and continued his professional activities without a break (*ESC A75* now obsolete). A performer entering the profession after 5 April 1987 was taxed as being in receipt of employment income in respect of performances under standard Equity contracts, but not necessarily in respect of other performances. Similarly, taxed was one already in the profession who did not meet either of the above tests or fell behind with his tax affairs. As the Schedule D treatment was, in the Revenue's eyes, a non-statutory concession there was no right of appeal to the Commissioners against a decision that a person's tax record has ceased to be 'satisfactory'.

4.66   Although the Revenue did not appeal the *McCowan* and *West* decisions, Ian Lorimer, a film technician (a vision mixer) took his own case to the Court of Appeal where it was held, albeit on *Edward v Bairstow* principles, that he was self-employed (*Hall v Lorimer* [*1994*] *STC 23*). The Revenue decided not to take the case to the House of Lords.

4.67   A single judgment was given by Nolan LJ. 'The case has been argued before us . . . on the agreed basis that the critical issue is whether or not the contracts from which the taxpayer derived his earnings were contracts of service . . . The detailed facts of the matter, which are so important in a case of this sort are set out with admirable thoroughness and clarity in the case stated . . .'.

4.68   The Crown submitted that 'an employment property so called is not the less an employment because it is casual rather than regular' and that 'the nature and degree of skill involved in the work cannot alone be decisive'. Nolan LJ accepted both of these propositions. He was hesitant about the Crown's suggestion that he should follow the approach taken in *Market Investigations* (see 4.22) and affirmed in *Lee Ting Sang* (see 4.33), as 'In cases of this sort there is no single path to a correct decision. An approach which suits the facts and arguments of one case may be unhelpful in another.' He endorsed the view of Mummery J in the High Court that 'In order to decide whether a person carries on business on his own account it is necessary to consider many different aspects of that person's work activity. This is not a mechanical exercise of running through items on a check list to see whether they are present in, or absent from, a given situation. The object of the exercise is to paint a picture from the accumulation of detail. The overall effect can only be appreciated by standing back from the detailed picture which has been painted, by viewing it from a distance and by making an informed, considered, qualitative appreciation of the whole . . . Not all details are of equal weight or importance in any given situation. The details may also vary in importance from one situation to another . . . It is . . . impossible in a field where a very large number of factors have to be weighed to gain any real assistance by looking at the facts of another case and comparing them one by one to see what facts are common, what are different and what particular weight is given by another tribunal to the common facts. The facts as a whole must be looked at, and a factor which may be compelling in one case in the light of the facts of that case may not be compelling in the context of another case.'

4.69   He found the distinction between an employee selling his labour and a contractor selling the product of his labour 'very hard to apply in the case of a professional man. Surely the self-employed barrister advising in his chambers or the doctor advising in his surgery is selling his skill and labour and not its product. If the scene shifts to the court or to the operating theatre can the client or patient really be said to be buying the product which may be disastrous in spite of the best efforts of the advocate or the surgeon . . . Again the question, whether the individual is in business on his own account, though often helpful, may be of little assistance in the case of one carrying on a profession or vocation. A self-employed author working from home or an actor or singer may earn his living without any of the normal trappings of a business. For my part I would suggest there is much to be said in these cases for bearing in mind the traditional contrast between a servant and an independent contractor . . . it is, I think, in any event plain that Cooke J was not intending to lay down an all-purpose definition of employment. For example, his test does not mention the duration of the particular engagement or the number of people by whom the individual is engaged'.

4.70   Nolan J specifically upheld the continuing relevance of the *Davies v Braithwaite* decision and felt it 'not surprising that the Special Commissioners attached importance to the case because it concerned an actress . . . whose income-earning activities had much in common with those of the taxpayer'. It is worth noting that the Revenue were contending that Mr Lorimer had 580 different 'employments' during a four-year period! *Hall v Lorimer* arises from another extra-statutory approach by the Revenue to taxation based ostensibly on their interpretation of the decision in *Fall v Hitchen*—or, many think, based on a desire to extend PAYE to as many of the self-employed as they could get away with! In the early 1980s they adopted the view that it was impossible for casual and freelance film technicians and other behind-the-scene workers to be self-employed and insisted that film companies should apply PAYE to all payments to such people—their latest guidance requiring this even where the worker is an employee of someone else such as his own personal services company (although 'by concession' they do not actually require tax to be deducted for assignments lasting less than a week). They gradually relented, looking at the work done by different categories of workers, and accepted that certain types of work did not constitute an employment. As a result they published a list of 'Grades where PAYE need not be applied'. Most of these were agreed in the early 1980s. They have been extremely reluctant to add to the list since then. Mr Lorimer's grade was not included on the list—and since his victory has not been added to it!

4.71   Following consideration of the *Hall v Lorimer* decision the Revenue said the decision adds two further factors to be considered in determining whether someone is an employee. The engagements may need to be looked at in the context of the worker's business activities as a whole including such matters as his exposure to bad debts and the amount of time spent on organising, obtaining or carrying out the work; and it may be appropriate to take into account the length of the individual engagement and the number of other persons for whom similar work is performed. They also conclude that the *Market Investigation* test may not be very relevant to professional people who conduct their occupations without the usual trappings of business such as stock, premises, and equipment. Independence may be a useful pointer in such cases. The Revenue will also look at whether the person's services require the exercise of rare skill and judgement, the worker is engaged for a specific task, the worker incurs substantial unreimbursed expenditure in obtaining, organising and carrying out engagements requiring visits to various sites, there is a risk of delayed payment and bad debts, and the extent to which the worker is able to influence pay.

4.72   The Revenue have also agreed that in the light of the *McCowan* and *West* decision actors, ballet dancers, opera singers and other performers and artistes who appear in live theatre, etc. or film, TV and video productions under Equity or Musician's Union Contracts may well be engaged under contracts for services, i.e. self-employed. The terms of the contract may not be decisive in themselves. They have indicated that the same principal applies to stage managers. They notified theatres, etc. that PAYE need not be applied to earnings of such people from September 1994. The Revenue also announced that individuals accepted to be within Schedule D from 1994/95 onwards but previously assessed as being in receipt of employment income could apply to have their tax liabilities for 1990/91 to 1993/94 recomputed. This decision effectively rendered the Reserved Schedule D concept obsolete. The Revenue's current position is that a performer or artiste is normally assessable under Schedule D except where he is engaged for a regular salary to perform in a series of different productions over a period of time in such roles as may be stipulated from time to time by the engager, e.g. permanent members of an orchestra or a ballet, opera or theatre company. This applies also to stage managers but not normally to other non-performing theatrical staff. They also accept that musicians engaged to appear at theatrical performances, those engaged under 'first call' or 'guarantee' contracts, musicians who are shareholder performers in the London Philharmonic, London Symphony, New Philharmonia and Royal Philharmonic Orchestras and other orchestral players who are engaged for individual performances are self-employed *(Employment Status Manual, paras ESM 4.122–4.140)*. In the film and television industries front of camera performers are generally accepted as self-employed. So are certain categories of behind camera workers. The Revenue publish a grading list setting out which classes they accept as Schedule D.

4.73   In their booklet IR175 issued in connection with the IR35 or personal service company rules (see 19.33) the Revenue appear to accept that *Hall v Lorimer* is not confined to the entertainment industry but is part of the mainstream law on what is an employment.

Offices held by professionals

4.74   The next category of cases in which the same problem arises is in relation to offices held by professionals. The leading case here is *IRC v Brander and Cruickshank 46 TC 574*. A Scottish firm of advocates derived a substantial part of its income from acting as company secretaries and registrars. Following the takeover of one company they were paid compensation for losing their role as registrar. They successfully claimed that as a registrarship was an office the income should strictly not have been included in their Schedule D income and although they did not wish to disturb this treatment the compensation was not part of their Schedule D activities but assessable under Schedule E—and being less than £30,000 (see 11.21(a) below) not taxable. The House of Lords upheld this contention. In *Walker v Carnaby Harrower, Barham and Pykett 46 TC 561* a similar claim was upheld in relation to compensation received by a firm of accountants who were asked to resign as auditors of a group of companies.

4.75   In spite of these decisions the Revenue have never sought to contend that accountants must exclude audit fees from their Schedule D accounts or that other similar receipts by professional firms should be taxed as employment income. Indeed on the contrary they have introduced concessions to prevent some such receipts being taxed as employment income where an Inspector of Taxes might have sought to persuade the payer to apply PAYE (see 2.25 above).

Doctors

4.76   The third category in which the same problem arises concerns doctors. A doctor in general practice works for the National Health Service under a contract for services and is assessable on his earnings under Schedule D. If he has a private practice the receipts from it are obviously also part of his Schedule D income. If, however, a doctor also has a part-time hospital appointment with a local Health Authority this is an office or employment taxable as employment income and the hospital pays the earnings under deduction of PAYE. The case that established that the hospital earnings should not be included in the Schedule D profits was a House of Lords decision, *Mitchell and Edon v Ross 40 TC 11*. The Revenue insist that a doctor's hospital earnings should be distinguished in this way.

4.77   The bulk of the tax litigation involving doctors has not been concerned with the principle of whether hospital earnings are taxable as employment income, but rather with the resultant problem in relation to expenses. The difficulty is that expenses in relation to the hospital appointment are not an allowable deduction in calculating Schedule D profits as they are obviously not wholly and exclusively incurred in earning such profits. Indeed, they are nothing to do with earning such profits, except to the extent that it might be contended that the hospital appointment enhances the reputation of the doctor, and possibly his ability to refer patients to hospital colleagues, and that the holding of the employment (even if it were unpaid) would be a necessary part of practice public relations. Unfortunately, in most cases the expenses are not deductible in calculation net employment income either, as the duties of the employment will not normally start until the doctor arrives at the hospital. In the *Mitchell and Edon* case the expenses were disallowed completely, and this has generally been the outcome of subsequent cases also, the one success being another House of Lords decision, *Pook v Owen 45 TC 571*. This problem is considered in more detail in Chapter 5.

Chapter 5

Expenses

Introduction

5.1   Normally an employer can be expected to provide an employee with whatever facilities he needs to perform his tasks effectively. Accordingly, he will either incur all necessary business expenses or will reimburse the employee for the cost of such expenditure. However, this is not always the case. In many businesses, such as the building or engineering trades, an employee will be expected to bring with him to the job his own basic tools and sometimes even quite expensive equipment. In others, the employee may invent his own equipment to do a job effectively and his employer may be happy for him to use such individual equipment on the job, and may be prepared to reflect the value of such equipment in the wage he pays. Sometimes, while accepting that a job could be done far more effectively if certain expenditure was to be incurred, the employer may feel that he cannot justify that expenditure in the context of his other commitments and the employee may decide to incur it himself. In some instances an employer will agree to pay a general expense allowance (which is effectively treated as part of the employee's salary for tax purposes) but out of which he expects the employee to pay for the expenses he incurs for the purpose of his work.

Statutory provisions

5.2   Specific provisions would therefore be expected to allow an employee to deduct from his salary expenses that he incurs in the course of his employment. These are to be found in *ITEPA 2003, ss 327–377*. Unfortunately, *section 336*, the general rule, is very narrowly drawn and over the years the courts have interpreted it extremely restrictively. Because of this a paraphrase of *section 336* would be dangerous and it is accordingly set out in full below:

'The general rule is that a deduction from earnings is allowed for an amount if:

(a)   the employee is obliged to incur and pay it as holder of the employment; and

(b)   the amount is incurred wholly, exclusively and necessarily in the performance of the duties of the employment'.

5.3   There are then in *sections 337* (travel in performance of duties) and *338* (travel for necessary attendance) two separate general rules for travel expenses.

'A deduction from earnings is allowed for travel expenses if:

(*a*)   the employee is obliged to incur and pay them as holder of the employment; and

(*b*)   the expenses are necessarily incurred on travelling in the performance of the duties of the employment'; and

'A deduction from earnings is allowed for travel expenses if:

(*a*)   the employee is obliged to incur and pay them as holder of the employment; and

(*b*)   the expenses are attributable to the employee's necessary attendance at any place in the performance of the duties of the employment'.

5.4   Prior to 2003/04 the wording read 'If the holder of an office or employment is *obliged* to incur and defray out of the emoluments of that office or employment:

(*a*)   qualifying travelling expenses; or

(*b*)   any amount (other than qualifying travelling expenses) expended wholly, exclusively and necessarily in the performance of the duties of the office or employment;

there may be deducted from the emoluments to be assessed the amount so incurred and defrayed.' [*ICTA 1988, s 198(1)*].

5.5   ' "Qualifying travelling expenses" means:

(*a*)   amounts necessarily expended on travelling in the performance of the duties of the office or employment; or

(*b*)   other expenses of travelling which:

   (i)   are attributable to the necessary attendance at any place of the holder of the office or employment in the performance of the duties of the office or employment; and

   (ii)   are not expenses of ordinary commuting or private travel.' [*ICTA 1988, s 198(1A)*].

From 2002/03 onwards a deduction against employment income cannot be claimed for qualifying travelling expenses in respect of the use of a car if mileage allowance payments (see 7.68) are made to the taxpayer in respect of use of the vehicle or mileage allowance relief (see 7.70) is available (*ICTA 1988, s 198(5)*).

5.6   Up to 1997/98 the text read:

'If the holder of an office or employment is *necessarily obliged*:

(*a*)   to incur and defray out of the emoluments of that office or employment the expenses:

    (i)   of travelling *in the performance* of the duties of the office or employment; or

    (ii)   of keeping and maintaining a horse to enable him to perform those duties; or

(*b*)   otherwise to expend money *wholly, exclusively and necessarily in the performance of those duties*;

there may be deducted from the emoluments to be assessed the expenses so necessarily incurred and defrayed.'

It will be seen that the changes from 1998/99 related wholly to travelling expenses apart from the consignment to history of the relief for keeping and maintaining a horse.

5.7   If the wording seems a little old-fashioned it is because the provision is virtually unchanged since the time of its original embodiment as the *Income Tax Act 1853, s 51*. The wording of most of the provisions tends to alter on consolidation of the tax statutes (which occurred in 1918, 1952, 1970 and 1988). It is no accident that the draftsman has not sought to make alterations here beyond what is necessary to deal with the new relief for employment-related travelling expenses which do not meet the condition of being in the performance of the duties. It is because there is a great deal of judicial guidance on its interpretation which the draftsman wished to preserve and which any alteration might invalidate.

The three requirements

5.8   There are three main hurdles that need to be overcome to obtain a deduction for an expense.

(*a*)   The employee must be 'obliged' to incur it.

(*b*)   It must be incurred 'in the performance of' the duties of the employment (other than travelling expenses within *section 198(1A)(b)*).

(*c*)   Except for travelling expenses, it must be 'wholly, exclusively and necessarily' incurred.

5.9   It is very difficult to meet all three of these tests. 'Obliged' has been held to connote an expense that is not personal to the employee but that each and every holder of the office or employment would have to incur. The leading case is *Ricketts v Colquhoun 10 TC 118*. A barrister who lived and worked in London was appointed to the office of Recorder of Portsmouth. He claimed to deduct his travelling expenses to Portsmouth. It was held that he could not do so as he would not have incurred the expense had he lived in Portsmouth. 'In the performance of the duties' is an equally hard test to satisfy.

Travelling expenses

5.10   It will be seen that there are two distinct categories of deductible travelling expenses. Travel in performance of duties and travel attributable to necessary attendance at a place in performance of the duties. The test of travelling in the performance of the duties of the employment can be hard to satisfy. Travelling expenses to one's place of employment are not incurred 'in the performance of' the duties of the employment; they are incurred in order to put the employee in a position to carry out his employment in order to apply this test. Sometimes a person has more than one place of employment. In such circumstances it is necessary to determine which, if any, is the base of the employment in order to apply this test. Travel from the base is travel in the performance of the duties of the employment, as once a person has reached his employment base he has commenced his duties. Many employees claim that their home is their base, so that all travel is in the course of the employment. Where a person, such as a travelling salesman, has no fixed place of employment, and rarely visits his company's premises, it may well be possible to show this. In most cases, however, it will not be possible.

5.11   This is well illustrated by *Miners v Atkinson* [*1997*] *STC 58* (see 5.36). The Revenue contended that Mr Miners' place of work was the office of a client of his employer company, so the travelling expenses from Mr Miners' home (the company's registered office) was not allowable. The Special Commissioner said that this ignored the fact that the taxpayer was employed by his company not the third party. However, he went on to hold that there was no evidence that the taxpayer's house had been specially designed or adopted as the company's office. Accordingly, it was not necessary for the work of the taxpayer to be carried out from that precise address. The taxpayer and his wife could have moved the registered office closer to the third party's premises. In these circumstances, costs of travel from the registered office/home were not 'necessarily' incurred for the purpose of the employment. Arden J endorsed this view. He suggested that the starting point is that the company's premises was the taxpayer's home. This required one to ask whether the taxpayer is working at home out of choice. He answered that question by quoting the Special Commissioners' view that it was not necessary for the work to be done at that precise address. This actually does not answer whether the taxpayer is working at home out of choice; it answers whether the particular location of the company's office was at the choice of its directors. Once the question is posed in that form it is difficult to see how travelling expenses of a director can ever be allowable, as the location of the business premises will always be at the choice of the board of directors. It is hard to see that it can make any difference whether the choice of location of the offices coincides with the choice of location of the home. It seems an extraordinary concept that a business could move its office closer to its customer, so travel to the customer is not allowable!

5.12   The Revenue accept that where travel is in the course of the employee's duties allowable expenses 'can include the cost of a reasonable level of refreshments (both alcoholic and non-alcoholic) with the meal and refreshments such as tea, coffee or soft drinks taken between meals'. (*IR Press Release 16 May 1995*). They also accept that travel includes 'the cost of any attributable subsistence, for example an evening meal and hotel room where the employee has to stay away overnight' (*Tax Bulletin 32, December 1997*). It also includes, for example, toll fees, the cost of hiring a car and parking charges. It will not include private expenses such as newspapers and laundry (but see 5.38 for the special relief for personal overnight expenses).

5.13 One interesting case on this theme is *Taylor v Provan 49 TC 579*. A Canadian resident was appointed a director of a UK brewery group. His only responsibility was to bring about a major merger. Most of his work was done from his home in Canada. He received no remuneration but was reimbursed for travel between Canada and the UK. Evidence was given that he was unique and no-one else could have done the job, which was specially created for him. It was held that the job required two places of work, his home in Canada and the company's offices in England, so that the air fares were for travel between the two and thus incurred in the course of the employment.

5.14 Home to work travel is not regarded as private use of a company car—and presumably is regarded as a business expense where public transport is used:

(*a*)   where the employee has a travelling appointment;

(*b*)   where the employee travels from home to a temporary place of work and the distance travelled is less than that between the normal place of work and the temporary place of work;

(*c*)   where, exceptionally, the home qualifies as a place of work and the employee travels from home to another place or work in the performance of his duties, and, by concession;

(*d*)   where a disabled person is provided with a car for home to work travel and there is no other private use;

(*e*)   where public transport is disrupted; and

(*f*)   for late-night journeys within the terms of *ITEPA 2003, s 248* (formerly *ESC A66*) (see 9.115(*t*)) (*Hansard 12 May 1993, col 472*).

5.15 The second category is travel which is attributable to the necessary attendance of the employee at a place in the performance of the duties, provided that the expense is not excluded as ordinary commuting or private travel. That word 'necessary' should be noted; but it is not the travelling expense that needs to be necessary in this case, it is the attendance of the employee at a particular place. It remains to be seen how this will be interpreted by the courts. It is not 'necessary' for a director of an English engineering company to do design work from his villa in the South of France; he does it there out of personal choice, so the expense, quite properly, will not be deductible. But what about the worker who is asked to go once a month to deliver stock to the branch office in his home town? It is necessary for someone to undertake that job, but it is not necessary for that particular employee to do it. And what about the employee who delivers an urgent and important document to the office in his home town? It is necessary for the document to be delivered, but in many cases this could have been achieved by consigning the document to a courier company. It is to be hoped that once a business need for something to be done in a particular place is identified the Revenue will accept that the 'necessary attendance' test is met and will not seek to become involved in the commercial management decision as to whose attendance it should be.

5.16   The main relaxation for this category of travel is that the travel does not have to be in the performance of the duties; all that has to be shown is that the employee needs to be at the particular place in order to perform duties of the employment there. The main exclusions are for ordinary commuting and private travel. Ordinary commuting is travel between the employee's home (or some other place that is not a workplace in relation to the employment) and a place which is a permanent workplace. [*ITEPA 2003, s 338(3)*]. Private travel is:

(*a*)   travel between the employee's home and a place that is not a workplace in relation to the employment (i.e. a place at which the employee's attendance is necessary in the performance of the duties of the employment); or

(*b*)   travel between two places neither of which is a workplace in relation to the employment.

[*ITEPA 2003, s 338(5)*, formerly *ICTA 1988, 12A Sch 2(2)(3)*].

Travel that is 'for practical purposes' substantially ordinary commuting or private travel is treated as such commuting or travel. [*ITEPA 2003, s 338(4)*]. This appears designed to exclude from relief travel where there is a minimal business need and the substantial reason for the travel is a non-business one. It will exclude relief for the employee who is sent to Australia to deliver a letter that could have easily been sent by post but was hand-delivered solely to provide the employee with a 'perk'.

5.17   Ordinary commuting is commuting to or from a 'permanent workplace'. This is defined as a place which the employee regularly attends in the performance of his duties and which is not a temporary workplace. [*ITEPA 2003, s 339(2)*] A temporary workplace is a place which the employee attends in the performance of the duties of the employment for the purpose of performing a task of limited duration or for some other temporary purpose. [*ITEPA 2003, s 339(3)*].

5.18   The distinction between a permanent and a temporary workplace is an important one. Travel from home to a permanent workplace is always disallowable as ordinary commuting. Travel from home to a temporary workplace is neither ordinary commuting nor private travel and is accordingly deductible provided that the necessary attendance in the performance of the duties test is satisfied.

5.19   A place cannot be a temporary workplace if the employee's attendance there is in the course of 'a period of continuous work' at the place which either lasts more than 24 months or comprises all (or almost all) of the total period for which the employee is likely to hold the employment or the attendance there is 'at a time when it is reasonable to assume' that it will be in the course of such a period. [*ITEPA 2003, s 339(5)*]. A 'period of continuous work' at a place means a period over which, looking at the whole period and considering all the duties of the employment, the duties of the employment fall to be performed to a significant extent at that place. [*ITEPA 2003, s 339(6)*]. The Revenue have said that they will regard duties as performed to a significant extent at a place if the employee spends 40 per cent or more of his working time at that place. The converse does not hold true. A place can be a permanent workplace even though the employee spends less than 40 per cent of his time there, with the result that travel to that place falls to be disallowed as ordinary commuting (*Tax Bulletin 33, February 1998*).

5.20   Note especially the phrase 'at a time when it is reasonable to assume'. This applies the test prospectively as well as historically. If when the travelling expenses are incurred there is an intention, or even a likelihood, that the work at a particular place will extend over more than 24 months, that place cannot be a temporary workplace, even though the period of employment there actually turns out to be less than 24 months. The Revenue have said that the converse holds true also. Although the legislation prevents a place being a temporary workplace if the employee in fact spends a period there in excess of 24 months, the Revenue have indicated that they propose to ignore this. If when the employee first attends that site he expects to be working there for 24 months or less, they do not regard it as a permanent workplace until either there is a change of intention or the employee has in fact worked there for over 24 months.

5.21   An actual or contemplated modification of the place at which the duties of the employment fall to be performed is disregarded in applying the 24-month rule if it does not have, or would not have, any substantial effect on the employee's journey or on the expenses of travelling to and from the place where the duties are to be performed. [*ITEPA 2003, s 339(7)*]. For example, suppose an employee is sent from London to Edinburgh to open an office, commuting back to London at weekends. He takes premises on a 12-months lease, intending to move to larger premises in Edinburgh after that time. He intends to spend a further 18 months at the new office. It is not permissible to say that the period in the first office will last less than 24 months and so will that at the second. As the journey from London to the new office will be roughly the same as at the old, the two must be looked at as one. As the employee anticipates spending 30 months in Edinburgh the Edinburgh office will not be a temporary workplace, with the result that the whole of the travel will be disallowed as ordinary commuting.

5.22 Mr Phillips was a construction worker. During 2000/01 he had three separate assignments, each with a separate contract, obtained through an agency. The Special Commissioners held that commuting to and from work at a temporary job was ordinary commuting because the place where the work was performed was a permanent workplace. Mr Phillips accordingly had three separate employments. His attendance at each was in the course of a period of continuous work at that place which comprised all of the period for which he held the employment. Accordingly the travel was ordinary commuting (*Phillips v Hamilton* [*2003*] *STC (SCD) 286*). Mr Macken was also a construction worker. During 1998/99 he worked for a construction company at a site in Bristol through an agency. The company offered him a permanent job at the same site. It was held that although he had had two jobs he had nevertheless worked continuously at the same site for more than 24 months for the purpose of the 24-month rule (*Macken v Hamilton* [*2003*] *STC (SCD) 286*).

5.23 A place which the employee regularly attends in the performance of his duties and which forms the base from which those duties are performed, or which is the place at which the tasks to be carried out in the performance of the duties are allocated, cannot be a temporary workplace. [*ITEPA 2003, s 339(4)*]. For example, suppose a repairman has to go into his employer's office every Monday morning where he obtains his instructions for the week. That will be a permanent workplace, so his travelling expenses to and from the office will be ordinary commuting and disallowed, albeit that the remainder of his travelling expenses are likely to be deductible. If he is passed his instructions by telephone at his home instead of attending the office there would, in contrast, be no disallowance.

5.24 In certain circumstances a person is treated as having a permanent workplace consisting of an area, in which case travel to the edge of that area would be ordinary commuting but travel within it would be deductible. This applies where:

(*a*)   the duties are defined by reference to that area (whether or not they also require attendance at a place outside that area);

(*b*)   in the performance of the duties the employee attends different places within that area; and

(*c*)   none of the places that he so attends within that area is a permanent workplace [*ITEPA 2003, s 339(8)*].

There is no restriction on the size of the defined area. In theory it could be 'the UK' or even 'the world'. However, if it is defined more broadly than the area in which the employee normally works the Revenue are likely to contend that the defined area is a sham.

5.25 Travel between two workplaces in the course of a single employment is normally travel in the course of that employment. The position is different where there are separate employers at the two workplaces—and probably even if there are two separate employments with the same employer. There is an exception for expenses of travel between two places at which a person performs duties of different offices or employments under companies in the same group (i.e. where one is a 51 per cent subsidiary (= 50+ per cent) of the other or both are 51 per cent subsidiaries of a third company). Such expenses are treated as necessarily expended in the performance of the duties which that person is to perform at his destination. [*ITEPA 2003, s 340*]. It should be noted that this only applies within a group. If two companies are associated but do not form a group, travel between the two needs to meet the ordinary tests. Similarly if a person has employments with two partnerships or with a partnership and an associated company, the normal tests need to be met.

5.26   There is still potentially a problem where an employee works from home, particularly where he is the controlling director of a one-man company. The Revenue say that 'where employees work at home they usually do so because it is convenient rather than because the nature of the job actually requires them to carry out the duties of their employment there. However, where it is an objective requirement of the employee's duties to carry out substantive duties at the home address then his or her home is a workplace for tax purposes—with the result that travel between there and another permanent workplace in respect of the same employment is in the performance of the duties of the employment (*Tax Bulletin 32, December 1997*). The problem is that this 'objective requirement' test (which is not in the legislation) does not reflect modern practices. It is becoming increasingly common for employees to spend part of their working time at home by agreement with their employer. Indeed it is becoming fairly common for certain 'hot-desking' in large organisations (even including the Inland Revenue). This is where the employer has agreed that office employees can work from home so that he does not provide accommodation for all of them at his own premises on the basis that there is likely always to be a 'spare' desk available. The nature of the job does not require such staff to work from home. It is for the convenience of both the employee and the employer. Currently most employees are probably content in such circumstances to accept that travel to the employer's premises is ordinary commuting because that is normally a regular requirement. However, as home-working increases people are likely to increasingly question whether the Revenue's view is correct.

5.27   *Warner v Prior (2003 STC (SCD) 109* exemplifies the problem. Ms Warner was employed by Kent County Council as a supply teacher. She was required to do two types of duty, 'directed time' (actual teaching) and 'additional time' (marking work, writing reports and preparing lessons). Because there was rarely a place to do additional time work in a school (as a supply teacher had fewer facilities than permanent teachers) she carried out the bulk of her additional time in an office she maintained at home. The Special Commissioner held that her home office was a place of work and that it was objectively necessary having regard to her duties for her to have such a place of work somewhere other than the schools. However, he held that that fact of itself did not mean that she was entitled to deduct travelling expenses between her two places of work. Where she lived, at least within Kent, had no bearing on her appointment or her ability to perform it. Her secondary place of work at home was dictated by where she lived and not by the requirements of the job itself. The travelling expenses were accordingly not 'necessarily incurred' and were not deductible.

5.28   The position of the director of the one-man company is likely to depend on the facts. The new rules do not negate the *Miners v Atkinson* case (see 5.11 and 5.36). However, Mr Miners worked largely for one client, so there was a site that the court could·discern as his base. If a one-man company has a number of clients none of which can be categorised as the main one, it is probable that if the director's home is not his base and he will be a site-based employee—in which case all his travel will be from home to a temporary workplace and therefore fully deductible. Support for this view can be found in the parliamentary debates on the IR35 legislation (see 19.33) and the guidance in that legislation given in *Tax Bulletin 47 (June 2000)*.

5.29   It will be seen that the tests look at the status of the journey, not the nature of the expense. Once the application of the test gives rise to a deduction, the cost of the travel is allowable irrespective of the mode of transport. There is also no territorial limitation. If a temporary workplace is in Australia, the travel costs will be deductible as much as if it is in Manchester. The Revenue say that they will not normally deny relief simply because the employee could have used an alternative cheaper route or could have travelled standard class but went first class. However, if the travel arrangements are 'unusually lavish' they will want to consider whether, on the facts, the expenditure is really attributable to business travel or is, for example, some sort of reward—or perhaps motivated by a private whim of a director (*Tax Bulletin 32, December 1997*).

5.30   Under the rule that applied up to 1997/98, the Revenue distinguished between three types of work; normal, site-based employees and those with travelling appointments. A person had a travelling appointment if he had no fixed base but his work required him to travel to customers' premises, within a defined area, spending a very short time at each location. The obvious example is the travelling salesman. Another example is a TV repairman. All of the travelling expenses of such a person were deductible if he lived within the defined area; in effect his home was his base. If he did not, all of the travelling expenses within the defined area were deductible. A person was site-based if he had no fixed base but worked at a succession of different sites. The individual site where he was working at any particular time was regarded as his place of work. Accordingly no travelling expenses were allowable, everything was regarded as home to office travel. The concept of the site-based employee was recognised in *Elderkin v Hindmarsh 60 TC 651*. A consulting engineer was required to work at premises of clients around the country. His employer would telephone him at home and give him details of his next appointment. The engineer would attend the client's premises, for days or weeks at a time, carry out tests or other work and write a report from home. He was paid a living allowance by his employer when working away from home. This was held to be taxable. The living costs were not incurred in the performance of his duties as the duties did not commence until he reached a client's premises. The Inland Revenue were increasingly seeking to categorise itinerant workers as site-based, particularly in the construction and computer programming industries. Even where an employee had a fixed base, e.g. an office, the Revenue tended to ask where the substance of the work fell to be performed. If this was mainly outside the office, they frequently contended that the employment was nevertheless site-based. This was a particular problem with 'one-man' companies where the office is frequently a room set aside at the employee's home.

5.31   The employee who had a fixed base was not free from problems. A difficulty arose with what the Revenue call triangular travel. The Revenue considered that strictly speaking, where an employee went to a business engagement direct from home instead of going to his office or other work-base first, then no part of such travel was in the course of the performance of the duties of the employment. If, however, he went to his fixed base, travel from that base to the business engagement was properly deductible—although the Revenue have been known to question that where there was no business purpose for visiting the base other than to seek to make the onward travel allowable. The Revenue's approach was to allow as business travel the cost of the shorter of the journey from home to the business engagement or the journey from the office or other base to the business engagement.

5.32   The Revenue have entered into various Working Rule Agreements with Trade Associations relating to travel and subsistence payments in the construction and allied industries which contain limited concessionary elements. The benefit of such agreements are available to all employees in the industry that meet the relevant conditions, irrespective of whether or not the employer is a member of the relevant trade association (*Taxline, January 1995, item 17*). There are specific exemptions for travel where public transport is disrupted (see 9.115(t)), travel by disabled persons (see 9.115(u)) and occasional late night travel and breakdown in car sharing arrangements (see 9.115(t)). There is also an exemption for offshore oil and gas workers. Where such a person has a permanent workplace at an offshore installation no tax is charged on the provision of transport by sea or air between the UK mainland and the offshore installation provided that the place of arrival and departure on the mainland is one for which such transport is provided for employees generally. The exemption also covers overnight accommodation in the vicinity of the place of arrival and departure on the mainland where that is necessary because of the time that the transfer transport from the installation takes place, local transport to and from the place of accommodation, and the reimbursement of reasonable expenses incurred by the employee on such transport, accommodation or subsistence. [*ITEPA 2003, s 305*]. This replaces an earlier concession (*ESC A65*).

Case law

5.33   The allowability of travelling expenses has spawned a great deal of litigation. In *Nolder v Walters 15 TC 380* an airline pilot was liable to be called for duty at any time. He unsuccessfully sought a deduction for travel between his home and the airport on the basis that once he was called he was on duty and that accordingly his home was his base. It was held that his duties did not start until after he had reached the airport. In *Pook v Owen 45 TC 571*, by contrast, a doctor was allowed a deduction for travel between his home and a hospital. He demonstrated that he had two employment bases, his home and the hospital, so that travel between the two was in the course of his duties. He could show this because he took responsibility for a patient from the moment he received a call at home. He instructed the hospital staff on the telephone as to what treatment to give, jumped in his car, and continued the treatment when he reached the hospital. On the other hand, in *Bhadra v Ellam 60 TC 466* the duties of a relief doctor were held not to start until he reached the hospital. A similar disallowance was made in *Hamerton v Overy 35 TC 73* where the duties of a consultant anaesthetist were held not to start until he reached the hospital. A general practitioner who acted as a clinical officer at three separate hospitals was also denied relief for travelling expenses both to and between the hospitals (*Parikh v Sleeman [1990] STC 233*).

5.34   A non-executive director of an NHS trust with several hospitals received and read trust papers at home. He claimed that reading papers was part and parcel of his duties as a director. The Special Commissioners held that such reading was merely preparatory to carrying out his duties. Furthermore the need to read them at home did not arise from the nature of the duties, it arose from personal choice. The taxpayer was therefore not necessarily obliged to defray travelling expenses from his home to the trust sites in the performance of his duties (*Knapp v Morton, [1999] STC (SCD) 13*).

5.35   The fact that it is impossible to live near one's place of work will not help. In *Andrews v Astley 8 TC 589* an employee was compelled by a housing shortage to live outside the town where he worked but was refused a deduction for the cost of maintaining a motorbike to get to work. A deduction was also refused in *Phillips v Keane 1 ITC 69*, an Irish case where the identical tests of deductibility apply. Even if the employee cannot choose his place of work, as in the wartime case where the Government directed a married woman to work for a particular company, travel from home will still not be allowable (*Phillips v Emery 27 TC 90*).

5.36   A worrying decision that will add weight to what appears to be a concerted attack by the Inland Revenue on travelling expenses of shareholder/directors of one-man companies based at their homes is that in *Miners v Atkinson* [*1997*] *STC 58*. Mr Miners was a computer consultant employed by a one-man company, WCLA, based at his home. During the period in dispute it appears that the only client of WCLA was another company, Lombard, some 80 miles away. It was not disputed that Mr Miners was not an employee of Lombard. He did some of the Lombard work at WCLA's office (at his home) but much of it at Lombard's premises. The Special Commissioner accepted that Mr Miners' base was at WCLA's office but nevertheless held that the travelling expenses to Lombard's offices were not necessarily incurred in the performance of his duties with WCLA. 'Mr and Mrs Miners were the only directors and the shareholders of WCLA. Had they wished they could have moved to Croydon or anywhere else and re-established the registered office of WCLA wherever they wished'. This was upheld by Arden J very succinctly: 'The starting point is that 4 Sandringham Road was the taxpayer's home. On the authorities, it seems to me that one must ask whether the taxpayer was working at home out of choice. The Special Commissioners answered that question against the taxpayer. "It was not necessary for the work which Mr and Mrs Miners carried out at 4 Sandringham Road to be done at that precise address. It could have been done anywhere". In the light of Lord Reid's speech particularly in *Taylor v Provan* (see 5.12). . . . in my judgment the Special Commissioner was correct in concluding that the taxpayer's travelling expenses were not deductible.' The passage from Lord Reid's speech in *Taylor v Provan* to which the Judge refers is, 'If the holder of an office or employment has to do part of his work at home the place where he resides is generally still his personal choice. If he could do his home work equally well wherever he lives then I do not see how the mere fact that his home is also a place of work could justify a departure from the Ricketts ratio', i.e. that the expenses with which *section 198* is concerned are only those which each and every occupant of the particular office is necessarily obliged to incur in the performance of his duties. There is, however, a big difference between Mr Taylor and Mr Ricketts and the case of Mr Miners. Their employer had an office elsewhere; they did not have to work at home. In Mr Miners' case the only place of business of WCLA was at Sandringham Road. Thus, while it was true that he was based at home, he was actually based at the sole place of business of his employer. If the suggestion that a two person company can move its place of business near to its major customer if it wishes is carried to its logical conclusion, that similarly applies to any company under the control of one person even where it has established an office away from the home of the controlling shareholder. Where does the dividing line fall? Would Mr Miners have succeeded if he had converted his garage into an office? Or if he had bought the house next door and turned it into an office? Or if he had rented a purpose built office a few streets away? On the test adopted by the Commissioner and the judge it is hard to see that any of these would have made a difference. Some people think that a separate office a few streets away would have been acceptable, but it is illogical that the trader who can afford to rent an office should be treated more favourably than one who does not have the money to do so.

5.37   An equally worrying case is *Kirkwood v Evans ([2002] EWHC 30(Ch)), (2002 STC 231)* which seems to undermine the growing trend towards homeworking. Mr Evans was a civil servant employed by the DSS in King's Lynn until June 1991. He was then employed on detached duty in Southampton. In June 1991 the DSS decided to transfer the work to Leeds. For five years Mr Evans commuted between King's Lynn and Leeds, for which he received an allowance from the DSS towards his travel costs. The DSS introduced a voluntary homeworking scheme in 1996 at which time they appear to have told Mr Evans that he should either work from home or seek alternative employment. Mr Evans opted for homeworking, which made his home his main work place. He agreed with the DSS that he would attend their office in Leeds once a week to deliver the work he had done and collect new work for the forthcoming week. It was held that:

(*a*)   Mr Evans had two work places, one in King's Lynn and the other in Leeds and travelling between the two was dictated by the place where he chose to live not by the nature of the work;

(*b*)   the office in Leeds was a permanent workplace as the terms of the homeworking scheme required him to attend there on one day a week; and

(*c*)   the travel was ordinary commuting (see 5.17) because it was between the employee's home and a place which is a permanent workplace and could not therefore fall within *section 198(1A)* (see 5.5); it was irrelevant that Mr Evan's home was also a workplace.

For good measure the judge also disallowed the costs of heating and lighting the workspace in Mr Evans' home on the grounds that these were not wholly exclusively and necessarily incurred in the performance of his duties. That seems particularly harsh. He needed the light to work by. He would not have switched it on were he not working. Accordingly, it is hard to see why the cost of the units of electricity consumed whilst he worked there did not meet that test. It is generally accepted that items like telephone calls and electricity where the cost depends on usage do not have a dual purpose where individual units are consumed for a specific business purpose. The judge also said that as homeworking was optional under the scheme it was not necessary for Mr Evans to incur the expense, as he had chosen to work from home. He could have continued to commute to Leeds albeit that it appears that his employer was no longer prepared to subsidise such commuting.

Lorry drivers

5.38   There are also special concessions for lorry drivers. No tax charge will arise if an employer reimburses to the driver the extra cost of travelling and subsistence which the employee incurs because he is away on duty. Where a driver travels full-time in the course of his duty the additional cost of meals at restaurants and cafes over what he would have spent if he were able to get home for meals can similarly be reimbursed—unless the driver travels only in a limited area. The driver is expected to produce bills or vouchers (*SP 16/80*).

5.39 Even where travel is in the course of the employment it is not sufficient for it to be convenient to use a particular mode of transport. Thus, where a civil servant claimed to deduct the excess of the cost of using his car when travelling on official business over the mileage allowance he received, it was held that he was not 'necessarily obliged' to incur this expense as it was not a condition of his employment that he had to use the car and there was no evidence that he could not have travelled by public transport (*Marsden v IRC 42 TC 326*).

Temporary absence

5.40 As explained at 5.19 an employee who is temporarily sent to work away from his normal place of work can claim a deduction of expenses necessarily incurred in travelling to the temporary place and also for accommodation and subsistence at that place. Two conditions must be met: the absence must not be expected to exceed twenty-four months (and must not do so in fact) and the employee must return to his normal place of work at the end of the temporary assignment. This rule is not limited to a temporary workplace in the UK and will, accordingly, cover hotel and subsistence expenses if an employee is sent by his employer to work overseas for, say, three or four months.

Personal incidental overnight expenses

5.41 There is a specific exemption from tax for incidental overnight expenses of up to £5 a night in the UK and £10 a night elsewhere. It covers sums paid to, or on behalf of, a director or employee wholly and exclusively for the purpose of defraying any expenses which are incidental to the employee being away from his usual place of abode during a qualifying absence from home and which would not otherwise be deductible as an expense. A qualifying absence from home means a continuous period throughout which the employee is obliged to stay away from his usual place of abode and during which he has at least one overnight stay and all of such stays are at places to which the travelling expenses are deductible in calculating taxable employment income (other than under the special provisions in *sections 371* (see 13.45), *374* (see 12.34) and *376* (see 13.38)) or, if there are no travelling expenses (e.g. because he travels with someone else at no extra cost), such expenses would have been deductible had they been incurred (*ITEPA 2003, ss 240, 241*). From 1997/98 the exemption also applies where the stay is at a place to which the employee has gone for training, education, etc. within *ITEPA 2003, s 250* (see 9.69). From 2000/01 it applies where it is at a place to which he has gone for education or training within *ITEPA 2003, s 255* (see 9.72). [*ITEPA 2003, s 240(6)*].

5.42 The relief does not apply to expenses borne by the employee; they must be either reimbursed to him or incurred by the employer. The

£5 and £10 limits are *de minimis* figures. If the expense is £5.01 the whole amount is taxable. The limit applies to the total payment, aggregating cash payments, payments by non-cash vouchers, credit tokens and payments of expenses (*ITEPA 2003, s 241(2)*). Where the stay covers a number of consecutive nights the aggregate expenses are compared with £5 or £10 multiplied by the total number of nights; each night cannot be considered on its own (*ITEPA 2003, s 241(3)*). A night and an overnight stay are not defined. However, the £5 figure applies if the whole of the night is spent in the UK and the £10 figure if any part of the night is spent outside the UK. As the legislation refers to at least one overnight 'stay' the position on nights' travelling is unclear.

Example

Jack and Jill, two employees of Aquarian Enterprises Ltd, went on a business trip to New York. Jack caught a flight on Monday afternoon which got him into New York at 5.00 pm (New York time) as he had a preliminary meeting at 9.00 am Tuesday morning. Jill caught a flight on Tuesday morning which got her to New York at 2.30 pm local time for their afternoon meeting. They both caught the 9.00 pm flight to London on Tuesday night which arrives at Heathrow at 9.00 am Wednesday morning.

Jack had an overnight stay in New York on Monday. He had a continuous period from Monday afternoon to Wednesday morning throughout which he was obliged to stay away from his UK place of abode. This absence included two nights, Monday and Tuesday, spent at least partly outside the UK (as most of Tuesday night was spent either in New York or over the Atlantic). His allowance is accordingly £20.

Jill's position is unclear. Depending on how one defines night—as when night starts in the UK it is mid-afternoon in New York—she could be said to have spent part of the night in New York as it would have been about 2.00 am London time when her flight home left. She certainly spent part of the night on the aircraft. But is that sufficient? Did she have an overnight stay anywhere? Probably, as she stayed away from her UK home overnight even if she did not stay in any one place during that time.

5.43 This exemption covers personal expenses such as newspapers, hotel videos, telephone calls home, etc. that are not incurred for business purposes. The idea is to relieve employers of the obligation to scrutinise hotel bills and isolate such personal expenses on the form P11D. The limit is so small that it is doubtful whether it achieves that objective. It is likely that in most cases the detailed scrutiny will still be needed to check if the *de minimis* limit is breached. If the employer has a policy requiring repayment of any excess personal expense over the £5 or £10 limit no tax liability will arise provided the excess is actually repaid. The Revenue say that in such circumstances there may be reporting consequences, i.e. the amount needs to be shown on the P11D, if the refund is not made within a reasonable time of the payment (*IR Press Release 16 May 1995*). Where an item is covered by the exemption it does not need to be shown on the P11D.

Directors

5.44   By concession, a director of two or more companies in a group or a collection of associated companies (or a person who is a director of one company and an employee of another) is regarded as having one place at which he normally acts as a director of all the companies concerned. This enables travel between the offices or places of business of all the companies to be allowable as being necessarily incurred in the course of his duties. This concession applies only to UK travel (*ESC A4*). It is not expressed to apply to mere employees.

5.45   A director who gives his services free to a company 'not managed with a view to dividends' (which probably means with a view to profit—the Revenue instance a company that owns a hall or sports ground or runs a club) is not taxed on any travelling expenses reimbursed to him, even if they are from home to the company's premises (*ESC A4*).

5.46   By concession, if a director or higher-paid employee on an overseas business trip takes his wife with him because his health is so precarious that he cannot undertake foreign travel unaccompanied, and the employer pays the wife's expenses, these are not assessed on the husband (*ESC A4*).

5.47   The expenses of a county surveyor in attending a world road conference in Tokyo were held not to be allowable even though he wanted to discuss with other experts there a problem arising from his work. He went at his own expense and in his own time. His employer did not require him to attend and thus the expense was not necessarily incurred (*Owen v Burden 47 TC 476*).

Expense allowances

5.48   The Inland Revenue frequently contend that if an employer does not pay for an expense, that is *prima facie* evidence that the employee was not necessarily obliged to incur it. Whilst there would appear to be no legal basis for this, it is probably a reasonable starting point in most cases. If an employee is likely to incur expenses that, for one reason or another, he does not wish to ask his employer to reimburse, he should ask his employer to designate part of his salary as an expense allowance. Such an allowance would at least rebut the Revenue's *prima facie* inference, as the very payment of the allowance suggests that the employee is expected to incur expenses that will not be specifically reimbursed.

In the performance of duties

5.49   The second hurdle is whether an expense is incurred in the performance of the duties of the employment. The problems with travel
expenses have already been considered but similar problems arise with
other expenses. The question that the courts normally pose is whether the
person was performing his duties at the time he was reaping the fruits of
the expenditure. In *Humbles v Brooks 40 TC 500*, where a history teacher
attended weekend lectures to update his knowledge of history, it was held
that while he was sitting in the lecture room he was not teaching and
thus while the expenditure was of benefit to his duties it was not in the
performance of them. Even where a student laboratory assistant was
required at his employer's expense to attend classes in preparation for a
university degree he was denied relief for travelling expenses and text
books as it was held that his attendance at the classes, although a condition of his employment, was not in the performance of it (*Blackwell v
Mills 26 TC 468*). In *Lupton v Potts 45 TC 643* examination fees paid by
a solicitor's articled clerk were disallowed. He did not need to pass the
examination to carry out his duties and the expenditure was not incurred
in the course of them. Employment agency fees to obtain a job are to
place a person in a position to perform the duties of that job, not incurred
in the performance of it (*Shortt v McIlgorm 26 TC 262*). In *Ansell v
Brown [2001] STC 1166* dietary supplements taken by a professional
Rugby Union player were held, reversing the decision of the General
Commissioners, not to have been incurred in the performance of his
duties. The employment contract required Mr Brown 'to maintain at all
times a high standard of physical fitness'. The judge thought it plain that
'the expenditure on supplements was incurred for the purpose of achiev-
ing and maintaining the required level of fitness and the required size and
physique for a back-row forward', but held that was expenditure to
enable him to perform the duties and not in the performance itself. He
also added that in any event the need for the expenditure arose from Mr
Brown's own personal circumstances, namely his need to increase his
weight, which would have meant that the 'necessary' test was not met
either. In *Ben Nevis v IRC (2001 STC (SCD) 144) (SpC 281)* an
employee could work for his employer only if he were registered with
the Securities Association. The Association declined to register him
because he was under investigation by his previous employer. The new
employer agreed to allow his employment to continue but on condition
that he kept it informed of developments in the investigation. The taxpayer was ultimately exonerated by the investigation. The legal fees
incurred by the employee were held not to be in the performance of the
duties of the new employment; the taxpayer was merely putting himself
in a position to perform those duties.

5.50   A particularly harsh case is *Snowdon v Charnock (2001 STC
(SCD 152) (SpC 282)*. Dr Snowdon was a doctor and a psychiatrist. This
qualification enabled him to act as a psychotherapist. He was employed
as a Higher Specialist Registrar in Psychotherapy. This is a training post
including supervised clinical work. The taxpayer incurred psychotherapy

fees for personal analysis, half of the cost of which was reimbursed by his employer. The Revenue accepted that that half was not taxable on Dr Snowdon by virtue of *section 251* (see 9.67), i.e. work-related training. Dr Snowdon claimed a deduction for the other 50 per cent. His employment contract required him to undergo personal therapy and described this both as a duty of the post and a condition of the employment. The personal therapy was required to enable Dr Snowdon to put himself in the shoes of a patient so as to be able to realise the likely effect of his clinical advice. Although the judge felt the case to be a borderline one, he held that the taxpayer was not required to spend the money in the performance of his duties. 'While he was undergoing personal therapy he was not performing the duties under the contract of employment'. It is hard to see why not if it was a specific duty, but the judge was clearly swayed by the fact that the job was a training post and that the psychotherapy was a training requirement of the Royal College of Psychiatrists and thus enabled the taxpayer to become better qualified to perform his duties.

Domestic help

5.51   Domestic help to enable a person to take up or continue in employment is not an allowable expense as the employee is neither necessarily obliged to incur the expense, nor incurs it in the performance of the duties. A married couple employed jointly at a single salary as master and mistress of a school could not deduct the cost of a housekeeper engaged to carry out the household duties while the wife was working (*Bowers v Harding 3 TC 22*). A widower could not deduct a payment to a housekeeper to look after his children while he was at work (*Halstead v Condon 46 TC 289*). The costs of a child minder or of putting a child in a crèche so that the mother can work will similarly not be deductible although, in fairly limited circumstances, there is now an exemption from tax in relation to the provision of crèche facilities by the employer (see 6.41(*m*) below).

Duality of purpose

5.52   The third hurdle is that to qualify for a deduction an expense must be wholly and exclusively incurred in the performance of the duties (the word 'necessarily' does not seem to add much in this context as once a person is necessarily obliged to incur an expense, that expense is likely automatically to be necessarily incurred).

Mallalieu v Drummond

5.53   The most important case in this area is the Schedule D case of *Mallalieu v Drummond 57 TC 330*. Under Schedule D, expenditure has to meet the 'wholly and exclusively' test (but not the 'necessarily obliged' one). This case is particularly important because it is a House of Lords decision and a fairly recent one (1983). Miss Mallalieu was a barrister. The Bar Council requires that in court a lady barrister should wear black dresses, suits, tights and shoes and white shirts or blouses. Miss Mallalieu did not wear black and white on social occasions. She had an extensive, colourful wardrobe. She gave evidence that when buying clothes for court work her only motive was to comply with the bar's rules of professional conduct. It was held that the expenditure was not wholly and exclusively incurred in the performance of the duties as she had a dual motive for incurring it. The secondary motive was to meet the normal human requirements of warmth and decency. Although she may have consciously only had in her mind the rules of professional conduct she must have subconsciously realised that she could not have appeared in court naked. In the House of Lords, Lord Brightman sought to draw a distinction between the *Mallalieu* circumstances and cases where a person is required to wear a uniform or a costume, but as he thought the difference was self-evident did not bother to explain it. This is unfortunate. It is by no means self-evident, at least to the author, that a waitress required to wear a uniform or an entertainer wearing a costume do not thereby satisfy their needs of warmth and decency.

5.54   The real answer probably lies in the *Edwards v Bairstow 36 TC 207* principle that the courts can disturb a finding of fact by the Commissioners only if no reasonable body of Commissioners properly instructed in the law could have arrived at it. The General Commissioners having found that Miss Mallalieu had a (subconscious) motive of the preservation of warmth and decency, even though there was no specific evidence presented to this effect, were entitled to reach that conclusion—indeed Lord Brightman was of the opinion that he would have found it impossible to reach any other conclusion. The clothes were 'ordinary' clothes and Miss Mallalieu not only wore them in court but also in her chambers and on the way to and from court. She therefore in practice satisfied to a significant degree her need for warmth and decency. A uniform or a costume is not normally suitable for wear outside the work environment so it is unlikely that a body of Commissioners would find a dual motive in such expenditure. However, some uniforms are suitable for wear outside work—shop assistants employed by Marks & Spencer, for example, frequently wear their uniforms to and from the shop—but these do not seem to have been attacked by the Revenue.

Clothing

5.55   The other practical explanation, of course, is that uniform or costume cases are unlikely, in general, to come before the courts. The Inland Revenue have long adopted the stance that if clothing is suitable for everyday use it cannot be wholly and exclusively incurred for business purposes. If it is not suitable for everyday use any non-business benefit is incidental to the business purpose. It is improbable, even in the light of *Mallalieu v Drummond*, that suitability or unsuitability for everyday use can be the statutory test as to whether expenditure is incurred wholly and exclusively for business purposes. If, for example, an actor buys a lounge suit to wear in a play and only ever wears it on stage, the fact that he could have worn it on other occasions is unlikely to detract from the fact that his professional use of it is likely to have been the motive for its acquisition. Equally, the fact that clothing is specially reinforced to meet the rigours of a stage performance is likely to support a motive that the expenditure was wholly and exclusively for business purposes even though in outward appearance it may be indistinguishable from a suit for everyday wear. Nevertheless, the *Mallalieu v Drummond* decision has in practice resulted in the Revenue challenging expenditure on clothing—and indeed on other expenditure that satisfies a personal need—far more rigorously than before. On the other hand, they seem to have adopted a test that if a logo or the name of the employer is permanently affixed to the clothes that will satisfy the test of deductibility. It is difficult to discern a statutory justification for this distinction. The Revenue seem content for the company's name to be in fairly small lettering. The *Mallalieu v Drummond* principle is not confined to clothing. The Revenue are increasingly putting it forward as an argument over a wide range of cases.

Entertainers

5.56   The problem is, in practice, particularly acute in the entertainment professions as the modern trend is for musicians to wear everyday casual clothing, for many plays to be performed in everyday wear, rather than in period costume, and for other entertainers to adopt an everyday, casual look. Fortunately, many Inspectors of Taxes seem to adopt a commonsense approach to stage clothing, although not all do. Few seem to be sympathetic, however, to the problem that to support a public image a person often has to adopt a far more expensive mode of dress than he or she would ordinarily have chosen on occasions when they are in the public eye, such as at press receptions, film premieres, industry get-togethers, etc.

Earlier court cases

5.57   *Mallalieu v Drummond* was not, of course, the first case where a deduction for clothing was in dispute. A computer engineer who wore a suit and tie only at work because his employer required him to be presentably dressed when working at customers' premises, was refused a deduction for the cost of such clothing seven years before the *Mallalieu* case was heard on the same grounds, namely that he wore the clothing for the private purpose of warmth and decency as well as for a working purpose (*Hillyer v Leeke 51 TC 90*). An engineer who claimed the cost of suits and other clothing for everyday wear on the basis that his expenditure was heavier than normal because of damage by oil from the machinery he was servicing was denied this, although he was allowed a deduction for the cost of overalls (*Woodcock v IRC 51 TC 698*). Similarly a surveyor was refused a deduction for everyday clothing he wore on site visits (*Ward v Dunn 52 TC 517*) and a plainclothes policeman was taxed on a clothing allowance paid to him, while being refused a deduction for the expenditure (*Fergusson v Noble 7 TC 176*).

5.58   Similarly in *Sanderson v Durbidge 36 TC 238*, a local government officer was refused a deduction for the excess of the cost of evening meals eaten out when he attended council meetings over what he would normally have spent on meals. A claim to deduct only part of an expense, as in this case, is invariably fatal as it amounts to an admission of duality of purpose. A civil servant living at an overseas naval base was refused a deduction for the extra costs of living abroad as compared with living in the UK (and was taxed on the allowance the Government paid him towards such costs) (*Robinson v Corry 18 TC 411*).

5.59   The extra cost to a water board employee who was required to live near his work in central London over what he would have paid had he lived in the suburbs was disallowed in *Bolam v Barlow 31 TC 136*, as was the cost of a London flat (provided by the company) for a company director who was required by his employer to move to London (*McKie v Warner 40 TC 65*). Mess expenses of Army officers were held not to be deductible in *Lomax v Newton 34 TC 558* and *Griffiths v Mockler 35 TC 135* and lodging expenses of an army officer allotted a civilian billet in lieu of accommodation at barracks was held not deductible—and the lodging allowance paid to him was held to constitute taxable income—in *Nagley v Spilsbury 37 TC 178*.

5.60   Perhaps one of the unluckiest cases in the duality of purpose area is the Schedule D case of *Prince v Mapp 46 TC 169*. The taxpayer, a professional guitarist, was also an architect. He cut his finger sharpening a pencil and the guitar strings kept catching in the cut. He claimed the cost of plastic surgery to remedy the problem to enable him to play the guitar properly. This was refused because in cross-examination he admitted that he sometimes played the guitar when with friends—which enabled the Commissioners to find duality of purpose: although the operation was wholly and exclusively to enable him to play the guitar it was not wholly and exclusively to enable him to play it professionally.

Telephone costs

5.61   Another area to fall foul of the duality of purpose test—and one where the Revenue are now usually challenging claims for a deduction— is the telephone rental charge. Even where a telephone is installed specifically at an employee's home so that he can be contacted by his employer outside normal working hours, the cost of rental is incurred so that the telephone is available to make and receive both business and private calls and thus has a dual purpose (*Lucas v Cattell 48 TC 353*). A disallowance similarly arose in *Nolder v Walters 15 TC 380* where telephone rental was claimed and in *Hamerton v Overy 35 TC 73* where a proportion of the rental was claimed. Even if an employer were to install a telephone in an employee's home and forbid him to use it for personal calls it is likely that the Revenue would still refuse a deduction on the basis that the telephone is available for incoming personal calls. The fear of abuse by allowing a deduction for the, normally, very minor cost of private telephone calls is exemplified by the rules for mobile telephones (see 9.35). If a mobile telephone is provided by the employer the government are willing to accept that private use is likely to be *de minimis* and have exempted such calls. However if the employee provides his own mobile telephone and the employer picks up the bill any rental or similar cost will be taxable on the employee in the same way as with a fixed phone and the cost of personal calls will constitute a benefit in kind.

5.62 Telephone costs illustrate two important principles in relation to duality of purpose. The first is that the *Act* will not allow a deduction for part of an expense; it is all or nothing. Accordingly, rental costs are, strictly speaking, disallowable in full even if the telephone is used predominantly for business purposes. In practice, the Revenue's approach to the 'all or nothing' principle varies considerably from Inspector to Inspector and from one expense to another but they generally adopt a commonsense approach. If an expense is predominantly for business a proportion will normally be allowed; if it is mainly for personal reasons the Revenue will generally resist a deduction for any part of the expenses.

The 'motive' test

5.63 It should be borne in mind that the test is a motive test, 'Why was the expenditure incurred?' If the motive was solely a business motive it does not matter that the taxpayer may obtain a personal benefit as a side effect of the expenditure. For example, if an employee is sent to Manchester to visit his company's branch and takes the opportunity to have lunch with a friend who lives there, there is little doubt that the fare was wholly and exclusively incurred for the business purpose and that meeting the friend was not a secondary motive of going to Manchester, but merely an opportunity resulting from the wholly business expenditure. Even the *Mallalieu* decision does not breach this principle; it merely stresses that the professed motive for incurring an expense may not be the sole motive. The test is a subjective one. What matters is why the expenditure was actually incurred rather than why the taxpayer thought that he was incurring it. As indicated earlier, a claim to deduct part of an expense is effectively an admission of duality of purpose. In many cases such a claim might be put forward as a compromise. The possibility of deriving some personal advantage from an expense frequently calls into question whether there may have been a dual motive in incurring it or whether the private benefit merely resulted from the business needs. Neither the Revenue nor taxpayers generally want to take disputes over small amounts of expenditure to appeal and the allowance of part of the expenditure is normally a compromise that satisfies both sides. Nevertheless, an initial claim for part will not necessarily be perceived by an

Inspector as an offer of a compromise; it is more likely to be seen as an admission of a dual purpose.

Apportionment of expenditure

5.64   The second principle illustrated by telephone expenses is that some expenses are in reality a totality of a series of separate expenditures, each of which might be wholly and exclusively for a specific purpose. In such circumstances it is permissible to break the expense down into its constituent parts. Thus, telephone calls are charged by the call. If a person makes 50 telephone calls in a quarter, of which 30 are for business, a claim to deduct 60 per cent of the cost of calls is not a statement that there was a dual purpose in making any individual call. It merely seeks to segregate the cost of business calls from the extraneous cost of personal calls which, for convenience, the telephone company has included on the same bill. As indicated at 5.37, the decision in *Kirkwood v Evans ([2002] EWHC 30(Ch)), (2002 STC 231)* may have cast doubt on this principle.

5.65   There are a great many other expenses which vary with usage, such as electricity, gas, petrol, etc. Such items may not be purchased by the unit but nevertheless, where it is possible to attribute part of the cost of an item to wholly business use, it is permissible to do so. Where apportionment is not strictly possible, although it frequently occurs in practice, is with items (such as a television licence) where the expenditure permits an item to be used for a fixed period and part of the usage during that period is for non-business purposes. In such a case the Revenue consider that the expenditure is incurred to make the item available for the mixed business and private use.

5.66   A chink in the duality of purpose wall was disclosed in *Westcott v Bryan 45 TC 476*. Mr Bryan, the managing director of a major public company, was required by the company to live in a house that reflected his position, as they regarded it as of paramount importance that overseas visitors should be entertained by him at his home. The company purchased a very large house, far larger than Mr Bryan would have chosen, for his occupation and paid all the expenses of it. The Revenue sought to tax him on the expenses. The Commissioners found that there was a genuine business use of the house and that Mr Bryan's personal use was restricted in that he was not free to discriminate as to his guests. They allowed 25 per cent of the expenses as being for business purposes and held that Mr Bryan was taxable on the other 75 per cent. The Inland Revenue appealed (as far as the Court of Appeal) on the basis that expenses can only be apportioned if the benefit to the company is severable from that to the director, for example, where there is a specific room set aside for business purposes. It was held that this was too strict a test. 'Some part of the expense is for the company's benefit, and not for the director's benefit. It may not be a severable part, but it is undoubtedly some part and there should be an apportionment' (Lord Denning MR, *45*

TC at p. 490). This case illustrates that where there is more than one motive for expenditure this may not be fatal if the reason is that the motive of the employer differs from that of the employee.

Claims disallowed by the courts

5.67　Other claims for deductions for expenses that have been disallowed include the cost of subscription by a bank manager to a club, even though membership was required by the employer, as the employee was not performing the duties of his employment while he was at the club (*Brown v Bullock 40 TC 1*); costs of lighting and heating a separate room in which an insurance agent's sons could do their homework while he interviewed clients at his home (*Roskams v Bennett 32 TC 129*); the expenses of the directors of a family farming company of taking part in an overseas tour organised for British farmers, partly to visit farms and partly for sightseeing, as there was a dual purpose for the expense (*Thomson v White 43 TC 256*); and the costs borne by the employer of defending a company director against a dangerous driving charge which could have led to him going to prison, thus depriving the company of his services (*Rendell v Went 41 TC 641*). If the taxpayer in *Roskams v Bennett* had set aside a room to interview clients, rather than setting aside one for his children, he would undoubtedly have obtained his deduction.

5.68　In *Smith v Abbott* and *Fitzpatrick v IRC* [*1994*] *STC 237*, two cases on similar facts which were heard together by the House of Lords, it was held that the expenses incurred by journalists in buying newspapers were not incurred in the performance of their duties, in spite of a finding of fact that a newspaper proprietor expected or required his journalists to read widely.

5.69　Some of the reasoning is difficult to follow. Particularly worrying is Lord Templeman's comment that 'If deductions of this kind were allowed in one case every journalist or other similar employee would claim to be entitled to deduct the payment made by him for every newspaper and periodical which he chose to purchase and there would be no end to it. A sports reporter is employed to report sport, not to read newspapers . . . A journalist who reads newspapers does so in order to be able to perform his duties to the highest possible standard but he does not read in performance of his duties . . . there was some dispute as to whether a journalist was required as a condition of his employment to read newspapers . . . But it appears from *Blackwell v Mills* that this dispute is not relevant . . . It seems to me impossible to say that when the sports reporter was reading newspapers in the quiet of his home he was performing the duties of a sports reporter either at the offices of the newspaper or on location . . . It does not matter therefore whether . . . the journalists were contractually bound by their employers to expend money in the purchase of other newspapers and magazines . . . Whether or not a journalist thinks it is necessary to read one or more newspaper and periodical his duty is the production of his employer's newspaper and he is not carrying out that duty when he is reading other newspapers.'

5.70 This goes far beyond anything that the Revenue have ever sought to claim. It is difficult to see any reason why the duties of a job should have to be performed either at the office or on location. There is no logical reason why an employer should not require a person to carry out a number of duties leaving him free to determine where they are carried out. Nor is it clear why a sports reporter should have only a single duty, to report sport, so that other things that he is required to do which are peripheral or supplementary to that function cease to be duties of the employment. The distinction drawn by Lord Templeman, between the performance of the duties and preparatory work seems suspect as he does not appear to even consider the full scope of the duty. In a dissenting judgment Lord Browne-Wilkinson poses the test that 'whether or not a particular operation is a duty of the employment has to be determined objectively, i.e. by answering the question "Does the nature of the job require the doing of the act which gives rise to the expenditure?"', which seems a far more satisfactory approach and does at least give weight to the finding of fact of the extent of the duties.

Schedule D cases

5.71 Schedule D cases where a claim to deduct expenses was disallowed and which have relevance for Schedule E taxpayers include the cost of a visit to North America partly to attend a professional conference and partly for a holiday (*Bowden v Russell and Russell 42 TC 301*); the cost of medical expenses where the ill health arose from the taxpayer's working conditions (*Norman v Golder 26 TC 293*); medical expenses of an architect and guitarist (*Prince v Mapp 46 TC 169*—see 5.60) and the cost of a private room in a nursing home so that the taxpayer could carry on his business whilst recovering from medical treatment (*Murgatroyd v Evans-Jackson 43 TC 581*). The problem in each case was duality of purpose.

5.72 One item that the taxpayer succeeded in deducting was the cost to a solicitor of business lunches with clients (the food and drink of the partner was a side benefit derived from the solely business purpose of entertaining the client) (*Bentleys, Stokes and Lowless v Beeson 33 TC 491*). Unfortunately, such expenditure is now non-deductible by statute.

Expenses where remittance basis applies

5.73 If the income is assessable on a remittance the expense must either have been paid out of the earnings (i.e. out of the amount remitted) or must have been paid in the UK either in the year of remittance or an earlier year in which the employer was a UK resident and must be such that it would have qualified as a deductible expense if the earnings of the year in which the expense was incurred had been taxable when received.

[*ITEPA 2003, s 353*]. Obviously the same expense cannot be deducted twice if part of the emoluments from an employment are taxable on a remittance basis and part on a receipts basis. [*ITEPA 2003, s 354*].

Members of Parliament

5.74   A Member of Parliament cannot claim a deduction for expenditure on (or in connection with) the provision or use of residential or overnight accommodation to enable him to perform his duties as an MP, whether that accommodation is in his constituency or near the Houses of Parliament. [*ITEPA 2003, s 360*]. This is because he is paid an allowance to cover the additional expenses necessarily incurred in staying overnight away from his main residence for the purpose of performing his parliamentary duties and that allowance is exempt from tax. [*ITEPA 2003, s 292*].

5.75   Expenses paid to an MP in accordance with a resolution of the House of Commons to reimburse European travel expenses, namely the cost of travel between the UK and either a European Union institution or agency or the national parliament of another EU country, a candidate or applicant country or a member of the European Free Trade Association, do not constitute taxable income. Nor does any additional expenses incurred in such travel. [*ITEPA 2003, s 294* as amended by *FA 2004, s 82*]. This is because the Government regard such travel as in the course of the MP's parliamentary business so that it should be exempt from tax in the same way as expenses of travel on parliamentary duties within the UK. Up to March 1999 the relief was limited to travel to EU institutions or agencies. The extension to the national parliaments of EU countries and candidate countries apply from that date and that to the national parliaments of applicant countries and EFTA countries from 6 April 2004.

5.76   There is a special exemption from some of the benefits in kind rules for government Ministers and holders of other salaried office under the *Ministerial and other Salaries Act 1975*, i.e. the Speaker and Opposition office-holders. The exemption covers:

(*a*)   transport or subsistence provided by the Crown to the office-holder or to any member of his family or household; and

(*b*)   the payment (or reimbursement) by the Crown of any expenses incurred in connection with the provision of transport or subsistence to the office-holder or members of his family.

The exemption applies even if the Minister is not actually paid a salary, as long as he is entitled to one. Head (*b*) includes the provision of a car (with or without a driver), the provision of car fuel and of any other benefit in connection with the car. It also includes food, drink and temporary living accommodation. The exemption did not, however, extend to the benefit in respect of a mobile phone prior to 1999/00.

5.77   *Expenses*

[*ITEPA 2003, s 295*]. This provision was introduced 'to clarify the treatment of such items to avoid any uncertainty'.

5.77   All of these exemptions also apply to members of the Scottish Parliament, the National Assembly for Wales and the Northern Ireland Assembly (*ITEPA 2003, ss 293, 294, 295*, formerly *FA 1999, s 52* and *5 Sch*).

Detached national experts

5.78   For 2003/04 onwards the daily subsistence allowances paid by the European Commission to persons whose services are made available by the Commission by their employers under the 'detached national experts scheme' established by the Commission on 26 July 1988 (or any replacement scheme) is exempt from tax. [*ITEPA 2003, s 304*]. Such allowances were previously not taxed by virtue of *ESC A84*.

Resettlement grants

5.79   There is also an exemption from tax for any grant or payment made or authorised by parliament:

(*a*)   to a person ceasing to be a member of the House of Commons on a dissolution of parliament;

(*b*)   to a person ceasing to hold certain ministerial and other offices;

(*c*)   as a resettlement grant for persons ceasing to be an MEP; or

(*d*)   to a person ceasing to be a member of the Scottish, Welsh or Northern Irish parliaments on a dissolution or ceasing to hold certain ministerial or other offices.

[*ITEPA 2003, s 241*].

Flat rate deductions

5.80   The Treasury are given power to fix a sum which in their opinion is a fair average annual expenditure by persons in a class that they specify, being people in receipt of earnings payable out of the public revenue, who are obliged to lay out and expend money wholly, exclusively and necessarily in the performance of their duties. That sum can then automatically be deducted as allowable expenses irrespective of the amount actually spent. If the employee can show that his actual expenditure exceeds the fixed sum he can deduct the actual expenditure instead. [*ITEPA 2003, s 368*]. This provision will apply to civil servants, to members of the armed forces and to people such as judges or MPs holding public offices. The idea is obviously to avoid a profusion of claims.

5.81   For 2003/04 onwards the Treasury also have power to fix a round sum deduction which in their opinion represents the average annual expenses incurred by a class of employees in respect of the repair and maintenance of work equipment, i.e. tools and special clothing. The Treasury must be satisfied that the employees are generally responsible for incurring the expense and that they could have claimed a deduction for the actual expense. No deduction can be claimed if the employer pays or reimburses the expense to which the lump sum relates, or would do so if requested. [*ITEPA 2003, s 367*]. This enacts a previous concession, *ESC A1*. The Revenue agree such fixed expense allowances with trade unions and similar bodies. An employee can either claim this agreed figure irrespective of his actual expenditure or can make a *section 336* claim for his actual expenditure. However, if he opts to make a *section 336* claim, rather than accept the flat rate deduction, the Inland Revenue may be reluctant to allow a claim to the flat rate deduction in later years. The amounts agreed under such arrangements are normally relatively small and the figures are not regularly revised.

Professional subscriptions

5.82   Subscriptions to professional and similar bodies will not normally meet the requirements of *section 336* as the expense will not normally be incurred in the performance of the duties of the employment. Accordingly, it is specifically provided that certain fees or subscriptions can be deducted from the emoluments of an employment if they are defrayed out of those emoluments. [*ITEPA 2003, ss 343–345*].

The fees are those payable for registration, licensing or other matters payable as a condition of being able to practice the profession and can be deducted only if the duties of the employment involve the practice of the relevant profession. The professions concerned are:

Health Professionals

> Chartered Psychologists (including the practising certificate fee)
> Chiropractors
> Dental auxiliaries (1)
> Dentists (1)
> Dispensing Opticians (1)
> Members of the Health Professions Council
> Members of the Hearing Aid Council
> Medical Practitioners
> Members of the Nursing and Midwifery Council
> Ophthalmic Opticians (1)
> Osteopaths
> Pharmaceutical Chemists (1)

Animal Health Professionals

> Farmers
> Veterinary Surgeons (1)
> Entrants on the supplementary veterinary register (1)

Legal Professionals

Licensed Conveyancers
Solicitors (fee for practising certificate) (1)

Architects (1)
Teachers (General Teaching Council Register)
Patent and Trade Mark agents

Patent agents (registration and practising fees) (1)
Trade Mark agents (registration and practising fees)

Transport Sector

Driving instructors
Aircraft maintenance engineers (2) (3)
Air traffic controllers (and student air traffic controllers) (2) (3)
Aircraft flight crew (2) (3)
Flight information service officers (2) (3)
Drivers of large goods vehicles or passenger carrying vehicles (2)

From 1 July 2003, the fee payable by a person employed (or to be employed) at a UK airport for a criminal records check required for the issue of a security pass

Seamen (certificate of competence or licence)
Seafarers (cost of medical fitness certificate)

Security

Fees payable in applying for a licence from the Security Industry Authority under the *Private Security Industry Act 2001*.

The list was substantially expanded in the *ITEPA 2003*. Only those fees marked (1) qualified up to 2002/03. For the professionals marked (2) the cost of the related medical examination is also allowable. So is the cost of the technical examination for those marked (3). The Revenue have power to add items to the above list. [*ITEPA 2003, s 343*]. They added airport criminal record checks by the *Income Tax (Professional Fees) Order 2003 (SI 2003 No 1652)* and fees for those in the private security industry by the *Income Tax (Professional Fees) Order 2004 (SI 2004 No 1360)*.

5.83   The deduction for annual subscriptions is for subscriptions paid to a body of persons approved by the Inland Revenue. They can approve a body, only if it applies for approval, its activities are not of a mainly local character, they are carried on otherwise than for profit, and they are mainly directed to all or any of:

(*a*)   the advancement or spreading of knowledge—either generally or among persons belonging to the same or similar professions (or occupying the same or similar positions);

(*b*)   the maintenance or improvement of standards of conduct and competence among the members of a profession; and (*c*) the indemnification or protection of members of any profession against claims in respect of liabilities incurred by them in the exercise of their profession.

[*ITEPA 2003, s 344(1)–(3)*].

5.84 If the activities of a body are directed mainly to such a purpose but are also to a significant extent directed to some other purpose, the Revenue can approve the deduction of such part of the annual subscription as they think fit (having regard to all relevant circumstances and in particular the amount of the body's expenditure or its different activities). [*ITEPA 2003, s 344(5) (6)*]. Approval can be given with effect from the beginning of the tax year in which the body applies for approval. The Revenue have power to withdraw or vary approval. [*ITEPA 2003, s 345(1)*]. The body has a right of appeal against a refusal of approval. [*ITEPA 2003, s 345(2)*].

5.85 As well as the body qualifying for approval, the employee has to show that membership of it is relevant to the employment. A fee within 5.82 above is deductible if it is a condition, or one of the alternative conditions, of the performance of the duties of the employment that the employee's name is maintained on the register or that he holds the practising certificate. [*ITEPA 2003, ss 343(1), 344(1)*]. A subscription is deductible only if the activities of the professional or other body are relevant to the employment, i.e. the performance of the duties of the employment is directly affected by the knowledge concerned or involves the exercise of the profession concerned. [*ITEPA 2003, s 344(1)(b)*]. In *Singh v Williams [2000] STC (SCD) 404* a retired medical practitioner sought to set a professional subscription against his civil service pension but the Commissioner felt that although on first sight the word 'profits' in *ITEPA 2003, s 62(2)* (see 3.1) might encompass pension payments it is plain that the scheme of the legislation in respect of expenses excludes pensions from being emoluments for that purpose.

5.86 The Inland Revenue periodically publish a list of bodies approved under *section 344* above the latest of which was issued in December 2002 and can be found in the Revenue's website. If a body is not on this list Inspectors of Taxes are likely to refuse a deduction. However, *section 344* does not override *section 336*; it supplements it. If a subscription to a professional or other body can be brought within *section 336* the taxpayer is entitled to deduct it as an expense irrespective of whether that body has applied for approval under *section 344*.

Overseas professional bodies

5.87 A particular difficulty arises with subscriptions to overseas professional bodies as they do not, in general, seek approval under *section 344*. Most, but not all, Inspectors of Taxes generally use their common-sense and allow a deduction if the activities are similar to those of a UK approved body. However, it needs to be realised that this is a concessional treatment. If a body is not on the Revenue's list, irrespective of the reason, it is for the taxpayer either to persuade the body to seek approval or to bring his expenditure within the tight rules of *section 336*.

5.88   It should also be noted that *section 344* applies only to an annual subscription to an approved body; it does not grant relief for an initial admission fee or for other payments such as examination fees for post-qualification examinations where these are not specifically allowed by *section 343*.

Forces' travel

5.89   Travel facilities provided for army, navy or air force personnel going on leave or returning from it are specifically exempted from tax. [*ITEPA 2003, s 296*]. This applies not only to travel vouchers and warrants for specific journeys but also to allowances irrespective of leave travel. The exemption applies regardless of whether the tax charge would otherwise have arisen under *section 62(2)* (see 3.1 above), *84* (see 6.20 below) or *201* (see 6.41 below). Travel for leave is, of course, equivalent to home to office travel for a civilian.

5.90   There is also an exemption from tax for armed forces' food, drink and mess allowances payable out of the public revenue to (or in respect of) any description of members of the armed forces of the Crown which the Treasury certifies are payable either instead of food or drink normally supplied to members of the armed forces or as a contribution to the expenses of a mess. [*ITEPA 2003, s 297*].

5.91   There is also an exemption from tax for training expenses allowances and bounties payable in consideration of undertaking certain training and attaining a particular standard of efficiency which are payable out of the public revenue to members of the reserve and auxiliary forces of the Crown. [*ITEPA 2003, s 218*].

Crown employee foreign service allowance

5.92   Any allowance paid to a person in employment under the Crown is tax free if it is certified (by the Treasury or certain specified ministers) to represent compensation for the extra cost of being obliged to live outside the UK in order to perform the duties of the employment. [*ITEPA 2003, s 299*].

Agent's commission paid by entertainers

5.93   Where a person is employed as an actor, singer, musician, dancer or theatrical artist, a deduction can be claimed for agent's commission—up to a maximum of 17.5 per cent—and VAT thereon. The commission must be paid by the employee under an agency contract to a properly licensed agent (under the *Employment Agencies Act*) and must be calculated as a percentage of the emoluments (or part thereof). The emoluments must obviously themselves be taxable. It should be noted that if an agent agrees to accept a round sum fee instead of a percentage that fee will not be deductible. Such commission paid to a *bona fide* non-profit co-operative society which acts as the agent will also qualify. [*ITEPA 2003, s 352*]. This did not apply prior to 1990/91.

Capital allowances

5.94   An employee can claim capital allowances for his expenditure on plant and machinery which is 'necessarily provided' for use in the performance of his duties (unless the earnings are taxable on a remittance basis). [*CAA 2001, s 36* formerly *CAA 1990, s 27(1)(2)*]. The 'necessarily provided' test does not apply to cars, vans or other mechanically propelled road vehicles if the expenditure is incurred partly for the purpose of the employment and partly for other purposes. [*CAA 2001, s 36(3), s 80*]. From 6 April 2002 expenditure on the provision of a mechanically propelled road vehicle or a cycle cannot attract capital allowances even if it meets the necessarily provided test. [*CAA 2001, s 36(1)(a)* substituted by *FA 2001, s 59*]. Where capital allowances were being claimed on such items there is a deemed disposal of the asset at market value at 6 April 2002. [*CAA 2001, s 59(4)*]. This deemed disposal will of course trigger a balancing charge or allowance. The Revenue have indicated that if it creates a charge they will in practice not seek to collect the tax until the vehicle is sold, albeit that they are statutorily entitled to collect it in 2002/03. It is understood that the Revenue regard equipment as necessarily provided only if:

(*a*)   the taxpayer is paid entirely or largely by results (for example, by commission);

(*b*)   the method by which the employee is to achieve the results is not stereotyped; and

(*c*)   the employee is required to bear the cost of such equipment performing functions or activities intended to achieve his objective in his job and the employer does not provide or pay for such equipment. (*Taxation, 10 March 1994, p. 507*).

There is no statutory basis for these three tests and they seem of doubtful validity.

Employee liability and indemnity insurance

5.95   A specific deduction is allowed for expenditure in relation to certain employee liabilities which are defrayed out of the emoluments, i.e., the deduction cannot exceed the emoluments. It covers:

(*a*)   a payment of (or towards) damages or compensation or in settlement of a claim for damages or compensation;

(*b*)   costs or expenses in relation to such a claim and proceedings arising from it;

(*c*)   indemnity insurance premiums, but only to the extent that the premium relates to indemnifying the employee against the above matters.

[*ITEPA 2003, s 346(1)*].

However, no deduction can be made for liabilities or costs which the employer could not lawfully insure against, e.g., costs arising from a criminal conviction (*ITEPA 2003, s 346(2)*).

5.96   The liability must be imposed in respect of some act or omission (or of proceedings arising out of a claim) in the director's or employee's capacity as employee, or in some other capacity in which he acts in the performance of the duties of his employment, e.g. as an employee of a subsidiary company to which his services are seconded. In the case of indemnity insurance premiums the policy must not be for a period exceeding two years, must not entitle the employee to receive any benefit in addition to the risks insured against and the right to renew the policy (other than a benefit to which no significant part of the premium can be attributed), must not be connected with any other contract, and must relate exclusively to one or more of:

(*a*)   indemnifying a person (which will include both the employer and employee) against a liability in one of the above capacities;

(*b*)   indemnifying a person against any vicarious liability in such a capacity in relation to acts or omissions of someone else;

(*c*)   the payment of costs or expenses (including those incurred by a third party) in relation to a claim under the policy;

(*d*)   indemnifying an employer against any loss from the payment by him to an employee of his in relation to a liability within (*a*) or (*b*).

[*ITEPA 2003, s 346, 348, 349*].

5.97   An insurance contract is connected with another if one is entered into by reference to the other or with a view to enabling (or facilitating) the other to be entered into on particular terms, and the terms of either would otherwise have been significantly different. If the two contracts are both indemnity insurance contracts (satisfying 5.95) and the difference in terms simply reflects a reasonable reduction of premium either because they are entered into together and cover different proportions of the same risks or the second is entered into under a renewal right in the first, they are not regarded as connected (*ITEPA 2003, s 350*).

5.98   Relief is also given—in this case against total income—for such expenditure by an ex-director or employee. The payment must be made within six years following the end of the year of assessment in which the employment ceased and the amount must have been deductible under *section 346* had the employment continued and the payment been defrayed out of emoluments for the year in which the payment was in fact made. [*ITEPA 2003, ss 555–564*, formerly *FA 1995, s 92(1)–(3)*]. This appears to limit the deduction to what the emolument would have been had the employment continued, although it is unclear how such a limitation is to be calculated. Obviously, relief cannot be claimed if the expenditure is covered by insurance or is reimbursed by the ex-employer, a successor to his business, or a connected person of the ex-employer or a successor. [*ITEPA 2003, s 557*, formerly *FA 1995, s 92(4)*]. If such a reimbursement itself constitutes an unapproved retirement benefit under *s 596A* (see 10.60) or is taxable as an emolument of the former employment, the expenditure can be deducted from the taxable amount [*ITEPA 2003, s 555(1)(b)*, formerly *FA 1995, s 92(5)*]. If the expenditure exceeds the amount from which it is deductible—as indicated above, it is not clear if this means the ex-employee's total income for the year of payment or the salary he would have earned for that year had the employment continued—the ex-employee can claim to set the excess against any capital gains of the same tax year (before off-setting any brought forward losses or deducting trading losses under *FA 1991, s 72* or *FA 1995, s 90(4)*).

Chapter 6

Benefits in Kind

Quantum of the benefit

6.1   As indicated in Chapter 3, a payment to an employee of 'money's worth' constitutes emoluments. However, the quantum of such emoluments is the amount of money into which the benefit or payment in kind can be converted. This is generally far below the cost of providing the benefit, either because the market price of second-hand goods, even if unused, is generally well below the original retail price of those goods, or because the benefit is not easily saleable because a vendor cannot pass the legal title, there is no evidence of title, or the benefit is of a restrictive nature. Accordingly, in the absence of special provisions there would be a great incentive to ask to be paid in kind, either in whole or in part, by the employer purchasing goods or services and assigning these to the employee.

6.2   It is therefore not surprising to find specific rules covering the taxation of benefits in kind. Where a benefit falls within these special rules its money's worth value will of course cease to constitute emoluments.

Three categories of benefit

6.3   Benefits in kind effectively fall into three categories.

(*a*)   Those that apply to all employees.

(*b*)   Those that apply only to 'higher-paid' employees and company directors.

(*c*)   Those for which there are no special provisions, and are thus taxable only to the extent that they constitute emoluments, and which can be taxed on their money's worth value.

Who are 'higher-paid employees'?

6.4   Before considering how a benefit is to be taxed it is obviously necessary to determine whether the employee is a director or is 'higher-paid' and thus within the special rules applicable to such people. The expression 'higher-paid' is used below for convenience. It was a statutory term from 1976 to 1989 but was replaced in the *Finance Act 1989* by the more accurate, but very much more unwieldly, expression 'employees earning £8,500 per annum or more' and 'employment to which Chapter II of Part V of the principal Act applies'. [*FA 1989, s 53*]. This change of nomenclature was made because the Government felt that 'the expression "higher paid employment" has become inappropriate, and can be misleading, since £8,500 is well below the national average for full time earnings and the benefit rules now apply to the great majority of employees'. The *Rewrite Act* has taken the reverse approach. It provides that benefits are taxable on everyone unless they are in excluded employment. [*ITEPA 2003, s 63*]. It then calls those in excluded employment 'lower-paid'. [*ITEPA 2003, s 216(1)*].

6.5   In considering whether a person who is not a director (or who is a full-time working director) earns over £8,500 per annum, or rather, to be precise, is in an employment with emoluments at the rate of £8,500 a year or more, emoluments must be calculated as if they include all benefits (and other amounts) taxable under the higher-paid employee rules, and also all those benefits that are taxable on all employees. Furthermore, no deduction can be made for mileage allowances, most allowable expenses, professional subscriptions or under the special rules for ministers of religion in *section 290*. [*ITEPA 2003, s 218*]. Where a car is made available for private use (as mentioned in *s 114*—see 7.2) and an alternative to the benefit is offered the amount to be included in respect of the benefit is the higher of the scale charge or the value of the alternative, plus any non-cash vouchers, credit tokens or expenses payments given in respect of the car (even though such sums are excluded from tax by *ITEPA 2003, s 269(1)*) (*ITEPA 2003, s 219*). This can lead to unfairness as is illustrated by *Allcock v King (2004 STC (SCD) 122, Sp C 396)*. Mrs Allcock had a salary for 1998/99 of £3,440. She was also provided with a car. This was available for private use. Petrol was provided by the company and some at least was paid for using a company credit card. The Revenue contended that the car use and car fuel benefit (£4,680 in aggregate) brought the earnings up to £8,120. To this had to be added the credit card payments of £491 giving a total of £8,611. As this was over £8,500 Mrs Allcock fell within the benefit legislation. The Commissioner, Graham Aaronson QC, thought this 'an anomaly – and a very unfair one – in the benefits-in-kind provisions'. Nevertheless with the greatest reluctance he concluded that the Revenue were correct in law and that 'there is in law no escape from the trap that the statutory language has set'. If a person has two or more employments with the same employer they must all be treated as higher-paid if either the higher-paid rules apply to one of them by virtue of holding a directorship or the aggregate emoluments exceed £8,500 per annum. [*ITEPA 2003, s 220*]. If an individual, partnership, company or other body has control of another partnership, company or other body, all employees of the controlling body are to be treated (for the purpose of *section 218* only) as if they were employees of the individual or the controlling body—so that if they have employments with both the controlling and controlled entity such employments need to be looked at together. [*ITEPA 2003, s 220(3)*].

6.6   These special rules were introduced in 1979 and the figure of £8,500 has never been changed, despite a 317 per cent increase in inflation and a more than threefold increase in average male earnings between 1979 and 2002. They replaced a previous system of taxing benefits of higher-paid employees that started in 1948 when higher-paid meant earning £2,000 per annum or more. The limit was increased to £5,000 in 1975 and to £7,500 in 1978. It appears that the intention is that, in time, these special provisions will apply to all employees. Presumably it is politically inexpedient to be seen to impose additional tax burdens on the lower-paid, so this ultimate intention will be achieved by allowing inflation to continually whittle away the number of employees who are not covered by these rules.

Directors

6.7   It should be noted that employment as a director is automatically within the special rules irrespective of the level of earnings—and even if the director has no earnings—unless the director does not have a 'material interest' in the company and either:

(*a*)   his employment is as a full-time working director; or

(*b*)   the company is non-profit making (i.e. does not carry on a trade and its functions do not consist wholly or mainly in the holding of investments or other property) or it is established for charitable purposes only.

[*ITEPA 2003, s 216(1)–(3)*].

6.8   References below to higher-paid employees should be read as including directors brought within the higher-paid employee rules under these provisions.

Meaning of 'director'

6.9   Some of the expressions used above are specially defined for the purpose of these rules. A 'director' means:

(*a*)   in relation to a company whose affairs are managed by a board of directors or similar body, a member of that board;

(*b*)   in relation to a company whose affairs are managed by a single director or similar person, that person; and

(*c*)   in relation to a company whose affairs are managed by the members themselves, a member of the company.

[*ITEPA 2003, s 67*].

6.10   Any person in accordance with whose directions or instructions the directors (as defined above) are accustomed to act is also a director of the company, unless the directors merely act on advice given by him in a professional capacity. [*ITEPA 2003, s 67(1)(2)*]. The application of this provision was challenged unsuccessfully in the House of Lords in *R v Allen (2001 STC 1537) ([2001] UKHL 45)*. It was admitted in that case that Mr Allen was a 'shadow director' of a non-UK company that owned a house that he occupied. However, he contended that the benefit provisions (and the special rules on accommodation described in Chapter 8 which adopt the same definition) did not apply, as although *section 67* states that a director includes a shadow director it does not deem such a person to hold an office, so unless the individual holds an employment the benefit rules could not apply. Alternatively if he did hold an office it is not one the emoluments of which fall to be taxed as employment income as it would be a non-UK one with no UK duties and to construe a benefit from it as taxable would breach the territorial limitation of the UK's taxing jurisdiction. Both of these arguments were dismissed fairly briefly on the basis that the legislative intent was clearly that accommodation and benefits received by a shadow director should be taxed in the same way as those received by a director.

Meaning of 'full-time'

6.11   A director is a full-time working director if he is required to devote substantially the whole of his time to the service of the company in a managerial or technical capacity. [*ITEPA 2003, s 67(3)*]. The *Act* does not say what is meant by 'substantially the whole of his time'. It presumably does not mean 20-odd hours a day seven days a week. The Revenue's *Employment Income Manual* states that 'substantially the whole' has its normal meaning. It will allow for the director working slightly less than the full normal working hours of the company. They also refer their staff to *IRC v D Devine & Sons Ltd 41 TC 210* where the Court of Appeal held that a taxpayer who worked three full days a week was not a full-time director (although that case dealt with different legislation). They also say that a director of several companies can be regarded as a full-time working director of the company which occupies the largest proportion of his time provided that he works for that company for more than 50 per cent of its full normal working hours and works in aggregate for all the companies for at least 75 per cent of those normal working hours (*Employment Income Manual, para 20202*). If an employee-type director does not have a managerial or technical role—as can happen with a small company where, say, the company's only salesman is appointed a director—he cannot qualify as a full-time working director. It is unclear why Parliament should have wanted to discriminate in favour of people with management responsibilities and against those without. One might have expected that if a class of person was to be excluded from the special rules the latter had a stronger claim than the former rather than the other way around.

6.12   In early 1993 the Revenue expressed the view that 'full-time' in the context of full-time employment abroad under *ESC A11* means something like a 35–40 hour week (*Tax Bulletin, Issue 6, page 57*). However, they specifically stated that this view 'is not concerned with other instances where the term "full-time" appears in statute, for example "full-time working director" in the benefit in kind rules'. Their Employee Share Schemes manual tells staff that they should not accept schemes which define a full-time employee or a full-time director by reference to a working week in excess of 25 hours (excluding meal breaks) (*para 26010*), but as their concern is that a company should not be able to exclude too many people from all-employee share schemes it is probably unwise to rely on this test in different circumstances. The same manual later says that they should also not accept a scheme that defines a full-time director by reference to a working week of less than 25 hours excluding meal breaks (or 30 hours including meal breaks) (*para 27015*). It also says that a person who works for 25 hours per week as a director of two companies is unlikely to be a full-time director of both (*para 27016*)—but if they are all scheme companies the time can be aggregated (*para 27017*). Capital gains tax retirement relief and taper relief contain a definition of full-time, namely that the person 'must be required to devote substantially the whole of his time to the service of the company' (*TCGA 1992, A1 Schedule 22(1), 6 Schedule 1(2)*). In *Palmer v Maloney* [1999] STC 890 the Court of Appeal found it hard to put a meaning on this, one judge interpreting the words literally and the other two stating that whatever it meant Mr Palmer, who worked 42 hours a week for one company, was required to devote substantially the whole of his time to it but disagreeing on any general principle. Aldous LJ thought it a jury question to be decided on the facts of each case as, while the Revenue's test of 75 per cent of the full hours worked by other employees (*Capital Gains Manual 63621*) may be appropriate as a matter of pragmatism, he doubted that it always gives the right answer. Clarke LJ thought 'there seems to be much to be said for a rule of thumb such as that adopted by the Inland Revenue'.

Meaning of 'material interest'

6.13   A person has a material interest in a company if, either on his own or with one or more of his associates:

(*a*)   he is the beneficial owner of (or able directly or indirectly to control) more than five per cent of the ordinary share capital of the company; or

(*b*)   he possesses (or is entitled to acquire) such rights as would in the event of a winding up of the company or in any other circumstances, give an entitlement to receive more than five per cent of the assets which would then be available for distribution among the participators, and the company is a close company,

or if any associate of his (with or without other associates) fulfils either of the above conditions. [*ITEPA 2003, s 68(2)(3)*].

Meaning of 'participator'

6.14   For this purpose the definition of participator in *section 417(1)* and that of associate in *section 417(3)* apply with the modification that (as well as such relatives of the employee himself) the parents or remoter forebear, child or remoter issue or brother or sister of the director's spouse, and the spouses of such relatives of either the director or his spouse, are also associates (such persons are not associates under *section 417(3)*). The definition of control in *section 840* applies, and it also applies (with the necessary modifications) in relation to an unincorporated association. [*ITEPA 2003, s 69*].

The provisions applicable to all employees

6.15   The special provisions that apply to all employees, lower-paid as well as higher-paid, cover cash vouchers, non-cash vouchers, credit tokens and living accommodation. The first three of these are considered below. Living accommodation is dealt with in Chapter 8.

Cash vouchers

6.16   A cash voucher is any voucher, stamp or similar document capable of being exchanged (either on its own or together with other vouchers, stamps or documents) for a sum of money equal to (or greater than, or not substantially less than) the expense incurred in providing the voucher. It includes a voucher exchangeable only after a time and also a voucher that is capable of being exchanged either for cash or for goods or services. [*ITEPA 2003, s 75*]. As a cash voucher can be exchanged for cash it is, not surprisingly, treated as cash and the employee taxed at the time he receives it as if he had received a cash sum equal to the amount for which the voucher can be exchanged. [*ITEPA 2003, s 81*]. The cash itself is, of course, not then taxable as a benefit or under the basic definition of emoluments. [*ITEPA 2003, s 95*]. If a person incurs an expense in or in connection with cash vouchers for two or more employees as members of a group, it must be apportioned amongst them on a just and reasonable basis. [*ITEPA 2003, s 77*].

6.17   A document intended to enable a person to obtain payment of a sum mentioned in it is not a cash voucher if that sum would not have been constituted employment income had the cash been paid direct without the interposition of the voucher. [*ITEPA 2003, s 80(a)*]. This ensures that, for example, an expenses claim or a petty cash slip cannot be regarded as a cash voucher and create an unanticipated tax charge. Similarly, a savings certificate, the accumulated interest on which is exempt from tax (or would be exempt if certain conditions were satisfied) is not a cash voucher. [*ITEPA 2003, s 80(b)*]. It is obviously not the Government's intention that a person given a national savings certificate by his employer should immediately be taxed on its face value, which includes a large element of tax-free growth that is obtainable only by holding the certificate for five years. For 2003/04 onwards there is also an exclusion for a cash voucher which is of a kind made available to the public generally and which is provided to the employee or a member of the employee's family on no more favourable terms than to the public generally. [*ITEPA 2003, s 78*].

6.18   If a voucher is capable of being exchanged for cash but for an amount substantially less than its cost and the difference represents (in whole or part) the cost of providing sickness, personal injury or death benefits (a sickness benefits-related voucher), the cost of providing such benefits is ignored for the purpose of determining whether the voucher is a cash voucher. [*ITEPA 2003, s 76*]. Once it is established that the voucher is a cash voucher PAYE is still applied only to the sum for which the voucher can be exchanged. [*ITEPA 2003, s 81(2)*]. This provision will ensure that industry-wide holiday stamp schemes where the stamp also provides insurance cover against sickness, etc. are brought within the cash voucher rules so that PAYE is applied to the holiday pay element. The Revenue are given power to exempt such schemes from the cash voucher provisions entirely if they are satisfied that PAYE can be (and, presumably, will be) applied when the voucher is actually exchanged for cash. [*ITEPA 2003, s 79*]. It appears that if a scheme is so exempted the employee is doubly taxable to a degree as he is then not entitled to the benefit of *ITEPA 2003, s 95(2)*, which prevents the market value of the voucher being an emolument. Undoubtedly, the Revenue would not collect such tax by concession.

6.19   If a cash voucher is appropriated to an employee without being given to him, for example, a stamp is attached to a card held for him, the tax charge will arise at the time of such appropriation. [*ITEPA 2003, s 73(3)*]. If a cash voucher is given not to an employee but to his spouse, parent, child, the spouse of one of his children, or a dependant of the employee it must of course be treated as having been given to the employee. [*ITEPA 2003, s 74*].

Non-cash vouchers

6.20   A 'non-cash voucher' is any voucher, stamp or similar document or token capable of being exchanged for money, goods or services (or any combination of the three) and which is not a cash voucher. It includes a transport voucher, which is a ticket, pass or other document or token intended to enable a person to obtain passenger transport services, even though the voucher does not have to be given up. The most common type of transport voucher is, of course, a Rail or London Transport season ticket or travelcard. It also includes a cheque voucher, which is a cheque provided for an employee and intended for use by him wholly or mainly for payment for particular goods or services or for goods or services of one or more particular classes. The most common type of cheque voucher will be a cheque given to an employee to pay for goods or services ordered on behalf of the employer for the benefit of the employer. A voucher does not cease to be a non-cash voucher if it can only be exchanged together with other vouchers, etc. or if it can be exchanged only after some time has elapsed. [*ITEPA 2003, s 84*].

6.21   If an employee is given a non-cash voucher he must be treated as having received emoluments from his employment equal to the cost of the voucher (or of the money, goods or services for which it can be exchanged) to the employer (or the person who provided it, or, from 1994/95, the person at whose cost it was provided). [*ITEPA 2003, s 87(1)–(3)*]. If the employee makes any payment for the voucher, the assessable amount is reduced by that payment. [*ITEPA 2003, s 87(2)(b)*]. The chargeable amount is deemed to be emoluments for the year of assessment in which the voucher is given to the employee or, if later, in which the employer incurs the expense—unless it is a cheque voucher in which case it is the year in which the cheque is handed over to the shop, or is posted to it. [*ITEPA 2003, s 88*]. A curious result of this provision is that only the employee and not the employer will know the year in which a cheque voucher is assessable, and only the employer—not the employee—will know when any other non-cash voucher is assessable. A non-cash voucher does not of itself trigger a PAYE liability.

Exemptions from charge

6.22   Because of these special rules to tax the cost of a cash voucher the goods or services obtained with the voucher are of course excluded from being earnings to avoid double taxation. [*ITEPA 2003, s 95(2)*]. Where specific benefits are exempted from tax the legislation normally also exempts the use of a voucher to provide that benefit. Such provisions are:

s 269	– use of a voucher to obtain goods or services in connection with a car, van or heavy goods vehicle (see 7.2);
s 296	– travel facilities for the armed forces;
s 242	– works bus services;
s 243	– employer subsidised public transport services;
s 244	– cycles and safety equipment;
s 261	– sporting and recreational facilities;
s 210	– minor exempt benefits;
s 237(1)	– parking provision (see 7.92);
s 246	– transport for disabled employees;
s 247	– cars for disabled employees;
s 248	– transport home in certain cases;
s 265	– third party entertainment;
s 345	– travel during transport strikes;
s 264	– annual parties; and
s 317	– subsidised meals

[*ITEPA 2003, s 266* – previously each section included the exemption].

6.23   If a non-cash voucher is used to pay business expenses the employee can claim a deduction of the lessor of the amount treated as earnings under the non cash voucher rules or the amount that would have been deductible under *ITEPA 2003, ss 336, 337* or *370–376* if he had paid the expenditure himself. [*ITEPA 2003, s 362*]. Prior to 2003/04 the relief was given by treating the taxable amount in respect of the voucher as an expense which could qualify for relief under *ICTA 1988, ss 198, 201, 201AA* or *832(3)*. [*ICTA 1988, s 141(3)*]. If a non-cash voucher is appropriated to a person without being given to him, e.g. it is attached to a card for his benefit or is retained by the employer for safekeeping, it is treated as being received by the employee at the time of such appropriation. [*ITEPA 2003, s 82(3)*].

6.24 A non-cash voucher is also exempted from tax to the extent that it is used to obtain entertainment (including hospitality of any kind) for the employee or a member of his family or household (prior to 2003/04 a relation of his) if it is provided at the cost of someone other than his employer (or a connected person of the employer); the employer (or a connected person) has not directly or indirectly procured the provision of the voucher; and the entertainment is not provided in recognition of particular services which have been performed by him in the course of his employment (or in anticipation of particular services to be so performed). [*ITEPA 2003, ss 265, 266(1)*]. This will cover such things as the provision to an employee by a customer of his employer of an admission ticket to a football match or other sporting event in the course of entertainment by the customer. A member of a person's family (or a relation), for this purpose, means the spouse, parent, child or dependant of the employee or the spouse of an employee's child. [*ITEPA 2003, s 721(4)*]. *Section 839* applies to determine whether a person is connected with the employer.

6.25 There is also an exemption in relation to transport vouchers provided for an employee of a passenger-transport undertaking (such as British Airways and the privatised railway companies although as they did not exist in 1982 they cannot satisfy the second test—but see 6.52) under arrangements in operation on 25 March 1982 and intended to enable that employee or a relation of his (as defined above) to obtain passenger transport services provided by his employer, its subsidiary or parent company, or another passenger transport undertaking. [*ITEPA 2003, s 86*]. This was intended to ensure that where an airline pilot gets cheap flights for his family or a train driver cheap travel on continental railways, the document by which he achieves it would continue to escape tax. This concession was based on the premise that there is probably no cost to the transport undertaking in any event as the marginal cost of transporting an extra passenger is probably nil.

6.26 There is also an exemption for non-cash vouchers used for incidental overnight expenses while the employee is working away from home. The goods or services in question must be incidental to the employee being away from his usual place of abode for a period including at least one overnight stay, must not otherwise be deductible as a Schedule E expense and must not exceed an average £5 a night in the

UK or £10 a night elsewhere. [*ITEPA 2003, s 268*]. The detailed rules are the same as apply to expenses and are considered at 5.41.

6.27 Where a person incurs expense in relation to the provision of non-cash vouchers for a group of employees the amount must be apportioned in such manner as is just and reasonable. [*ITEPA 2003, s 77*]. A non-cash voucher is automatically deemed to be provided by reason of a person's employment—which is, of course, essential for it to be taxable as employment income—if it is provided by his employer. [*ITEPA 2003, s 82(2)*]. Prior to 2003/04, no exception was made where the employer was an individual. Accordingly, if a father employed his son in his business and outside the business gave the son a cheque as a birthday present made out to the supplier of, say, a hi-fi, the cost of the hi-fi constituted emoluments of the employment even though it is in fact nothing to do with the employment. There is now an exception where the employer is an individual and the provision is made in the normal course of the employer's domestic, family or personal relationships. [*ITEPA 2003, s 83(2)*]. A non-cash voucher provided for a member of the employee's family (within 6.19 above) must be treated as having been provided for the employee. [*ITEPA 2003, s 83*]. For 2003/04 onwards a non-cash voucher is also not taxable if it is of a kind made available to the public generally and is not provided to the employee or relative on more favourable terms than to the public generally. [*ITEPA 2003, s 85*]. There is also a reduction in the taxable amount for a meal voucher where it is provided for an employee for use on a working day if meal vouchers are made available to all employees who are employed by the same employer and in lower-paid employment. The cash equivalent of the benefit is to be reduced by 15p for each working day for which the voucher is provided. A meal voucher is a non-cash voucher which can only be used to obtain meals, is not transferable and is not of the kind in respect of which no liability to income tax arises under *section 317* (subsidised meals) (see 9.63). The relief does not extend to a meal voucher provided for a relative of the employee. [*ITEPA 2003, s 89*]. This gives statutory effect to a long-standing Revenue concession, *ESC A2*, on luncheon vouchers.

6.28 *Section 87* has virtually blocked the provision of benefits to lower-paid employees in a tax advantageous form. It requires a great deal of ingenuity (and a lot of administrative trouble) for most employers to provide benefits to employees without bringing some sort of voucher into existence to evidence to the supplier that the employee is entitled to the goods or services and that the employer will pay for them.

Credit tokens

6.29 A 'credit token' is a credit card, debit card or other card, token, document or other thing given to a person by another person who undertakes either that on the production of it he will supply money, goods or services on credit, or that, if on the production of it to a third party that third party supplies money, goods or services, he will pay that third party for them. [*ITEPA 2003, s 92(1)*]. A cash voucher or non-cash voucher is not a credit token. The use of an object to operate a machine is treated as the production of that object, e.g. if an employer provides his staff with tokens to operate the firm's coffee machine they will be credit tokens. [*ITEPA 2003, s 92(3)*]. A document will still be a credit token even if some other action is required in addition to its production to obtain the money, goods or services and even if the employer gets a commission from the third party who accepts the voucher. [*ITEPA 2003, s 92(2)*].

6.30   On each occasion that an employee (or for 2002/03 onwards a relation of the employee within 6.19 above) uses a credit token to obtain money, goods or services the employee is treated as having received employment income equal to the expense incurred by the employer (or other person providing the credit token or the person at whose cost it was provided) in connection with the provision of the money, goods or services obtained. [*ITEPA 2003, s 94*]. It is irrelevant when the credit token is given to the employee. In theory, if an employee does not drink coffee very often he needs to count up the coffee machine tokens sitting in his drawer at 5 April and notify the Revenue of their total value as the employer will doubtless declare to the Revenue the issue of them to the employee not their usage. It seems improbable that this happens in practice. The most obvious example of a credit token is a company credit card. Where goods are obtained using a credit card it should be noted that the assessable date is the time the card is used, not the later date when the employer settles the bill.

6.31   Where the use of a credit token is taxable under *section 94* no charge on the goods or services obtained by that use will arise under any other provision. [*ITEPA 2003, s 95*]. If a credit token is used to pay business expenses the employee can submit a *section 336* claim (see 5.2 above) or one under *ITEPA 2003, ss 343–346, 351* (see 5.82 and 5.95 above and 19.16 below) and in the same way as if he had incurred the expense himself. [*ITEPA 2003, s 363*]. If the employee reimburses any part of the cost, such as where he has to pay for personal expenditure on his company credit card, the assessable amount is reduced by the payment he makes. [*ITEPA 2003, s 94(2)*]. PAYE does not apply on the use of credit tokens.

6.32   No assessment will arise to the extent that a credit token is used by the employee to obtain the use of a car parking space at or near his place of work, or to obtain entertainment (including hospitality) provided at the cost of a third party without any prompting by the employer, i.e. which qualifies for the same exemption under the non-cash voucher rules (see 6.22 above). [*ITEPA 2003, s 267*].

6.33   There is also an exemption for credit tokens used for incidental overnight expenses while the employee is working away from home. The goods or services in question must be incidental to the employee being away from his usual place of abode for a period including at least one overnight stay, must not otherwise be deductible as a Schedule E expense and must not exceed an average £5 a night in the UK or £10 a night elsewhere. [*ITEPA 2003, s 268*]. The detailed rules are the same as apply to expenses and are considered at 5.41.

6.34 Where a person incurs expense in relation to the provision of credit tokens for more than one employee the amount must be apportioned in such manner as is just and reasonable. [*ITEPA 2003, s 94(4)*]. A credit token is automatically deemed to be provided by reason of a person's employment if it is provided by his employer. [*ITEPA 2003, s 90(2)*]. Prior to 2003/04 no exception was made where the employer is an individual. Accordingly, if a father employed his son in his business and outside the business the son was provided with a family member's card on his father's credit card, the cost of purchases on that card constituted emoluments of the employment even though it was, in fact, nothing to do with the employment. This anomaly has now been corrected. No benefit now arises where the employer is an individual and the provision is made in the normal course of the employer's domestic family or personal relationships. [*ITEPA 2003, s 90(2)*]. A credit token provided for a relation of the employee (as defined at 6.19 above) must be treated as having been provided for the employee. [*ITEPA 2003, s 91*]. For 2003/04 onwards no benefit arises if the credit token is of a kind made available to the public generally and it is not provided to the employee on more favourable terms than to the public generally. [*ITEPA 2003, s 93*].

Dispensations

6.35 An employer (or any other person) can apply, in effect, for a dispensation from the non-cash voucher and credit token provisions. To do this he must send to the Inspector of Taxes a statement of the cases and circumstances in which such vouchers or tokens are provided for employees. If the Inspector is satisfied that no tax would be payable on them, e.g. because they can only be used to meet bona fide business expenses or because the employee will reimburse the full cost of personal expenses, he can exempt them from these provisions. The Inspector may revoke such a dispensation at any time if in his opinion it is reasonable to do so. He can revoke it with retrospective effect to the day it was originally given if he thinks fit, or with effect from any later date that he feels appropriate. [*ITEPA 2003, s 96*]. Dispensations are considered in more detail at 6.77 onwards.

Benefits applicable only to higher-paid employees

The basic rules

6.36 If by reason of his employment any payments are made to a higher-paid employee (see 6.4 above) in respect of expenses and those amounts are not otherwise taxable on him as income, they must be treated as earnings from his employment and taxed on him accordingly. [*ITEPA 2003, ss 70(1)*]. For this purpose any sum put at an employee's disposal and paid away by him is treated as paid to him in respect of expenses. [*ITEPA 2003, s 70(2)*]. This is, on the face of it, a somewhat startling proposition. It is tempered to some extent by the fact that the employee is entitled to make any appropriate claim to deduct expenses under *ITEPA 2003, s 336* (see 5.2 above) (or under *ITEPA 2003, s 351* if he is a clergyman) or for relief for subscriptions under *ITEPA 2003, s 343*, (see 5.82) or for employee liability payments (see 5.95) under *ITEPA 2003, s 346* as if he had expended the money himself. [*ITEPA 2003, s 72(2)*]. Mileage allowance payments (see 7.68) and passenger payments (see 7.72) in respect of an employee's own car were specifically excluded from *section 153* but the format of *ITEPA 2003* no longer makes such a provision necessary.

6.37   In *Wicks v Firth* [*1983*] *STC 25* Lord Denning expressed the view that the words 'by reason of' are far wider than the word 'therefrom' used in *ICTA 1988, s 19(1)* and are deliberately designed to close the gap in taxability left by the House of Lords in *Hochstrasser v Mayes*. Oliver LJ agreed but suggested that the words require one to ask the question 'What is it that enables the person concerned to enjoy the benefit?'. This question was adopted in *Mairs v Haughey* (see 11.59) and also in *Wilcock v Eve* (see 3.17), in both of which the disputed item was held not to be taxable as a benefit in kind.

Treatment of expenses

6.38   In other words, all expenses paid to higher-paid employees are treated with suspicion, and are assumed not to be business expenses. It is then up to the employee to displace that presumption by showing that the expenses meet the strict rules to attract a deduction.

6.39   Strictly speaking, as payments to the employee are assessable income, such expense payments should be subject to PAYE but the Inland Revenue have not been known to take the point.

Payments to third parties

6.40   It should be noted that *section 70* applies only to payments made to the employee (or into an account under his control). It does not apply to payments to third parties. If payments to third parties in respect of expenses satisfy an existing liability of the employee it should not be overlooked that such payments already constitute emoluments under general principles as they constitute amounts of money's worth provided for the employee by reason of his employment. This is emphasised by the decision in *Sports Club plc v Inspector of Taxes* [*2000*] *STC (SCD) 443* which is considered at 3.9–3.11.

The assessable amount

6.41   Where a person is in higher-paid employment and by reason of his employment any benefit is provided for him or for members of his family or household an amount equal to the cash equivalent of the benefit must be treated as income from his employment. [*ITEPA 2003, s 201*]. If the same benefit would give rise to an amount taxable as earnings under the basic rules and an amount being treated as earnings under the benefits code the earnings rule takes precedence and the amount taxed under the benefit code is limited to the excess of the benefit code figure over the amount already taxed as earnings. [*ITEPA 2003, s 64*].

Exceptions

6.42   There are a number of exceptions.

(*a*)   The right to receive (or the prospect of receiving) a sum which is itself taxable under *section 221* (sick pay under industry-wide arrangements) see 2.36 above). [*ITEPA 2003, s 202(1)(c)*].

(*b*)   A benefit to which the round sum car use (see 7.2 below), van use (see 7.94 below) or petrol (see 7.46 below) benefits apply. [*ITEPA 2003, s 202(1)(a)*].

(*c*)   A benefit which is taxable under the special rules applying to beneficial loans (see 9.1 below) and employee shareholdings (see Chapter 14). [*ITEPA 2003, s 202(1)(a)*].

(*d*)   If a person is taxable on the car use benefit (see 7.2 below), or van use benefit (see 7.94 below) *ITEPA 2003, s 201* does not apply to any benefit in connection with that car, other than a benefit in connection with a driver for the car, i.e. the car use benefit does not cover the wages, uniform, subsistence, etc. of a chauffeur. [*ITEPA 2003, s 239(4) (5)*]. It also does not cover a car telephone, if it is portable (but does so if it is fixed: see 7.93 and 9.35 below).

(*e*)   The provision of a car parking space at or near the employee's place of work. [*ITEPA 2003, s 237*].

(*f*)   If living accommodation is provided for a person by reason of his employment *ITEPA 2003, s 201* does not apply to:

   (i)   alterations and additions to the premises which are of a structural nature—as these are really expenses of the company as 'landlord' rather than of the employee as occupier; and

   (ii)   repairs to the premises such that if the premises were let under a lease to which *section 11, Landlord and Tenant Act 1985* applies they would be obligations of the landlord, not the occupier. *Section 11* imposes on the landlord the obligation, at his own cost, to keep in repair the structure and exterior of the dwelling including the drains, gutters and external pipes; and to keep in repair and proper working order the installations in the dwelling for the supply of water, gas, electricity, sanitation, space heating and hot water. [*ITEPA 2003, s 313*].

(*g*) The provision by the employer for either the employee himself or his spouse, children or dependants, of any pension, annuity, lump sum, gratuity or similar benefit to be given on the employee's death or retirement. This will cover not only an actual payment on retirement but also, for example, the payment of an insurance premium on a policy to provide for such a payment (or by *ESC A72* any other member of the employee's family or household, i.e. spouse, children, children's spouses, parents, servants, dependants or guests). [*ITEPA 2003, s 307* and *ESC A72*].

(*h*) The provision by the employer of meals in a canteen in which meals are provided for the staff generally. [*ITEPA 2003, s 317(1)(a)*]. For 2003/04 onwards the exemption also applies if the meals are provided for the employees at a particular location. [*ITEPA 2003, s 317(1)(a)*]. It also covers other meals provided on the employee's business premises if:

  (i) the meals are on a reasonable scale;

  (ii) all of the employees (or all of them at a particular location) can obtain either a free or subsidised meal or a meal voucher or token enabling them to obtain a meal; and

  (iii) if the meals are provided in the restaurant or dining room of a hotel or catering business at a time when meals are being served to the public, the employees eat only in a part of the room designated for staff only.

[*ITEPA 2003, s 317(1)(b), (2)–(5)*]. This gives statutory effect to a prior extra-statutory concession, *ESC A74*.

(*j*) The provision for the employee of medical treatment outside the UK (or of insurance cover against the cost of such treatment) where the need for the treatment arises while the employee is outside the UK for the purpose of performing the duties of the employment. Medical treatment for this purpose includes all forms of treatment for, and all procedures for diagnosing, any physical or mental ailment, infirmity or defect, and the cost of such treatment includes the costs of providing for the employee to be an in-patient in a hospital. [*ITEPA 2003, s 325*]. If the employee is so ill that his doctors feel that he should be flown back to the UK for treatment, this exception would not cover the cost of treatment in the UK or the cost of flying him back. It would, however, cover the cost of treatment in a different overseas country to that in which he was initially taken ill.

(*k*) The provision of entertainment (including hospitality of any kind) for the employee, or for members of his family or household, if:

(i) the person providing the benefit is not his employer, nor a connected person of the employer within *section 839*;

(ii) neither the employer (nor a connected person of his) has directly or indirectly procured its provision; and

(iii) it is not provided either in recognition of particular services which have been performed by the employee in the course of his employment or in anticipation of his performing such services. [*ITEPA 2003, s 265*].

This exempts, for example, the cost incurred by a customer or supplier of the employer who entertains the employee for his own, rather than the employer's, purposes.

(*l*) If an asset or service which improves personal security is provided for an employee by his employer by reason of his employment the cost is not taxed on the employee (or, to be precise, it is taxed on him but offset by an equivalent deduction). Similarly, no charge arises if the employer reimburses such expenditure by the employee. [*ITEPA 2003, s 377(2)*]. This exemption applies only if the asset or service is provided to meet a special threat to the employee's personal security which arises wholly or mainly from the employment concerned. [*ITEPA 2003, s 377(1)*]. The meeting of the threat must be the sole object of the employer in bearing the cost. The asset must be intended for use solely to improve personal physical security (e.g. not partly to improve security to property of the employee) and the benefit resulting from a security service must consist wholly or mainly of an improvement to the employee's personal physical security. [*ITEPA 2003, s 377(3)*]. A proportion of the cost is exempted from tax if the asset is partly provided to meet a threat to the employee's personal security. [*ITEPA 2003, s 377(4)*]. The fact that the expenditure also improves the physical security of the employee's family or household as well as himself will not restrict the relief. [*ITEPA 2003, s 377(7)*]. Relief is not given for the cost of a car, ship, aircraft or a dwelling-house and its grounds. [*ITEPA 2003, s 377(8)*]. It will be given for additions to such assets, e.g. bulletproof windows for a car, a perimeter wall round the house, etc. This relief is intended to be very restrictive. It is intended to meet threats from terrorists and other extremist groups. It will not apply, therefore, to such things such as rape alarms provided to female staff who work late or similar items for protection against the criminal activities that the average citizen may have to face.

These provisions were considered by the Special Commissioners in *Lord Hanson v Mansworth (Sp C 410, 2004, STI 1365)*. Hanson plc expanded into Northern Ireland in 1978. Lord Hanson was perceived to be close to the Conservative Party although he did not make any contributions to it. The company was concerned about his safety and provided him with a 24-hour security service at his country home (eight dog handlers and dogs and three guards) from

1989/90 to 1997/98. He was put on the police 'reserve' list in 1990. The Commissioners held that Lord Hanson met the profile of the type of person who could well be an IRA target. There was therefore a threat. They thought that 'special' means 'out of the ordinary' and a terrorist threat is out of the ordinary. The threat arose wholly or mainly by reason of Lord Hanson's employment as his high profile arose only by virtue of his name and role in Hanson plc. They thought that the test of whether meeting the threat was the sole object of the provider is a subjective one, i.e. what was the employer's belief. They further held that the security service was clearly not provided to protect the house from a generalised criminal threat (it already had a burglar alarm system) and that the benefit to Lord Hanson was certainly mainly an improvement in his personal physical security. The Commissioners also held that although the relief is automatic and does not have to be claimed Lord Hanson was negligent in not having shown the benefit of the security services on his tax return and an offsetting deduction. This is, at least a little, startling as there is no box for such a deduction on the tax return.

(*m*) The provision by an employer of workplace nurseries and similar facilities for children of employees (up to the age of 18), although only in fairly limited circumstances. The facilities must provide some form of care or supervised activities, but this must not be supervised activity provided for educational purposes, e.g. nursery schools for pre-school age children are excluded. It must be provided under arrangements made by persons who include the employer, on premises made available by one of those persons (which must not be domestic premises), any local authority registration requirements for the crèche must be complied with, and the employer must be wholly or partly responsible for financing and managing the provision of the care. [*ITEPA 2003, s 318*]. It is not sufficient for an employer to book a number of places in an existing, commercially run child care facility. He must have a say in the management. In practice, only large employers are likely to set up crèches in the light of these restrictions, although the Government apparently hope that groups of small employers will get together to engage a child minder and set up a crèche jointly on one of their premises. From 2005/06 this relief will be replaced by the broader relief described at 9.100 onwards.

(*n*) There are also specific exemptions for the first £8,000 of certain removal expenses (see 9.87), sports and recreation facilities (see 9.46) redundancy counselling (see 9.84), and the payment by an employer on behalf of an employee of amounts in respect of employee liabilities or officers' indemnity insurance (see 5.95). [*ITEPA 2003, s 334*].

(*o*) Incidental overnight expenses where a person is working away from home for a period which includes at least one overnight stay. The expenditure must not exceed an average of £5 a night in the

UK or £10 a night elsewhere. [*ITEPA 2003, s 240, 241*]. The detailed rules that must be met are the same as for such reimbursed expenses and are considered at 5.41.

(*p*)   The provision in premises occupied by the employer (or others providing it) of accommodation, supplies or services used by the employee solely in performing the duties of the employment. [*ITEPA 2003, s 316(1)*].

(*q*)   From 1999/00, making available the use of a mobile telephone to the employee or to a member of his family or household (see 9.35).

(*r*)   From 1999/00 making available computer equipment provided that specified conditions are met (see 9.89).

(*s*)   From 1990/00 the use of a works bus provided that certain conditions are met (see 9.93).

(*t*)   From 1999/00 there are some exemptions for cycles (see 9.97).

(*u*)   From 2000/01 onwards the provision of accommodation, supplies or services used by the employee in performing the duties of his employment. If the benefit is provided on premises occupied by the employer (or by the provider of the benefit if different) any use of it for private purposes by the employee or members of his family or household must not be significant. Use is for private purposes if it is not in performing the duties of the employment and simultaneous use for performing the duties of the employment and for some other purpose is treated as private. [*ITEPA 2003, s 316(2)(3)*]. No guidance has been given as to the meaning of not significant. If the benefit is not provided on the employer's premises it needs to be shown that the sole purpose of providing the benefit is to enable the employee to perform the duties of his employment, that any use for private purposes is not significant and that the benefit is not an excluded benefit [*ITEPA 2003, s 316(4)*]. A motor vehicle, boat, aircraft, or any benefit that involves the extension, conversion or alteration of any living accommodation (or the construction, extension, conversion or alteration of a building or other structure on land adjacent to and enjoyed with such accommodation) are excluded benefits. [*ITEPA 2003, s 316(5)*]. The Treasury has power to amend this list of excluded benefits. [*ITEPA 2003, s 316(6)*]. This provision exempts incidental private use of business assets. It is likely that before 2000/01 most people did not recognise that a benefit arose in such circumstances in any event.

(*v*)   From 2003/04 where an employer makes a payment to an employee in respect of reasonable additional household expenses which the employee incurs in carrying out duties of the employment at home under homeworking arrangements the payment is exempt from income tax. Household expenses are expenses connected with the day to day running of the employee's home. Homeworking arrangements are arrangements between the employee and the employer under which the employee regularly performs some or all of the duties of the employment at home. [*ITEPA 2003, s 316A* inserted by *FA 2003, s 137*]. It should be noted that it is only the additional expenses (e.g. light, heat, telephone) caused by the homeworking that qualifies for relief, not a proportion of any expenses that would have been incurred in any event. The Revenue have said that they will accept an amount of up to £2 a week (£104 a year) as reasonable without supporting evidence. If the employer pays more than this amount they will expect to see evidence to demonstrate that the payment is wholly in respect of additional expenses (IR Press Release, 9 April 2003).

(*w*)   From 2000/01 onwards the Treasury are given power by Regulation to exempt from *section 154* such minor benefit as they may specify. They cannot exempt a benefit under this power unless it is made available to an employer's employees generally on the same terms. [*ITEPA 2003, s 210*]. With effect from 21 August 2000 they have exempted welfare counselling (counselling of any kind, other than medical treatment of any kind or advice on finance (other than debt problems), on tax, on leisure or recreation, or legal advice) provided that it is made available to an employer's employees generally on similar terms (*Income Tax (Benefits in Kind) (Exemption for Welfare Counselling) Regulations 2000—SI 2000 No 2080*). For 2002/03 they exempted the first six cyclist's breakfasts ('qualifying meals') provided for an employee in a tax year. This is food or drink provided by an employer in recognition of the employee having used a cycle on a designated day to make a journey between their home and their workplace, and which is provided for consumption by the employee on their arrival at the workplace on that day. They removed the limitation to six meals from 25 June 2003. They have also exempted the benefit from the provision of a bus or minibus for conveying employees on a relevant journey, i.e. one which is a single journey of a distance of up to 10 miles made between the workplace and shops or other amenities and made on a working day. (*Income Tax (Exemption of Minor Benefits) Regulations 2002) (SI 2002 No 205*).

(*x*)   From 9 July 2002, the provision of a benefit to a disabled employee if the main purpose of providing the benefit is to enable the employee to perform the duties of the employment, it consists in the provision of a hearing aid or other equipment, services or facilities (other than an excluded benefit under (a) above), it is provided under (or within the terms of) the *Disability Discrimination Act 1995*, the Access to Work programme (under the *Employment and Training Act 1973, s 2* or its Scottish or Northern Irish equivalent) or some other statutory provisions (whether or not the employer has a legal duty to provide the benefit) and the benefit is made available to the employer's employees generally on similar terms. [*Income Tax (Benefits in Kind) (Exemption for Employment Costs resulting from Disability) Regulations 2002 [SI 2002 No 1596)*].

Payments to the employee's family

6.43   For the purpose of the benefit in kind provisions, all sums paid to an employee by his employer himself, and all benefits provided for an employee (or for members of his family or household) by his employer, must be treated as paid or provided by reason of the employment—even if it can be demonstrated that they are made for entirely unconnected reasons. There is an exception where the employer is an individual (but not if it is a partnership) and it can be shown that the payment or provision was made in the normal course of that individual's domestic, family or personal relationships. [*ITEPA 2003, s 201(3)*].

6.44   The people regarded as members of a person's family or household are his spouse, his sons and daughters, spouses of his sons and daughters, his parents, and his dependants, domestic staff and guests. [*ITEPA 2003, s 721(4)*].

6.45   As indicated at 6.40 above, the assessable amount is the cash equivalent of the benefit. This is the 'cost of the benefit' less any part of that cost which is made good by the employee to the person providing the benefit. [*ITEPA 2003, s 203*]. If the benefit is provided to a member of the employee's family there does not appear to be a right to reduce the cost by any payment made by the family member, but the Revenue will undoubtedly allow this by concession.

The cost of the benefit

6.46   The 'cost of a benefit' is normally the amount of any expense incurred in (or in connection with) its provision. A proper proportion of any expense relating partly to the benefit and partly to other matters must be included. [*ITEPA 2003, s 204*]. Where an employee sells or transfers an asset to his employer or to a person nominated by the employer and the right or opportunity to make the transfer arose by reason of the employment, the employee is not taxable on the payment or reimbursement of expenses which are incidental to, and incurred wholly and exclusively as a result of, the transfer and which are of a kind not normally met by the transferor. [*ITEPA 2003, s 326* enacting *ESC A35*]. This excludes from the cost of the benefit the employer's legal and other costs of acquisition. It would not exclude any expense paid by the employer which would normally be borne by the vendor (*IR Press Release 27 April 1994*). There is no corresponding concession where the employer transfers an asset to the employee.

6.47   Where the benefit consists in the provision to the employee of a service provided by the employer in the normal course of its business, or the transfer to him of goods produced by the company, commonly called 'in-house' benefits, the cost of providing the benefit is the marginal cost. This was settled by the House of Lords in *Pepper v Hart [1992] STC 898*. That case was concerned with the provision by a private school of education for children of its teachers—a standard perk in the education field. The school argued that the cost to it of providing the education was the marginal cost and it cost virtually nothing to add another child to an existing class of children where there were vacancies in the class. The Revenue contended that the total cost of running the school had to be apportioned amongst all the pupils, including the children of teachers, to arrive at the cost of the benefit. This would give a figure roughly equal to the standard fees charged by the school less the profit element included in such fees.

6.48   The Revenue contention was upheld in both the High Court and the Court of Appeal. In an exceptional seven-man hearing before the House of Lords, five of their Lordships supported the Revenue's interpretation and two, including the Lord Chancellor, the taxpayer's, on a simple consideration of the statutory language. However, the House, in a landmark decision, opted to set aside the tradition that the courts could not consult Hansard to assist in determining what Parliament has intended in enacting the legislation. It felt that this should be permissible where:

(*a*)   legislation is ambiguous or obscure, or leads to an absurdity;

(*b*)   the materials relied on are statements by a Minister or other promoter of the *Bill*; and

(*c*)   the statements relied on are clear.

6.49   When what is now *section 204* was introduced in 1976 the original Bill contained a clause which sought to tax in-house benefits by reference to the price which the public would pay for the item. However, the Government withdrew that provision, the Minister stating, 'I will give some reasons which weigh heavily in favour of the withdrawal of this provision. The first is the large difference between the cost of providing some services and the amount of benefit which under the *Bill* would be held to be received . . . I would point out that air and rail journeys are only two of a number of service benefits which have a number of problems attached to them. But there is a large difference between the cost of the benefit to the employer and the value of that benefit as assessed. It could lead to unjustifiable situations resulting in a great number of injustices and I do not think we should continue with it . . . The second reason for withdrawing Clause 54(4) is that these services would tend to be much less used . . . The third reason is the difficulty of enforcement and administration which both give rise to certain problems. Finally it was possible to withdraw this part of the legislation as the services cover not only a more difficult area, but a quite distinct area of these provisions, without having repercussions on some of the other areas . . . .' (*Hansard Standing Committee E 17 June 1976, cols 893–895*).

6.50   He was then asked, 'Is he saying that these benefits will remain taxable but that the equivalent cost of the benefit will be calculated on some different basis? Or is he saying that these benefits will not be taxable at all?' The Minister responded, 'The existing law which applies to the taxation of some of these benefits will be retained. The position will subsequently be unchanged from what it is now before the introduction of the legislation'. He later said, 'The employee earning more than £5,000 or the director will be assessed on the benefit received by him on the basis of the cost to the employer . . . If a company provides a service to the kind of employee which we have been talking about, and the company subsidises that service, the benefit assessable on the employee is the cost to the employer of providing that service . . . Some companies provide services of a kind where the cost to them is very little. For example, an airline ticket, allowing occupation of an empty seat, costs an airline nothing—in fact, in such a case there could be a negative cost, as it might be an advantage to the airline to have an experienced crew member on the flight. The cost to the company, then, would be nothing . . . sub-section (2) only re-states the existing position. It does not produce anything new.' (*Cols 930–932*).

6.51   On 22 June 1976 the Minister told the standing committee in response to a question on travel concessions for merchant seamen, 'This proposal concerns the employee of a company and his wife . . . and the concession of a free passage or voyage in a company ship . . . I think that I can satisfy the hon Gentlemen that these voyages will not now be subject to tax as a result of the withdrawal of sub-clause (4) apart from the nominal charge for food which is normally made and which would be assessable . . . the only basis for charge would be on the cost to the employer, and in the example that we are considering that would be very small.' He was then specifically asked about concessionary fees for children of teachers at fee paying schools and replied, 'now the benefit will be assessed on the cost to the employer, which would be very small indeed in this case'. As indicated earlier, in *Pepper v Hart* itself the Revenue were seeking to value the benefit to a teacher at a private school of cheap education of his child at the school, the very situation that had been envisaged in that question.

6.52   The previous rules had been explained to the Finance Bill standing committee by the Minister in 1975 in response to a question on the imposition of tax on certain vouchers. The railwayman travelling on his normal voucher will not be taxable either '. . . because the provision of the service that he provides falls upon the employer. Clearly, the railways will run in precisely the same way whether the railwaymen use this facility or not, so there is no extra charge to the Railways Board itself, therefore there would be no taxable benefits'.

6.53   Faced with these repeated assurances the House of Lords had no trouble in finding that, with the benefit of being able to consult *Hansard*, the reference to cost must be to marginal cost.

6.54   Following the decision in *Pepper v Hart* the Revenue announced that its effect 'was that in the case of all in-house benefits the cost of the benefit to the employer is the additional or marginal cost only' (*IR Press*

Release 21 January 1993). This Press Release made clear that in-house benefits include goods as well as services and facilities. It went on to state that the marginal cost depends on each employer's particular circumstances but that as a general guide the Revenue accept that:

(*a*) rail or bus travel on terms which do not displace fare-paying passengers involves no or negligible additional costs;

(*b*) goods sold at a discount which leave employees paying at least the wholesale price involve no or negligible net benefit;

(*c*) where teachers pay 15 per cent or more of a school's normal fees there is no net benefit; and

(*d*) professional services which do not require additional employees or partners (e.g. legal and financial services) have no or negligible cost to the employer provided the employee reimburses any disbursements.

Transfer of assets

6.55 If the benefit consists of the transfer of an asset to the employee (or a member of his family or household) and the asset has been used or has otherwise depreciated since it was acquired by the employer (or other person who provides the benefit) the cost of the benefit is not the cost of the asset to the employer but its market value at the time of transfer, i.e. the price which it might reasonably have been expected to fetch on a sale in the open market at that time [*ITEPA 2003, s 206*], subject to 6.56 below. This works both ways. It would be unreasonable to tax an employee on the amount he paid for, say, a computer which has been used by the company for five years and is now obsolete and of very little value. It is only fair that if the employee buys the computer from the company at its current value no benefit should arise, and that if he does not pay for it the benefit should be limited to its current value, as the real benefit is what the employee has saved by not having to buy a machine in the same state from a second-hand shop. On the other hand some assets increase in value. If the employee takes home the painting that cost £500 and has been on his office wall for five years he may well find that he has a benefit charge on £1,200 or some similar figure because the painting has increased in value.

6.56 If the second-hand asset has previously been used by the company to provide a benefit to the employee, or to another higher-paid employee, by allowing him the use of it, the cost of the benefit is the higher of:

(*a*) its market value at the time of transfer; or

(*b*) the original cost of the asset (its market value at the time when it was first used by the employer (or other provider of the benefit) to provide benefits) less the aggregate of the amounts previously assessed on higher-paid employees in relation to the use of the asset. [*ITEPA 2003, s 206(5)*].

Example

On 5 July 2002 M Ployer Ltd purchased a video recorder for £800 which
it installed at the house of Arthur, a higher-paid employee. On 5 December
2005 it sold the recorder to Ben, another higher-paid employee, at its then
market value of £60.

Benefit charge on Arthur

		£
2002/03	20% of £800 × 9 months	120
2003/04	20% of £800	160
2004/05	20% of £800	160
2005/06	20% of £800 × 8 months	107
		£547

Benefit charge on Ben

	£	£	£
2005/06			
Higher of: Market value:		60	
Cost	800		
Less: Assessed on Arthur	(547)		
		253	253
Less: Payment by Ben			60
Benefit charge			£193

In this example Ben suffers a very heavy benefit charge even though he
buys the asset at full market value. He would have been wiser to have
let the employer sell the asset and bought a second-hand machine from
a shop. Although the benefit has been pro-rated for parts of a year—
which happens in practice—the *Act* appears to impose a full 20 per cent
of cost charge even though the asset is not made available to the
employee throughout the year. If Arthur had continued to have use of
the asset for over five years the benefit would continue at 20 per cent
of cost, so overall he would have been assessed on a figure greater than
cost. An employee should be wary of his employer making very expensive assets with a long life, such as antiques or works of art, available
for his use.

6.57   This charge does not apply to cars. [*ITEPA 2003, s 206(3)(a)*].
Nor does it apply to an asset first used to provide benefits to higher-paid
employees before 6 April 1980. [*ITEPA 2003, s 206(3)(c)*]. If such an
asset, or a second-hand car, is transferred to an employee after having
been used by the company, the cost of the benefit will be its market
value at the time of the transfer, even if that use was by the employee
himself.

6.58   It should not be overlooked that if the asset transferred is within
the scope of capital gains tax the transfer will give rise to a capital gains
tax charge on the employer. Where an asset is acquired in consideration

for or in recognition of a person's (or another's) services or past services in any office or employment *TCGA 1992, s 17(1)(b)* requires the capital gain on the disposal to be calculated by reference to the market value at the time of the transfer. In practice the Revenue normally used to calculate the gain by reference only to any consideration actually paid by the employee but this concession was withdrawn from 1995/96 (*Tax Bulletin, Issue 14, December 1994*).

Assets placed at the employee's disposal

6.59   If an asset is placed at the disposal of the employee (or of other members of his family or household) for his use without any transfer of the ownership of the asset, the cost of the benefit is the aggregate of:

(*a*)   the annual value of the use of the asset, namely (in most cases) 20 per cent of its market value at the time when it was first applied by the employer (or other provider of the benefit) in the provision of any benefit for any person; and

(*b*)   any expense incurred in (or in connection with) the provision of the benefit other than the cost of acquiring or producing it incurred by the owner, and any rent or hire charge payable for it by the person providing the benefit.

[*ITEPA 2003, s 205*].

6.60   In most cases the figure at (*a*) will be 20 per cent of the cost of the asset. If the asset is land the annual rental value of the use of the asset is its annual value under *ITEPA 2003, s 110* (see 8.5 below). If the asset was first used to provide benefits for higher-paid employees before 6 April 1980 only 10 per cent of the cost of the asset is charged instead of 20 per cent. [*ITEPA 2003, s 205(3)*]. If the asset is leased or rented and the rent exceeds the 20 per cent of cost figure (or in the case of land the annual value) the figure to be used at (*a*) will instead be the rent or leasing charges paid. [*ITEPA 2003, s 205(2)*].

6.61   If the service or asset is used in whole or part for business purposes the taxpayer can make an expenses claim under *ITEPA 2003, s 336* (and *section 343* if he is a clergyman), *section 346* if it is an employee liability payment (see 5.95), or *section 343* if the benefit is the payment of a qualifying subscription, as if he had incurred expenditure out of his emoluments equal to the cost of the benefit from the asset. [*ITEPA 2003, s 365*].

6.62   Where an asset is used both in the business and for an employee's private purposes some fixed costs, such as road tax for a van, do not need to be taken into account where the private use of the asset is incidental to business use as it is only any additional expense incurred in connection with the provision of the asset that gives rise to a benefit (*IR Press Release 21 January 1993*).

Former employees

6.63   The main benefit in kind rules apply where the person is an employee at some point in the tax year in which the benefit is provided [*ITEPA 2003, s 201(4)*]. They accordingly cannot apply to benefits payable to a former employee after the end of the year of assessment in which the employment ceases. Indeed, the Revenue used to take the view that they cannot apply to a benefit provided after the employment has ended but later in the same year of assessment. This does not mean such benefits escape tax. The Revenue view was that the value of the benefit is part of the termination package and assessable as such and this view has been given statutory effect from 1998/99 (see 11.41). A charge can also arise under other provisions. *ITEPA 2003, s 394* imposes tax on employment income (for the year the benefit is received) on a benefit in kind which is provided under a retirement benefits scheme. The Revenue interpret 'retirement benefits scheme' very widely (see 11.38). Any payment made as a result of a person's retirement—which could be deemed to occur if he leaves his job within a few years prior to retirement age—is likely to be within *section 394*. Benefits payable as part of a redundancy package would not normally be within *section 394*. The amount of such a benefit is calculated in the same way as for benefits in kind. [*ITEPA 2003, s 398*].

6.64   If the recipient of the benefit is a shareholder or an associate of a shareholder the benefit can also be a distribution, calculated on the same basis as for tax on employment income. [*ICTA 1988, s 418(1)(4)*]. Although the same benefit cannot be taxed under both *ITEPA 2003, s 203* and *ICTA 1988, s 418* [*ICTA 1988, s 418(3)*] there is no such limitation where the benefit is taxable under *ITEPA 2003, s 394* or (see 10.60) *section 402* (see 11.16).

Time when benefit is provided

6.65   An interesting question arose in *Templeton v Jacobs* [*1996*] *STC 991*. The taxpayer, who lived in London, was offered employment from 1 May 1991 by a company in Kenilworth. He was not prepared to move and it was agreed that the taxpayer would, at the company's expense, convert his loft to an office. The builder sent his invoices to the company. These were all paid in full before 1 April 1991. The Revenue sought to tax the whole cost of the loft conversion as a benefit in kind. The taxpayer contended that the benefit had been provided on 1 April 1991 and as the employment did not exist in 1990/91 could not be taxed under *section 203*. The High Court, reversing the decision of the Special Commissioners, held that no benefit is provided until it becomes available to be enjoyed by the taxpayer. In this case the work was not completed until after the employment had started so was not available until then. The judge also rejected an alternate claim that as the loft was rented to the company it was occupied by it and thus exempt under *section 316(1)* (see 6.42(*p*)), holding that the benefit was the carrying out of the work, not the occupation of the office.

Lower-paid employees

6.66   The benefit in kind provisions (other than those described at 6.14–6.34 above, and 8.1–8.29 below do not apply to those in lower paid employment, i.e. where the earnings for the years are at a rate of less than £8,500. [*ITEPA 2003, s 217*]. In practice, with the average wage at April 2003 now £24,752 per annum, the number of lower-paid employees is diminishing and there are very few for whom employers might wish to provide benefits.

6.67   Furthermore, except for major companies that can provide in-house facilities for staff, a certain amount of ingenuity is needed, or a significant degree of inconvenience must be tolerated, to provide benefits for lower-paid employees without generating a tax charge on the cost of providing the benefit. This is because it is essential to avoid bringing into existence anything that might constitute a non-cash voucher (see 6.20 above) or a credit token (see 6.28 above). For example, suppose an employer enters into an arrangement with a local tailor to supply suits to his staff. How is the tailor to know who is entitled to a suit? If the employer gives the employee a letter addressed to the tailor saying that if he supplies a suit to the employee the employer will pay for it, the letter will be a non-cash voucher. If the employer says to the tailor that all his staff have official identification cards and he should supply a suit to whoever shows one, and send the employer a bill stating the name on the identity card, the card is probably a credit token. If the employee simply orders the suit himself and takes a cheque from the employer with him when he collects it, the cheque is a non-cash voucher—and in any event the cost of the suit is an emolument of the employee as he will have incurred the liability to pay for the suit. The employer could personally accompany the employee to the tailor and order the suit himself, but this does involve a certain amount of inconvenience.

6.68   If an employer does contrive to provide benefits to lower-paid employees without triggering a charge under the benefit rules the benefit does not, in theory at least, escape tax. The employee is taxable under general principles (see 3.2 above) on the money's worth into which the benefit can be converted. The leading case is *Wilkins v Rogerson 39 TC 344* where the employer arranged for an employee to collect a new suit from a tailor. It was held that he was taxable on the second-hand value of the suit, which was £5, and not its cost of £14.75. Whilst goods can normally be converted into cash—albeit at a figure significantly below cost—the same is not always true of services. For example, if an employer says to an employee, 'Come to the hairdressers with me and I will arrange for you to have your hair cut and styled', it is impossible for the employee to convert that benefit into cash because, by seeking to assign it, the employer would be aware that the person claiming the benefit was not the employee and would refuse to provide the benefit. Accordingly, the money's worth of the benefit would be nil.

Remuneration packages

6.69 Apart from company cars, where the quantum of the benefit has in the past been significantly below the cost of providing it and in some, but by no means all, cases still is, most benefits provided to higher-paid employees attract a tax charge equal to the cost of providing the benefit. In these circumstances the provision of benefits might be thought somewhat pointless. Admittedly, there is a national insurance saving but in most cases this is only 9 per cent of the employee's salary (12.8 per cent less 30 per cent tax relief) or 10.2 per cent with a 19 per cent corporation tax rate, and it is questionable whether this is a sufficient benefit to justify the administrative costs. Probably the most common reason for providing benefits is that such provision is widespread in the UK and if other employers provide benefits it may be necessary to follow suit to attract the right calibre of staff. An employee may perceive the benefit to be worth more than an equivalent sum in cash even though he will suffer tax on it. He may also perceive an employer who provides benefits as having a more caring attitude towards staff than one who does not, although often such a perception is far from the case.

6.70 If an employer does decide that he wants to provide benefits it is obviously important to give staff the right benefits; those that will attract them to the employer or will motivate them in their work. Unfortunately, it is often difficult to determine what benefit to provide. It is also difficult to know whether the cost of the benefit is justifiable in terms of the incentive effect on staff. For example, an employee who does not drive, or one whose spouse already has a company car, would probably appreciate a rise far more than a company car. Many employees may be happier with a cash increase than a benefit. Other things being equal, it is better to have 60p in one's pocket to spend as one may wish than £1 spent on a benefit which generates a 40p tax charge that has to be met out of one's own pocket, and which may not be a benefit that one might have chosen for oneself. Even where an employee may appreciate a benefit, such as family medical insurance, if the expenditure on such an item is low on his list of priorities it is unlikely to motivate him significantly. These problems can be minimised by the use of remuneration packages.

6.71 The basic concept of a remuneration package is that the employer is prepared to pay a certain sum to obtain the services of the employee. This could be paid wholly in cash or it could be spent partly in cash and partly in the provision of benefits. In theory, provided that the total cost is the same, it should make no difference to the employer how the money is laid out but the provision of benefits could be advantageous to the employee.

Fixed packages

6.72 A remuneration package can be fixed or flexible. A fixed remuneration package generally comprises a standard package, the components of which the employer is normally prepared to convert into cash if the employee wishes. For example, he may say to the prospective employee, 'We will offer you £20,000 a year, plus a Ford Escort car, plus a non-contributory pension scheme; we think the car is worth £2,000 a year and we will put £1,000 a year into the pension scheme so we are really offering you £23,000'. If the employee were to say he would prefer to be paid £23,000 with no benefits, the employer ought to be prepared to accede to this. With a fixed remuneration package, therefore, the employer has to try to assess what benefits he thinks might be attractive to the employee and consequently takes a gamble on whether the employee might be indifferent to them. For example, whilst an employee is unlikely to actually refuse a company car unless he is positively offered extra salary in lieu, if the employee values the use of the car at £800 whereas the employer values it at £2,000, the cost of providing the car will have been largely wasted. The employee would find the job more attractive if he were given a £1,000 rise instead of the car.

Flexible packages

6.73 With a flexible remuneration package the employer fixes the amount he is prepared to spend to obtain or keep the employee and leaves the employee to decide how much of that he would like as salary and how much as benefits and what benefits he would like provided. This has a number of obvious advantages. It ensures that the employee realises what it costs to provide the benefit. It may also give the employer a competitive advantage, as some of the benefit he may be prepared to provide, if he is willing to respond positively to the employee's wishes, may not be available to the employee from other prospective employers.

6.74 There are dangers. If a large number of staff are involved, the administration costs of providing a range of benefits can be enormous. The provision of benefits could also give rise to staff jealousies. If one employee chooses an expensive car and a colleague a cheaper car and a larger salary, there is a risk that after a time the second employee may forget that his contemporary has a bigger car because he chose to forgo part of his salary and may come to see the difference in cars as reflecting a difference in status and thus become dissatisfied. What if an employee changes his mind? Should he be able to change the make up of his remuneration package and, if so, how frequently? There may be practical problems in ceasing to provide a benefit if the employer has had to enter into a long term contractual relationship with someone else to provide it. Consideration also needs to be given to the VAT position. Customs and Excise have been known to contend that there is a VATable supply to an employee if he has an entitlement to exchange his use of an asset for a cash sum. Although they have retreated from this in relation to cars (see 7.45) they did so by changing the law so their argument could still run for other assets.

6.75 For these reasons fully flexible remuneration packages are rare. An employer would normally be wise to set some parameters on the employee's choice. He could have a limited list of benefits that he is prepared to provide, any or all of which the employee can opt to take as part of his remuneration package. Such schemes are often called 'cafeteria schemes' to reflect the fact that the employee chooses what he wants from the menu. If an employer opts for such a scheme, he should probably be prepared to consider the provision of benefits that are not on his list where these could be provided without undue trouble. He probably ought to provide a minimum amount that must be taken as salary, e.g. if the remuneration package is a total of £30,000 perhaps at least £20,000 must be salary. He also ought to set limits to avoid an undue risk of jealousy between employees, e.g. an employee with a £30,000 remuneration package might not be permitted to choose a company car costing more than say £20,000. He also ought to set limits to ease administration. For example, an employee could be allowed to choose what car he wants, provided that it is one that can be provided and serviced by one of the motor suppliers with which the employer already has an account.

6.76 Provided that these factors are borne in mind and both employer and employee are prepared to approach the provision of benefits with a degree of commonsense, the remuneration package can become an important tool in motivating employees. The choice of benefits that might be considered for inclusion in a remuneration package is very wide. The obvious ones are company cars, employee shareholdings and similar incentives, pensions and medical insurance. Some less obvious ones are considered at 9.115 below.

Form P11D, dispensations and PSAs

6.77 Where an employer provides benefits for, or reimburses expenses of a higher-paid employee, he must complete an annual return of expenses paid to each such employee by 7 July following the year of assessment concerned. [*TMA 1970, s 15(6)–(8)* and *Regulation 85* of the *PAYE Regulations*]. This return is provided on a form P11D. A separate form strictly needs to be completed for each employee, but if there is a dispensation for travelling and subsistence payments, then P11D lists of, typically, cars, car fuel and medical insurance are perfectly acceptable to the Inland Revenue, and indeed may be preferred for large employers.

6.78 *FA 1995, s 106* introduced a new *TMA 1970, s 15* from the start of self-assessment in 1996/97. This is broadly similar to the previous section but *subsections (5), (9)* and *(11)* impose additional obligations. *Subsections (5)* and *(9)* allow the P11D to require details of payments by third parties. If the provision of the benefit or payment has been arranged or guaranteed or in any way facilitated by the employer he must provide particulars of the payment or benefit and the name and address of the third party. If they were not arranged by him but he is aware of their existence he must provide the name and address of the third party. *Subsections (9)* and *(11)* require the employer to calculate the amount of any benefit and to determine the amount of any expenses, etc. that are chargeable to tax. In doing so, he cannot make any deductions, e.g. for allowable expenses under *ITEPA 2003, s 336*, which he is unable to substantiate by reference to information in his possession and—even if he can do this he must not make any deductions due under *ITEPA 2003, s 328(1), 362, 363, 364* or *365*. [*TMA 1970, s 15(11)(a)*].

6.79   Prior to 1990/91 the Revenue were content for forms P11D to be completed on the basis of the expenses in a company's accounting year ending in the fiscal year. However, they now refuse to accept this practice, insisting that forms P11D must reflect the expenses paid in the fiscal year.

Purpose of the form

6.80   Prior to 1996/97 the form P11D was solely an information return. The inclusion of an item on it was not an indication that it was taxable. All expenses reimbursed to the employee or incurred on his behalf had to be included on the return even if the expenditure was clearly for *bona fide* business reasons. It now tries to combine several things. It is a report of taxable benefits—or at least the employer's perception of the nature and amounts of taxable benefits. In addition, it is a report of expenses made to and on behalf of the employee. This is a report of total expenses, not merely of taxable expenses. It is for the employee to submit a *section 198* claim to establish the amount that is taxable in relation to expenses.

Dispensations

6.81   The Revenue has power to grant a dispensation from including expenses on a form P11D if the Inspector of Taxes is satisfied that they will not give rise to a tax charge on the employee. [*ITEPA 2003, s 65*]. The procedure is that the employer (or other person who incurs the expenditure) applies to the Inspector for a dispensation. The application, which can be done by way of letter, must list the employees, or categories of employee in respect of whom the dispensation is sought, the type of expenses concerned and the circumstances in which the expenditure is incurred. If the dispensation is granted, expenses of the agreed type paid to the person or class of person concerned do not have to be included on the form P11D in future years. A form P11D obviously still has to be completed if any expenditure is incurred in relation to the employee of a type not covered by the dispensation. However, only such expenditure need then be shown on the form. The Revenue must grant the dispensation if they are satisfied that no tax is payable under the relevant parts of the benefit code. [*ITEPA 2003, s 65(2)*]. Where a dispensation is given nothing in that provision is to apply to the payments or benefits covered by it. [*ITEPA 2003, s 65(5)*].

6.82   The Inland Revenue will not normally grant a dispensation for round sum allowances. They are granted for such things as travelling and subsistence, home telephones where the employer reimburses business calls only, and similar items where no personal benefit is likely to arise. The Inspector will need to be satisfied that the employer has a satisfactory system for authorising expenses and controlling reimbursements to employees. The Inspector is obviously unlikely to entertain any consideration of a dispensation if there are outstanding P11Ds for earlier years. There is a separate dispensation for non-cash vouchers and credit tokens. This is dealt with at 6.34. Where a dispensation granted before 6 April 2002 covered car mileage allowance that part of it ceases to have effect from that date if mileage allowance payments (see 7.68) are made to the employee. [*FA 2001, s 58*]. The dispensation is unnecessary as the mileage allowance payments are not taxable up to a statutory limit and the intention is to tax any payments in excess of that limit.

Director's expenses

6.83   There is no reason why dispensations should not be claimed by small private companies for director's expenses, but the Inspector is likely to be reluctant to grant a dispensation in such cases unless similar types of expense are also paid to employees and the system used for controlling reimbursements to employees is also applied to the directors. The Revenue booklet on dispensations (*IR69*) used to state that 'employees or directors who authorise their own expenses may have to be excluded' but the latest version (1996) no longer does so. As the concept of a dispensation is to cover recurrent expenses that are clearly of a business nature and which are properly authorised this is not unduly surprising. The expenses of a director tend to be more variable and, in most cases, there is no independent scrutiny of the validity and reasonableness of such expenses.

6.84   The Inspector of Taxes has power to revoke a dispensation either retrospectively to the time it was granted or from such later date as he may specify. [*ITEPA 2003, s 65(6)–(9)*].

Form P11D(a)

6.85   Where all the expenses paid to higher-paid employees are covered by a dispensation—or none are paid in relation to particular employees—the employer does not need to complete a form P11D showing nil expenses. He can instead complete a form P11D(a) which is a list of employees with a certificate appended stating that no forms P11D are due in respect of such people.

Form P9D

6.86   If benefits or round sum expenses are provided to lower-paid employees or payments in kind are made to such people, the employer has to complete another form, P9D, in relation to each such employee.

Again, this is an information return. It gives details of the items concerned so that the Revenue are aware of them and can determine what sum, if any, is assessable on the employee in relation to such expenditure.

PAYE Settlement Agreements (PSAs)

6.87   There is a procedure under which an employee can settle in a single payment the income tax liabilities of his employees on minor or non-recurrent benefits in kind and expenses payments. The employer agrees to accept responsibility for the tax, and the amounts covered by the PSA then cease to be income of the employees concerned. The legislation is contained in *Regulations 105–117* of the *PAYE Regulations* on the authority of *ITEPA 2003, ss 703–707*.

6.88   The items that can be covered by a PSA are expenses and benefits that are agreed by the Revenue to be either:

(i)   minor as regards the amounts of the sums paid or the type of benefit provided;

(ii)   irregular as regards the frequency in which (or the times at which) the sums are paid or the benefit is provided; or

(iii)   paid provided or made available where:

    (*a*)   in the case of a payment it is impracticable to apply PAYE; and

    (*b*)   in the case of a benefit it is shared by more than one employee and apportionment between them is impracticable.

[*Regulation 106*].

The Regulations are deliberately vague to allow the Revenue and employers scope to be reasonable in agreeing what should be included in a PSA (*SP 5/96, para 6*). The Revenue do not wish to dictate to Inspectors what can and cannot be included in a PSA and say that even the items shown as eligible in *SP 5/96* will not always be appropriate for inclusion *(para 7)*.

6.89   The Revenue say that an objective judgement must be made in applying head (i); they interpret minor as meaning minor in value, not a small part of the individual's earnings. Items that could fall into this category might include:

long service awards outside *ESC A22* (see 9.113(*w*))
incentive awards
reimbursement of late night taxis home outside *ITEPA 2003 s 248* (see 9.113(*t*))
personal incidental overnight hotel expenses in excess of the statutory daily limit
a present for an employee in hospital
staff entertaining such as a ticket to Wimbledon

use of a company van
use of a pool car where the conditions for exemption are not met
subscription to gyms, sports clubs, etc.
telephone bills
gift vouchers and small gifts

(*SP 5/96, para 10*)

6.90   If an item is not minor it could still be irregular. In deciding
whether something is irregular the Revenue will take account of the
nature of the item, the normal frequency of its payment and how often it
was given to the employee in question. A payment could be irregular in
relation to employee B even if it is regular in relation to employee A.
Normally, the Revenue will look only at the year, but something provided
to an employee once a year every year would probably be regarded as
regular. The sort of things the Revenue believe this head might cover are:

occasional attendance at an overseas conference where the whole
expense does not satisfy the test under *ITEPA ss 336–338* (see 5.2)
expenses of a spouse occasionally accompanying an employee abroad
occasional use of a company holiday flat
one-off gifts which are not minor

(*SP 5/96, para 13*).

Another obvious example is removal expenses in excess of the statutory
limit.

6.91   To come within head (iii) the employer will need to show that it
is not possible to apply PAYE or enter the item on form P11D without a
disproportionate amount of effort or record-keeping taking account of the
value of the item concerned, the number of employees involved and the
nature of the item. The Revenue give as examples:

free chiropody care
hairdressing services
shared use of the firm's bus to work
Christmas parties and similar entertainment outside *ESC A70*
(see 9.115(*s*))
the cost of shared taxi fares home outside *ITEPA 2003 s 248* (see
9.115(*t*))
shared cars

(*SP 5/96, para 15*)

6.92   A PSA is incorporated in a formal written agreement between
the employer and the Revenue. [*Regulation 111*]. It can be entered into
before the start of a tax year, during the year or between 6 April and
5 July following the end of the tax year. [*Regulation 112*]. However, it
cannot cover emoluments paid before the agreement is made or benefits
already reflected in the PAYE coding for the year. [*Regulation 112(2)*].
An agreement can be varied within the same time limits. [*Regulation
113*]. *Regulation 108* lays down rules for the calculation of the tax. This

must be paid by 19 October following the end of the tax year. [*Regulation 109*]. Interest runs on tax paid late [*Regulation 115*] and interest is payable from the 19 October date on any overpayment. [*Regulation 116*]. The employer must keep specified records and make them available for inspection by the Revenue. [*Regulation 117*]. Any serious breach of this requirement, or a serious failure to pay the tax on the PSA or pay over PAYE regularly, will entitle the Revenue to cancel the PSA. [*Regulation 114*].

6.93　It should be stressed that once an item is included in a PSA it ceases to be income of the employee for all tax purposes—and the employee is not entitled to credit for any of the tax or repayment of it (*Regulation 107*). Unfortunately, there is no obligation to tell employees what is covered by a PSA or even that one has been entered into. If the employee incorrectly puts the amount on his return as income the Revenue will collect tax on it; they cannot tell him that the employer has already paid tax on the item under a PSA. *Section 53* of the *Social Security Act 1998* introduced a new Class 1B National Insurance to be payable by employers for 1998/99 onwards in respect of a PSA. For 1996/97 and 1997/98 the DSS considered the NIC needed to be applied in the normal way, i.e. the amounts applicable to each of the employees had to be identified and NIC accounted for both on those items in the PSA which attract NIC and on the proportion attributable to each employee of the tax liability of the employer under the PSA. This NIC charge makes a PSA unattractive as the employer still needs to do much of the administrative work that the PSA is designed to avoid.

Chapter 7

Benefits in Relation to Cars and Vans

Introduction

7.1   Probably the most popular benefit in kind in the UK is the company car. The tax treatment of cars provided to employees may conveniently be approached in five parts:

(*a*)   company cars for the exclusive use of a single higher-paid employee;

(*b*)   car fuel for company cars;

(*c*)   pool cars for higher-paid employees;

(*d*)   contributions to the running costs of an employee's own car; and

(*e*)   cars provided for lower-paid employees.

The calculation of the benefit in respect of the use of a car changed radically from 6 April 1994 and again from 6 April 2002. The rules up to 2001/02 are considered at paragraphs 7.38–7.43.

Company cars for exclusive use

7.2   The vast majority of company cars are provided for the exclusive or primary use of a single executive director or employee. Such cars attract a scale charge if they are available for private use and the employee is higher-paid (see 6.4 above), as most are. The scale charge figure is treated as earnings from the employment (*ITEPA 2003, s 120*). The scale charge applies to a car made available (without any transfer of ownership) for the use of the employee (or of members of his family or household); if the car is made available by reason of the employment; is available for private use, and the benefit is not otherwise chargeable to tax as the employee's income. [*ITEPA 2003, s 114(1)(3)*]. As with other benefits for higher-paid employees, if the car is provided by the employer himself it is automatically deemed to have been made available by reason of the employment unless the employer is an individual and it can be shown that it was made available to the employee or other person in the normal course of the employer's domestic, family or personal relationships. [*ITEPA 2003, s 117*].

7.3   Mr Vasilis sought to take himself out of the scope of these special rules by arranging for his company to sell him a 5% interest in the car. He contended that the car had not been 'made available (without any transfer of ownership)' as there had been a transfer of ownership of the 5%. Accordingly *section 114* could not apply and the benefit fell to be calculated under *section 205* (see 6.58) (which in the case of an expensive car gave a more favourable result). This argument found favour with the Commissioners but Pumfrey J reversed their decision, holding that the words in parenthesis were not to be construed as taking the car outside the special regime for cars (*Christensen v Vasilis (2004) STC 935*).

Private use

7.4   'What is meant by a car being available for private use?' If a car is made available to an employee or members of his family or household by reason of his employment it is deemed to be available for private use as well as business use unless both:

(*a*)   the terms on which it is made available prohibit any private use; and

(*b*)   there was in fact no private use in the year of assessment.

[*ITEPA 2003, s 118*].

7.5   'Private use' means any use other than for the employer's business travel. [*ITEPA 2003, s 118(2)*]. The meaning of business travel is considered at 5.9 above. In *Gurney v Richards [1989] STC 682* a fire officer was required by his employment contract to be on call at all times and to drive his official car—equipped with a fixed flashing blue light—whenever he was on duty. He was forbidden from using the car for private use. The employer accepted that he had to use the car to drive to work (so as to be in it if he was called), but this did not prevent the High Court ruling that, as such travel was not in the course of his duties, it constituted private use so that car benefit was assessable on the employee. However, the case was remitted to the Commissioners to determine whether the existence of the flashing light might prevent the vehicle being a car at all, i.e. was it unsuitable to be used as a private vehicle? It is not known what the Commissioners decided. It is to be hoped that they held that it was a car, as the scale benefit is likely to be far less than 20 per cent of the cost of the car. The unfairness has to a huge extent been remedied from 2004/05 onwards by the introduction of a special relief for emergency vehicles where the only private use is while the employee is on call (see 7.64).

Business travel

7.6   Business travel is travel for which the expense if incurred by an employee would be deductible under *ITEPA 2003, ss 337–342* (see 5.3). [*ITEPA 2003, s 117(1)*]. Travel from a person's home to his place of employment is not normally travel in the performance of the duties. It is undertaken to put a person in a position to perform such duties, and as such is private mileage.

7.7   Where a chauffeur driven car is provided to take an employee to and from work so that he can work on confidential papers in the car the Revenue do not accept that such work can of itself change the essentially private nature of the travel. They consider that the work being done is only one of the factors to be considered when deciding whether the journey is either a business one or is merely incidental to business use (*SP 2/96*). The Statement of Practice hints that it could well be business use if papers are needed for a meeting at the employee's home or have to be delivered to a client. This seems an odd test. It seems to be saying that if there is a business need to transport the papers then the fact that the employee goes with them does not prevent the transport having a business purpose. On the other hand, if there is a business need for the employee to work on the papers the fact that he chooses (or is obliged) to do this in his own time when he is travelling to work does not necessarily mean that this is a business need.

The current system

7.8   A new, environmentally more friendly, system of taxing company cars was introduced from 6 April 2002. [*FA 2000, s 58* and *11 Schedule*]. The cash equivalent of the benefit is a percentage of the original list price of the car. Where the original list price exceeds £80,000 the benefit is based on £80,000 only. [*ITEPA 2003, s 121*]. The Treasury have power to increase (but not reduce) this figure. [*ITEPA 2003, s 170(1)(a)*]. For most new cars this percentage is based on the carbon dioxide emission rating for the car. All cars sold in the EC that were first registered after 30 September 1999 have had to be sold with an EC or UK certificate that specifies a carbon dioxide emissions figure in terms of grams per kilometre driven. From November 2000 this figure has had to be shown on the car's log book (Vehicle Registration Document). Some cars registered between 1 January 1998 and 1 October 1999 also had to carry an emissions certificate. The car use charge for such cars is based on the emissions figure shown on the certificate. [*ITEPA 2003, ss 135, 136*].

7.9   For cars without an EC or UK emissions figure of (defined in *ITEPA 2003, s 134*) the percentage is based on the engine capacity of the car, as under the system that applied up to 5 April 2002, but using a lesser percentage for older cars and for smaller cars first registered after 1 January 1998. This alternative basis must be used for all cars first registered before 1 January 1998 and for imported cars without an official EC or UK emissions certificate even if the emissions figure is known. [*ITEPA 2003, s 140*].

Cars with a UK or EC emissions certificate

7.10   The percentages for 2004/05 are as follows.

Emissions up to	145 g/km	15%
	150 g/km	16%
	155 g/km	17%

and so on rising by 1% point per
5 additional g/km (rounded down to
the nearest multiple of 5) to

Emissions up to   240 g/km   34%
                   245 g/km   35%

If the car's emissions figure is not a multiple of five it is rounded down.

[*ITEPA 2003, s 139(4)*]. For 2003/04 the 15% rate applied where the emission level was below 155g/km.

7.11   For 2005/06 and 2006/07 the 15% rate will apply only where the emissions level does not exceed 140g/km. The increase in steps of 1 percentage point per 5g/km of emissions will continue so the 35% maximum will apply where the emissions level is 240g/km or more. [*ITEPA 2003, s 139(2)*]. The Revenue are given power by statutory instrument to reduce the level at which the 15% figure applies for 2007/08 and subsequent years. [*ITEPA 2003, s 170(3)*].

Cars with no UK or EC emissions certificate

7.12

	First registered Before 1.1.1998	*First registered After 31.12.1997*
Up to 1400 cc	15%	15%
1401–2000 cc	22%	25%
over 2000 cc	32%	35%

If the car does not have an internal combustion engine with one or more reciprocating pistons the percentage is 15 per cent for an electrically propelled car and 32 per cent or 35 per cent (as applicable) in any other case i.e. the reduced percentages for cars under 2000 cc do not apply. [*ITEPA 2003, ss 140, 142*]. A car is an electronically propelled vehicle for this purpose only if it is propelled solely by electrical power and that power is either derived from a source external to the vehicle or from an electrical storage battery which is not connected to any source of power when the vehicle is in motion. [*ITEPA 2003, s 140(4)*].

Diesel Cars

7.13   A supplement of three percentage points is added to the scale figures subject to a cut off of 35 per cent. [*ITEPA 2003, s 141*]. This applies irrespective of whether or not the car has an emissions certificate but does not apply to cars first registered before 1 January 1998. Thus, for example, a diesel car with 168 g/km emissions attracts a scale charge of 22 per cent of original cost (19 + 3); one with 252 g/km would attract a scale charge of 38 per cent (35 + 3) but this is limited to 35 per cent); a post-1 January 1998 imported 2000 cc car attracts a scale charge of 28 per cent (25 + 3) but a slightly larger car attracts the basic charge of 35 per cent (as the surcharge cannot increase the scale figure above 35 per cent, it will be ineffective).

Bi-fuel Cars

7.14   Where a car which was first registered after 31 December 2000 is registered on the basis of an EC or UK emissions certificate that specifies different emissions figures for different fuel the scale charge is based on the lowest figure (if there is more than one figure specified in relation to each fuel it is the lowest 'emissions (combined)' figure specified. [*ITEPA 2003, 137(2)*].

Automatic Cars for Disabled Drivers

7.15   If:

(*a*)   the car has an official emissions figure;

(*b*)   the car has automatic transmission;

(*c*)   at any time in the tax year concerned the employee has a disabled person's badge;

(*d*)   by reason of his disability the employee can only drive a car with automatic transmission; and

(*e*)   the emissions figure for the car is greater than it would have been if the car had been an equivalent manual car,

the emissions figure applicable to the equivalent manual car can be used instead. [*ITEPA 2003, s 138*].

7.16   An equivalent manual car is one that is first registered on or about the same time as the employee's car and which is the closest variant available of the make and model of the employee's car (but does not have automatic transmission). [*ITEPA 2003, s 138(3)*]. A car has automatic transmission for the purpose of this provision only if the driver is not provided with any means whereby he can vary the gear ratio between the engine and road whether independently of the accelerator and brakes or, if he is provided with such means, these do not include a clutch pedal or lever that he can operate manually. [*ITEPA 2003, s 138(4)*].

Discounts

7.17   The Treasury can by regulation reduce all or any of the above percentage figures other than those for cars first registered before 1 January 1998. [*ITEPA 2003, s 170(4)*].

Original list price

7.18   It is important to note that the benefit is based on the original list price of the car, not its cost, even if it was bought new. In the past it has often been relatively easy to obtain discounts from list price so the benefit figure will often be based on a significantly greater figure than the cost of the car. The list price is the price published by the car's manufacturer, importer or distributor, as the case may be, as the inclusive price appropriate for a car of that kind if sold in the UK singly in a retail sale in the open market on the day immediately before the date of its first registration, i.e. the date on which it was first registered under the *Vehicle Excise and Registration Act 1994* or under corresponding legislation of any country or territory. [*ITEPA 2003, ss 123(1), 171(2)*]. The inclusive price is the price including delivery to the showroom (or other place of business of the seller), tax and fitting standard accessories. [*ITEPA 2003, s 123(2)*]. Special rules apply where a car has no list price, e.g. it was not offered for sale in the UK at the time of first registration. A notional list price has to be used instead (see 7.24).

7.19   The original list price has to include qualifying accessories. These are accessories which are made available for use with the car and by reason of the employee's employment, and are attached to the car but not necessarily provided for use in the performance of the employee's duties. [*ITEPA 2003, s 125*]. A mobile phone is not an accessory, but any other kind of equipment can be. [*ITEPA 2003, s 125(2)(d)*]. Accessories for the disabled are also excluded. This covers equipment designed solely for use by a chronically sick or disabled person, and also any other equipment which was made available for use with the car because it enabled the employee to use the car in spite of a disability which entitled him to hold a disabled person's badge, i.e. one issued to him under the *Chronically Sick and Disabled Persons Act 1970* (or its Northern Ireland equivalent) and which is not required to be returned to the issuing authority under that provision (the familiar orange disabled sticker). The employee must actually hold a disabled person's badge, not merely be entitled to it, at the time the car is first made available to him. This exclusion does not extend to a car made available for a disabled member of the employee's family. [*ITEPA 2003, ss 125(2)(c), 171(4), 172*]. If at the time the car was first made available to the employee the only qualifying accessories available with the car were standard accessories, the list price of the car covers such accessories even if they were fitted after first registration, but to be a standard accessory it must have been available as such at the time of first registration. [*ITEPA 2003, ss 125(4), 126*]. If any qualifying accessory was available with the car as an optional extra (even if factually the accessory was not supplied with the car) then the list price to be used is that for a car which includes the accessory in question. [*ITEPA 2003, s 126(2)*]. If the accessory in question was available with the car when it was originally registered but there was no list price for such an accessory when supplied with the car, the list price is in the sum of that of the car without the accessory plus the list price of the accessory at that time (including fitting, delivery charges, customs duty, car tax and VAT). [*ITEPA 2003, ss 127(1)(a), 129*].

7.20   If there was no list price including such charges a notional list price for the accessory has to be adopted instead. This is the price (inclusive of fitting, delivery and taxes) which the accessory might reasonably have been expected to fetch if sold in the UK singly in a retail sale in the open market immediately before it was first made available for use with the car—which will be either the time of its first sale or, if it was fitted between then and its first becoming available to the employee in question, the date it was fitted. [*ITEPA 2003, s 130*]. Where an accessory is fitted after the car was first made available to the employee, the list price (or notional list price) of that accessory, presumably at the time the accessory was fitted, must be added to the list price of the car. If the price of any such accessory was less than £100 it can be ignored. [*ITEPA 2003, s 126(3)*].

7.21   The Revenue view on 'cherished' number plates is that although the cost of the plate itself is a qualifying accessory, to be included in the value of the car, most of the value of a cherished number plate lies in the intangible right to use a particular registration mark, i.e. the cost of the number plate must be apportioned, the part attributable to the plate being part of the value of the car and the balance (the bulk) being the cost of a separate intangible right. Where the car is a company car *ITEPA 2003, s 239* it will prevent the value of that right being taxable as it is provided in connection with the provision of the car (*Tax Bulletin, Issue 14, December 1994*).

7.22   Equipment by means of which the car is capable of running on road fuel gas is not regarded as an accessory (although it was prior to 1998/89). [*ITEPA 2003, s 125(2)(b)*]. This removes a disincentive from converting cars to run on road fuel gases (i.e. compressed natural gas or liquid petroleum gas). If a car is manufactured so as to be capable of running on road fuel gases, the benefit is not calculated on the full list price of the car. It is on that figure less so much of that price as it is reasonable to attribute to the car being manufactured in that way rather than in such a way as to be capable of running only on petrol. [*ITEPA 2003, s 146*]. In most cases this is likely to give a figure equal to the list price of the equivalent petrol model. Road fuel gas is defined as any substance which is gaseous at a temperature of 15°C under a pressure of 1013.25 millibars and which is for use as fuel in road vehicles. [*ITEPA 2003, s 171(1)*]. Any new types of gases which do not meet this tight test will therefore not qualify for this relaxation. From 2002/03 this does not apply to bi-fuel cars taxed by reference to carbon dioxide emissions (see 7.14). [*ITEPA 2003, s 146(1)(b)*].

7.23   If an accessory replaces a previous one of the same kind and it is not superior to the old one the change is ignored in calculating the benefit. If the new accessory is superior to the old the value of the old accessory is excluded and the price of the new substituted. A new accessory is superior to the old if its price exceeds the price of the old (or if greater, the price of an equivalent accessory to the old. [*ITEPA 2003, s 131*, formerly the *Income Tax (Car Benefits) (Replacement Accessories) Regulations 1994 (SI 1994 No. 777)*].

Cars with no original list price

7.24   Where a car does not have an original list price a notional price must be adopted instead. [*ITEPA 2003, s 122(b)*]. This is the price which might reasonably have been expected to be its list price if the manufacturer, importer or distributor (as the case may be) had published an inclusive price appropriate for a car of the same kind (and with the same qualifying accessories as were fitted when the car was first made available to the employee in question, even if such accessories did not exist when the car was originally sold) if sold in the UK singly in a retail sale in the open market on the day immediately before the date of the car's first registration. [*ITEPA 2003, s 124*].

Practical solutions

7.25   Many employers do not have readily available the original list price of employees' cars or of any accessories bought before 5 April 1994. The Revenue have said they will accept prices for such cars taken from published guides of actual list prices where the manufacturer's price is not available. The Revenue have also said that for such cars only major optional extras such as automatic gearboxes, air conditioning, etc. need be priced. Minor accessories can be treated as *de minimis* (*IR Press Release 27 September 1993*). Nevertheless, there is of course a legal obligation on the employer to provide the correct list price and a potential liability for penalties if he does not. Where a car does not have a list price—or despite all efforts the employer cannot discover it—it is apparently up to the employer to make his own estimate—and to be able to defend it if it is challenged by the Inland Revenue.

Classic cars

7.26   Special rules apply for classic cars. If the market value of the car and any qualifying accessories on the last day of the tax year (or if earlier the last day it is made available to the employee) exceeds the original list price the scale benefit must be based on that market value. [*ITEPA 2003, s 147(2)*]. A classic car for this purpose is one that has a market value of £15,000 or more and is 15 years old or more at the end of the fiscal year. [*ITEPA 2003, s 147(1)*,]. It should particularly be noted that the value has to be recalculated—and if necessary agreed with the Revenue—every year.

Capital contributions

7.27   If the employee contributes a capital sum towards the cost of the car or towards the cost of accessories whose value is added to the list price of the car, such contribution (or the aggregate of all such contributions) can be deducted from the list price but subject to a maximum deduction of £5,000. [*ITEPA 2003, s 132*]. The limitation is to prevent a full reimbursement eliminating any benefit in relation to the running costs of the car. In the case of a classic car the £5,000 is deducted from the market value calculated each year. [*ITEPA 2003, s 147(5)–(7)*]. If the employee is entitled to a repayment of part of the capital contribution on the sale of the car by reference to the disposal value in the same proportion as the original contribution bore to the cost of the car, this does not require a recalculation of the *section 168D* contribution figure, and does not give rise to a charge to tax as employment income on the amount repaid. If the agreement provides for the contribution to be repaid in full on the disposal of the car, however, the Revenue do not regard it as a capital contribution at all (*Tax Bulletin, Issue 14, December 1994*).

Shared cars

7.28   If two employees have shared use of a car, a double charge strictly arose prior to 2003/04, but by concession the Revenue apportioned one scale benefit between the two (*IR Press Release 2 August 1989* and *ESC A71*). This practice is given statutory effect for 2003/04 onwards by *ITEPA 2003, s 148*. The apportionment must be done on a just and reasonable basis. The car must be made available to all sharers by the same employer and it must be concurrently available to them.

What is a car?

7.29   A car is defined as any mechanically propelled road vehicle except:

(*a*)   a vehicle of a construction primarily suited for the conveyance of goods or burden of any description;

(*b*)   a vehicle of a type not commonly used as a private vehicle and unsuitable to be so used;

(*c*)   a motor cycle as defined in *section 190(4)* of the *Road Traffic Act 1972*; and

(*d*)   an invalid carriage as defined in *section 190(5)* of that *Act*.

[*ITEPA 2003, s 115*].

Income Tax liability

7.30   If the scale benefit charge applies to a car, the tax on the charge satisfies the employee's income tax liability in respect of the use of the car (other than for car fuel or in connection with the provision of a chauffeur). He cannot be taxed in relation to the discharge of any liability of his in connection with the car (where, for example, the employee personally incurs a liability for repairs, insurance or road-fund licence and the employer reimburses it to him or pays the cost direct); nor under the provisions relating to non-cash vouchers and credit tokens in respect of items or services acquired in relation to the car; nor under *section 203* (see 6.44 above) in respect of expenses incurred by him in connection with the car. [*ITEPA 2003, s 239*].

7.31   Where two members of a family or household, e.g. father and son, are both employees of a family company, the Revenue in the past took the view that they could assess either of them on a car made available by reason of either employment, i.e. they can assess the father both on his car and the son's although the son's car is clearly provided by reason of the son's employment (indeed strictly they can assess both on both cars but in practice do not do so) (see also 6.43 above). In such circumstances the car is regarded as provided by reason of the son's employment if it can be shown that the car is actually provided by reason of the son's employment and that either equivalent cars are made available to other employees holding similar posts with the employer or the provision of an equivalent car is in accordance with normal commercial practice for a job of that kind. [*ITEPA 2003, s 169*, enacting *ESC A71*].

7.32   Some people felt that the decision in *Heaton v Bell* (see 7.90) could be used in reverse to avoid the car benefit charge. The theory was that if a car is made available on terms that it could be surrendered at any time in exchange for a £1 a week salary increase, a charge would arise under *ITEPA 2003, s 62* based on the money's worth of the use of the car being £1 a week. Whether the courts would accept this argument seems questionable—although the Revenue themselves seemed to do so—but for 1995/96 onwards at least such a device will not work as *ITEPA 2003, s 119* now provides that the mere fact that an alternative to the benefit of the car is offered does not make the benefit taxable under *section 62*. There is a similar anti-avoidance rule for living accommodation (see 8.2). It is not clear if the concession continues to apply after 2002/03. The car appears to fall within *section 148* (see 7.28) i.e. it is available to father and son concurrently. It is available to the father because it is available to a member of his family, i.e. the son, and is available to the son by reason of his own employment. To continue with the concession it would need to be just and reasonable to apportion the entire benefit to the son and nothing to the father.

Car unavailable for part of the year

7.33   No benefit arises for any part of the year of assessment in which the car was unavailable for use. The scale figure is multiplied by the fraction that the number of days in the tax year on which the car is available bears to the number of days in that year (which will be 365 or 366 in a leap year). However, a car can only be regarded as unavailable on a particular day in three circumstances:

(*a*)   if it was not made available until after that date, e.g. a car provided to an employee on 1 October 2004 is unavailable to him from 6 April 2004 to 30 September 2004;

(*b*)   if it ceased before that date to be available, e.g. if a car is sold on 4 August 2004 it is unavailable to the employee from 5 August 2004 to 5 April 2005; or (*c*)   the day falls within a period of 30 days or more throughout which it is not available to the employee.

[*ITEPA 2003, s 143*].

It appears that a car remains available to the employee even if it is incapable of being used throughout a period of more than 365 days. The test is if it has been made available to the employee or to members of his family or household, not whether it is capable of use. [*ITEPA 2003, s 116*]. It may well be unavailable if the employer specifically forbids the employee to use the car during a specified period though.

Replacement cars

7.34   If a car normally available to the employee is not available to him for a period of under 30 days and a second car is made available to replace the normal car during that period, the replacement car is treated as unavailable on the days on which it replaces the normal car, i.e. it is ignored. The replacement car must not be materially better than the normal car and must not be made available to the employee under an arrangement one of the main purposes of which is to provide the employee with the benefit of a car which is materially better than the normal car. A car is materially better for this purpose if it is materially better in quality or its cost (original list price plus accessories) is materially higher than that of the normal car. [*ITEPA 2003, 145*, formerly the *Income Tax (Replacement Cars) Regulations 1994*].

Payments for private use

7.35   If as a condition of the car being available for the employee's private use he is required to pay an amount of money for such use (whether by deduction from earnings or otherwise) the payment by the employee is deducted from what would otherwise have been the cash equivalent of the car. [*ITEPA 2003, s 144*].

Business Use

7.36   Unlike with the rules that applied up to 2001/02 the scale figures are based solely on the costs and emissions level of the car; the amount of the benefit does not vary according to the level of business mileage. The previous rules sometimes created an incentive to use the car for business purposes even if public transport would have been more sensible as the benefit reduced if business mileage exceeded 2,500 miles in a year, and reduced further if it exceeded 18,000 miles. The above scale figures also apply unaltered to second cars. Previously such cars attracted a higher benefit.

7.37   This does not mean that an expense claim cannot be made in respect of business use of the car although it seems probable that it will only be in rare circumstances that such a claim will be competent as the scale figure is a rough and ready way of arriving at a benefit where there is mixed use of the car. A reduction for business use was allowed in *Kerr v Brown and Boyd v Brown* ([2002] STC (SCD) 434 and 2003 STC (SCD) 266). Mr Kerr and Mr Boyd were senior officers in the fire brigade. They were each provided with a car which he was required to use in the performance of his duties. They worked in 24 hour shifts consisting of 8 or 12 hours of managerial duties and 16 or 12 hours of standby duties (during which they had to be in their local area and available immediately in the case of fire). The cars were used to store and convey firefighting equipment. They were fitted with flashing blue lights and a sign reading 'Fire'. They were not used for personal use other than home to work travel when on duty. They were used for other brigade purposes when the officers were on leave. The taxpayers contended that the need to have their equipment at all times meant that the cars were not available for private use in the ordinary sense of that expression. Alternatively, their homes were their base as when they were on duty they undertook responsibility immediately they were called. The Special Commissioners considered the case with respect to *Gurney v Richards* (see 7.5). They accordingly held that there was private use. However, they also accepted that on rest days and leave the cars were unavailable for private use. They accordingly held that the benefit should be reduced in the proportion that the days the cars were not available for private use bore to the total number of days in the year. At a later hearing they amplified this. An unbroken period of 24 hours should be treated as a day. A day should be regarded as a rest day even if part of it was spent in the car commuting. If a person does not work a full 24-hour shift (Mr Boyd did not always have to do stand by duty) the shift actually worked should be regarded as a day. It was not realistic to take the total hours worked and divide by 24.

The rules for 1994/95 to 2001/02

The scale charge

7.38   Prior to 2002/03 the amount of the charge depended on the original list price of the car, its age and the business mileage during the year of assessment. Different rules applied prior to 1994/95.

7.39   For 1999/00 to 2001/02 the charge was normally 25 per cent of the original list price if the car was new or 18.75 per cent (75 per cent of 35 per cent) if it was four or more years old at the end of the tax year. Higher percentages applied for second cars and those used for less than 2,500 business miles during the year of assessment, and there was a reduced percentage for cars used for over 18,000 business miles—other than a second car. Curiously, it was not sufficient merely to show more than 18,000 business miles. It had also also be shown that such mileage was 'required by the nature of his employment'. [6 *Schedule 2(1)*]. The actual percentages were as below but for cars with an original list price exceeding £80,000 the benefit was based on £80,000 only. [*Section 157(2)* and *6 Schedule* inserted by *FA 1993, 3 Schedule*]:

	Under 4 years old	Over 4 years old
Business use under 2,500 miles	35%	26.5%
" " 2,500–17,999 miles	25%	18.75%
" " 18,000 miles or more	15%	11.25%
Second cars up to 17,999 miles	35%	35%
" " 18,000 miles or more	25%	25%

For 1994/95 to 1998/99 the percentages were:

	Under 4 years old	Over 4 years old
Business use under 2,500 miles	35%	23.33%
" " 2,500–17,999 miles ($\frac{2}{3} \times 35\%$)	23.33%	15.56% ($\frac{2}{3} \times 35\%$)
" " 18,000 miles or more ($\frac{1}{3} \times 35\%$)	11.67%	7.78% ($\frac{1}{3} \times 35\%$)
Second cars up to 17,999 miles	35%	23.33%
" " 18,000 miles or more ($\frac{2}{3} \times 35\%$)	23.33%	15.56%

Second cars

7.40   Where the employee (together with members of his family or household) was provided with more than one car, the one to which the basic scale charge applied was the one that was used to the greatest extent for the employee's business travel. [*6 Schedule 4*]. This of course gave an incentive to use the more expensive one predominantly for business travel whereas, other things being equal, the employee would probably have chosen to use the cheaper one, which was likely to be more efficient on fuel.

Change of car

7.41   Where there was a change of car during the year the 18,000 miles p.a. and 2,500 miles p.a. tests were applied to each car separately, the mileage ceilings being pro-rated on a daily basis for the period of use of each car. [*6 Schedule 3*]. It was confirmed in *Henward v Clarke* [*1997*] *STI 638* that this could result in the higher scale figure applying to a car which was used at the rate of less than 2,500 miles a year during the period for which it was available even though the combined usage of the two cars during the year was well over the 2,500 mile figure.

Age of the car

7.42   'How old is a car?' The age at any time is the interval between the date of its first registration and that time. [*Section 168(5)(b)*]. The scale charge to be adopted for a car was that applicable to its age at the end of the relevant year of assessment. [*Section 157(2)*]. This was so even if the car had been sold or scrapped or otherwise ceased to exist during the year—it was then the age the car would have been if it had been kept until the end of the year of assessment. For example, a car first registered on 5 April 1998 attracted the lower scale benefit for 2001/02 as it was over four-years-old on 5 April 2002. One first registered on 7 April 1998 was only three years, 364-days-old on 5 April 2002 and will attract the higher benefit for 2001/02. The date of a UK car's first registration was the date that it was first registered under the *Vehicles (Excise) Act 1971*. If a car was first registered overseas, the relevant date was the date of its first registration under the corresponding legislation of the country or territory where that registration took place. [*Section 168(5)(d)*].

Other Matters

7.43   The rules described earlier in relation to the determination of the original list price of a car (7.18–7.25), classic cars (7.26), capital contributions (7.27), shared cars (7.28), the meaning of a car (7.29), running costs in relation to the car (7.29–7.32), cars unavailable for part of the year (7.33), and replacement cars (7.34) also applied under the pre-2002/03 system.

Salary sacrifice arrangements

7.44   A salary sacrifice arrangement under which an employee agrees to reduce his salary if his employer will provide him with a company car, or with a car of a better standard than it would otherwise have provided has no particular implications provided that there is no arrangement under which the car can be surrendered and the salary restored (see 7.90 below). A mere understanding that the salary will be restored if employer and employee were to agree at some future date that the company will no longer provide a car should not fall foul of *Heaton v Bell 46 TC 211*. The salary surrendered will not constitute either a contribution towards the cost of the car or a payment for its use. All that has happened is that the employee's remuneration package has been varied. As with salary waivers, once an entitlement to income has arisen, i.e. the work has been done to earn the salary, it is probably not possible to sacrifice part of the salary. Only future salary can be sacrificed.

7.45   At one stage Customs and Excise contended that where a salary sacrifice was made VAT was chargeable by reference to the salary given up as this constituted consideration for the right to use the car. No such charge arises now, however (*VAT (Treatment of Transactions) Order 1992, SI 1992 No 630*). This applies irrespective of whether what is sacrificed is cash or other benefits provided that no specific charge is made for the use of the car. (*Business Brief 9/92*).

Car fuel for company cars

7.46   If a higher-paid employee is provided with a car to which the scale benefit rules described above apply and he is also provided with fuel for that car by reason of his employment, he is also assessable on a fuel benefit. The cash equivalent of the benefit is the 'appropriate percentage' of £14,400 [*ITEPA 2003, s 150(1)*]. This is the percentage used to calculate the benefit in relation to the use of the car (see 7.8–7.17). [*ITEPA 2003, s 150(2)*].

7.47   No fuel benefit arises if either the employee is required to make good to the employer the whole of the expenses incurred in connection with the provision of the fuel for private use or fuel is made available only for business travel. [*ITEPA 2003, s 151*]. In practice, many Inspectors of Taxes contend that it is impossible to meet the first of these conditions as the employee cannot demonstrate that he has not used any of his employer's petrol at any time during the year of assessment to drive home from work or for some similar private purpose. The benefit is not reduced at all if the employee reimburses some, but not the whole, of the cost of petrol for private use. Accordingly, if an employee is required to reimburse the cost of fuel for private motoring, detailed mileage records may need to be kept so as to be able to demonstrate that the full cost has in fact been reimbursed. It may be better to require the employee to pay for the fuel as a condition of the car being made available for his private use so that the payments can reduce the car use benefit (see 7.35 above). It appears that if the employee is required to reimburse the cost of all private petrol as a condition of the car being made available for private use and can show that he has reimbursed the full cost of such petrol the same payments will both eliminate the car fuel benefit and reduce the car use benefits. However, the Revenue can be expected to resist such a contention.

7.48   The benefit is proportionately reduced if the car is unavailable for part of the tax year. [*ITEPA 2003, s 152(1)*]. It is also proportionately reduced if for part of the tax year either the facility for the provision of fuel for private use is not available, fuel is made available only for business travel or the employee is required to reimburse the cost of providing the fuel for private use. [*ITEPA 2003, s 152(2)*]. This latter reduction applies only if there is no time later in the year when one of these conditions is not met, i.e. it applies only where the employer stops providing fuel for private use in the tax year and does not recommence doing so in the same tax year. [*ITEPA 2003, s 152(3)*]. Where the cash equivalent is proportionately reduced it is reduced in the proportion that the days in the year for which fuel is made available bears to the number of days in the tax year. [*ITEPA 2003, s 152(4)*]. Where the use benefit in relation to a shared car is apportioned between two or more employees a corresponding reduction is also made in relation to the fuel benefit. [*ITEPA 2003, s 149(4)*]. Accordingly there will be no taxable fuel benefit in the provision of electrical power as *section 239(1)(e)* excludes from tax the actual expenses incurred in connection with a taxable car.

7.49   A different system applied prior to 2003/04. The benefit was a fixed sum dependent on the engine size of the car, with lower rates applying for diesel engined cars. For 2002/03 the amounts were:

Size	Petrol car	Diesel car	
	£		£
up to 1400cc	2,240	up to 2000cc	2,850
1401–2000cc	2,850		
over 2000cc	4,200	over 2000cc	4,200

The figures for 1994/95 to 2001/02 were:

1994/95	petrol cars: £640, £810, £1,200	diesel cars: £580, £750
1995/96	petrol cars: £670, £850, £1,260	diesel cars: £605, £780
1996/97	petrol cars: £710, £890, £1,320	diesel cars: £640, £820
1997/98	petrol cars: £800, £1,010, £1,490	diesel cars: £740, £940
1998/99	petrol cars: £1,010, £1,280, £1,890	diesel cars: £1,280, £1,890
1999/00	petrol cars: £1,210, £1,540, £2,270	diesel cars: £1,540, £2,270
2000/01	petrol cars: £1,700, £2,170, £3,200	diesel cars: £2,170, £3,200
2001/02	petrol cars: £1,930, £2,460, £3,620	diesel cars: £2,850, £4,200

The figures for earlier years are shown in the Appendix.

7.50   If the car did not have an internal combustion engine with one or more reciprocating pistons, e.g. it was an electric car or a rotary engined car, the benefit for 2002/03 was £4,200 irrespective of the size of the car. [*ICTA 1988, s 158*]. For 1996/97 the benefit was £1,320, for 1997/98 it was £1,490, for 1998/99 it was £1,890, for 1999/00 it was £2,270 for 2000/01 it was £3,200 and for 2001/02 it was £3,620. It is not readily apparent why a Chancellor pledged to reduce carbon emissions should have opted to penalise rather than encourage the use of electric cars.

7.51   There was no reduction for cars over four years old as the age of the car did not reduce petrol consumption. Surprisingly, the £4,200 maximum applied even to the most expensive cars. More surprisingly still, it also applied to second cars and those used for less than 2,500 business miles. If the car use benefit was reduced because the car is unavailable for use for part of the year (see 7.33 above) the car fuel benefit was also reduced in the same proportion. [*Section 158(5)*]. Up to 1992/93 the benefit was also reduced where mileage exceeded 18,000 business miles but no such reduction applied for 1993/94 onwards.

7.52   If the employee was required to make good to the person providing the fuel the *whole* of the expense incurred in connection with his private use (and in fact did so) the car fuel benefit was reduced to nil. There was no benefit charge where fuel was made available to the employee only for business travel. [*ICTA 1988, s 158(6)(b)*].

Discharge of employee's liability

7.53   If a liability in respect of fuel for a car is discharged (e.g. by the employer paying the garage bills), or a non-cash voucher or a credit token (such as a company credit card) is used to obtain fuel for the car or to obtain money which is spent on such fuel, or any sum is paid in respect of expenses incurred in providing fuel for the car, this must be regarded as constituting the provision of fuel for the car. [*ITEPA 2003, s 149(3)*].

7.54   Curiously, although *ITEPA 2003, s 239* prevents an employee being assessed both to the car use benefit and on the cost of repairs, etc. to the car, this is specifically expressed not to apply to a liability arising by virtue of *section 149*. In *Richardson v Worrall 58 TC 642* it was held that at the moment an employee filled his car with petrol he had incurred a liability to pay for that petrol and a subsequent payment for it by use of a company credit card amounted to the employer discharging that liability of the employee, so that the amount paid constituted emoluments. In practice the Revenue are unlikely to seek to tax the employee on the cost of providing the fuel where the scale fuel benefit applies.

Pool cars

Meaning of 'pool car'

7.55   Neither the car use nor the car fuel benefit apply where an employee has the use of a pool car, i.e. one which has been included in a car pool for the use of the employees of one or more employers. [*ITEPA 2003, s 167(2)*]. A car can, however, only be treated as a pool car for a year of assessment if:

(*a*)   in that year it was made available to (and actually used by) more than one employee;

(*b*)   it was made available to each of those employees by reason of his employment (see 6.43 above);

(*c*)   it was not in that year ordinarily used by one of the employees to the exclusion of the others;

(*d*)   any private use of the car made by any of the employees entitled to use the car in that year was merely incidental to his business use of it; and

(*e*)   during that year the car was not normally kept overnight in (or in the vicinity of) any residential premises where any of the employees was residing (unless the place where it was kept was occupied by the employer or other person making the car available to the employees). [*ITEPA 2003, s 167(3)*].

7.56   If a car qualifies as a pool car it is treated as not being available for the private use of any of the employees entitled to use it, so that neither the car use nor the car fuel benefit will apply to any of the employees in relation to the car. [*ITEPA 2003, s 167(2)*]. Nor will there be any charge for the provision of a chauffeur (*Hansard 14 May 1993, col 585*).

7.57   When the provisions were introduced, the Minister gave as an example of head (*d*) above that if an employee takes a pool car home so that he can make an early start for a business meeting the next morning the private use, driving from the office to his home, would be merely incidental to the following day's business use. Whether such a journey is 'purely incidental' as interpreted in a different context in *Robson v Dixon 48 TC 527* seems questionable.

7.58   Some years later the Revenue set out in *SP 2/96* what they believe parliament meant by 'merely incidental to', namely that it is necessary to consider whether:

(*a*)   the private use of the car is independent of the employee's business use; or

(*b*)   the private use follows from the business use.

They regard this as 'a qualitative test which means that it is necessary to look at the nature of private use, over the year, by each employee who uses the car'. It is not clear what this means; logically such a test ought to be applied on a journey by journey basis so that only if every single journey falls within (*b*) could the car constitute a pool car. Applying their test, the Revenue say that where an employee takes a car home in order to make an early start on a business journey the following morning, where that journey could not reasonably be undertaken the next day starting from the normal place of work, the journey home in the evening is purely incidental to the business travel next morning. Where an employee staying overnight on a business trip drives to a nearby restaurant such use is also merely incidental to the business use even though it is not necessary to use the car for the trip to the restaurant. They consider the incidental use of the car for an annual holiday as something falling within (*a*) and thus not incidental. This suggests that, once a business need to use a car is established, any private use while that business need subsists is likely to be incidental but any journey where there is no business need cannot be incidental. Where a chauffeur driven car is provided so that the employee can work in the car the Revenue do not accept that travel between work and home is necessarily incidental to business use (see 7.6).

7.59   Head (*c*) in 7.55 above seeks to ensure that, say, the managing director's Rolls Royce is not included in a car pool when, in reality, anyone other than the managing director using it does so at his peril.

7.60   It is not clear what happens if there is occasional use of a car for private purposes of an employee (not falling within 7.55(*d*) above) but the employee is required to pay for such use. It is arguable whether such use can be 'private use' at all as the company is exploiting the car for payment in the course of its business. Furthermore, a charge in respect of a car can only arise if a benefit is provided to the employee; *section 157* (car available for private use) merely sets out a formula for calculating any benefit that arises under *ICTA 1988, s 154(2)*. It would be odd if use which does not in any event give rise to a benefit could prevent a car from being a pool car. It is also worth noting that *paragraph 10* of *SP 5/96* (see 6.89) envisages a taxable benefit being provided from the use of a pool car, which is impossible if 7.55(*d*) above is read literally.

Home to office travel

7.61 It should particularly be noted that a car cannot qualify as a pool car if it is used by any of the employees for home to office travel or for other private use except where such use is purely incidental to business use. There is accordingly no scope for avoiding the scale benefit charges by having a pool of similar cars none of which is allocated specifically to an individual but any of which can be used by the employees concerned as they wish. The pool car rules apply only where use of the cars is restricted to business use. There is an exception to this rule for government Ministers (see 5.76). The Revenue also accepts that if a chauffeur is required to take a pool car home for retention overnight that will not disqualify the car from being a pool car (*SP 2/96*).

7.62 It is a question of fact whether or not a car is a pool car. Prior to 1996/97 it was possible to clear the position in advance by making a claim to the Inspector of Taxes for the car to be accepted as a pool car. [*ICTA 1988, s 159(4)*]. There was a right of appeal against the refusal of such a claim. However, this procedure was abolished in the *FA 1996*.

Emergency vehicles

7.63 For 2004/05 onwards there is an exemption from the benefit rules for emergency vehicles. An emergency vehicle is defined as a vehicle which is used to respond to emergencies and which has fixed to it a lamp designed to emit a flashing light for use in emergencies (or which would have such a lamp but for the fact that if it did that would give rise to a special threat to the personal physical security of those using it by making it apparent that they were employed in an emergency service). [*ITEPA 2003, s 248A(3)* inserted by *FA 2004, s 81*].

7.64 The exemption applies only where:

(*a*) an emergency vehicle is made available to a person employed in an emergency service for the person's private use,

(*b*) the terms on which it is made available prohibit its private use otherwise than when the person is on call or engaged in on-call commuting; and

(*c*) the person does not make private use of it otherwise than in such circumstances [*ITEPA 2003, s 248A(1)(2)* inserted by *FA 2004 s 81*].

7.65 For this purpose private use means use other than for the person's business travel (i.e. travel the expenses of which, if incurred and paid by the employee would (if the rules on mileage allowances (see 7.68) did not apply) be deductible in an expenses claim in relation to the employment. [*ITEPA 2003, s 171(1)*]. A person is employed in an emergency service if he is a constable or other person employed for police purposes, employed for the purposes of a fire or a fire and rescue service, or employed in the provision of ambulance or paramedic services. A person is on call when he is liable, as part of normal duties, to be called on to use the emergency vehicle to respond to emergencies. He is engaged in on-call commuting when he is using the vehicle for ordinary commuting (see 5.16), or for travel between two places that is for practical purposes substantially ordinary commuting, and is required to do so in order that the vehicle is available for his use, as part of his normal duties, for responding to emergencies [*ITEPA 2003, s 248A(3)–(8)* inserted by *FA 2004, s 81*].

7.66   Mileage allowance payments (see 7.68) cannot be claimed in relation to such a vehicle. [*ITEPA 2003, s 236(2)(c)* as amended by *FA 2004, s 81(2)*].

Employee-owned cars

7.67   Prior to 2002/03 no special rules applied to payments by an employer in relation to a car owned by a higher-paid employee. If the payment was to settle bills incurred in respect of the car the amount paid was assessable on the employee as a benefit under *ICTA 1988, s 154* (see 6.40 above). If the payment was a mileage allowance it was not taxed to the extent that it was a mere reimbursement of the cost of business motoring. If, however, it exceeded such cost the excess was taxable as a benefit. In practice, the Revenue published non-statutory authorised mileage rates (see 7.77). A payment of such a rate was accepted as being mere reimbursement of the cost incurred. A new system of approved mileage allowance payments was introduced from 2002/03. If an employee used his car for private use after that date he could not claim a deduction for a greater amount than such payments even if he could establish that the actual running costs were higher.

Mileage allowance payments

7.68   From 2002/03 onwards there is an exemption from income tax for approved mileage allowance payments. [*ITEPA 2003, s 229(1)*]. These are amounts paid to an employee in respect of expenses in connection with the use for business travel (see 7.6) of a qualifying vehicle. [*ITEPA 2003, s 229(2)*]. The employee must obviously be the driver of the vehicle and it must not be a company vehicle. [*ITEPA 2003, s 229(4)*].

7.69   Mileage allowances are approved to the extent that they do not exceed in total specified limits. [*ITEPA 2003, s 229(3)*,]. These are as follows:

Cars and Vans	
On the first 10,000 miles	40p per mile
On the excess over 10,000 miles	25p per mile
Motorcycles	24p per mile
Cycles	20p per mile

[*ITEPA 2003, s 230(2)*]

The Treasury have power by statutory instrument to amend these figures. [*ITEPA 2003, s 230(6)*].

7.70   If an employee uses his own vehicle for business travel and either is not paid mileage allowance payments (for example, because his employer does not make such payments or the employee does not claim them) or the mileage allowance payments that he receives are less than the statutory limits he can claim a deduction (mileage allowance relief) for the shortfall against the emoluments from the employment. [*ITEPA 2003, ss 231, 232*]. If the emoluments are taxable (i.e. on a remittance basis) mileage allowances for an earlier year in which the employee was UK resident can also be deducted. [*ITEPA 2003, s 232(3)*]. This ensures that the relief is given when the remuneration is remitted if remittances during the year to which the allowances relate were insufficient. It should be noted that the relief can only be given against earning from the relevant employment; it is not given against employment income generally.

7.71   Business travel is of course travel for which expenses incurred by the employee would be deductible under *sections 337* to *342* (see 5.2). [*ITEPA 2003, s 236(1)*]. A qualifying vehicle is a car, van, motorcycle or cycle. [*ITEPA 2003, s 235(1)*]. A car for this purpose is defined as a mechanically propelled road vehicle which is not a goods vehicle, a motor vehicle or a vehicle not commonly used as a private vehicle and unsuitable to be so used. [*ITEPA 2003, s 235(2)*]. It could, for example, therefore include a mobile home. A van is a mechanically propelled goods vehicle with a design weight not exceeding 3,500 kilograms and which is not a motorcycle. [*ITEPA 2003, s 235(3)*]. The *Road Traffic Act 1988* definitions of a motorcycle (a mechanically propelled vehicle, not being an invalid carriage, with less than four wheels and the weight of which unladen does not exceed 410 kilograms) and a cycle—see 9.117— are adopted. [*ITEPA 2003, s 235(4)*]. The allowance is not tied to an individual vehicle. What is looked at is the use of any vehicle of the particular kind during the year. [*ITEPA 2003, s 230(3)*]. For example, if an employee sometimes uses a van, sometimes uses his own car and sometimes uses his wife's car it is the combined business mileage for all three that needs to be looked at to determine whether the 10,000 mile limit is exceeded.

7.72   Furthermore, the 10,000-mile figure applies to the total number of business miles in relation to the employment or any associated employment (i.e. where the employer is the same, is an associated company (within *ICTA 1988, s 416*) or if the employers are partnerships or companies and controlled (within *ICTA 1988, s 840*) by the same person (or partnership)). [*ITEPA 2003, s 230(4)(5)*]. There are a couple of oddities in this definition. If a company controls two other companies the mileage in all three employments are aggregated. However, if an individual controls two companies, whilst mileage in the employments by the two companies is aggregated, mileage in an employment with the individual as a sole trader does not appear to be from an associated employment and is therefore not aggregated. Similarly, an employment with a partnership and one with a company owned by that partnership appear to have to be aggregated if a single individual (or another partnership) controls the partnership, but not otherwise. The legislation gives no guidance as to how the limit is to be applied where there are associated employments. This could be important in a 'double Schedule E' arrangement for a non-UK domiciled taxpayer where remuneration from the overseas employment is not remitted to the UK. The normal rule is that where the legislation is silent the taxpayer is entitled to adopt whatever treatment is most favourable to him. This would enable him to treat mileage by his UK car attributable to his UK employment as being the first 10,000 miles of business travel and mileage by his overseas car attributable to his overseas employment as being the top slice of the total mileage. It also appears that business travel includes travel in a company car. As the benefit in respect of a company car is not affected by the proportion of business mileage, it appears that where a person owns a second car personally he could claim the 40p a mile for use of his own vehicle even where his business mileage in the company car exceeds 10,000 miles. A vehicle is a company vehicle (so no mileage allowance can be claimed for travel in it) even if it is a pool car or van, so that no taxable benefit arises on it. A cycle is a company vehicle if it is provided by the employer and the employee would have been taxable on its provision but for *section 244* (see 9.97) [*ITEPA 2003, s 236(2)*]. Accordingly, an employee ought not to pay any of the maintenance costs of his company bicycle but these should be incurred direct by the company as only the company can obtain any tax relief (the employee would not be able to satisfy the wholly and exclusively test for, say, new tyres).

7.73   The statutory rates are maxima. Even if the employee can show that the actual costs applicable to business mileage exceed these mileage rates he/she cannot claim a deduction for the excess.

Mileage allowances for carrying passengers

7.74   For 2002/03 onwards there is an additional relief for an employee who carries a fellow employee with him or her in a car or van (but not on a motorcycle or cycle). No income tax charge will arise on a 'passenger payment' made to him by his employer. [*ITEPA 2003, ss 233, 234*]. A passenger payment is an amount paid to an employee because, while using a car or van (other than a company vehicle) for business travel, he carries one or more qualifying passengers in it. [*ITEPA 2003, s 233(3)*].

7.75   The passenger payment for 2002/03 and 2003/04 is 5p per mile. [*ITEPA 2003, s 234(1)*]. If the employee carries more than one qualifying passenger the allowance is 5p per passenger. The Treasury have power by regulation to alter the rate. [*ITEPA 2003, s 234(3)*]. It should be particularly noted that, unlike with the mileage allowance for the driver, the relief is dependent on the employer making a payment to the driver; it is not possible to claim a deduction against earnings where no payment is made. As the relief is intended to encourage car-sharing it is unclear why a passenger payment cannot be made if an employee carries a colleague in a company car.

7.76   A qualifying passenger is a passenger who is also an employee for whom the travel is business travel. [*ITEPA 2003, s 233(3)*]. It does not appear that the passenger has to be an employee of the driver's employer. The requirements that the travel must be business travel for the passenger probably means that in practice there will be few cases where it will apply in other circumstances, although it is possible to imagine some. For example, an employee who uses their own car to go to a business conference in another town might take with them friends who are going to the same conference. It is improbable that the employer would make him a passenger payment in such circumstances but the employers of the friends might do so. The definitions in 7.68 to 7.73 above also apply to passenger payments. So does *ITEPA 2003, s 117* (see 7.2).

Mileage allowances up to 2001/02

7.77   The Revenue published non-statutory authorised mileage rates from 1990. Prior to that both the AA and RAC published average annual running costs for different sizes of cars and taxpayers tended to use these. However, the Revenue did not consider them to be reliable rates for tax purposes because they included an element for interest on capital and also AA/RAC membership fees. The Revenue had themselves for some years operated an administrative arrangement, the Fixed Profit Car Scheme (FPCS), with major employers under which the employer undertook to apply PAYE to any excess of the mileage payment he made over the FPCS figures. The Revenue decides to publish (and rename) those rates (their Authorised Mileage Rates, or AMR) so that they could be used by all employers (who were apparently supposed to call the scheme the Car Allowances Enhanced Reporting Scheme (CAERS) not the FPCS). If a higher figure was adopted the Revenue were likely to assess a benefit (normally by a coding adjustment) on mileage allowances paid to an employee who used his own car for business purposes to the extent that they exceeded the CAERS figures unless actual running costs can be proved. The authorised mileage rates for 2001/02 were:

Engine size	up to 1500cc	1501–2000cc	over 2000cc
First 4,000 business miles	40p	45p	63p
Excess:	25p	25p	36p

7.78 The figures for previous years were:

	up to 1000cc	1001–1500cc	1501–2000cc	over 2000cc
First 4,000 business miles:				
1990/91	24.5p	30p	34p	43p
1991/92	24.5p	30p	34p	45p
1992/93	25p	30p	38p	51p
1993/94	26p	32p	40p	54p
1994/95	27p	33p	41p	56p
1995/96	27p	34p	43p	60p
1996/97	27p	34p	43p	61p
1997/98 to 2000/01	28p	35p	45p	63p
Excess:				
1990/91	9.5p	11.5p	13.5p	16.5p
1991/92	11p	13p	16p	20.5p
1992/93	14p	17p	21p	27p
1993/94	15p	18p	22p	30p
1994/95	15p	19p	23p	31p
1995/96	15p	19p	23p	32p
1996/97	16p	19p	23p	33p
1997/98 to 2000/01	17p	20p	25p	36p

7.79 If an employer paid the same mileage allowance whatever size of car is used the tax free rate for 1997/98 to 2000/01 was 40p for the first 4,000 miles and 22.5p for the excess. It is not clear if such an average rate could be used for 2001/02. If it could, it was 45p and 25p.

For earlier years the rates were:

	First 4,000 business miles:	Excess:
1990/91	32p	12.5p
1991/92	32p	14.5p
1992/93	34p	19p
1993/94	36p	20p
1994/95	37p	21p
1995/96	38.5p	21p
1996/97	38.5p	21p

7.80 If the mileage allowance paid by the employer was less than the above figures, the employee could claim a deduction for the difference against his earnings under *ICTA 1988, s 198* (see 5.2) (*IR Press Release 14 December 1999, para 14*). Where the average rate was used by the employer and the scale rate for the car was greater it was not clear if the employee could claim a Schedule E deduction for the difference. If the employer did not reimburse business mileage at all the employee could not adopt the average figure though.

7.81 In addition to the mileage allowance the employee could claim capital allowances and interest on a loan taken out to acquire the car. For these purposes the employee did not need to show that the car was 'necessarily' provided for use in the performance of his duties. [*CAA 1990, s 27(2A)*]. Where the car was used for the employment at 5 April 1990, but was not 'necessarily' so used, the employee was treated for capital allowance purposes as having acquired it at 6 April 1990 at its market value at that date. [*FA 1990, s 87(3)*]. However, where the CAERS scheme was used, the employee effectively has to waive his claim for capital allowances as this relief was already included in the mileage allowances. He could still make a claim for loan interest though (*IR Press Release 26 March 1991*). These extra allowances do not apply under the new system for 2002/03 onwards.

7.82 If the employee hired the car he could claim relief for the hire charges only if they could qualify under the normal wholly, exclusively and necessarily rules. Even then a restriction applied if the car was not a qualifying hire car and the retail price when new exceeded £12,000. The deductible amount was reduced by multiplying it by £12,000 plus the retail price when new, divided by twice the retail price. For example, suppose that the hire charge was £800 and the retail price of the car when new was £20,000.

The deduction was limited to

$$£800 \times \frac{(12,000 + 20,000)}{2 \times 20,000} = £640$$

(*ICTA 1988, s 578A* inserted by *CAA 2001, 2 Sch 52* replacing *CAA 1990, s 35(2)*—although it is not readily apparent that the former wording applied to Schedule E). For this purpose a car was a qualifying hire car if it was hired under a HP agreement under which there was an option to purchase exercisable on the payment of not more than 1 per cent of the retail value of the car when new, or it was a qualifying hire car under *CAA 2001, s 82* (*ICTA 1988, s 578B*). This provision ceased to apply from 2002/03 because from that date payments for the use of a car ceased to be deductible from earnings as they were being replaced by mileage allowance payments (see 7.68) and mileage allowance relief (see 7.70).

7.83 It should be stressed that the AMR figures were concessions designed to reduce administrative work. An employee was not obliged to adopt these scale figures. Alternatively, for example, he could claim a mileage allowance from his employer based on the actual running cost of the car. This could well give a greater tax-free figure than the AMR. However, the availability of the AMR is likely to mean that the Revenue would want detailed running cost figures—possibly backed up by vouchers—from those who chose not to use it.

7.84 The percentage benefit figures were intended to reflect the average costs of running a car. In practice the average was likely to be less than the true average cost as the benefit was based on historic value and thus was unlikely to reflect the impact of inflation on running costs. An average is bound to produce winners and losers.

Is it better to have a company car?

7.85   The decision as to whether a person should be provided with a company car or whether he should provide his own car and claim a mileage allowance is not wholly tax-driven. Even where the decision will be dependent on which alternative is more beneficial from a tax point of view, it is not always an easy one to make. The answer depends on many factors such as the cost of the car, the likely running costs, the total mileage, the proportion represented by private mileage, and the records that the employee is prepared to maintain. Furthermore, the decision needs to be made at the start of the year: it cannot be made retrospectively. Accordingly, it will need to be made on the basis of estimates. There are a number of computer programmes available which will point to the correct decision for a particular car but, even so, the need to use estimates is likely to prevent the answer being wholly reliable. There are some simple rules that are likely to produce the right answer in many cases.

(*a*)   Is the employee prepared to keep detailed mileage records?

(*b*)   If he is not prepared to keep such records the car should probably be owned by the company. It is improbable that the Revenue will accept a claim for a deduction for a privately owned car based on estimates.

(*c*)   Whilst mileage allowance payments can sometimes be realistic for the first 4,000 miles they are poor where business mileage exceeds that level. Accordingly, this method of recharging will not normally be attractive unless business mileage is low. It is in any event always necessary to know the actual business mileage in order to claim the mileage allowance from the company.

(*d*)   As mileage allowance payments are a fixed figure they are more attractive for small cars then for large, expensives ones.

(*e*)   If the employee is prepared to keep detailed records, whether or not it is better for the car to be owned by him or the company depends on:

    (i)   the proportion of business to private mileage;

    (ii)   the running costs; and

    (iii)   the emissions level of the car, or its original list price if it does not have an emission certificate.

Unfortunately, the decision has to be made before the start of the tax year and at that stage the first two of these factors are unknown so must be guessed. Whilst an estimate, or informed guess, can normally be made of (i) it is not normally possible to guess the size of repair bills with any degree of accuracy, particularly if insurance cover against accidents is limited. Nevertheless the estimate will give a ball park figure for the total cost of running the car. From this can be deducted the estimated mileage allowance payments for the estimated business mileage to produce the likely cost of private motoring if the car is owned personally.

One thing that can be calculated in advance is the benefit figure. This is a known percentage of the emissions figure plus the same percentage of £14,400 (or a known percentage of the original list price plus £14,400) to cover both the use and car fuel. It will normally be sensible to pay for private fuel on a company car unless business mileage is very high and private mileage (including home to work exceptionally low). The resultant figure can be divided by the estimated private mileage to produce a benefit figure per mile of private motoring.

Advisory fuel rates for company cars

7.86   In January 2002 for the first time the Revenue published guidelines on fuel only mileage rates for company cars. These can be used for 2001/02 to 2004/05 both where employers reimbursed employees for business travel in their company cars, and where they required employees to repay the cost of fuel used for private travel so as to avoid the fuel scale charge. It was open to an employer to seek to justify a higher figure in any particular case. The rates were:

engine size	rate per mile
petrol cars	
up to 1400 cc	10p
1401–2000 cc	12p
over 2000 cc	14p
diesel cars	
up to 2000 cc	9p
over 2000 cc	12p

Lower rates apply for LPG cars, namely for 2001/02 to 2003/04, up to 1400cc 6p, 1401–2000cc, 7p and over 2000cc 9p rising for 2004/05 to 7p 8p and 10p respectively.

It should be stressed that these rates apply only to fuel for company cars. If an employee uses his own car for business travel the higher mileage allowance payments considered at 7.69 apply. The rates cannot be used for any other purpose. If an employer pays a higher rate for fuel used for business travel in a company car and can show that the cost of business travel is higher, e.g. where employees need to use particular types of car to cover rough terrain, there will be no benefit. If he cannot show this the excess will not trigger a need to pay the fuel scale charge provided that reimbursement is solely for miles of business travel but the excess will be taxed and charged to NIC as employment income. Similarly, the Revenue will accept that no benefit arises where the employee reimburses the above rates (or higher) for private travel. The Revenue do, however, reserve the right to contend that 'in exceptional cases', such as where a very large-engined company car achieves fewer than 16 miles to the gallon, a higher repayment rate should apply.

Volunteer drivers

7.87   Prior to 6 October 1991 the Revenue generally turned a blind eye to any profit element in the motor mileage allowance paid to people who drive for the hospital car service and other volunteer organisations. Strictly speaking, any difference between the allowance received and the actual running costs is taxable, and the Revenue, in consultation with Treasury Ministers, decided to tax such profits from that date. 'To ensure that, so far as possible, neither people running volunteer car services nor drivers themselves are troubled at all when the tax liability, if any, is likely to be trivial' they have given such volunteers a choice between:

(*a*)   paying tax on the difference between the mileage allowance they receive and the fixed profit car scheme rates; or

(*b*)   paying tax on the difference between the mileage allowance they receive and their actual running costs.

'To ensure that . . . voluntary work done by drivers . . . should [not] be put at risk by sudden changes in tax liabilities or misunderstandings about them,' i.e. because no one dreamt that the Government would be so petty as to tax such amounts, the introduction of the new arrangements was phased in. Only a quarter of the profit element was taxed for the period 6 October 1991 to 5 April 1992 and the year to 5 April 1993; ½ was taxed for 1993/94; ¾ for 1994/95 and the full amount is exacted for 1995/96 onwards. This is subject to the exception that the full tax will be charged for all years affected for taxi and mini-cab drivers and similar operators who drive for the hospital car service and other voluntary organisations, as the Government regards the reimbursed expenses as normal trading income for such people (*IR Press Releases 13 November 1991* and *30 March 1993* and *ESC A77* but obsolete after 1994/95).

Lower-paid employees

7.88   The car use and car fuel scale benefits apply only to higher-paid employees (and company directors). If a car is provided for a lower-paid employee no tax charge will arise except to the extent that the right to use the car represents 'money's worth'. Although in theory an employee could hire out his company car to a neighbour, even if expressly forbidden to do so by his employer, in practice he could not normally do so as the need to have the car available for business travel would prevent any meaningful bargain being struck. It might therefore be difficult for the Revenue to show that there is any monetary value into which the right to use the car can be converted. If petrol is provided for the car, that will have a money's worth equivalent although it is likely to be below the retail price.

7.89   There are three problems in providing cars for lower-paid employees. The first is that the scale benefit must be assumed to apply for the purpose of determining whether or not the employee is lower-paid.

There are likely to be very few employees earning under £8,500 less the benefit figure for whom employers might wish to provide cars.

7.90   Secondly, there must be no arrangements in existence under which the employee would be entitled to a salary increase if he were to give up the right to use the car. In *Heaton v Bell 46 TC 211* lower-paid employees were able to borrow a car from their employer in return for agreeing to a reduction of £2 a week in their salary. It was held that an employee was assessable on a benefit of £2 per week as even if the deduction reduced the salary (rather than being an agreed deduction paid out of it) the employee could convert the right to use the car into a £2 a week salary increase at any time and this constituted money's worth.

7.91   Finally, the expenditure needs to be incurred by the employer. If it is incurred by the employee and merely paid by the employer the payments will themselves constitute emoluments. Care accordingly needs to be taken to ensure that repairs, etc. are clearly contracted for by the employer and that the garage is aware that it is carrying out the work for the employer not the employee.

Car parking

7.92   Expenditure incurred in paying (or reimbursing) expenses in connection with the provision of a car parking space at or near the employee's place of work is not regarded as an emolument of his employment. [*ITEPA 2003, s 237*]. This applies to the use of a company's own car park, a season ticket at a public car park, garage space rented for a specific executive and, it appears, even the reimbursement of one-off car park charges and parking meter charges including the excess charge but not a penalty charge. It applies irrespective of whether the employer or the employee provides the car. It also extends to parking for cycles (see 9.97) and motorcycles. For 2005/06 onwards this exemption also applies to parking for a van. [*ITEPA 2003, s 237* as amended by *FA 2004, 14 Schedule 7*].

Car telephones

7.93   The Inland Revenue consider that the car scale charge covers the provision of a car telephone in the company car provided that the telephone cannot be used separately from the car (*SP 5/88* now obsolete). In the past this did not apply to a portable telephone even though it may in practice only be used in the car. It also does not apply to a car telephone installed by the employer in a car owned by the employee. In such a case a benefit will arise unless either the employee is prohibited from using the telephone for private calls or he reimburses to the employer the full cost of private calls. The full cost for this purpose is not simply the call charges. An appropriate part of the rental charges, or the cash equivalent of the benefit in relation to the telephone (20 per cent of the cost), and of any administrative costs connected with the telephone, must also be included. From 1991/92 to 1998/99, a £200 scale charge applied to portable telephones and from 1999/00 no benefit arises where ownership of the telephone remains with the employer (see 9.35 below).

Vans and lorries

7.94   Prior to 1993/94 the Revenue did not normally seek to discern a benefit in kind in the private use of company vans or lorries. From that date, a round sum benefit is introduced in relation to vans, i.e. mechanically propelled road vehicles of a construction primarily suited for the conveyance of goods or burden, of a design weight of up to 3,500 kilograms, and which are not motorbikes [*ITEPA 2003, s 115(1)*]—and an exemption is given for heavy goods vehicles, i.e. vans of a design weight exceeding 3,500 kilograms. [*ITEPA 2003, s 238*]. The design weight is the weight the vehicle is designed (or adapted) not to exceed when in normal use and laden. [*ITEPA 2003, s 115(2)*].

7.95   The exemption for lorries extends to the discharge of a liability of the employee in connection with the vehicle, to credit tokens used to obtain goods or services in connection with it, and to benefits and expenses incurred in connection with it. [*ITEPA 2003, s 239*]. The exemption does not, however, apply if the employee's use of the lorry is wholly or mainly for private use, e.g. he is a steam enthusiast and uses it to transport a steam engine to fairs. [*ITEPA 2003, s 238(3)*]. Nor does it apply to the provision of a chauffeur for the lorry! [*ITEPA 2003, s 239(5)*].

7.96   The scale benefit for a van, regardless of size, is £500 if it is less than four years old or £350 if it is four or more years old at the end of the year of assessment. [*ITEPA 2003, s 157*]. The benefit is reduced proportionately in the same way as the car benefit if the van is unavailable for use—but only if the period of unavailability is a continuous period of 30 days or more or fell before the van was made available or after it ceased to be available. [*ITEPA 2003, s 158*]. The amount of the benefit is also reduced by any payment that the employee is required to make (and makes) as a condition of the van being available for private use. [*ITEPA 2003, s 159*]. The scale benefit covers all expenditure in connection with the van. Unlike with cars, this includes the provision of fuel. [*ITEPA 2003, s 239*].

7.97   Special, extremely complex, rules apply to shared vans. [*ITEPA 2003, ss 160–166*]. A van is a shared van for a period if throughout that period it is available either:

(*a*)   concurrently to more than one employee of the same employer; or

(*b*)   to different employees of the same employer but so that the employee or employees to whom it is available at any given time are not necessarily the same people as those to whom it is available at other times. [*ITEPA 2003, s 156*].

7.98 If a van is available only to one employee for a period exceeding 30 days, it cannot be a shared van for that period. [*ITEPA 2003, s 156(4)*]. A period can apparently be a few hours, as it is specifically provided that if a van would be treated as shared during part of a day it is to be treated as a shared van for the entire day. [*ITEPA 2003, s 156(5)*].

7.99 The benefit to an employee in respect of the use of a shared van is calculated by dividing the basic £500 or £350 figure equally between all employees to whom that van is available during the period for which it is a shared van. [*ITEPA 2003, ss 161–163*].

Example

A Builder Ltd makes a van available to a group of employees, A, B, C, D and E on 6 August 2004. On 6 November 2004 he sends A to do a special job lasting until 6 December and A takes the van with him. The van is over four years old on 5 April 2005. B is promoted on 10 August and ceases to use the van. C leaves on 30 November 2004 and is replaced by F from 4 February 2005.

The van is a shared van from 5 August 2004 to 5 November 2004 (92 days). It is not a shared van from 6 November to 6 December as it is available exclusively to A during that period. (If A had finished the special job a day earlier the van would have been a shared van throughout as the exclusive period would have been only 30 days.) The van is then a shared van again from 7 December to 5 April. The total benefit to be shared is accordingly $92 + 120 = {}^{212}/_{365} \times £350 = £203$. During the year of assessment the van was available to A, B, C, D, E and F at some time. Accordingly, each is assessable on ⅙ of £203, or £33. In addition, A is assessable on ${}^{31}/_{365} \times £350 = £29$ for the 31 days that he had exclusive use of the van.

7.100 It will be noted that in the above example each employee was assessable on £33 even though the actual periods of use differed, i.e. A, D and E had its use for the entire 212 days, B for only 4 days, C for 92 days and F for 60 days. Accordingly, an alternative calculation is available. An employee can claim to adopt instead a fixed daily benefit of £5 for each day that he (or members of his family or household) actually used the van. [*ITEPA 2003, s 164*]. There is no reduced figure where the van is over four years old. Use for any part of a day must be treated as use for the entire day. In the above example it will pay B to claim the use of the alternative method as this will reduce his benefit from £33 to £20 (4 × £5). It is unlikely to be sensible for the other employees to make the claim, although it should be noted that the standard method looks at availability for use whereas the alternative method looks at only days of actual use.

7.101 Where more than one shared van is made available by the employer the calculation is done on a global basis [*ITEPA 2003, s 161*]—

or perhaps it is not as *section 155(7)* (formerly *para 5(6)*) envisages the benefit for an individual employee who has use of only one of the vans being calculated by reference only to the particular van concerned.

Example

Con Tractor has a fleet of six vans, four of which are over four years old on 5 April 2004. Each van is allocated to a foreman. Con employed a maximum of 30 staff (including the foremen) during 2004/05. The staff work as a pool. On each job the foreman selects a team of workers from the pool and picks them up each day in his van from a mutually agreed collection point to take them to the work site. Although most employees worked for different foremen during the year, Pat and Sean worked for Mick only; Pat because all the other foremen knew that he worked best for Mick and Sean because he was employed for five days only during which he worked on one job only.

The basic benefits for the vans are two at £500 and 4 at £350 = £2,400. This is divided amongst the 30 staff giving £80 benefit per person. It is irrelevant that the foremen used only one of the vans. It is also irrelevant that Sean only ever used one of them (all of them were available to Pat even though in practice he used only one). Sean should obviously elect to opt for the alternative basis so reducing his benefit to £25 (5 × £5).

7.102   Other points to note are as follows:

(*a*)   An employee is taken into account only if he or a member of his family or household actually makes private use of one of the vans at least once during the year; mere availability for use is not enough. [*ITEPA 2003, s 162(1)*].

(*b*)   It is irrelevant how many different vans in the fleet an individual actually uses—or is entitled to use. [*ITEPA 2003, s 162(2)*].

(*c*)   If Mick, in the above example, always tells his team to meet at his house, and is forbidden to use the van other than to drive the team to sites, it is probable that the van is not available for Mick's private use. This is because while the others are probably journeying from home to work, a private use (unless it can be shown that their duties begin at Mick's house), Mick could well be driving to the site in the course of his duties, of which one of these is to drive the others to the site.

(*d*)   With cars the Revenue do not normally seek to impose a benefit on passengers, other than for chauffeur-driven cars, whereas with vans they regard use as a passenger as attracting a benefit.

(*e*)   It appears that all employees, including lower-paid employees, who have private usage of the van or vans are taken into account in arriving at the amount of the benefit, although only higher-paid employees are assessable.

(*f*)   The calculation is based on the total fleet for the entire year (excluding any non-shared use period); separate calculations are not done for different periods of shared use, where the usage of a van varies during a tax year.

(*g*)   Separate calculations are needed if the vans are made available by different employers, e.g. use of vans is shared by companies in a group.

(*h*)   Where the van is not a shared van for part of the year, or is incapable of being used for a period of 30 days or more, the £500 or £350 figure is reduced accordingly. [*ITEPA 2003, s 163*].

(*j*)   The total benefit for any one employee is limited to £500. [*ITEPA 2003, s 166*]. This limitation will only come into play if there are more vans than employees who use them.

(*k*)   If an employer uses a van as a shared van for part of the year, and it is available only to him for another part, the two benefits are calculated separately and then aggregated. [*ITEPA 2003, s 155(4)*].

(*l*)   Where an employee is required to make a payment as a condition of a van being available for his private use, that payment is deducted from his individual benefit figure. [*ITEPA 2003, s 159*]. Where he makes such a payment for private use of one van but not for private use of another, the calculations are still done on an aggregate basis so if the payment is large enough it can eliminate the entire benefit in relation to both vans.

(*m*)   The normal six-year time limit applies to a claim to use the alternative basis.

(*n*)   For 2002/03 if an employee used their own van for business journeys the authorised mileage rates that applied to cars (40p for the first 10,000 miles and 22.5p thereafter) also applied to vans. No authorised mileage rates for vans were announced for earlier years.

7.103   A new system of benefits in respect of vans will apply for 2005/06 onwards. There will be no benefit charge at all if the private use of the van during the tax year is 'insignificant'. Insignificant is not defined, [*ITEPA 2003, s 114(3A)*, inserted by *FA 2004, 14 Schedule 2*]. In addition, the cash equivalent of the benefit will be nil if throughout the tax year (or the part of it for which the van is made available to the employee):

(*a*)   the terms on which the van is available to the employee prohibit its private use otherwise than for ordinary commuting (as defined in *ITEPA 2003, s 338(3)* – see 5.16) or travel between two places that is for practical purposes substantially ordinary commuting;

(*b*)   neither the employee nor a member of the employee's family or household makes private use of the van otherwise than for such purposes; and

(*c*)   the van is available to the employee mainly for use for the purposes of the employee's business travel (as defined in *ITEPA 2003, s 171(1)* namely the travel costs of which would be deductible for tax purposes if the mileage allowance rules (see 7.78) did not apply)

[*ITEPA 2003, s 155(1)–(7)* as substituted by *FA 2004, 14 Schedule 5*].

7.104   In all other cases the benefit will be:

For 2005/06 and 2006/07	£500 if the age of the van is less than four-years-old at the end of the tax year or £350 if it is older, i.e. the current rules continue to apply.
For 2007/08	£3,000.

It will be seen that the benefit will be very substantially increased from 2007/08 onwards where a van is made available for private use. Furthermore, the current figures include fuel where this is made available by the employer. From 2007/08 onwards there will be a van fuel benefit of £500, so for a van that is over four-years-old the benefit charge is effectively ten times the current charge. As with the current rules, the benefit is reduced for periods where the van is unavailable for private use, it is shared, or the employee makes a payment in relation to private use.

7.105   The calculation of the reduction where the van is unavailable for private use will continue to follow the rules on car benefits (see 7.33), including the requirement that a car is treated as unavailable only if it is unavailable throughout a continuous period of 30 days (or during a period before or after which it was supplied to the employee). [*ITEPA 2003, s 156* as substituted by *FA 2004, 14 Schedule 5*]. If a van is available to the employee for a period of less than 30 days and during the period of unavailability a replacement van is provided, in order to avoid double taxation the replacement van is deemed not to have been made available on those days for which a benefit continues to accrue in relation to the original van. [*ITEPA 2003, s 159* as substituted by *FA 2004, 14 Schedule 5*].

7.106   The current complex rules on shared vans will disappear. Instead, the benefit for each employee to whom the van is available for private use will be calculated in the normal way and then reduced on a just and reasonable basis. However, if one of the employees who shares the van is a lower paid employee (i.e. outside the scope of the benefit code) and another who is within the benefit code is higher paid and is a member of the same family or household as the lower paid employee the availability to the lower paid employee is ignored in making this reduction. For example, suppose Jack who is a higher paid employee and his son Joe who is a lower paid employee have shared use of the van. Its availability to Joe must be ignored in arriving at Jack's benefit, so Jack will be regarded as having the entire private use of the van [*ITEPA 2003, s 157* as substituted by *FA 2004, 14 Schedule 5*]. It remains to be seen what will happen in circumstances in which Jack and Joe share the van with another employee, Fred. It is probably just and reasonable for Fred's benefit to be reduced by two-thirds. But is it then just and reasonable for Jack's benefit to be reduced by 50% (on the basis that the van is deemed to be available only to him and Fred) or by a third (on the basis that if the availability to Joe is disregarded the use by Joe becomes use by virtue of the van being made available to Joe as a member of Jack's family)? The latter is more logical but it is difficult to fit into the clear wording that the availability of the van to Joe (not its availability to Joe by virtue of Joe's own employment) is to be disregarded. See also 7.112.

7.107 If the employee is required to pay an amount of money as a condition of the van being available for his private use (or that of a member of his family or household) the payment can be deducted from the cash equivalent under *section 155* (after any reduction under *sections 156* and *157*) but cannot reduce the benefit below nil [*ITEPA 2003, s 158* as substituted by *FA 2004, 14 Schedule 5*].

7.108 As indicated at 7.104, for 2007/08 onwards a van fuel benefit charge also arises if fuel is provided for the van by reason of an employment and the £3,000 cash equivalent benefit applies in respect of the van. Fuel is treated as provided for a van if (in addition to any other way it may be provided) a liability in respect of the provision of fuel is discharged, a non-cash voucher or credit token is used to obtain fuel (or to obtain money which is spent on fuel), or a sum is paid in respect of expenses incurred in providing fuel. However, no van fuel benefit will arise in relation to any facility or means for supplying electricity for an electrically propelled van. [*ITEPA 2003, s 160* as substituted by *FA 2004, 14 Schedule 5*].

7.109 The benefit is normally £500 but this is proportionately reduced if the van use benefit is reduced under *section 156* (van unavailable) or *section 157* (shared vans). Where a replacement van is supplied during a period of unavailability fuel supplied for the replacement van is obviously treated as relating to the normal van. The benefit is also proportionately reduced if for any part of the tax year the facility for the provision of fuel is not available, fuel is made available only for business travel (see 7.104) or the employee is required to (and does) make good the whole of the expense incurred in connection with the provision of fuel for his private use, but only if there is no later time in the tax year in which that situation applies, i.e. a reduction can be made only if one of these three circumstances either applies for the entire tax year or starts to apply during the year and continues for the rest of the year. Where the benefit is proportionately reduced this is done on a daily basis, i.e. in the proportion in which the number of days for which the car is unavailable (or one of the other three circumstances applies) bears to the number of days in the tax year [*ITEPA 2003, s 163* inserted by *FA 2004, 14 Schedule 5*].

7.110 In the case of a shared van the reduction in the fuel benefit follows that which applies to the use benefit. [*ITEPA 2003, s 164* inserted by *FA 2004, 14 Schedule 5*].

7.111   No fuel benefit of course arises if the employee is required to make good the whole of the expense of providing the fuel for private use throughout the tax year or if fuel is made available only for business travel. [*ITEPA 2003, s 162* inserted by *FA 2004, 14 Schedule 5*].

7.112   If a van or vans are made available to two persons who are both employees of the same employer and are members of the same family or household there is a potential for double taxation, i.e. A is taxable by reference to both his own and B's use and B is taxable by reference to both his and A's use. To avoid this A is not chargeable to either a van use or van fuel benefit by reference to B's use of the van if either B is chargeable in relation to the van or B:

(*a*)   is a lower paid employee;

(*b*)   has the use of the van in his own right as an employee (not by virtue of A's employment); and

(*c*)   either

   (i)   equivalent vans are made available to employees who are in similar employment to B with the same employer and who are not members of the family or household of higher paid employees of the employer; or

   (ii)   the making available of an equivalent van is in accordance with the normal commercial practice for an employment of the kind held by B.

[*ITEPA 2003, s 169A* inserted by *FA 2004, 14 Schedule 6*].

Motor cycles

7.113   There are few special rules for motor cycles. The Revenue say that a motor cycle is a car for capital allowance purposes so that if it costs more than £12,000 the capital allowances may be restricted (Capital Allowance Manual, para 2398). On the other hand, they say that the CGT exemption for cars does not apply to motor cycles even with a sidecar (Capital Gains Manual, para 76907). It is unclear why, as that exemption applies to a mechanically propelled road vehicle constructed or adapted for the carriage of passengers and most motor cycles are designed to carry a passenger.

7.114   The Revenue state that for industrial life agents the cost of protective clothing for business travel by motor cycle qualifies as a business expense (Schedule E Manual, para 7544). There is no logical reason why this should not equally apply to other employees who use a motor cycle for business travel.

7.115   For 2000/01 and 2002/03 a tax-free mileage allowance of 24p per mile could be paid for employees who used their own motorcycles for business travel (IR Press Release 14 December 1999). Unlike with the CAERS rates for cars (see 7.77) this 24p rate applied to total business mileage where this exceeded 4,000 miles. The employee could adopt the actual cost if this was greater and he was prepared to maintain the records necessary to show this. The new system introduced for cars from 2002/03 onwards (see 7.67) also applies to motorcycles, although the mileage rate for 2003/04 remains 24p per mile.

Chapter 8

Benefits in Relation to Accommodation

Occasions of charge

8.1   Where living accommodation is provided for an employee, a charge to tax can arise under three headings.

(*a*)   There is a basic charge in relation to the accommodation that applies, irrespective of whether the employee is higher- or lower-paid, unless it can be shown that he is in 'representative occupation' of the property (i.e. he is occupying it on behalf of his employer, generally as an integral part of his duties).

(*b*)   There is an additional charge if the cost of the accommodation exceeds £75,000.

(*c*)   If the employee is in higher-paid employment the payment by the employer of the running costs of the property, such as rates, light and heat will give rise to a benefit in kind.

8.2   In certain circumstances a charge could arise under the basic rules for taxing employment income applying the *Heaton v Bell 46 TC 211* principle (see 7.90). From 1996/97 the charges described below under *ITEPA 2003, ss 105, 106* applies in priority to any charge under other provisions and tax under the basic charging provision for employment income (*section 62*) is chargeable only to the extent, if any, that it would produce a greater taxable amount than *sections 105* and *106*. [*ITEPA 2003, s 109*]. This is an anti-avoidance provision.

The basic charge

8.3   If a person is provided with living accommodation by reason of his employment he is taxable on an amount equal to the 'rental value of the accommodation' less, if he pays rent or makes any other payment, so much as is made good to the employer (or other person who provides the accommodation) and less such amount as could have been deducted in an expenses claim under *section 336* (or *section 351* in the case of a clergyman) if the employer had paid for the accommodation himself. [*ITEPA 2003, ss 105, 327*].

Rental value

8.4   The rental value of the accommodation is the higher of:

(*a*)   any rent paid by the employer (or other person who provides the benefit) for the premises for the period they are provided to the employee; and

(*b*)   the rent that the employee would have paid for the period of occupation if the premises had been let to him at an annual rent equal to their annual value.

[*ITEPA 2003, s 105(3)(4)*].

Annual value

8.5   The annual value for this purpose is the rent which might reasonably be expected to be obtained on a letting from year to year if the tenant undertook to pay all usual tenant's rates and taxes and the landlord undertook to bear the cost of repairs, insurance and any other expenses necessary for maintaining the property in a state to command that rent. [*ITEPA 2003, s 110(1)*]. For this purpose the assumed rent is to be calculated on the basis that the only amounts that may be deducted in respect of services provided by the landlord are the costs to him of providing any relevant service, namely any service other than the repair, insurance or maintenance of the accommodation or of any other premises. [*ITEPA 2003, s 110(2)*]. If the accommodation is of a kind that might reasonably be expected to be let on terms that the landlord is to provide services which are either relevant services or the repairs, insurance or maintenance of any premises which do not form part of the accommodation but are occupied by the landlord, the notional rent is to be increased by the excess of the charge that could have been made for the relevant services over the cost of providing them plus the amount that could have been charged in respect of the repair etc of the other premises (with no deduction for any costs of such work). [*ITEPA 2003, s 110(3)–(5)*]. In practice, the Revenue used to adopt the rateable value where the property was in the UK, as the definition of annual value for rating purposes was the same. Domestic rates were abolished from 1 April 1990 (1989 in Scotland). Despite this the Revenue continue to base the benefit of living accommodation on the gross annual value for rating purposes—which actually represents 1973 values. For new, or materially altered buildings, employers are asked to supply an estimate of what the gross annual value would have been had domestic rates continued. The Revenue will liaise as necessary with the District Valuer's office to confirm the employer's estimate. Unfortunately, *ITEPA 2003, s 110*, unlike the *ICTA 1988* provision which it replaced, makes no mention of the *Rating Act* so it is hard to see how *section 110* can legitimately be interpreted as requiring one to arrive at a notional rental value over 30 years ago! Nevertheless the Revenue have said that they will continue with this practice. The charge under *section 106* (see 8.18) was originally introduced as a rough and ready method of approximating the benefit to the market rent. Accordingly if the Revenue were to seek to apply *section 110* to the charge under *section 105* it would create a double tax charge.

Representative occupation

8.6   As indicated earlier, the charge does not apply if the employee is in representative occupation. This can occur in three circumstances only.

(*a*)   Where it is necessary for the proper performance of the employee's duties that he should reside in the accommodation, e.g. the caretaker of a block of flats will need to live in one of the flats to do his job properly so that he is on hand when the occupiers of other flats need him. [*ITEPA 2003, s 99(1)*].

(*b*)   Where the accommodation is provided for the better perform-ance of the duties of his employment, and it is one of the kinds of employment in which it is customary to provide living accommo-dation for employees, e.g. a school caretaker does not need to live on or near the premises but because of the need to inspect the premises at intervals to ensure that they are secure, it makes sense for him to do so, and he will normally be provided with a house in the vicinity of the school. [*ITEPA 2003, s 99(2)*].

(*c*)   Where there is a special threat to the employee's security, and security arrangements are in force, and he resides in the accom-modation as part of those arrangements, e.g. the Prime Minister does not have to live at 10 Downing Street to carry out his job (Harold Wilson did not) but because of the risk of terrorism the pre-sent Prime Minister needs to live there as special security arrange-ments have been made to protect the property. [*ITEPA 2003, s 100*].

8.7   Where one of these exemptions applies not only is there no charge in relation to the provision of the accommodation but no assess-ment could be made on the employee in respect of rates paid by the employer (or any other person other than the employee), irrespective of whether these were paid by the employer or they were paid by the employee and reimbursed to him. [*ICTA 1988, s 145(4)*]. By concession no assessment is made where the employer pays the employee's council tax either (*IR Press Release 16 March 1993*).

8.8   The Revenue draw a distinction between board and lodging and living accommodation. They say that the exemption does not apply where the employee is provided with board and lodging (*Schedule E Manual SE 11322*). They interpret living accommodation as 'something which gives the occupant the necessary facilities to live domestic life independently without reliance on others to supply basic needs'. They say that at a minimum they would expect an individual to have the use of a refrigera-tor and full cooking facilities, even if such facilities are shared (*para SE 11321*). It seems questionable whether the term 'living accommodation' would be given such a narrow meaning by the courts rather than the broader interpretation of a place where someone lives.

8.9   The Revenue gives as examples of employees (who live on the premises concerned) who might be exempted under para 8.6 –

(*a*)   (*para SE 11342*)

agricultural workers who live on farms or agricultural estates;

lock-gate and level crossing gate keepers;

caretakers (with a genuine full-time caretaking job);

stewards and green keepers;

managers of pubs;

wardens of sheltered housing schemes.

(*b*)   (*paras SE 11351* and *11352*)

police officers;

Ministry of Defence police;

Prison Governors, officers and chaplains;

clergymen and ministers of religion;

members of HM Forces;

members of the Diplomatic Service;

managers of newsagents shops that have paper rounds;

managers of traditional off-licence shops (i.e. which keep pub hours);

head teacher, bursar, matron, nurse and doctor of boarding schools and other teachers at such schools with pastoral or other irregular contractual responsibilities outside normal school hours;

stable staff of racehorse trainers;

vets assisting in veterinary practices (but only if the better performance test can be individually justified);

managers of camping and caravan sites (but only if the better performance test can be individually justified).

(*c*)   (*para SE 11362*)

an employee under a genuine terrorist threat to his life—although they warn that the conditions are 'very difficult' to meet.

This is not of course an exhaustive list. Anyone in different circumstances who believes that they falls within one of the three circumstances is entitled to claim relief.

Council Housing

8.10   No benefit arises to an employee of a local authority if accommodation is provided to him by that authority and the terms on which it is provided are no more favourable than those on which similar accommodation is provided by the authority for persons who are not their employees but whose circumstances are otherwise similar to those of the employee. [*ITEPA 2003, s 98*]. This ensures that a person who lives in a council house or flat and happens to be a council employee will not be charged to a benefit if the rent he pays is less than a market rent, provided that he pays the same rent as he would have done had he not been a council employee.

Directors

8.11   The exemption conferred by heads (*a*) and (*b*) in 8.6 above does not apply if the accommodation is provided by a company and the employee is a director of that company (or of an associated company) unless:

(*a*)   he does not have a material interest in the company; and

(*b*)   either:

    (i)   he is a full-time working director;

    (ii)   the company neither carries on a trade nor does its business consist wholly or mainly in the holding of investments or other property; or

    (iii)   the company is established for charitable purposes only.

[*ITEPA 2003, s 99(3)–(5)*].

8.12   The definition of director considered at 6.9 above applies. A person has a material interest in a company if he or associates of his (or he and his associates) is the beneficial owner of, or able to control, more than 5 per cent of the ordinary share capital or, if the company is a close company, possesses (or is entitled to acquire) such rights as would entitle him to more than 5 per cent of the assets on a winding-up. [*ITEPA 2003, s 68*]. A full-time working director is a director who is required to devote substantially the whole of his time to the service of the company in a managerial or technical capacity. [*ITEPA 2003, s 66(3)*]. The Revenue interpret 'substantially the whole of his time' as meaning a normal working day (see 6.11).

8.13   The restriction in 8.11 above also applies if the employee is a director of an associated company (i.e. one company controls the other or the two are under common control). [*ITEPA 2003, s 99(3)(5)*]. If he is a director of a number of associated companies the above tests must be met in relation to all such directorships. [*ITEPA 2003, s 99(3)*]. It is likely that in practice the Revenue will look at all associated employments together in deciding whether or not the employee is a full-time working director, but there is no requirement for them to do so.

The employee's family

8.14   If living accommodation is provided for members of an employee's family or household, i.e. his spouse, his children and their spouses, his parents and his domestic staff (servants up to 2002/03), dependants or guests [*ITEPA 2003, s 721(5)*] by reason of the employee's job it must be treated as having been provided to him, so as to bring these provisions into operation. [*ITEPA 2003, s 97(1)*]. Living accommodation provided by the employer is automatically deemed to have been provided by reason of the employment unless either:

(*a*)   the employer is an individual and it can be shown that he has provided the accommodation in the normal course of his domestic, family or personal relationships; or

(*b*)   the employer is a local authority and the terms on which the accommodation is provided are no more favourable than those which apply to council tenants for similar accommodation in similar personal circumstances to the employee.

[*ITEPA 2003, s 97(2)*].

It should be noted that (*a*) will not include a partnership, even a husband and wife partnership, so other members of the family who live at the family home and work in the partnership business would be taxable if the home is a partnership asset—which could well be the case with a flat above the business premises.

Agricultural workers

8.15   By concession the Revenue do not tax an agricultural worker on the value of free board and lodging (as opposed to a gross wage from which he agrees to a deduction to cover board and lodging) provided that, if the lodging is not in the farmhouse, it is in premises which the employer has contracted to use and for which he pays the cost direct (*ESC A60*).

Ministers of religion

8.16   Where a clergyman or minister of religion is provided with a residence in premises owned or leased by a charity or ecclesiastical corporation from which to perform his duties and he is not a higherpaid employee, he is not taxed in respect of expenditure on heating, lighting, cleaning and gardening even though these are his contractual liability. This applies whether the church pays the sums on his behalf, reimburses them to him, or pays him an allowance towards such costs (*ESC A61*).

Chevening House

8.17   The charges under *section 105* and *106* do not apply in relation to the occupation of Chevening House which was put into trust for occupation by members of the Royal Family, or any other premises held on the trusts set out in the *Chevening Estate Act 1959*. [*ITEPA 2003, s 101*].

Accommodation costing over £75,000

8.18   The last domestic rating revaluation in England and Wales was in 1973 and the previous one was in 1963. Accordingly, while it was convenient for the Revenue to adopt rateable values as the rental value for the purpose of what is now *section 105*, that figure long ago ceased to reflect the market rent that was envisaged by the legislature when the provision was first introduced. Therefore, in 1977 it was decided to supplement the basic charge with a further charge based on the cost of the property. If the Revenue were to change their (non-statutory) practice and base the *section 105* charge on the actual market rental value of the property as the statute requires, the additional charge will become a penal impost if it is not repealed. However, the Revenue have indicated that they will continue to use rateable values. In November 1995 the Revenue recognised the inequity that arises where the charge under what is now *section 105* is based on the open market value of the property, for example because it is situated overseas so does not have a rateable value or an equivalent value. In such circumstances they will not seek to collect tax under *section 106* (*ESC A91*). If the *section 105* charge is greater than would apply with a UK property, but nevertheless below a market rent, it does not appear that the concession will allow a reduction in the *section 106* charge.

Occasions of additional charge

8.19   The additional charge arises where:

(*a*)   living accommodation is provided for a person in any period by reason of his employment (which has the same meaning as in 6.40 above); and

(*b*)   the cost of the accommodation exceeds £75,000.

[*ITEPA 2003, s 106*].

Prior to 2003/04 the employee also had to be taxable under *ICTA 1988, s 145* (the predecessor of *section 105*) in relation to the accommodation (or would have been so taxable had the rent paid equalled or exceeded the annual value). However, under the rewrite where the cost exceeds £75,000 both charges are now contained within *section 106*.

Amount of charge

8.20   The amount of the additional charge is the rent that would have been payable (for the period that the accommodation is made available to the employee) if the property had been let at an annual rent equal to the appropriate percentage of the excess of the cost of providing the accommodation over £75,000. [*ITEPA 2003, s 106*]. If the employee pays rent, etc. to the employer (or other provider of the accommodation) this is deducted first from the charge calculated under *section 105* but, to the extent that it exceeds the annual value, the balance is deducted from the amount that would otherwise have been chargeable under *section 106*. [*ITEPA 2003, s 106(3)*].

The appropriate percentage

8.21   The appropriate percentage of the cost of providing the accommodation is the rate prescribed by the Treasury under *section 181* (beneficial loans—see 9.4 below) at the *beginning* of the year of assessment. This is:

1985/86	12%	1995/96	8.0%
1986/87	12%	1996/97	7.25%
1987/88	11.5%	1997/98	6.75%
1988/89	10.5%	1998/99	7.25%
1989/90	14.5%	1999/00	6.25%
1990/91	16.5%	2000/01	6.25%
1991/92	13.5%	2001/02	6.25%
1992/93	10.75%	2002/03	5.0%
1993/94	7.75%	2003/04	5.0%
1994/95	7.5%	2004/05	5.0%

Cost of the accommodation

8.22   The 'cost of providing the accommodation' means the aggregate of:

(*a*)   the expenditure (including legal and other acquisition costs) incurred in acquiring the interest in the property held by a 'person involved in providing the accommodation'; and

(*b*)   any expenditure on improvements incurred by such a person before the year of assessment in relation to which the benefit arises.

[*ITEPA 2003, s 104*].

8.23   In other words, it is the cost of the property plus the cost of improvements up to the end of the previous year of assessment. A small benefit can be obtained by deferring until after 5 April improvements that are planned in February or March so that the cost does not increase the benefit for the next year of assessment.

Relevant persons

8.24   The following are 'person involved in providing the accommo-dation':

(*a*)   the person providing the accommodation;

(*b*)   the employer (if he is not the provider of the accommodation); and

(c)   any person who is connected (within the meaning of *section 839*) with a person falling within (*a*) or (*b*) above.

[*ITEPA 2003, s 112*].

8.25   Where more than one relevant person has an interest in the property, e.g. one holds a lease and another the freehold reversion, the expenditure incurred by each of them will need to be aggregated to arrive at the cost of providing the accommodation.

Property already owned by the employer

8.26   If an estate or interest in the property was held by a relevant person throughout the six years up to the date when the accommodation was first occupied by the employee, the cost of providing the accommodation is calculated differently. In these circumstances it is the aggregate of the market value of the property at the date when the employee first occupied the property plus expenditure on improvements by relevant persons between that date and the end of the year of assessment before that for which the benefit arises. This applies irrespective of whether during the six-year period the property was owned by the person who makes it available to the employee or by a different relevant person, or even by a succession of relevant persons. [*ITEPA 2003, s 107*]. The original cost of the accommodation in such circumstances was felt to be a historical figure unrelated to the need to acquire the property for occupation by the employee, and it would be unfair for the employee to be put in a substantially better position, by having his benefit calculated by reference to an out-of-date figure, than he would have been in had the house had to be bought specifically for his occupation. The market value of the property at the time it is first made available to the employee is the price which it might reasonably be expected to fetch on a sale in the open market with vacant possession. In arriving at this value any option in respect of the property held by the employee, or a connected person of his, or by a relevant person (as defined at 8.24 above) which would depress the value must be ignored. [*ITEPA 2003, s 107(3)(4)*].

8.27   If the employee reimburses any part of the cost of acquisition of, or improvements to, the premises to the employer (or another relevant person), or pays a premium for the grant of a lease or sub-lease of the premises, that payment is deducted from the aggregate amount referred to at 8.20 above (or at 8.26 above, where the market value figure is adopted). [*ITEPA 2003, s 104*].

More than one property provided

8.28   If an employee is provided with more than one property, the Inland Revenue initially considered that the *section 106* charge was on the excess of the aggregate cost of both properties over £75,000. But they now accept that the two properties can be looked at separately so that a charge will only arise on the excess of the cost of an individual property over £75,000.

Property provided to more than one employee

8.29   Where a property is provided as living accommodation to more then one employee in the same period, the total charge under *sections 105* and *106* on all of the employees concerned is limited to the amount that would have been taxable if it had been provided to a single employee during that period. The apportionment of the reduction between the employees must be done on a just and reasonable basis. [*ITEPA 2003, s 108*, enacting *ESC A91*].

Running costs

8.30   If the employee is in a representative occupation (see 8.6 above) there is a limit on the amount on which he can be assessed in respect of running costs. This applies to expenditure on:

(*a*)   heating, lighting or cleaning the premises;

(*b*)   repairs, maintenance and decoration; and

(*c*)   the provision of furniture and other appurtenances or effects which are normal for domestic occupation.

[*ITEPA 2003, s 315*].

Amount of charge

8.31   The total benefit in relation to all of the above items is limited to 10 per cent of the net amount of the emoluments of the employment for the year of assessment. If the property is not available for the employee for the entire year the figure is reduced proportionately. [*ITEPA 2003, s 315(4)*].

8.32   Expenditure incurred by the employee and reimbursed to him is treated as if it were expenditure by the employer for applying this limitation. On the other hand, if the employee reimburses expenditure by the employer (or anyone else other than the employee himself), the amount reimbursed is deductible from the 10 per cent of the emoluments figure. [*ITEPA 2003, s 315(4)*].

Net emoluments

8.33   The net amount of the employee's emoluments is the amount of those emoluments (excluding the expenditure at heads (*a*) to (*c*) in 8.30 above) less:

(*a*)   any capital allowances deductible from the emoluments;

(*b*)   any deduction for expenses under *sections 198, 199* and *332(3)*;

(*c*)   any deduction for fees and subscriptions under *section 201*;

(*d*)   contributions by the employee to a company pension scheme deductible under *sections 592(7)* and *594*; and

(*e*)   contributions to retirement annuities deductible under *section 619(1)(a)*.

(*f*)   mileage allowance relief (see 7.70).

[*ITEPA 2003, s 315(5)*].

8.34   When personal pensions were introduced the need to amend this list to include payment to a personal pension scheme allowable under *section 639* seems to have been overlooked.

Associated companies

8.35   If the employer is a company, emoluments of any employment by an associated company (i.e. one which controls, or is controlled by, the employer company or is under common control with it) must be brought into account in calculating the 10 per cent limit as if they were emoluments of the employment in relation to which the accommodation is provided. [*ITEPA 2003, s 315(5)*].

8.36   This limitation of the benefit figure in respect of running costs applies only where a charge would arise under *section 105* (see 8.3 above) but for being excluded under the representative occupation rules (see 8.6 above). [*ITEPA 2003, s 315(2)*]. It will not apply if the employer pays the heating, lighting, etc. of a property owned by the employee himself.

Exceptions

8.37   It should be noted that telephone expenses are not included in the list of items to which the 10% limit applies. Furthermore, only a proportion of gas and electricity bills are covered by this limitation, i.e. the part which relates to lighting, heating, and powering cleaning equipment. The part relating to cooking, heating hot water, powering TV, hi-fi equipment, power tools, etc. should be excluded from the calculation and assessed on the employee in full in addition to the 10 per cent figure.

8.38   It must also be remembered that expenditure on structural alterations and certain repairs does not give rise to a benefit at all (see head (*f*) at 6.42 above) and is therefore excluded from the expenditure under head (*b*) at 8.30 above. Where the employee is in a representative occupation, no charge arises in respect of rates or, by concession, council tax (see 8.7 above). A charge will arise in relation to the community charge, however, if this was paid by the employer (and the 10 per cent limitation will presumably not apply to it).

Council tax

8.39　　If the employer pays an employee's council tax the payment will be taxable on him as a benefit in kind unless he is in a representative occupation (see 8.7). The payment will also attract both employer's and employee's national insurance. If the employee's duties require him to work at home and he is entitled to deduct a proportion of his domestic expenses under *section 336* he may be able to deduct an appropriate proportion of his council tax if he has a room or rooms set aside exclusively for work (*IR Press Release 16 March 1993* and *DSS Press Release 9 November 1993*).

8.40　　Different rules applied to the community charge, the predecessor of council tax. The community charge was a tax on individuals. Accordingly, the Revenue considered it taxable even where the employee was in a representative occupation, such as a nanny or an au pair, and would not allow any part as a business expense or to be included in reimbursable removal expenses (see 9.46) (except in the case of the standard community charge on, for example, second homes, which was a tax on property). Council tax in contrast is a property tax so the Revenue treat it in the same way as rates (which were payable prior to 1 April 1990).

Chapter 9

Other Benefits

Beneficial loan arrangements

Notional interest

9.1   If a higher-paid employee is granted an interest-free loan by reason of his employment, he is treated as receiving earnings from the employment of an amount equal to interest on the loan at 'the official rate' for the period that the loan is outstanding during each year of assessment. [*ITEPA 2003, s 175*]. Similarly, if a loan carries interest at a rate below the official rate, a tax as employment income charge arises on the difference between interest at the official rate and that actually paid. [*ITEPA 2003, s 175*]. There is an option to aggregate all loans by the same lender and borrower where the lender is a close company, the borrower is a director of that company, the benefit of each loan is obtained by reason of his employment, the rate of interest on none of the loans exceeds the official rate at any time in the tax year, the loans are in the same currency, and none of them are qualifying loans. An election to aggregate must be made by 7 July after the end of the tax year. If there are several loans either all must be aggregated or none. [*ITEPA 2003, s 187*].

9.2   A replacement loan is treated as remaining the same loan as the original one if it is replaced, directly or indirectly by either a further employment-related loan from the same employer or a person connected with him, or by a third party loan which is itself replaced by such a further employment-related loan within the next 40 days. [*ITEPA 2003, s 186*].

9.3   An interesting issue arose in *Harvey v Williams* [*1998*] *STC (SCD) 215*. Mr Harvey was employed by Supergas Ltd. The company asked him to move from Newark to their Sittingbourne branch. He could not find a suitable house in Kent within his price range. Supergas agreed to 'lend' Mr Harvey £10,000 interest free to buy a £70,000 house on the basis that when the house was sold they would receive 10/70ths of the sale proceeds. Mr Harvey contended that the £10,000 was not a loan, it was an investment by Supergas. The Special Commissioner held that as Supergas had agreed to make a loan, he had to hold it was a loan. Accordingly, *section 175* applied. This is a harsh decision. There seems

no doubt that Supergas Ltd was obtaining a full commercial consideration for the outlay of its money. In no sense was it providing any benefit
to Mr Harvey. It emphasises that great care needs to be taken if slightly
unusual answers are found to commercial problems, as the Revenue will
not be slow to enforce a tax charge even in circumstances where there is
little doubt that had parliament foreseen them it would not have imposed
a charge. It also emphasises the importance of getting the documents
right.

The official rate

9.4   The official rate is fixed from time to time by the Treasury by
statutory instrument. [*ITEPA 2003, s 181*]. It is arrived at by taking the
average base rates of the main High Street banks, rounding this to the
nearest whole number and adding 1.5 per cent. The rates initially changed
infrequently. In 1997 the Treasury adopted a policy of amending the rate
more often to keep it in line with market interest rates but from January
2000 reverted to changing it infrequently. The rates that have applied from
time to time are as follows:

06.04.1978 – 05.05.1980	9.0%	06.08.1991 – 05.10.1991	11.75%
06.05.1980 – 05.10.1982	15.0%	06.10.1991 – 05.03.1992	11.25%
06.10.1982 – 05.04.1987	12.0%	06.03.1992 – 05.06.1992	10.75%
06.04.1987 – 05.06.1987	11.5%	06.06.1992 – 05.11.1992	10.5%
06.06.1987 – 05.09.1987	10.5%	06.11.1992 – 05.12.1992	9.75%
06.09.1987 – 05.12.1987	11.5%	06.12.1992 – 05.01.1993	9%
06.12.1987 – 05.05.1988	10.5%	06.01.1993 – 05.03.1993	8.25%
06.05.1988 – 05.08.1988	9.5%	06.03.1993 – 05.01.1994	7.75%
06.08.1988 – 05.01.1989	12.0%	06.01.1994 – 05.11.1994	7.5%
06.01.1989 – 05.07.1989	14.5%	06.11.1994 – 05.10.1995	8%
06.07.1989 – 05.11.1989	15.5%	06.10.1995 – 05.02.1996	7.75%
06.11.1989 – 05.11.1990	16.5%	06.02.1996 – 05.06.1996	7.25%
06.11.1990 – 05.03.1991	15.5%	06.06.1996 – 05.11.1996	7.00%
06.03.1991 – 05.04.1991	14.5%	06.11.1996 – 05.08.1997	6.75%
06.04.1991 – 05.05.1991	13.5%	06.08.1997 – 05.03.1999	7.25%
06.05.1991 – 05.07.1991	12.75%	06.03.1999 – 05.01.2002	6.25%
06.07.1991 – 05.08.1991	12.25%	06.01.2002 – to date	5.00%

The Revenue have said that the 5% rate will apply throughout 2004/05,
subject to review in the event of significant rate changes (Press Release
12.1.2004).

9.5   Between 18 August 1989 and January 2000 the rate was supposed to be automatically recalculated each time one of the six main
High Street banks changed its base lending rate. The new rate came into
effect from the 6th of the month following that change (*SI 1989 No
1297*). However, Barclays Bank PLC reduced its base rate on
22 September 1992 (as well as the reduction on 16 October 1992 which

gave rise to the 6 November 1992 reduction in the official rate). Barclays Bank again reduced it on 8 February 1994 and increased it on 7 December 1994, 2 February 1995, 8 March 1996, 6 May 1997 and altered it on various other dates during 1997 to 1999 with none of these changes giving rise to an alteration in the official rate.

9.6   The Revenue announced in January 2000 that in order to simplify record-keeping, valuation and reporting requirements in future, the official rate will be set in advance for the whole of the following tax year and will not be increased during that year even if typical mortgage rates (on which they say it is based) are increased. Accordingly the 5 per cent rate will apply throughout 2004/05. They recognise that 'this policy would need to be reviewed if typical mortgage rates were to fall sharply during a future tax year' (*IR Press Release 25 January 2000*).

9.7   The Treasury are empowered to prescribe a different 'official rate' or rates for foreign currency loans. Such special rates can apply only where both the employee normally lives in the foreign country concerned and he has actually lived there at some time in the six years prior to the year of assessment concerned. [*ITEPA 2003, s 181(2)*]. The Revenue consider that a holiday in the home country would not of itself be sufficient to show that the employee has actually 'lived' there; they consider that living connotes a degree of continuance (*Tax Bulletin, Issue 13, October 1994*). To date they have prescribed rates only for loans in Japanese Yen and Swiss Francs, i.e.:

	Yen	Francs
06.06.1994 – 06.07.1994	3.9%	5.7%
06.07.1994 – to date	3.9%	5.5%

These rates have not changed since 1994.

The employee's family

9.8   These provisions (and those in relation to waivers—see 9.28 below) apply not only to a loan to the employee himself but also to a loan to any relative of his. For this purpose a relative means the employee's spouse, his or his spouse's parents or remoter forebears, his or his spouse's children or remoter issue, his brothers and sisters, brothers or sisters of the employee's spouse, and a spouse of any of the above. [*ITEPA 2003, s 174(6)*]. This definition of relative is far wider than that which applies generally to the benefit in kind provisions.

Meaning of loan

9.9   The Revenue interpret 'loan' very widely. It includes 'any form of credit'. [*ITEPA 2003, s 173(2)(a)*]. However, advances against expenses need not be treated as a loan provided that the maximum amount outstanding does not exceed £1,000, the advances are spent within six months, and the employee accounts to his employer regularly for his expenditure. If any of these conditions are not met it must be treated as a loan. Up to 2002/03 there was no statutory authority for this but the relevant Statement of Practice, SP7/79, has now been codified in *ITEPA 2003, s 179(1)(2)*. The Revenue have power to increase the £1,000 and six months limit in relation to an individual loan on the application of the employer. [*ITEPA 2003, s 179(3)(4)*]. The advance must be for the purpose of paying either necessary expenses (those which the employee is obliged to incur and pay as holder of the employment and are necessarily incurred in the performance of its duties) or incidental overnight expenses (expenses that are incidental to the employee's absence from the place where he normally lives, relate to a continuous period of absence within *section 240* (see 5.41) and would not be deductible as an expense if the employee incurred and paid them [*ITEPA 2003, s 179(1)(5)(6)*]. The inclusion of the word 'not' in *section 179(6)(c)* looks odd. It may be because if the expenses were deductible they would constitute necessary expenses.

9.10   Particular care needs to be taken with partnership service companies, as the case of *Andrew Grant Services Ltd v Walton (1999 STC 330)* demonstrates. Mr Grant and his brother were in partnership as estate agents. Andrew Grant Services Ltd provided services to the partnership in return for a management charge. This was calculated annually by the company's accountants based on the expenses of the service company. The annual fee was the expenses of the company plus a mark-up. Sound familiar? That is how most such service companies operate. The Revenue successfully contended that this was a form of credit. When the partnership consumed services it incurred a liability to pay for them. Such credit was extended from day to day (i.e. even before the service company paid its supplier!) Accordingly, there was a 'loan' from the time the services were consumed until the time the services were paid for. It appears from this that the only way to avoid a *section 175* liability in respect of a partnership service company is to pay for the services in advance! It may be relevant that in this case there was no agreement as to payment. The position may be different if there is an agreement between the partnership and the service company that the company will bill on a specific date.

Exceptions to the charge

9.11   There are a number of exceptions to this tax charge on notional interest.

(*a*)   There is no charge if the amount outstanding on the loan (or the aggregate of all the loans within *section 175*) does not exceed £5,000 at any time in the tax year.

(*b*)   There is also no charge in respect of non-qualifying loans if the £5,000 limit is breached only because of the existence of qualifying loans (all or part of the interest on which is eligible for tax relief either under *section 353* (relief for interest paid), or as a trading expense) and the £5,000 figure would not be exceeded if such loans are ignored. [*ITEPA 2003, s 180*].

Example

John has the following loans outstanding from his employer throughout 1999/00.

(i)   A second mortgage of £20,000 towards the purchase of his principal residence. (John also has a building society mortgage of £25,000.)

(ii) A season ticket loan which has averaged £2,300 during the year. The maximum amount was £4,800 in October 1999 and John is repaying it at the rate of £400 a month.

(iii) A temporary loan of £1,000 made in February 2000 to clear credit card balances.

As loan (i) was a qualifying loan (though it would not be after 5 April 2000) it did not need to be aggregated with loans (ii) and (iii). The highest amount of loan (ii), £4,800 was in October when loan (iii) did not exist. In February 2000 the amount of loan (ii) was £3,600 (£4,800 less three monthly repayments) and loan (iii) was £1,000, a total of £4,600. Accordingly, the *de minimis* exemption applies to loans (ii) and (iii) (but not loan (i)) because there was no point in the year at which the aggregate amount outstanding on the non-qualifying loans exceeded £5,000.

(*c*) If a loan is made for a fixed and unvariable period and at a fixed and unvariable rate of interest, and 'the amount of interest paid on' the loan for the tax year in which it was made 'was equal to or greater than the interest that would have been payable at the official rate for that year', no charge arises merely because the official rate of interest in a subsequent year is higher than the fixed rate (although a charge could arise if, for example, the employee defaults in payment of the interest). [*ITEPA 2003, s 177*]. The words in inverted commas are taken from the legislation, as it appears to be defective. The concept of the relief was to confer exemption where the interest payable is at least equal to interest at the official rate at the time the loan was made. However, the wording seems to assume that the same official rate will apply throughout a year of assessment, which, of course, is not necessarily the case. Furthermore, the relief does not appear to apply at all if no interest was actually paid on the loan in the year it was taken out, e.g. if the interest is payable quarterly and the loan was made on 1 February, no interest would have been payable until 1 May in the following tax year. It may be that the courts would interpret 'paid ... for the year' as allowing one to accrue the interest on a day-to-day basis provided that it is actually paid at some time. If a loan is made at the official rate of interest and that rate increases before the end of the tax year, it will be apparent that the conditions for the relief cannot be met as interest calculated on a day-to-day basis at the official rate must exceed interest at the fixed rate actually applying to the loan.

(*d*)   Where a loan was made before 6 April 1978 (when there was no official rate) but is for a fixed and unvariable period and at a fixed and unvariable rate of interest, no charge will arise if it can be shown that the rate of interest payable is such as could have been expected to apply to a loan on the same terms (other than the rate of interest) made at that time between persons not connected with one another (within *section 839*) dealing at arm's length. [*ICTA 1988, s 161(3)*]. Unlike the exception in head (*c*) above, this rule seems to apply even if no interest is actually paid on the loan, e.g. because the employer opts not to pursue collection.

(*e*)   Where the loan is made not to the employee but to a relative, no tax charge will arise if the employee can show that he personally derived no benefit from it. [*ITEPA 2003, s 174(5)(b)*].

(*f*)   If the employee dies, the charge on notional interest ceases at the date of his death (i.e. the loan is deemed to have been repaid at that date). [*ITEPA 2003, s 190*].

(*g*)   For 1994/95 to 1999/00 there was no charge if at the time the loan was made it was made by the lender in the ordinary course of a business carried on by him which includes the lending of money and

(i)   comparable loans, i.e. loans for the same or similar purposes and on the same terms and conditions, were available to all those who might be expected to avail themselves of the lender's services in the course of its business;

(ii)   a substantial proportion of the comparable loans was made to members of the public at large with whom the lender was dealing at arm's length; and

(iii)   in the year of assessment concerned the employee's loan and the comparable loans made around the same time are held on the same terms, and any changes in the terms imposed since the employee's loan was made were imposed in the ordinary course of the lender's business.

[*ICTA 1988, s 161(1A)(1B)*]. This was intended to exempt mortgages and loans by banks, building societies and other financial institutions where the loan to the employee is made on the same terms as loans to members of the public generally. Whether it achieved this is questionable. Banks do not have a single basis for lending money to all customers as is envisaged in (i). Their terms and the availability of some types of loan, will depend on their assessment of the risk involved so the 'same terms' will not be available to all their customers. Loans are made on the same terms only if the same fees, commissions and other incidental expenses are charged to staff. [*FA 1994, s 88(5)*]. The Revenue stressed that 'the same terms' does not mean 'broadly the same'. A loan did not qualify if the loan-to-income or loan-to-value ratio is relaxed for employees. However, they consider head (ii) above will be satisfied if over 50 per cent of the comparable loans are to the public at large and could be met at a lower figure. They say the public at large means the public in general as opposed to a specific section of the public, but does not require the loans to be available 'to everyone on the Clapham omnibus' (*Tax Bulletin, Issue 12, August 1994*). The question in *West v Crossland (1999 STC 147)* was when is a loan not making a loan. Mr Crossland was an employee of Nationwide Building Society. He took a variable rate mortgage on preferential terms. He accepted that *section 160* applied. In early 1994 he asked the Nationwide to switch his mortgage into a fixcd rate loan on the same terms as were available to the general public and claimed that henceforth the above exemption applied. 'No', said the Revenue, 'at the time it was made the loan was on preferential terms. Those terms have changed; it is still the same loan and the test has to be applied at the time the loan was made'. 'I agree' said Lindsay J. 'Mr Crossland could have avoided the tax charge by repaying the loan and reborrowing on the new terms. The fact that Mr Crossland could so easily have satisfied the provisions . . . does not point to any manifest injustice in the Revenue's requirements that those demarcations apparently required by Parliament, have, indeed to be satisfied.'

(*h*)   For 2000/01 onwards head (*g*) was replaced by an exemption from the charge on notional interest on a loan made on ordinary commercial terms [*ITEPA 2003, s 176*]. For this purpose a loan is made on ordinary commercial terms if it is made by the lender in the ordinary course of a business carried on by him which includes the lending of money or the supplying of goods or services on credit provided that either:

(i)   at the time it was made comparable loans were available to all those who might be expected to avail themselves of the services provided by the lender, a substantial proportion of comparable loans made by the lender at or about the time the loan was made were made to members of the public at large with whom the lender dealt at arm's length, comparable loans generally made to the public at that time are (i.e. at the current time, not when the loan was made) still held on the same terms, and if those terms differ from those applicable immediately after the loan was made the changes were imposed in the ordinary course of the lender's business [*ITEPA 2003, s 176(3)*];

(ii)   if the loan has been varied since it was made but before 6 April 2000, at the time of that variation a substantial proportion of the aggregate of any existing loans were varied around the same time so as to be held on the same terms as the employee's loan after it was varied and any new loans by the lender around that time on the same terms were made to members of the public, a significant number of those loans and the employee's loan are now held on the same terms, and if those terms differ from those applicable immediately after the time of the variation the changes were imposed in the ordinary course of the lender's business [*ITEPA 2003, s 176(5)*]; or

(iii) if the loan has been varied after 5 April 2000, at the time of that variation members of the public that had loans from the lender for similar purposes had a right to vary their loans on the same terms and conditions as the employee, any existing loans so varied are now held on the same terms, if those terms differ from those that applied immediately after the variation the changes were imposed in the ordinary course of the lender's business, and a substantial proportion of the aggregate of the loans varied at around the same time so as to be held on the same terms as the employee's loan after it was varied (and any new loans made by the lender at around that time which are held on those terms) were made to members of the public [*ITEPA 2003, s 176(6)*].

For the purpose of (i) above a loan is comparable to another if it is made for the same or similar purposes and on the same terms and conditions as the loan in question. [*ITEPA 2003, s 176(4)*] In determining whether loans made before 1 June 1994 were made (or are held) on the same terms and conditions, any fees, commission or other incidental expenses incurred by the borrower are ignored [*ITEPA 2003, s 176(8)*]. Similarly, in making the comparison for the purposes of (ii) and (iii) above, payments by a borrower or penalties, interest or similar amounts incurred as a result of varying the loan or on fees, commissions, or other incidental expenses incurred for the purpose of obtaining the loan are ignored to determine whether rights to vary loans are exercisable on the same terms or conditions or loans are held on the same terms. [*ITEPA 2003, s 176(9)*].

(*i*) For 2000/01 onwards there is no charge on notional interest if, had interest been paid, the whole amount would have been either eligible for tax relief under *ICTA 1988, s 353* (relief for interest paid) or deductible in computing the profits of a trade, profession or vocation or of a Schedule A business. [*ITEPA 2003, s 178*]. Between 1994/95 and 1999/2000 such loans were within what is now *section 175* but a corresponding deduction was allowed for the notional interest (see 9.26). This cumbersome procedure was needed because interest on a mortgage on a private residence attracted a reduced relief. The abolition of that relief enables the rules to be simplified.

Calculation of charge

The 'normal' method

9.12 There are two alternate methods of calculating the taxable amount. The first, the 'normal method', is to multiply the average amount outstanding in the year of assessment by the number of whole months during which the loan was outstanding, divide by twelve, and multiply the result by the official rate of interest in force during the period the loan was outstanding. [*ITEPA 2003, s 182*].

9.13 Where a loan was outstanding for the entire year the average rate is:

1989/90		15.67%
1990/91		16.00%
1991/92		11.81%
1992/93		9.75%
1993/94		7.688%
1994/95	(Sterling)	7.70%
	(Sw.Fr.)	5.85%
	(Yen)	4.50%
1995/96		7.79%
1996/97		6.93%
1997/98		7.08%
1998/99		7.16%
1999/00 and 2000/01		6.25%
2001/02		5.937%
2002/03–2004/05		5.00%

The average rate for all of the years from 1995/96 to date for Sw. Fr. loans is 5.5% and for Yen loans 3.9%.

9.14 The average amount outstanding is arrived at by adding the amount of the loan outstanding on 5 April preceding the year of assessment and the amount outstanding on 5 April in the year of assessment and dividing by two, i.e. in most cases, by adding the loan at the beginning of the year and that at the end of the year, and dividing by two. If the loan commenced during the year the balance at the date the loan was made is used in place of that at the preceding 5 April, and if it is fully repaid in the year the balance at the date of such repayment is adopted in place of the balance at the following 5 April. If the amount of the loan varied on one of the two days used, i.e. because the loan was either increased or partly repaid on that day, the highest amount outstanding at any time on the relevant day must be used.

9.15 The number of whole months for which a loan is outstanding means tax months, i.e. months ending on the fifth day of a calendar month, not calendar months or 31-day periods. The average official rate is determined on a day-to-day basis.

Example

Joe is a higher-paid employee, and on 18 July 1996 his employer lent him £15,000. Joe repaid £5,000 on 5 April 1997, £4,000 on 16 June 1997and the balance on 20 October 1997.

1996/97

		£
Loan at 18.07.1996		15,000
Loan at 05.04.1997	—the highest balance on that day	15,000
		30,000
	half thereof	15,000

Complete tax months outstanding
(from 6 August 1996)   8

Official rate in force for period loan
outstanding (262 days)

		%
18.07.96 – 05.11.96	111/262 × 7%	2.966
06.11.96 – 05.04.97	123/262 × 7.75%	3.890
		6.856

Taxable amount £15,000 × 8/12 × 6.856% =   £686

1997/98

		£
Loan at 05.04.1997	— the highest balance on that day (even though the loan was not that high at any time in 1997/98)	15,000
Loan at 20.10.1997	— the highest balance on that day	5,000
		20,000
	half thereof	10,000

Complete tax months outstanding
(to 5 September 1997)   5

Official rate in force for period
loan outstanding (198 days)

		£
06.04.97 – 05.08.97	122/198 × 6.75%	4,159
06.08.97 – 20.10.97	76/198 × 7.25%	2,783
		6,942

Taxable amount £10,000 × 5/12 × 6.942% =   £289

9.16 It will be seen that this is a somewhat rough and ready calculation. Either the taxpayer or the Inspector of Taxes can elect to use 'the alternative method' which is more accurate—but more time-consuming to compute. The election must be made by 31 January following the end of the tax year—so that the employee can use the correct calculation in his tax return. Prior to 1996/97, there was no time limit for the Inspector to exercise this option, apart from the practical one that if the Schedule E assessment is appealed against, the settlement of the appeal (either by agreement or after a hearing) normally determines the taxable amount. If the taxpayer wished to use the alternative method, on the other hand, he had to do so within 30 days after the issue of a notice of assessment using the normal method of calculation (or such later time as the Inspector may allow) or, if no assessment has been raised (or one has been raised but this does not include the notional interest), within six years after the end of the year of assessment. [*ICTA 1988, 7 Schedule 5(1)(2)*].

The 'alternative' method

9.17 The alternative method involves taking each period for which the official rate remains fixed, taking the maximum amount of the loan outstanding on each day in that period, aggregating those figures, dividing by 365, multiplying by the official rate for the period, and adding together the results for each such period in the tax year. [*ITEPA 2003, s 183*].

Example

Using the same facts as the previous example, the calculation under the alternative method is as follows:

1996/97: there are three periods for which the official rate remains fixed and the loan is outstanding.

18.07.96 – 05.11.96	111 days	7%
06.11.96 – 05.04.97	151 days	6.75%

In this example the maximum amount outstanding remained at £15,000 on each day in the period. The calculations are therefore:

	£
£15,000 × (111/8%) days ÷ 365	319.32
£15,000 × (151/6.75%) days ÷ 365	418.87
	738.19

1997/98: there are two periods for which the official rate is fixed and the loan is outstanding.

06.04.97 – 05.08.97	122 days	6.75%
06.08.97 – 20.10.97	76 days	7.25%

The loan was £10,000 from 06.04.97 to 16.06.97 (the highest figure on that day) and £6,000 from 17.06.97 to 20.10.97. The calculation is accordingly:

06.04.97 – 16.06.97	73 days	6.75%
17.06.97 – 05.08.97	49 days	6.75%
06.08.97 – 20.10.97	76 days	7.25%

	£
£10,000 × (73 days × 6.75%) ÷ 365	135.00
£6,000 × (49 days × 6.75%) ÷ 365	54.37
£6,000 × (76 days × 7.25%) ÷ 365	90.58
	279.95

9.18 It will be seen that in this example it is not in the taxpayer's interest to opt to adopt the alternative method in 1996/97 but in 1997/98 in this example it is in the taxpayer's interest to adopt the alternative method.

9.19 If two or more employees are chargeable to tax in respect of the same loan for 2000/01 onwards the cash equivalent must be apportioned between them in a fair and reasonable manner and the part apportioned to each is treated as the cash equivalent of the loan so far as he is concerned [*ITEPA 2003, s 185*].

Payment of interest

9.20 Where interest is actually paid on a loan for a year of assessment it can be deducted from the figure calculated above to determine the taxable amount. [*ITEPA 2003, s 175(3)*]. This is so even if the interest is paid in a subsequent year of assessment. The Revenue take the view that a payment after the end of the tax year can be an amount 'paid on the loan for that year' only if the loan agreement specifically allows the employer to charge interest. It is difficult to see how they can read this requirement into the statutory wording though.

9.21 Up to 5 April 1991 for the purpose of making the above calculations, all the loans between the same lender and borrower for which a cash equivalent fell to be ascertained (i.e. which did not come within any of the exemptions and for which any interest paid was below the official rate) had to be treated as a single loan. [*ICTA 1988, 7 Schedule 3(3)*].

Loan made by reason of employment

9.22 Both for the purpose of the charge on notional interest and the charge on loan waivers, etc. described below, a loan must be regarded as made by reason of a person's employment if either:

(*a*)   it is made by his employer—unless the employer is an individual and the loan can be shown to have been made in the normal course of his domestic, family or personal relationships;

(*b*)   it is made by a company or partnership;

    (i)   over which his employer has control; or

    (ii)   by which his employer (if it is a company) is controlled; or

    (iii)   is controlled by the same person that controls his employer (if it is a company); or

(*c*)   if the employer is (or controls, or is controlled by) a close company, it is made by a person who has a material interest in that company (or the company which controls it)—unless, for 1994/95 onwards, that person is an individual and it can be shown that the loan was made in the normal course of his domestic, family or personal relationships.

[*ITEPA 2003, s 174(2)(5)*].

9.23   For the purpose of determining whether a loan was made by reason of a person's employment a company includes a partnership (but the expression 'close company' does not) and references to the employer include a prospective employer. [*ITEPA 2003, s 174(2)*]. Furthermore, an employer or other person is deemed to have made a loan if either money was lent by someone else and the rights assigned to the employer etc., or the employer etc. arranges, guarantees or in any way facilitates the continuation of a loan already in existence. [*ITEPA 2003, s 174(4), 7 Schedule 2*].

9.24   The Revenue regard a loan by an overseas employer to a foreign employee who comes to work in the UK as within the scope of this provision if it was made at a time when the employee's emoluments were taxable in the UK as employment income, it was made in contemplation of the employee working or living in the UK, or the loan was already in existence before the employee had UK taxable emoluments and the employer facilitated its continuation. They do not regard the employer as facilitating the loan merely because it is conditional on the employment continuing or the employer deducts the interest and repayments from the employee's salary and pays it over to the lender (*Tax Bulletin, Issue 13, October 1994*).

9.25   In applying the provisions on notional interest and on loan waivers, etc. references to a loan must be taken to include any form of credit, and a loan obtained by reason of a person's employment must be taken to include a fresh loan applied directly or indirectly in repaying an earlier loan obtained by reason of the employment. References to making a loan include arranging, guaranteeing or in any way facilitating a loan. [*ITEPA 2003, s 173(2)*].

9.26   In *Grant v Watton* ([*1999*] *STC 330*) it was held that a loan by the employer company to a partnership of which the employee is a member gives rise to a benefit charge on the employee. Furthermore if the arrangement between the company and the partnership provides for services to be provided by the company on the basis of its costs plus a percentage mark-up and those arrangements contain no provisions regarding the date of payments for such services, the company gives credit to the partnership each time it makes a payment to its suppliers, as that payment triggers the right to recover the sum plus the mark-up from the partnership.

Qualification for tax relief

9.27 For 1994/95 to 1999/00 where the loan qualified in whole or part for tax relief the employee was treated as having paid interest on the loan in the same tax year equal to the taxable cash equivalent (although the employer or other lender was not treated as receiving such notional interest). Such notional interest was deemed to be paid on the last day of the tax year or where relevant, the earlier of the date the loan was repaid or the employment ceased. [*ICTA 1988, s 160(1A)(b)*]. This eliminated the need for special rules to exempt from the benefit provisions loans where the interest wholly or partly qualified for tax relief. It also coped with the limitation of mortgage interest relief to 20 per cent for 1994/95, 15 per cent for 1995/96–1997/98 and 10 per cent for 1998/99 and 1999/00, when the relief was abolished. This provision has been retained in the rewrite. [*ITEPA 2003, s 184*]. It is not readily apparent why, as it appears to be spent. Relief is now given under *section 178* (see 9.11(j)).

Example

The tax effect of the loan to John in the example in 9.11(*b*) above is as follows.

	£	£	£
Average amount outstanding	20,000		
Cash equivalent of the loan		1,386	
Tax thereon at 40%	(20,000 × 6.93%)		554
Notional loan interest		1,386	
Qualifying for relief under			
sections 353 and *357*	30,000		
Less building society loan	25,000		
	5,000		
Notional interest thereon			
£5,000/£20,000 × £1,386		346	
Tax relief at 15%			52
Net tax payable			502

Waivers, etc. of the loan

9.28 If a loan to (or to a relative of) a higher-paid employee which was obtained by reason of the employment is released or written off (in whole or in part) the amount written off is taxable as income from the employment in the year it is written off. [*ITEPA 2003, s 188(1)*]. This charge applies not only to a loan within the charge to notional interest but also to one where interest was paid at or above the official rate, or which fell into one of the exceptions given at 9.11 above. If the loan is written off after the employment has ceased, the employment is deemed to have continued in existence so as to trigger the tax charge at the time it is written off. [*ITEPA 2003, s 188(2)*]. This charge cannot be avoided by arranging for a replacement loan to the ex-employee to repay the employment-related one, with the replacement loan being waived or written off. [*ITEPA 2003, s 188(3)*]. As the deemed remuneration from such deemed employment is taxable as earnings it might perhaps be possible to pay real personal pension or retirement annuity payments against it even if the real former employment was a pensionable employment.

Exceptions to the charge

9.29 There are some exceptions to this charge.

(*a*) It does not apply if the loan was made to a relative of the employee and the employee can show that he derived no benefit from it (as such a loan is not an employment-related loan). [*ITEPA 2003, 174(5)(b)*].

(*b*) It does not normally apply if the amount written off is already deemed to be income and chargeable to income tax under some other provision. However, if that other provision is *section 403* (payment of compensation, etc. on termination of employment) so that there is a risk that no tax might actually be paid because of the exemption for the first £30,000 of compensation (see 11.21 below) then the charge under *section 188* will apply. Prior to 2003/04 there was nothing to prevent double taxation—other than the Revenue's goodwill. Any amount taxed under *section 188* could be taxed again under *section 403*. However, the charge under *section 403* is excluded for 2003/04 onwards. [*ITEPA 2003, s 189(2)(b)*]. The exemption from the charge under *section 188* also does not apply where the other provision is *ICTA 1998, s 677* (sums paid to a settlor otherwise than as income) and the tax charge under that section is a future charge—which may never crystallise. In certain circumstances, *section 677* (as extended by *section 678*) treats a loan to a settlor by a company connected with the settlement (one in which the settlement holds shares) as income of the settlor up to the amount of the accumulated income of the settlement. If the loan exceeds such income the excess will cause undistributed income of future years to be regarded as income of the settlor until he has been taxed on the full amount of the loan. If a settlement has no income or no prospect of any (or all its income is distributed as it arises) no charge on the settlor can arise, which is why the Revenue needs to be able to extract tax on a waiver of the loan. If tax is paid under *section 188* there is no exemption from tax under *section 677* in future years so double taxation can result.

(*c*) No charge will be made if the loan is written off or released on or after the death of the taxpayer. [*ITEPA 2003, s 190(2)*].

(*d*) If the loan is released in pursuance of arrangements made with a view to protecting the holder of shares acquired before 6 April 1976 from a fall in their market value no charge will arise. Before the law was altered on that date a popular form of employee incentives was the issue to executives of shares in the company in which they worked, the cost being financed by way of an interest-free loan repayable only when the executive wished to dispose of the shares. Such schemes often contained a provision that if the price of the shares fell, the difference between the amount of the loan and the market value of the shares would be waived so that the executive would not suffer a loss. [*ITEPA 2003, 7 Schedule 25(2)*].

Director's tax paid by employer

9.30   If a payment which attracts tax under PAYE is made to a person employed as a director of a company (but not otherwise), and the employer does not deduct the tax but it is paid to the Revenue by some person other than the director, the amount so paid must be treated as emoluments of the director unless it is made good by him to that other person. [*ITEPA 2003, s 223*, formerly *ICTA 1988, s 164(1)*].

9.31   This is aimed at the situation where the Revenue collect the tax by assessing the company under *Regulation 80* of the *PAYE Regulations*. As this is an assessment on the company the payment of the tax is not settling an obligation of the director—as a *Regulation 80* assessment is a liability of the company—and would not therefore be emoluments of his under general principles. It is also probably not a payment for the director's benefit as it is paid to settle an obligation of the company itself.

9.32   Accordingly, without this special provision the payment could escape tax (and was apparently held by the Commissioners to do so prior to the introduction of this provision) thus enabling the director to extract from the company his gross salary free of tax. By treating the payment as additional remuneration—the tax on which will be collected by the Revenue from the director—the *section* restores the position.

9.33   If the company debits the payment to a director's current account, rather than treating it as a tax liability of the company, the Revenue will normally regard the amount as having been made good by the director so no charge will arise. Strictly speaking, it has probably not been made good until the current account balance has been cleared.

9.34 The *section* does not apply at all to higher-paid employees who are not directors (within the meaning given at 6.9 above) or to a director who does not have a material interest in the company, and is not automatically brought into the higher-paid net simply by virtue of holding the directorship (see 6.7 above). [*ITEPA 2003, s 223(7)*]. It also does not apply to a director if he has died before the tax is paid over to the Inland Revenue. [*ITEPA 2003, s 223(6)*]. If he has ceased to be a director before the tax is paid over the payment must be treated as having been made in the year the employment ceased and will thus form part of the director's income for that year. [*ITEPA 2003, s 223(5)*].

Mobile telephones

9.35 From 1999/00 onwards there is no benefit charge in relation to a mobile telephone being made available (without any transfer of the property in it) to the employee or to a member of his family or household. [*ITEPA 2003, s 319*]. A mobile telephone for this purpose is 'wireless telegraphy apparatus designed or adapted for the purpose of transmitting and receiving spoken messages so as to provide a telephone which is connected to a public telecommunication system (within the meaning of the *Telecommunications Act 1984*) and is not physically connected to a land-line'. It does not include a cordless telephone (i.e. one designed or adapted so as to provide a wireless extension to a telephone and which is used only as such an extension to a telephone that is physically connected to a land-line) or a telepoint telephone (i.e. one used for the purpose of a short-range radio communications service utilising frequencies between 864 and 868 megahertz).

9.36 The exemption extends to a telephone provided in connection with a car, van or other heavier commercial vehicle.

9.37 The exemption applies not only to the provision of the phone but also to the cost of calls (*Hansard, Standing Committee B, col 369*). However it appears that the exemption applies only where the mobile telephone is owned or rented by the employer. If the employee buys his own telephone and charges the cost of calls to the employer a benefit will arise. Care accordingly needs to be taken. If the phone account is in the name of the employee he will be taxable on the full cost of calls.

9.38 Where an employee needs a telephone for business use it is now more attractive to provide him with a mobile phone (completely tax free) than with a fixed one on which he will be taxed on the full rental charge plus the cost of private calls.

9.39 From 1991/92 to 1998/99 a scale charge of £200 applied to the provision of the use of a mobile telephone. [See below and *ICTA 1988, s 159A(1)(2)*]. The benefit for a year of assessment was nil if, in that year, either there was no private use of the telephone or the employee was required to, and did, make good (to the person providing it) the full cost of any private use. [*ICTA 1988, s 159A(3)*]. The 'full cost' was defined as the aggregate of the cost of private calls and any other cost of the benefit provided determined in accordance with *ICTA 1988, s 156(2), (5)–(7)*. The Revenue stated that this means the cost of any private telephone calls and a proper proportion of the cost of hiring the telephone or of 20 per cent per annum of its purchase price if it was owned by the employer. They originally said that there was no need to pay a proportion of the cost of line rental or any other standing charges (*IR Press Release 21 January 1993*) but subsequently stated that this applied only if the purpose of the provision of the telephone was to make it available for business use (*Tax Bulletin, Issue 12, August 1994*). 'Private use' was defined as use of the telephone to make calls other than calls made wholly, exclusively and necessarily in the performance of the duties of the employment. Use of the telephone solely to receive calls will not attract a charge—either under *section 159A* or the general benefit rules—as *section 159A(3)* specifically provided for a benefit of nil. To thwart avoidance the Government provided that the acceptance of a reverse charge call had to be treated as equivalent to making the call! It was difficult to fall within this exemption as the *Act* gave no guidance as to how the cost was to be apportioned between private and business calls and if the employee got the apportionment wrong he suffered the £200 benefit. The Revenue indicated that simply banning the employee from making private calls did not render the telephone unavailable for private use, but nevertheless they would not expect employers to analyse telephone bills to check that no private use has in fact taken place.

9.40   If the telephone was unavailable for private use for part of the year, the £200 figure was reduced accordingly. The meaning of 'unavailable' was the same as is used for cars (see 7.33 above). If different mobile telephones were made available to the employee on different days he was treated as having the same telephone available throughout, but if two or more were made available concurrently each attracted its own benefit charge. [*ICTA 1988, s 159A(2), (4)–(6)*].

9.41   A mobile telephone under the old legislation was one connected to a public telecommunication system but which was not connected to a land-line. It did not, however, include a cordless telephone which was used only as an extension to a telephone which was itself connected to a land-line. Nor did it include a 'telepoint' telephone, i.e. apparatus used for the purpose of a short-range radio communications service utilising frequencies between 864 and 868 megahertz inclusive. It is understood that companies such as Rabbit, Phonepoint and Zone Phone used such frequencies, although as far as the author is aware no such systems are any longer in operation.

Scholarships

9.42   A scholarship provided for a child of an employee (or any other member of his family or household) must be treated as provided by reason of the employee's employment if it is provided under arrangements entered into by his employer or by any person connected with the employer. [*ITEPA 2003, s 212*]. This applies irrespective of whether or not the employer or a connected person contributes directly or indirectly to the cost of providing the scholarship. [*ITEPA 2003, s 212(2)*]. The *section 839* definition of connected persons applies. [*ITEPA 2003, s 718*].

9.43   No benefit will, however, arise in relation to a payment in respect of a scholarship which:

(*a*)   is provided from a trust fund or under a scheme;

(*b*)   is held by a person receiving full-time instruction at a university, college, school or other educational establishment; and

(*c*)   would not be regarded as provided by reason of the employment if *section 201(3)* and *section 212* (which deem any payment, etc. by the employer to have been made by reason of the employment—see 6.42 above) had not been enacted,

provided that in the year it is paid, no more than 25 per cent of the total payments from the fund (or under the scheme) in respect of scholarships held by persons within (*b*) above is attributable to scholarships provided by reason of a person's employment. [*ITEPA 2003, s 213*].

9.44   A scholarship includes an exhibition, bursary or similar educational endowment. An employment includes one where the employee is lower-paid and also an employment not assessable to UK tax which would be so assessable had the employee been resident and ordinarily resident in the UK and all of the duties performed in the UK. [*ITEPA 2003, ss 211(3), 213(7)*]. This definition of employment does not enable the Revenue to assess lower-paid employees or non-residents working overseas; it is needed to ensure that children of such employees are taken into account in determining whether the 25 per cent limit for relevant scholarships is breached. The exemption is intended primarily to cover scholarships provided by a company for children of the general public, or the public in a specified area, where the fact that one of the scholarships is won by a child of an employee is fortuitous.

9.45   *Section 331* (which exempts from income tax income arising from a scholarship held by a person receiving full-time instruction at a university, college, school or other educational establishment) must not be construed so as to confer an exemption from tax under the benefit in kind rules on anyone other than the scholar himself. [*ITEPA 2003, s 215*].

Removal expenses

9.46   A special relief applies to removal expenses, under which up to £8,000 can be paid tax-free to assist an employee with a move. The payment must be paid to the employee or to a third party on his behalf and be in respect of qualifying removal expenses, or must be incurred in the provision of a qualifying removal benefit for the employee or for members of his family or household. [*ITEPA 2003, s 271*]. The expense is ignored for employment income purposes, i.e. it does not create income and an offsetting deduction. [*ITEPA 2003, s 271(1)*]. Where the reimbursed expenses exceed the £8,000 limit, tax on the excess is collectible by direct assessment not under PAYE provided the reimbursement relates to qualifying removal expenses. [*Regulation 4 of the PAYE Regulations*]. See IR leaflet *IR134* (*Income Tax and Relocation Packages*).

9.47   Qualifying removal expenses are 'those' reasonably incurred by the employee in connection with a change of residence and incurred on or before the end of the year of assessment following that in which the trigger event takes place. [*ITEPA 2003, ss 272(3), 274(1)*]. Qualifying removal benefits are benefits meeting the same conditions. The Revenue have power in relation to individual cases to extend the period by another (or more) year of assessment. [*ITEPA 2003, s 274(2)*].

9.48   The change of residence must result from one of the following trigger events:

(*a*)   taking up employment with a new employer;

(*b*)   an alteration of the duties of an existing employment (which probably includes entering into a new employment with the same employer); or

(*c*)   an alteration of the place where the employee normally performs the duties of his employment.

In each case the time of the trigger event is when the employee begins to perform the new duties at the new place, not when he enters into the contract of employment. [*ITEPA 2003, s 273(2)*].

9.49   The change of residence must be made wholly or mainly to allow the employee to have his residence within a reasonable daily travelling distance of the place where he will normally perform his new duties (or the new place where he will perform his existing duties). [*ITEPA 2003, s 273(3)*]. The employee also needs to show that his previous residence was not already within a reasonable daily travelling distance of that place. [*ITEPA 2003, s 273(4)*].

9.50   To qualify as an eligible removal expense, expenditure must fall within one of the heads set out in paragraphs 9.51 to 9.61 below. [*ITEPA 2003, s 272(1)*]. The Treasury have power by *regulations* to add items to these categories (but not to delete items). [*ITEPA 2003, s 286*].

Expenses of disposal

9.51   Where the employee (and/or a member of his family or house-hold) has an interest in his current home and that interest is disposed of (or intended to be disposed of) in consequence of the move.

(*a*)   Legal expenses connected with the disposal of the employee's interest (including in relation to the redemption of a mortgage relating to the residence, i.e. either one for money borrowed to acquire it or one secured on it).

(*b*)   Any early redemption penalty on such a mortgage.

(*c*)   Fees of an estate agent or auctioneer.

(*d*)   Expenses of advertising the intended disposal.

(*e*)   Charges for disconnecting gas, electricity, telephone and other public utilities serving the residence.

(*f*)   Expenses of maintaining, insuring or preserving the security of the residence whilst it is unoccupied pending disposal.

(*g*)   Rent paid in respect of the residence whilst it is unoccupied pending disposal.

[*ITEPA 2003, s 279*].

Expenses of acquisition

9.52   Provided that the employee (and/or members of his family or household) acquires an interest in the new residence.

(*a*)   Legal expenses in connection with the acquisition (including in connection with a loan raised to acquire it).

(*b*)   Procurement fees in relation to a loan to acquire the interest in the new residence.

(*c*)   Mortgage indemnity insurance to protect a lender who lends the whole or a substantial part of the value of the employee's interest in the residence.

(*d*)   Survey or inspection fees in connection with the acquisition.

(*e*)   Land registry fees (or the Northern Ireland equivalent).

(*f*)   Stamp duty.

(*g*)   Connection fees for gas, electricity, telephone and other public utilities.

[*ITEPA 2003, s 277*].

Expenses of abortive acquisition

9.53   Where expenses are incurred with a view to the acquisition of an interest in a residence which would have been the employee's new residence but where the employee (or other potential acquirer) reasonably declined to proceed with the acquisition or was prevented from doing so through circumstances beyond his control. The expense must have fallen within (*a*)–(*g*) in paragraph 9.52 had the acquisition proceeded. [*ITEPA 2003, s 278*].

Expenses of transporting belongings

9.54 Provided they are connected with transporting domestic belongings (of the employee and members of his family or household) from the employee's existing residence to the new one, or are insurance covering such transport. It is not clear whether assets of a hobby or other interest of the taxpayer qualify as domestic, i.e. whether belongings of the employee are automatically 'domestic', or if the test is first, are the items of a domestic nature and, if so, do they belong to the employee or his family or household.

(*a*)   Packing and unpacking.

(*b*)   Temporary storage if a direct move from the old to a new residence is not made (it is not clear what is temporary, it probably does not cover continuing storage where the new residence is too small to take all of the furniture and this is put in store because a further transfer is envisaged at a future date).

(*c*)   Detaching fittings from the old residence—but only if they are to be taken to the new, not if they will be sold or otherwise disposed of.

(*d*)   Attaching fittings at the new residence, and also adapting them if they are brought from the old residence—but not if they are brought from elsewhere such as a second home.

[*ITEPA 2003, s 280*].

Travelling and subsistence

9.55

(*a*)   Travelling and subsistence of the employee and members of his family or household while making temporary visits to the new area (i.e. the area around or near the place where the employee's future duties will normally be performed) for purposes connected with the change of residence.

(*b*)   The employee's costs of travelling between his former residence and the place where he will normally perform his future duties.

(*c*)   Except where he is taking up employment with a new employer, the employee's costs of travelling between his new residence and his original place of work—if he will be employed in the new location by a different group company, consideration ought to be given to his being seconded by the original employer for an initial period.

(*d*)   Costs of the employee's subsistence (i.e. food, drink and temporary living accommodation).

(*e*)   The employee's costs of travelling between his former residence and any temporary living accommodation.

(*f*)   Except where he is taking up employment with a new employer, the employee's costs of travelling, prior to his change of residence, between his new residence and any temporary living accommodation.

(*g*)   Costs of travel of the employee and members of his family or household from his former residence to the new one provided that they are made in connection with the change.

(*h*)   The cost of subsistence of a child under 19 who is a member of the employee's family or household while staying in living accommodation around or near the former residence for the purpose of securing continuity of his education.

(*j*)   Such a child's cost of travelling between that accommodation and the employee's new residence.

(*k*)   The costs of subsistence for such a child while staying in living accommodation around or near the employee's new place of work before the change of residence in order to secure continuity of education. (Subsistence means food, drink and temporary living accommodation; boarding school fees at a school near the new residence for one or two terms may well be 'temporary' if the child will thereafter become a day pupil, but is probably not if the child will continue to board there.)

(*l*)   The costs of travel by such a child between such temporary accommodation in the new locality and the employee's former residence.

[*ITEPA 2003, s 281*].

9.56   **Bridging loan expenses** i.e. interest payable by the employee (and/or members of his family or household) in respect of a loan raised by him wholly or partly because there was a gap between the time of acquisition of the new residence and the disposal of the old. The employee (and/or members of his family or household) must have had an interest in the old residence, dispose of it in consequence of the change of residence, and acquire an interest in the new one. If the new loan exceeds the market value of the interest in the old residence, interest on the excess does not qualify. Nor does interest on any part of the loan used for some purpose other than redeeming a loan on the old residence (i.e. one used to acquire it or for which the residence formed security) or acquiring the new one. [*ITEPA 2003, s 284*].

9.57   **Replacement of domestic goods** i.e. expenditure on the purchase of domestic goods intended to replace items used at the former residence but which are not suitable for use in the new. The employee (and/or members of his family or household) must have had an interest in the old residence, dispose of it in consequence of the move, acquire an interest in the new residence, and incur the expense as a result of the move. Any sale proceeds of the replaced goods must be deducted from the expenditure—although there is no requirement to deduct their market value if they are disposed of otherwise than by sale. [*(ITEPA 2003, s 285]*.

Benefits and expenses do not however fall into this head if they are deductible under *sections 341* (travel at start or finish of overseas employment), *342* (travel between employments), *370–372* (travel costs where duties performed abroad), or *373–375* (travel costs of non-domiciled employees). In other words if an expense can qualify as a deduction under some other provision it does not need to be included in the £8,000 limit. [*ITEPA 2003, s 282*]. Making a car or van available to the employee or members of his family or household for private use by reason of his employment is also excluded from this head (as it attracts a tax charge under other provisions). [*ITEPA 2003, s 283*].

9.58 Broadly speaking, the items that can constitute eligible removal benefits are the same as those in paragraphs 9.51 (disposal costs), 9.52 (acquisition costs), 9.53 (abortive acquisition costs), 9.54 (transport of belongings), 9.55 (travelling and subsistence) and 9.57 (duplicate expenses) above. However, if a car or van would otherwise constitute an eligible facility for travel it cannot do so if it is also available for other private use, i.e. it attracts the normal scale car and van use benefits. Also, if travel expenses already qualify for the special reliefs for overseas travel (see 13.36 and 13.45) those reliefs take precedence and the expense is not to be treated as a removal expense.

9.59 Bridging loan expenses do not have an exact parallel in eligible removal benefits. However, there is a separate relief where a loan is raised by the employee (and/or members of his family or household) in connection with a move that satisfies the conditions in paragraph 9.56 above and *section 175* (beneficial loans, see 9.1) would otherwise apply to the loan. [*ITEPA 2003, s 288*]. For this purpose a loan qualifies if the employee (and/or members of his family or household) had an interest in a former residence, disposed of it in consequence of the move, acquired an interest in the new residence, and raised the loan wholly or partly because of a gap between the acquisition of the new residence and the disposal of the old. [*ITEPA 2003, s 288(2)*]. Relief under *section 288* can be given only to the extent that qualifying removal expenses and qualifying removal benefits together fall short of the £8,000 maximum. [*ITEPA 2003, s 288(1)(3)*]. Where *section 288* applies the beneficial loan rules of *section 175* do not apply to that unrelieved amount for the 'exempted loan discharge period'. The number of days in this period is that produced by the formula:

$$\frac{\text{unrelieved amount} \times 365}{\text{maximum amount of loan} \times \text{official rate}}$$

where: the unrelieved amount is the unrelieved balance of the £8,000;

the maximum amount of the loan is the maximum in the period from making the loan to, normally, the end of the year of assessment following that in which the change of employment occurs; and

the official rate is that in force at the time the loan is actually made.

If the formula produces a fraction it is rounded up. [*ITEPA 2003, ss 288(1)(4), 289*].

Overall limit

9.60 There is an overriding limit of relief on £8,000 for any change of residence. If husband and wife are both employees they can each attract £8,000 of relief on the same move. The Treasury have power to vary this figure. The benefit in kind rules apply for calculating the value of a qualifying removal benefit. [*ITEPA 2003, ss 287, 716(2)(d)*].

Interpretation

9.61 References in paragraphs 9.46 to 9.60 above to a person's residence means his sole or main residence. [*ITEPA 2003, s 276*]. A member of a person's family or household means that person's spouse; son and his spouse; daughter and her spouse; parent; domestic staff; dependant or guest. [*ITEPA 2003, s 721(5)*]. It should be particularly noted that this does not include a 'common law wife' or other 'partner' who is not a spouse, unless such a person can qualify as a dependant or guest—which would probably not be the case if he contributes his share of the running costs of the residence. Nor does it appear to include a mother-in-law or father-in-law unless that person qualifies as a dependant or guest. Subsistence means food, drink and temporary living accommodation. [*ITEPA 2003, s 281(6)*].

Arrangements with relocation companies

9.62 If an employer operates an arrangement under which employees are able to sell their homes to either their employer or a relocation company for its current market value plus a share in any profit made by the relocation company when it resells the house, the profit share is, by concession, treated as covered by the capital gains tax private residence exemption even though it is a separate asset from the house. The house must be sold by the relocation company within three years of the employee's sale to that company. If the employee owns the property jointly with someone else, e.g. his spouse, the concession also applies to the profit share received by that other person (*ESC D37*). The sale to the relocation company must be made under arm's length arrangements set up by the employer and the employee must have to sell his house because he has to move home, for example, on a transfer within the employer's organisation. Where the employee owns the home jointly with others, e.g. with his spouse, the concession also applies to the other joint holders. In addition, the costs borne by the employer or the relocation company will not be assessed as a benefit on the employee (*ESC A85*). This does not apply to any costs of the employee's transfer which would normally be borne by the vendor though.

Provision of meals

9.63   The provision by the employer (but not in theory at least, by a third party such as the employer's holding company) of free or subsidised meals (or light refreshments) in a canteen or on the employer's business premises does not attract a tax charge on the employee provided that:

(*a*)   they are provided on a reasonable scale;

(*b*)   all employees, or all of them at a particular location, can obtain either (or both) a free or subsidised meal or an equivalent meal voucher or token; and

(*c*)   if the meals are provided in the restaurant or dining room of a hotel, catering or similar business at a time when meals are being served to the public, the meals are taken in a part of the restaurant which is designated for the use of employees only.

[*ITEPA 2003, s 317* and *ESC A74* as amended by *FA 2004, 17 Schedule 1*]. Prior to 2004/05 the exemption for meals in a canteen did not require the provision to be on a reasonable scale and did not permit the issue of meal tokens or vouchers. Prior to 2003/04 the exemption applied only where meals were provided for employees generally so did not apply if a business had staff at a number of locations all of which did not include canteen facilities.

9.64   A canteen does not have to be on the employer's premises. The Revenue are sometimes prepared to treat the provision by the employer of meals at a local restaurant as within this exemption if the employer does not have his own canteen and has entered into an arrangement with the restaurateur to provide meals for his staff. The Revenue is unlikely to allow directors—and possibly higher-paid employees—to benefit from this concession, however. The Revenue say that the word 'canteen' has its ordinary meaning.

9.65   Where a company has both a staff canteen and a directors' or executive dining room the Revenue will normally regard the dining room as part of the canteen provided that the lunches are on a reasonable scale. If the two do not share the same kitchen the Revenue might resist this treatment.

Luncheon vouchers

9.66   The Revenue do not tax luncheon vouchers if their value does not exceed 15p per working day. When the concession was introduced an employee could buy a reasonable meal for 15p. Today he would be lucky to get a cup of tea! The vouchers must be non-transferable, used only for meals, and available to lower-paid staff if they are not given to all staff. [*(ITEPA 2003, s 89*, formerly *ESC A2)*].

Training

Work-related training

9.67   No tax liability arises by virtue of the provision for an employee of work-related training or any benefit incidental thereto. [*ITEPA 2003, s 250(1)(a)*]. The exemption applies both where the cost is paid direct by the employer and where it is reimbursed by the employer to the employee. [*ITEPA 2003, s 250(1)*]. Work-related training is any training course or other activity designed to impart, instil, improve or reinforce any knowledge, skills or personal qualities which:

(*a*)   are likely to prove useful to the employee when performing the duties of the employment (or a related employment); or

(*b*)   will qualify, or better qualify, the employee to perform those duties (or to participate in any charitable or voluntary activities that are available to be performed in association with the employment).

[*ITEPA 2003, s 251(1)*].

9.68   A related employment for this purpose is another employment with either the same employer or with a person connected with the employer and which the employee is to hold, has a serious opportunity of holding or can reasonably expect to have such an opportunity to hold so in due course. [*ITEPA 2003, s 251(2)*].

9.69   The exemption also covers the payment of costs which are incidental to the employee undertaking the training, expenses incurred in connection with examinations (or other assessment of what the employee has gained from the training), and the cost of obtaining any qualification, registration or award to which the employee becomes (or may become) entitled as a result of the training or examination. [*ITEPA 2003, s 250(2)*]. It covers travelling and subsistence (which includes food, drink and temporary living accommodation) only to the extent that such expenses would either have qualified for relief under *sections 336* or *337* (see 5.2) or attracted mileage allowance relief (see 7.70) if the employee had undertaken the training as one of the duties of his employment and the employee had incurred and paid the expense. [*ITEPA 2003, s 253*].

9.70   It does not however extend to facilities or other benefits that are provided to the employee:

(*a*)   to enable him to enjoy the facilities or benefits for entertainment or recreational purposes which are unconnected with imparting skills or personal qualities within *section 251*;

(*b*)   to provide him with an inducement to remain in his employment (or to accept a new employment with the same or a related employer) where that inducement is unconnected with imparting such skills or personal qualities; or

(*c*)   to reward the employee for performing duties of his employment or performing them in a particular way.

[*ITEPA 2003, s 253*].

9.71   Nor does it extend to the cost of providing an employee with an asset (or the use of an asset) unless:

(*a*)   it is provided or made available for use only in the course of the training;

(*b*)   it is provided or made available both for such use and for use in the performance of the employee's duties but not for any other use;

(*c*)   it consists of training materials provided in the course of the training; or

(*d*)   it consists of, or is incorporated into, something made by the employee in the course of the training.

[*ITEPA 2003, s 254*].

This is very restrictive. If there is any possibility of the asset being used by the employee for leisure or at home, heads (*a*) and (*b*) cannot apply so a benefit will arise. Training materials means stationery, books or other written material, audio or video tapes, compact discs or floppy disks. [*ICTA 1988, s 200C(7)*]. It will not include, say, a bricklayer's trowel or similar small items. Nor would it include a personal stereo on which to play the training tapes.

Individual learning account training

9.72   From 2000/01 the relief was extended to cover much non-work-related education and training funded by the employer both for employees and ex-employees but only where the individual holds an account that qualifies under *section 104* of the *Learning and Skills Act 2000* or was a party to arrangements qualifying under *sections 104* or *106* of that *Act* (or its Scottish equivalent). [*ITEPA 2003, s 255*]. If an employer incurs expenditure in making a payment to a training provider in respect of the costs of qualifying education or training provided by that person, or pays or reimburses any related costs, such payment will not constitute earnings of the employee or give rise to a benefit on him. [*ITEPA 2003, s 255(1)(2)*].

Retraining courses

9.73   If an employer incurs expenditure in paying for (or reimbursing) expenses incurred in connection with a qualifying training course undertaken by an employee or ex-employee with a view to retraining the employee, the cost is not assessable on that employee. [*Section 588(1)*]. To qualify, a course must:

(*a*)   be designed to impart or improve skills or knowledge relevant to (and intended to be used in the course of) gainful employment or self-employment of any description;

(*b*)   be entirely devoted to the teaching or practical application of these skills and knowledge;

(*c*)   not exceed one year's duration; and

(*d*)   take place wholly within the UK.

[*ITEPA 2003, s 311(1)(3)*].

9.74   The employee must attend the course on a full-time or substantially full-time basis. [*ITEPA 2003, s 311(3)(d)*]. The expenses qualifying for this relief are:

(*a*)   the course fees;

(*b*)   fees for any examination taken during, or at the end of, the course;

(*c*)   the cost of books which are essential for the course; and

(*d*)   such travel expenses as would have been allowable if attendance at the course had been one of the duties of the employment (or, from 2002/03, mileage allowance relief (see 7.70) would have been available).

[*ITEPA 2003, s 311(2)(5)–(7)*].

9.75   The employee must have been employed full-time by the employer for at least two years prior to starting the course (or prior to his ceasing the employment if earlier); the opportunity to take the course must have been available on similar terms to all employees or ex-employees (or all in the same category as the employee concerned); when the employee starts the course his employment must not have ceased more than twelve months earlier, and his employment must cease not later than two years after completing the course (and he must not be re-employed by the same employer within two years). [*ITEPA 2003, s 311(4)*].

9.76   Qualifying education or training for this purpose means training of a kind that qualifies for grants authorised by regulations under *sections*

108 or *109* of the *Learning and Skills Act 2000* (or the corresponding Scottish enactment). The related costs of such training are:

(*a*)   any costs incidental to the employee's undertaking the training which are incurred wholly and exclusively as a result of his doing so;

(*b*)   any expenses incurred in connection with an assessment (by examination or some other means) of what the employee has gained from the training; and

(*c*)   the cost of obtaining for the employee any qualification, registration or award to which he has (or may) become entitled as a result of the training or assessment.

[*ITEPA 2003, s 255(3)*].

9.77   The object of this relief is to encourage the retraining of redundant employees so that they can rejoin the labour market with a skill to facilitate the finding of new employment.

Other courses

9.78   In addition to this statutory relief the Revenue by concession do not tax an employee on the costs (and associated expenses) of an external training course in the UK which is paid for by the employer, provided that the course either:

(*a*)   leads to the acquisition of job-related knowledge or skills; or

(*b*)   is a course of general education for people under 21 of a type commonly undertaken at school (*ESC A63*).

9.79   From 1992/93 to 31 August 2000 any UK resident individual over school-leaving age (and, if under 19, not in full-time education) could claim relief against total income for the costs of a qualifying course of vocational training (other than one taken for leisure purposes). A qualifying course was one accredited as a National Vocational Qualification (prior to 1 January 1994 other than at level five which relates to management skills) by the National Council for Vocational Qualifications or its Scottish equivalent. [*FA 1991, s 32* and *Vocational Training (Tax Relief) Regulations 1992 (SI 1992 No 746)*]. From 6 May 1996, *section 31* also granted relief to a person aged 30 or over for the costs of any other training course that satisfied the conditions of *ICTA 1988, s 589(1)*, required participation on a full-time or substantially full-time basis, and extended for a period which consisted of or included four consecutive weeks. [*FA 1991, s 32* as amended by *FA 1996, s 144*]. *Section 32* was repealed by *FA 1999, s 59(2)* and the *FA 1999, Section 59(3)(b), (Appointed Day) Order 2000 (SI 2000 No 2004)* with effect from 1 September 2000. It was no longer felt necessary following the introduction of Individual Learning Accounts by the *Learning and Skills Act 2000* (see 9.72).

9.80 If the employee paid the costs himself and could not obtain relief under *FA 1999, s 32* he could still deduct these from his remuneration provided that the conditions in 9.79 were met, the course was full-time, it lasted at least four weeks, took place during normal working hours and he continued to receive his full salary (*ESC A64* and *SP4/86*). This concession was withdrawn on 31 August 2000.

Exceptions

9.81 Again the relief does not apply:

(*a*) to the extent that the expenditure is incurred in paying or reimbursing the costs of any facilities or other benefits for the purpose of:

　(i) enabling the employee to enjoy the facilities or benefits for entertainment or recreational purposes or in the course of any leisure activity; or

　(ii) rewarding the employee for the performance of his duties or for the manner in which he has performed them. [*ITEPA 2003, s 258*].

(*b*) to expenditure on reimbursing expenses of travelling or subsistence (including food and drink and temporary living accommodation) unless such expenses would have been deductible under *ITEPA 2003, s 336* or *337* (see 5.3) (or mileage allowance relief (see 7.70) would be available) if the employee had undertaken the training in the performance of the duties of his employment. [*ITEPA 2003, s 257*].

(*c*) to expenditure incurred in paying or reimbursing the cost of providing the employee with (or with the use of) any asset other than:

　(i) one made available for use only in the course of the training;

　(ii) one made available for use both in the course of the training and in the performance of the duties of the employment but not to any significant extent for any other use;

　(iii) one consisting in training materials (which is limited to stationery, books or other written material, audio or video tapes, compact discs and floppy disks) provided in the course of the training; or

　(iv) one consisting in something made by the employee in the course of the training, or incorporated into something so made.

[*ITEPA 2003, s 259, ICTA 1988, s 200F(3)(5)*].

9.82 The employer must also have 'fair opportunity arrangements' in place at the time he incurs the expenditure and the training costs must give effect to such arrangements. These must provide:

(*a*) for the making of contributions by the employer to costs arising from qualifying education or training being undertaken by employees or ex-employees; and (*b*)   for such contributions to be generally available, on similar terms, to all employees.

[*ITEPA 2003, s 260(1)(2)*].

The Treasury have power by regulation to specify the 'employer' of Crown servants for this purpose. [*ITEPA 2003, s 260(3)–(5)*]. They have done so by the *Individual Learning Accounts (Separate Employers Under the Crown) Regulations 2000 (SI 2000 No 2076)* that provides that employment under or for the purposes of a Government Department is to be treated as employment under the organisation concerned (although it is not clear if that organisation is HM Government or the individual Government department) and employment as a member of one of the Armed Forces is to be treated as employment with the particular force concerned.

9.83   In practice the Revenue also do not normally assess the employee on the cost of courses or examinations which are directly related to his work provided that the cost is borne by the employer and he requires the employee to attend the course. In *Clayton v Gothorp (47 TC 168)*, where an employer made a loan to an employee to enable her to take a nine-month training course (to enable her to gain promotion in her job) on terms that it would be waived if the employee served the employer for at least 18 months after the course, the amount waived was held to be taxable as remuneration.

Sporting and recreational facilities

9.84   There is an exemption from income tax in respect of any benefit consisting of a right or opportunity to make use of sporting or other recreational facilities provided by the employer for the use of employees generally. [*ITEPA 2003, s 261(1)–(3)*]. The exemption extends to vouchers which are exchangeable for such a benefit, and covers the provision of the benefit not only to employees but also to other members of their family or household, i.e. their spouse; children and their spouses; parents; servants; dependants and guests. [*ITEPA 2003, s 261(1)*]. A benefit will still arise to the employee if such benefits are provided to his grandchildren, or to his common law spouse or 'partner' unless that person qualifies as a dependant. In practice such benefits were frequently not assessed in earlier years either.

9.85   The relief does not cover:

(*a*)   A benefit consisting of the provision of, or of the use of, any mechanically propelled vehicle. As vehicle includes a ship, boat, aircraft or hovercraft this would normally include a yacht—even a sailing yacht normally uses its engine to get in and out of harbour. It would also seem to cover the use of a golf buggy at the company golf course.

(*b*)   The provision of, or use of, holiday or overnight accommodation, or of accommodation provided in association with a right to make use of such accommodation. This would not impose a benefit in relation to the use of the hotel pool table when attending a training course as the Revenue would regard the use as incidental to the course, not the course as incidental to the pool table, and would not seek to impose a benefit charge under normal rules provided, of course, that they accept that the course is wholly, exclusively and necessarily for the purpose of the employment.

(c)   A facility provided on domestic premises—which includes land belonging to, or enjoyed with, a private dwelling. This seems to discriminate against small companies. If a major company can provide a company billiard room and company swimming pool on its premises without giving rise to a benefit on its employees it is not clear why a benefit should arise if the managing director of a small firm allows his employees to use his personal swimming pool, tennis court or billiard room at his home.

(d)   A facility provided so as to be available to, or for use by, members of the public generally. This will prevent the exemption applying to subscriptions to commercial sports or health clubs. However, it seems to go much further than that. If a company erects a sports complex which it makes available without charge to the local community it is unclear why there should be a benefit on its own employees who use it, whereas if it is not public spirited and limits use to its employees they will cease to be taxable. In practice, it may be that the marginal cost of the employees' usage is nil as the cost is incurred in providing the facility to the public—although the company would argue otherwise, as to obtain tax relief for the cost it may well need to show that use by the public is incidental to the provision for employees.

(e)   A facility which is not used, either wholly or mainly, by people whose right or opportunity to use it derives from employment (whether with the same or with different employers). It derives from employment only if the facility is provided so as to be available generally to employees of a specific employer and the person using it is an employee or ex-employee of his or a member of the employee's family or household. The distinction between (d) and (e) seems to be that (d) excludes facilities provided for the benefit of the general public whereas (e) looks at facilities provided for employees but which in practice are also used by other people. It is not clear how the employer is supposed to monitor the facility's usage; how much public use is necessary to prevent the facility being mainly used by employees, although mainly is normally interpreted as meaning over 50 per cent; or whether mainly refers to the number of people who use the facility or the amount of time it is in use by employees and others respectively. A local amateur Olympic swimming hopeful who is allowed to use the company swimming pool for training is likely to use it far more intensively than any of the employees. Allowing the company sports ground to be used for the local village fête could well bring in a far greater number of non-employees than the company's total workforce.

[*ITEPA 2003, ss 261(4)–(6), 262*].

9.86 The Treasury have power both to limit these exclusions and to further restrict the scope of the exemption. [*ITEPA 2003, s 263*]. Sports facilities probably include sports kit and equipment, e.g. where the firm's football team plays on public pitches, as well as the provision of the pitch itself.

Redundancy, etc. counselling

9.87 Expenditure on the provision of qualifying counselling services to an employee is exempted from tax. [*ITEPA 2003, s 310*]. To qualify:

(*a*) the main purpose of the counselling must be to enable the employee to adjust to the termination of his office or employment, or to help him to find other gainful employment or self-employment, or both;

(*b*) the counselling services must be either:

    (i) giving advice or guidance;

    (ii) imparting or improving skills; or

    (iii) making available the use of office equipment or similar facilities;

(*c*) the employee must have been employed by the employer for at least two years (ending with the earlier of the termination of the employment or the commencement of the counselling);

(*d*) the opportunity to receive counselling on similar terms must be available generally either to all employees or to a particular class of employee—although the Revenue accept that one person can form a class if his job is unique within the company; and

[*ITEPA 2003, s 310(2)–(5)*].

9.88 The exemption extends not only to expenditure on the counselling services themselves (including the reimbursement of counselling fees incurred direct by the employee) but also to the payment or reimbursement of travelling expenses incurred in connection with the services—although only if such travel costs would have been deductible under *ss 336* or *337* (see 5.2) if the receipt of the counselling services had formed part of the duties of the employment and the employment had continued (or from 2002/03 mileage allowance relief (see 7.70) would have been available). [*ITEPA 2003, s 310(6)–(8)*]. The exemption covers counselling provided by a third party, e.g. the employer's holding company, as well as that provided by the employer itself. [*ITEPA 2003, s 310(1)*].

Computer equipment

9.89 For 1999/00 onwards there is a limited exemption where the benefit consists of the provision of computer equipment which is made available (without any transfer of the property in it) to a higher paid employee or a member of his family or household. [*ITEPA 2003, s 320*]. Computer equipment for this purpose includes printers, scanners, modems, discs, and other peripheral devices designed to be used by being connected to or inserted in a computer. [*ITEPA 2003, s 320(7)*]. The exemption does not extend to the cost of access to, or the use of, public telecommunications systems. [*ITEPA 2003, s 320(7)(c)(ii)*]. Accordingly if the computer is used for internet access the charges of the Internet Service Provider (ISP) will be covered but the cost of the telephone company which links the computer to the ISP will not. The logic of this distinction is not readily apparent.

9.90   The computer equipment must be made available under arrangements that do not favour directors of the company. [*ITEPA 2003, s 320(3)*]. If directors are included in the arrangements computer equipment must not be made available to directors (or their families or household) on terms which favour directors. Arrangements are taken to favour directors if, and only if, either under the arrangements the employee is required to be a director or, taking all such arrangements together, the terms on which the equipment is made available are more favourable in some cases where the employee is a director than in one or more cases where he is not. [*ITEPA 2003, s 320(6)*]. Under the original wording the effect seemed to be that the exemption could never apply if the only employees were directors or if, although there were other employees, only directors were provided with computer equipment. The new wording seems to permit relief when the only employees are directors as the person is not 'required' to be a director. Curiously, if both employees and directors are provided with such equipment and a director is offered better terms (such as more expensive equipment) than any one of the other employees covered by the arrangements, it is not only the director who loses the exemption but all of the employees as well.

9.91   The exemption applies only to the first £500 of cash equivalent of the benefit made available in aggregate to an employee and members of his family or household. [*ITEPA 2003, s 320(5)*].

There is no requirement that the computer must be used even partly for business. The idea is to encourage computer literacy generally. Where computer equipment or software is used solely for business it can be excluded in calculating the £500 figure.

9.92   For 2004/05 onwards the exemption also applies where the use of a computer would be taxed under the general employment income charging provision rather than as a benefit, as where the employee has the choice of the use of a computer or extra salary. [*ITEPA 2003, s 320(1)* inserted by *FA 2004, s 79*]. Curiously it appears that in such a case the £500 limit does not apply, although this appears to be unintentional.

Works transport services

9.93   For 1999/00 onwards no benefit charge arises in relation to an employee's use of a works transport service. [*ITEPA 2003, s 242*]. This is a service for conveying employees of one or more employers on qualifying journeys which is provided by means of a bus (a road passenger vehicle with a seating capacity of twelve or more) or, for 2002/03 onwards, a minibus (a vehicle constructed or adapted for the carriage of passengers which has a seating capacity of nine, ten or eleven – but ignoring any seats which do not meet the construction and use requirement of the *Road Traffic Act 1988*). [*ITEPA 2003, s 242*]. A qualifying journey is one between the employee's home and workplace, or between one workplace (any place at which the employee's presence is necessary in the performance of the duties of the employment) and another, which is made in connection with the performance of the employment. [*ITEPA 2003, s 249*]. The idea is to encourage employers to provide works buses for commuting to dissuade employees from driving. The government envisage that small employers could club together to hire a bus but this seems unlikely in practice. The government have said that a qualifying journey will include one that covers only part of the distance between the employee's home and his workplace (*Hansard, Standing Committee B, col 411*).

9.94 The transport service must be available generally to employees of the employer (or employers) concerned and the main use of the service must be for qualifying journeys by those employees. [*ITEPA 2003, s 242(1)(b)(c)*]. The exemption is subject to compliance with the conditions that the service must be used only by the employees for whom it is provided or their infant children (including step children and illegitimate children but only those aged under 18). [*ITEPA 2003, s 242(1)(c)*].

Support for public bus services

9.95 If an employer gives financial or other support to a public transport road service (a public passenger transport service provided by means of a road vehicle) no benefit in kind charge arises for 1999/00 onwards on employees of that employer who happen to use the transport service. [*ITEPA 2003, s 243*]. Most people outside the Inland Revenue would be surprised at the suggestion that a benefit might arise on an employee simply because his employer chooses to subsidise or otherwise support a public bus service. A road vehicle is not defined. It could include a rural post office bus or even, presumably, a cycle rickshaw!

9.96 With the exception for 2002/03 onwards of local bus services, the transport service must not be available on favourable terms to employees of the employer concerned, i.e. they must pay the same fares as members of the general public, and the service must be available generally to employees of the employer concerned (it is hard to see how this condition could not be met if it is a public bus service). [*ITEPA 2003, s 243(4)*]. For 2002/03 onwards, if the transport service is a local bus service as defined in *section 2* of the *TA 1985*, i.e. a local stopping bus service, employees of the employer can receive free or reduced price travel provided of course that the service is available to employees generally.

Cycles

9.97   From 1999/00 some specific exemptions were introduced to encourage cycling. No benefit arises in relation to facilities for parking a cycle provided that the parking space is at or near the employee's place of work. [*ITEPA 2003, s 237*]. In addition, no benefit charge arises in respect of the provision of:

(a)   a cycle (within *s 192(1), Road Traffic Act 1988*, i.e. a bicycle, a tricycle or a cycle having four or more wheels, not being in any case a motor vehicle); or

(b)   cyclists safety equipment

provided that there is no transfer of the property in the cycle or equipment, i.e. provided that ownership remains with the employer (or the employer has contracted to hire the bicycle). [*ITEPA 2003, s 244*]. The benefit or facility in question must be available generally to all employees of the employer concerned and the employee must use the bike mainly for qualifying journeys (i.e. from home to work and between one workplace and another). [*ITEPA 2003, ss 244(4), 249*]. It is not clear how the employer is to check that the bike is used mainly for business as he is obliged to do when he completes the employee's P11D. The answer apparently is that the government expects him to ignore the responsibility that it has placed on him to do so. As the Minister put it 'there is no intention to withdraw the relief if the employee also uses the bike for private or leisure use. Provided that the bike is mainly used for the commuting journey, the tax exemption will remain. By concession, employers will not be expected to check up on their employees' other cycling journeys (*Hansard 6 July 1999, Col 873*).

9.98   If an employee uses his own bike partly for the purposes of his employment he could claim capital allowances on it for 1999/00 to 2001/02 without having to show that he 'necessarily' provided the bike for the purpose of his employment. He could not of course claim full capital allowances; he could only claim the proportion that use of the bike for the purpose of his employment (which did not include home to work travel) bores to total use in the tax year. [*CAA 1990, s 27(2B)* as amended by *FA 1999, s 50(2)*]. This relief ceased at 5 April 2002.

An employee is entitled to a tax-free mileage allowance payment of 20p a mile for business cycling. [*ITEPA 2003, s 230*]. Between 6 April 1999 and 5 April 2002 an employee was entitled to a tax-free mileage rate for business cycling of 12p a mile and if his employer did not make such a payment could claim a deduction for the 12p a mile (or the balance of the allowance if the employer pays him at a lower rate) in calculating his taxable income.

9.99   For 2002/03 onwards there is also an exemption from the benefit in kind charge for cyclists' breakfasts. This is dealt with at 6.41(*w*).

Childcare

9.100 From 2005/06 onwards the limited relief for childcare nurseries described at 6.41(*m*) is replaced by two new reliefs. There is an exemption from tax under the benefit in kind rules where childcare is provided by an employer. [*ICTA 1988, new s 318* inserted by *FA 2004, 13 Schedule 1*]. There is a further exemption for up to £50 a week in respect of payments by the employer in respect of childcare provided by others or of childcare vouchers. [*ICTA 1988, s 318A* inserted by *FA 2004, 13 Schedule 1*].

9.101 In both cases the child must be a child or stepchild of the employee. In the case of childcare provision the child must be either resident with the employee or a person in respect of which the employee has parental responsibility. In the case of vouchers and payments the child must both be resident with the employee and the employee must have parental responsibility. [*ICTA 1988, s 318(3), 318A(3)*].

9.102 A person remains a child for the purpose of these provisions until the last day of the week which contains 1 September following the child's 15th birthday – or 16th if the child is disabled. A child is regarded as disabled if either:

(*a*) a disability living allowance is payable in respect of him (or has ceased to be payable solely because he is receiving free in-patient treatment within the meaning of the *Social Security (Hospital In-Patients) Regulations 1975* and is not serving a sentence imposed by a court in a prison or youth custody institution);

(*b*) he is registered as blind by a local authority under *National Assistance Act 1948* (welfare services) *s 29* or the corresponding Scottish or Northern Irish provisions;

(*c*) he was formerly registered blind but has ceased to be so registered within the previous 26 weeks.

[*ICTA 1988, s 318B(2)–(4)*].

9.103 Parental responsibility means all of the rights duties, powers, responsibilities and authority which by law a parent of a child has in relation to the child and the child's property. [*ICTA 1988, s 318(5)*]. It is clear from the context however that 'all' is not to be read literally, i.e. that relief will be due even if the parental authority is shared with the other parent [*ICTA 1988, s 318B(5)*]. In both cases childcare means any form of care or supervised activity that is not provided in the course of the child's compulsory education [*ICTA 1988, s 318B(1)*].

9.104 The relief for employer provided childcare is unlimited. However, it applies only if

(*a*) the premises on which the care is provided are not used wholly or mainly as a private dwelling;

(*b*)   any applicable registration requirement under the *Children Act 1989, Part 10A* (or the Scottish or Northern Irish equivalents) is met;

(*c*)   the premises on which the care is provided is either made available by the scheme employee or in the case of 'partnership arrangements' by one or more of the partners;

(*d*)   the childcare scheme is open to the scheme employer's employees generally (or generally to those of its employees at a particular location); and

(*e*)   the employee to whom the childcare is provided is either an employee of the scheme employer or is an employee working at the same location as those employees of the scheme employer to whom the scheme is open.

[*ICTA 1988, s 318(3)–(8)*].

9.105   If the qualifying conditions are met in relation to part only of the costs the exemption applies to that part. [*ICTA 1988, s 318(2)*]. Partnership arrangements exist where childcare is provided under arrangements made by two or more persons (including the scheme employer), the premises on which the care is provided are made available by one or more of those persons, and under the arrangements the scheme employer is wholly or partly responsible for financing and managing the provision of the care. [*ICTA 1988, s 318(7)*].

9.106   The exemption is aimed at creches and workplace nurseries – although the nursery does not have to be on the employer's premises. Partnership arrangements allow a group of neighbouring employees either to jointly set up a creche or for other employers to contribute to the cost of one employer's creche in return for it looking after children of the contributors' employees. However, as all of the users of the creche must be employees of someone, it probably does not permit an employer to enter into an arrangement with a nearby commercial creche. Head 9.104(*e*) will cover not only partnership arrangements but also cases where an employer allows his creche to be used by neighbouring employers without requiring a contribution from them. The requirement that all the employees must work at the same location is an odd one. It seems to severely limit the scope for partnership arrangements. For example, two businesses adjacent to one another are clearly in the same location but it seems doubtful if two businesses half a mile from each other can meet this test.

9.107   One snag with a workplace creche is that parents who commute do not necessarily wish to subject their young children to the delights of rush hour travel. They would prefer to use a childcare facility near where they live. The £50 a week relief helps in such cases – although £50 will not purchase much care.

9.108   The conditions that must be met (in addition to that at 9.102) are:

(*a*)   that the care is qualifying childcare; and

(*b*)   that it is provided under a scheme that is open either to the employer's employees generally or generally to those at a particular location.

[*ITEPA 2003, s 318A(4)(5)*]. It should also be noted that the childcare must be 'provided' by the employer [*ITEPA 2003, s 318A(1)*]. In other words, the contract with the nursery must be entered into by the employer. The relief does not apply if the employer merely reimburses the employee for payments by the employee or even makes a direct payment to the nursery if the contract is between the nursery and the employee. An employer contemplating using this relief ought to take legal advice on his liability, if any, if an employee's child is injured at the nursery. An employer who does not wish to undertake such a responsibility should use childcare vouchers (see 9.113) as these can be used to settle a liability entered into by the employee.

9.109   Qualifying childcare means registered or approved care, i.e. it must be provided either by:

(*a*)   a person registered under the *Children Act 1989, Part 10A*;

(*b*)   a school or establishment that is exempt from registration under *paras 1* or *2* of *Schedule 9A* to that *Act*;

(*c*)   a school or school premises (or by a local authority) out of school hours if the child is eight or over;

(*d*)   a childcare provider approved by an accredited organisation (within the *Tax Credit (New Category of Child Care Provider) Regulations 1999*;

(*e*)   a childcare provider approved in accordance with the *Tax Credits (Approval of Home Child Care Providers) Scheme 2003* if the child care is provided wholly or mainly in the child's home;

(*f*)   a domicilary care worker under the *Domicilary Care Agency Regulations 2002* [*ITEPA 2003, s 318C(1)(2)(3)*].

Heads (*e*) and (*f*) do not apply in Wales. The definition is different in Scotland and Northern Ireland, which have different child care laws. The rules there can be found in *ITEPA 2003, s 318C(4)(5)*. Care provided for a child outside the UK qualifies only if it is provided by a child care provider approved by an organisation accredited under the *Tax Credit (New Category of Child Care Provider) Regulations 2002* [*ITEPA 2003, s 318C(6)*].

9.110   However, the exemption does not apply to child care which is either:

(*a*)   provided by the partner (i.e. one of a married or unmarried couple) of the employee; or

(*b*)   provided by a relative of the child (parent, grandparent, aunt, uncle, brother or sister, whether by blood, half blood or marriage) if the care is provided wholly or mainly in the child's home or the home of the person having parental responsibility for the child

even if that person is a registered or approved carer. *[ITEPA 2003, s 318C(7)(8)]*.

9.111   The exempt amount is £50 for each qualifying week. A qualifying week is a tax week in which qualifying care is provided for a child. An employee is only entitled to one exempt payment, i.e. £50 per week, even if care is provided for more than one child. However, if both husband and wife is employed each can receive £50 even if there is only one child. *[ITEPA 2003, s 318C(6)–(8)]*. If the payment in a week exceeds £50, the first £50 is exempt and the balance is taxable as a benefit. *[ITEPA 2003, s 318A(1)]*. If there are several payments some of which meet the qualifying conditions and some of which do not the exemption will be given for the qualifying payments (up to the £50 limit). *[ITEPA 2003, s 318A(2)]*.

9.112   The Treasury have power to vary the £50 figure by statutory instrument. They can similarly amend the qualifying conditions under both *sections 318* and *318A* as appears to them to be appropriate having regard to the corresponding regulations relating to the child care element of working tax credit.

9.113   As mentioned earlier there is also an exemption of up to £50 a week for child care vouchers. *[ITEPA 2003, s 270A inserted by FA 2004, 13 Schedule 3]*. The qualifying conditions are identical to those under *section 318A*. A childcare voucher is a non-cash voucher, stamp or similar document or token intended to enable a person to obtain the provision of care for a child (whether or not in exchange for it). *[ITEPA 2003, s 84(2A) inserted by FA 2004, 13 Schedule 2]*.

9.114   An employee is obviously not entitled both to exempt child care provision under *section 318A* and exempt vouchers under *section 270A* in the same week.

Miscellaneous

9.115   Other benefits that an employer might consider are as follows.

(a)   *Health insurance*: The cost of BUPA, PPP, etc. premiums paid by the employer is taxable on the employee (unless he is lower-paid). The employer can normally obtain the cover cheaper than the employee himself through group scheme discounts, so this is a popular benefit. There is also an incidental benefit to the employer that an employee who is taken ill may be able to obtain the treatment quicker at a time convenient to him and the employer, and in a private room where he can be available for consultation by other staff.

(*b*)   *Death in service life assurance*: This will not give rise to a benefit in kind charge even if the policy is written in favour of the employee's spouse or dependants. [*ITEPA 2003, s 307*]. In practice, no charge will be made even if the nominated beneficiary is not strictly a dependant (*ESC A72*).

(*c*)   *Permanent health insurance or serious illness insurance*: Whilst the premium is taxable on the employee, the employer can often buy the cover more cheaply, as a group scheme can benefit from the spread of risk that it provides.

(*d*)   *Professional subscriptions*: No benefit in kind charge arises if the employee pays on the employer's behalf a subscription that would qualify for tax relief under *ITEPA 2003, s 343* (see 5.78 above) if it were paid by the employee.

(*e*)   *Private minibus or coach*: Unless the works transport exemption (see 9.93) applies, a benefit in kind will arise on higher-paid employees if the employer provides a bus or coach to collect staff near their houses and bring them to and from work. However, the cost is likely to be well below the cost of equivalent public transport and the non-monetary benefit of avoiding changes of trains, etc. and avoiding the rush hour crush can be significant.

(*f*)   *Foreign travel*: If there is a business need for someone to take a trip abroad it may not always matter who goes. Accordingly, there might be scope for spreading this perk around the staff or for awarding the assignment to a specific employee who could derive an incidental benefit from it, e.g. if someone has to visit Australia to pay a goodwill visit to the company's agents there the employee with relatives there could be chosen, or the one who has long expressed a desire to visit Australia, so he can take a few days holiday (at his own expense) while he is in Australia.

(*g*)   *Secondment to overseas branches*: Many staff like the concept of spending some months working overseas. If there is a need to second someone to an overseas office should it be such a person? There is no cost of providing such benefits, as the fare and accommodation has to be incurred for the business need that gives rise to the secondment. The incidental benefit can be very valuable to the employee but, because it has no cost and no money's worth, will not give rise to a tax charge on him.

(*h*)   *Flexible hours*: Many people value being able to choose—within limits, of course—the hours they work. If the business is such that they can be given this choice without disrupting the business, this can provide a significant benefit, but again with no cost or money's worth. A problem is that in most organisations it is difficult to allow senior staff this flexibility.

(*j*)   *Longer holidays*: Extra holidays are very important to some people and can accordingly be used to motivate them—particularly if the extra time has to be earned by meeting specific targets. It needs to be borne in mind that giving time off has a cost in lost productivity, unless, of course, it is given in recognition of increased productivity or the employee is not working at full capacity throughout the year, e.g. in a seasonal business extra time off in the off-season may have little or no real cost.

(*k*) *'No questions asked expense allowance'*: Although such an allowance is taxable on the employee as emoluments it can have a morale-boosting effect as it can be seen as a recognition that an employee is thought responsible enough to be expected to incur some business expenditure on his own initiative, and can make it easier for the employee to claim tax relief for business-related expenditure that he chooses to incur but does not feel able to ask his employer to reimburse.

(*l*) *Staff discounts on the employer's own goods, etc.*: The tax charge on higher-paid employees is the marginal cost, which will often be very low (*Pepper v Hart [1992] STC 898*). The Revenue accept that there is no benefit if the price paid is at least wholesale price. However, in most cases there should be no benefit (or a fairly nominal one) even if the price paid is significantly below that figure. Customs and Excise used to contend that VAT was due on the retail price of the goods where an employee had a contractual entitlement to the discount under his employment contract but now accept that it is only the price actually paid that attracts VAT (*Business Brief 8/92*).

(*m*) *Other staff discounts*: The employer may be in a position to negotiate significant discounts for his staff with suppliers and others—particularly if he is willing to give their staff discounts in return. There is little or no cost to the employer in providing such benefits.

(*n*) *Directors' indemnity insurance*: This does not normally give rise to a tax charge for 1995/96 onwards. The detailed rules are considered at 5.95–5.98.

(*o*) *Medical check-ups*: The provision of routine health checks or medical screening for employees does not confer a chargeable benefit and does not need to be included on form P11D whether the check-ups are carried out in house or by an outside firm. This contrasts with a payment by the employer for an employee's medical treatment or for diagnosis, where a benefit does arise (*Tax Bulletin, Issue 7*).

(*p*) *Free legal, financial or tax advice*: Although the employee will be taxable on the cost of such advice the employer will normally be able to negotiate special terms from his own accountant or solicitor to provide advice to his staff—particularly if this is provided on the employer's premises and there is a reasonable number of people involved so the professional adviser can obtain the benefit of economies of scale.

(*q*) *Use of office facilities*: If an employee is involved in outside interests, such as charities or community organisations, he may value being allowed to handle correspondence for such private activities from his office using the firm's photocopier, telephone, typing facilities, etc. Although in theory he is taxable on the cost this is likely to be negligible. The real benefit lies in the ability to handle such correspondence, etc. during working hours when it can often be done more effectively.

(r) *Use of other facilities*: In some types of business employees may be able to benefit from using the business facilities in 'down' time, e.g. a recording engineer may welcome the chance to use his employer's recording studio for personal projects when it is not booked by customers.

(s) *Christmas parties*: No tax is payable by an employee in relation to expenditure by his employer on a Christmas party or other annual function which is available to employees generally or available generally to those at a particular location provided that the cost per head of the party or function does not exceed £150 (£75 up to 2002/03). If two or more functions are provided in a tax year and the total exceeds £150 but the aggregate of two or more does not, the cost of those functions is not taxed but that of other functions is. The cost per head includes VAT and transport or accommodation incidentally provided for persons attending the party (whether or not they are employees). [*ITEPA 2003, s 264*, formerly *ESC A70*]. It should be noted that the £150 is a *de minimis* figure, i.e. if the cost is £151 a head the entire £101 will be taxable. If expenditure is near the limit it should be carefully monitored to ensure that the £150 figure is not accidentally breached because of 'no shows' at a function for one reason or another.

(t) No income tax liability arises from 2003/04 onwards on:

   (a) the provision for the employee of overnight accommodation at or near the employee's permanent workplace (or a payment to the employee to reimburse such an expense); or

   (b) the provision for the employee of transport for the purpose of ordinary commuting (or travel between two places that is for practical purposes substantially ordinary commuting) (or the reimbursement of such an expense).

where a strike or other industrial action disrupts a public transport service normally used by the employee. [*ITEPA 2003, s 345*]. This replaces a concession (*ESC A58*) under which the Revenue did not tax the provision of travel or accommation and subsistence during a period when public transport was disrupted due to industrial action.

There is also an exemption from 2003/04 for the provision or transport (or the payment or reimbursement of the expense) where the journey is from the employee's workplace to his home and either:

   (a) the journey is made when the employee is required to work later than usual and until at least 9pm, such occasions occur irregularly, by the time the employee ceases work either public transport home is no longer available or it would not be

251

reasonable to expect the employee to use it, and the transport is by taxi or similar private road transport; or

(b)   the employee regularly travels to work in a car with one or more other employees of the same employer under arrangements for the sharing of the car with them and the journey is made on an occasion when the employee is unable to use the car because of unforeseen and exceptional circumstances.

This exemption applies only to the first 60 journeys in the tax year. [*ITEPA 2003, s 248*]. It replaces a previous concession (*ESC A66*) which had applied to late night working for many years and was extended to the breakdown of car sharing arrangements from 6 April 1999. Apparently, the Revenue consider that where a supermarket manager is called out in the middle of the night because of the burglar alarm being triggered the taxi fare to the supermarket is taxable but the return fare is exempt under (a) above (*Taxline*, September 1994, item 108). For the purpose of (b) unforeseen circumstances include where the employee travels home at the same time but cannot travel in the shared car, e.g. he has to use a taxi as he needs to take home with him files or computer equipment and there is insufficient room in the car for that equipment. It will not cover a case where inability to travel home in the shared car could reasonably have been anticipated. Nor curiously will it cover a journey from home to office, such as where the car breaks down and the employee needs to be in the office for an important meeting.

(u)   *Disabled employees*: There is also an exemption from 2003/04 onwards for the provision of transport for a disabled employee (or the payment or reimbursement of expenses incurred on such transport) where that transport is for the purpose of ordinary commuting (or travel between two places that is for practical purposes substantially ordinary commuting). A disabled employee for this purpose is one who has a physical or mental impairment with a substantial and long-term adverse effect on the employee's ability to carry out normal day to day activities. [*ITEPA 2003, s 246*]. *Section 246* does not apply to the provision of the use of a car. Instead no car use or petrol benefit will apply (and there will be no benefit in respect of the payment or reimbursement of expenses incurred in connection with the car) provided that:

(a)   the car has been adapted for the employee's special needs (or it has automatic transmission if the disability means that the employee can only drive such a car);

(b)   the car is made available on terms prohibiting its use otherwise than for business travel, ordinary commuting (or substantially ordinary commuting) or travel to a place that would be covered by one of the training exemptions (see 9.67); and

(c)   in the tax year concerned the car is only used in accordance with those terms.

[*ITEPA 2003, s 247*]. These provisions replace a prior concession, *ESC A59*, which exempted home to work transport for disabled employees.

(v) *Suggestion scheme award*: No tax charge arises in relation to certain awards under suggestion schemes. The scheme must be open on the same terms to employees of the employer generally (or to a particular description of them), the suggestion must relate to the activities carried on by the employer, the employee must not have been reasonably expected to have made the suggestion in the course of his duties (having regard to his experience) and the suggestion must not be made at a meeting held for the purpose of proposing suggestions. [*ITEPA 2003, s 321*]. In the case of an encouragement award (i.e. one made for a suggestion with intrinsic merit or showing special effort) any excess over £25 is taxable. In relation to a financial benefit award (i.e. one for a suggestion relating to an improvement in efficiency or effectiveness which the employer has decided to adopt and reasonably expects will result in a financial benefit) the reward is exempt, subject to a cap of £5,000, if it does not exceed the greater of:

  (a) 50% of the financial benefit reasonably expected to result from the adoption of the suggestion for the first year after its adoption; or

  (b) 10% of the financial benefit reasonably expected to result for the first five years after its adoption.

If two or more awards are made on the same occasion for the same suggestion the maximum exempt amount is apportioned between them in proportion to their awards. If two or more awards for the suggestion are made to the same person on different occasions the limit is applied on a cumulative basis. [*ITEPA 2003, s 322*]. This replaces an earlier concession (*ESC A57*).

(w) *Long service awards*: No tax liability arises from 2003/04 in respect of a long service award (i.e. one to mark at least 20 years' service with the same employer) provided that:

  (a) it takes the form of either tangible moveable property, shares in the employer company (or another company in the same 51% group) or the provision of a benefit other than cash, a cash voucher, a credit token, securities, shares other than in the employer company, or an interest in or rights over securities or shares (including in the employer company); and

  (b) the chargeable amount does not exceed £50 for each year of service in respect of which the award is made (£20 for payments before 6 April 2004).

[*ITEPA 2003, s 323(1)–(3)*]. If the amount exceeds the limit at (b) only the excess is taxable. The exemption does not apply if a prior award was made to the same employee within the previous 10 years. Service with two or more employers can be aggregated if one is a successor to the other or both are or have been in the same group or in the same group as a predecessor or successor of the other. [*ITEPA 2003, s 323(2)(4)(5)*]. This replaces a previous concession (*ESC A22*). The taxability of award is, in any event, questionable. It was held in *Ball v Johnson 47 TC 155* that a cash award made by a bank to employees who passed their banking examination did not constitute emoluments of the employment. However, the Revenue consider that *Wicks v Firth 56 TC 318* has over-ruled this case as far as higher-paid employees are concerned. It is not clear how they have reached this conclusion!

9.116   No tax charge arises on employees in relation to the cost of an annual party or similar annual function provided for an employer's employees which is available to them generally (or available generally to those at a particular location). [*ITEPA 2003, s 264(1)*]. The cost of the function must not exceed £75 per head. This is arrived at by dividing the total cost of providing the function (including VAT and transport or accommodation incidentally provided for persons attending it) by the total number of attendees. [*ITEPA 2003, s 264(2)(4)*]. If there is more than one function in a year the £75 test applies to the aggregate cost. [*ITEPA 2003, s 264(3)*]. *Section 264* replaces from 6 April 2003 a previous concession, *ESC A70*. The limit was £50 a head up to 1994/95.

9.117   The Revenue consider that if an employee receives commission (from his employment) in respect of his or her own insurance policy such commission is taxable remuneration, not a reduction in the cost of the policy. If he does not take the commission but requests, or allows, it to be invested for his or her benefit (e.g. to augment the policy) the commission that could have been taken is an emolument. If the employee is never entitled to commission but the employer forgoes commission due to him and it is used to augment the employee's policy, the value of such augmentation may not be an emolument. If the employee pays a net discounted insurance premium to his employer the amount of the discount is a benefit. If the benefit obtained by the employee is available to members of the general public on the same basis the Revenue accept that no benefit arises (*SP 5/95*).

9.118   Although not a benefit that most employers are in a position to provide it should be mentioned for completeness that there is an exemption from income tax for 2003/04 onwards for the provision of coal or smokeless fuel or an allowance paid in lieu of such provision if the employee is a colliery worker and the amount of coal or fuel provided (or in respect of which the allowance is paid) does not substantially exceed the amount reasonably required for personal use. Curiously, it is for the Revenue to prove that it exceeds such an amount, not for the taxpayer to show that it does not. A colliery worker for this purpose is a coal miner or any other person employed at or about a colliery otherwise than in clerical, administrative or technical work. [*ITEPA 2003, s 306*]. This replaces an earlier concession (*ESC A6*).

Chapter 10

Pension Provision

Introduction

10.1 To encourage saving towards one's retirement, tax relief is given for payments by both an employer and his employees to provide for pensions and other retirement benefits for employees. This pension provision obviously has to be in accordance with an approved scheme and there are limits on the contributions that can qualify for tax relief. A new system of tax relief for pension contributions is being introduced from 6 April 2006. This will replace the whole of the current rules outlined in this Chapter. The primary legislation is contained in the *Finance Act 2004* but much of the detail will be fleshed out by regulation, so the legislation is not yet complete. A summary of the new rules is given at 10.65 onwards.

Types of pension scheme

10.2 There are two distinct types of approved arrangements, occupational pension schemes (retirement benefit schemes) and personal pensions. Prior to July 1988, when the personal pension rules were introduced, pension provision could be made by way of approved retirement annuities. Although new retirement annuity contracts cannot now be taken out, contributions can continue to be made to those in force at 1 July 1988 (provided that the contract terms so permit). The retirement annuity rules are similar to those which apply to personal pensions. In many respects retirement annuities are more attractive than personal pensions and an employee who has the ability to contribute to either is normally better advised to make further contributions to his retirement annuity plan.

10.3 From April 2001 the new stakeholder pension schemes introduced by the *Welfare Reform and Pensions Act 1999* came into being. For tax purposes these are a form of personal pension and operate under the personal pension scheme rules. That Act also introduced greater interchangeability between defined contribution (i.e. money purchase) occupational pension schemes and personal pensions.

Individual Pension Accounts

10.4 *ICTA 1988, s 638A* gives the Revenue power to prescribe restrictions on approval of pension arrangements. They have used this power to permit the use of Individual Pension Accounts from 6 April 2001.

[Personal Pension Scheme (Restriction on Discretion to Approve)
(Permitted Investments) Regulations 2001, SI 2001 No 117]. This is a
form of self-administered personal pension. The funds must be held by a
trustee manager or administrator not by the individual. It can invest only
in authorised unit trusts, shares in qualifying EEA open-ended investment
companies, units in UCITS formed under the laws of another EC country, shares in a qualifying UK (or EEA) investment company, shares in
an investment company with variable capital, and government and public
securities. It is also possible to have a self-invested personal pension
scheme with wider investment powers.

10.5   It is also possible to provide for a pension by way of an unapproved scheme. However, the employee is chargeable to income tax on
contributions made by his employer to an unapproved pension fund.
[ITEPA 2003, s 386(1)]. Accordingly, such schemes are far less attractive
than approved schemes. There is, however, often a role for them where
the maximum contributions have already been made to an approved
scheme. Unapproved schemes are considered at 10.56 *et seq*. If such a
payment relates to more than one employee it is apportioned between
them in the proportion that the cost of providing the benefits to a single
employee bears to the aggregate cost of providing the benefits separately
for all of the employees concerned. *[ITEPA 2003, s 388]. Section 386*
does not apply if the actual earnings from the employment are taxable on
a remittance basis (or from 2004/05 onwards not taxable at all) in the
year that the pension scheme contribution is paid, or if the employee is
non-UK domiciled, employed by a foreign employer and the Revenue
accept that the pension scheme corresponds to an approved scheme.
[ITEPA 2003, ss 389, 390 as amended by *FA 2004, 17 Schedule 2]*.

10.6   This chapter looks at pension provision from the viewpoint of
the employer and employee only. The detailed rules relating to the operation of a pension scheme itself are outside the scope of this book and are
not considered here. It should be mentioned, however, that all three types
of approved pension fund (four if stakeholder pensions are regarded as
different from personal pensions) are exempt from tax on investment
income (although not on any trading income that they may generate) and
capital gains. Contributions towards retirement via such funds ought
therefore to be capable of producing a far higher return than the investment of the funds by the employee himself out of taxed income. To the
extent that a taxpayer invests via an Individual Savings Account (ISA),
he ought to be able to match or beat the growth in an approved pension
scheme as an ISA is itself a tax-free fund, the investment policy of which
can (in theory at least) be better matched to the needs of the individual.

Occupational pensions

10.7   The Inland Revenue must approve a retirement benefit scheme,
and thus enable the scheme itself to qualify for tax exemption and confer

tax relief for qualifying contributions by both employer and employee, if the scheme meets the ten specified conditions set out in *section 590*. These conditions are not repeated here as, in practice, very few schemes are approved under *ICTA 1988, s 590*. The conditions are very stringent and the benefits that can be provided are poor. If the employer is an investment company the Inland Revenue will not generally approve a retirement benefit scheme under their discretionary powers described below and, accordingly, if pension provision is to be made for employees of such a company by way of an occupational pension scheme this can only be done by way of a scheme under *section 590*.

Discretionary power of Inland Revenue

10.8   The Inland Revenue have discretionary power to approve a retirement benefit scheme even though it does not comply with the requirements of *section 590*. [*ICTA 1988, s 591*]. They can attach such conditions to the approval as they think fit. The vast majority of occupational pension schemes are set up with approval under *section 591*. The Inland Revenue have laid down detailed guidelines as to how they will normally exercise this discretion in their *Booklet IR12*. Since 6 April 2001 they can approve different parts of a single scheme under the retirement benefit and personal pension legislation and approve a split of a scheme into a number of sub-schemes. The scheme will have to make clear for each member to which part of the scheme he belongs. [*ICTA 1988, s 611*]. This will give employers greater flexibility.

10.9   *ICTA 1988, s 591(6)* enables the Board to make regulations (by statutory instrument) to limit their own discretionary powers. Where such regulations are made (other than if they relate only to the benefits provided by the scheme), existing schemes must amend their rules within the following three years so that they would be eligible for approval as a new scheme—but need not dispose of any prohibited investments held at the time the regulations are made. [*ICTA 1988, s 591A*]. The Board made regulations under this provision on 15 July 1991 in relation to small self-administered schemes (see 10.19 below) and on 3 December 1993 to restrict payment of refunds from schemes to which an employee pays additional voluntary contributions. [*Retirement Benefit Schemes (Restriction on Discretion to Approve) (Additional Voluntary Contributions) Regulations 1993 (SI 1993 No 3016)*].

10.10   From 10 May 2000 the approval or continued approval of a retirement benefits scheme is dependent on the inclusion of the statutory rules for pension sharing on divorce. [*FA 1999, 10 Schedule 2,3 (b)*]. Pension sharing itself came into effect from 1 December 2000. From that date a court can order a pension entitlement to be split between the spouses. The amount allocated to the non-earner can either be earmarked within the scheme or transferred to a different scheme. In most cases the earner is not be able rebuild his pension to counter the funds transferred.

Maximum benefits

10.11   The Revenue stipulate that the maximum benefits that can be provided by the pension scheme are, in general, the following.

(*a*)   A pension of two-thirds of the employee's final salary. If the scheme was set up after 13 March 1989 (or if the individual employee became a member of the scheme after 31 May 1989) approved pension provision cannot be made in relation to an employee's earnings in excess of £102,000 per annum (£60,000 up to 5 April 1990, £64,800 to 5 April 1991, £71,400 to 5 April 1992, £75,000 to 5 April 1993 and 1994, £76,800 to 5 April 1995, £78,600 to 5 April 1996, £82,200 to 5 April 1997, £84,000 to 5 April 1998, £87,600 to 5 April 1999, £90,600 to 5 April 2000, £91,800 to 5 April 2001, £95,400 to 5 April 2002, £97,200 to 5 April 2003 and £99,000 to 5 April 2004). [*FA 1989, 6 Sch 20*]. Accordingly, the maximum permitted pension for such a person is £66,000 per annum. This maximum can only be paid if the employee has at least 20 years' service with the employer company.

The employee's final salary can be either:

(i)   the employee's basic salary for one of the five years preceding his normal retirement age plus an average over a suitable period (generally three years) ending on the last day of that selected year of fluctuating pay such as commission and bonuses; or

(ii)   the average of the employee's total earnings over a period of three or more consecutive years ending within the ten years prior to his normal retirement age.

A director who controls 20 per cent or more of the employer company must adopt method (ii). The actual earnings figures can be increased in line with the retail prices index before this average is calculated. Special rules apply where a person ceases employment before normal retirement age. Earnings for this purpose excludes compensation and ex gratia payments taxable under *ITEPA 2003, s 401* and amounts taxable as income from employment which arise from the acquisition or disposal of shares (or an interest in shares) or from a right to acquire shares. [*ICTA 1988, s 612(1)*]. The Revenue apparently consider that compensation paid for the loss of rights due to cancellation of a share option scheme is not excluded from being remuneration by this provision—except possibly if the scheme is cancelled specifically to boost pensionable earnings. (*Taxline, January 1995, Item 20*).

(*b*)   An addition to the pension to take account of cost of living increases. This can either be a fixed increase of 3 per cent per annum compound, the actual increase in the retail prices index (but not more than 8 per cent per annum), or a discretionary increase not exceeding the rise in the retail prices index since the pension started to be paid.

(*c*)   A widow's pension equal to two-thirds of the employee's own pension, i.e. four-ninths of his final salary.

(*d*)   A lump sum payment if the employee dies whilst employed by the company, of four times his salary.

Commutation of lump sum

10.12   Part of the pension can be 'commuted' to a lump sum on retirement, i.e. the employee can elect to take a tax-free lump sum on retirement and a reduced pension. If the money in the pension scheme is insufficient to pay the maximum lump sum the whole fund could be withdrawn tax free, i.e. there is no need to restrict the lump sum to enable any minimum amount of pension to remain payable. The maximum lump sum is 1½ times the employee's final salary but limited to £148,500, i.e. 1½ times £99,000. Forty years' service with the employer is needed to be able to take such a sum. For shorter periods of employment the lump sum is the greater of ³⁄₈₀ of final salary for each year of service or 2¼ times the pension that would otherwise be payable for the first year. These limits are the maximum permissible. The pension scheme itself can provide lower limits if it wishes to do so.

10.13   Different—generally more generous—limits apply to pension schemes set up before 14 March 1989 (if the employee joined the scheme before 1 July 1989).

Retirement age

10.14   An employee's normal retirement age is any age that the employee may select between 50 and 75. An earlier retirement age may be allowed for people in certain occupations (scc 10.52). Obviously the lower the retirement age selected, the lower an employee's pension is likely to be as it will be payable for a longer period. Similarly, the maximum benefits can only be drawn if the pension fund has sufficient assets.

It is nevertheless often sensible to select as low a retirement age as possible. Retirement can be deferred to increase the size of the pension if the individual does not wish to retire when he reaches the selected age. If a high age is initially selected and the individual wishes to cease working earlier he will either have to wait until he reaches the selected retirement age before he can draw his pension or take early retirement, which will normally result in a restricted pension. Also, the earlier the retirement age the higher the contributions that the employer will be permitted to pay into the scheme—but if retirement is deferred there may not be scope for further contributions after the selected retirement age has been reached.

Employer's contributions

10.15   The contributions that an employer can make into an occupational pension scheme are limited only by reference to actuarial valuations. In other words, the scheme's actuary determines (on the basis of criteria laid down by the Inland Revenue) what contributions are necessary to generate at the employee's normal retirement age a fund of sufficient size to provide the pension benefits to which he is entitled. This will depend on the employee's age, his length of service up to normal retirement age, the normal retirement age selected, the benefits to which the employee will be entitled under the scheme on reaching normal retirement age, and the existing size of the pension fund. The actuary must revalue the assets in the fund—and revise the maximum contribution levels—periodically. This is usually done every three years. For a person in his forties with little or no previous pension provision the maximum contribution can be very high—often 80 per cent to 100 per cent of the employee's salary or even higher. Most employers do not make the maximum permissible contribution to occupational pension schemes.

Employee's contributions

10.16 The employee can himself contribute up to 15 per cent of his salary towards his occupational pension—assuming that the scheme rules permit this. However, there is no requirement for the employee to contribute anything. The Inland Revenue have power to permit higher contributions but are unlikely to do so. The Inland Revenue generally require contributions by employees to be regular and to continue for at least five years.

Additional voluntary contributions

10.17 If the scheme rules do not permit contributions from the employee, or if the employee does not wish to contribute to his employer's retirement benefit scheme, the employee can augment his pension from his employer's scheme by making contributions to a different pension provider. Such contributions—free-standing AVCs (additional voluntary contributions)—are subject to the overriding limit that the total contributions payable by the employee are limited to 15 per cent of his salary. Where an employee pays free-standing AVCs the limit on benefits set out at 10.11 above is applied to the aggregate pension. This is achieved by providing that the employee's entitlement under his AVC scheme must be deducted from the maximum benefit otherwise payable under the employer's scheme. No part of the pension under the AVC scheme can be commuted into a lump sum. If a pension scheme becomes over-funded, i.e. the value of its assets exceeds the amount that the actuary calculates is needed to meet the pension benefits, the excess must be refunded to the company. If the employer is prepared to make the maximum possible contributions there is little point in the employee contributing anything, either to the employer's scheme or as free-standing AVCs, as such contributions will reduce the amount that the employer can contribute (or cause the scheme to become over-funded). There is one advantage to the employee contributing, namely if he dies while still in the employment, his contributions (plus interest) can be repaid in addition to the normal four-times salary death in service benefit, but this is not normally a major benefit.

Small self-administered pension schemes

10.18   An occupational pension scheme normally takes the form of a trust. This can be set up by the company itself or can be part of an insurance company fund. Where annual contributions are likely to exceed around £10,000 per annum (some people put the cut-off point as low as £5,000), it is worth considering using a small self-administered pension scheme (SSAS). This has all the tax benefits of an insurance company administered scheme (although it is subject to closer scrutiny by the Inland Revenue) but the investment policy can be in the hands of the employee himself. In general, properly managed, this is likely to enable the fund to grow at a faster rate, partly because the investment policy can be geared specifically to the employee's anticipated retirement date, and partly because the employee could well be prepared to accept a greater degree of risk than an insurance company.

10.19   *The Retirement Benefits Schemes (Restriction on Discretion to Approve) (Small Self-administered Schemes) Regulations 1991 (SI 1991 No 1614)* prohibit the Revenue approving a small self-administered pension scheme unless it is the only such scheme in which the employer participates, the administrator has agreed in writing to notify the Revenue within 90 days of certain types of transaction and the trust deed prohibits the trustees from:

(*a*)   borrowing in excess of three times the ordinary annual contribution paid by the employer plus three times the contractual annual contributions of employees plus 45 per cent of the market value of the scheme's investments (*Regulation 4*);

(*b*)   investing in personal chattels (other than *choses in action*), residential property (other than property to be occupied by an employee who is not connected with his employer and is required as a condition of his employment to occupy it, or property occupied by a person who is neither a scheme member or connected with one and which is occupied in connection with the occupation of business premises held by the trustees, e.g. a caretaker's flat), or shares in a private company which carries more than 30 per cent of the voting power or entitles the holder to more than 30 per cent of any dividends declared by the company (*Regulation 5*);

(*c*)   lending money (even on arm's length terms) to a scheme member or a connected person of a member (other than to the employer itself) (*Regulation 6*);

(*d*)   lending money to the employer unless the loan is necessary for the purposes of the employer's business, it is for a fixed term, at a commercial rate of interest, evidenced by a written agreement, and contains a provision for immediate repayment if the employer breaches the agreement, ceases to carry on business or becomes insolvent (*Regulation 6*);

(*e*)   making loans to the employer and investments in shares in the employer which, at the time the loan is made, exceed in aggregate:

(i)   when the loan is made within two years of the establishment of the scheme, 25 per cent of the market value of the assets of the scheme derived from contributions made by the employer and employees (this appears to mean gross assets);

(ii)   when the loan is made more than two years after the establishment of the scheme, 50 per cent of the market value of all the assets of the scheme (*Regulation 7*);

(*f*)   directly or indirectly buying or selling property from or to a scheme member or a connected person of a member (other than the employer itself) (*Regulation 8(1)(a)*); or

(*g*)   directly or indirectly buying or selling property from or to the employer without first obtaining independent professional advice in writing and acting in accordance with such advice (*Regulation 8(1)(b)*).

The reference to the employer in heads (*e*) and (*f*) above appears to prohibit loans to and transactions with a subsidiary or associated company of the employer. A scheme in existence at 15 July 1991 had to amend its rules by 14 July 1994 to introduce these prohibitions or its approval lapsed. [*ICTA 1988, s 591A(2)*]. Accordingly, the above rules now apply to all SSASs. These *regulations* codify the Revenue's previous practice.

In applying the limit in head (*e*) any portion of scheme funds notionally underpinning retired members (and their prospective widowers/widows), ex-spouses', widowers'/widows' or dependants' benefits in payment where the purchase of an annuity has been deferred must be ignored (PSO Update 143, March 2003). For the purpose of head (*d*) the fixed term must be realistic; it is not acceptable for a series of short-term loans to be made when in reality it is intended that the loan should be outstanding for several years. The Revenue will not question whether an interest rate is commercial if it is at least bank base rate plus 3%. The Revenue say that the commerciality of a loan may be in doubt if the borrower is currently in arrears on an earlier loan or on rent due to the SSAS or has at any time defaulted on an earlier loan (PSO Update 143, March 2003).

10.20   *The Retirement Benefits Schemes (Restriction on Discretion to Approve) (Small Self-Administered Schemes) (Amendment) Regulations 1998 (SI 1998 No 728)* further restricts the 45 per cent element of the borrowing limit from 7 April 1998 to 45 per cent of the amount that results from deducting from the market value of the scheme assets (other than any franking pensions in payment) at the time of the loan the aggregate of any sums borrowed to purchase those assets and other scheme liabilities. It also restricts the limit on an investment in an unquoted company to 30 per cent of the shares of any one class. It however relaxes the prohibition on investing in residential property to allow investments in ground rents and rent charges.

Payments to employees

10.21   The payment of pension is of course income taxable on the employee as pension income. [*ITEPA 2003, ss 567, 580*]. A tax charge can also arise on other payments to an employee out of an approved scheme in two circumstances. The first is under *ITEPA 2003, s 623* where a payment is made to or for the benefit of an employee in pursuance of a duty to return surplus funds. Normally, the duty is to return such funds to the employer. A payment to the employee can however arise in relation to additional voluntary contributions (AVCs). The administrator of the scheme is taxable under Case VI of Schedule D at the relevant rate on the grossed up amount of the payment. The relevant rate was initially 35 per cent but was reduced to 32 per cent in respect of payments after 5 April 2000 by the *Income Tax (Charge to Tax) (Payments out of Surplus Funds) (Relevant Rate) Order 2000 (SI 2000 No 600)*. The grossed up amount is regarded as income of the employee (taxable under Case VI) but he cannot claim repayment of any part of the 32 per cent. [*ITEPA 2003, s 624*].

10.22   The second is under *ITEPA 2003, s 583* which imposes an income tax charge as pension income on unauthorised payments to or for the benefit of an employee (or an ex-spouse). If the payment (or any transfer of assets or other transfer of money's worth) is not expressly authorised by the rules of the scheme, the employee (or the ex-spouse if she receives the payment) is taxable on the amount as if it were employment income for the year of assessment in which the payment was made. The sort of payments that might trigger a charge under *section 583* are a refund of contributions on the discontinuance of a scheme, the payment in cash of the full proceeds of an insurance policy on withdrawal from service and transfers of funds to an unapproved scheme (*PSO Manual 17.2.31*). There has been a great deal of concern in recent years that the Revenue are applying *section 583* where an individual ceases full-time employment with the company but continues as a non-executive director or in a different role to that which he previously held. The Revenue used to treat the cessation of the full-time job as 'retirement' but has changed its view and now requires the individual to cease working for the company. It is likely that a number of such cases will come before the courts.

10.23   The first to have done so is *Venables v Hornby* [*2004*] *STC 84*. Mr Venables was a director and substantial shareholder in Ven Holdings Ltd. He 'retired' from the company at the end of June 1994 aged 53. Thereafter he spent most of his time in Florida. However he remained an unpaid non-executive director of the company. The family would telephone him from time to time to seek advice on a wide range of company issues. However, he ceased to attend the company's offices or to visit its building sites as he had done before June 1994. The trustees had discretion to award an immediate pension to a member of the scheme 'who retires in normal health at or after the age of 50'. The trustees duly opted to pay Mr Venables his full pension, part of which he commuted, as he was entitled to do, for a lump sum of approximately £580,000. In June 1994 Mr Venables was not in the best of health but that was not the reason for his retirement. The Revenue contended that as Mr Venables remained a non-executive director he was still an employee and so could not have retired. The Special Commissioner thought it fallacious to argue that because the term 'employee' includes someone who is a director, any non-executive director had not retired from whatever he was doing as an executive director. He pointed out that *section 583* does not refer to retirement but to payments not authorised by the rules of the pension scheme. If as a matter of fact the taxpayer had retired when he received the payment, the circumstances of having a non-executive directorship cannot alter the fact of his retirement as an employee and executive of the company. However, he upheld the assessment on Mr Venables as he considered that he was not 'in normal health' in June 1994 and accordingly the conditions for the exercise of the trustees' discretion did not operate. Fortunately, for Mr Venables the House of Lords disagreed. It felt that 'in normal health' was not intended as a condition but merely as words of exposition (i.e. a member who retires (even in normal health) at or after the age of 50). They went on to hold on the facts that 'given the hours he worked before June 1994 and the extent of his duties as a director of a small family company, it is far-fetched to attribute his remuneration to his office rather than his employment'. Accordingly, as the pension contributions related to his employment, not his office, and he had ceased to hold that employment he had 'retired' in the context of the pension scheme trust deed at the time he received the payment, so it was not taxable on him.

10.24   It is reassuring to see the House of Lords confirm that there is a distinction between what a person does as a director and what he does in some other capacity. The Revenue sometimes seek to contend that if a person is a director of a company he cannot provide services to the company as a sole trader. This is clearly wrong. All that a director is statutorily required to do is comply with his obligations under the *Companies Acts*. He is not required to provide executive services. The company is free to determine from whom it wishes to purchase services. This case reinforces the view that if it decides to purchase them from the director in a different capacity that does not make the cost of such services earnings from the directorship.

Withdrawal of approval

10.25   If an approved company pension scheme ceases to meet the conditions for approval the Revenue can withdraw approval retrospectively, but only as far back as the date when the facts ceased to warrant approval. [*ICTA 1988, s 591B(1)*]. In some cases this was exploited by SSASs, the trustees deliberately breaching the rules and then treating the fund as an ordinary trust, but retaining the benefit of the past tax relief. To prevent this, where approval of a company pension scheme is withdrawn, tax at 40 per cent is now chargeable on the value of the fund at the date of its withdrawal. The tax is payable by the administrator. This charge does not apply only to SSASs. It applies to any scheme with less than twelve members at the date approval is withdrawn and to any larger scheme of which a person who is (or had been) a controlling director is a member, or was a member at any time in the twelve months prior to the withdrawal of approval. [*ICTA 1988, s 591C*]. No tax charge will apply if the reason that a scheme ceases to be approved as a retirement benefit scheme is that it has been converted to a group personal pension scheme in accordance with *ICTA 1988, s 631A* and *23ZA Schedule*. [*ICTA 1988, s 591C(2)*]. *Schedule 23ZA* allows a money purchase occupational scheme to change to a group personal pension scheme. Such a change is irreversible. It was inserted with effect from 2001/02 by *FA 2000, 13 Schedule 7, 27*. The capital gains tax rules in *TCGA 1992, s 272* apply for valuing the assets with the exception that a loan to any scheme employer, former scheme employee, company connected with a scheme (or former scheme) employer, member or person connected with a member, must be valued at face value (plus any unpaid interest); it cannot be reduced to market value if less. [*ICTA 1988, s 591D(1)–(3)*]. This could result in the tax charge exceeding the fund's assets if a former scheme employer has become insolvent and a 'loan-back' had been made to it. The trustees are personally liable for the tax, with the exception that a person approved by the Revenue to act as a trustee of the scheme (which is probably limited to a pensioner trustee of an SSAS, or an insurance company or similar pension provider) is not liable provided he is not a connected person of one of the other trustees, a scheme member or a contributing employer. In *R v IRC, ex p Roux Waterside Inn Ltd [1997] STC 781* an artificial arrangement was entered into under which a pension scheme transferred the bulk of its assets to a new scheme with Revenue approval and steps were taken to prevent the second scheme attracting approval. The Revenue withdrew their approval of the old scheme retrospectively to the day before the transfer to the new. It was held that they were entitled to do so even though there was a beneficiary of the old scheme whose benefits were not transferred and who would suffer from the withdrawal.

10.26   This charge is in addition to any charge under *ITEPA 2003, s 394* (see 10.61) on the distribution of the scheme assets to the beneficiaries and does not affect the amount of that charge. [*ICTA 1988, s 591D(6)*]. However, the CGT base cost of the assets within the trust is uplifted to the value on which tax was charged under *ICTA 1988, s 591C*. [*TCGA 1992, s 239A*]. It must be stressed that the *ICTA 1988, s 591C* charge is on the total assets of the fund, not merely on its unrealised gains and untaxed income.

Personal pensions

10.27   A personal pension scheme must be established by an approved pension provider—an insurance company, bank, building society and certain other financial institutions. The only benefits that it can provide are the following.

(*a*)   The payment of an annuity (a pension) to the employee. This must be payable by an authorised insurance company (not necessarily the one that established the personal pension scheme) and must normally commence between the employee's 50th and 75th birthdays. It must not be capable of assignment or surrender and must be for the life of the employee—although it can be payable for a minimum term of not more than ten years instead of ceasing on the death of the employee. [*ICTA 1988, ss 633(1)(a), 634*]. The annuity can be taken before age 50 in the event of incapacity or if the occupation is one in which the Revenue are satisfied it is customary to retire before that age. The approved early retirement ages of which the author is aware are set out in 10.52. From 1 May 1995 income can be drawn from the fund and the purchase of the annuity deferred, but not beyond age 75 (see 10.28).

(*b*)   The payment of a lump sum in commutation of part of the annuity if the employee so elects. The lump sum must be taken before the annuity or any income withdrawal (see 10.28) commences and must not exceed 25 per cent of the amount of the pension fund. The right to the lump sum must not be capable of being assigned or surrendered. [*ICTA 1988, s 633(1)(b), 635*].

(*c*)   The payment after the employee's death of an annuity (or income withdrawals) to his spouse or dependants. This annuity must be payable by an authorised insurance company and must not exceed the employee's own pension (or, if he dies before pensionable age, what that pension would have been if an annuity had been purchased on the day before his death). It must normally be payable for the life of the annuitant but can cease on the annuitant's marriage. An annuity payable to the surviving spouse can be deferred until that spouse's 60th birthday (or, if later, until the expiration of any fixed term for which the employee's own pension was payable) or can cease before the spouse's death if she is under 45 when the employee dies and there are infant children who will all reach 18 before the spouse's 45th birthday. If the annuity is payable to a dependant under 18 it must cease on the dependant reaching 18 or, if later, ceasing full-time education. Any annuity can incorporate a minimum fixed term of up to ten years. The annuity must not be capable of being assigned or surrendered. [*ICTA 1988, ss 633(1)(c), 636*].

(*d*)   The payment (by an authorised insurance company) of a lump sum on the employee's death before the age of 75. The pension scheme cannot pay any annuity (to either the employee before his death or to his dependants) in addition to such a lump sum. The lump sum cannot exceed the return of contributions together with interest or bonuses thereon and allowing for any previous income withdrawals (see 10.23). If the fund consists of units in a unit trust scheme the lump sum can equal the sale proceeds of the units. [*ICTA 1988, ss 633(1)(d), 637*]. From 1 May 1995 if the member's death occurs after the employee's normal pension date (in which case he will probably have been taking income withdrawals, as otherwise he would have deferred his pension date), the lump sum must be payable within two years of the death. A lump sum cannot be drawn if the surviving spouse has elected to defer taking an annuity (see (c) above). [*ICTA 1988, s 637A*]. From 29 April 1996 if the surviving spouse takes income withdrawals (see 10.28) and dies before the annuity is purchased the funds remaining can pass as a lump sum to her heirs even though the death is outside the two-year period. [*ICTA 1988, s 637A*].

(e) Up to 2000/01 the scheme could incorporate insurance against a risk relating to the non-payment of contributions. [*ICTA 1988, s 633(2)*]. Waiver of premiums insurance is not permitted from 2001/02. [*FA 2000, 13 Schedule 9*].

(f) From 2001/02 shares which an employee has acquired under an approved SAYE option scheme (see 16.35) or which has been appropriated to him under an approved profit sharing scheme (see 16.35) can be transferred as a non-monetary contribution into a personal pension scheme at their market value. The transfer must take place within 90 days of the employee receiving the shares. [*ICTA 1988, s 638*].

10.28 From 1 May 1995, if the scheme permits it, where a scheme member elects to defer the purchase of an annuity, he can take income withdrawals from the scheme. These cannot start earlier than the member's normal retirement date nor extend beyond his 75th birthday. The annual income withdrawals do not have to be fixed amounts but must exceed a statutory minimum. For the three years from the member's normal retirement date the annual minimum is 35 per cent of the annual annuity that could have been purchased for him on his normal retirement date. For the next three years it must not be less than 35 per cent or greater than 100 per cent of the annuity that could have been purchased on the third anniversary of the retirement date, and so on. The income withdrawals in any one year cannot exceed the annuity that could have been purchased. [*ICTA 1988, s 634A*]. Where the member elects to take a lump sum he must do so at normal retirement date, i.e. before he takes any income withdrawals; he cannot defer the decision until the purchase of the annuity. [*FA 1995, 11 Sch 5*]. The employee's spouse or dependants can also elect to take income withdrawals after his death (but not after the earlier of age 75 or the date the employee would have become 75). If the surviving spouse is under 60 and elects to defer the purchase of an annuity until age 60 this will debar him/her from making income withdrawals. The 35 per cent and 100 per cent limits set out above also apply to income withdrawals by a spouse or dependant, but, of course, based on the spouse's annuity entitlement not the deceased employee's. [*ICTA 1988, s 636A*]. Once a member starts to take income withdrawals the scheme cannot accept further contributions or make a transfer payment to a different scheme. [*ICTA 1988, s 638(7A)*].

10.29   From 2001/02 a single income withdrawal review date can be fixed for all of an individual's personal pension arrangements. There is a 60-day window preceding each three-yearly valuation period in which to make the decision. [*ICTA 1988, s 634A*]. Schemes started before 1 October 2000 will need to amend their rules to permit this. It is a requirement of policies taken out after that date. From the same date it has been possible to buy two or more annuities with the fund instead of a single one. [*ICTA 1988, s 634A*]. This also applies to annuities under *ICTA 1988, s 636A*. [*ICTA 1988, s 636A*].

10.30   It will be seen that personal pensions differ from occupational pensions in that there is no limit on the size of the annuity or the lump sum. This is because the Inland Revenue's control over personal pensions is not achieved by limiting what can come out of the fund but rather by restricting the contributions that go into it.

Allowable contributions

10.31   Contributions to a personal pension scheme can be made by either the employer or the employee or both. If the employee opts out of the state earnings-related pension scheme contributions to the personal pension fund will also be made by the state. The maximum contribution in any year of assessment is the allowable percentage of the employee's 'net relevant earnings' (see 10.46 below) for that year.

Employee's age at beginning of the year of assessment	Allowable percentage
up to 35	17½
36–45	20
46–50	25
51–55	30
56–60	35
61 or over	40

Contributions by the employer are not of course treated as emoluments of the employee. [*ITEPA 2003, s 308*].

10.32   However, contributions cannot be paid in relation to any excess of net relevant earnings over £102,000 (£60,000 before 6 April 1990, £64,800 for 1990/91, £71,400 for 1991/92, £75,000 for 1992/93 and 1993/94, £76,800 for 1994/95, £78,600 for 1995/96, £82,200 for 1996/97, £84,000 for 1997/98, £87,600 for 1998/99, £90,600 for 1999/00, £91,800 for 2000/01, £95,400 for 2001/02, £97,200 for 2002/03 and £99,000 for

2003/04). If a person has more than one personal pension scheme this limit applies to the aggregate payments under all such schemes.

Lump sum on death

10.33   Not more than 10 per cent of the aggregate pension contributions (5 per cent of net relevant earnings before 2001/02) can be used to provide a lump sum on death (within (*d*) at 10.27 above). The 10 per cent limit applies whatever the age of the employee. [*ICTA 1988, s 640(3)*].

Carry back of contributions

10.34   Prior to 2001/02 if the contributions by the employee in any of the prior six years were less than the allowable percentage for that year, further contributions equal to that unused relief could be paid. These qualified for tax relief in the year of payment, not that in which the earnings arose. Where such contributions were paid in excess of the limit for the current year they were set against earnings for the earliest possible year in the six-year period. [*ICTA 1988, s 642*]. This carry forward relief ceased at 5 April 2001, i.e. unused relief cannot be carried forward into 2001/02 or subsequent years. [*FA 2000, 13 Schedule 13*].

Tax relief

10.35   Tax relief is given for the full amount of an employee's contribution to a personal pension scheme. However, it can be deducted only from his relevant earnings for the year of assessment in which the payment is made. [*ICTA 1988, s 639(1)*]. Accordingly, even where there is unused relief for earlier years, there is an overriding limitation on premiums payable equal to the amount of the employee's relevant earnings for that year.

10.36   An election can be made (within three months after the end of the year in which the contribution is paid) to treat all or a specified part of a contribution paid by the employer (but not that paid by the employer) as having been paid in the previous tax year (or the year before that if there were no relevant earnings in the previous year). [*ICTA 1988, s 641 as amended by FA 2003, s 174(3)*]. The tax relief will then be given against that previous year's income. For contributions paid after 5 April 2001 the carry back election applies only to contributions paid by 31 January in the tax year and the election must be made on or before the date the premium is paid. [*ICTA 1988, s 641A*].

10.37   Tax relief at the basic rate is given by deduction at source: the employee only pays the insurance company, etc. 78 per cent of his premium, and the insurance company reclaims from the Inland Revenue the 22 per cent deducted. [*ICTA 1988, s 639(3)*]. If the employee is taxable at the 40 per cent higher rate of tax, relief for the additional 18 per cent is given in the taxing the earnings or in the PAYE coding. Because personal pension payments by an employee are paid under deduction of tax whereas the self-employed used to pay their premiums gross, the Revenue considered that it was not possible for a single policy to cover both employed and self-employed earnings. This is because *ICTA 1988, s 639(2)* provides that relief for an employee 'shall' be given in accordance with *subsection (3)* (deduction of tax), and *subsection (7)* denies relief for any other premium under the same policy. This restriction ceased to apply from 2001/02. All personal pension contributions are now payable under deduction of tax at the basic rate, and contributions can be made even if a person has no earnings. Accordingly, there is no longer any cause to differentiate payments in relation to different types of earnings. [*Section 639* as amended by *FA 2000, 13 Schedule 15* and the *Personal Pension Schemes (Relief at Source) Regulations 1988 (SI 1988 No 1013)* as amended by the *Personal Pension Schemes (Relief at Source) Amendment Regulations 2000 (SI 2000 No 2315)*].

Employer's contributions

10.38   Payments by the employer are set against the contribution limits first, so that they reduce the amount that can be paid by the employee. [*ICTA 1988, s 640(4)*]. The employer's contributions are limited to the appropriate percentage of the employee's net relevant earnings for the year; he cannot make contributions in relation to unused relief of earlier years [*ICTA 1988, s 642(1)*]; and an election cannot be made to treat the employer's contributions as paid in the previous year. [*ICTA 1988, s 641(1)*].

10.39   If the total contributions paid (by the employer and employee combined) exceed the limits set out in 10.31 above, the excess must be repaid to the employee (or to the employer to the extent to which it exceeds the employee's contributions). [*ICTA 1988, s 638(4)*].

Meaning of relevant earnings

10.40   An employee's relevant earnings are the aggregate of his:

(*a*)   earnings taxable as employment income from an office or employment which is not a pensionable employment;

(*b*)   income from any property which is attached to (or forms part of) the earnings from such an employment;

(*c*)   income taxable under Schedule D which is immediately derived by the taxpayer from the carrying on of a trade, profession or vocation (either as an individual or as a partner); and

(*d*)   income from patent rights treated as income under *section 529.*

[*ICTA 1988, s 644(2)*].

10.41 For 2001/02 onwards anyone can make contributions of up to £3,600 in a tax year whether or not he has net relevant earnings. The only conditions are that at some point in the year the person must not be a member of a company superannuation scheme and either he must be resident and ordinarily resident in the UK at some time during the tax year (or at some time during the previous five years and also at the time that he took out the personal pension policy), or he or his spouse must be treated under *ITEPA 2003, s 38(2)* (see 2.21) as performing duties in the UK. [*ICTA 1988, s 632A*].

10.42 A gain on the acquisition or disposal of shares (or an interest in shares or option or other right to acquire shares) which is taxable as employment income is not relevant earnings for this purpose (although it is under the retirement annuity rules). The Pension Schemes Office (formerly the Superannuation Funds Office) have apparently accepted that this does not exclude the value of shares issued to the employee as additional remuneration and thus taxable as emoluments under the rule in *Weight v Salmon 19 TC 174* (see 3.6 above) although the wording seems wide enough to exclude such shares. Nor is a payment for compensation for loss of office or other payment taxable under *ITEPA 2003, s 401* (see 11.14 below) excluded. [*ICTA 1988, s 644(4)*]. Earnings of a director (but not an employee) of an investment company are not relevant earnings if the company is under the control of its directors ('control' being defined in *ICTA 1988, s 840*). [*ICTA 1988, s 644(5)*].

10.43 For 2001/02 onwards contributions can be based on relevant earnings for a basis year (which need not be a year for which the employee made personal pension contributions but cannot be one in which he was prohibited from making such contributions), being any of the five previous years. Thus an employee can pay personal pension contributions for 2003/04 on his highest relevant earnings in any of the years 1998/99, 1999/00, 2000/01, 2001/02, 2002/03 or 2003/04. [*ICTA 1988, ss 646B, 646C*]. Where a person ceases to have relevant earnings he can continue to make contributions for the next five years. The maximum contribution is based on the net relevant earnings for either the last year in which he has such earnings or any of the five previous years. [*ICTA 1988, s 646D*].

Example

John was aged 58 when he was made redundant on 10 June 2002. He had the following relevant earnings:

Year	£
1996/97	46,000
1997/98	40,000
1998/99	38,000
1999/00	34,000
2000/01	39,000
2001/02	34,000
2002/03	6,000

The maximum contributions that John can make are:

Year	£	
2001/02	46,000 × 35% (based on 1996/97)	
2002/03	40,000 × 35% (based on 1997/98)	
2003/04	40,000 × 35%	(,, ,,)
2004/05	40,000 × 35%	(,, ,,)
2005/06	40,000 × 40%	(,, ,,)
2006/07	40,000 × 40%	(,, ,,)
2007/08	40,000 × 40%	(,, ,,)
2008/09	Nil (as no earnings in last 5 years)	

Meaning of pensionable employment

10.44   An employment is a pensionable employment (the earnings for which are not relevant earnings) if it is one to which an approved occupational pension scheme (or a statutory scheme, or a foreign government scheme) relates, and the employee is a participant in that scheme. However, an employment is not pensionable if the only benefits payable under the scheme are an annuity to the employee's spouse or dependants or a lump sum payable on death in service. [*ICTA 1988, s 645(1)–(3)*]. If the emoluments of an employment are foreign emoluments (see 12.9 below) membership of an overseas scheme which 'corresponds to' an occupational pension scheme will render the employment pensionable. [*ICTA 1988, s 645(4A)*]. From 2001/02 a member of an occupational money purchase pension scheme can make contributions to a personal pension scheme provided that the total contributions by him and his employer do not exceed the limits set out in 10.32 [*ICTA 1988, s 645*].

10.45   Emoluments from an employment are also not relevant earnings if the employer is a company of which the employee is, or has been, a controlling director at some time during the year of assessment, or the previous ten years, if during the year of assessment either:

(*a*)   he is in receipt of benefits in respect of past service with the company under an occupational pension scheme, etc.;

(*b*)   he is in receipt of benefits under a personal pension scheme and that scheme took a transfer payment from an occupational pension scheme in respect of past service with the company; or

(*c*)   he is in receipt of a benefit within (*a*) or (*b*) above in respect of past service with a different company which previously carried on the trade or business now carried on by the employer company at a time in relation to which the occupational pension scheme contributions were made. [*ICTA 1988, s 644(6A)–(6F)*].

Meaning of net relevant earnings

10.46   A person's net relevant earnings for a year of assessment are his relevant earnings (see 10.40 above) for that year less the following deductions:

(*a*) any annuity, annual payment, (other than interest), patent royalty, mining rent or electric line wayleave that would be deductible as a trading expense but for the fact that it is relieved as an annual payment;

(*b*) expenses deductible under *sections 197AG, 198, 201* and *332(3)* (see 5.2 above); and

(*c*) losses or capital allowances which are deducted in arriving at the total income for the year and which relate to a trade the earnings of which are relevant earnings of the employee or his spouse.

[*ICTA 1988, s 646*].

Retirement annuities

10.47 The retirement annuity rules are similar to those applying to personal pensions. The main differences are as follows.

(*a*) An employer cannot contribute to a retirement annuity.

(*b*) The maximum contributions are lower, i.e.

Age at start of year	Allowable percentage
up to 50	17½
51–55	20
56–60	22½
61 or over	27½

(*c*) The £99,000 earnings cap does not apply.

(*d*) The earliest permitted retirement age is 60 (not 50). An earlier retirement age was allowed for people in certain occupations (see 10.52).

(*e*) The amount that can be commuted to a lump sum is such a sum as does not exceed three times the remaining annuity. This normally produces a figure of around 28 per cent of the fund rather than the 25 per cent that applies for personal pensions.

(*f*) Gains on share options, etc. and compensation for loss of office can constitute relevant earnings.

(*g*) The carry forward relief described at 10.43 does not apply but that at 10.34 continues to do so.

10.48 It must be stressed that although payments can still be made into a retirement annuity scheme that was set up before 1 July 1988 (provided the scheme rules permit this) it is no longer possible to set up new retirement arrangements.

Relationship between retirement annuities and personal pensions

10.49   There is nothing to prevent an individual making contributions in the same year of assessment in relation to the same relevant earnings to both retirement annuities and personal pensions. However, the total contributions to both types of scheme cannot together exceed the maximum contribution levels. As these maxima are different for the two types of scheme rules are obviously needed to co-ordinate the operation of the two sets of rules. These are contained in *section 655*. Where an individual contributes to both types of scheme the maximum amount he could otherwise contribute to the personal pension scheme in a year of assessment is reduced by the amount of his allowable retirement annuity premiums paid in that same year. [*ICTA 1988, s 655(1)(a)*].

Example

Len has relevant earnings of £100,000 for 2003/04. He is aged 50 at 6 April 2003. He pays (*a*) £10,000, (*b*) £19,000 into retirement annuities. How much can he pay into a personal pension scheme?

(*a*)	Retirement annuity limit 17½% of £100,000	£17,500
	Personal pension limit 25% of £99,000 (capped)	£24,750
	Less: retirement annuity paid	£10,000
	Maximum personal pension contribution	£14,750
(*b*)	Personal pension limit 25% of £99,000	£24,750
	Less: retirement annuities paid £19,000, but	
	limited to relief allowed	£17,500
	Maximum personal pension contribution	£7,250

In circumstance (*a*) Len could either pay £14,750 into a personal pension or an additional £7,250 into a retirement annuity. He cannot do both.

10.50   Great care needs to be taken when paying personal pension contributions in these circumstances. It needs to be remembered that if such premiums are paid in excess of the allowable limit, the excess needs to be repaid (see 10.39 above). Accordingly, the reduction in the limit arising from the making of retirement annuity payments could disallow prior personal pension payments made earlier in the year of assessment so that they have to be refunded by the pension provider.

Some people feel that any payment into a personal pension will cause retirement annuity payments in the same year to be capped. However, there is no legislative basis for this. The contractual arrangements with the personal pension provider could, of course, contain an undertaking that the person will not do anything which would result in the premium having to be refunded, so effectively preventing retirement annuity payments being made in excess of the personal pension cap, but this is not a standard provision.

10.51 In ascertaining unused relief of earlier years for retirement annuity purposes personal pension contributions paid must be deducted. [*ICTA 1988, s 655(1)(b)*].

Retirement ages

10.52 In certain types of business a person's effective working life ends at a far younger age than normal. The Inland Revenue have power to agree an earlier retirement age, indicated below, for people in the following occupations, both for occupational pensions, personal pensions and retirement annuities.

Retirement age	*Profession or occupation*
30	Downhill skiers.
35	Athletes; badminton players; boxers; cyclists; dancers; footballers (excluding Football League players); ice hockey players; models; national hunt jockeys; Rugby League (and Union) players; squash players; table tennis players; wrestlers.
40	Cricketers; motocross motorcycle riders; motorcycle road racing riders; motor racing drivers; saturation, deep sea, and free swimming divers; speedway riders; tournament golfers; trapeze artists; WPBSA snooker players.
45	Flat racing jockeys; reserve forces members.
50	Circus animal trainers; croupiers; martial arts instructors; moneybroker dealers; newscasters (ITV); off-shore riggers; Royal Navy reservists; Rugby League referees.
55	Pilots (aircraft); brass instrumentalists; part-time firemen; inshore fishermen; moneybroker directors and managers; female nurses, physiotherapists, mid-wives and health visitors; certain part-time psychiatrists; singers.

These ages do not apply automatically. They are dependent on the facts of an individual case. The Revenue have said that they do not accept lack of success as a result of waning popularity as justifying a low normal retirement date for an entertainer. Where earnings of a sportsman are channelled through a company of which he is a director they will not normally agree an early retirement age unless the only income of the company arises from actually playing or taking part in the sport in question (PSO Update 120, 25.2.2002).

Making the choice

10.53 It is not always easy to decide whether to make pension provision by way of an occupational pension scheme or a personal pension (or retirement annuity). It depends very much on the circumstances. Both are tax-free funds, so if the contribution level proposed would be acceptable under either route the funds ought, in theory at least, to grow at the same rate.

10.54 The difference between the two types of scheme is that with an occupational pension scheme the main restriction is on what can come out of the fund whereas with personal pensions it is on the contributions that can be made. Both have a £102,000 earnings cap—although both pre-14 March 1989 occupational pension schemes and pre-1 July 1988 retirement annuity schemes can provide pensions based on the employee's full earnings where they exceed £102,000.

10.55 Factors to consider are as follows.

(a) Where a person has high earnings at a very young age the investment of 17½ per cent of earnings in a personal pension could well generate a higher pension than that permitted under an occupational scheme.

(b) Where a person is in his 30s or 40s the amount that can be paid into an occupational pension is likely to exceed that which can be put into personal pensions (although this is only relevant if the contributions actually paid exceed the personal pension limit).

(c) An occupational scheme is tied to employment with a particular company or group of companies. If the employment ceases no further contributions can be paid into the scheme and the benefits are likely to be restricted as the number of years service with the employer will be limited. A personal pension is not tied to a particular employment. The Revenue will allow an occupational pension fund to be transferred to another occupational scheme or a personal pension in many cases. However, in practice, the amount of the transfer payment tends to be much smaller than the value that would have been obtained in due course from the original scheme had it been allowed to continue.

(d) If a person's peak career earnings arise while he is young and then fall off, he may not have a high enough final salary to enable the whole pension fund to be utilised in paying pension benefits.

(e) There is greater investment choice with an occupational pension scheme than with a personal pension. In particular, the employee can determine his own investment policy by using a small self-administered pension scheme. Although it is possible to have a self-administered personal pension, the number of people who provide such a facility is far more limited.

(f) If an occupational pension scheme's investment performance is very successful this could result in the scheme becoming overfunded so that the surplus has to be repaid to the employer (and taxed in his hands at a special 40 per cent rate). If the investment policy of a personal pension scheme is very successful this increases the pension (and commuted lump sum) for the employee.

(*g*)   If the employee is not particularly interested in a pension it is often possible to draw a larger lump sum on retirement from an occupational scheme than from a personal pension scheme. With the latter, not more than 25 per cent of the pension can be commuted whereas with the former the entire pension could be commuted if the fund does not exceed 1½ times the employee's final salary.

(*h*)   The employer must contribute to an occupational scheme. It is optional whether he contributes to a personal pension.

10.56   The choice between personal pensions and retirement annuities (where the employee is eligible to subscribe to both) is simpler. The only areas where the personal pension is more attractive are that it is possible to have a retirement age of 50 whereas the minimum retirement age for retirement annuities is 60, and an individual may be able to contribute more to a personal pension in a year than to a retirement annuity by virtue of the increased contribution limits applicable for those aged 36 and over. However, it is possible to transfer a retirement annuity fund into a personal pension fund (but not vice versa). Accordingly, the best strategy is generally to continue to contribute to retirement annuities and, if the employee decides to take earlier retirement, to convert the fund into a personal pension at that stage—or to defer drawing any pension until the age of 60.

Unapproved schemes

10.57   Unapproved pension schemes can either be funded or unfunded, i.e. the employer does not make contributions to a pension provider but simply enters into a commitment with the employee to provide him with specific pension benefits on retirement. As mentioned at 10.5, a problem with funded schemes is that an income tax charge arises on the contributions, which is obviously unattractive to the employee. If there are no contributions there is nothing to which a tax charge can attach. When the pension is paid it will of course attract tax—but so will pension payments under an approved scheme. The major disadvantage is that an unfunded scheme provides little protection to the employee. His pension depends on the employer still being in existence at the time he retires, and on it then having the necessary financial resources to actually meet its commitments to ex-employees.

10.58   Although superficially unattractive a funded unapproved retirement benefits scheme (FURBS) can be used to provide significant benefits to directors and senior employees if the company is prepared to gross up the tax liability on the contribution.

Example

M Ployer Ltd is prepared to pay £100,000 for the benefit of an employee. It does this by paying £60,000 into a FURBS for the employee's benefit and paying him a bonus of £40,000 to enable him to meet the tax liability on it.

The net cost to M Ployer Ltd is as follows:

Assuming corporation tax at	19%	30%
	£	£
Contribution to FURBS	60,000	60,000
Bonus to meet the tax	40,000	40,000
Employer's NI on bonus	4,760	4,760
	104,760	104,760
Less corporation tax relief	19,904	31,428
Net cost	84,856	73,332
Amount held in pension fund	60,000	60,000
Net cost additional to extracting £60,000 from the company to be held for the employee in a tax-efficient form	24,856	13,332

10.59   This is of course not much different to the net cost of paying the whole £100,000 as a bonus—particularly as national insurance is payable on a contribution to a FURBS from 6 April 1999. *DSS Press Release 97/127, 22 July 1997.* The benefit lies in the fact that a FURBS is a relatively tax-efficient investment vehicle. In particular:

(*a*)   Provided that the only benefits payable under the FURBS are 'relevant benefits' within *ICTA 1988, s 612*, it pays tax at only 25 per cent on its income and capital gains. [*ICTA 1988, s 686(2)(c)(i)*]. Relevant benefits are any pension, lump sum, gratuity or other like benefits given (or to be given) on retirement or death, or in anticipation of retirement, or in connection with past service after retirement or death, or to be given on (or in connection with, or in anticipation of) any change in the nature of the employee's service. A benefit payable solely by reason of death in service or disablement by accident during service is not a relevant benefit though. The relevant benefit must be payable to the employee or to his wife, widow, children, dependants or personal representatives.

(*b*)   There is no limit on the contributions that can be made—other than that they have to be wholly and exclusively for the purpose of the employer's trade if they are to qualify for a corporation tax deduction.

(*c*)   There are no restrictions on the investments that can be made by the fund—although if it is wished to invest in shares in the employer company it is probably wise to seek clearance under *ICTA 1988, s 703*.

(*d*) There is no minimum or maximum retirement age. Accordingly, the FURBS can be used as a continuing inheritance tax shelter by selecting a very high retirement age, e.g. 99, as the funds are held outside the individual's estate until retirement.

(*e*) A FURBS can be a particularly attractive way to provide term life assurance. This is because if the employee can prove that no payment will be made to him out of an amount on which he has been taxed, the tax paid on that amount can be reclaimed. [*ITEPA 2003, s 392(1)*]. Once the term insured has expired, the money used to fund the premiums should meet this test. A claim for relief has to be made to the Revenue within six years of the occurrence of the event by reason of which no payment of benefit will be made. A claim obviously cannot be made if the reason that no payment will be made to the employee is that it will be made to a former spouse under a pension sharing order or provision under the *Welfare Reform and Pensions Act 1999*.

10.60 Other points to note are as follows.

(*a*) A FURBS can be run in conjunction with an approved scheme. Indeed it is normally sensible to make the maximum approvable provision first.

(*b*) There is no point in funding for a pension which will be taxable. A FURBS should only pay out a lump sum—which is normally tax-free. If a pension is required the lump sum can be used to purchase an annuity, which being a purchased annuity will have a substantial tax-free element.

(*c*) As there is no tax relief for employees' contributions there is no point in making them.

(*d*) If the FURBS is self-administered the costs of setting up and running the scheme do not give rise to benefits in kind provided that they are funded by the company as separately identifiable contributions (*IR Booklet, The Tax Treatment of Top-up Pension Schemes, paragraph 2.2.4*).

(*e*) The death benefit will attract inheritance tax if it is paid to the deceased's estate and may well do so if it is paid at the trustees discretion amongst a class that includes the estate (*IR Booklet, paragraph 2.5.5*).

(*f*) The settlement anti-avoidance provisions can apply to a FURBS, thus negating the income tax and capital gains tax benefit, but this is 'not likely to be the case where the structure and operation of a scheme are broadly similar to an approved pension scheme' (*CIR Booklet, paragraph 2.7.5*).

(*g*) There is an obligation to report to the Revenue the payment of a contribution to a FURBS within three months of its being paid. [*ICTA 1988, s 605(3)*]. The payment also needs to be shown on the employee's P11D.

10.61 Any benefit received under an unapproved pension scheme is chargeable to income tax if it is not already taxable as a pension. [*ITEPA 2003, s 394*]. In the case of a benefit in kind the taxable amount is normally the cash equivalent of the benefit. [*ITEPA 2003, s 398*]. This is calculated in the same way as under the benefit in kind rules (see Chapters 6–19). [*ITEPA 2003, s 398(2)(b)*]. There is, however, an exemption where the payment is a lump sum provided under a pension scheme to the employee (or his wife, widow, children, dependants, personal representative or any individual designated by the employee); the scheme is a FURBS; and the employee was taxed on the contributions to the scheme. [*ITEPA 2003, s 396*].

10.62 This exemption does not apply where any of the income and gains accruing to the FURBS were not charged to tax, unless the scheme was set up before 1 December 1993 and has not been varied since that date. Instead, tax is payable on the lump sum less the aggregate of contributions to the scheme on which the employee was taxed and contributions by the employee himself. [*ITEPA 2003, ss 395–396*]. Where the lump sum does not exhaust the employee's interest in the fund, only a proportion of the payments in it can be deducted in calculating the taxable amount. [*ITEPA 2003, s 397*]. The onus is on the employee to demonstrate that all of the income and gains of the FURBS have borne tax, and if they have not, that the contributions to the FURBS were taxed. [*ITEPA 2003, ss 395(5), 399(2)*].

10.63 Prior to 1 December 1993 tax on the income and gains arising within the FURBS could in theory at least, be avoided by establishing it outside the UK—although this significantly increased the risk that the Revenue might seek to apply the settlement provisions and a tax haven FURBS could also have been vulnerable to attack under *ICTA 1988, ss 739* or *740* and other existing anti-avoidance provisions. The amendments to *ICTA 1988, s 596A* made by the *Finance Act 1994* not only removed the benefits of offshore FURBS—although they still permit deferral of the tax—but can increase the overall tax as compared with the UK-based FURBS as the calculation makes no allowance for the fact that some types of income and gains, e.g. capital gains on government securities, attract exemption from tax.

Individual savings accounts

10.64 An alternative form of top-up pension provision is to contribute regularly into an Individual Savings Account (ISA) (or before 6 April 1999 to a personal equity plan). An individual could put £6,000 per annum into general PEPs and a further £3,000 per annum into a single company PEP up to 1998/99. For 1999/00 to 2005/06 he can put £7,000 per annum into an ISA and in subsequent years will be able to put £5,000 per annum into an ISA. Like FURBS there is no tax relief on contributions to a PEP or ISA. Unlike FURBS the growth within a PEP or ISA is tax-free as both its income and capital gains are exempt from tax. With an approved scheme tax relief is given for the contributions, growth within the fund is tax-free, but the funds ultimately come out in a taxable form apart from the tax-free allowance of 1½ times salary. With a PEP or ISA no tax relief is given for the contributions, growth within the fund is tax-free, and all withdrawals from the fund are tax-free also.

The New System from 2006/07

10.65   The new system will be far simpler than the current one. It does not seek to control how much can be contributed to a pension scheme or what the pension scheme does with the money. Instead it puts a limit on how much of the contributions to a scheme qualifies for tax relief and imposes a tax charge on money that comes out of the scheme other than in an approved form and non-pension benefits provided by the scheme.

10.66   There are three limits on contributions.

(*a*)   A lifetime allowance on the amount of pension savings that can benefit from tax relief. The lifetime allowance will rise annually, at least until 2010/11, as follows:

2006/07	£1,500,000
2007/08	£1,600,000
2008/09	£1,650,000
2009/10	£1,750,000
2010/11	£1,800,000

(*b*)   An annual allowance on the increase in value each year of an individual's pension fund. This will also rise annually as follows:

2006/07	£215,000
2007/08	£225,000
2008/09	£235,000
2009/10	£245,000
2010/11	£255,000

(*c*)   A contribution limit of the greater of:

(i)   100% of a person's earnings; or

(ii)   £3,600.

10.67   Pension schemes will be able to be established by employers and by financial institutions subject to regulation by the FSA. The Treasury has power by regulation to extend the class of providers [*FA 2004, s 151*]. It will not need the approval of the Inland Revenue to set up a pension scheme but the scheme will need to register with the Revenue to attract tax relief [*FA 2004, s 150*]. The Revenue will be able to withdraw the registration in the event of serious non-compliance with the tax rules

[*FA 2004, ss 154, 155*]. There will obviously be a right of appeal against both a refusal of registration and a decision to deregister [*FA 2004, ss 153, 156*].

10.68 Payments out of a pension scheme can fall into any of four categories, authorised member payments, unauthorised member payments, authorised employer payments and unauthorised employer payments. Unauthorised payments attract a tax charge. The Revenue will be entitled to withdraw a scheme's registration if the unauthorised payments in any 12-month period exceed 25% of the market value of the scheme's assets (although benefits-in-kind, compensation payments and payments made to comply with a court order are ignored in looking at the 25% figure) [*FA 2004, ss 155, 157, 237*].

10.69 The authorised (tax-free) member payments are:

(*a*) Payments of pension. The minimum age at which pensions can start will be 50 up to 6 April 2010 and 55 thereafter (or earlier in the event of ill-health). Pension benefit must commence at age 75 at the latest. There will be no limit on the size of the pension that can be paid. Control over this is in effect exercised by the tax charge where the employee's pension fund exceeds the lifetime allowance. The scheme rules will of course also be able to provide for payment of a pension to a pensioner's widow or dependant. Pension payments cannot normally continue beyond the date of the member's death with the exception that the scheme can provide for pension payments to continue for at least ten years (to cover a ten-year guaranteed annuity). If a scheme has fewer than 50 members the pension must normally be payable by an insurance company (i.e. by purchasing an annuity). The pensioner must be given an opportunity to select the insurance company. A short term annuity or income withdrawals from the scheme itself can be used up to age 75, when the final decision needs to be made. There is an alternative to buying an annuity at age 75, namely to continue with income withdrawals, but the maximum pension is then reduced to 70% of what would have been paid via an assurance company. Some commentators are already recommending this where the pensioner does not need his full pension to live on as after the pensioner's death the balance remaining in the fund can be used to fund a pension for someone else member who is also a member of the scheme. [*FA 2004, ss 161, 162, 164 & Schedule 28*].

(*b*) A lump sum on death (or in certain other circumstances). This cannot exceed 25% of the member's lifetime allowance. It will be possible to take the lump sum in instalments between the minimum pension age and age 75. [*FA 2004, ss 161, 163, 165 and Schedule 29*].

(*c*) A recognised transfer payment, i.e. a transfer of the funds to another registered pension scheme or to a recognised overseas pension scheme. [*FA 2004, ss 161, 166*].

(*d*)   A scheme administration member payments. This will be rare. It applies where a member is also involved in the administration of the scheme and is the arm's length salary for such work. [*FA 2004, ss 161, 167*].

(*e*)   A payment pursuant to a pension sharing order or provision, e.g. where there is an agreement or order to pass over pension rights to a spouse on a divorce. [*FA 2004, s 161*].

(*f*)   Such other payments as may be prescribed by regulation by the Revenue. [*FA 2004, s 161*].

10.70   An unauthorised member payment is any other payment by the scheme to a member. In addition the following transactions will be deemed to give rise to an unauthorised member payment.

(*a*)   If the member assigns or agrees to assign any of his pension benefits to a third party. The amount of the deemed payment is the consideration for the assignment (or the arm's length considering if the assignment is not at arm's length). Where a charge is triggered under this section the subsequent actual pension payments are not themselves unauthorised payments. Where an annuity is payable for the balance of a 10-year period after the pensioner's death the continuing pension payments are not caught by this rule. [*FA 2004, s 168*].

(*b*)   A benefit-in-kind provided out of the assets of the scheme (unless it is already taxable as employment income or would have been but for the employee earning less than £8,500 pa). The amount of the unauthorised payment is normally the benefit that would arise under the employment income benefit code rules. However, the Revenue have power by regulation to specify some different amount. [*FA 2004, s 169*]. Because a benefit will give rise to an unauthorised payment the current rules which limit the assets in which a scheme can invest as to prevent a risk of a benefit arising will no longer be needed.

(*c*)   An event that creates a shift in value from an asset owned by the pension scheme to one owned by the member. The amount of the deemed payment is the amount by which the value of the pension scheme asset is reduced (or is reduced by more than would have occurred had the transaction been an arm's length one). [*FA 2004, s 170*].

10.71   An unauthorised member payment attracts an unauthorised payment tax charge of 40%. The Treasury have power by regulation to vary this amount. The person liable for the tax is the member or, if the payment is made after his death, the recipient of the payment. If the total value of unauthorised payments in any 12-month period exceeds 25% of the value of the fund there will be in addition an unauthorised payment surcharge of 15%. If payments are made to more than one member they are jointly and severally liable for this surcharge. [*FA 2004, ss 204–208*].

10.72   The authorised employer payments are:

(*a*)   Public service scheme payments (which can only apply to a public service pension scheme). [*FA 2004, ss 171, 172*].

(*b*)   Authorised surplus payments. The Revenue will have power by regulation to permit (or presumably compel) a surplus to be repaid to the company—such a payment will however attract tax at 35% payable by the scheme administrator. [*FA 2004, ss 171, 173, 203*].

(*c*)   Compensation payments, i.e. a payment by the pension scheme to the employer to compensate the employer in respect of the member's liability for a criminal, fraudulent or negligent act or omission against the employer. [*FA 2004, ss 171, 174*]. Such a payment gives rise to a benefit to the employee of relieving him of the liability, so is of course taxable on the employee as an unauthorised member's payment.

(*d*)   Authorised employer loans. The pension fund will be able to lend up to 50% of the value of its assets to the employer. Such a loan must be secured by a first charge on assets of adequate value (i.e. to cover the loan plus interest), the loan must carry interest at least equal to a rate to be prescribed by regulation, the loan must be repayable within five years and must be repayable by equal annual instalments over its term. If any of these conditions are breached the breach will give rise to an unauthorised employer payment equal to the amount or value of the breach. If the company is unable to make loan repayments the repayments can be deferred for up to a further five years from the 5th anniversary of the loan. If the amount is still not repaid after ten years the outstanding amount becomes taxable as an unauthorised employer payment. [*FA 2004, ss 171, 175 and Schedule 30*].

(*e*)   Scheme administration employer payments, i.e. a payment to the employer to cover the arm's length cost of administering the scheme. [*FA 2004, ss 171, 176*].

(*f*)   The Revenue have power by regulation to prescribe other types of payment. [*FA 2004, s 171*].

10.73   Any other payment to the employer is an unauthorised payment. Value shifting transactions (i.e. which move value from an asset held by the scheme to one held by the employer) are also deemed to give rise to unauthorised employer payments.

10.74   An unauthorised employer payment gives rise to a 40% tax charge on the employer. It also gives rise to the additional 15% surcharge if total unauthorised employer payments in a 12-month period exceed 25% of the fund value. [*FA 2004 ss 204, 209*].

10.75   As at present, a registered pension scheme will be exempt from tax on its investment income and underwriting income (but not investment income held as a member of a property investment LLP). It will also be exempt from capital gains tax to the same extent as currently. [*FA 2004, ss 182, 183*].

10.76 Contributions by a member, or by a third party on behalf of the member, to the pension scheme (up to age 75 only) will attract tax relief in the year of payment to the extent that they do not exceed the limits at 10.65(*c*) above. Relief at the basic rate will be given by deduction at source (except for a net scheme where it will be given in full at source and a former retirement annuity scheme where payments can continue to be made gross). [*FA 2004, ss 184–190*].

10.77 An employee will be able to transfer shares acquired under an SAYE scheme or a SIP to the pension fund as contributions to the scheme (i.e. attracting tax relief) within 90 days of becoming entitled to the shares. [*FA 2004, s 191*].

10.78 Contributions to the scheme by an employer will be deductible in calculating its profits. A contribution will need to be spread forward if it both exceeds 210% of the contributions for the previous year and the excess is itself £500,000 or more. As at present relief is given only when the contributions are paid; they cannot be deducted on an accruals basis. [*FA 2004, ss 192 & 194*]. Statutory payments to make good a deficit in the scheme assets are also deductible. If the trade has ceased at the time of the payment they are deductible in the last period of trading. [*FA 2004, s 195*].

10.79 Contributions other than to a registered pension scheme, e.g. to a FURBS, will no longer be deductible but will no longer be taxable on the employer either. [*FA 2004, ss 196, 241*]. Pension payments from such a scheme will continue to be taxable on the employee though and a FURBS will not benefit from IHT relief. [*ITEPA 2003, ss 393-395* substituted by *FA 2004, s 243*].

10.80 The existing IHT relief for an interest in a pension fund that comes to an end on death will continue to apply to registered pension schemes and to certain schemes for non-residents. [*FA 2004, s 199*].

10.81 A charge to income tax will be imposed on the scheme administrator if a registered pension scheme pays a short service refund lump sum, i.e. if it refunds contributions to a member who is not entitled to short service benefit and which extinguishes the member's entitlement to benefit under the scheme. The tax charge is 20% on the first £10,800 of the payment and 40% on any excess. [*FA 2004, s 199* and *29 Schedule 5*].

10.82 An income tax charge of 35% is imposed on the scheme administrator if the scheme pays a pension protection lump sum death benefit (a benefit payable on death before 75 which the member has specified is to be treated as such a benefit—which he is allowed to do up to a specified limit), an annuity protection lump sum death benefit (a capital refund under an annuity where the member dies under 75) or an unsecured pension fund lump sum death benefit (a capital sum paid on death under 75 in respect of income withdrawal to which the member was entitled under an arrangement at the date of death). [*FA 2004, s 202* and *29 Schedule 14, 16, 17*].

10.83 If when benefit starts to be paid the value of the fund attributable to a member exceeds his lifetime allowance (see 10.65(*a*)) a lifetime allowance charge arises on the excess. The charge is 55% if the excess is paid to the employee as a lump sum or 25% if it will be paid in the form of pension. The tax is payable by the member if the excess is paid to him as a lump sum. If it is not the liability is a joint and several liability of the member and the scheme administrator. A benefit crystallisation event may not trigger a charge on the entire surplus (e.g. where a person is a member of a number of pension schemes and starts to draw from one only). In such a case the charge is of course calculated on a cumulative basis. [*FA 2004, ss 210–216*].

10.84 An individual who was a member of the scheme during a period of non-residence will have an enhanced lifetime allowance to reflect the fact the contributions during the period of non-residence will not attract tax relief. [*FA 2004, ss 217–222*].

10.85 If the total contributions by an individual in any one year exceed his annual allowance (see 10.65(*b*)) a tax charge at 40% is payable by the member in respect of the excess. The funds can remain in the pension scheme though. There are detailed rules for calculating the excess. [*FA 2004, ss 223–234*].

10.86 A scheme sanction charge of 40% applies where the scheme makes some types of unauthorised payment. If the payment has already attracted an unauthorised payment charge on either the member or the employer (see 10.69 and 10.73) the charge is reduced by the lower of the tax paid or 25% of the scheme chargeable payment. The charges does not arise if the unauthorised payment is a benefit-in-kind, a compensation payment, a payment by or in anticipation of a court order on a divorce or a payment of a type prescribed by the Revenue by regulation. The charge is a liability of the scheme administrator. [*FA 2004, ss 235–237*]. It should be noted that, apart from benefits, etc, the effective tax on unauthorised payments is 55% (i.e. a 40% unauthorised payment charge plus 15% (after deduction for the unauthorised payment charge)—scheme sanction charge) plus a further 15% unauthorised payment surcharge if the payment is over 25% of the scheme assets.

10.87 If the registration of a scheme is withdrawn there will be a deregistration charge of 40% of the assets of the scheme at the time of withdrawal. This is a liability of the scheme administrator.

10.88 If an employer adopts an unfunded registered scheme the benefit payments are deductible when paid, even though at that stage the member may no longer be an employee. If the benefits are taxable on the employee (but not otherwise) any expenses of providing them (other than contributions) are also deductible. [*FA 2004, ss 239, 240*]. If the employer under such a scheme insures against the risk that he may not be able to pay the pension because of his insolvency the cost of such insurance will be taxable on the employee as a benefit-in-kind. [*FA 2004, s 242*].

10.89 All existing approved pension schemes will automatically become registered schemes on 6 April 2006 (A day). If such a scheme does not wish to become a registered scheme it can opt out, but if it does so will suffer a tax charge of 40% on the value of the assets held on A day. [*FA 2004, 36 Schedule 1,2*].

10.90 If a member's fund in a scheme set up prior to A day exceeds the lifetime limit, the member can retain his existing pension rights (including rights to a lump sum) but will not be able to make further contributions to the scheme. [*FA 2004, 36 Schedule 7–18, 24–34*]. A member of a pre A day scheme will similarly retain his existing right to take a pension below age 55 after 2010. Where people in certain occupations currently have a retirement age under 50 (see 10.51) they can continue with that early retirement date but they will have to take a reduced pension entitlement. [*FA 2004, 36 Schedule 19*].

10.91 Pre A day approved loans to the employer can continue in force provided that there is no alteration in the repayment terms—and an extension for up to five years will not be regarded as such an alteration. [*FA 2004, Schedule 38*].

Chapter 11

Termination Payments and Signing-on Fees

Introduction

11.1   Particular difficulties arise with lump sum payments either at the commencement or termination of an employment. A payment made before the employment commences to induce a person to take up an employment is part of the emoluments from that employment. However, if it is made for some other reason, such as to induce the person to give up something else—a profitable professional position in *Pritchard v Arundale* (see 11.70 below), amateur status in *Jarrold v Boustead* (see 11.69 below), or something similar—then it is not remuneration of the prospective employment.

11.2   A payment on the termination of an employment, either as compensation for breach of the employment contract or ex gratia, is not normally emoluments unless there is a contractual entitlement to it. Such payments are nonetheless generally taxable as employment income by virtue of *ITEPA 2003, s 401*, but the tax treatment is more favourable than if the compensation itself constituted emoluments of the employment.

Compensation constituting emoluments

11.3   Compensation constitutes emoluments, and is thus taxable apart from the special provisions described below, if the employee is contractually entitled to it under the terms of his employment agreement.

Case law

Henry v Foster

11.4   Thus, in *Henry v Foster 16 TC 605*, the articles of association of the employer company provided that 'In the event of any director dying or resigning his office or in the event of any director ceasing to hold office for any cause ... the company shall pay to him or his representatives ... by way of compensation for the loss of office a sum equal to the total amount of the remuneration' for the previous five years. It was held that the substance of the matter was that in addition to his salary payments he became entitled to a further amount under the articles by way of deferred remuneration. Accordingly, the 'compensation' was taxable as employment income.

Hunter v Dewhurst

11.5   Another director of the same company, Mr Dewhurst wished to retire in 1923 but the other directors wished him to remain. He offered to stay on the board (but not as an executive) on the basis that he would be paid £10,000, would waive his right to future compensation under the articles, and would take a reduced salary. It was held, albeit on a three-to-two majority, that the £10,000 was not satisfying the payment due under the articles at a later date. Nor was it in respect of past services. Mr Dewhurst was not required to remain a director for any specific period, so it could not relate to future services. It was a payment to induce him not to retire. As such it was not part of his remuneration (*Hunter v Dewhurst 16 TC 605*).

Prendergast v Cameron

11.6   By contrast, in *Prendergast v Cameron 23 TC 122* a payment to induce a director not to resign was held to be taxable as remuneration as there is no difference between a promise not to resign and a promise to continue to serve as a director. Although Mr Cameron, like Mr Dewhurst, did not agree to continue as a director for any specific period, Viscount Caldecote thought it fair to assume that his fellow directors 'knew the man with whom they had to deal, and were confident that if he received the money they were prepared to pay him they would get good value for it'. He accordingly felt able to hold that the payment was remuneration for future services.

Hofman v Wadman

11.7   The importance of the documentation entered into is emphasised in *Hofman v Wadman 27 TC 192*. Mr Hofman had a five-year service agreement. The company wished to terminate his employment in order to facilitate a reorganisation but could not do so without breaching the contract. They entered into an agreement with him that the service agreement 'shall be cancelled forthwith, subject to the continuance of the fixed remuneration provided for in Clause 4 ... it is understood [Mr Hofman] agrees to render such assistance to our staff ... as may be requested'. It was held that this did not cancel the service agreement, it cancelled some elements but preserved the salary. 'Although Mr Hofman ceased to hold the office of works manager ... the continuation in the office ... does not affect the question of his liability to income tax under Schedule E (which used to be the

Schedule under which employment income was taxed).' Indeed McNaghten J indicated that even if the terms had been such that he was no longer under any obligation to render any services, he would still be liable to assessment in respect of all the payments made to him under the terms of the original service agreement.

Carter v Wadman

11.8   In *Carter v Wadman 28 TC 41* the taxpayer's employment agreement provided that in the event of the agreement being terminated he would be paid as compensation for loss of office £5 a week until the agreement would have expired. He was also entitled to a bonus of 25 per cent of the profits of the business. He could also prevent a sale of the business. On a disposal of the business he was paid £2,000 'in full settlement of all past, present and future claims under his service agreement'. It was held that this sum fell to be apportioned. To the extent that it related to giving up the claim to the £5 a week and the profit share, it was taxable; to the extent it related to giving up the ability to thwart a sale, it was not.

Dale v de Soissons

11.9   In *Dale v de Soissons 32 TC 118* the taxpayer's service agreement contained a provision that 'in the event of Mr de Soissons' appointment hereunder being so terminated there shall be paid to Mr de Soissons by way of compensation for loss of office the amounts following'. The compensation was held to be taxable. 'It seems to me the remuneration for the services took the form in part of a remuneration . . . for the period he in fact served plus a further sum which he was contractually entitled to get under the terms of his agreement and as part of the bargain which he made . . . The Colonel surrendered no rights. He got exactly what he was entitled to get under his contract of employment' (Sir Raymond Evershed, MR).

IR v Knight, Williams v Simmonds

11.10   In a Privy Council case, *Controller General of Inland Revenue v Knight [1973] AC 428*, Lord Wilberforce made the distinction 'Where a sum of money is paid under a contract of employment, it is taxable, even though it is received at or after the termination of the employment . . . Where a sum of money is paid as consideration for the abrogation of a contract of employment, or as damages for the breach of it, that sum is not taxable'. The agreement in *Williams v Simmonds 55 TC 17* provided that in the event of the company disposing of a substantial asset Mr Simmonds would be deemed to have lost his office as managing director and would be entitled to compensation calculated under a formula. It went on to say that Mr Simmonds could elect not to treat his office as terminated. He did not make such an election and was paid the compensation. It was held to be taxable. The judge described this result as 'unfortunate', as he pointed out that had Mr Simmons elected to treat his office as continuing and had then succumbed to pressure to resign, and had agreed to accept the same sum as compensation for the abrogation of his rights under the service agreement, it would probably not have been taxable.

Duff v Barlow

11.11   In *Duff v Barlow 23 TC 633* a payment to a director on the termination of his contract of employment was held not to be assessable as it was not for services rendered or to be rendered, the director having already received his agreed remuneration for such services. A similar decision was reached in *Hose v Warwick 27 TC 459* where a director of a company who was entitled to commission was paid to give up his rights to future commissions on being promoted to managing director of the company. Such items would now be taxable under *section 140* (see 11.14).

Wales v Tilley

11.12   Great care needs to be taken with lump sum payments where the employment continues on amended terms. In *Wales v Tilley 25 TC 136* the taxpayer was entitled to a salary of £6,000 per annum and, when his service ceased, to a pension of £4,000 per annum for a period of ten years. He was paid £40,000 to release the company from the prospective obligation to pay the pension and to agree to serve the company in future at a salary of £2,000 per annum. It was held that in so far as the payment related to giving up the right to the pension it was not taxable. A pension is a separate head of charge under Schedule E and accordingly neither the pension nor the sum paid to commute it constituted profit from the office. To the extent that it related to the reduction in salary it was taxable. 'The ordinary way of remunerating the . . . person employed is to make payments to him periodically, but I cannot think that such payments can escape the quality of income . . . because an arrangement is made to reduce for the future the annual payments while paying a lump sum down to represent the difference' (Viscount Simon).

Other cases

11.13   There is probably an inference that such a payment constitutes emoluments. Thus, in *Hamblett v Godfrey 59 TC 694* it was held that a payment to give up a right to be a member of a trade union was remuneration of the employment, as such rights were inseparable from the employment. In *Holland v Geoghegan 48 TC 482* payments to council dustmen to forego a right to sell materials salvaged from their collections were held to be emoluments. A payment to a director to relinquish a right under his employment agreement that the agreement could not be terminated without his consent was also held to be income under general principles (*Leeland v Boarland 27 TC 71*). So was a payment to a director to surrender his right to commissions due to him (*Bolam v Muller 28 TC 471*). In *McGregor v Randall 58 TC 110* a payment as compensation for the loss of future commission was held to be taxable.

Compensation not constituting emoluments

11.14   Where the compensation does not otherwise constitute emoluments it will not escape tax. *ITEPA 2003, s 401* imposes an income tax charge on any payment (not otherwise chargeable to tax) made in consideration of (or in consequence of, or otherwise in connection with) the termination of an office or employment or any change in its functions (whether or not under any legal obligation and either directly or indirectly). [*ITEPA 2003, s 401(1)*]. It was substantially recast from 1997/98 onwards. As recast it applies to all payments received, directly or indirectly, in consideration or in consequence of (or otherwise in connection with) the termination or change in the employment by either:

(*a*)   the employee (or office-holder) or former employee;

(*b*)   the spouse or any blood relative or dependant of the former employee; or

(*c*)   the personal representatives of the former employee.

Any payment or other benefit provided on behalf of (or to the order of) the employee or former employee is also treated as received by him. [*ITEPA 2003, s 401(4)(a)*]. The tax is chargeable on the employee, not the recipient, where (*b*) above applies. [*ITEPA 2003, s 403(1)*].

11.15   Compensation taxable under *section 401* is taxed in the year of assessment in which it is received. [*ITEPA 2003, s 403(2)*]. Prior to 1998/99 it was taxed in the year of assessment in which the employment or office terminated, or the duties changed, not that in which the payment was made if different.

11.16   The charge is specifically expressed to apply to benefit as well as payments. For this purpose a benefit includes anything which, if received for the performance of the duties of the employment, would be taxable as an emolument of the employment apart from any exemption. [*ITEPA 2003, s 402(1)*]. The right to receive the payment of compensation or benefit is obviously not itself regarded as a benefit for this purpose. [*ITEPA 2003, s 402(4)*]. A cash benefit is treated as received when it is paid (or a payment on account if it is made) or when the recipient becomes entitled to require payment of (or on account of) the benefit. A non-cash benefit is treated as received when it is used or enjoyed. [*ITEPA 2003, s 403(3)*].

Where compensation paid in connection with a change in the function of an employment includes benefits in kind, such benefits could be taxable under both *ITEPA 2003, s 201* (charge on benefits) and *ITEPA 2003, s 401*. In such circumstances the Revenue consider that the charge under *section 201* takes precedence (*Tax Bulletin 65*, June 2003).

11.17 For 2002/03 onwards there are specific exemptions for:

(*a*) a payment or benefit received in connection with a change in the duties of (or emoluments from) a person's employment which would have been exempt as qualifying removal expenses under *ITEPA 2003, s 271(1)* (see 9.46) if it had been paid for the performance of the duties of the employment [*ITEPA 2003, s 402(3)*]; and

(*b*) a payment or benefit received in connection with the termination of a person's employment, which, if it had been received in connection with the performance of the duties of the employment, would have been exempt under *ITEPA 2003*:

   (i) *section 269* expenses in relation to a car (see 6.42(*d*));

   (ii) *section 319* mobile telephones (see 9.35);

   (iii) *section 320* computer equipment (see 9.89);

   (iv) *section 239(4)* expenses in relation to a car (see 7.30), van (see 7.94), or lorry (see 7.95);

[*ITEPA 2003, s 402(2)*]

The specific exemptions under the following provisions of course also apply:

   (v) *section 317* meals in a canteen (see 6.42(h));

   (vi) *section 250* work related training (see 9.67);

   (vii) *section 255* individual learning accounts (see 9.72);

   (viii) *section 311* retraining courses (see 9.73);

   (ix) *section 310* redundancy counselling (see 9.87);

   (x) *section 308* employer's contributions under personal pension arrangements (see 10.31).

11.18 *ICTA 1988, s 148(5)* provided that *section 148* applied irrespective of whether the payment or other benefit was provided by the employer (or former employer) or by some other person and irrespective of whether or not the payment or benefit was provided in pursuance of a legal obligation. [*Section 148(5)*]. The wording of *ITEPA 2003, s 401* was felt to be so widely drawn that there was no need to specifically repeat this wording.

11.19 In *Walker v Adams* ([2003] STC 269) Mr Walker, a Northern Irish Protestant, was constructively dismissed based on religious discrimination. A severance agreement was negotiated. It was not disputed that this attracted a charge under what is now *ITEPA 2003, s 403*. However, Mr Walker subsequently made an application to the Fair Employment Tribunal under the *Fair Employment (Northern Ireland) Act 1989*. He was awarded £77,446, £12,500 for injury to feelings and £63,946 in respect of net income loss both to the date of the decision and in the future and in respect of the loss of pension rights. The Revenue accepted that the £12,500 was not a payment made 'in connection with' the termination of Mr Walker's employment but contended that the £63,946 was taxable. The Special Commissioner agreed. He accepted that the 1989 Act did not operate so as to import statutory terms into the contract of employment but created 'a free-standing right of action, basically tortious in nature, aimed against certain forms of discrimination'. Nevertheless, he felt that while the unlawful discrimination founded the tribunal's jurisdiction the chain of causation led back to the employment. 'The discrimination caused the termination of Mr Walker's employment; the termination caused the financial losses; and those losses gave rise to the £64,946 award'. He also felt that the words 'or otherwise' in what is now *ITEPA 2003, s 401* show that the relevant connection or link may be looser than would be required for a strict causation test.

11.20 The decision may well be wrong in the light of the later High Court decision in *Wilson v Clayton (2004 EWHC 898 (Ch) 2004 ST1 1121)*. Mr Clayton was employed by a local authority. His employment was terminated and he was offered a new contract on different terms. Mr Clayton claimed unfair dismissal. The Employment Tribunal upheld his claim and ordered the local authority to reinstate Mr Clayton and pay him the amount of lost remuneration (under his old terms) between the date of termination of his employment and the date of reinstatement, which came to £5,060. It was held that the £5,060 fell within *s 401*. It was received 'in connection with' the termination of the employment. The effect of the reinstatement order was not that the termination never took place.

11.21 There are a number of exemptions from the tax charge under *ITEPA 2003, s 401*:

(*a*) It applies only to the extent that the total payments and benefits in respect of an employment exceed £30,000. [*ITEPA 2003, s 403(1)*]. If an employee has different employments with the same employer or associated employers, a single £30,000 exemption applies in aggregate. [*ITEPA 2003, s 404*].

(*b*) It does not apply to a payment or benefit provided in connection with the termination of the employment by the death of the employee or on account of injury or disability of the employee. [*ITEPA 2003, s 406*].

(*c*) It does not apply to a payment or benefit under an approved retirement benefit scheme provided that either:

(i) the payment or other benefit is by way of compensation for loss of employment, or for loss or diminution of emoluments, due to ill health; or

(ii)   the payment or other benefit is properly regarded as earned by past service. [*ITEPA 2003, s 407*].

(*d*)   It does not apply to a payment or other benefit provided under a Royal Warrant, Queen's Order or Order in Council relating to members of Her Majesty's forces or by way of payment in commutation of annual or other periodical payments authorised by such a Warrant or Order. [*ITEPA 2003, s 411*].

(*e*)   It does not apply to:

(i)   any benefit provided under a superannuation scheme administered by the government of another Commonwealth territory (as defined in the *Overseas Development and Co-operation Act 1980*); or

(ii)   any payment of compensation for loss of career, interruption of service or disturbance made in connection with any change in the constitution of any such territory to a person who before that change was employed in the public service of that territory. [*ITEPA 2003, s 412*].

(*f*)   There is an exemption for foreign service (see 11.24).

(*g*)   It does not apply to a contribution to an unapproved pension scheme that is taxed on the employee under *ITEPA 2003, s 386*.

(*h*)   It does not apply to a contribution to a personal pension which would have been exempt from tax under *ITEPA 2003, s 308* had it been paid for the performance of duties of the employment. [*ITEPA 2003, ss 405(1), 408*].

(*i*)   Similarly it does not apply to a contribution to an approved pension scheme to provide benefits for the employee in accordance with the terms of the scheme. [*ITEPA 2003, s 408*].

11.22   The legislation contains detailed rules to identify the taxable payments where there are several payments and the aggregate exceeds £30,000. The £30,000 exemption must be set against receipts in earlier years before those of later years. If there is more than one payment or benefit in a single tax year, it is set first against cash payments in the order that they are received. If these do not exhaust the exemption, the balance is set against the aggregate of non-cash benefits received in the year. [*ITEPA 2003, s 404(4)(5)*].

11.23   Employers are associated for the purpose of aggregating payments if on the date of the termination or change in question in relation to any of the payments one of them is under the control of the other or one of them is under the control of a third person which either controls or is under the control of the other on that or any other date. The definition of control in *ICTA 1998, s 840* applies. References to any person include the successor of that person. [*ITEPA 2003, ss 404(2), 719*].

11.24 The exemption for foreign service applies:

(*a*) if such service comprises either 75 per cent or more of the whole period of service down to the date of the termination of the employment or change in its duties; or

(*b*) where the total period of service exceeds ten years, if the whole of the last ten are foreign service; or

(*c*) where the total period of service exceeds 20 years, if 50 per cent or more of the total period is foreign service and that period includes any ten of the last 20 years. [*ITEPA 2003, s 413(1)*].

Foreign service for this purpose is:

(i) employments from 2003/04 onwards for which the earnings are not general earnings (i.e. earnings for a year when the employee was resident or ordinarily resident in the UK) or, if they were, the individual is a seafarer and the whole of the earnings attracts the 100% deduction under *ITEPA 2003, s 378* (see 13.13).

(ii) employment from 1974/75 to 2002/03, the emoluments for which were not chargeable under Case I of Schedule E;

(iii) employment from 1974/75 to 1997/98 to which the 100 per cent foreign earnings deduction applied (this ceased from 16 March 1998);

(iv) employment before 1974/75 where the emoluments were not chargeable under Case I of Schedule E (or before 1956/57 were not chargeable under Schedule E). [*ITEPA 2003, s 413(2)–(6)*].

11.25 If an employment includes a period of foreign service but the above tests are not satisfied, a measure of relief is still due. The £30,000 standard exemption is first deducted from the compensation, etc. The balance is then reduced in the proportion that the length of foreign service bears to the whole period of service (up to the date of the termination or change). However, if the employee is entitled to deduct tax on making a payment to some other person (e.g. under a charitable covenant) the reduction is, if necessary, restricted to leave in charge to tax sufficient income to cover that deduction. [*ITEPA 2003, s 414*].

11.26 The value of a non-cash benefit is its cash equivalent. This is the greater of:

(*a*) the amount of earnings that the benefit would have given rise to if it were received by an employee for the performance of the duties of his employment; or

(*b*) the cash equivalent determined in accordance with *section 596B*, namely:

(i) in the case of a benefit other than living accommodation, the cash equivalent calculated under the benefit in kind rules for higher paid employees (see Chapters 6, 7 and 9);

(ii) in the case of living accommodation, the benefit calculated under the appropriate benefit rules (see Chapter 8).

[*ITEPA 2003, s 415*].

11.27 If a benefit consists of a cheap or interest-free loan the employee is treated as having paid interest on the loan—but only to the extent that the benefit is charged to tax (i.e. not if it is covered by the £30,000 exemption). This will enable him to claim a deduction against tax for that notional interest to the extent that the loan was one qualifying for tax relief on interest paid. [*ITEPA 2003, s 416*].

11.28 It is of course important to be able to evidence what a payment is for. The Revenue will normally look at the contract of employment. They will also look for minutes of the employer, correspondence between the parties and the wording of any termination agreement. The importance of ensuring that the termination agreement supports what the taxpayer intends to argue is emphasised by *Appellant v Inspector of Taxes* [*2001*] STC (SCD) 21. The appellant had a number of disputes with his employer about alleged racial discrimination and took these to an industrial tribunal. He won two of his appeals. He agreed to settle the third on the basis that his employer would pay him £20,000 and that the taxpayer would then take voluntary redundancy—for which he would be paid an additional lump sum of £65,684. The taxpayer claimed that this additional sum was for loss of his human and civil rights and was not taxable. Unfortunately, the termination agreement described it as consideration for the Appellant's voluntary termination of his employment. The taxpayer's fall-back was that at least part of it related to a confidentiality clause and an agreement not to institute further industrial tribunal claims that were included in the agreement. The Commissioner held that the substance and reality of the termination agreement was that it was paid for the voluntary termination. The parties had not attributed any part of it to the other obligations under the agreement. He also agreed with the Revenue that a payment that related to the confidentiality clause and the agreement not to institute proceedings would be taxable under *ITEPA 2003, s 225* (see 11.75) as those obligations constituted restrictive covenants.

The pre-1998/99 rules

11.29 The rules that applied prior to 1998/99 were substantially the same, the main difference being that they referred only to payments. However, the Special Commissioners held in *George v Ward* [*1995*] STC (SCD) 230 that ICTA 1988, s 148 was not limited to amounts convertible into money—in that case the right to use a car for an agreed period following the termination of the employment. The taxpayer contended that as the right was personal to him, non-assignable and non-devolvable it could not be converted into money. The Special Commissioners held that Mr George nevertheless received valuable consideration from the use of the car (as he would otherwise have to provide his own) and that this fell within *ICTA*

1988, s 148. The agreement provided for a car to be made available for nine years but it was in fact provided only for five. The Commissioner held that it was only the benefit actually received that was assessable. The Inspector and Mr George had agreed that the value of any benefit was the value in money terms that would be placed by a reasonable person on the right to use the car at the date of termination of the employment. This is relatively easy to calculate when the period of use had ended, as in that case, but in many cases the figure will fall to be calculated at a time when the period for which the benefit is actually provided is not yet ascertainable. The reporting obligation is extended from 6 April 1999 by the *Income Tax (Employments) (Amendment No 2) Regulations 1999 (SI 1999 No 70)*. This requires the employer (or former employer) to give details to the Revenue of any award of payments combined with other benefits or consisting solely of such benefits where the total amount of the payments and other benefits exceed £30,000 and to give the same details to the employee. There is no obligation to remind either the Revenue or the employee of benefits that are received by the employee in later years.

11.30   The old *ICTA 1988, s 148* was specifically stated to include any payment in commutation of annual or periodical payments which were payable in respect of such a termination (whether or not such payments would themselves have been taxable). [*Section 148(2)*]. In such a case the tax charge arose at the date on which the commutation was effected. [*ICTA 1988, s 148(4)(a)*]. This ensured that the charge could not be avoided by agreeing to pay compensation as a monthly sum, then, after a few months, paying a capital sum to rid oneself of the obligation, and contending that the payment was not connected with the employment but rather with the obligation to make the monthly payments.

11.31   A payment to the spouse of an employee or to a relative (not defined) or a dependant of his, or which was made on behalf of, or to the order of, the employee of course had to be treated as having been made to the employee. Any valuable consideration other than money had to be treated as being a 'payment' for the purpose of *section 148* (and *section 188*—see 11.32 below). [*Section 148(3)*].

11.32   *ICTA 1988, s 188* (which was repealed by *FA 1998*) provided a number of exceptions to the charge under *ICTA 1988, s 148* (but not to a charge on a lump sum which constitutes emoluments under general principles including a payment under a deemed retirement benefit scheme (see 10.55)). The charge did not apply to the following.

(*a*)   The first £30,000 of any payment within *ICTA 1988, s 148*. [*ICTA 1988, s 188(4)*]. In applying this exception, if two or more payments to the same person were chargeable under *section 148*, either in respect of the same employment or in respect of different employments under either the same or associated employers, these payments had to be aggregated. If the payments were income of different years of assessment, the £30,000 exemption was applied against the first payment, any excess against the second and so on. If they were income of the same year of assessment, the £30,000 was deducted rateably from all the payments. [*Section 188(5)*]. For this purpose, offices were held under associated employers if, at the date by reference to which any of the compensation payments became taxable, one of those employers (or his successor) was under the control of the other (or his successor), or of a third party who controlled (or was under the control of) the other one at that date or on any other date to which one of the compensation payments related. [*Section 188(7)*].

(*b*) A payment made in connection with the termination of the employment by the employee's death. [*Section 188(1)(a)*].

(*c*) A payment made on account of injury to (or disability of) the employee. [*ICTA 1988, s 188(1)(a)*]. In *Horner v Hasted* [*1995*] *STC 766* a senior employee was required to retire aged 58 years by his firm. His claim that a termination payment fell within this provision 'as it was made following the termination of his employment on account of a mental disability brought about by an obsessive campaign he had undertaken against the Inland Revenue' was dismissed. It was held that for the exemption to apply it has to be established both that the disability was a total or partial impairment of the employee's ability to perform the duties of his employment and that the person who made the payment had made it on account of the disability. The facts found by the Special Commissioner did not establish either of these conditions.

(*d*) A payment in respect of an employment, the duties of which included 'foreign service' if that foreign service covered at least three-quarters of the length of the service (or, if the period of employment was long enough, of the whole of the last ten years of the period of service, or half of the period of service provided that that half includes at least ten of the last 20 years service). [*ICTA 1988, s 188(3)*]. Foreign service, for this purpose, meant:

(i)   service before 1974/75 where tax was not chargeable on the emoluments under Case I of Schedule E (before 1956/57 under Schedule E); or

(ii) service from 1974/75 onwards, if either tax was not chargeable on the emoluments under Case I of Schedule E (or, if there were no emoluments, would not have been chargeable had any been paid), or it was chargeable but the 100 per cent deduction under the 365-day rule (see 13.8 below) applied to effectively exempt the emoluments from UK tax. [*ICTA 1988, 11 Schedule 10*].

The length of service to be taken into account is the period ending with the date of the termination of the employment (or of the change in the duties), or, in relation to a payment in commutation of periodical payments, the date of the termination or change in respect of which those payments would have been made. [*ICTA 1988, 11 Schedule 9*].

(*e*)   Where the foreign service exemption in (*d*) above did not apply but the period of service included foreign service (within the meaning set out above), part of the compensation payment was exempted, namely, the proportion of the payment that the length of the foreign service bore to the total length of the employment. [*ICTA 1988, 11 Schedule 3*]. This exemption had to be claimed. [*ICTA 1988, s 188(6)*]. The normal six-year time limit for claims applied. Relief under *ICTA 1988, 11 Schedule 3* was restricted if the full relief (combined with personal allowances) would result in the employee having insufficient UK taxable income to cover charges, etc. that he had to pay. [*ICTA 1988, 11 Schedule 2*].

(*f*)   A payment in respect of a restrictive undertaking, which was specifically taxable not under *section 148* but under *section 313* (see 11.66 below). [*ICTA 1988, s 188(1)(b)*].

(*g*)   Benefits provided in pursuance of an approved pension scheme. [*ICTA 1988, s 188(1)(c)*].

(*h*)   Benefits provided under an unapproved pension scheme where the employee was taxed on the amounts of the contributions to the scheme (or sums set aside for the purpose of the scheme) at the time they were paid (see 10.4 above). [*ICTA 1988, s 188(1)(c)*].

(*j*)   Benefits provided under certain other pension schemes—unless the benefit was compensation for loss of office or for loss or diminution of emoluments payable otherwise than because of ill health (this exclusion did not apply to a payment properly regarded as a benefit earned by past service). [*ICTA 1988, s 188(1)(d),(2)*].

(*k*)   A terminal grant, gratuity or other lump sum paid under any Royal Warrant, Queen's Order, or Order in Council relating to members of HM forces, or any payment in commutation of periodic payments authorised by such a Warrant or Order. [*ICTA 1988, s 188(1)(e)*].

(*l*)   A benefit under a superannuation scheme administered by the government of an overseas territory within the Commonwealth (within the meaning of the *Overseas Development and Cooperation Act 1980*), or a payment, to a person previously employed in the public service of such an overseas territory, of compensation for loss of career, interruption of service or disturbance which was made in connection with any change in the constitution of that territory. [*ICTA 1988, s 188(1)(f)*].

11.33   A greater relief than the £30,000 referred to in 11.32(*a*) above could sometimes be claimed where the compensation, etc. payment was made in pursuance of an obligation incurred before 10 March 1981. [*ICTA 1988, 11 Schedule 12–19*]. As it is difficult to envisage any circumstance in which a payment made now could be in pursuance of such an obligation and not be taxable under the normal Schedule E charging rules, rather than under *ICTA 1988, s 148*, these provisions are not considered further. In *O'Brien v Williams [2000] STC (SCD) 364* the Special Commissioner was called on to interpret this proviso and after considering the legislative history posited 'payment pursuant to an obligation which would be insufficient to enable one to say that the payment amounted to an emolument of the employment, but which would, apart from the exemption, attract a charge to tax under the new provisions'.

Other matters

11.34 As indicated in 11.14 above, *ITEPA 2003, s 401* applies to any payment in connection with the termination of an employment which is not otherwise chargeable as employment income whether or not it is made in pursuance of a legal obligation. It will apply to an ex gratia payment even where the employee has foregone his proper notice period or if he resigns. It will also apply to a payment made to compromise a legal action by the employee against his employer or to head off the threat of such an action. A payment in lieu of notice where someone is dismissed also falls within *ITEPA 2003, s 401*.

11.35 Tax cannot be avoided by the employee ceasing to be UK resident prior to the determination of his employment. In *Nichols v Gibson* *[1996] STC 1008* the taxpayer's employment was terminated on 6 April 1994 after 31 years' service. He had been given prior warning of the termination and obtained employment in Jamaica. With the leave of his existing employer he started this on 1 April 1984. He contended that the compensation he received was not taxable as he was not UK resident in 1984/85 when the employment terminated, and none of the cases of Schedule E applied to him that year. It was held that *ITEPA 2003, s 401* imposes a charge independently of the basic employment income charging rules so it is irrelevant whether the ex-employee is UK resident or working in the UK in the tax year that the employment ceases.

11.36 *ITEPA 2003, ss 409, 410* exclude from *ITEPA 2003, s 401* for 1995/96 onwards any reimbursement by the former employer of a payment in respect of an employee liability or indemnity insurance premium which would have been deductible by the employee under *ITEPA 2003, s 555* (see 5.95) had it not been reimbursed. If the employee has died a payment to his executors or administrators is similarly excluded. If the employer does not actually reimburse the expense but provides some other valuable consideration, the amount of such consideration is deemed to be a payment to the extent of the costs of the liability so as to preserve the exemption.

Information

11.37 The *PAYE Regulations* can require an employer or former employer to provide information in relation to these provisions. [*ITEPA 2003, s 684(4)*]. Up to 5 April 1998, where a termination payment within *ICTA 1988, s 148* was made, the payer had to send written particulars of the payment to the Inspector of Taxes not later than 30 days after the end of the year of assessment in which it was made. [*ICTA*

1988, s 148(7) before substitution by *FA 1998, s 58(1)*]. Failure to do so laid the payer open to a penalty of up to £300 (and a further £60 per day after the failure to deliver the particulars has been declared by the Courts or Commissioners). *[TMA 1970, s 98(1)(b)]*. The *PAYE Regulations* impose an obligation to deduct tax on the excess of the payment over £30,000.

11.38 The reporting obligation was reintroduced in an extended form from 6 April 1999 by what is now *Regulation 91* of the *PAYE Regulations*. This requires the employer (or former employer) to give details to the Revenue of any award of payments combined with other benefits or consisting solely of such benefits where the total amount of the payments and other benefits exceed £30,000 and to give the same details to the employee. There is no obligation to remind either the Revenue or the employee of benefits that are received by the employee in later years.

Ex gratia payments

11.39 Care needs to be taken with ex gratia payments to be able to demonstrate that the payment is not an emolument of the employee. The Inland Revenue will expect to see a minute authorising the payment and showing the reason for it. Many people recommend that the payment is made after the employment is terminated, to separate it from the employment. While it is doubtful if this is necessary, it is worth considering if it can be done without undue trouble. It remains a question of fact whether or not a payment is emoluments of an employment; the timing of the payment cannot change its nature.

11.40 The Revenue do however accept that it is unlikely that an implied contractual term to make a payment in lieu of notice can exist. This is because a contractual right to receive notice of termination of employment (whether specific or as a result of the *Employment Rights Act 1996*) would conflict with an implied right to receive a payment in lieu of notice. They do however say that in certain circumstances an exgratia payment can fall within the definition of earnings in *ITEPA 2003, s 7* because something can be an emolument even though it is non-contractual. If a payment in lieu of notice is paid as an automatic response to a termination, e.g. if every time there is a redundancy all employees receive a payment in lieu of any period of unworked notice, they consider that 'the payment is an integral part of the employer-employee relationship for the workplace, albeit non-contractual, and has its source in that relationship and nowhere else' (*Tax Bulletin 63*, Feb 2003).

11.41 In March 1991 the Pension Schemes Office (formerly the Superannuation Funds Office) stated (in *SFO/OPB Memorandum 104*) that the Revenue have been advised that an arrangement by an employer to pay ex gratia 'relevant benefits' to an employee constitutes a retirement benefit scheme. Such a scheme will not be an approved scheme, so the contribution to it, i.e. the ex gratia payment, will constitute emoluments taxable as employment income. Accordingly, *section 401* and, more importantly, the £30,000 exemption (see 11.21(*a*) above), will not apply to such a payment. 'Relevant benefits' are defined as 'any pension, lump sum, gratuity or other like benefit given or to be given on retirement or on death, or in anticipation of retirement, or in connection with past service, after retirement or death' or in connection with any change in the nature of the employee's service. [*ICTA 1988, s 612(1)*].

11.42   The Revenue say that 'self-evidently' there will be an 'arrangement' if the payment flows from any prior formal or informal arrangement with the employee. They also think that it includes any system, plan, pattern or policy for making such payments, such as a decision taken at a meeting to make an ex gratia payment, or where a personnel manager makes an ex gratia payment under a delegated authority or on the basis of some outline structure or policy, or where it is common practice for the employer to make ex gratia payments to a particular class of employee (*SP 13/91*).

11.43   The payment must be made in respect of death or retirement to be caught. The Revenue have said that an ex gratia payment on severance of the employment due to redundancy or loss of office (or because of death or disability due to an accident) is not affected 'where the arrangements for making the payment are designed solely to meet such a situation'. In particular, 'genuine redundancy payments' are not affected (*SP 13/91*).

11.44   They have also confirmed to the ICAEW (*Tax 15/92*) that:

(*a*)   a senior executive who changes jobs at age 45, obviously as part of his normal working career, is not retiring so any ex gratia payment is not affected by the approach;

(*b*)   if, however, at the time he changes jobs he is aged 60 'this might well be regarded as retirement', but would depend on the precise circumstances;

(*c*)   if a division of a company is sold and the 55-year-old manager responsible for running it leaves to take a job with the purchaser, this 'does not look to be consistent with retirement but with maximising his opportunities to continue working until normal retirement age' so it would probably not be caught;

(*d*)   if a person in his 50s has a heart attack and is advised by his doctor to leave work and seek a less stressful position that 'may well be viewed as retirement'—although if the ex gratia payment is made purely as compensation for the loss of health it would not be regarded as made in connection with the retirement; and

(*e*)   if an employee aged 50 leaves to take a job nearer home to be able to nurse her aged parents it would probably not be viewed as retirement bearing in mind the age of the employee and the fact that she obtains further work—but may well be regarded as retirement if she does not seek a further job.

11.45 They have told the Law Society (*Law Society Press Release 7 October 1992*) that whether an individual continues to work, or make him or herself available for work after employment is terminated is not conclusive. It is simply a factor to take into account. So is the age of the individual. 'An ex gratia payment made to a man moving on to a further full-time employment in his middle years will obviously not be made "on or in anticipation of retirement". However, an ex gratia payment to a man of older years who has no other full-time employment in prospect could fall on the other side of the line'. They also say that 'provided the situation has not been contrived for the purpose of obtaining favourable tax treatment, then termination of employment in circumstances which amount to unfair dismissal, whether that comes about because the employee is sacked or is forced to resign, will not constitute "retirement"'.

11.46 The Pension Schemes Office say the only benefits affected are lump sums, gratuities and similar benefits given:

(i) where a person retires or dies;

(ii) in anticipation of retirement;

(iii) after a person has retired or died (if the payment is in recognition of past services); or

(iv) as compensation for any change in the conditions of a continuing employment.

11.47 The Pension Schemes Office are willing to grant approval (so that the lump sum will become a non-taxable capital payment under an approved pension scheme) for an ex gratia lump sum payment if:

(*a*) it is the only lump sum relevant benefit potentially payable in respect of the employment (i.e. the employee is not a member of an approved pension scheme unless the payment is on retirement and the other scheme provides benefits only on death-in-service); and

(*b*) it satisfies the normal requirements for approval of a retirement benefit scheme; in particular the lump sum on retirement does not exceed 1½ times salary—or the appropriate lower figure where the employee has less than 40 years' service.

11.48 They are also prepared to accept, without formal approval, that a payment is tax-free if in addition to meeting those two conditions the payment (together with any other payments from associated employments) does not exceed ½ of the pensions earning cap, i.e. currently $\frac{1}{12}$ × £99,000 = £8,250 (*PSO Memorandum 111* and *SP 13/91*).

Payments in lieu of notice

11.49 Care also needs to be taken with payments in lieu of notice (PILONs). If the payment is compensation for a breach of the employment agreement or, probably, even agreed liquidated damages it will not be emoluments. However, if there is a contractual entitlement it will be general earnings within *ITEPA 2003, ss 7* and *62* to which the £30,000 exemption will not apply. The trap is well illustrated by the case of *EMI Electronics Ltd v Coldicott (1999) STC 803*, a Court of Appeal decision. The employment agreement provided for six months written notice but went on to say 'The company reserves the right to make payment of the equivalent of salary in lieu of notice'. It was held that this was sufficient to make the PILON a contractual payment assessable under *section 62*.

11.50   This principle was carried a step further in *Richardson v Delaney (2001 STC 1328)*. The employment agreement provided for an 18-month notice period but entitled the company to terminate the employment 'with immediate effect' by paying salary in lieu of notice. On 1 December 1995 it gave the 18-months notice and put the employee on garden leave. At the same time it suggested an alternative, namely that the employment should terminate by mutual agreement on 28 December 1995, and the company would make a payment to the employee of £68,001 in compensation for the premature termination of the employment. After negotiation the compensation payment was agreed at £75,000 plus the taxpayer would keep his company car worth £10,000. Lloyd J could see no breach of contract. The company was entitled to give notice to terminate the contract. It was entitled to make a payment in lieu of notice. That payment could not become compensation simply because the employment had continued for a month, and the payment in lieu covered only 17 months. Whilst that is logical, it is hard to reconcile with the terms of the employment agreement. The employment was not terminated by the company with immediate effect. It was terminated by notice and, as a separate agreement, it was subsequently mutually agreed that the notice period would not be worked and that a payment would be made. It may well be that this agreement varied the employment contract and would be taxable as such, but that was not the basis of the decision.

11.51   Lloyd J was strongly influenced by dicta of Lord Browne-Wilkinson in *Delaney v Staples [1992] 1 AC 687*, an unfair dismissal case. Lord Browne-Wilkinson had there identified four principle categories of case in which a payment is made that could be described as in lieu of notice:

(*a*)   where proper notice is given, the employee is put on garden leave, and he is paid the whole of his wages up-front instead of month by month;

(*b*)   where the contract of employment provides expressly that the employment may be terminated either by notice or on payment of a sum in lieu;

(*c*)   where at the end of the employment the employer and employee agree that the employment is to terminate forthwith on payment of a sum in lieu of notice; and (*d*) where without the agreement of the employee the employer summarily dismisses the employee and tenders a payment in lieu of proper notice.

Lord Browne-Wilkinson was concerned to determine whether or not a payment was wages, not if it was compensation. Lloyd J could not fit the payment to Mr Delaney into any of the four categories. He thought it was 'to some extent ... closer to Lord Browne-Wilkinson's third category although not entirely foreign to his second category'.

11.52 This is a somewhat worrying decision. Many terminations fall between categories (*c*) and (*d*). The employee agrees to prematurely terminate his employment by resigning and the employer agrees to make a payment. This is generally a cosmetic procedure as the employee is anxious to avert falling within category (*d*). If category (*d*) is the only true case of a breach of contract, as Lloyd J clearly implies, can the employee resign and yet still be within (*d*)? He probably could do if the employer summarily dismisses him and the payment (and the resignation) is made in settlement of a challenge by the employee against the validity of the purported dismissal and in settlement of his claim against that challenge.

11.53 The Revenue issued further guidance in *Tax Bulletin 63* (Feb 2003) in the light of a January 2001 employment case, *Cerberus Software Ltd v Rowley (2001 IRLR 160)*. In that case the Court of Appeal held that a provision in the contract that an employer 'may' make a PILON meant that the employer was free to give neither notice nor a PILON but instead to breach the contract and pay damages for the breach. The Revenue do not consider that this conflicts with the *EMI* decision, as in *EMI* 'the employer had exercised his discretion and so ensured that the source of the payment was the employer-employee relationship' whereas in *Cerberus* it had suited the employer to breach the contract as the ex-employee had found alternative employment during the notice period.

11.54 The Revenue say that it is crucial to establish and examine the facts to decide whether the discretion has been exercised. Factors that may be relevant include:

– A settlement that is substantially the same in value as an exercise of the discretion would have produced is likely to be viewed as made by exercise of the discretion, as happened in *Richardson v Delaney* (although each case will depend on its own facts).

– A payment resulting from a decision not to exercise discretion could be expected to have characteristics normally associated with compensation or damages for breach of contract (such as the employee by securing alternative employment had reduced the loss or damage caused by the employer's breach).

– Other adjustments are common when calculating payments for a breach (such as the application of the decision in *British Transport Commission v Gourley ([1955] 3 All ER 796)* that the real loss is the after-tax income that the employee would have received), and

–   A decision by an employer not to exercise its discretion might be evidenced in writing.

Legal expenses

11.55   Legal expenses incurred in connection with a claim for compensation for loss of office are not deductible from the compensation. The charge under *section 401* is on the actual amount of the payment (*Warnett v Jones 53 TC 283*). It will not help if the settlement requires the employer to pay the legal costs. As this relieves the employee of an obligation to settle an expense that he has incurred, the payment of such fees is itself a benefit within *section 401*. However, by concession the Revenue will not seek tax on the receipt of legal costs recovered by a successful ex-employee under a court order (including one following a compromise of action), or where a dispute is settled without court action on terms that include a specific undertaking to pay the ex-employee's costs. In the latter case the payment must be made direct to the ex-employee's solicitor and the costs to which it relates must be exclusively in connection with the termination of the employment (*ESC A81* and *Law Society Press Release 3 November 1993*). The concession does not apply to other professional fees—in particular, accountancy fees—but if the accountant, valuer or other professional is engaged by the solicitor and his fees are shown as disbursements on the solicitor's bill (or absorbed by the solicitor in his own costs) the Revenue accept that they form part of the legal costs (*Tax Bulletin, Issue 13, October 1994*).

Lump sums under approved pension schemes

11.56   Lump sums paid (whether on retirement or otherwise) either:

(*a*)   in pursuance of an approved pension scheme (except where it is compensation paid for loss of office or for loss or diminution of emoluments where such loss is not due to ill health);

(*b*)   in pursuance of a retirement benefits scheme within *ICTA 1988, s 611* (see 10.7 above); or

(*c*)   under approved personal pension arrangements within *ICTA 1988, ss 630–655* (10.27–10.56),

are specifically exempted from income tax. [*ITEPA 2003, s 637*]. This will exempt such payments not only from the general charging provisions but also from *section 401*. However, in the case of a personal pension scheme if the member's death occurred after his normal pension date, i.e. if he was taking income withdrawals from the fund, the lump sum is taxable. The tax is at a flat rate of 35 per cent, payable by the pension scheme administrator and is not income for any other tax purposes. [*ICTA 1988, s 648B*]. The reason for the charge is that the lump sum (which will be a return of contributions with interest) is in lieu of future annuity payments, which would themselves have been taxable.

Members of Parliament

11.57 Grants and payments made by the House of Commons to a person who ceases to be an MP on dissolution of Parliament, under *section 131* of the *Parliamentary Pensions Act 1984* to persons ceasing to hold certain ministerial and other offices, or under *section 3* of the *European Parliament (Pay and Pensions) Act 1979* which provides for resettlement grants to persons ceasing to be Euro MPs, are similarly exempted from tax. Curiously, such grants remain taxable under *section 401* to the extent they exceed £30,000. [*ITEPA 2003, s 291*].

Redundancy payments

11.58 Statutory redundancy payments are specifically exempted from tax as earnings, except under *section 401*. [*ITEPA 2003, s 309*]. So is any additional voluntary payment by the employer, but only up to a figure equal to the statutory payment, i.e. twice the statutory payment can be paid tax-free. [*ITEPA 2003, s 309(2)*].

11.59 On the privatisation of Harland & Wolff employees were offered new employment by a proposed buy-out company, Harland & Wolff 1989 Ltd. To induce him to accept, an employee was given an ex gratia payment consisting of two elements, 30 per cent of the sum to which he would have been entitled under Harland & Wolff's non-statutory redundancy scheme, and £100 per complete year of service with Harland & Wolff. The Revenue contended that the entire payment was an inducement to accept the new employment and as such was an emolument of it. The House of Lords unanimously held that the sum was severable; the 30 per cent element being a payment in reality to give up the employee's rights under the Harland & Wolff redundancy scheme and as such 'derives its character from the nature of the payment which it replaces', and the £100 per annum payment being taxable under Schedule E (*Mairs v Haughey* [*1993*] *STC 569*).

11.60 Their Lordships criticised the Revenue for not applying *SP 1/81* (which said that the Revenue would not assess the first £30,000 of non-statutory redundancy pay, even if it was part of the conditions under which the employees agreed to give their services or they had an expectation of it). They also held that in any event in law a redundancy payment is not an emolument. It has 'a real element of compensating or relieving an employee for the consequences of his not being able to earn a living in his former employment. The redundancy legislation reflects an appreciation that an employee who has remained in employment . . . has a stake in his employment which justifies his receiving compensation if he loses that stake. It is distinct from the damages to which he would be entitled if his employment were terminated lawfully. It is also unlike a deferred payment of wages in that the entitlement to a redundancy payment is never more than a contingent entitlement, which no doubt both the employer and employee normally hope will never accrue'. A redundancy payment is not a payment from being or becoming an employee (per *Shilton v Wilmshurst*—see 11.72); it is to compensate or relieve an employee for what can be the unfortunate consequences of becoming unemployed. It is also paid after the employment has come to an end, a *prima facie* indication that it is not an emolument from that employment.

11.61 Following that decision the Revenue withdrew *SP 1/81* and replaced it by *SP 1/94*. This accepts that non-statutory redundancy is taxable only under *ITEPA 2003, s 401* (i.e. only on the excess over £30,000) whether the scheme is a standing one which forms part of the terms on which the employees give their services or is an *ad hoc* scheme devised to meet a specific situation. It goes on to warn that payments 'which are not genuinely made to compensate for loss of employment through redundancy . . . In particular payments which are in reality a form of terminal bonus' are taxable in full. It instances as terminal bonuses payments for meeting production targets or doing extra work in the period leading up to a redundancy, and payments conditional on continual service in the employment for a time after the issue of the redundancy notice. It concludes by suggesting that employers might wish to submit redundancy schemes to their local Inspector (enclosing the scheme document plus the text of any intended letter to employees) for advance clearance as to whether the payments are taxable.

11.62 It is important that the employee actually becomes redundant as is shown by *Allan v IRC [1994] STC 943*. An old established company operating two stores decided to close down its business and sell its assets. It resolved to make redundancy payments to a number of employees. After closing the first store it received an offer for the company which was accepted. The shareholders felt that the redundancy payments should still be made irrespective of whether an employee was kept on by the purchaser. The company was sold in March 1982 and in May 1982 it paid a redundancy payment to Mr Allen. Mr Allen continued to be employed by the company. It was held that, although originally intended as a redundancy payment, the payment had changed its character by the time it was made. At that stage it was a payment by an employer to its employee. The payment arose from the employment and from nothing else as Mr. Allen had never, in fact, been made redundant.

11.63 In *Antelope v Ellis [1995] STC (SCD) 297* the taxpayer was employed as managing director of a subsidiary company within a group from around 1986. In 1991 the group wished him to relinquish that post and become managing director of a second group company. He did not want the new job but eventually agreed to the transfer on condition that if he were to leave the group before March 1993 he would receive a substantial redundancy payment. He ceased the employment within that period and received the payment. The Special Commissioner held that it was not a termination payment (to which the £30,000 exemption would apply) but an inducement to take the employment with the second company. It is hard to reconcile this decision with *Mairs v Haughey*. It does not appear that the case was cited to the Commissioner, who accepted the Crown's submission based on *Prendergast v Cameron 23 TC 122*—see 11.6.

11.64   Because of the difficulty of valuing such benefits—in particular the benefit of cheap mortgage until he finds another job when an employee of a bank is made redundant—the Revenue announced a concession applying where an employment terminated after 6 April 1996 and before 6 April 1998. The employee could, if he wished, show on his tax return for the year of termination any cash sum received plus the amount of the benefit enjoyed for that year only, calculated by reference to *ITEPA 2003, s 398* (see 10.61). In most cases these follow the benefit in kind rules for employees. No benefits need then be shown on the return in later years. Instead, the Revenue will raise an assessment on the taxpayer each year for the benefit enjoyed in that year. If the taxpayer can show that the aggregate amount assessed exceeds the amount that would have been taxable on the statutory basis the assessments will be limited to that amount. As this cut off depends on the valuation exercise which the concession is designed to circumvent it is unlikely that many people will claim it. If the taxpayer opts to adopt the statutory basis of valuing the right to the future benefit at the date of termination, the Revenue say that the amount adopted cannot subsequently be re-opened if it proves excessive, e.g. because the benefit ceases earlier than was anticipated. It is not wholly clear that such an incorrect assumption cannot be an error entitling the taxpayer to re-open the return under *TMA 1970, s 33*. This concession is no longer needed following the changes introduced in the *FA 1998* (see 11.14) which have broadly the same effect as the concession.

11.65   Where, as part of the arrangements for the termination of a person's employment, the employer agrees to make a special payment into an occupational pension scheme for the employee (or purchases an annuity from a life office, which is approved as a pension scheme) the Revenue will not seek to charge tax under *ITEPA 2003, s 401* in relation to the payment (*SP 2/81*).

Golden handcuffs

11.66   Particular problems arise where the employment is not the only reason for a payment. Thus, on the sale of a business the price to be paid for the goodwill or for shares could be tied to the length of the vendor's service with the purchasing company. This was a popular ploy when firms of stockbrokers were sold in the mid-1980s. The partners would be issued with loan stock or a similar security of the purchaser which would be redeemable at the time he ceased to work for the purchaser. The redemption terms would vary according to the length of service, e.g. the loan stock could be redeemable at par within the first year, at £1.20 if redeemed in the second, £1.40 if redeemed in the third, and so on. It was usually a term of the agreement that the company would be entitled to redeem the loan stock if the partner ceased to work for it.

11.67 This sort of arrangement has the same effect as paying the employee a loyalty bonus if he remains with the company for more than a year. Nevertheless, it is likely that, in normal circumstances, the full redemption price of the loan stock would be a capital gain, not income. Such arrangements are probably only viable in certain types of business. It would need to be established that the ultimate redemption price reflects the real value of the business at the time of acquisition and that the requirement for the vendor to remain with the company was felt necessary to enable that value to be fully realised. If this cannot be shown, the Revenue might well be able to show that the increase in the price to be paid for the loan stock arose from the employment.

Signing-on fees

Case law

Riley v Coglan

11.68 If a payment is made to a person on, or prior to, taking up an employment it is necessary to analyse the real reason for the payment. If it is to induce him to take up the job, the payment will be regarded as an emolument of that employment. This is particularly likely to be the case if the payment is tied to the employee remaining in the employment for a specified period. In *Riley v Coglan 44 TC 481* an amateur rugby player received a signing-on fee on joining a rugby league club as a professional. The agreement provided that part of the fee was to be returnable if he did not remain with the club for a specified period. It was held that the payment was remuneration, being a reward for remaining in the club's employment for the period.

Jarrold v Boustead

11.69 In contrast, if the payment is to induce the person to give up some existing benefit that is incompatible with the employment, that payment may not constitute emoluments. The leading case is *Jarrold v Boustead 41 TC 701*, another case where an amateur rugby player received a signing-on fee for joining a rugby league club. It was held that the payment was not a reward for his future services to the club; it was to compensate him for having to give up his amateur status. He attached value to this as, once lost, it could not be regained.

Pritchard v Arundale, Vaughan-Neil v CIR

11.70 In *Pritchard v Arundale 47 TC 680* a senior partner in a successful firm of accountants was approached to become managing director of a company. He was not prepared to give up his professional practice without the company showing sufficient commitment to him to give him the confidence to leave his partnership. The major shareholder of the company accordingly transferred to him a substantial block of shares in the company. The Revenue claimed that those shares were a reward for the future services he was to perform for the company. It was held that it was to induce him to give up professional practice and did not constitute emoluments. Similarly, in *Vaughan-Neil v IRC 54 TC 223* a payment to a practising barrister who gave up the bar and took employment with a company was held to be an inducement to accept the professional and social consequences flowing from taking up an employment. Interestingly, in that case the Revenue conceded that the payment was not remuneration of the employment but contended that it was assessable as a restrictive covenant as he agreed to cease his practice at the bar. The court did not feel this was tenable as the bar's rules of conduct prevent an employed barrister from continuing in practice, and the payment could not, in reality, be to prohibit him from doing something that he was powerless to do.

11.71   Unfortunately, this does not always hold good. Each case needs to be looked at on its own merits. In *Glantre Engineering Ltd v Goodhand 56 TC 165*, a payment of £10,000 made to Mr Wells, an employee of a leading firm of accountants, to induce him to take up employment with an engineering company was held to be taxable. Warner J distinguished the case from that of *Pritchard v Arundale* on three grounds. The payment to Mr Wells was made by the prospective employer; that to Mr Arundale was made by a third party. Mr Arundale was not merely changing from one employment to another; he was exchanging the status of senior partner in a firm of chartered accountants for that of joint managing director of, and shareholder in, a company. Mr Arundale was entitled to his shares on signing the agreement but was not to start work until some time later and if he had died in the interim his estate would have been entitled to retain the shares; Mr Well's payment was one of the specific terms of his new employment. As Warner J reversed the decision of the Commissioners this suggests that the circumstances in which an inducement payment is not taxable are likely to be fairly limited. Mr Wells did give up the security of working for a major firm of accountants and the likelihood of a future partnership with it and the payment was specifically stated to compensate for the losses.

Shilton v Wilmshurst

11.72   In *Shilton v Wilmshurst [1990] STC 55* Nottingham Forest FC agreed with Southampton FC to transfer to Southampton the contract of the footballer, Peter Shilton, in return for a substantial transfer fee. This transfer would only go through if Shilton himself agreed satisfactory terms of employment with Southampton. Nottingham Forest made a payment to Shilton to induce him to agree to join Southampton. The

Revenue contended that their payment was remuneration for his future services with Southampton, whereas Shilton claimed that it was taxable under *section 148* (subject to the first £30,000 being exempt) as a payment on the termination of his employment with Nottingham Forest. The Court of Appeal observed that Nottingham Forest would obtain no benefit from Shilton's services to Southampton so it was hard to see why they should remunerate him for such services. Their only interest was in obtaining the transfer fee from Southampton, and the payment was to induce Shilton to undertake the necessary steps to enable this to be paid to them. However, the House of Lords dismissed this distinction. The question to be asked was whether the payment was an emolument 'from employment', i.e. from being or becoming an employee. The fact that Nottingham Forest had a different motive for making the payment did not stop it being a payment in return for the taxpayer agreeing to become an employee of Southampton. It was made available to Shilton in return for his agreeing to render services to Southampton. It was putting a gloss on the legislation to suggest that payment by a third party could only be an emolument if that party has an interest in the performance of the duties.

Teward v CIR

11.73   In *Teward v IRC [2001] STC (SCD) 36* Mr Teward was employed by Glaxochem Ltd. That company sold one of its plants to Synpac Chemicals Ltd. The taxpayer agreed to join Synpac. A stumbling block was Mr Teward's share options in Glaxo Holdings plc, the parent company of Glaxochem. Synpac agreed to pay Mr Teward £24,103, the amount of the loss Mr Teward would suffer on being forced to abandon his share options, in consideration of his entering into a service agreement with Synpac. Mr Teward argued that the payment was compensation for giving up his advantages under the Glaxo share option schemes and was unconnected with his employment with Synpac. The Commissioners thought it clear from the evidence that the payment formed part of the package of arrangements whereby Mr Teward became an employee of Synpac. Accordingly the new employment was the source of the payment.

11.74   In spite of the above cases, it is unsafe to assume that a signing-on fee can be paid tax-free. The Inland Revenue are likely to take the stance that any such payment relates to future services and the taxpayer may well have to pursue his case before the courts if he is to show otherwise.

Payments for a restrictive covenant

11.75   If an employee, ex-employee or potential employee (or director) gives, in connection with holding that employment or office, an undertaking the tenor or effect of which is to restrict him as to his conduct or activities, any sum that is paid to him in respect of giving the undertaking (or of its total or partial fulfilment) must be treated as an emolument of the employment if it would not otherwise be so. [*ITEPA 2003, s 225(3)*]. This applies whether or not the undertaking is legally valid. It applies not only to a payment to the employee himself but also to a payment to any other person. If the employee dies before receiving the payment it must be treated as having been paid immediately before his death. [*ITEPA 2003, s 225(5)*]. This provision does not apply if the remuneration from the employment is taxable on the remittance basis, i.e. is not general earnings. [*ITEPA 2003, s 225(6)*]. Any valuable consideration given in relation to such an undertaking is taxed in the same way as a sum of money. [*ITEPA 2003, s 226*]. For this purpose, the mere assumption of an obligation to make over or provide valuable property, rights or advantages does not constitute valuable consideration—but anything done in the discharge of such an obligation does. [*ITEPA 2003, s 226(2)*].

11.76 It is, therefore, not possible to avoid income tax on a signing-on fee or termination payment by paying it for a restrictive covenant. In *RCI (Europe) Ltd v Woods (2004 STC 315)*, Mr Haylock agreed to be bound by a restrictive covenant up to December 1995. The agreement provided that he could elect for the restrictive covenant to continue to apply to December 1996 and December 1997, in which case he would be entitled to further payments. His contention that such further payments did not fall within *ITEPA 2003, s 226* as they were derived from the elections, not from the employment, was dismissed by Lightman J. The elections were a continuation of covenants given in relation to the termination of the office. The reason the continued undertakings were given was that Mr Haylock had held the office of director. Mr Haylock also contended that even if the payments arose from his employment he was not gainfully employed by RCI Europe at the time they were received so the payment could not be taxed. Lightman J held that the payment did not fall within what is now *Reg 8(5)* of the *Social Security (Contributions) Regulations 2001 (2001 SI 1004)* (earnings period for payments made after a person ceased to be a director in relation to periods in which he was a director to be the year in which they are paid) as the payment did not relate to any particular period. Accordingly the normal rules, which gave a one-week earnings period, applied.

11.77 At one stage there was evidence that some Inspectors were seeking to tax payments as termination of employment as consideration for a restrictive covenant on the basis that as part of the arrangements for the termination of the employment it is common for an employee to agree not to take any further action for damages against the employer—and fairly common for him to sign an acknowledgement that the compensation is in full and final settlement of all claims against the employer. The Revenue argue that this restricts the employee's future conduct and thus the payment is within *section 226 (Taxline, November 1994, Item 149)*. In most cases such an argument does not accord with the facts. The compensation is not paid 'in respect of the giving of the undertaking', it is paid in respect of the premature cessation of the employment. The

Revenue now accept that no chargeable value should be attributed to such undertakings. This applies not only where the employee accepts the termination settlement in full and final settlement of his claims but also where the agreement expressly provides that the employee should not commence, or should discontinue, legal action in respect of his claims, and where it re-affirms undertakings about the individual's conduct or activity after termination which formed part of the terms on which the employment was taken up (*SP 3/96*).

11.78 The Revenue still consider that a charge would arise if an employer were to make a payment specifically for an undertaking not to litigate. What if there is no such provision but the compromise agreement contains a 'repayment clause', i.e. a requirement for the employee to repay some or all of the compensation if he subsequently initiates litigation in respect of the employment or its termination? The Revenue say this should not trigger a tax charge. If the settlement sum is paid in consideration of settling the employee's genuine claim 'the settlement sum is exhausted by reference to those claims and no sum remains to be attributable to the undertaking not to litigate ... whether or not a repayment clause exists'. They will however challenge the entire arrangement if the employee's claims appear spurious. The Revenue also point out that if a repayment clause is activated that has no affect on the taxation of the original compromise payment; there is no provision to allow relief for the repayment (*Tax Bulletin 67*, Oct 2003).

Transfer of assets

11.79 If an asset is transferred to the employee as part of his termination arrangements the market value of the asset will be taxed in accordance with the above rules. In addition there may be capital gains tax or capital allowance consequences. *TCGA 1992, s 17(1)(b)* requires the capital gain to be calculated by reference to market value where an asset is disposed of in connection with a person's (not necessarily the transferee's) loss of office or employment or diminution of emoluments or otherwise in consideration for, or in recognition of, past services in an office or employment. If the asset has qualified for capital allowances as plant and machinery, e.g. it is a company car, and it is sold below market value the actual sale price is used as the disposal value for capital allowance purposes where there is a charge to tax under Schedule E on the disposal. [*CAA 2001, s 61(2)*]. This does not appear to envisage a Schedule E charge on the full amount of the undervalue, but if the whole amount is excepted from tax by *ITEPA 2003, 403(1)* (see 11.21(*a*)), the disposal value appears to be the market value, not the price paid if less.

Chapter 12

Foreign Nationals Working in the UK

Reliefs available

12.1   There are a number of special reliefs for foreign nationals working in the UK. Some of these can also apply to a UK national who is not domiciled in the UK or returns to the UK after having been resident and ordinarily resident overseas for a period of years.

Employment in the UK for short periods

12.2   If a person is neither resident nor ordinarily resident in the UK he will be taxable only on earnings for duties performed in the UK. Accordingly, if any duties of the employment are performed outside the UK the salary has to be apportioned between UK and non-UK work, with only the part attributable to the former being chargeable to UK tax.

12.3   The meaning of residence and ordinary residence is considered in Chapter 2 (see 2.12 above). It must also be borne in mind that the 'tie-breaker' clause of a double taxation agreement may prevent a person from being regarded as UK resident even though he would be resident in the UK under the normal rules (see 13.4 below). Although ordinary residence is a peculiarly British concept and as such is not normally referred to in double taxation agreements, it is sufficient to show that a person is not UK resident to take his non-UK earnings outside UK tax irrespective of whether or not he may be ordinarily resident in the UK.

12.4   Where a person comes to the UK to take up employment he is treated as resident from the date of his arrival if he comes to work for at least two years and ordinarily resident from the same date if it is clear that he intends to stay for at least three (*Booklet IR20 paragraphs 3.7, 3.8*). If these tests are not met at the time of his arrival the normal residence rules apply, i.e. he will normally be UK resident in the tax year of arrival only if he is physically present in the UK for over 183 days. He will be regarded as ordinarily resident from the start of the tax year following the third anniversary of his arrival, unless prior to then he makes a decision to remain in the UK for at least three years (from the date of his arrival) or buys accommodation or acquires it on a lease of three years or more—in which case he will be regarded as UK ordinarily resident from the start of the tax year in which the event occurs (or from the date of arrival in the UK if it occurs in the tax year in which he comes to the UK (*Booklet IR20 paragraphs 3.9–3.11*)).

Double taxation agreements

12.5   If a resident of a country with which the UK has entered into a double taxation agreement works in the UK the double tax agreement will usually exempt him from UK tax on his salary provided that:

(*a*)   he is not present in the UK for more than 183 days during the year of assessment (or a 12-month period commencing or ending in that year);

(*b*)   the remuneration is paid by, or on behalf of, an employer who is not a resident of the UK; and

(*c*)   the remuneration is not borne as such by a permanent establishment or a fixed base of the employer in the UK.

12.6   See, for example, *article 15* of the *UK/USA Double Taxation Convention* (*SI 2002 No 2648*). As the wording of double taxation agreements differs, the applicable agreement needs to be referred to in each case to ascertain the exact scope of the exemption. In particular, it will often not apply to artists, athletes and entertainers, or to merchant seamen crewing a UK registered ship or aircraft engaged in international trade.

12.7   In the past the Revenue accepted that head (*b*) was satisfied if the non-resident remained an employee of an overseas employer where he was seconded by that employer to a UK associated company. They now consider this wrong and interpret the reference to the employer as meaning the 'economic employer' rather than the legal one. Accordingly, they do not consider that the exemption applies when the cost of the employee's salary has been borne by a UK company that uses his services. This new approach applies for 1995/96 where the UK work assignment started after 1 July 1995 and from 1996/97 in all other cases (*Tax Bulletin, Issue 17, June 1995*).

12.8   Double taxation agreements can also exempt certain other types of earnings. For example, several of the UK's double tax agreements exempt earnings of professors or teachers who visit the UK for a period of up to two years for the purpose of teaching or research, although it was suggested in the case of *IRC v Vas* [*1990*] *STC 137* that this relief can apply only to earnings in the 24 months from the time of the person's first such visit to the UK even if that was of very short duration. In any event, if a visit exceeds two years the exemption does not apply at all; the earnings for the whole period, not merely the excess over two years, will be taxable. Payments to students who are in the UK for the purpose of full-time education or training are also generally exempted. So, normally, is remuneration of employees of the foreign government (or a political subdivision thereof) unless they are UK nationals.

Overseas Earnings

12.9   Overseas earnings (formerly called 'foreign emoluments') are earnings of a person not domiciled in the UK from an office or employment with an employer resident outside the UK and the Republic of Ireland (provided he is not also UK resident—i.e. is not dual resident). [*ITEPA 2003, s 22*].

12.10   If the duties of an office or employment are performed wholly outside the UK and the emoluments therefrom are foreign emoluments, the income is excepted from the basic rules on taxing earnings under *ITEPA 2003, s 9* (see 2.5), but it will then be assessable under *Section 23* (see 2.6) on a remittance basis.

12.11   Where an employee is resident and ordinarily resident in the UK but not UK domiciled he is taxable on a remittance basis in relation to 'chargeable overseas earnings'. [*ITEPA 2003, s 22(2)*]. 'Overseas earnings' for this purpose are earnings from an employment with a foreign employer the duties of which are performed wholly outside the UK. A foreign employer for this purpose is an individual, partnership or body of persons resident outside the UK and not resident in the UK (i.e. not dual resident) or in the Republic of Ireland. [*ITEPA 2003, ss 23(2), 721(1)*]. Prior to 2003/04 such earnings were called 'foreign emoluments'. If the duties are not performed wholly outside the UK, or if the employer is a UK company, partnership or individual, the whole of the earnings from the employment are taxable in the UK whether or not they are remitted to the UK.

12.12   If an employee is resident but not ordinarily resident in the UK (irrespective of where he is domiciled) he is also taxable on a remittance basis but only in respect of earnings for duties performed outside the UK (other than an overseas Crown employment subject to UK tax). [*ITEPA 2003, s 26(2)*]. Such a person is taxable on his earnings for work performed in the UK irrespective of whether or not he is paid in the UK or remits the earnings to the UK.

12.13   It should be stressed that in such a case the earnings – or at least the part attributable to non-UK work – need to be paid outside the UK. If the salary is paid in the UK this will have the effect of remitting the part attributable to non-UK work and thus bringing it within the charge to UK tax.

12.14   As indicated at 12.2, if the employee is neither resident nor ordinarily resident in the UK he is taxable in the UK only on earnings from work done in the UK.

Associated employments

12.15   If during a tax year an employee holds an associated employment as well as the employment with a foreign employer which gives rise to overseas earnings, and the duties of the associated employment (or employments) are performed wholly or partly in the UK, the earnings from the two employments need to be aggregated and re-apportioned on a reasonable basis if that would result in a lower amount being regarded as overseas earnings within 12.9 above. [*ITEPA 2003, s 24*]. The detailed rules are considered at 13.24 below.

Payments out of foreign emoluments

12.16 If an employee makes payments out of his overseas earnings or foreign emoluments in circumstances corresponding to those in which the payments would have reduced his liability to income tax, the Board of Inland Revenue can allow those payments as a deduction in calculating the amount of the emoluments. [*ITEPA 2003, s 355*]. In the past they exercised this discretion to allow a deduction for foreign alimony or maintenance payments, mortgage interest relief and pension contributions, to the extent that such payments would have been deducted if they had been made in the UK under a UK source agreement. For 1992/93 onwards a deduction for an annuity or other annual payment cannot be allowed unless it would have been within the charge to Schedule D, Case III had it arisen in the UK. [*F(No 2)A 1992, s 60*]. This prevents a deduction being given for, in particular, foreign maintenance where a deduction would not be allowed for UK maintenance. The main item to which this relief now applies is foreign pension contributions to a scheme whose terms correspond to a UK approved pension scheme. Where such deductions, or a deduction for foreign travel expenses, other expenses incurred in relation to the employment, or for pension payments under a UK pension scheme, are allowed the emoluments are treated as reduced by those deductions (so only the net amount is capable of being remitted within Case III). If the 25 per cent deduction referred to at 12.12 above applied, this was given on the net salary after such deductions. [*ICTA 1988, s 192(5)*].

The remittance basis

12.17 As indicated at 12.10 above, some earnings are taxable only to the extent, and at the time, that they are remitted to the UK. An amount is treated as remitted to the UK if it is:

(*a*)   paid in the UK;

(*b*)   used or enjoyed in the UK; or

(*c*)   in any manner or form transmitted or brought to the UK.

[*ITEPA 2003, s 33(2)*].

Treatment of debts

12.18 It is specifically provided that income must be treated as having been remitted to the UK if it is applied outside the UK by a person who is ordinarily resident in the UK in (or towards) satisfaction of a 'UK-linked debt', namely:

(*a*)   any debt for money lent to him in the UK (or for interest on such a debt);

(*b*)   any debt for money lent to him outside the UK which has itself been brought into the UK (presumably only by the taxpayer); or

(*c*)   any debt incurred for satisfying in whole or in part a debt falling within (*a*) or (*b*) (or a prior replacement debt).

[*ITEPA 2003, s 33(3)(4)*].

12.19   If the employee brings into the UK money lent to him overseas, but the overseas debt is satisfied out of the remuneration before he brings in the funds, (*a*) to (*c*) above apply as if the money had been brought into the UK before the debt was satisfied—but the remittance will be deemed to take place at the time the money is actually brought into the UK. [*ITEPA 2003, s 33(5)*].

12.20   If a mortgage is raised overseas to buy a UK property the repayment of the principal will amount to a remittance but the payment of the interest will not if it is paid overseas out of funds left overseas.

12.21   If the employee borrows money and income is applied by him in such a way that the money (or property representing it) is held by the lender on behalf of (or to the account of) the borrower in such circumstances that it is available to the lender for the purpose of reducing the debt (by set-off or otherwise), the income must be treated as applied by the employee in satisfaction of the debt—but only if, under the arrangement between the lender and the employee, the amount for the time being of the employee's indebtedness to the lender (or the time at which the debt is to be repaid or reduced) depends in any respect directly or indirectly on the amount or value so held by the lender. [*ITEPA 2003, s 34(2)–(4)*]. This would not deem salary accumulating in the employee's deposit account in Bank A overseas to have been used to settle a loan from Bank A merely because the bank have a right of set-off under the general law. If, however, there is an arrangement that the bank will lend the employee 80 per cent of the balance from time to time on his deposit account, the payments into the deposit account (or at least 80 per cent of them) will be treated as remitted to the UK when the employee brings the loan moneys into the UK.

12.22   A loan is deemed to have been incurred for the purpose of satisfying a prior debt to the extent to which it is so used, and if a lender assigns or transmits the right to repayment the person for the time being entitled to the debt is treated as the lender. [*ITEPA 2003, s 34(5)(6)*].

12.23   Heads (*b*) and (*c*) in 12.18 above are very widely drawn. They appear to treat as a remittance bringing into the UK an asset bought overseas. However, the Revenue's consultative document on residence issued in July 1988 indicated a more relaxed attitude. They do not regard bringing a foreign asset, such as a car, into the UK as a remittance, but if it is sold whilst in the UK they regard the proceeds as a remittance. In contrast while many people would not regard using a credit card outside the UK and paying the bill overseas as a remittance the Revenue consider that it is if the credit card company is a UK company. They apparently consider this to be the case even if the credit card company obtains payment by exercising a direct debit authority on a foreign bank account (*Inspector's Manual, para 1569*). It is highly questionable whether that is a correct analysis.

Overseas savings, etc.

12.24   Where an employee has overseas earnings or foreign emoluments outside the UK and also has other funds, such as savings from a period before he came to the UK, it should be noted that the onus is on the taxpayer to disprove an assessment. Once the funds become mixed, for example, by putting the savings and the earnings, or amounts derived from the sale of investments made out of the earnings, into the same bank account, it becomes impossible to show that remittances out of that account are not remittances of the earnings. Accordingly, the foreign emoluments should be paid into a separate overseas bank account from other funds. It would be sensible to use the earnings account to meet non-UK expenditure, so maximising the amount of savings that are available to be remitted to the UK.

Relief for delayed remittances

12.25   Where a person who is taxable on the remittance basis and brings earnings into the UK in a particular year and could not have remitted them earlier because of either:

(*a*)   the laws of the country or territory where the earnings were received;

(*b*)   executive action of its government; or

(*c*)   the impossibility of obtaining in that country currency (other than the currency of that country or territory) that could be transferred to the UK;

he can claim to treat the earnings as having been remitted to the UK in the year in which they were received in the overseas country. [*ITEPA 2003, s 35*]. Such an election would avoid a bunching of taxable income.

12.26   If the taxpayer already has unremittable earnings for an earlier year or years he can choose which year's earnings his deemed remittance represents (up to the amount of the previously unremitted earnings for each particular year). Such an election must be included in the *ITEPA 2003, s 35* claim and is irrevocable. If the person has died before the earnings become remittable the election can be made by personal representatives. [*ITEPA 2003, s 36*].

12.27   A claim under *ITEPA 2003, s 35* must be made by the fifth anniver-sary of 31 January following the tax year in which the funds are remitted to the UK. The resultant adjustments to earlier year's tax can be made even though the normal time limit for doing so has expired. If the taxpayer has died before the funds become remittable the claim can be made by his personal representatives and the personal representatives are liable for the tax as a debt due from and payable out of the estate. [*ITEPA 2003, s 36*]. It should be noted that the relief applies only to the extent that the funds are actually remitted to the UK in the tax year in which the restrictions on remitting them cease to apply. There is no relief if the remittance is delayed to a later year.

Travelling expenses

Special relief

12.28   There is a special relief for travelling expenses of an employee who is not domiciled in the UK and is in receipt of emoluments for duties performed in the UK. [*ITEPA 2003, s 337(1)*]. It applies if one of the following conditions is satisfied on the date on which the employee arrives in the UK to perform duties of the office or employment, (the qualifying arrival date), namely:

(a)   the employee was not resident in the UK in either of the two years of assessment immediately prior to that in which the qualifying arrival date (or the first such date in the year of assessment if there is more than one) falls; or

(b)   he was not in the UK for any purpose at any time during the period of two years ending immediately prior to that arrival in the UK.

[*ITEPA 2003, s 375*].

12.29   Once one of these conditions is met, the reliefs set out below apply for a period of five years beginning with that date. [*ITEPA 2003, s 373(3)*].

12.30   It is difficult to envisage when head (b) might apply. It seems to assume that the person was resident in the UK in the two preceding years of assessment but nonetheless did not visit the UK at all for a period of two years. It is unlikely that he would be held to be UK resident in the year immediately prior to the start of the employment in such circumstances.

Amounts exempted

12.31   During the five-year period for which *section 373* applies, the employee is not taxed on travelling expenses for any journey made either:

(a)   from the country (outside the UK) in which he normally lives to any place in the UK in order to perform any duties of the office or employment there; or (*b*)   to the country in which he normally lives from any place in the UK after performing duties there,

provided that the cost of the travel facilities is borne by his employer or is paid by the employee and reimbursed by his employer (and that the expenses form part of the earnings from the employment). [*ITEPA 2003, s 373(4)*].

Meaning of 'usual place of abode'

12.32   It should be noted that if the employee comes from Paris but takes his summer holiday in Nice, the travel to and from Nice would qualify for relief. If he takes his holiday in Barcelona, travel to and from Barcelona would not qualify as Spain is a different country. If he flies to and from Nice and motors to Barcelona the cost of the travel to and from Nice will qualify but the expenses from Nice to Barcelona will not. It appears that if the employee flies to Paris to catch another plane to Nice, only the expenses of the flight to Paris will qualify as it is the cost of returning to the country where the employee normally lives, not to any particular place in that country, that are relieved.

12.33   The purpose of these reliefs is to allow a non-UK national to visit his family and friends during his early years of residence in the UK without having to do so out of taxed income. Once the employee has been working in the UK for five years he ought to have adjusted his life sufficiently so that this special relief is no longer needed. The requirement for the expense to be borne, or reimbursed, by the employer arose because the Government in 1986, at the time the relief was introduced, felt that the employer would not be prepared to meet the cost unless in all the circumstances it were reasonable. Accordingly, this would reduce the risk of abuse.

The employee's family

12.34   The relief that is given for visits by an employee's spouse and infant children when he is working abroad for a continuous period of at least 60 days (see 13.45–13.49 below) also applies where a non-UK domiciled employee is working in the UK and is himself entitled to relief under *section 373*, i.e. during the five years from the time he first meets the qualifying conditions. This relief for journeys by the spouse and children is given for journeys:

(*a*)   made to accompany the employee at the beginning of the continuous 60-day period, or to visit him during it; or

(*b*)   to return to the home country following a journey within (*a*).

[*ITEPA 2003, s 374*].

12.35   The rules set out in 13.45–13.49 below, apply to this relief. As with the employee's own travel expenses, the cost must be borne by the employer or incurred by the employee and reimbursed to him by his employer. [*ITEPA 2003, s 374(1)*].

12.36   If a journey within either 12.28 above, or 13.45 below, is made partly for the purpose specified therein and partly for some other purpose, only so much of the expenses as is attributable to the specified purpose can be deducted from the emoluments (so the balance will give rise to a benefit in kind). [*ITEPA 2003, ss 373(6), 374(7)*].

12.37   If an expense qualifies as a deduction under both *section 373* and some other provision it obviously cannot be deducted twice. [*ITEPA 2003, s 330*].

Administrative procedure

12.38   In the past there were practical problems in handling the affairs of people coming to work temporarily in the UK as many Inspectors of Taxes insisted on obtaining formal domicile rulings even though it was clear that the person was in the UK for a temporary purpose only. The residence form, P86, now includes a section on domicile so that 'in straightforward cases' an individual's residence and domicile status will be dealt with together. The Revenue have indicated that this will apply where a person who has never been UK domiciled has come here only to work and intends to leave the UK once the employment ceases. (*IR Press Release, 8 September 1994*). Following the introduction of self-assessment it is less important to know one's residence and domicile position in advance of completing a tax return—although it is of course desirable in order to plan one's finances effectively. Pre-self-assessment there was a special return, form 11K, for non-UK domiciled taxpayers. This is no longer the case. Now a non-UK domiciled or non-UK resident taxpayer completes the normal tax return form (if asked to complete a return) and attaches to it a 'Residence' page on which the taxpayer claims his non-UK domiciled or non-UK resident status.

Tax Equalisation Payments

12.39   It is common for multi-national employers to operate tax equalisation schemes where a foreign national is sent to work in the UK. Under such a scheme the employer pays the employee, in addition to his salary, the difference, if any, between the tax that he would have paid on his salary in his home country and the tax that he pays in the UK. In effect it indemnifies him again, his UK tax burden exceeding that in his home country. It is well-established that such payments are taxable as additional salary. Where the employee has both emoluments for work performed in the UK and earnings taxable on a remittance basis for overseas work the Revenue have always considered that to the extent that a tax equalisation payment is to meet a tax liability in respect of earnings for UK work it is itself taxable as UK earnings. The alternative view is that as it relates to the employee's overall income it should be apportioned between UK and overseas income in proportion to such income. For 1994/95 to 1996/97 the Revenue were prepared to compromise and treat the taxable amount as their figure plus half the difference between the two bases, but said that anyone who wished to dispute their approach for 1997/98 onwards would need to litigate the position (*Tax Bulletin 27, Feb 1997*). See also *SA Help sheet 212* and *Tax Bulletin, Issue 31, pages 467–469*. Miss Perro duly did so *(Perro v Mansworth [2001] STC (SCD) 179) (SpC 286)*. The Special Commissioner upheld the Revenue view, holding that the payment was in respect of the UK duties.

Chapter 13

Working Overseas

Introduction

13.1   Special reliefs apply to UK residents working overseas. It should be borne in mind that these only apply if the employee remains resident or ordinarily resident in the UK. If he is working overseas for several years he is likely to have become non-UK resident in which case his salary will be outside the scope of UK tax.

13.2   It should also be noted that earnings from a Crown employment for duties performed outside the UK is normally subject to UK tax as if the duties were performed in the UK. [*ITEPA 2003, ss 25(1)(b), 26(1)(b), 27(1)(b), 28*]. A Crown employment is employment under the Crown which is of a public nature and the earnings from which are payable out of the public revenues of the UK or of Northern Ireland. [*ITEPA 2003, s 28(2)*]. The Revenue have power to make an order excepting from the operation of *ITEPA 2003, ss 25(2)* and *27(2)* general earnings of any description of employee (or any description of employment) specified in the order. This can be done if they consider that such earnings should not be subject to UK tax having regard to the international obligations of the government and such other matters as appears to the Revenue to be relevant. [*ITEPA 2003, s 28(5)(6)*]. The intention is to make such an order to give statutory effect to *ESC A25* which exempts from UK tax the earnings of locally engaged (as distinct from UK based) unestablished staff working abroad who are not resident in the UK if the maximum rate of pay for their grade is less than that of an executive officer in the UK Civil Service working in Inner London.

Year of departure

13.3   Where a person goes overseas to take up full-time employment under a contract of employment for a period that includes a complete tax year, the Revenue's practice is to regard him as ceasing to be both resident and ordinarily resident in the UK from the time of his departure (*Booklet IR20, paragraph 2.2*). Obviously, if his employment terminates prematurely and he comes back within that tax year this concession will not be applied. The same applies to his spouse if she goes with him, or if she joins him later (in which case her non-residence will date from the time of her departure (*paragraph 2.4*)). The Revenue say 'full-time' for this purpose must be interpreted in accordance with its ordinary non-technical meaning, i.e. putting in what a layman would clearly recognise as a full working week. They also consider that where someone has several part-time jobs overseas concurrently, or an employment and self-employment concurrently, it might be reasonable to aggregate the total working time (*Tax Bulletin, Issue 6, page 57*).

Advantages of non-residence

13.4 When a person works overseas but continues to spend a significant time in the UK he may be resident in both countries. In such a case thought may need to be given to whether it is sensible to seek to give up his UK residence and, if so, how this might be done. If he is working in a country with which the UK has a double taxation agreement that agreement probably prevents him being resident in both of the contracting countries at the same time.

13.5 For example, if a person would be regarded as US resident under US law and as UK resident under UK law the UK/US double taxation agreement contains the following rules to determine which country is entitled to treat him as a resident—with the other country agreeing to treat him as non-resident in relation to income covered by the double taxation agreement.

(*a*) If he has a permanent home available to him in only one of the countries he is treated as a resident of that country.

(*b*) If he has a permanent home in neither or both countries he is treated as resident in the country with which his personal and economic relations are closest (his centre of vital interests).

(*c*) If his centre of vital interests cannot be determined he is treated as a resident of the country in which he has a habitual abode.

(*d*) If he has a habitual abode in both countries, or neither of them, he is treated as being a resident of the country of which he is a national.

(*e*) If he is a national of both countries, the Inland Revenue and Internal Revenue Service must agree between themselves which country is to treat him as a resident.

(*Article 4(4), UK/USA Double Taxation Convention, SI 2002 No 2648*).

13.6 This 'tie-breaker' clause is not the same in all of the UK's double taxation agreements although they broadly follow this pattern.

13.7 If a UK resident intends to work in the USA for two years and will also have significant earnings in another country it may sometimes be sensible to try to arrange his affairs so that the above tests will result in his remaining UK resident. This is not difficult to achieve provided that he meets the UK tests of residence, as such a person's centre of vital interests is likely to remain in the UK. It used to be easy to ensure that a person met the UK residence requirement by ensuring that he retained a UK house and a UK directorship and visited the UK every year for a board meeting. Now that the retention of available accommodation is no longer a test of UK residence, this has become far more difficult to achieve.

13.8   Establishing UK residence will not take the US earnings out of charge to US tax as the US is entitled under the agreement to tax US earnings if a UK resident is present in the US for more than 183 days in a calendar year (or he is present for a shorter period but the salary is claimed as a deduction in calculating US taxable profits of his employer). It will, however, take non-US income, such as the third-country salary, out of US tax.

Relief for long absences abroad

13.9   Prior to 17 March 1998 the earnings of a UK resident from work performed overseas effectively escaped UK tax if that person was working overseas for a period of 365 days or more (with fairly generous visits back to the UK being permitted during the period). This special relief was abolished by *section 63(1)* of the *Finance Act 1998* except for seafarers (see below). There was no transitional relief. If an employee was working overseas at 17 March 1998 he retained the right to his relief in respect of earnings paid before that date in respect of work done before that date, provided that he remained overseas for as long as was necessary to complete the requisite 365-day period. However, earnings for work done after 16 March 1998 and for work done before that date but paid after 16 March became taxable in full.

13.10   In determining whether emoluments relate to periods before or after 17 March 1998, any arrangements entered into after that date are ignored. [*FA 1998, s 63(7)*]. This will prevent a payment on account of emoluments for a period spanning that date being retrospectively attributed wholly to the part of that period which fell before 17 March.

13.11   The relief was initially introduced in 1977 by a Labour government to encourage businesses to go overseas and develop export markets. It is ironic that it was another Labour government that decided that was no longer a worthy cause. The relief had been exploited by entertainers and other high earners at whom it had not been directed, so it is understandable that the Chancellor wished to deny the relief to such high earners. It could clearly have been retargeted to assist the businessman, the labourers on construction projects overseas and similar cases which it was initially intended to encourage, but the Chancellor, Gordon Brown, opted not to do this.

Seafarers

13.12   The relief (with some modifications) does continue to apply to employment as a seafarer. This is defined as an employment (other than Crown employment) consisting of the performance of duties on a ship (or of such duties and others incidental to them). [*ITEPA 2003, s 384(1)*]. A ship for this purpose is not defined, but is expressed not to include any offshore installation within the meaning of the *Mineral Workings (Offshore*

Installations) Act 1971 or what would be such an installation if the reference in that *Act* to controlled waters was to any waters. [*ITEPA 2003, s 385*]. This excludes those employed on oil rigs and gas installations—or at least on some of them! In *Clark v Perks [2001] STC 1254* the Court of Appeal had to consider the meaning of a ship. It was held that this is an ordinary English word and its application to the facts of a particular case is a question of fact for the Commissioners to decide. In that case the General Commissioners had held that a moveable 'jack-up' oil rig which had no motive power of its own and had to be towed by tugs was a ship. It was held that this was a decision that they were entitled to come to. In *Lavery v Macleod [2000] STC (SCD) 118* the Special Commissioners held that a different jack-up rig had sufficient characteristics to be a ship. They noted that the Revenue accept that two other types of moveable drilling rigs, a drill-ship and a semi-submersible unit are ships. They were also clearly impressed that the jack-up rig has been moved several times including one journey of 2,500 miles which took 27 days. They emphasised that their decision depended on the individual facts of that case.

13.13   If in any year of assessment the duties of an employment as a seafarer are performed wholly or partly outside the UK and any of those duties are performed in the course of a qualifying period which falls wholly or partly in that year and consists of at least 365 days, a deduction of 100 per cent of the emoluments attributable to the chargeable period, or to so much of it as falls within the year of assessment, is allowed from those emoluments. [*ITEPA 2003, ss 378, 379*].

13.14   The relief for seafarers under *section 378* applies from 17 March 1998 only. Prior to that seafarers were included with other taxpayers in *ICTA 1988, s 193*. It appears that the 365-day qualifying period under *section 378* could not start before 17 March 1998, i.e. the seafarer had to complete a full year from that date to qualify for relief; time spent overseas before 17 March 1988 could not count towards that qualifying period. The detailed rules are the same as those which formerly applied to the general relief.

The relief up to 16 March 1998

13.15   The general relief applied where in a year of assessment:

(*a*)   the duties of an office or employment were performed wholly or partly outside the UK; and

(*b*)   any of those duties were performed in the course of a 'qualifying period' which fell wholly or partly in that year and consisted of at least 365 days.

A deduction equal to the whole of the emoluments from that employment which were attributable to that period (or the part of it that fell within the year of assessment) was allowed in charging tax under Case I of Schedule E. [*ICTA 1988, s 193(1)*].

Nature of the relief

13.16 A deduction from earnings of 100 per cent of such earnings is, of course, equivalent to exempting them from UK tax. In fact it is better! Because the earnings are still taxable they will constitute relevant earnings for personal pension and retirement annuity purposes (although effectively not under an occupational pension scheme).

13.17 This relief (and the continuing relief for seafarers), often referred to as 'relief under the 365 day rule', applied only to earnings where the employee is taxable in the UK on the worldwide earnings from his employment. It could not apply, for example, to foreign emoluments (see 12.9 above) taxable on a remittance basis, even if the earnings were all received in the UK in the year of assessment.

Meaning of 'qualifying period'

13.18 A 'qualifying period' for the purpose of this relief was a period of consecutive days which either:

(*a*) consisted entirely of days of absence from the UK; or

(*b*) consisted partly of such days and partly of intervening days included by virtue of *12 Schedule 3(2)*.

[*ICTA 1988, 12 Schedule 3(1)*].

Time permitted in UK

13.19 *12 Schedule 3(2)* provides that where a period consisting entirely of days of absence from the UK (called 'the relevant period') comes to an end and there have previously been one or more qualifying periods (i.e. within (*a*) or (*b*) in 13.17 above) the relevant period, the last qualifying period and the intervening days may be treated as a single qualifying period, provided that:

(*a*) there are no more than 62 intervening days; and

(*b*) the number of days in the resulting period which are not days of absence from the UK does not exceed one-sixth of the total number of days in that period.

[*ICTA 1988, 12 Schedule 3(2)*].

13.20 For seafarers, the proviso is that:

(*a*) there are no more than 183 intervening days; and

(*b*) the number of days in the resultant period which are not days of absence from the UK does not exceed half of the total number of days in that period.

[*ITEPA 2003, s 378(2)(3)*]. This allows the seafarer to return to the UK for up to six months a year on average and still qualify for the 100 per cent deduction. This increased limit also applied before 17 March 1998. [*ICTA 1988, 12 Schedule 3(2A)*].

13.21 Up to 1990/91, the total permitted days was one-quarter and the limit for any one trip 90 days. Where the continuous period straddles 6 April 1991 the new test can be applied to the entire period (but, it appears, only for the purpose of determining if the qualifying conditions are met for 1991/92). [*FA 1991, s 45*].

13.22 This was a very generous relief. Not surprisingly, the Revenue applied the rules rigidly. Great care needed to be taken with the timing of visits to the UK.

Example

Joe left the UK on 12 May 2000 to take up a one-year contract in Singapore. He returned to the UK on 18 July 2000 for 30 days during his children's school holiday, on 18 December for 13 days over Christmas, on 4 February 2001 for nine days for his wife's birthday, on 29 March 2001 for eight days for Easter, and finally returned to the UK on 14 May 2001.

(*a*) The period 12 May 2000 to 17 July 2000 is a qualifying period under *12 Schedule 3(1)(a)*.

(*b*) The period 17 August 2000 to 17 December 2000 is a relevant period under *12 Schedule 3(2)*. Accordingly, provided that the 30 intervening days in the UK do not exceed the one-sixth maximum, the whole period from 12 May 2000 to 17 December 2000 can be treated as a single qualifying period. That period consists of 220 days. One-sixth of 220 is 37. As the 30 intervening days are less than 37 the period counts as a single qualifying period.

(*c*) The period 31 December 2000 to 3 February 2001 is a relevant period under *12 Schedule 3(2)*. There is a previous qualifying period from 12 May 2000. Accordingly, the entire period 12 May 2000 to 3 February 2001 will be treated as a qualifying period provided the one-sixth maximum is not exceeded. The total days in that period is 268, one-sixth of which is 44. The total days in the UK are 30 on the first trip and 13 on the second, a total of 43. As this is less than 44 the entire period from 12 May 2000 is a single qualifying period.

(*d*) The period 13 February 2001 to 28 March 2001 is a relevant period. There is a previous qualifying period. Accordingly, the entire period 12 May 2000 to 28 March 2001 will be treated as a qualifying period provided that the one-sixth limit is not breached. The total days in that period is 321, one-sixth of which is 53. The cumulative total of days in the UK is 52, so again the limit is not breached.

(*e*) The period 10 March 2001 to 14 May 2001 is a relevant period. As there is a previous qualifying period the entire period 12 May 2000 to 14 May 2001 will be a qualifying period provided that the one-sixth limit is not breached. Joe had spent a total of 60 days in the UK, which is less than one-sixth of 368 (61 days), so the entire period may be treated as a single qualifying period. The Revenue say in their booklet *IR58, Going to Work Abroad*, that if the calculation does not give a whole number it must be rounded down.

13.23 There are a number of points that need to be borne in mind.

(*a*) The legislation looked at days of absence from the UK, not days spent working overseas. It does not matter what the taxpayer was doing while he was overseas.

(*b*) The 62-day figure applied only to days in a single trip. If a person was overseas for, say, 540 days he could return to the UK for up to 90 days provided that no single trip exceeded 62 days.

(*c*) The one-sixth test was applied by reference to days up to the time when the person returned to the UK for his second or subsequent trip, not the time he left the UK to go abroad again. Thus it did not matter that when Joe went to Singapore after Easter he had at that stage spent 60 days in the UK out of a total of 338 days since 12 May 2000 (one-sixth of which is 56). Accordingly, it did not really matter how many days a person spent in the UK on a visit (provided, of course, it was less than 63) if he then stayed abroad for a sufficient period to bring the cumulative UK days below one-sixth of the total.

(*d*) Going abroad for a short period and then returning to the UK could be very dangerous. Suppose that Joe had taken his wife to Paris on February 8th and 9th as a birthday treat. Those two days would form a relevant period so the one-sixth test would have to be applied after that trip. At that stage the total period from 12 May 2000 would be 272 days of which 47 were spent in the UK. This is greater than one-sixth of 272 (45). Therefore, the period 12 May 2000 to 9 February 2001 cannot be a qualifying period. The effect is that the earnings for the period 12 May 2000 to 3 February 2001 would be fully taxable as that qualifying period is one of less than 365 days. A new qualifying period would start from 31 December 2000 as the four UK days in the 41-day period 31 December 2000 to 9 February 2001 is less than one-sixth of that period. However, unless Joe remained overseas until 31 December 2001 that new qualifying period would again be less than 365 days, so no relief would be due.

(*e*) There does not appear to be any requirement for the employment to exist throughout the qualifying period. All that is required is that overseas duties are performed 'in the course of' the qualifying period. In theory, therefore, Joe could simply have stayed overseas after his employment ceased in May 2001 until such time as he had built up a 365-day qualifying period and thus at least have obtained relief for his earnings from 31 December 2000 onwards.

(*f*) It was specifically provided (and still is for seafarers by *ITEPA 2003, s 378(4)*) that a person could not be regarded as absent from the UK on any day unless he was absent at the end of it, i.e. at midnight. [*12 Schedule 4*]. It did not matter that the taxpayer did a full day's work overseas; if he caught a late flight arriving in the UK that evening, the day was treated as a day of presence in the UK. The converse did not hold good. If a person was overseas at midnight it was a question of fact whether or not the day was a day of absence from the UK. If he left in the early morning it probably was; if he left late at night it probably was not. In practice, the Revenue treated any day on which a person was overseas at midnight as a day of absence.

Emoluments attributable to the qualifying period

13.24   Once a 365-day qualifying period was established, it was next necessary to ascertain the emoluments attributable to that period. The legislation gave some guidance where the duties of the employment (the relevant employment) or of any other employment held by the taxpayer which was associated with the relevant employment were not performed wholly outside the UK. The amount of the emoluments for the year of assessment from the relevant employment, in respect of which a deduction was allowed, was not to exceed such proportion of the emoluments for that year from the relevant employment and the other employment (if any) as was shown to be reasonable, having regard to the nature of, and time devoted to, the duties performed outside and in the UK respectively and to all other relevant circumstances. [*ICTA 1988, 12 Sch 2(1)(2)*]. This is still the rule for seafarers. [*ITEPA 2003, s 380(2)*]. For this purpose two employments are associated if they are with the same person or with persons associated with each other. Two companies are associated with one another if one has control of the other (within *section 416*) or both of them are under the control of the same person or persons. A sole trader or partnership is associated with another person (including a company) if one of them had control of the other (within *section 840*) or both are under the control of the same person or persons, but in applying this test a sole trader is not to be treated as under the control of any other person. [*ITEPA 2003, ss 24(5)(6), 380(3)(4)*].

Apportionment of UK and non-UK duties

13.25   In practice, if a person had a single employment embracing both UK and overseas duties the Inland Revenue rarely accepted that any method other than a straight time apportionment was appropriate to ascertain the earnings qualifying for the deduction. If there were separate employments for UK and non-UK duties it was more difficult for the Revenue to mount a challenge under this provision, particularly if the earnings from the non-UK employment could be shown to be directly related to the profits of the overseas employer, where, for example, the employee was paid on a commission basis.

13.26 It has been held that the attribution of the emoluments of a single employment between UK and overseas duties must be made by reference to the employee's contractual rights (subject to the ceiling in *12 Schedule 2*). When the contract does not specifically allocate part of the remuneration to the overseas duties, the remuneration contractually accrues on a day-to-day basis under the *Apportionment Act 1870.* (*Varnam v Deeble 58 TC 501*). For this purpose the daily salary is $\frac{1}{365}$ of the annual salary, irrespective of the number of days in the year that an employee is contractually required to work (*Platten v Brown 59 TC 408; Leonard v Blanchard [1993] STC 259*).

Emoluments qualifying for deduction

13.27 Where there was a single employment with both UK and non-UK duties, what qualified for the deduction was the amount of the emoluments attributable to the qualifying period, not the emoluments attributable to the duties performed abroad. [*ITEPA 2003, s 379(1)*]. In other words, the earnings for intervening days spent in the UK qualified for the 100 per cent deduction (and still do so for a seafarer), even if the employee worked in the UK on those days. For this reason it was often better to have a single employment for both UK and overseas work if the job involved UK duties and there were no special circumstances which could justify a far higher proportion of the emoluments as attributable to overseas work than would apply on a strict time basis.

13.28 It should be noted that the deduction applies to emoluments attributable to (i.e. earned in) the qualifying period. The relief will, of course, be given in the year that those earnings are assessed where they are received in a later year than that in which they were earned.

13.29 For 1992/93 onwards the emoluments qualifying for relief are the net amount after deduction of capital allowances; overseas travel expenses within *ICTA 1988, s 193(4)* or *s 194(1)*; allowable expenses under *section 198* or *199*; professional subscriptions under *section 201*; the special relief for expenditure by ministers of religion under *section 332*; contributions to an occupational pension scheme under *section 592* or *594*; and the special reliefs for corresponding payments out of foreign emoluments under *section 192* and travel expenses for non-UK domiciled individuals under *section 195*. [*ITEPA 2003, s 381*]. It is not clear in what circumstances *section 192* can apply as foreign emoluments do not attract the relief. In practice, the Revenue applied this restriction in earlier years too—with the exception of 1990/91 and 1991/92—so any late claims in respect of such years will not be accepted on the basis that that was the 'practice generally prevailing' within the terms of *TMA 1970, s 33(1)* and *ICTA 1988, s 206* (*IR Press Release 8 June 1992*). From 2002/03 mileage allowance relief under *section 197AG* (see 7.78) also needs to be deducted. [*FA 2001, 12 Sch Part II, 15*].

13.30 Earnings for a period of leave immediately after the qualifying (or eligible) period are treated as attributable to the eligible period if (or to the extent that) they are earnings for the tax year in which that qualifying period ends. [*ITEPA 2003, s 379(2)*].

Incidental duties

13.31 If an employment was, in substance, one where the duties fell in the year of assessment to be performed in the UK, any duties performed overseas which were merely incidental to UK duties had to be treated for the purpose of *ICTA 1988, s 193(1)* as if they were performed in the UK. [*12 Schedule 6*]. However, it is difficult to envisage a person spending a continuous period of 365 days abroad if the substance of his employment consists of UK duties.

13.32 Duties which a seafarer performs on a ship (prior to 17 March 1998 a vessel or aircraft) engaged on a voyage beginning or ending outside the UK (or on part of a journey beginning or ending outside the UK) are to be treated as performed abroad notwithstanding that they may be performed on a UK registered ship (or aircraft). However, where the journey, or any part of it, both begins and ends in the UK (including the Continental shelf), those duties will not be covered by *section 193(1)* to the extent that they are actually performed in the UK. [*ITEPA 2003, s 382*].

13.33 Duties of a seafarer performed outside the UK must be treated as performed in the UK if in the tax year in which they are performed the employment is in substance one whose duties fall to be performed in the UK and the work outside the UK is merely incidental to the performance of UK duties. [*ITEPA 2003, s 383*].

Share options

13.34 Prior to 1994/95 the Revenue accepted that where the earnings of an employee qualified for the foreign earnings deduction, the gain on exercise of a share option would also attract that deduction if it is exercised in the appropriate year. They now take the view that a gain on a share option is not an 'emolument' and therefore cannot attract the deduction (*IR Press Release 7 March 1994*). This is unlikely to be a problem except where the individual normally works in the UK for the same employer and is temporarily sent overseas. This is because the tax charge on the exercise of an option (see 14.13) applies only where at the time the option is granted the employee is taxable under Case I of Schedule E. [*ICTA 1988, s 140(1)*]. Accordingly the only Schedule E charge will be on the value of the option at the time of its grant in accordance with *Abbott v Philbin* (see 3.19). This is usually a very low figure.

Returning expatriates

13.35 The Revenue interpreted the legislation as requiring the employee to be UK resident and ordinarily resident throughout the qualifying period. The Revenue's view was challenged, unsuccessfully, in *Carstairs v Sykes [2000] STC 1103*. It was held there that the statutory context was that *ICTA 1988, s 193* was an exception to *ICTA 1988, s 19*, which provided that tax is chargeable under Case I of Schedule E where an individual is resident and ordinarily resident in the UK. Accordingly the most natural construction of 'absent' from the UK is 'not physically present in the UK as the country of residence and ordinary residence'. There was an anomaly with terminal leave pay. If a person worked abroad for a qualifying period and returned to the UK for his terminal leave, the terminal leave pay was regarded as relating to the qualifying period and thus escaped tax (see 13.30). If the employee was non-resident during the period overseas the terminal leave pay was taxable under Case I of Schedule E as earnings from an employment carried on in the UK (*SP 18/91*).

Deduction for travelling expenses

Expenditure qualifying for deduction

13.36   If a person who is resident and ordinarily resident in the UK holds an employment the duties of which are performed *wholly* outside the UK (and the emoluments are not overseas earnings or foreign emoluments, see 12.9 above) expenses of the employee:

(*a*)   in travelling from any place in the UK to take up the employment; or

(*b*)   in travelling to any place in the UK on its termination,

are deductible from the earnings (up to 2002/03 they are treated as having been necessarily incurred in the performance of the duties of the overseas employment).

[*ITEPA 2003, s 341(1)–(4)*, formerly *ICTA 1988, s 193(3)*].

13.37   Accordingly, travel from the UK to take up the overseas employment and travel back to the UK following its termination will not give rise to a benefit in kind if paid by the employer (and will qualify for a deduction if paid by the employee). At least, that is the intention and what happens in practice. Prior to 2003/04 it was not wholly clear that deeming expenses to be necessarily incurred in the performance of the duties implied that the employee is necessarily obliged to incur such expense. If travel is partly for one of the above purposes and partly for another purpose the deduction obviously applies only to the part that is properly attributable to the employment. [*ITEPA 2003, s 341(5)*].

Board and lodging expenses

13.38   If, for the purpose of enabling an employee within 13.36 above, to perform the duties of the overseas employment:

(*a*)   board and lodging outside the UK is provided for him and the cost is borne by or on behalf of his employer; or

(*b*)   he incurs expenses out of his emoluments on such board and lodging and those expenses are reimbursed by or on behalf of his employer,

the amount of such expenditure can be deducted from the emoluments (provided, of course, that such expenses are taxed as part of the emoluments). [*ITEPA 2003, s 376*]. If board and lodging is partly to enable the employee to perform the duties of the overseas employment and partly for some other purpose, only the part attributable to the former qualifies for a deduction. [*ITEPA 2003, s 376(3)*].

Multiple employments

13.39   If a person who is resident and ordinarily resident in the UK holds two or more employments, the duties of at least one of which are performed *wholly or partly* outside the UK, and travels from one place (having performed there duties of one office or employment) to another place for the purpose of performing duties of another office or employment (the emoluments from which are not overseas earnings or foreign emoluments), and either or both of those places are outside the UK, a deduction from the earnings of the employment to which he is travelling so as to trigger the right to claim the travel as deductible expenses is given for the travel expenses. [*ITEPA 2003, s 342(1)–(7)*]. Prior to 2003/04 relief was given instead by treating the travel expenses as having been necessarily incurred in the performance of the duties which the person was to perform at his destination. [*ICTA 1988, s 193(5)(6)*]. If travel is partly for the purpose of performing the duties and partly for some other purpose, only the part of the expense attributable to the employment is allowable. [*ITEPA 2003, s 342(8)*]. The intention of this deeming is to ensure that the travel expenses do not give rise to a benefit in kind if paid by the employer and that they qualify for a deduction if paid by the employee.

Duties performed partly outside UK

13.40   Where a person holds an employment the duties of which are performed partly outside the UK travel expenses borne by his employer (or incurred by him and reimbursed by his employer) on any journey by him:

(*a*)   from any place in the UK to the place of performance of any of the duties outside the UK; or

(*b*)   from the overseas place of performance of any of the duties to any place in the UK,

he can deduct the expenses from the earnings (or up to 2002/03 was not taxable on the travel expenses) provided that the duties concerned can only be performed outside the UK and the expense was incurred wholly and exclusively for the purpose of performing the duties (for expenditure within (*a*)) or of returning after performing the duties (for expenditure within (*b*)). [*ITEPA 2003, s 370(1)(2)(4)*].

13.41 The requirement that the duties can only be performed outside the UK is obviously to prevent the controlling director of a family company opening an office overlooking the beach in the south of France and choosing to work from that office in the summer. The requirement that the expenditure must be borne or reimbursed by the employer is because the Chancellor of the Exchequer at that time believed that if the employer pays for the expenditure he will ensure that it is a reasonable amount. This assumption is of dubious validity in many cases, particularly where the employer is a company controlled by the employee.

13.42 If a person is absent from the UK for the purpose of performing the duties of one or more offices or employments (whether or not performed wholly overseas) he is similarly not assessable on travel expenses borne by his employer (or incurred by him and reimbursed by his employer) in respect of:

(*a*)   any journey by him from the place of performance of the overseas duties to any place in the UK; or

(*b*)   any return journey following a journey within (*a*),

provided that the duties concerned can only be performed outside the UK and the absence from the UK was occasioned wholly and exclusively for the purpose of performing the overseas duties. [*ITEPA 2003, s 370(1)–(3)*].

Duties performed on a vessel

13.43 For the purpose of *section 370* (and *371* below), duties which are performed on a vessel cannot be treated as performed outside the UK if the voyage is simply from one UK port to another [*ITEPA 2003, ss 40(1), 372*] but the relief under *section 370* (see 13.40 above) applies if the reason for the travel was not merely to perform the duties concerned (i.e. the overseas duties) but also if it was to perform those duties and other duties of the employment, e.g. it was to join the vessel overseas for a voyage to a UK port. [*ITEPA 2003, s 370(5)(e)*].

13.44 If an expense qualifies for relief under both *section 342* and *section 370* it obviously cannot be deducted twice. However, the taxpayer can choose under which *section* he wants the relief to be given. [*ITEPA 2003, s 330(1)*].

Family travel

13.45 A special relief is given for expenses of an employee's family in visiting him, where the employee is working overseas for 60 days or more. The employee must be absent from the UK for a continuous period of 60 days or more for the purpose of performing the duties of one or more offices or employments. [*ITEPA 2003, s 371(1)–(4)*]. 'Continuous' means that even a single day back in the UK, for whatever reason, will debar the relief (or start a fresh 60-day period after the employee returns overseas).

13.46 If travel facilities are provided for travel for the employee's spouse or infant children and the cost is borne by or on behalf of the employer (or the expense is incurred by the employee and reimbursed to him by the employer) the expenditure is allowed as a deduction in calculating the earnings from the employment (provided it constitutes part of such earnings). [*ITEPA 2003, 371(1)*]. The effect is that the employee will not be assessed on a benefit in kind in relation to the expenditure.

Travel eligible for relief

13.47 This relief applies only to travel between a place in the UK and the place of performance of the duties (or any of them) outside the UK, being either:

(*a*)   a journey by the employee's spouse or any infant child of his accompanying him at the beginning of the 60-day period or to visit him during that period; or

(*b*)   a return journey following a journey falling within (*a*).

[*ITEPA 2003, s 371(5)*].

13.48 It applies to not more than two outward and two return journeys by the same person in the same year of assessment. A child includes a stepchild and an illegitimate child, but the child must be under 18 at the beginning of the outward journey. [*ITEPA 2003, s 371(6)(7)*].

Example

On 1 January 2004 Keith is sent by his employer to work on a contract in Indonesia. The contract lasts until 31 October 2004. Keith's employer pays for the following trips for Keith's wife, Katie, and his children Ken and Kelly. Ken is 16 and Kelly's 18th birthday is on 12 September 2004.

1 January 2004 initial visit by Katie and Ken

15 January 2004 return trip by Katie and Ken

10 February 2004 visit by Ken and Kelly

21 February 2004 return trip by Ken and Kelly

31 March 2004 visit by Ken and Kelly

14 April 2004 return trip by Ken and Kelly

9 September 2004 visit by Katie and Kelly

18 September 2004 return trip by Katie and Kelly

(1) Travel for both Katie and Ken on 1 January 2004 and 15 January 2004 qualifies for relief.

(2) Travel for both Ken and Kelly on 10 February 2004 and 21 February 2004 qualifies for relief.

(3) Travel by Kelly on 31 March 2004 qualifies for relief. That by Ken does not as Ken has already made two return journeys in 2003/04. It is assumed that there was no previous overseas tour (in the same or a different country) by Keith in 2003/04. If Keith had been on an earlier tour, any trips by Katie, Ken or Kelly during that previous tour would have to be taken into account to determine which visits breached the two-trip limit.

(4) Travel by Kelly on 14 April 2004 qualifies for relief. It is not clear whether Ken's travel does. Although it is his first trip in 2004/05 the expression 'two outward and two return journeys' could be interpreted as requiring both the outward and return journey to qualify to obtain relief for either.

(5) Travel by both Katie and Kelly on 9 September 2004 and 18 September 2004 qualifies for relief. It does not matter that Kelly is over 18 on 18 September 2004 as she was under that age on 9 September.

13.49 It should be noted that the visit must be to the place of performance of the duties. Thus, if Keith had been worried about Ken and Kelly coming to Indonesia and had suggested that instead they all fly to Singapore to see one another, the relief would not apply and Keith would be assessed on the cost of Ken and Kelly's fares. Indeed, if he had suggested they visit him in Djakarta, the capital of Indonesia, rather than going to the remote jungle site where Keith was actually working it again appears that the relief would not apply as Djakarta would not be 'the place of performance' of the duties. *Section 371* does not give relief for the employee's own travel expenses if he comes back to the UK to visit his family. However, in most cases such expenses will fall within *ITEPA 2003, s 370* (see 13.40). *Section 370* does not contain any limit to the number of journeys. It does however carry an additional requirement that the duties performed outside the UK can only be performed there.

Pensions

13.50 Normally, where a person receives a relevant benefit from an unapproved retirement benefit scheme it is chargeable to tax unless the contributions to the scheme were themselves taxed as a benefit in kind. [*ITEPA 2003, ss 394, 396*]. Obviously, this provision was not intended to apply to pension provision for overseas work where the pension scheme was established abroad. Accordingly, by concession the Revenue do not seek tax on a lump sum benefit receivable by an employee (or his personal representative or a dependant) from an overseas pension scheme if his foreign service (see 11.24) comprises either:

(*a*) at least 75 per cent of his total service in the employment;

(*b*) the whole of the last ten years' service in the employment (where it exceeds ten); or

(*c*) at least 50 per cent of his total service where that exceeds 20 years and the foreign service includes at least ten of the last 20 years.

Where these conditions are not met only the proportion of the lump sum that the period of UK service in the employment bears to the total period of the employment will be taxed (*ESC A10*).

13.51 A UK company that pays pension contributions under an unapproved scheme in relation to an employee working overseas will not be denied relief for the payment under *FA 1989, s 76* (which denies a deduction unless the employee is taxable on it) if the payment is made either:

(i) to a fund within *section 615(3)* (pension schemes in respect of certain overseas government service where the employee is non-UK resident); or

(ii) to a non-UK pension scheme which is accepted as a corresponding scheme under *ITEPA 2003, s 390*, and the payment is for the benefit of employees in receipt of foreign emoluments or who are not UK resident and whose duties are performed wholly outside the UK (*IR Press Release 8 October 1991*).

Chapter 14

Employee Shareholdings

Introduction

14.1   There is a great deal of legislation in relation to employee share-holdings. This can be split into two broad categories: approved share schemes, and other transactions.

14.2   Approved share schemes are considered in Chapters 15 and 16. These enable limited benefits to be provided to employees without attracting a tax charge provided that a large number of fairly stringent conditions are complied with. There are five types of approved share scheme. Approved profit sharing schemes and savings-related share option schemes cannot be used to provide benefits to selected employees, they must be directed at virtually the entire work force. Accordingly, whilst they encourage wide share ownership they are not generally suitable as employee incentives. They cannot be targeted to specific employees and cannot be tied to the performance of the employee. Share option schemes of the kind introduced by the *Finance Act 1984* (which are often called executive share option schemes) can often provide an attractive benefit to selected employees but other than for start-ups this is fairly modest, is limited to future growth in the value of the shares, and will not enable the employee to actually obtain a shareholding in the company for at least three years. Enterprise Management Incentives, whilst selective, are limited to a small number of employees and are aimed primarily at unquoted companies, where there is normally a share valuation problem and the tax incentive could turn out to be an incentive to leave the company rather than to tie the employee to it. Employee Share Ownership Plans are attractive and flexible. However they are all-employee schemes and most growing companies are not attracted to such schemes. Furthermore it is question-able whether there is a real incentive in giving financially unsophisti-cated employees unmarketable shares whose value is not readily apparent.

14.3   Because of the severe limitations on the use of approved schemes, many employers and their employees who wish to use share ownership as a means of providing incentives for senior executives, opt to accept the tax charges that arise where benefits from shares in the employer company are provided without resort to an approved scheme. Unapproved share schemes can be particularly attractive in a start-up situation where the shares have little value. If any tax charge can be triggered immediately, such as by giving the employee shares immediately—or preferably by selling them to him at a very low market value—with an obligation to resell them at a low price should the employee leave the company within a specified period, it is attractive to accept that tax charge and avoid any inhibitions on the development of the business that the need to comply with conditions for approval would otherwise generate.

Occasions of charge on unapproved schemes

14.4   There are a number of potential occasions of charge to income tax in relation to unapproved employee share schemes:

(*a*)   If the shares are restricted securities (see 14.22) an income tax charge arises:

    (i)   if they cease to be restricted securities (other than on a transfer to an associated person;

    (ii)   the restrictions are varied; or

    (iii)   the shares or securities are sold (see 14.22).

(*b*)   If the shares are convertible securities (see 14.50) an income tax charge arises on:

    (i)   their conversion;

    (ii)   their disposal (other than to an associated person);

    (iii)   a sale of the right to convert; or

    (iv)   the receipt of any other benefit in respect of the entitlement to convert (see 14.52).

(*c*)   If the initial market value of the shares is artificially depressed (see 14.59) an income tax charge arises at the time of acquisition of the securities (see 14.60).

(*d*)   If such shares are restricted securities an income tax charge arises at the end of the first tax year in which they are held as if the restrictions had been lifted at that time (see 14.62).

(*e*)   If the value of the shares is artificially enhanced an income tax charge arises at the end of the tax year in which such enhancement takes place (see 14.71).

(*f*)   If the shares are acquired at an undervalue a tax charge will either arise:

    (i)   at the time of acquisition under the basic employment income charging provision (*ITEPA 2003, s 62*) on the amount of the undervalue; or

    (ii)   if the payment due at that time is less than the market value of the securities, as if a notional interest free loan equal to the amount of the undervalue had been made to the employee by the employer at that time (see 14.78).

(*g*)   Where (*f*)(ii) applies there is an annul income tax charge on notional interest on the notional loan (unless had interest been paid it would have qualified as a charge on income) (see 14.79 and 9.1).

(*h*)   In such a case if the shares are sold or no further payment becomes due in respect of them and at that time all or part of the notional loan is still outstanding an income tax charge arises at that time on the outstanding amount (see 14.84).

(*i*)   If the shares are sold for a consideration greater than their market value an income tax charge arises on the excess (see 14.86).

(*j*)   If the employee receives any benefit by virtue of holding the shares that benefit is taxed as income (see 14.87).

(*k*)   If the shares are acquired under an option no tax charge arises on the grant of the option but an income tax charge can arise on:

    (i)   the exercise of the option;

    (ii)   an assignment or release of the option;

    (iii)   receipt of a benefit in connection with the option (see 14.89).

Effect of the provisions

14.5   Accordingly, the effect of most of these provisions is to subject to income tax gains that would otherwise have been liable to capital gains tax. Where the rate of tax is the same for both taxes, treating the amount as income usually merely results in a loss of the ability to utilise the employee's £8,200 annual capital gains tax exemption against the gain (if he has not already utilised it on other transactions). A more serious problem is that share options (other than under the EMI scheme—see 16.72) defer the start of taper relief on the shares themselves until the option is exercised. With a two-year indexation period for business assets, which includes all unquoted shares and virtually all quoted shares held by employees, the sooner the taper period starts the better from the employee's point of view, although it may not be a great hardship for an employee to have to hold the shares for two years after exercising their option—unless they do not have the necessary outside finance to acquire the shares in the first place. From the company's perspective a three-year option period ties the employee to the company for five years if he wants the full 90 per cent taper relief, but the loss of the employee's goodwill by extending the period in this way needs to be weighed against this benefit. In most cases the tax is collected from the employee. There is in general no obligation on the employer to apply PAYE, although the decision of the Special Commissioners in *Paul Dunstall Organisation Ltd v Hedges (Sp C 179, [1999] STC SCD 26)* (see 2.27) has cast doubt on this. PAYE does need to be applied where the shares are readily convertible assets (see 2.88 onwards). Normally this will only apply on an acquistion of shares, not on one of the other transactions described below which trigger a tax charge. However, it is specifically provided that PAYE must be applied on the trigger events under the employee share scheme rules (see 2.102).

Share acquisitions included

14.6   Many people expect tax charges to arise where an employee subscribes for shares at an undervalue. It should not be overlooked, however, that the various provisions outlined below apply not only where an employee subscribes for new shares or is granted an option to do so. They equally apply if he acquires existing shares from one of the shareholders or is granted an option by a shareholder to acquire shares from him.

Phantom shares

14.7   Before considering the legislative provisions in detail, mention should be made of phantom shares (sometimes called shadow shares), which are becoming increasingly popular. As the name suggests these are notional shares. The employee is allotted an agreed number of phantom shares. When the company declares a dividend he is paid a bonus equal to the dividend he would have received had he held that number of shares. When he wants to 'dispose' of his shares the company will pay him a bonus equal to the gain he would have made had that number of actual shares been sold on the open market. If the company makes a scrip issue the employee will be 'issued' with further phantom shares. In the event of a rights issue, as he is not expected to make a cash payment, he will either receive the cash sum for which he could have sold his rights, or such additional shares as could have been acquired with the proceeds of the sale of the rights attaching to the remainder. If desired the company's articles of association can give the holder of phantom shares the right to vote at general meetings.

14.8   The concept is, of course, that if the employee is going to pay income tax on all the benefits he would obtain from ownership of the shares he might as well simply be paid income. This is convenient for the employee as the 'gain' can be taxed under the PAYE system at the time he receives the income rather than face a large tax bill at a later date when he may well have already spent the funds. It is convenient to the employer because it simplifies administration and does not affect the size of holdings of other shareholders. As share incentives generally aim to give the employee a stake in the growth of the company, phantom shares meet this objective as well as actual shares. The main difference is that the cost of the incentive is met by the company (but as such triggers a corporation tax deduction for the company) whereas with real shares the cost is effectively met by the shareholders (as they are giving the employee part of the growth that would otherwise have accrued to their own shares). With an unquoted company the interests of the shareholders and the company are usually identical and the shareholders will usually realise that they are providing the value of share options, whereas with a listed company many shareholders probably do not realise this.

Shares in private companies

14.9   Employee shareholdings are not generally of great incentive value in private companies except in two circumstances. The first is where there is a strong likelihood that the company will be sold or a public quotation obtained for its shares in the reasonably near future. In such circumstances very substantial benefits can be obtained by the employee as the sale or flotation will itself result in a significant increase in the value of the shares. The second is that the ownership of shares in the employer company can have a strong psychological effect on some employees, even though the shares have little real value.

14.10   The reason that such shares are not generally of value to employees in other circumstances is, of course, that, as there is no market for the shares, the employee cannot realise their value. If he wishes to dispose of them, the only potential purchasers are likely to be the other shareholders, and the size of the employee's holding is likely to be such that those other shareholders will be indifferent as to whether or not they acquire those shares. Furthermore, many private companies do not pay dividends so the employee is unlikely to receive any other benefit from his ownership of the shares.

14.11   Although the value of the employee's shares—both on acquisition and disposal—is likely to be small, that value has to be agreed with the Shares Valuation Division of the Inland Revenue, which can be both time-consuming and costly, and if the Revenue's figure differs significantly from the company's, a tax charge under one of the provisions outlined below will arise in relation to that difference in value.

Simple share acquisitions

14.12   It also needs to be borne in mind that in most cases the special rules considered below do not displace the charge under the basic charging provision, *ITEPA 2003, s 62*. This states that earnings includes 'any ... other profit or incidental benefit of any kind obtained by the employee if it is money or money's worth'. [*ITEPA 2003, s 62(2)(b)*]. Money's worth is the monetary value at the time of receipt of something that is capable of being converted into money. For example, if a person is given ordinary shares in the company for which he works at a time when they have a value of £1,000 he will in most cases be taxable under *section 62* on that £1,000. The special rules described below are intended to impose an additional tax charge in circumstances where the value of the shares, or in the case of shares acquired under an option the value of the option, at the time of acquisition does not properly represent the benefit obtained by the employee.

14.13   In many cases the charge under *section 62* will be the only charge. This is likely to be the case where the shares are ordinary shares not subject to any restrictions and not attracting any rights other than those attaching to all of the shares. It is only if there is something unusual about the shares as a result of which they are likely to increase in value disproportionately to those shares held by other shareholders that the special rules considered below are likely to bite.

Unapproved employee share schemes: the current rules

14.14   The special rules that apply to unapproved employee share schemes were substantially recast by *section 139* and *Schedule 22* to the FA 2000. These are now contained in *ITEPA 2003*, new *ss 417–484*.

14.15   They impose an income tax charge where:

(*a*)   securities or an interest in securities is acquired by a person;

(*b*)   the right or opportunity to acquire the securities (or interest) is available by reason of an employment of either the acquirer or of any other person; and

(*c*)   that person does not pay the full, unrestricted market value for the security (*Hansard*, SCB, 22.5 2003, col 256).

[*ITEPA 2003, s 421B(1)*]

14.16   For this purpose:

(*a*)   securities (or an interest) are acquired at the time when the person becomes beneficially entitled to the securities or interest in them (if that is different from the time when the securities are conveyed or transferred) [*ITEPA 2003, s 421B(2)(a)*];

(*b*)   references to an employment include a former employment and a prospective employment [*ITEPA 2003, s 421B(2)(b)*];

(*c*)   a right or opportunity to acquire securities (or an interest in securities) which is made available by a person's employer (or a person connected with his employer) is deemed to have made available by reason of his employment (unless the person who makes the opportunity available is an individual and that opportunity is made available in the normal course of his domestic, family or personal relationships) [*ITEPA 2003, s 421(3)*]; and

(*d*)   an interest in shares or securities means an interest which is less than full beneficial ownership (including an interest in the proceeds of sale) but excluding a right to acquire the shares or securities. [*ITEPA 2003, s 420(8)*].

There is a potential problem in relation to earn-outs where a company is sold to another with the price payable dependant on profit targets over the next few years being met. It is usual for at least some of the existing management to remain with the company or become employees of the new company. Despite the wording of (*c*) above the Revenue have said that where it can be shown that the earn-out is further consideration for the disposal of the target company rather than value obtained by reason of employment the value of the shares of the new company received under the earn-out will be taken to be equal to the value of the shares sold so that no liability to income tax will arise (Press Release 22.7.2003). The press release sets out the sort of factors that the Revenue will take into consideration.

14.17   *Chapters 2* to *4 (sections 422–450)* (see 14.22–14.88) cease to apply to securities or an interest in securities:

(*a*)   immediately after the securities are disposed of (other than to an associated person. [*ITEPA 2003, s 421B(5)*];

(*b*)   immediately before the death of the employee [*ITEPA 2003, s 421B(6)*]; or

(*c*)   seven years after the first date following the acquisition of the securities on which the employee is no longer an employee of either the employer, if the securities are issued by a company that company, or a person connected with the employer or such a company. [*ITEPA 2003, s 421B(7)*].

14.18   'Securities' for the purpose of these provisions includes:

(*a*)   shares (or stock) in a body corporate, wherever incorporated, or in an unincorporated body constituted under the laws of a foreign country or territory;

(*b*)   debentures, debenture stock, loan stock, bonds, certificates of deposit and other instruments creating or acknowledging indebtedness;

- the Revenue say that this includes gifts (Press Release 2.7.2003).

(*c*)   warrants and other instruments entitling their holder to subscribe for securities (whether or not in existence or identifiable);

- the Revenue say that where a warrant simply gives a right to acquire shares it will be excluded under 14.19(*e*) but if a warrant gives other rights, such as a current right to receive dividends in respect of the shares to which it relates, it will be a security (Press Release 2.7.2003).

(*d*)   certificates or other instruments conferring rights in respect of securities held by third parties and the transfer of which may be effected without the consent of such third parties;

(*e*)   units in collective investment scheme (i.e. arrangements which are made with effect to property of any description (including money) the purpose of which is to enable people taking part in the arrangements to participate in any way from (or receive profits or income arising from) the acquisition, holding, management or disposal of the property or sums paid out of such profits or income);

(*f*)   futures (i.e. rights under a contract for the sale of a commodity, or other property, under which delivery is to be made at a future date at a price agreed when the contract is made – which includes where the contract is expressed to be by reference to a standard lot or quality with the price being variable to take account of such variations and also where the price is not specified in the contract but is left to be determined by reference to the price at which a contract is to be entered into on a market or exchange (or could be entered into at a time and place specified in the contract)); and

(*g*)   rights under a contract for differences (or similar contract the purpose or pretended purpose of which is to secure a profit or avoid a loss by reference to fluctuations in the value or price of property or of an index or some other factors designated in the contract). [*ITEPA 2003, (s 420(1)–(4)), (8)*].

14.19   However, the following are not securities:

(*a*)   cheques (and bills of exchange other than bills accepted by a banker), banker's drafts and letters of credit;

(*b*)   money and statements showing balances on a current, deposit or savings account;

(*c*)   leases and other dispositions of property and saleable securities;

(*d*)   rights under contracts of insurance (within the *Financial Services and Markets Act 2000 (Regulated Activities) Order 2001* (SI 2001 No 544); and

(*e*)   options.

[*ITEPA 2003, s 420(5)*].

14.20   The Treasury have power to amend by statutory instrument the definition of what is and is not a security for the purpose of the unapproved share schemes legislation. [*ITEPA 2003, s 420(6)(7)*].

14.21   The amount of the tax charge depends on the trigger. Different rules apply to:

(*a*)   restricted securities (*Chapter 2* of *Part 7* of *ITEPA 2003* – see 14.22)

(*b*)   convertible securities (*Chapter 3* – see 14.50)

(*c*)   securities with artificially depressed market value (*Chapter 3A* – see 14.59)

(*d*)   securities with artificially enhanced market value (*Chapter 3B* – see 14.71)

(*e*)   securities acquired for less than market value (*Chapter 3C* – see 14.78)

(*f*)   securities disposed of for more than market value (*Chapter 3D* – see 14.86)

(*g*)   post acquisition benefit from securities (*Chapter 4* – see 14.87)

(*h*)   shares acquired under securities options (*Chapter 5* – see 14.89).

Some of these new provisions apply only to securities acquired on or after 16 April 2003 whereas others affect shares acquired before that date also.

Chapter 2:	Does not apply to securities or interests in securities acquired before 16 April 2003. It applies to securities acquired after that date from a date to be appointed by the Treasury by statutory instrument [*FA 2003, 22 Schedule 3(2)*]. This was fixed as 1 September 2003 (*Finance Act 2003, Schedule 22, para 3(1)* (Appointed Day) Order 2003 (SI 2003 No 1997).
Chapter 3:	Applies irrespective of the date of acquisition of the securities but only applies from 1 September 2003. [*FA 2003, 22 Schedule 4(2)*].
Chapter 3A:	Generally applies irrespective of the date of acquisition of the securities but *sections 446E* (see 14.62) and *446I(1)(a)* (see 14.69) do not apply to securities or interests in securities acquired before 16 April 2003 and for securities acquired from that date apply only from 1 September 2003. [*FA 2003, 22 Schedule 5(2)(3)*].
Chapter 3B:	Generally applies irrespective of the date of acquisition of the securities but *sections 446M* (see 14.76) and *446N* (see 14.75) do not affect securities or interests in securities acquired before 16 April 2003 and for securities acquired from that date apply only from 1 September 2003. [*FA 2003, 22 Schedule 6(2)(3)*].
Chapter 3C:	Does not apply to securities acquired before 16 April 2003. [*FA 2003, 22 Schedule 7(2)*].
Chapter 3D:	Applies to securities and interests in securities disposed of after 15 April 2003 irrespective of when they were acquired. [*FA 2003, 22 Schedule 8(2)*].
Chapter 4:	Applies from 16 April 2003 irrespective of when the securities were acquired, but for shares acquired before 16 April 2003 the following provisions of *ITEPA 2003* as originally enacted continue to apply: *section 450* (other than *subsections 3(b)–(e)*, and *6(b)*) (see 14.159), and as far as is relevant for the purposes of *section 450*, *sections 447–449, 451, 452* (other than *subsection (4)* and *(5)*) *461* (other than *subsection (3)*), *464–466* and *468–470*. [*FA 2003, 22 Schedule 9(3)(a),(4)*]. These provisions also apply up to 1 September 2003 for shares acquired after 15 April 2003. [*FA 2003, 22 Schedule 9(3)(b), (4)*].
Chapter 5:	Applies to share options as originally defined under *ICTA 1988, s 254(1)* (see 14.128) from 1 September 2003 and to other options from 16 April 2003. [*FA 2003, 22 Schedule 10(2)*].

Restricted securities

14.22   If the securities concerned are restricted securities a tax charge arises when a chargeable event occurs in relation to the securities (see 14.29).

[*ITEPA 2003, s 422*]. The chargeable amount is of course income for the year in which the chargeable event occurs. [*ITEPA 2003, s 426*]. The issue of the securities is not a chargeable event.

14.23 'Employment related' shares or securities are restricted securities if there is any contract, agreement, arrangement or condition which reduces the market value of the securities and which either:

(1)   provides for:

  (*a*)   transfer, reversion, or forfeiture of the employment-related securities (or the interest in them) if certain circumstances arise (or do not arise);

  (*b*)   as a result of that transfer, reversion or forfeiture the person by whom the employment-related securities are held will cease to be beneficially entitled to them; and

  (*c*)   that person will not be entitled to receive an amount which would have been at least equal to that market value at the time of the transfer, reversion or forfeiture if there had been no such provision for transfer, reversion or forfeiture [*s 423(2)*]; or

(2)   restricts:

  (*a*)   the freedom of the holder of the securities to dispose of them or of their sale proceeds;

  (*b*)   the right of the holder to retain the securities or their sale proceeds; or

  (*c*)   any other right conferred by the securities [*s 423(3)*], or

(3)   creates a disadvantage (or possible disadvantage) to the holder, the employee (if different) or any person connected with either as a result of either retaining or disposing of the shares [*s 423(4)*].

[*ITEPA 2003, s 423*].

This definition potentially creates a problem with 'ratchet' shares. These normally provide for the shares to increase in value if performance targets are met. Such shares are commonly used in management buy-outs. Such shares were not within the scope of *FA 1988, s 78* (see 14.159) as the right giving rise to the increase is not created or varied after issue; it is inherent in the shares from the outset. They do however seem to fall within 14.23(3). The Revenue have entered into a Memorandum of Understanding with the British Venture Capital Association (dated 25 July 2003) covering various aspects of *section 423*. In it they accept that where the management of an investee company hold ratchet shares the ratchet arrangement should be taken into account in arriving at the unrestricted market value of the shares (see 14.33) provided that:

(*a*)   the ratchet rights of the managers depend on the overall performance of the company not on the individual performance of any particular shareholder;

(*b*)   the ratchet arrangements of the managers are in place when the Venture Capitalists acquire their shares;

(*c*)   the price the managers pay for their shares reflects, at the time of acquisition, their maximum economic entitlement (which the Revenue accept is met if the managers pay the same price as the venture capitalists); and

(*d*)   the managers' shares are ordinary shares.

Although the Memorandum does not deal with other ratchet shares the principle seems to be that if the price paid for ratchet shares is at least the full market value of ordinary shares having the same rights apart from the ratchet no tax will arise. Further guidance is given in the Revenue Press release of 22.7.2003.

14.24   However employment-related securities are not restricted securities by reason only that:

(*a*)   they are unpaid or partly paid and as such are liable to forfeiture for non-payment of calls (and there is no restriction on the holder's right to meet such calls);

(*b*)   the holder can be required to sell the securities (or offer them for sale) if he ceases to be employed by the employer (or a person connected with the employer) as a result of misconduct; or

(*c*)   the securities can be redeemed on payment of any amount.

[*ITEPA 2003, s 424*].

14.25   It will be apparent that the market value of a restricted security is usually very low as the restrictions artificially depress that value. The legislation accordingly aims to impose a tax charge when the restriction is lifted.

14.26   There can still be a tax charge on acquisition if the securities fall within heads 2 or 3 of paragraph 14.23. However, the restrictions within head 1 are likely to render the shares completely valueless (or almost so). Accordingly, no charge arises on the issue of such shares. There is no initial charge even if the shares would still be restricted under heads 2 or 3 following the lifting of the head 1 restrictions (as the lifting of those restrictions will trigger a tax charge by reference to the value at that time of the shares subject to the head 2 or 3 restrictions). [*ITEPA 2003, s 425(1)*].

14.27   This is subject to two caveats. Any charge imposed under *Chapter 3*, (see 14.47) *3C* (see 14.50) or *5* (see 14.89) of *Part 7* to the *Act* will still arise. [*ITEPA 2003, s 425(2)*]. Secondly the employer and employee can jointly elect for the normal charge to arise on acquisition. [*ITEPA 2003, s 425(3)*]. Such an election is irrevocable, must be made within 14 days of the acquisition of the shares and must be in a form approved by the Revenue. [*ITEPA 2003, s 425(4)(5)*]. The Revenue have said that there is no scope for accepting an election made outside the 14-day period. They have published the form of election on their website. They have not given it a number. The easiest way to find it is to search under '*s 425*'. The election does not need to be sent to the Revenue. They only want to see it in the context of an enquiry. If an employer wishes to make any amendments to this form they need to be approved in advance by the Revenue (Press Release 2.7.2003).

14.28 At first sight it is hard to imagine why anyone should want to avail themselves of this election, but it can give a saving overall. The government say that an employee may prefer to pay some tax on acquisition to reduce the charge on a future chargeable event. The reason is that the rules seek to tax as income the part of the growth in value after the time of acquisition of the shares that is attributable to the restrictions. If there is no initial tax charge the growth in value up to the time of the removal of the restrictions (or the first occasion on which any of them is removed) is split between the part attributable to the actual cost of the shares and the part attributable to the restrictions. Any amount taxed on acquisition is added to the actual cost and this increases the proportion of the growth that is attributable to such cost. In the vast majority of cases falling within head 1 in para 14.23 the initial value of the restricted shares is likely to be very low, with the result that any initial undervalue by reference to the value of the shares in the light of the restrictions is also likely to be very low. Accordingly, although electing to trigger a tax charge on that undervalue is likely to create a small benefit when the restrictions are removed, the tax saving will normally be so small that it is unlikely to justify the administrative costs of triggering the charge on acquisition of the shares.

14.29 There are three chargeable events that can trigger an income tax charge subsequent to the acquisition of the securities. These are:

(*a*) the securities (or interest) ceasing to be restricted securities in circumstances in which an associated person is beneficially entitled to them (or to the interest) after the event;

(*b*) the variation (or removal) of any restriction relating to the securities in such circumstances; and

(*c*) the disposal for consideration of the securities (or any interest in them) by an associated person (otherwise than to another associated person) at a time when they are still restricted securities.

[*ITEPA 2003, s 427(3)*]. There are, however, a number of exceptions to the basic rule. These are considered at 14.47.

14.30 The reference to an associated person is confusing as most people would assume this to mean someone who is not the employee but has some connection with him. That is not however the case. Associated persons are defined as:

(*a*) the person who acquired the securities on the acquisition;

(*b*) the employee (if different); and

(c)   any relevant linked person (a person who either is (or has been) connected with or is (or has been) a member of the same household as, either the employee or the person who initially acquired the shares – but a company is not a relevant linked person if it is the employer, the issuer (or original vendor) of the shares, or the person by whom the opportunity to acquire them was made available).

[*ITEPA 2003, s 421C* as amended by *FA 2004, s 90(2)*]. A former connected person or member of the employee's household was not a linked person prior to 18 June 2004 but is from that date even if the shares were acquired earlier.

14.31   Accordingly the tax charge will in most cases be triggered by:

(a)   the shares ceasing to be restricted securities at a time when they are still held by the employee (or a connected person);

(b)   some or all of the restrictions being varied or removed at a time when the shares are still held by the employee (or a connected person); or

(c)   the shares being sold by the employee to an unconnected person at a time when they are still restricted shares.

14.32   The definition of a connected person in *ICTA 1988, s 839* applies. [*ITEPA 2003, s 718*]. The extension to members of the same household as the employee or as the person who holds the shares should be noted. It might well make a common-law spouse a relevant linked person so that a disposal to such a person will not trigger the charge but the later removal of the restrictions will do so.

14.33   The taxable amount is:

$$\text{UMV} \times (\text{IUP} - \text{PCP} - \text{OP}) - \text{CE}$$

Where:

UMV = Unrestricted Market Value = the market value of the securities immediately after the chargeable event but for any restrictions.

IUP = Initial Uncharged Portion = the proportion of what would have been the market value at the time of the acquisition but for any restrictions that were either not initially paid for or not previously charged to tax.

PCP = Previously Charged Proportion = the amount charged to tax on a previous chargeable event.

OP = Outstanding Proportion = the proportion of the share value that is still reduced by restrictions.

CE = Consideration and expenses = any amount paid (or expenses incurred) in connection with the lifting or variation of the restrictions. [*ITEPA 2003, s 428(1)(2)* new].

14.34   The *Act* requires the calculation of the IUP, PCP, and OP by reference to further formulae and further terms IUMV (Initial Unrestricted Market Value), DA (Deductible Amounts) and AMV (Actual Market Value). The following are Deductible Amounts:

(*a*)   any consideration given for the acquisition of the shares (which presumably includes any amounts given for the acquisition of any shares from which they derived including any payments pursuant to an option in respect of such shares);

(*b*)   any amount that constituted earnings from the employment in respect of the acquisition of the shares (see 14.13);

(*c*)   any amount that constituted earnings from the employment under *Chapter 2* (conditional interest in shares) or *Chapter 4* (post-acquisition benefits from shares) as originally enacted (or their predecessors, *ICTA 1988, ss 140A–140C*, and *FA 1988, ss 78–87*);

(*d*)   if the shares were acquired on a conversion of other employment-related securities, any amount taxed on the employee as employment income on the conversion; and

(*e*)   if the acquisition of the shares was pursuant to an option, any amount taxed on the employee as income of the employment on the exercise of the option [*ITEPA 2003, s 428(3)*].

It should be noted that the amount taxed on a previous application of the current rules where the restrictions are withdrawn in stages is not deducted. This is because the formula effectively allows for this.

14.35   The formula to arrive at IUP is:

$$\frac{IUMV - DA}{IUMV}$$

That to arrive at PCP is the aggregate of the results of the application of the formula IUP – PCP – OP on each previous chargeable events (or nil if there were no previous chargeable events).

That to arrive at OP is:

$$\frac{UMV - AMV}{UMV}$$

AMV is of course the actual market value of the shares immediately after the chargeable event. [*ITEPA 2003, s 428(4)(5)*].

14.36

Example

Fred Bloggs is issued with A shares in Wonder Consultants Ltd on 10 August 2003. The A shares rank pari passu with the ordinary shares with the exception that they are subject to the following restrictions.

14.36 *Employee Shareholdings*

(*a*)   Wonder Consultants Ltd. is entitled to forfeit the shares without compensation at any time within the first three years; and

(*b*)   If the holder wishes to dispose of the shares at any time within the first five years he must first offer them for sale to employees of Wonder Consultants Ltd at par.

Fred acquired 5,000 shares at 10p a share. The value of the ordinary shares on 10 August 2003 was £5 a share. The value subject to the restrictions was 15p a share. The value of ordinary shares at 9 August 2006 is £8 per share and that at 9 August 2008 £10 per share. The value of the A shares immediately after the removal of restriction (a) was £3 a share.

There is no charge on Fred on the acquisition of the A shares (see 14.22) but there are two chargeable events, on the cessation of the (*a*) restriction on 9 August 2006 and on the cessation of the (*b*) restriction on 9 August 2008.

Taxable on 9 August 2006

UMV $= 5,000 \times £8 = £40,000$

IUP $= \dfrac{\text{IUMV } (5,000 \times £5 = £25,000) - \text{DA } (5,000 \times 10p = £500)}{\text{IUMV } (£25,000)}$

         $= 0.98$

PCP $= \text{nil}$ (as there were no previous chargeable events)

OP $= \dfrac{\text{UMV } (£4,000) - \text{AMV } (5,000 \times £3 = £15,000)}{\text{UMV } (£40,000)}$

         $= 0.625$

CE $= \text{nil}$ (as no payment is required to remove the restriction).

The taxable amount is therefore

$£40,000 \times (0.98 - \text{nil} - 0.625) - \text{nil}$
$£40,000 \times 0.355 = £14,200$

Taxable on 9 August 2008

UMV $= 5,000 \times £10 = £50,000$
IUP $= \dfrac{\text{IUMV } (£25,000 \text{ as before}) - \text{DA } (£500 + £14,200 = £14,700)}{\text{IUMV } (£25,000)}$

         $= 0.412$

PCP = 0.355 (as above)

OP = $\dfrac{\text{UMV £50,000} - \text{AMV (5,000} \times \text{£10,000} = \text{£50,000)}}{\text{UMV (£50,000)}}$

CE = nil (no payment is required to remove the restrictions).

The taxable amount is therefore
£50,000 × (0.98 – 0.355 – nil) – nil
£50,000 × 0.625 = £31,250

14.37 The calculation effectively splits the increase in value of the shares as follows:

part of value initially paid for	2.0%
part taxed in 2006/07	62.5%
part taxed in 2008/09	35.5%
	100%

2% of growth in value is accordingly subject only to capital gains tax.

The growth of the remaining 98% up to 2006/07 is subject to income tax, part in 2006/07 and the rest in 2008/09. The growth between August 2006 and 2008 in value of the 62.5% charged to income tax in 2006/07 attracts only capital gains tax because once it attracts the income tax charge on removal of the relevant restrictions that part of the value ceases to be regarded as employment related.

14.38 If Fred and Wonder Consultants had elected under *s 425(3)* (see 14.27) to trigger the charge on the real undervalue in August 2003 when the shares were issued to Fred the charge would have been on £250 (5,000 × 15p value less 10p cost). However, that £250 would then have been become part of DA making DA £750 and IUMV 0.97%. This would have reduced the tax charge in 2006/07 to £40,000 x 0.345% or £13,800 but left that in 2008/09 unchanged. In effect the formula apportions the part of the initial value attributable to the restrictions not 'paid for' between the events that trigger a cessation of those restrictions. Nevertheless it will be seen that by paying tax on £250 up front Fred would have reduced the taxable amount on the removal of the first restrictions by £400. Whether a £150 overall saving would have justified the extra work is another question.

14.39 The employer and employee can jointly elect to calculate the gain on a chargeable event by ignoring the reference to OP (which effectively means ignoring the existence of any restrictions that continue to attach to the shares after that chargeable event). [*ITEPA 2003, s 430(1)(a)*]. This triggers the entire charge as if all of the restrictions on the shares had been removed at the time of the chargeable event. In return it treats the shares as ceasing to be restricted securities for the future.

14.40 It might be sensible to make such an election if the remaining restrictions are unlikely to have much effect on the value of the shares. A good example is a provision that in the event of the person ceasing to be an employee the shares must be offered for sale to other employees or the company before they are offered to other people. In reality it is unlikely that anyone who is not an employee would be in the market for the shares in such circumstances so the restriction is unlikely to significantly affect the value of the shares. It would probably be worthwhile in such circumstances to trigger the tax charge and save the administrative costs of having to do a second calculation when the shares are eventually sold.

14.41   The employer and employee can also jointly elect either:

(*a*)   to calculate the tax charge under *ITEPA 2003, s 62*, on the issue of the employment related securities by ignoring the restrictions in valuing these securities. [*ITEPA 2003, s 431(1)*]; or

(*b*)   to calculate the tax charge under *section 62* by ignoring some but not all of the restrictions, specifying in the election which are to be ignored. [*ITEPA 2003, s 431(2)*].

14.42   Such an election results in tax being paid at the time of issue of the shares on the amount by which the restrictions (or the specified restrictions) reduce the market value of the shares. It might be sensible to make the election if the shares are expected to grow rapidly in value. If the company is newly formed the shares may well have little or no value at the time the shares are issued irrespective of whether they are restricted or not. In such circumstances it would clearly be worth triggering the charge at a time when it will result in little or no tax becoming due, so as to be able to treat the shares as unrestricted shares for the future for tax purposes. If the restrictions were not included in an attempt to avoid tax, but were attached to the shares for good commercial reasons, the restricted value is unlikely in most cases to be much different to the unrestricted value so again it might make sense to trigger any tax charge at the time of issue of the shares to avoid having to cope with the legislation for the future.

14.43   The Revenue have said that where shares are issued under an EMI option an election under *s 431* to ignore any restrictions on the shares acquired will increase the acquisition cost of the shares but will not normally result in a tax charge because of the exemption in *s 530* (see 16.111). As the election will prevent any future charge to income tax if the restrictions are lifted or varied, it will normally be in the employee's interest to make the election. They warn, however, that while they are happy with normal commercially driven restrictions on such shares, such as employee pre-emption rights, 'one would not expect to see an EMI option linked to other restrictions that materially depress the market value of the shares under option ... the purpose of the option would need to be considered and the option would not be a qualifying EMI option if it was issued as part of a scheme or arrangement one of the main purposes of which was the avoidance of tax through the use of restrictions' (Press Release 5.9.2003). If the market price on exercise is lower than the market value at the time the option was granted a *section 431* election will increase the tax payable on exercise as the limit on the charge under *section 531* (see 16.112) will then operate by reference to the unrestricted market value, not the actual value (Press Release 10.9.2003).

14.44 An election under both *sections 430* and *431* is irrevocable, must be made within 14 days of the acquisition of the shares (or of the charge-able event if it is under *section 460*), and must be in a form approved by the Board of Inland Revenue. [*ITEPA 2003, ss 430(2)(3), 431(4)(5)*]. There is a form of election on the Revenue's website. The comments at 14.27 apply equally to this form. The Explanatory Notes to the Finance Bill state that the election does not need to be notified to the Revenue at the time. Presumably it merely needs to be reflected in the employee's tax return and in the return that needs to be made to the Revenue by the company under *section 421K* (see 14.115). For shares or securities issued between 16 April 2003 and 1 September 2003 (the appointed day) the election needed to be made within 14 days after 1 September 2003. [*ITEPA 2003, s 432(3)*].

14.45 Where employment-related securities are restricted securities (or a restricted interest in securities) the employer and employee are deemed to have made an election under *section 431* if the acquisition occurs after 17 June 2004, and the securities are shares (or an interest in shares) which are either:

(a) awarded or acquired under an approved SIP (see 15.1) in circumstances in which no liability to tax arises because of s *490* (see 15.43);

(b) acquired by the exercise of an option under an approved SAYE option scheme (see 16.5) in circumstances in which no liability to income tax arises because of *s 519* (see 16.11(*b*));

(c) acquired by the exercise of an option under an approved CSOP scheme (see 16.8) in circumstances in which no liability to income tax arises because of *s 524* (see 16.11); or

(d) acquired by the exercise of an EMI option (see 16.72) in circumstances in which no liability to income tax arises because of *s 530* (see 16.112)

[*ITEPA 2003, s 431A* inserted by *FA 2004, s 88(3)*]. Where the shares were acquired before 18 June 2004 the deemed election is treated as made on that date and where applicable *s 446O* (see 14.73) has effect as if the shares were acquired on that date [*FA 2004, s 88(12)(13)*].

14.46 If the shares are convertible securities (see 14.50) or an interest in convertible securities the market value for the purpose of the above calculation is to be determined as if they were not. [*ITEPA 2003, s 428(8)*] It is not wholly clear what this means. The explanatory notes to the Finance Bill stated that it is 'the value ignoring those conversion rights' which suggests that the conversion rights are to be ignored completely although the wording appears equally apposite to require an assumption to be made that the conversion had already taken place. The former interpretation is undoubtedly the intention as the conversion will trigger a charge under *Chapter 3* (see 14.50). If the chargeable event occurs on a disposal within *section 427(3)(c)* (see 14.29) and the consideration for the securities is less than their actual market value an appropriate proportion of the taxable amount calculated at 14.33 is taxable (i.e. that amount multiplied by the consideration over the actual market value). [*ITEPA 2003, s 428(9)*].

14.47   The occurrence of a chargeable event does not trigger a tax charge if:

(*a*)   the employment-related securities are shares (or an interest in shares) [*s 429(1)(a)*];

(*b*)   the restrictions attaching to the employment-related securities attach to all of the company's shares of the same class [*s 429(1)(b)*];

(*c*)   all of the shares of that class (other than the employment related securities in question) are affected by an event similar to the event that is the chargeable event in relation to the employment related securities (i.e. the restrictions are removed, or varied, or the shares are disposed of (depending on which type of chargeable event triggers the occasion of charge to tax) [*s 429(1)(c),(2)*];

(*d*)   immediately before the trigger event either:

  (i)   the company is 'employee-controlled by virtue of holdings of shares of that class' [*s 429(3)*]; or

  (ii)   the majority of the shares of that class are not employment-related securities (for events prior to 7 May 2004 the test was that the majority was not held by (or for the benefit of) employees of the company, persons who are related to employees of the company, associated companies of the company, employees of any 'associated company' of the company or persons who are related to an employee of any such associated company). [*s 429(4)* as amended by *FA 2004, s 86(5)*].

(*e*)   for events after 6 May 2004 the avoidance of tax or NIC was not the main purpose, or one of the main purposes, of the arrangement under which the opportunity to acquire the securities was made available [*s 429(1)(ba)(1A) inserted by FA 2004, s 86*].

[*ITEPA 2003, s 429*]. This exemption is disapplied in certain cases – see 14.70.

14.48   For the above purpose a company is employee-controlled by virtue of shares of a class if:

(*a*)   the majority of the shares of that class (other than any held by, or for the benefit of, any associated company) are held by, or for the benefit of, employees of the company or of a company controlled by the company (or ex-employees or prospective employees of such companies); and

(*b*)   those employees are together able as holders of the shares to control the company.

[*ITEPA 2003, s 421H(1)*].

The definition of associated company contained in *ICTA 1988, s 416* applies [*ITEPA 2003, s 421H(2)*]. For events prior to 7 May 2004 a person was related to an employee if either he acquired the shares pursuant to a right or opportunity available by reason of the employee's employment or he was connected with a person who so acquired the shares (or with the employee) and acquired the shares from the employee or from another person who was related to the employee other than under a disposal made by way of a bargain at arm's length. [*ITEPA 2003, s 429(5)*].

14.49   The *National Insurance Contributions and Statutory Payments Act 2004, s 3* amends *SSCBA 1992, Schedule 3A* to permit an employer to recover employers NIC from an employee if the employer and employee agree and the NIC relates to deemed income under *ITEPA 2003, s 426* or s *438* (see 14.50). This election mirrors that for share options (see 14.102). It needs Revenue approval. From a date to be announced, where such an agreement is entered into the amount taxable under *section 426* will be reduced by any amount recovered from the employee before 5 June following the end of the tax year (and any amount that has become the employee's liability as a result of the election). The deduction is obviously not to be taken into account in determining the NIC itself. If the Revenue withdraw approval of the election the liability transferred to the employee is limited to any amount actually paid before 5 June following the end of the tax year. [*ITEPA 2003, s 428A*, inserted by *FA 2004, 15 Schedule 1*].

Convertible securities

14.50   If the employment-related securities are convertible securities:

(*a*)   the conversion rights are ignored in ascertaining the market value of the shares for income tax purposes at the time of their acquisition – and thus in ascertaining any tax payable under *ITEPA 2003, s 62*; but

(*b*)   a tax charge arises if a chargeable event occurs in relation to the securities.

[*ITEPA 2003, ss 437, 438*].

14.51   Securities are convertible for this purpose if:

(*a*)   they confer on the holder an immediate or conditional entitlement to convert them into securities of a different description;

(*b*)   a contract, agreement, arrangement or condition authorises or requires the grant of such an entitlement to the holder if certain circumstances arise (or do not arise); or

(*c*)   a contract, agreement, arrangement or condition makes provision for the conversion of the securities (otherwise than by the holder) (e.g. automatically on the happening of a specified event) into securities of a different description.

[*ITEPA 2003, s 436*].

14.52   There are four possible chargeable events:

(*a*)   the conversion of the employment-related securities into securities of a different description in circumstances in which the employee (or an associated person) is beneficially entitled to the new securities [*s 439(3)(a)*];

(*b*)   the disposal for consideration of the employment-related securities (or any interest in them) by the employee (or an associated person) otherwise than to another associated person at a time when they are still convertible securities [*s 439(3)(b)*];

(*c*)   the release for consideration of the entitlement to convert [*s 493(3)(c)*]; and

(*d*)   the receipt by the employee (or an associated person) of a benefit in money or money's worth in connection with the entitlement to convert (but ignoring the benefit of a conversion within (*a*) to (*c*) and a benefit received on account of any disability of the employee within the meaning of the *Disability Discrimination Act 1995*). [*s 493(3)(d), (4)*].

[*ITEPA 2003, s 439*].

Associated person has the meaning considered at 14.30 above.

14.53   The taxable amount on the occurrence of a chargeable event is the difference between the gain realised on that event and the aggregate of any consideration given for the entitlement to convert and any expenses incurred by the holder of the securities in connection with the conversion, disposal or receipt. However both of these items have special meanings.

14.54   The amount of gain realised on the occurrence of a chargeable event within *s 439(3)(a)* (an actual conversion) is calculated using the formula:

$$CMVCS - (CMVERS + CC)$$

where:

CMVCS = Current Market Value of the Converted Securities = the market value at the time of the chargeable event of the securities into which they are converted (ignoring any conversion rights that those new securities may themselves have).

In the case of an interest in securities it is the proportion of the market value of the securities which the value of the interest bears to the value of the securities.

CMVERS = Current Market Value of the Employment Related Securities = what would have been the market value of the securities at the time of the chargeable event if they were not convertible securities.

CC = Consideration for Conversion = the amount of any consideration given for the conversion.

The amount of gain realised on an event within *s 439(3)(b)* (disposal prior to conversion) is calculated using the formula:

$$DC - CMVERS$$

where:

$$DC = Disposal\ Consideration$$

The amount of gain realised on an event within *s 439(3)(c)* (sale of the right) or *(d)* (receipt of a benefit) is the consideration received or the market value of the benefit as the case may be. [*ITEPA 2003, s 441*].

14.55 The consideration given for the entitlement to convert is the excess, if any, of the consideration given to acquire the securities (AES) over what the market value of the securities would have been at the time of the acquisition if the conversion rights had not existed (NCMV). [*ITEPA 2003, s 442*]. In other words the employee is treated as having bought the conversion rights only if and to the extent that his actual acquisition price exceeded the then value of the shares ignoring the right to convert. If the shares were restricted shares and an election was made under *s 431* (see 14.41) to ignore the restrictions in valuing the shares it is that uplifted value that has to be compared with the subscription price. In effect, there will be no consideration within *section 442* if any income tax charge arose on the issue of the shares.

Example

14.56 Peter Pan acquired 1,000 A shares in Wendy Enterprises Ltd on 5 October 2003 for £2,000. The shares were subject to restrictions and convertible to ordinary shares on 5 October 2008. The value of the A shares on 5 October 2003 was £1,800. The value ignoring the conversion rights was £300 and that ignoring both the conversion rights and the restrictions was £1,400. The value on 5 October 2005 of the ordinary shares into which Peter's A shares were converted was £10,000. The value of the A shares immediately prior to conversion was £7,000. The restrictions were removed in June 2006 at which time the unrestricted value ignoring the conversion rights was £6,000.

Peter paid £2,000 for shares that, ignoring the conversion rights, were worth £300. Accordingly he has given consideration of £2,000 – £300 = £1,700.

The gain realised on conversion is:

CMVCS – CMVERS + CC
£10,000 – £7,000 + nil (as no consideration was given for the conversion)

= £3,000

The taxable amount on conversion is:

Gain realised – consideration given
£3,000 – £1,700 = £1,300

Peter will have also suffered a charge on the removal of the restrictions of:

$$\text{UMV} \times (\text{IUP} - \text{PCP} - \text{OP})$$
$$\frac{£6,000 \times (1,400 - 300 - nil - nil)}{1,400}$$

$$= £6,000 \times 78.57\% = £4,714$$

If Peter had elected under *section 431* to ignore all of the restrictions the position would have been:

taxable on acquisition = value of unrestricted shares – consideration paid
ignoring conversion rights
£1,400 – £2,000
= nil

taxable on removal of restrictions = nil
taxable on conversion = gain realised – consideration given
£3,000 – (£2,000 – £1,400 = £600)
£2,400

14.57   No charge arises on the happening of a chargeable event if:

(*a*)   the employment related securities are shares in a company;

(*b*)   all the company's shares of the same class are convertible;

(*c*)   all of the company's remaining shares of that class are affected by an event similar to that which is the chargeable event in relation to the employment related securities (i.e. converted, disposed of, the conversion right is released or a benefit is received as the case may be); and

(*d*)   immediately before the trigger event either:

   (i)   the company was employee-controlled by virtue of holdings of shares of that class; or

   (ii)   the majority of the company's shares of that class were not employment-related securities (for events prior to 7 May 2004 the test was that the majority was not held by (or for the benefit of), employees of the company, persons who are related to such employees, associated companies of the company, employees of any associated company of the company and persons who are related to such employees.

and

(*e*)   for events after 6 May 2004 the avoidance of tax or NIC was not the main purpose, or one of the main purposes, of the arrangement under which the opportunity to acquire the securities was made available [*s 443(1)(ba),(1A)*, inserted by *FA 2004, s 86*].

[*ITEPA 2003, s 443*].

The definitions of employee-controlled, associated company and related person considered at 14.48 above again apply. [*ITEPA 2003, ss 443(5), 444(6)*].

14.58   If an election under *SSCBA 1992 Sch 3A* is made for the employee to bear the employer's NIC liability in relation to the deemed income under *section 438* the taxable amount can be reduced by that NIC. The detailed rules are the same as apply to *section 426*. These are considered at 14.49. [*ITEPA 2003, s 442A* inserted by *FA 2004, 16 Schedule 2*].

Securities with artificially depressed market value

14.59   Further charges can arise where the market value of employment related securities (or other relevant securities) is reduced by things done other than for genuine commercial reasons. [*ITEPA 2003, s 446A(1)*]. This applies in particular to:

(*a*)   anything done as part of a scheme or arrangement the main purpose, or one of the main purposes, of which is the avoidance of tax or NIC; and

(*b*)   any transaction between companies which are members of the same group (51% subsidiaries) on terms which are not such as might have been expected to be agreed between persons acting at arm's length (other than a payment for group relief).

[*ITEPA 2003, s 446A(2)(3)*].

14.60   A charge to income tax arises on the acquisition of such an artificially depreciated security if at the time of acquisition the market value has been reduced by at least 10% as a result of things done other than for genuine commercial purposes within seven years prior to the time of the acquisition. [*ITEPA 2003, s 446B(1)(2)*]. The charge is additional to that arising under any other provision. [*ITEPA 2003, s 446B(4)*]. The amount is calculated by the formula FMV – MV, where FMV is what the market value at the time of acquisition would have been if those things had not been done and MV is the actual market value of the securities at that time (or, if greater, the amount of the consideration given for the acquisition of the securities). [*ITEPA 2003, s 446C*].

14.61   If the artificially depreciated securities are restricted securities (see 14.23) (or in interest in such securities) the full market value (but not the market value) must be determined as if the employment related securities were not restricted securities. [*ITEPA 2003, s 446D(1)*]. This effectively taxes the full value of the restriction. Accordingly the charge on the removal of the restrictions (or other chargeable event) will not apply in such a case. [*ITEPA 2003, s 446D(1)*]. If the artificially depreciated securities are convertible securities (or an interest in convertible securities) both the full market value and market value are determined as if they were not (so the charge on conversion will also apply in such a case). [*ITEPA 2003, s 446D(2)*].

14.62   If the market value of employment-related securities which are restricted securities (or an interest in such securities) is artificially low immediately after an event which is a chargeable event for the purpose of *s 426* (charge on restricted securities – see 14.22) the UMV (market value of the securities) for the purpose of *s 428(2)* (see 14.33) is calculated as if the depreciating events had not taken place (as well as ignoring the restrictions) and on events after 6 May 2004 the event that gave rise to the reduction and the fact that the employment related securities are about to be disposed of or cancelled. [*ITEPA 2003, s 446E(1)(a),(6)–(8)* as amended by *FA 2004, s 87*]. The market value is artificially low for this purpose if it has been reduced by at least 10% as a result of anything done otherwise than for genuine commercial reasons within seven years prior to the occurrence of the chargeable event (and if *s 425(2)* (see 14.27) precludes a tax charge arising on acquisition, the seven-year period instead runs to the date of acquisition of the shares). [*ITEPA 2003, s 446E(2)–(5)* as amended by *FA 2004, s 87*].

14.63   If the market value is artificially low on 5 April in any year a chargeable event is deemed to occur on that 5 April under *s 427(3)(a)* (lifting of restrictions) (see 14.29) in respect of the securities. The seven-year period to determine whether the value is artificially low in such a case is the seven year to the 5 April concerned (or to the date of acquisition where *s 425(2)* applies). [*ITEPA 2003, s 446E(1)(b),(2–6)* as amended by *FA 2004 s 87*]. This does not mean that there is an annual charge. Once the charge under *section 427(3)(a)* has been triggered the shares are no longer regarded as restricted shares (see 14.29) so no further charges can arise under that provision. This provision applies only to shares acquired after 15 April 2003 and applies to such shares only from 1 September 2003 [*ITEPA 2003, s 446J(3)*]. *Section 446J(3)* does not apply to securities acquired before 16 April 2003. [*FA 2003, 22 Schedule 5(3)*].

14.64   From 7 May 2004 if immediately before the employment-related securities are disposed of (other than by a chargeable event), or are cancelled without being disposed of, the market value of the securities is artificially low, a chargeable event under *section 427(3)(a)* (see 14.29) is treated as occurring on the date on which the disposal or cancellation occurs. In such a case no deduction for OP can be made in the calculation under *section 428* (see 14.33).

14.65   If the securities were acquired before 7 May 2004 a charge under *section 446E(1)(aa)* is triggered only if their market value would be artificially low immediately before the disposal or cancellation if the seven-year relevant period began on 7 May 2004 (if that is later than its normal starting date). [*FA 2004, s 87(5)*].

14.66 If the market value of an employee's interest in shares which is only conditional (see 14.195) is artificially low immediately after a chargeable event under *ITEPA 2003, s 427*, as originally enacted the reference to market value in *s 428(1)* as originally enacted must be taken as referring to what that value would have been but for the action giving rise to the depreciation in value. The market value of shares is artificially low for this purpose if it has been reduced by at least 10% as a result of things done otherwise than for genuine commercial purposes within the seven years before the chargeable event or, if later, within the period beginning with 16 April 2003. [*ITEPA 2003, s 446F*].

14.67 If the market value of employment related shares which are convertible securities (see 14.50) (or an interest in such securities) has been reduced by at least 10% as a result of things done otherwise than for genuine commercial purposes in the seven years preceding the acquisition, the market value of the securities in the definition of NCMV in s 442(5) (value of convertible securities at time of acquisition) (see 14.54) is what the value would have been but for those depreciatory events (as well as ignoring the conversion rights). [*ITEPA 2003, s 446G*].

14.68 If the market value of securities into which employment related securities are converted is artificially low at the time of a chargeable event under *s 439(3)(a)* (conversion) (see 14.52) the references to market value in the definition of CMVCS in *s 441(6)* (amount of gain realised by conversion) (see 14.54) must be taken to refer to what that market value would have been had the depreciatory events not taken place. The market value of such securities is artificially low for this purpose if it has been reduced by at least 10% as a result of things done other than for genuine commercial reasons in the seven years prior to the occurrence of the chargeable event. [*ITEPA 2003, s 446H*].

14.69 If any consideration or benefit mentioned in:

(*a*)   *s 428(9)* (consideration on disposal of restricted securities) (see 14.46)

(*b*)   *s 441(4),(5)* or *(9)* (consideration for disposal of convertible securities, release of entitlement to convert, or benefit received in respect of entitlement to convert) (see 14.54)

(*c*)   *s 446C(4)* (securities with artificially depressed market value) (see 14.60)

(*d*)   *ss 446X* and *446Y(3)* (consideration for disposal of securities exceeding market value) (see 14.86) or

(*e*)   *s 448* (securities benefit not otherwise subject to tax) (see 14.87)

consists in whole or part in the provisions of securities or an interest in securities the market value of which is artificially low, the market value of the consideration or benefit must be taken to be what it would have been if the depreciatory event had not taken place. The seven-year period in this case ends with the receipt of the consideration or benefit. [*ITEPA 2003, s 446I*]. Head (*a*) does not apply if the securities were acquired before 16 April 2003. [*FA 2003, 22 Schedule 5(3)*].

14.70   From 6 May 2004

(*a*)   *section 429* (see 14.45) does not apply where *sections 446E* (see 14.47) or *446I(1)(a)* applies;

(*b*)   *section 443* (see 14.57) does not apply where *sections 446G* (see 14.61), *446H* (see 14.67) or *446I(1)(b)* applies;

(*c*)   *section 446R* (see 14.77) does not apply where *section 446B* (see 14.56) applies; and

(*d*)   *section 449* (see 14.85) does not apply if *section 446I(1)(c)* applies.

[*ITEPA 2003, s 446IA* inserted by *FA 2004, s 86(6)*].

Securities with artificially enhanced market value

14.71   Adjustments may also be required to be made where the market value of an employment-related security is increased by things done otherwise than for genuine commercial purposes (a non-commercial increase), including in particular:

(*a*)   something done as part of a scheme or arrangement the main purpose, or one of the main purposes, of which is the avoidance of tax or NIC; and

(*b*)   a transaction between companies in a group (51% subsidiaries) on terms which are not such as might be expected to be agreed between persons acting at arm's length (other than a payment for group relief).

[*ITEPA 2003, s 446K*].

14.72   If the market value of the securities (IMV = Increased Market Value) is at least 10% more than what that value would have been if the non-commercial increase had been disregarded (the MV) on a 'valuation date' in relation to a 'relevant period' (normally 5 April), the employee is taxable on employment income of the difference between the two amounts (IMV – MV) for the tax year in which the valuation date falls. [*ITEPA 2003, s 446L (1)–(6)*]. In arriving at both the IMV and MV of the securities any restrictions having effect in relation to the employment-related securities and any non-commercial reductions (i.e. reduction in the market value as a result of something done otherwise than for genuine commercial purposes) must both be ignored. [*ITEPA 2003, ss 446L(6)(7), 446K(4)*].

14.73   A relevant period is a tax year. In the first year it is the period from the acquisition of the securities (or from 16 April 2003 if they were acquired before that date) to the following 5 April. In the year in which the securities cease to be within the charge to income tax (e.g. because they are sold or all restrictions are removed, etc.) it is the period from 6 April to the date that the securities cease to be taxable. A valuation date is the last day of a relevant period. [*ITEPA 2003, s 446O; FA 2003, 22 Schedule 6(4)*].

14.74 If on the valuation date the securities are relevant restricted securities (i.e. restricted securities in respect of which no election has been made under *s 430* or *431(1)* to crystallise the tax charge up-front – see 14.39–14.41) the above amount determined under *s 446L* (see 14.72) must be multiplied by CP(Chargeable Proportion) where CP = I – OP

OP (Outstanding Proportion) is the amount that would be determined under *s 428(5)* on the valuation date if there had been a chargeable event on that date (see 14.35). If an election has been made under *s 431(2)* (to crystallise up front part of the tax charge in relation to the restriction) the reference above to the amount under *s 428(6)* is of course what that amount would be applying, *s 431(2)*. [*ITEPA 2003, s 446M*]. *Section 446M* does not apply to securities acquired before 16 April 2003. [*FA 2003, 22 Schedule 6(3)*].

14.75 If the employment related securities have been restricted securities (or an interest in such securities) at any time during the relevant period a deduction needs to be made from the amount determined under *s 446L* (where applicable applying *s 446M*). This Deductible Amount (DA) is TA – ARTA, where

TA = Taxable Amount = the amount determined under *s 428* in relation to the chargeable event (see 14.35).

ARTA =   Artificially Reduced Taxable Amount = the figure that would have been the taxable amount under *s 428* in relation to the chargeable event if any non-commercial increases during the period beginning at the same time as the relevant period and ending immediately before the chargeable event had been disregarded.

[*ITEPA 2003, s 446N*]. *Section 446N* does not apply to securities acquired before 16 April 2003. [*FA 2003, 22 Schedule 6(3)*].

14.76 From 7 May 2004 none of the exemptions in *section 429* (see 14.47), *s 443* (see 14.57), *s 446R* (see 14.88) or *s 449* (see 14.88) apply if the market value of the employment related securities at the time of the acquisition has been increased by 10% or more by non-commercial increases within the seven years prior to the acquisition of the securities. If a charge arises under section *s 446L* (see 14.72) *section 429* cannot subsequently apply in relation to those securities. [*ITEPA 2003, s 446NA* inserted by *FA 2004, s 86(7)*].

14.77 It will be seen that *section 446L* imposes an annual charge. However, this is not cumulative as the MV disregards only those non-commercial increases that take place during the tax year itself. The 10% de minimis limit is applied on a cumulative basis though. The adjustment under *section 446N* is designed to eliminate amounts already taxed under *s 446L* from the taxable increase in value on the removal of the restrictions (or other trigger event).

Securities acquired for less than market value

14.78   Where no payment is made for employment-related securities at or before the time of the acquisition, or the payment made is less than the market value of the securities, a notional interest-free loan is treated as having been made to the employee by the employer at the time of the acquisition. [*ITEPA 2003, ss 446Q(1), 446S(1)*]. This is based on *ITEPA 2003, s 175* (see 9.1) but goes wider as it is not restricted to higher paid employees. At first sight it would appear to apply to a situation where an employee is gifted unrestricted ordinary shares. However that is not the case because 'employment-related securities' is defined to mean securities or an interest in securities to which *Chapters 2–4* of *Part 7, ITEPA 2003, (ss 442–470)* apply (*ITEPA 2003, s 421B(8)*). Accordingly it applies only where the securities already fall within the rules described at 14.15 onwards.

14.79   The notional loan is treated as an employment-related one, which brings into play the rules on such loans set out in *ITEPA 2003, ss 175–187* (see 9.1) [*ITEPA 2003, s 446S(2)(3)*].

14.80   The amount of the notional loan is of course the difference between the market value of the securities at the time of the acquisition and the total of any 'deductible amounts'. [*ITEPA 2003, s 446T(1)*]. If the securities are not fully paid the market value is what the value would have been if they were fully paid. [*ITEPA 2003, s 446T(2)*].

14.81   The deductible amounts are:

(*a*)   any payment made by the employee (and or if different by the person who acquired the securities) at or before the time of the acquisition;

(*b*)   any amount taxed as earnings on the employee under *ITEPA 2003, s 62* (the basic charging provision on earnings) in respect of the acquisition of the securities;

(*c*)   where *ITEPA 2003 s 425(2)* (see 14.27) applies, any amount taxed as employment income under *s 426* on the first chargeable event in relation to the securities (*s 425(2)* defers the tax charge on the issue of restricted securities until the happening of a chargeable event);

(*d*)   if the securities were acquired on a conversion of other employment on related securities any amount taxed as employment income under *ITEPA 2003, s 438* (see 14.50) on the conversion; and

(*e*)   if the securities were acquired under an option any amount taxed as employment income under *ITEPA 2003, s 476* (see 14.94).

[*ITEPA 2003, s 446T(2)*].

14.82   The amount of the notional loan outstanding at any later time is obviously the difference between the amount initially outstanding and the amount of any further payments made for the securities up to that time. [*ITEPA 2003, s 446T(4)*].

14.83   The notional loan is treated as discharged when either:

(*a*)   the securities are disposed of (other than to an associated person within the meaning given in *ITEPA 2003, s 421C* (see 14.30); or

(*b*)   if the securities were not fully paid up at the time of acquisition, the outstanding or contingent liability to pay for them is released, transferred, or adjusted so as to no longer to bind the holder or any associated person;

(*d*)   the total payments for the securities come to equal the amount initially outstanding, i.e. the notional loan is 'repaid' by an associated person; or

(*e*)   the employee dies.

[*ITEPA 2003, s 446U(1)(4)*].

14.84   Where the loan is treated as discharged under (*a*) or (*b*) above (but not (*c*) or (*d*)) the balance of the notional loan outstanding at the time of the trigger event is treated as employment income of the employee for the tax year in which that event occurs. [*ITEPA 2003, s 446U(2)(3)*]. This applies even if the employment has terminated by that time.

14.85   No charge in relation to such a notional loan arises if the securities are shares, all of the shares of the same class are acquired for a payment below their market value (or for no payment) and at the time of their acquisition either the company is employee-controlled (within *ITEPA 2003, s 421H,* – see 14.48) by virtue of holdings of shares of that class or the majority of the company's shares of the same class are not employment-related securities (for events prior to 7 May 2004 the test was that the majority was not held by, or for the benefit of, employees, related persons of employees, associated companies of the company, employees of such associated companies and related persons of such employees). [*ITEPA 2003, s 446R as amended by FA 2004, s 86*]. A person was related to an employee for this purpose if either that person acquired his shares pursuant to a right or opportunity available by reason of the employee's employment or he was connected (within *ICTA 1988, s 839*) with such a person or with the employee and acquired his shares from the employee or another person who was related to the employee other than by way of a bargain at arm's length. [*ITEPA 2003, s 446R(5)*]. For events after 6 May 2004 the exemption applies only if the avoidance of tax or NIC was not the main purpose, or one of the main purposes, of the arrangement under which the opportunity to acquire the securities was made available. [*s 446R(1)(ba),(1A)* inserted by *FA 2004, s 86*].

Securities disposed of for more than market value

14.86   If employment-related securities are disposed of by the employee (or an associated person within *s 421C* – see 14.30), other than to another associated person, for a consideration which exceeds the market value at the time of the disposal the excess gain is taxed as income for the tax year in which the disposal takes place. *[ITEPA 2003, ss 446X, 446Y(1)(2)]*. The amount of the excess gain is the difference between the consideration received on the disposal and the aggregate of the market value of the securities at the time of the disposal plus any expenses incurred in connection with the disposal. *[s 446Y(3)]*.

Post-acquisition benefits from securities

14.87   If the employee or an associated person (within *ITEPA 2003, s 421C,* – see 14.30) receives a benefit by virtue of the ownership of employment-related securities the amount or market value of that benefit is taxed as employment income of the tax year in which it is received. *[ITEPA 2003, ss 447, 448]*.

14.88   The charge on benefits does not apply if the securities are shares, a similar benefit is received by the owners of all of the shares of the same class and, immediately before the receipt of the benefit, either the company is employee-controlled by virtue of holdings of shares of that class or the majority of the company's shares of that class are not employment-related securities (for events prior to 7 May 2004 the test was that the majority was not held by or for the benefit of employees of the company or the other persons described in *s 446R*) (see 14.85 above). *[ITEPA 2003, s 449]*. For events after 6 May 2004 the exemption applies only if the avoidance of tax or NIC was not the main purpose, or one of the main purposes, of the arrangement under which the opportunity to acquire the securities was made available. *[s 449(1)(ba),(1A)* inserted by *FA 2004, s 86]*.

Securities options (including share options)

14.89   The next set of rules applies where a securities option is acquired by a person and the right or opportunity to acquire the option is available by reason of an employment (or former or prospective employment) of that or any other person. *[ITEPA 2003, s 471(1)(2)]*. A securities option is any right to acquire securities. *[ITEPA 2003, s 420(8)]*. A right or opportunity to acquire a securities option which is made available by a person's employer (or a connected employer within *ICTA 1988, s 839*) must be regarded as being made available by reason of that person's employment unless it is provided by an individual in the normal course of his domestic, family or personal relationships. *[ITEPA 2003, s 471(3)]*. A right or opportunity to acquire a securities option which is available by reason of holding employment-related securities must be regarded as being available by reason of the same employment as gave rise to the opportunity to acquire the employment-related securities. *[ITEPA 2003, s 471(4)]*.

14.90   The basic rule is that no income tax charge arises in respect of the acquisition of the option (other than the charge under *ITEPA 2003, s 526*, on an option under an approved CSOP scheme which was granted at a discount). *[ITEPA 2003, s 475]*.

14.91   An income tax charge can however arise:

(*a*)   on the acquisition of the securities pursuant to the option, under any of *ITEPA 2003*:

    (i)   *s 446B* (see 14.60)

    (ii)   *s 446S* (see 14.78)

    (iii)   *s 476* (see 14.94)

(*b*)   under *ITEPA 2003, s 476* on an assignment or release of the option;

(*c*)   under *ITEPA 2003, s 476* on the receipt of a benefit in connection with the option.

[*ITEPA 2003, s 473(2)(3)*].

14.92   Special rules relate to options acquired under:

(*a*)   an approved SAYE option scheme (see 16.11);

(*b*)   an approved CSOP scheme (see 16.11);

(*c*)   an enterprise management incentive scheme (see 16.73).

[*ITEPA 2003, s 473(4)*].

14.93   No income tax charge (other than any charge under *ITEPA 2003, s 66*) arises in relation to the acquisition or exercise of an employment-related securities option if either:

(*a*)   at the time of the acquisition the employee was not both resident and ordinarily resident in the UK;

(*b*)   the option is employment-related by reason of a former employment and no charge would have arisen if the acquisition of the option had taken place in the last tax year in which the employment was held;

(*c*)   the option is employment-related by reason of a prospective employment and no charge would arise if the acquisition of the option had taken place in the first tax year in which the employment is held; or

(*d*)   the option is a new option (within *ITEPA 2003, s 483* – see 14.104) and one of the above exceptions applies in relation to the old option.

[*ITEPA 2003, s 474*].

14.94   Subject to these exceptions an income tax charge arises on the acquisition of securities under the option (or the happening of some other chargeable event). [*ITEPA 2003, s 476(1)(2)*]. The following are chargeable events:

(*a*)   the acquisition of securities pursuant to the option by either the employee or some other associated person (see 14.30);

(*b*)   the assignment or release of the option for consideration by the employee or another associated person (other than to another associated person or for payment by an associated person);

(c) the receipt by the employee (or an associated person) of any other benefit in money or money's worth in connection with the option.

[*ITEPA 2003, s 477 (3)* as amended by *FA 2004, s 90(4)*].

However, such an event is not a chargeable event if it occurs after the death of the employee. [*ITEPA 2003, s 477(2)*]. If the employee was resident and ordinarily resident at the time the option was granted a tax charge will arise on its exercise even if at that stage the employee has ceased to be resident and ordinarily resident in the UK.

14.95 For the purpose of (a) above securities are acquired at the time when a beneficial interest in them is acquired. [*ITEPA 2003, s 477(4)*]. For the purpose of (c) above:

(i) a benefit received on account of any disability (within the *Disability Discrimination Act 1995*) is ignored; and

(ii) a benefit in money or money's worth received as consideration for (or in connection with) either failing to exercise the option (or undertaking not to do so) or granting to another person a right to acquire the securities which are the subject of the option, must be regarded as having been received in connection with the option.

[*ITEPA 2003, s 477(5)(6)*].

14.96 For the purpose of the share option rules the person who initially acquired the option, the employee (if different) and any relevant linked person are associated persons. [*ITEPA 2003, s 472(1)*]. A person is a relevant linked person if he either is (or has been) connected with or is (or has been) a member of the same household as the employee (or if different the person who initially acquired the option). However, a company is not a relevant linked person if it is the employer (or, if different, the person who granted the option or the person by whom the right or opportunity to acquire it was made available). [*ITEPA 2003, s 472(2)(3)* as amended by *FA 2004, s 90(3)*]. A former connected person or member of the employee's household was not a linked person prior to 18 June 2004 but is from that date even if the options were acquired earlier. The *ICTA 1988, s 839* definition of connected persons applies. [*ITEPA 2003, s 718*].

14.97 If the employee has been divested of the option by operation of law, e.g. he has become bankrupt, the person who exercises the option or receives the consideration is the taxable person rather than the employee. In such a case the tax charge is under Case VI of Schedule D. [*ITEPA 2003, ss 476(5), 477(7)*].

14.98 The taxable amount is:

$$AG - DA$$

Where   AG = the gain realised on the occurrence of the chargeable event (see 14.91); and

DA = the total of any deductible amounts (see 14.100).

[*ITEPA 2003, s 478*].

14.99   The amount of gain realised on the exercise of the option is the market value of the shares at the date of such exercise less the price payable for the shares under the option. [*ITEPA 2003, s 479(2)(3)*]. This does not of course apply if the option is an enterprise management incentive option as *ITEPA 2003, ss 531* and *532* contains different rules in relation to such options (see 16.111). [*ITEPA 2003, s 479(4)*]. The amount of gain realised on an assignment or release of the option is the consideration received for the assignment or release. The amount of gain realised on the receipt of any other benefit is the amount received or the market value of the benefit. [*ITEPA 2003, s 479(5)(6)*]. This is subject to the proviso that if a benefit, or the consideration for realising or assigning an option, consists in whole or part in the receipt of securities (or an interest in securities) the market value of which has been reduced by at least 10% as a result of something done otherwise than for genuine commercial purposes within the prior seven years, the market value of such securities must be taken as what it would have been but for the reduction. In particular anything done as part of a scheme or arrangement, one of the main purpose of which is the avoidance of tax or NIC, must be treated as not having been done for genuine commercial purposes. So must any transaction (other than a payment for group relief) between companies which are members of the same group (51% subsidiaries) on terms which are not such as might be expected to be agreed between persons acting at arm's length. [*ITEPA 2003, s 479(7)–(9)*].

14.100   The deductible amounts are:

(*a*)   any consideration given for the acquisition of the option itself [*s 480(2)(a)*];

(*b*)   any expenses incurred in connection with the acquisition of the securities or the assignment, release or receipt which gives rise to the chargeable event [*s 480(2)(b)*];

(*c*)   any amount taxed as employment income under *ITEPA 2003, s 526* (option under approved CSOP scheme granted at a discount – see 16.11) to the extent that it is attributable to the shares in question [*s 480(4)*];

(*d*)   any amount taxed as earnings under *ITEPA 2003, s 66* (the basic charging provision on employment income) in respect of the acquisition of the option [*s 480(5)(a)*];

(*e*)   any amount charged to income tax as a benefit in kind in respect of the option [*s 480(5)(b)*];

(*f*)   the amount of any gain by a previous holder on an assignment of the option which would have been a deductible cost under *s 479(2)(c)* as originally enacted (see 14.120) on an exercise of the option at a time when that section was in force [*s 480(5)(c)*]; and

(*g*)   any amount deductible under *sections 481* or *482* (see 14.102) in relation to employer's National Insurance contributions borne by the employee. [*s 480(7)*].

[*ITEPA 2003, s 480(2)(4)(5)(7)*].

Curiously there seems to be no relief for any expenses in connection with the grant of the option.

14.101   If there is more than one chargeable event in relation to an option (including if *sections 476* or *477* as originally enacted applied to that earlier event) amounts deducted in calculating the gain realised on an earlier event obviously cannot be deducted again. [*ITEPA 2003, s 480(6)*].

14.102   If the employer and employee have entered into an agreement under *Contributions and Benefits Act 1992, 1 Schedule 3A,* for the employee to reimburse the employer's NIC on the exercise of the option, or made an election under *1 Schedule 3B* to that *Act* to transfer responsibility for payment of such NIC to the employee, any amount reimbursed to the employer under that agreement before 5 June following the tax year in which the gain is realised, and the amount of any liability transferred to the employee, are deductible under 14.100(*g*) above. [*ITEPA 2003, s 481(1)(2)*]. If the Revenue withdraw their approval to an election under *1 Schedule 3B* the amount deductible is limited to any NIC liability actually met by the employee before 5 June in the tax year following that in which the gain is realised. [*ITEPA 2003, s 481(3)*]. The deduction obviously cannot be made to arrive at the amount chargeable to the NIC. [*ITEPA 2003, s 481(4B)* inserted by *FA 2004, 16 Schedule 3*].

14.103   If the employee becomes liable to pay a special contribution under *Social Security Contributions (Share Options) Act 2001, s 2* in respect of the option that contribution is deductible under 14.100(*g*) above. Such a contribution can be payable only where the option was granted between 6 April 1999 and 19 May 2000. The special contribution was an amount equal to employer's NIC on the gain that would have been made had the option been exercised on 7 November 2000. In return for that payment no NIC is payable on exercise of the option. The appropriate notice of the election must have been given to the Revenue by 11 August 2001, the person (or one of the persons) who gave the notice must have been liable for the employer's NIC (either as the employer or by virtue of an election under *Contributions and Benefits Act 1992, 1 Schedule 3B*), and the special contribution must actually have been paid by 11 August 2001 (or such later date as the Revenue may have agreed). [*ITEPA 2003, s 482*].

14.104   If an employment-related securities option (the old option) is assigned or released and all or part of the consideration for that assignment or release consists of another securities option (the new option), the value of the new option is not treated as consideration for the assignment or release of the old. Instead the above rules apply to the new option as they applied to the old. [*ITEPA 2003, s 483(1)–(3)*]. In such a case the amount of the consideration given for the acquisition of the new option is the sum of:

(*a*)   the consideration given for the old option (or if any amount (other than the new option) was received for its assignment or release, the amount if any by which the cost of the old option exceeded such receipt); and (*b*) any valuable consideration (other than the old option) given for the acquisition of the new option.

[*ITEPA 2003, s 483(4)*].

14.105 Two or more transactions must be treated as being a single transaction by which one option is assigned for a consideration which consists of or includes another option if they result in a person ceasing to hold an option and either that person or a connected person (within *ICTA 1988, s 839*) coming to hold another option, and one or more of those transactions is effected under arrangements to which two or more persons holding employment-related securities options which would attract income tax under the above rules are parties. [*ITEPA 2003, s 483(5)*].

The rules prior to 2003/04 that still apply

14.106 The changes made by the *FA 2003* had a two-fold aim, to block some avoidance opportunities in the existing legislation and to simplify the rules so that they would operate more fairly. As indicated at 14.21 some of these provisions are still relevant as they continue to apply to securities issued before 16 April 2003 and in some cases to securities issued between that date and the appointed day under *FA 2003, 22 Schedule 3(2)*. These are:

Options: paragraphs 14.118–14.140 continued to apply to options granted before 16 April 2003, but only until 1 September 2003. They have been replaced by the provisions considered at 14.89 to 14.105 above.

Acquisitions at an undervalue: paragraphs 14.141–14.152 continue to apply to securities acquired before 16 April 2003. They have been replaced by the provisions considered at 14.78–14.85 above for acquisitions after that date.

Disposals at an overvalue: paragraphs 14.153–14.155 ceased to apply from 16 April 2003. They have been replaced by the provision considered at 14.86 above.

Unapproved share schemes: paragraphs 14.156–14.178 ceased to apply from 16 April 2003 with the exception that the charge on the removal or variation of a restriction applying to the shares under *ITEPA 2003, s 450(3)(a)* (as originally enacted) (see 14.159(*a*)) and *s 450(1)(3)(4)* and *(5)* which relate to it, continue to apply in relation to shares and interests in shares acquired before 16 April 2003 (and to other shares until 1 September 2003). To the extent that they relate to *section 450, sections 447–449, 451(1)* to *(3), 461(1)(e), 464–466* and *468–470* also continue to apply so far as relevant. They have been replaced by the provisions considered at 14.59–14.70 above.

Special benefits: paragraphs 14.179–14.181 ceased to apply from 16 April 2003. They have been replaced by the provisions considered at 14.87 and 14.88 above.

Ancillary provisions: paragraphs 14.182–14.189 ceased to apply from 16 April 2003 except to the extent that they relate to the provisions listed above under unapproved share schemes.

Conditional shares: paragraphs 14.190–14.200 continue to apply to shares acquired before 16 April 2003 and to other securities until 1 September 2003. These provisions have been replaced by those considered at 14.22–14.49 for securities acquired after 16 April 2003.

Convertible shares: paragraphs 14.201–14.207 cease to apply from 1 September 2003. They have been replaced by the provisions considered at 14.50–14.58 for securities acquired after that date.

Additional matters

14.107 For the purpose of *Chapters 2–4* (14.22–14.88) but not *5* (options), 'associated persons' in relation to employment related securities means the person who acquired the securities on the acquisition, or if different, the employee and any relevant linked person. A person is a linked person if he and either the person who acquired the securities on the acquisition or, if different, the employee are connected (within *ICTA 1988, s 839*) or are members of the same household (the person's domestic staff and guests – *ITEPA 2003, s 721(5)*). A company is not however a relevant linked person if it is the employee, the person from whom the employment-related securities were acquired), the person by whom the right or opportunity to acquire the employment-related securities was made available, or the person by whom the securities were issued. [*ITEPA 2003, s 421C* inserted by *FA 2003, 22 Schedule 2*].

14.108 If an associated person is entitled to employment-related securities and either:

(*a*) as a result of the conversion of those securities (or of any other transaction or series of transactions) he ceases to be entitled to the original securities but he or another person acquires replacement securities; or

(*b*) by virtue of his being entitled to the original securities he or an associated person acquire other securities (the additional securities);

the replacement securities or the additional securities must be treated as acquired pursuant to the same right or opportunity as the original securities. [*ITEPA 2003, s 421D(1)(2)* inserted by *FA 2003, 22 Schedule 2*]. If the market value of the original securities is reduced by reason of the issue of the replacement securities or additional securities (or the securities in which they are an interest) that reduction is treated for the purposes of *Chapters 2* (restricted securities) (see 14.22) and *3* (convertible securities) (see 14.50) as consideration or additional consideration given for the acquisition of the additional securities or the replacement securities. [*ITEPA 2003, s 421D(3)*]. *Subsections (2)* and *(3)* apply irrespective of whether or not any actual consideration was given for the additional or replacement securities [*ITEPA 2003, s 421D(4)*]. Where *Chapters 2* to *4* (14.22–14.88) apply to an interest in securities an increase of that interest is treated as a separate interest acquired pursuant to the same right or opportunity as the original interest and a reduction of that interest (other than by a disposal to an associated person) is treated as a disposal otherwise than to an associated person of a separate interest proportionate to the reduction [*ITEPA 2003, s 421D(5), (6)*]. Such a disposal is a chargeable event which potentially triggers a tax charge.

14.109 *Chapters 2, 3* and *4* of *Part 7* of *ITEPA 2003* do not apply in relation to employment-related securities if, at the time of acquisition, the employee was not both resident and ordinarily resident in the UK and *Chapters 3A* to *3D* do not apply if at that time the earnings from the employment were not taxable in the UK (or would not have been taxable if there had been any earnings). [*ITEPA 2003, s 421E(1)(2)*]. None of *Chapters 2* to *4* apply to a former employment if they would not have applied if the acquisition of the securities had taken place in the tax year in which the employment was held, or to a prospective employment if they would not have applied to an acquisition in the first year in which the employment was held. [*ITEPA 2003, s 421E(3)(4)*]. In the case of additional and replacement securities this residence test applies to the acquisition of the original securities. [*ITEPA 2003, s 421E(5)*].

14.110 There is an exemption from *Chapter 2* (restricted securities – see 14.22), *3* (convertible securities – see 14.50) and *3C* (securities acquired at an undervalue – see 14.78). For employment-related securities that are shares acquired under the terms of an offer to the public (or an interest in shares so acquired), but only if the avoidance of tax or NIC was not the main purpose (or one of the main purposes) of the arrangements under which the right or opportunity under which the shares were acquired or for which they are held arose. Up to 18 June 2004 the exemption also extended to *Chapters 3A, 3B, 3D* and *4* and the main purpose test did not apply. Where shares within *Chapter 3B* (securities with artificially enhanced value – see 14.71) were acquired before 18 June 2004 they are treated for the purpose of *section 446* (see 14.73) as if they had been acquired on that date. [*ITEPA 2003, s 421F(1)* as amended by *FA 2004, s 89*]. The rules on priority share allocations set out at 14.151 continue to apply to shares issued under the new rules. In a case within *ITEPA 2003, s 544(1)* (exemption for priority share allocations where different offers are made to public and employees) (see 14.151) the exemption covers an acquisition made under the terms of either the public or the employee offer, irrespective of whether or not there is any benefit within *section 544(2)*. [*ITEPA 2003, s 421F(2)(3)*].

14.111 Prior to 18 June 2004 none of *Chapters 2* to *4* of *Part 7* of *ITEPA 2003* applied to:

(*a*)   shares awarded or acquired under an approved Share Incentive Plan (see Chapter 16);

(*b*)   shares acquired by the exercise of a share option granted under an approved SAYE option scheme; or (*c*) shares acquired by the exercise of a share option granted under an approved CSOP scheme.

[*ITEPA 2003, s 421G* inserted by *FA 2003, 22 Schedule 2* and repealed by *FA 2004, s 88(2)*].

14.112 For the purposes of *Chapters 2* to *4* a company is employee-controlled by virtue of shares of a class if the majority of the company's shares of that class (other than any held by or for the benefit of any associated company – within *ICTA 1988, s 416*) are held for the benefit of employees (or ex-employees or prospective employees) of the company or of a company controlled by that company, and those employees are together able as holders of the shares to control the company. [*ITEPA 2003, s 421H*].

14.113 For the purposes of *Chapters 2*, (see 14.22) *3*, (see 14.50) and *3A* (see 14.59) references to consideration given for the acquisition of the employment-related securities cover consideration given both by the employee and, if different, the person by whom the securities were acquired. [*ITEPA 2003, s 421I(1)(2)*]. Consideration given for a right to acquire the securities is regarded as part of the consideration for their acquisition. [*ITEPA 2003, s 421I(2)*]. If the right to acquire the securities (the new option) is the whole or part of the consideration for the assignment or release (or for agreeing to a restriction of the exercise of the right) of another right to acquire them (the old option), the consideration given for the new option is the sum of the amount by which the consideration for the old option exceeds any consideration received for the assignment or release of the old option (apart from the new option) and any valuable consideration given for the new option (apart from the old one). [*ITEPA 2003, s 421I(4)(7)*]. For this purpose two or more transactions are treated as a single transaction by which a right to acquire the securities is assigned for a consideration which consists of or includes another right to acquire the securities if:

(*a*) the transactions result in a person ceasing to hold a right to acquire the securities and that person or a connected person coming to hold another right to acquire them; and

(*b*) one or more of the transactions is effected under arrangements to which two or more persons who hold rights to acquire the securities in respect of which a tax liability could arise under *Chapter 5* (options) (see 14.89) are parties.

[*ITEPA 2003, s 421I(5)*].

Information

14.114 Every 'responsible person' in relation to a 'reportable event' must provide written particulars of that event to the Revenue by 7 July in the tax year following that in which the event takes place. [*ITEPA 2003, s 421J(3)* inserted by *ITEPA 2003, 22 Schedule 2*]. Once a report has been made that absolves all other responsible persons from making a report. [*ITEPA 2003, s 421J(7)*]. The responsible persons are:

(*a*) the employer;

(*b*) any 'host employer' of the employee;

(*c*) the person from whom the securities (or interest or option) was acquired; and

(*d*) if the securities are not 'excluded securities' the person by whom the securities were issued.

[*ITEPA 2003, s 421L(2)(3)*]. A host employer is a person for whom the employee works at the time of the reportable event and who would be treated for PAYE purposes under *ITEPA 2003, s 689(2)* (see 2.59) as making a payment of PAYE income of the employee in question if a payment were made by the employer in respect of the period in which the employee works for the employer and the conditions of *s 689(1)(c)(d)* were satisfied in relation to the payment. [*ITEPA 2003, s 421L(4)(5)*]. Excluded securities are:

(i) loan stock, bonds or other instruments creating or acknowledging indebtedness issued by (or on behalf of) a national or regional government or local authority (of the UK or elsewhere) or any body whose members consist of states, national or regional governments or local authorities, or

(ii) securities which are listed or dealt in on a recognised stock exchange and were issued by a person who (at the time of the reportable event) is not connected with the employer in question

[*ITEPA 2003, s 421I(6)*].

14.115 The reportable events are:

(*a*) an acquisition of securities, an interest in securities or a securities option pursuant to a right or opportunity available by reason of the employment of the person who acquires the securities, interest or option or of any other person (or an event which is treated a such an acquisition);

(*b*) an event which is a chargeable event within *ITEPA 2003, s 426* (restricted securities) (see 14.22);

(*c*) an event which is a chargeable event for the purposes of *ITEPA 2003, s 438* (convertible securities) (see 14.50);

(*d*) the doing of something which gives rise to a taxable amount under *ITEPA 2003, s 446L* (artificial enhancement of value) (see 14.72);

(*e*) an event which discharges a notional loan under *ITEPA 2003, s 446U* (securities acquired at an undervalue) (see 14.83);

(*f*) a disposal of securities or an interest in securities within *ITEPA 2003, s 446X* (disposal at an overvalue) (see 14.86);

(*g*)   the receipt of a benefit which gives rise to a taxable amount under *ITEPA 2003, s 447* (benefits from securities) (see 14.87);

(*h*)   the assignment or release of a securities option acquired pursuant to a right or opportunity available by reason of the employment of the person who acquires the option or of any other person (see 14.91); and

(*i*)   the receipt of a benefit in money or money's worth which is received in connection with such a securities option (or treated as being so received under *ITEPA 2003, s 477(6)*) (see 14.95).

[*ITEPA 2003, s 421K* inserted by *FA 2003, 22 Schedule 2*].

14.116   In addition, the Revenue can by notice require a responsible person to provide them with such particulars of any reportable event which takes place in a period specified in the notice as are required by the notice, or if no reportable events in relation to which person served with the notice is a responsible person have taken place in that period, to state that fact. [*ITEPA 2003, s 421J(4)*]. Any such notice must specify a date within which it must be complied with. This must not be less than 30 days after the date when the notice is given. [*ITEPA 2003, s 421J(5)(6)*]. Once a person has complied with such a notice this absolves any other responsible person from the obligation to notify the chargeable event. [*ITEPA 2003, s 421J(8)*].

14.117   The Revenue have power to prescribe the form of a notice under both *subsections (3)* and *(4)*. The prescribed form is the Revenue's Form 42. It is important to realise the very wide scope of the wording of 14.107(*a*). The Revenue say that this is not intended merely to require a report of share etc issues within the rules outlined above. It requires details of all share issues where the right or opportunity to acquire the shares arose or was deemed to arise, 'by reason of the individual's employment (or prospective employment). A right or opportunity made available by a person's employer, or a connected person of the employer, is automatically deemed to be by reason of the employment (subject to an exception where the employer is an individual) (see 14.16(*c*)). Accordingly, in the Revenue's view the paragraph requires details of all issues of shares in family companies where the recipient is or will become a director of the company. It probably also requires details of transfers of shares by an existing controlling shareholder, e.g. to his children, if the recipient is, or will become, a director. Whether the Revenue's view is right seems questionable. The structure of the rewrite legislation is that the opening section of a Chapter, in this case *section 417*, sets out the scope of the Chapter and the later provisions define that scope. Accordingly, there is a strong argument that *section 421K* can only require details of transactions within the scope of *sections 417–548*. Unfortunately, the penalty for not completing the return is up to £300 (plus daily penalties of up to £60 a day) and that for completing it negligently (which the Commissioners might well hold includes omitting something which the Revenue had publicly said needs to be included) is up to £3,000, so it is probably wisest to comply with the Revenue's view.

The rules up to 2002/03

Unapproved share options

14.118 If a director or employee realised a gain from the exercise of an option (or other right) to acquire shares in a company (not necessarily his employer company) which he obtained as a director or employee within Case I of Schedule E he was taxable on the amount of his 'gain' under Schedule E. [*ITEPA 2003, s 479* (old)]. There was an exemption for approved share option schemes (see 16.11 below). A Schedule E charge similarly arose if the employee did not exercise the option but made a gain from its assignment or release. The amount taxed of course then formed part of the base cost of the shares for capital gains tax purposes. [*TCGA 1992, s 120(4)*].

14.119 If the employee was UK resident when the option was granted, the Revenue consider that it is taxable even though he has ceased to be resident and ordinarily resident in the UK before it is exercised. Prior to 1994/95 they did not seek to charge tax in such circumstances if the employee was not normally UK resident, normally worked outside the UK, was granted the option while working in the UK for a brief period, and the option was over shares in the overseas parent company of the UK employer company (*IR Press Release 7 March 1994*).

Meaning of 'gain'

14.120 The 'gain' realised by the exercise of an option was the difference between the market value of the shares acquired under the option (i.e. the amount that the employee might reasonably expect to obtain for them on a sale in the open market at the time the option was exercised) and the amount or value of the consideration given for both the shares and the option itself. [*ITEPA 2003, s 479* (old)]. The gain realised by the assignment or release of an option was the difference between the consideration received for the assignment or release and the price paid for the option. [*ITEPA 2003, s 480* (old)]. Where the option was over a greater number of shares than those being acquired (or the option money was for the grant of the option plus something else) a just apportionment of the option money had to be made.

Options granted to third parties

14.121 If the option was granted not to the director or employee but to some other person (and was granted by reason of the employment) a tax charge still arose on the employee even though he did not obtain the benefit. [*ITEPA 2003, s 471(2)* (old)]. Similarly, if the director or employee gifted the option to someone else (or otherwise disposed of it not by way of a bargain at arm's length) or disposed of it to a connected person (i.e. one who was connected with him at the time the option was exercised) the gain was again taxable on the employee himself. In this case, the taxable gain was reduced to exclude any amount on which the employee was previously taxed on the assignment of the option to the connected person. [*ITEPA 2003, s 477* (old)]. If the 'assignment' of the option arose by operation of law on the bankruptcy of the employee (or otherwise) a tax charge was not made on the employee (who would be unlikely to be able to pay it) but the person who realised the gain was instead himself taxed on it under Case VI of Schedule D. [*ITEPA 2003, s 477(5)* (old)].

Assignment or release of option

14.122 If the option-holder omitted (or undertook to omit) to exercise the option, or himself granted (or undertook to grant) an option to someone else to acquire the shares or any interest in them, he was treated as realising a gain by the assignment or release of the option, so that any consideration or other benefit in money or money's worth that he received for the omission or the sub-option becomes taxable under Schedule E. [*ITEPA 2003, s 476* (old)]. This did not prevent a further charge arising on the employee when the option was exercised (even though the employee may not have been entitled to the benefit of such exercise) but if the consideration for the grant of the option was deducted in calculating the first charge it could not be deducted again.

Example

In 1997/98 Joe paid £1,000 for an option to acquire 10,000 shares in his employer company at a price of £5 per share at any time in the next five years. He wished to exercise the option in 1999/00. The major shareholder was at that time in dispute with his fellow shareholders and he asked Joe to defer exercising the option until the dispute was resolved. He paid Joe £3,000 as consideration for his not exercising the option. Joe eventually exercised the option in 2001/02 when the shares were worth £10 each.

1999/00

	£
Consideration for omitting to exercise option	3,000
Less: cost of option	1,000
Taxable under Schedule E	2,000

2001/02

	£	£
Value of shares acquired (10,000 × £10)		100,000
Less: cost of option	1,000	
Less: already deducted in 1999/00	(1,000)	—
Less: cost of shares (10,000 × £5)		(50,000)
Taxable under Schedule E		50,000

In *Bluck v Salton (2003 STC (SCD) 439 Sp C 378)* Mr Bluck received a payment for the cancellation of his options in January 1997. His employment had ceased in April 1995 due to redundancy and ill health but he had been allowed to retain his options, albeit that under the option scheme they lapsed on the cessation of his employment. Unfortunately, he could not demonstrate on what terms he had been allowed to do so. It was held, not surprisingly, that *section 135* applied to impose a charge to tax.

Acquisition of new option

14.123 If the option was assigned or released (in whole or part) in consideration of another option to acquire shares in either the same or a different company, the new option was not treated as consideration for the release or assignment of the old. Instead the new option was treated as if it had been granted by reason of the employment that subsisted when the old option was granted and as if the consideration for its acquisition consisted of (or included, if there was any additional consideration for it other than the old option) anything paid for the old option, except of course to the extent that such consideration had already been offset against a prior receipt. [*ITEPA 2003, s 485* (old)].

Example

Kenny was granted an option by his employer, Target Ltd, to acquire 4,000 shares in Target at a price of £8 per share. He paid £400 option money. In 1999/00 Bidder Ltd acquired Target. As part of the takeover terms Kenny exchanged his option for an immediate payment of £200 plus an option to acquire 2,000 shares in Bidder at £12 per share. At the time Kenny's option was valued at £900. In 2001/02 Kenny exercised the new option. He immediately sold the Bidder shares for £25 per share.

1999/00

	£	£
Consideration for release of option		
Cash	200	
Value of new option		ignored
		200
Less: option money		400
Taxable under Schedule E		—

2001/02

	£	£
Value of shares acquired 2,000 × £25		50,000
Less: cost of option over Target shares	400	
Part utilised in 1999/00	200	
	200	
Cost of Bidder shares 2,000 × £12	24,000	24,200
Taxable under Schedule E		25,800

Multiple transactions

14.124 If as a result of two or more transactions a person ceased to hold a share option and either he or a connected person of his came to hold another right to acquire shares in the same or any other company (whether or not such a right came from a person to whom the original option was assigned), and any of the transactions involved were effected under an arrangement to which two or more people holding employee share options were parties, the series of transactions had to be treated as a single transaction under which the original option was assigned for a consideration consisting of the new option (so as to bring 14.123 above, into effect). [*ITEPA 2003, s 485(5)* (old)]. This applied irrespective of whether the original option was assigned before the grant of the new option, at the same time as it, or subsequently. [*ITEPA 2003, s 485(6)* (old)].

Options granted before 3 May 1966

14.125 If the option was granted before 3 May 1966 the taxable gain was limited to the difference between the market value of the shares at the time the option was exercised and the market value of similar shares on 3 May 1966. [*ICTA 1988, s 136(4)(a)*].

14.126 For the purpose of this legislation an agreement to restrict the exercise of an option was treated as if it were a release of the option. [*ITEPA 2003, s 483(2)* (old)]. The definition of a director was the same as under the benefit in kind legislation (see 6.9 above) except that it also included a prospective director and a former director. [*ITEPA 2003, s 487(1)* (old)]. An employee included any person taking part in the management of the company's affairs and also included a prospective employee and an ex-employee. [*ITEPA 2003, s 487(1)* (old)]. Shares included stock (so far as the context permitted) and also corporate securities. [*ITEPA 2003, s 487(1)* (old)]. References to an option included any other right to acquire shares. [*ITEPA 2003, s 471(4)* (old)], did not actually refer to 'options' at all but these are the most common manifestation of such a right.

Test on acquisition of option

14.127 An option (or other right) to acquire shares was obtained by a person as a director or employee if either:

(a)   it was granted to him by reason of his office or employment as such a director or employee who was chargeable to tax on worldwide earnings in respect of the employment (i.e. *section 135* did not apply at all if the employee was taxable only in respect of UK work while he was non-UK-resident or on a remittance basis); or

(b)   the option was assigned to him and was originally granted (by reason of the employee's office or employment not the grantee's) to some other person.

[*ITEPA 2003, s 471(1)(3)* (old)].

If an option was granted to an ex-director or employee the test at heads (*a*) and (*b*) were applied by reference to the time at which he ceased to be an employee.

14.128 The capital gains tax definition of market value (contained in *TCGA 1992, s 272*) applied for the purpose of these provisions. [*ITEPA 2003, s 475(3)* (old)]. 'Securities' included securities not creating or evidencing a charge on assets. [*ITEPA 2003, s 487(1)* (old)]. The definition of connected person given by *ICTA 1988, s 839* applied. [*ITEPA 2003, s 718*].

Tyrer v Smart

14.129 In *Tyrer v Smart 52 TC 533* the courts had to consider whether shares were obtained 'as a director or employee'. In 1969 a company made a public offer of shares by tender. Employees were given a preferential right to acquire shares at the minimum tender price of £1. Mr Tyrer applied for and was allotted 5,000 such shares. The striking price was £1.25 and dealing commenced at £1.30. The High Court and the Court of Appeal held that Mr Tyrer had obtained his shares not as an employee but as the result of his willingness to take a commercial risk in investing. This was reversed by the House of Lords who held that the Special Commissioners were entitled to find that he had acquired the shares as an employee.

Tax payable by instalments on options granted before 6 April 1984

14.130 Where a Schedule E charge arose under *ICTA 1988, s 135* in relation to an option granted before 6 April 1984 the tax could be paid by instalments in certain circumstances. The consideration payable for the shares had to at least equal the market value of shares of the same class (adjusted for scrip and rights issues, etc.) at the time the option was granted (90 per cent of such value if the option was granted before 6 April 1982). The tax involved had to exceed £250. [*ICTA 1988, s 137(1)(2)*]. An election to pay by instalments had to be made to the Inspector of Taxes within 60 days of the end of the year in which the gain arose. [*ICTA 1988, s 137(3)*]. It is unlikely that any such options are still unexercised. *Section 137* was repealed by *ITEPA 2003* and not re-enacted.

14.131 Where the election was made, the tax was payable by five equal instalments:

(*a*) the first due 14 days after the Collector issued a demand note for the tax;

(*b*) the fifth on the last day of the fifth year following the end of the year of assessment in which the gain arose; and

(*c*) the others on such dates that the intervals between the five instalments was the same.

If the date at (*a*) was later than at (*b*) all five instalments were payable on the later date. [*ICTA 1988, s 137(4)(5)*].

Example

Len was granted a share option in 1983 exercisable at any time in the following 15 years. He exercised it in 1997/98. He gave notice that he wished to pay the tax, which amounted to £6,500, by instalments. It took some time to resolve his Schedule E assessment but this was eventually agreed on 10 June 1999 and the Collector issued a demand note for the first instalment of the tax on 20 June 1999.

First instalment due 3 July 1999
Fifth instalment due 5 April 2003.

There are 1,373 days between these two dates. Accordingly, each instalment will be 343 days apart (one will be 342). The due dates of the intermediate instalments are therefore:

Second instalment due 10 June 2000
Third instalment due 21 May 2001
Fourth instalment due 28 April 2002.

14.132 The taxpayer could, if he wished, pay the tax earlier notwithstanding that he had elected to pay by instalments. If the taxpayer becomes bankrupt after having made the election all the tax became immediately payable. [*ICTA 1988, s 137(6)*]. In calculating what tax was attributable to a gain on a share option, the gain had to be treated as the highest part of the employee's income (except to the extent that some other provision has already required that assumption to be made in relation to another source of income. [*ICTA 1988, s 137(7)*]. However, the amount that could be paid by instalments was limited to the balance owed on the Schedule E assessment where this was less than tax on the gain (*Hunt v Murphy* [*1992*] *STC 41*).

Information

14.133 When a company granted options to employees or directors that would give rise to a charge under *ITEPA 2003, s 471* if they were exercised, it had to send particulars to the Inspector within 30 days after the end of the year of assessment in which the options were granted. It similarly had to give details of shares allotted or transferred during the year in respect of options, of any assignment of an option of which it had received notice, and of any benefit in money or money's worth that it (i.e. the company itself—but not any other person even if the company has notice of it) provided for the assignment or release of any option, or in connection with the omission to exercise an option or otherwise in connection with the option or the shares. [*ITEPA 2003, s 486* (old)].

Options exercisable more than ten years after grant

14.134 In most cases the charge under *section 471* was the only tax charge that could be made in relation to an option [*ITEPA 2003, s 474* (old)], although Schedule E charges could arise under other provisions in relation to the shares themselves.

14.135 If, however, the option was capable of being exercised later than ten years after it was granted (seven years where the grant was before 6 April 1998) an immediate tax charge on the market value of the option arose at the time the option was granted. It arose because the value of an option had been held to constitute remuneration under general principles (*Abbott v Philbin 39 TC 82*) (see 3.16). The amount of this charge was generally very small. What is now *section 471* was introduced specifically because the result of the *Abbott v Philbin* decision was to exclude from tax most of the benefit from the exercise of the option, which the government of the day felt ought to constitute remuneration.

Williamson v Dalton

14.136 In *Williamson v Dalton 55 TC 575* it was held that an option must have some value even where it was contingent on certain conditions and difficult to assign. *Prima facie*, that value was the difference between the market price of the shares at the time the option was granted and the consideration payable under the option plus any option moneys. In fact, the market value is probably higher than that as it ignores completely the prospect that the value of the shares will grow between the time of the grant of the option and its exercise.

Value of the option

14.137 This *prima facie* assumption was subsequently given statutory effect. The value of the option had to be taken to be not less than the market value at the time it was granted of the shares which could be obtained on its exercise (or of any other shares into which such shares could be converted), less the consideration for which the shares could be acquired. [*ITEPA 2003, s 475* (old)]. If the consideration was variable, the least amount or value had to be used.

Example

Mike is granted an option to acquire 5,000 shares at 40p a share. At the time these are granted the shares are worth £1 each.

The value of the option cannot be less than:

	£
5,000 shares at £1	5,000
Option price 5,000 shares at 40p	2,000
	3,000

If Mike's option had been at £1 a share the presumption would not have applied. The value of the option would have been what someone would pay to acquire the option, which is likely to be a very small figure. It should be noted that in the above example the value of the option is £3,000, not £3,000 plus the price that someone would have paid to acquire the option if the price had been £1 a share.

14.138 Where an option was exercisable more than ten years after its grant, so that a liability to tax arose at the time of its grant, a charge under *ITEPA 2003, s 479* still arose when the option was exercised (or assigned or released). However, the amount of the gain on exercise was reduced by the amount taxed on the grant of the option. [*ITEPA 2003, s 478(2)* (old)]. Up to 2001/02 the tax paid on the grant was deducted from the tax payable on exercise but this was felt to give rise to arbitrary results.

Example

On 6 June 1995 Mary was granted for £100 an option to acquire £5,000 ordinary shares in Contrary Enterprises Ltd at any time up to 31 December 2008 at a price equal to 80 per cent of the market value of the shares at the time the option was exercised, subject to a minimum of £1 per share. The market value of Contrary Enterprises shares at 6 June 1995 was £12 per share. Mary exercised the option on 10 November 2002 when the market price of the shares was £18 per share and Mary's marginal rate of tax (after tax relief) was 35 per cent.

1995/96 charge on grant of option

	£
Value of option	
Market price of shares 5,000 × £12	60,000
Least amount of value for which the shares may be acquired (NB: not the price that would have to be paid to acquire them on 6 June 1995)	
5,000 × £1	5,000
Value of option (or open market value if higher)	55,000
Less: cost of option	100
	54,900
Tax thereon at 40%	22,360

2002/03 charge on exercise

	£	£
Market value of shares 5,000 × £18		90,000
Less: option money	100	
Cost of shares 5,000 × (£18 × 80%)	72,000	72,100
Taxable gain		£17,900
Less taxed on grant		£54,900
		NIL

14.139 The initial 'overpayment' of tax was not refundable. It will be seen that in this example the tax payable has exceeded the overall benefit obtained from the exercise of the option.

Options granted before 3 May 1966

14.140 Where an option was granted before 3 May 1966 a tax charge would also have arisen on the grant. The amount on which tax was paid in relation to such an option is treated as part of the consideration for the grant of the option in calculating the tax payable under *ICTA 1988, s 135*. [*ICTA 1988, s 136(4)(b)*]. If the tax paid on the grant exceeds that payable on the exercise, no part can be refunded.

Shares acquired at an undervalue (continues to apply to shares acquired before 16 April 2003)

14.141 If a person who was employed (or about to be employed) in director's or higher-paid employment (as defined at 6.4–6.6 above), or a person connected with him, acquired shares 'at an undervalue' before 16 April 2003 (whether in his employer or some other company) in pursuance of a right or opportunity available by reason of his employment, and the undervalue was not otherwise taxable under Schedule E, he was treated as having received a notional loan equal to the amount of the undervalue by reason of the employment. [*ITEPA 2003, s 194, s 193*]. The effect is to bring the beneficial loan provisions into play (see 9.1 above). These impose a Schedule E charge on the notional interest that would have had to be paid if the notional loan had carried real interest at a market rate (fixed by the Treasury). In practice, the charge on notional interest would not normally arise if the company is a close company. This is because there is an exemption if the loan was used for a qualifying purpose (see 9.11 above) and, in most cases, the purchase of shares in a close company by an employee of the company will come within this exemption.

14.142 However, the beneficial loan provisions also impose an income tax charge on the waiver of a loan obtained by reason of a person's employment (whether or not it was on beneficial terms) (see 9.34 above). This is far more significant in relation to employee shareholdings because the notional loan under *ITEPA 2003, s 193* is treated as remaining outstanding until one of a number of specified events occurs, with any outstanding balance at that time regarded as then being written off or waived. [*ITEPA 2003, s 195*]. In other words, an income tax charge will arise at that stage on the amount of the undervalue. The chargeable amount is then treated as part of the cost of the shares in such circumstances. [*TCGA 1992, s 120(3)*].

14.143 When were shares acquired at an undervalue? This expression was far wider than the day-to-day meaning of the words might imply. Shares could be acquired at an undervalue for the purpose of *ITEPA*

2003, s 193 even though a liability to pay the full market price arose—or indeed even if the price was greater than the market value of the shares, perhaps to reflect the fact that payment would not be made immediately. Shares were acquired at an undervalue for the purpose of the section if they were acquired either:

(*a*)   without payment for them at the time of acquisition; or

(*b*)   for an amount paid at the time of acquisition which was less than the market value of fully paid up shares of the same class.

[*ITEPA 2003, s 193(1)*].

14.144 In considering whether an acquisition fell into one of the above heads, the value of any obligation to make further payments for the shares at a later date had to be ignored. The amount of the undervalue on acquisition was the market value of fully paid up shares of the same class, less any payment made for the shares at the time of acquisition. [*ITEPA 2003, ss 193(2), 194*].

14.145 *ITEPA 2003, s 193* did not apply to a straightforward acquisition of shares with the price being immediately payable, or to a gift of shares as, in such circumstances, the difference between the market value of the shares and the price paid for them, if any, is taxable under general principles. It will represent money's worth in accordance with *Weight v Salmon 19 TC 174* (see 3.6 above).

Occasions of charge

14.146 It will be apparent that many common transactions under which employees or potential employees frequently acquire shares will be within *ITEPA 2003, s 193*. For example:

(*a*)   the acquisition of partly paid shares; and

(*b*)   the purchase of shares from an existing shareholder with the price being payable at a future date or by instalments.

14.147 If payments in respect of the shares, such as calls or payments of instalments on the purchase price, are made subsequent to the acquisition of the shares (and before the notional loan is deemed to terminate) such payments are regarded as repayment of part of the notional loan and deducted from it. [*ITEPA 2003, s 194(3)*]. *ITEPA 2003, s 193* will not apply where shares are given to an employee or are sold to him at an undervalue with the price being immediately payable, as the benefit obtained by the employee in such circumstances will already be taxable under the basic income tax rules on earnings.

Deemed waiver of the loan

14.148 The events that bring about the termination (and deemed waiver) of the notional loan are as follows.

(*a*)   The whole of the outstanding amount being made good by means of payment for the shares. If the price for the shares is at least equal to their market value at the time of their acquisition by the employee, payment for the shares will wholly extinguish the notional loan. Accordingly, the only effect of *ITEPA 2003, s 193*, will be the charge to notional interest which, as indicated above, will normally only create a tax liability if either the company is a non-close company or the employee does not work full-time for it and does not, (with his associates) own at least 5 per cent of the ordinary shares. [*ITEPA 2003, s 195(1)(a)*].

(*b*)   If the shares were initially partly paid, an occasion on which any outstanding obligation to pay for them is released (or is transferred or adjusted so as to no longer bind the employee or a connected person of his). For example, suppose an employee is issued with shares at a price of £2 per share of which 10p is payable initially and that the market price of ordinary shares at the time was £2 per share. The market price of the shares subsequently falls to 50p and the company agrees to reduce the price of the employee's shares to £1 per share, in other words, it waives the premium. A tax charge will arise at the time that the company agrees to reduce the price. It appears that the charge will be on £1.90 per share (as that will be the notional loan still outstanding at the time) even though the employee has a continuing obligation to pay a further 90p per share when the company makes a further call on them. [*ITEPA 2003, s 195(1)(b)*].

(*c*)   The disposal of the shares (including a surrender of the right to them) so that neither the employee nor a connected person of his has a beneficial interest in the shares. A disposal to a connected person, even by way of an arm's length sale, will not bring about a deemed waiver of the notional loan (see 9.28 above). A sale of partly paid shares (at arm's length to a non-connected person) will trigger a tax charge on the full amount of the undervalue even though the price received for the shares will reflect the fact that the purchaser is assuming the obligation to meet future calls. [*ITEPA 2003, s 195(1)(c)*].

(*d*)   The death of the employee—but no Schedule E charge in relation to the deemed waiver is imposed in this instance. [*ITEPA 2003, s 195(1)(2)*]. If the shares are acquired (or held) not by the employee but by a connected person of his the death of that connected person will not give rise to a deemed waiver of the loan.

Cessation of employment

14.149   If the employment has ceased at the time the notional loan is deemed to terminate, it is treated as continuing so that the tax charge can be made. [*ITEPA 2003, s 195(3)*]. *ITEPA 2003, s 192* applies to the acquisition and disposal of an interest in shares, such as an interest in the proceeds of sale of part of the shares, in the same way as to shares. Obviously, in such a case, the market value to be used is not the value of fully paid shares, but the proportion of such value attributable to the interest that the employee holds in the shares. [*ITEPA 2003, s 194*]. The *section* did not apply to share options—which were dealt with by *ICTA 1988, s 135*. [*ITEPA 2003, s 197(1)*].

14.150 References to shares includes stock and also securities (as defined in *ICTA 1988, s 254(1)*: see 14.128 above). An acquisition of shares includes their receipt by way of allotment or assignment. Reference to payment for shares includes giving any consideration in money or money's worth or making any subscription, whether in pursuance of a legal liability or not. The capital gains tax definition of market value [*CGTA 1979, s 150*] applies, as does the *section 839* definition of connected person. [*ITEPA 2003, s 197(1)*]. The *section* does not apply to any amount which is already liable to tax under some other provision. [*ITEPA 2003, ss 64(1)(2), 196*].

Priority allocation of shares

14.151 It is specifically provided that where there was an offer to the public of shares in a company at a fixed price or by tender and a director or employee (of that or any other company) was entitled to an allocation of shares in priority to members of the public, the benefit of that priority was not to be treated as an emolument (either under general principles or the benefit in kind rules). [*ITEPA 2003, s 542*]. This did not apply to the extent that the price payable by the employee was below the fixed offer price or the lowest successful tender price (or, in a case falling within 14.152 below, the appropriate notional price). [*ITEPA 2003, s 543*]. The total number of shares allocated as priority shares to employees could not exceed 10 per cent of the shares on offer, all the persons entitled to priority allocations had to be entitled on similar terms, and the priority applicants could not be restricted to directors or those whose remuneration exceeded a particular level. [*ITEPA 2003, s 542(3)(5)*]. If the offer was one of a series of offers to the public of shares of the same class the 10 per cent limit applied to the aggregate of all the offers, and the priority shares in an individual offer could not exceed 40 per cent of the shares in that offer. [*ITEPA 2003, s 544(3)*]. From August 1990 the fact that directors or employees of the company were entitled to a larger allocation per person than others (e.g. employees of a related company) was not to be taken to mean that they were not entitled on similar terms, provided that those other persons were similarly entitled to a larger allocation of shares in a different company which was offered to the public at the same time and the aggregate value of the package offered to both sets of people was comparable. [*ITEPA 2003, s 546(3)–(6)*]. This extension was to cover employee shares issued on the electricity privatisation.

14.152 Offers made after 15 January 1991 had to be genuine (*'bona fide'* in *FA 1988*). [*ITEPA 2003, s 542(1)(a), s 68(1)(a); FA 1991,* *s 44(2)]*. It is not clear what this means; it is hard to envisage an offer to the public not being genuine. From the same date, in determining whether the price payable by the employee is less than the offer price to the public, any 'registrant discount' made to the employee is ignored, provided that at least 40 per cent of the shares issued to the public attract a discount or other benefit of a similar value. A 'registrant discount' is a discount (or other benefit) given to employees who comply with the same conditions as members of the public who are entitled to a discount, and is given in the same circumstances as to members of the public. *[ITEPA 2003, ss 543(1)(b), 545(1)(b), 547]*. If the public are offered a combination of shares in two or more companies (as happened with Powergen and National Power) and a separate offer is made to employees which does not extend to shares in both (or all) companies, the public offer and the offer to employees are regarded as together constituting a single offer of shares to the public. *[ITEPA 2003, ss 544, 545(2)]*. In such a case the exemption has to be calculated by reference to 'the appropriate notional price'. This is the price at which the shares might reasonably have been offered to the public if they had been offered individually instead of as a package. *[ITEPA 2003, s 545(3)(5)]*. If such prices for all of the shares do not come to the aggregate price for the combined offer (as will almost always be the case as the shares would probably not have been offered as a package unless one component of it was unattractive on its own), the notional price of each is to be reduced or increased in proportion to the difference. *[ITEPA 2003, s 545(4)]*.

Disposals at an overvalue

14.153 If shares were disposed of for a consideration which exceeded their market value that excess was chargeable to income tax as earnings. *[ITEPA 2003, s 199]*. The shares had to be acquired after 6 April 1976 by a person employed (or about to be employed) in director's or higher-paid employment (or a person connected with him) in pursuance of a right or opportunity available by reason of the employment.

14.154 It was irrelevant whether the shares were acquired at a preferential price or at full market value, whether or not immediate payment was made for them, and whether they were acquired from the employer or from some other person. No income tax charge arose, however, if the shares were disposed of after the employee's death. *[ITEPA 2003, s 199(2)]*.

Unquoted companies

14.155 Where an employee has a small minority interest in an unquoted company the market value of his holding is likely to be very low. Most private companies contain a formula in their Articles of Association to fix the value at which shares are to be sold in certain specified circumstances. The formula under many, if not most, such pre-emption rights will ignore the fact that the shares constitute a minority interest. Accordingly, a disposal under the pre-emption rights was invariably at an overvalue.

Unapproved employee share schemes

14.156 A further tax charge could arise where, on or after 26 October 1987, a person acquired shares (or an interest in shares) in a company in pursuance of a right conferred on him, or an opportunity offered to him, by reason of a directorship or an employment. [*ITEPA 2003, ss 447, 449* (old)]. These provisions applied to lower-paid as well as higher-paid employees. They did not, however, apply if the employment was not within Case I of Schedule E. [*ITEPA 2003, s 447(4)* (old)]. Nor did they apply to an acquisition which was made in pursuance of an offer to the public or, after 16 January 1991, was treated as an offer to the public under *ITEPA 2003, s 544* (see 14.152 above) or which would have been so treated if no benefit had been given to the employee. [*ITEPA 2003, s 448(2)* (old)]. Where a tax charge arose under *ITEPA 2003, s 422* (see 14.22), this obviously displaced the *section 449* charge.

Occasions of charge

14.157 There were three occasions of potential tax charges:

(*a*) where restrictions were removed;

(*b*) where the shares were in a dependent subsidiary; and

(*c*) where a special benefit was received.

Charge where restrictions were removed

14.158 A charge to tax was triggered under this head if a 'chargeable event' occurred in relation to the shares at a time when the employee still had a beneficial interest in them. [*ITEPA 2003, s 449* (old)]. If the company was a dependent subsidiary at the time of the chargeable event (or was one at the time the shares were acquired), *section 449* (old) did not apply, but a charge under *section 453* (old) (see 14.166–14.178 below) arose instead. [*ITEPA 2003, s 445(4)* (old)].

Meaning of 'chargeable event'

14.159 A 'chargeable event' was the occurrence of any of the following, but only if it increased the value of the shares (or would have done so but for something else happening at the same time):

(*a*)   the removal or variation of a restriction to which the shares were subject;

(*b*)   the creation or variation of rights relating to the shares;

(*c*)   the imposition of a restriction on other shares in the company (which could increase the value of the employee's shares);

(*d*)   the variation of a restriction to which such other shares were subject; and

(*e*)   the removal or variation of a right relating to other shares in the company.

[*ITEPA 2003, s 450(1)(3)* (old)].

Exceptions

14.160 There were a number of exceptions. The above events were chargeable events only if the shareholder has been a director or employee of the company (or, if different, of the company which gave rise to the acquisition of the shares, or of an associated company) at some time during the seven years ending with the occurrence of the event. In other words, a removal of restrictions, etc. did not trigger a tax charge if the shareholder ceased to be a director or employee more than seven years earlier. [*ITEPA 2003, s 452(3)* (old)]. It is difficult to envisage a company that wants to provide a benefit to an ex-employee by varying rights attaching to his shares waiting to do so until three or four years after he has left, let alone seven!

14.161 A removal of restrictions or variation of rights was not a chargeable event if it affects all of the shares of the same class (and falls into one of the following categories) and at the time of the variation, etc., either:

(*a*)   the majority of the shares of the same class as were held by the employee were not held by (or for the benefit of):

(i)   directors or employees of the company,

(ii)   an associated company of the company (such as its parent company), or

(iii)   directors or employees of any such associated company;

(*b*)   the company was employee-controlled by virtue of holdings of shares of the same class as were held by the employee; or

(*c*)   the company was a subsidiary which was not a dependent subsidiary and its shares were of a single class.

[*ITEPA 2003, s 450(4)* (old)].

Associated companies

14.162 For the purpose of head (*a*) in 14.161 above a company was an associated company of another at a given time if at that time (or at any other time in the previous year) one had control of the other or both were under the control of the same person or persons. [*ITEPA 2003, s 470(1)* (old)]. Head (*a*) was aimed at the situation where a variation affected a class of shares mainly held by non-employees and the increase in value accrued to all, so that it could not have been designed as a benefit for employees as such. If the company was a subsidiary it was not normally possible to meet head (*a*) as the majority of the shares of the class held by employees would have been held by the parent company within (*a*)(ii).

Employee-controlled companies

14.163 A company was employee-controlled by virtue of holdings of shares of the same class (and thus within head (*b*) of 14.161) if the majority of the shares of that class (excluding any held by or for the benefit of an associated company, such as the parent company) were held by (or for the benefit of) employees or directors of the company or of another company under its control (i.e. shares held by employees of a subsidiary of the company could be included), and those people were together able as holders of the shares to control the company. [*ITEPA 2003, s 468* (old)]. Shares in a subsidiary could not normally satisfy this test as the shares held by the parent did not count towards the shares which controlled the company. It is possible to envisage a single class of shares in a subsidiary which have, say, double the voting rights attaching to them when they are held by employees than when they are held by other people, so that employees could control the company even though it is a subsidiary of another company, although this would be somewhat unusual.

14.164 Where a chargeable event took place, an income tax charge arose on the amount by which the value of the shares was increased by that event (or would have increased but for the occurrence of some other event such as a coincidental fall in the Stock Exchange value of the shares (*ICAEW Memorandum 739 13 December 1989*)). [*ITEPA 2003, ss 449(2), 451* (old)]. If the employee's interest in the shares was less than their full beneficial ownership, the charge was on an appropriate part of such amount only. [*ITEPA 2003, ss 451(2), 455(4)* (old)].

Restrictions on shares

14.165 References above to restrictions to which shares were subject, or to rights relating to shares, included restrictions imposed (or rights inferred) by any contract or arrangement or in any other way. [*ITEPA 2003, s 450(6)* (old)]. They did not have to be restrictions inherent in the shares themselves. Thus, if the shares were pledged as security for a loan, restrictions in the loan agreement needed to be considered. Restrictions in dealing with the shares might be imposed by an employee's service agreement or by a shareholders' agreement.

Charge on shares in dependent subsidiaries

14.166 If the company in which the employee has shares was a dependent subsidiary at the time he acquired his shares, a Schedule E charge arose in any year of assessment in which there was a chargeable increase in the value of the shares. [*ITEPA 2003, s 453(1)(2)* (old)]. The amount chargeable was the amount of such increase (or an appropriate part of that amount if the employee's interest was less than the full beneficial ownership of the shares). [*ITEPA 2003, s 455* (old)]. If a charge had already arisen under *ITEPA 2003, s 427* (old) (see 14.195) on the shares having previously ceased to be only conditional, or *section 435* (old) (see 14.201) on the shares having previously been converted from convertible shares, the amount of that charge was deducted. [*ITEPA 2003, s 455(2)(a)* (old)].

14.167 If the consideration for the acquisition of the shares was increased, in accordance with the terms on which the acquisition was made, the chargeable amount was reduced by the amount of such increased consideration. [*ITEPA 2003, s 455(2)(b)* (old)].

14.168 This ensured that if the shares were partly paid initially, an amount paid on a future call was deductible, and if the purchase price was dependent on a contingency, e.g. it is £x or such greater sum as may be agreed in due course with the Shares Valuation Division of the Inland Revenue as being the market value of the shares, the increase on the occurrence of that contingency formed part of the cost. It is not clear if this applied only to consideration becoming payable before the tax charge crystallises or if it included an amount becoming due subsequent to that event. As the subsection did not enable an agreed assessment to be adjusted it is probably the former.

14.169 If, in accordance with the terms on which the shares were acquired, the holder disposed of them at a price below their market value at the time of their disposal, the tax was recalculated to limit the charge to the excess of that consideration over the value of the shares at the time of their acquisition. [*ITEPA 2003, s 455(3)* (old)].

Example

Joe is appointed managing director of Sub-Manufacturing on 1 June 1993. He is given the opportunity to acquire 15 per cent of the company for £15,000, the other 85 per cent being owned by the parent company. The agreement is that if Joe leaves or ceases to work for the company before 31 May 2008 he must sell his shares to the holding company under a formula. Joe leaves the company on 31 March 2003. The market value of his shares on 1 June 2000 was £100,000. The price at which Joe was required to sell his shares in March 2003 was £70,000.

Joe is taxable under Schedule E in 2000/01

	£
Value of shares at seventh anniversary (1 June 2000)	100,000
Less: cost	15,000
	85,000

This amount is recalculated when Joe leaves, to become

	£
Disposal consideration	70,000
Less: cost	15,000
	55,000

Joe is entitled to a refund of the tax that he paid on the £30,000 difference. Unfortunately, under self-assessment it is unclear how he can obtain this. By March 2003 he is too late to amend his self-assessment for 2000/01 (as he has only until 31 January 2002 to do this). The reduction is not due to an error or mistake in Joe's 2000/01 tax return so *TMA 1970, s 33* will not apply. The reduction under *section 79(6)* is automatic; it is not a claim, so *TMA 1970, Schedule 1A* cannot operate. The tax is excessive, not too little, so the Revenue cannot make a discovery under *TMA 1970, s 29*. Presumably the Revenue will have to make a repayment to Joe under their care and management powers.

Occasions of charge

14.170 There was a chargeable increase in the value of the shares at the earlier of:

(*a*)   the seventh anniversary of the acquisition of the shares; and

(*b*)   the time when the employee ceased to have any beneficial interest in the shares,

if at that time the value of the shares exceeded their cost (or rather their value at the time of their acquisition). [*ITEPA 2003, s 454(2)(3)* (old)].

14.171 A charge also arose if, although the company was not a dependent subsidiary when the shares were issued, it became one at a later date but before the employee ceased to have any beneficial interest in the shares. [*ITEPA 2003, ss 453(1)(b), 454(4)* (old)].

14.172 In this case there was a chargeable increase in the value of the shares at the earliest of:

(*a*)   seven years from the time the company became a dependent subsidiary;

(*b*)   the time when the employee ceased to have any beneficial interest in the shares; and (*c*)   the time the company ceased to be a dependent subsidiary (if it so ceased),

if at that time the value of the employee's shares exceeded their value when the company became a dependent subsidiary. [*ITEPA 2003, s 454(4)(5)* (old)]. However, such a charge arose only if the shareholder was a director or employee of the company (or the company by virtue of employment with which he became entitled to acquire the shares, or an associated company of either) at some time during the seven years prior to the company becoming a dependent subsidiary, i.e. no charge arose if the person ceased to be an employee more than seven years before the company became a dependent subsidiary. [*ITEPA 2003, s 456(3)* (old)].

14.173 This was a penal provision. The charge was not limited to any increase in value brought about by a change in the rights attaching to the shares. What was taxed was the full increase in value of the shares over the seven years from the date of acquisition (or the company becoming a dependent subsidiary) or over the entire length of ownership of the shares if shorter. Most, if not all, of this growth was, of course, attributable to the commercial success of the company, and part to the effect of inflation.

14.174 It should particularly be noted that if a company was a dependent subsidiary at the time of acquisition of the shares but subsequently ceased to be one, that change did not trigger a charge. The future increase in value over the seven years from acquisition remained within the scope of the provision, whereas if it became a dependent subsidiary subsequent to the acquisition of the shares, the cessation triggered a charge on the then value.

Takeovers

14.175 *ITEPA 2003, s 453* also needed to be borne in mind on takeovers. If a majority holding in a company which was not a dependent subsidiary but was controlled by its directors was acquired by a second company, the first could well become a dependent subsidiary of the second by virtue of the acquisition. If employees or directors retained any shares in the first company, which is not uncommon where the purchaser, in order to provide incentives for the management, buys the shares in stages, those shares would be brought into the scope of *section 453* even though they may have been acquired ten or 20 years earlier.

Meaning of 'dependent subsidiary'

14.176 Every subsidiary company was assumed to be a dependent subsidiary throughout every period for which it made up accounts unless all of the following conditions were met.

(*a*)   The whole, or substantially the whole, of the company's business during that period of account (taken as a whole) was business carried on with persons who were not members of the same group as the company. [*ITEPA 2003, s 467(2)* (old)]. It is not clear what this required. For example, if all of the company's sales were to outside parties but the bulk of its purchases were from group companies, was its business carried on substantially with persons who were not members of the same group?

Business carried on with a subsidiary of the company itself (i.e. the subsidiary whose status is under enquiry) had to be treated as carried on with a person who was *not* a member of the same group, unless the whole or substantially the whole of the business of that and other subsidiaries of the company under enquiry during the period of account was carried on with other members of the group. [*ITEPA 2003, s 467(6)(7)* (old)]. In other words, the company under enquiry and all of its subsidiaries were effectively looked on as a single entity; it did not matter that there was trading between them: only business with other group members outside that entity was taken into account in applying the 'substantially the whole' test.

(*b*) During the period of account either the value of the company had not increased at all as a result of intra-group transactions, or any such increase did not exceed 5 per cent of the value of the company at the beginning of the period of account (or a proportionally higher percentage if the accounts were for over twelve months and lower if they were less than twelve months). [*ITEPA 2003, s 467(3)* (old)].

For this purpose intra-group transactions had a special, limited, meaning, namely 'transactions between companies which are members of the same group on terms which are not such as might be expected to be agreed between persons acting at arm's length (other than any payment for group relief)'. [*ITEPA 2003, s 467(8)* (old)]. The words in brackets presumably mean that a payment for group relief was not an intra-group transaction. More importantly, it will be seen that transactions between group companies that can be shown to have been carried out on arm's length terms were not intra-group transactions either (although they were, of course, still transactions carried on with persons who were members of the same group for the purpose of (*a*) above).

(*c*) The directors of the principal company of the group sent to the Inspector of Taxes, within two years after the end of the period of account, a certificate that in their opinion both conditions (*a*) and (*b*) above were met. [*ITEPA 2003, s 467(4)* (old)].

(*d*) That certificate had attached to it a report (addressed to the directors) by the auditors of the subsidiary (not those of the parent, if different) that they had enquired into the state of affairs of the company with particular reference to the conditions of (*a*) and (*b*) above, and were not aware of anything to indicate that the opinion expressed by the directors in their certificate was unreasonable in all the circumstances. [*ITEPA 2003, s 467(5)* (old)].

14.177 The requirement at (*c*) and (*d*) of 14.176 for a directors' certificate and auditors' report to be submitted within two years after the end of the accounting year (or other period) was easy to overlook. The Revenue did not have power to extend this two-year period. If the certificate was not duly submitted, the company would be a dependent subsidiary for that period even though conditions (*a*) and (*b*) of 14.176 may have been met throughout. There was no right of appeal against a refusal by the auditor to give the certificate, whether because he was not convinced that the opinion of the directors was not unreasonable or for any other reason. It appears that it was the auditor at the time that the certificate was submitted to the Revenue who had to give the report, not the one who audited the accounts for the period of account in question if different. If the auditor declined to carry out the review, e.g. because funds were not available to pay him, the company could not meet the requisite test, even if it could find someone else who was qualified to act as auditor who was willing to do the report!

14.178 Once a company was a dependent subsidiary, for however short a period, *ITEPA 2003, s 453(1)(b)* (old) came into play and thus brought the whole of the increase in value of the shares until the company ceased to be a dependent subsidiary (or over the following seven years or until disposal, if earlier) into the charge to income tax. The earliest that the company could cease to be a dependent subsidiary was at the start of its next accounting period so, in most cases, if the certificate was overlooked, the company would be a dependent subsidiary for at least a year. If the certificate was overlooked for the year the option was granted the position was far worse; the whole of the future increase in value remained in charge to income tax for the entire period of ownership (or seven-year period) (see 14.181 above).

Charge on special benefits

14.179 If the employee received at any time a 'special benefit' by virtue of his ownership of (or of an interest in) the shares, that benefit was taxable as earnings for the year in which it was received unless it was already taxable under some other provision. [*ITEPA 2003, s 457* (old)]. This applied irrespective of whether or not the shares were subject to restrictions or were shares in a dependent subsidiary, or were simply normal ordinary shares in a stand-alone company.

14.180 Every benefit was a special benefit for this purpose unless both:

(*a*) when it became available it was available to at least 90 per cent of the shareholders of the same class as those held by the employee; and (*b*)   when the benefit was received, either:

    (i)   the majority of the shares of the class concerned were held otherwise than by (or for the benefit of) directors or employees of the company, an associated company of the company, or directors or employees of such an associated company;

    (ii)   the company was employee-controlled by virtue of holdings of shares of the class concerned (see 14.163 above); or

    (iii)   the company was a subsidiary which was not a dependent subsidiary and the majority of the shares in respect of which the benefit was received were held otherwise than by directors or employees, an associated company (other than the company's parent), or directors of employees of an associated company (including the company's parent).

[*ITEPA 2003, s 458* (old)].

These exceptions did not apply where the company was a dependent subsidiary and had only one class of shares. [*ITEPA 2003, s 458(4)* (old)]. The rules were slightly different in relation to benefits received before 12 November 1991. They were amended to exempt benefits such as an entitlement to subscribe to a rights issue, or to shareholder priority in a public offer, where such rights are available generally to substantially all shareholders.

14.181   A charge under *section 457* did not arise if the shareholder ceased to be a director or employee of the company (or his employer company, if different, or an associated company of either) more than seven years before the date on which the benefit was received. [*ITEPA 2003, s 460* (old)].

Ancillary provisions

14.182   For the purposes of *ITEPA 2003, ss 447–460* (old), if a person's interest in shares was increased (or reduced) he was treated as acquiring (or disposing of) a separate interest proportionate to the increase or reduction. [*ITEPA 2003, s 464* (old)]. If a person acquired shares (or an interest in shares) in pursuance of a right conferred on him or an opportunity offered to him as a person connected with a director or employee, his shares were deemed to have been acquired by that director or employee. [*ITEPA 2003, s 447(5)* (old)]. If a director or employee disposed of his shares other than by way of a bargain at arm's length with an unconnected person, he was treated as continuing to have a beneficial interest in those shares until such time as they were ultimately disposed of at arm's length. [*ITEPA 2003, s 463(1)* (old)]. This did not apply if the shares were disposed of to the company in accordance with the terms on which the shares were acquired, e.g. if they were acquired on the condition that they had to be resold to the company on the termination of the employment. [*ITEPA 2003, s 463(2)* (old)].

14.183 If a connected person of a director or employee acquired the shares and received special benefit by virtue of his ownership of the shares, or such a benefit was received by a transferee of the shares who acquired them other than by way of a bargain at arm's length, it was treated as having been received by the employee. [*ITEPA 2003, ss 447(5), 457(2)* (old)]. If a right to acquire shares or an interest in shares was assigned to an employee and that right was conferred on some other person by reason of the assignee's employment, the assignee was treated as having acquired the shares (or the interest in them) in pursuance of a right conferred on him by reason of his employment. [*ITEPA 2003, s 447(4)(b)* (old)].

14.184 References above to an employee included a director (the author's shorthand, not the *Act's*). They also included a prospective employee or director and an ex-employee or director. [*ITEPA 2003, s 470(1)* (old)]. References to shares included securities of a company (see 14.128 above) and also stock. [*ITEPA 2003, s 470(1)* (old)]. A subsidiary meant a 51 per cent subsidiary (as defined in *section 838(1)*), i.e. where more than 50 per cent of the ordinary share capital was owned directly or indirectly by another company. [*ITEPA 2003, ss 450(4), 458(7), 467(8)* (old), *1 Schedule*]. References to an interest in shares included an interest in the proceeds of sale of part of the shares. [*ITEPA 2003, s 470(1)* (old)]. The value of a share or of a benefit was the amount which might reasonably be expected to be obtained from a sale of the share or benefit on the open market. [*ITEPA 2003, s 470(1)* (old)].

14.185 If, after a person had acquired shares (or an interest in shares) in pursuance of a right conferred on him (or opportunity offered to him) as an employee ('the originally-acquired shares'), he acquired additional shares or an interest in such shares ('the additional shares') by virtue of his holding of the originally-acquired shares, e.g. on a scrip or rights issue, the additional shares were treated as having been acquired at the same time as the originally-acquired shares and also as having been acquired by virtue of the employment. [*ITEPA 2003, s 461* (old)]. For the purpose of the charge on shares in a dependent subsidiary all of the shares were treated as a single holding—the cost of the originally acquired shares being treated as the cost of the entire holding and any payment for the additional shares being taken as an increase in the consideration for the original holding. [*ITEPA 2003, s 461(3)* (old)]. This prevented attempts to circumvent the provision by diluting the original holding by a scrip or rights issue and claiming that the right to the additional shares arose *qua* shareholder not *qua* employee.

14.186 If a person ceased to hold his shares as a result of a share exchange or similar reorganisation within *TCGA 1992, ss 127–130*, it was not regarded as a disposal but rather the new shares and the original shares were treated as a single holding (acquired when the original shares were acquired) with any consideration paid by the employee on the reorganisation being treated as an increase in the cost of that holding. If the employee received any consideration on the reorganisation, no immediate tax charge arose on it but that consideration was apportioned among the shares comprised in the new holding and added to the value of those shares when the income tax charge was triggered by *ITEPA 2003, ss 447–456* (old), formerly *FA 1988, ss 78, 79*, i.e. the charge was increased by the amount of such receipt. [*ITEPA 2003, s 462* (old)].

Information

14.187 When a person acquired shares, or an interest in shares, which fell within these provisions, i.e. they were acquired by virtue of his or someone else's employment, both the company whose shares were acquired and, if different, the employing company, had an obligation to send particulars of the acquisition to the Inspector of Taxes within 90 days after the end of the year of assessment in which the acquisition took place. [(30 days pre-6 April 2003) *ITEPA 2003, s 465* (old)]. This assumes that the company was aware of the acquisition, which was not always the case. Nevertheless, the requirement seems to be absolute. It was no defence against a penalty charge on the company to claim that it was not aware of the acquisition. Fortunately, the Revenue believed that 'as a general matter a company could not be required to provide information which it did not have and which was not within its (reasonable) power to obtain' (*ICAEW TR 739 13 December 1989*).

14.188 Similarly, both companies had to give notice to the Inspector of the occurrence of a chargeable event (see 14.157 above) or the receipt of a special benefit (see 14.179 above). In this case the time limit was 90 days (60 prior to 5 April 2003) after the occurrence of that event or the provision of the benefit (not of the end of the year of assessment). [*ITEPA 2003, s 466*]. There was no obligation on the company to give notice of the triggering of a charge under *ITEPA 2003, s 453* (charge on increase in value of shares in dependent subsidiary).

14.189 Failure to comply with the above requirements rendered the company liable to a penalty of up to £300 plus a further penalty of up to £60 a day if the failure continued after it has been declared by the Court or Commissioners, once penalty proceedings had been commenced. There were higher penalties if the failure to comply was fraudulent or negligent. [*TMA 1970, ss 53, 98*].

Shares subject to forfeiture, etc (continues to apply to shares acquired before 16 April 2003)

14.190 Although *ITEPA 2003, ss 447–452* (old) are fairly widely drawn, there was felt to be a risk of avoidance in two specific areas. Further legislation was accordingly introduced in the *Finance Act 1998* to cover two specific situations. The first was shares issued subject to a risk of forfeiture. It was not clear that this risk could properly be categorised as a restriction attaching to the shares. The Revenue initially believed it was and taxed the lifting of the risk under *FA 1988, s 78* (later *ITEPA 2003, s 447*) (see 14.156), but by 1998 were no longer confident that they were entitled to do so. The second was certain types of convertible shares. By 1998 they had come to the conclusion that the conversion of a share with no rights and thus a low value into a different class of shares with substantially increased rights was not a lifting of restrictions. These new provisions, like *sections 447–452*, applied only where the director or employee was taxable under Case I of Schedule E, i.e. he was both resident and ordinarily resident in the UK and was either domiciled in the UK or, if not UK domiciled, was employed by a UK resident employer to work wholly or partly within the UK.

14.191 *ITEPA 2003, s 422* as originally drafted, formerly *ICTA 1988, s 140A* applied where after 16 March 1998 a person acquired a beneficial interest in shares or securities in a company as a director or employee of that or any other company (called the 'employee's interest') on terms that his interest in the shares was 'only conditional'. [*ITEPA 2003, ss 422(1), 423(2), 428(3)* (old)].

14.192 A beneficial interest in shares was only conditional for this purpose so long as the terms on which the holder was entitled to the interest (whether imposed by contract or by any arrangement or in any other way):

(*a*)   provided that if certain circumstances arose (or did not arise) that person would cease to be entitled to any beneficial interest in the shares—either by way of transfer, reversion or forfeiture; and

(*b*)   on that event he would not be entitled to receive by virtue of his interest an amount equal to (or exceeding) the then open market value of the shares (or, to be precise, the amount that might reasonably be expected to be obtained from a sale of his interest in the shares in the open market if there were no provision for transfer, reversion or forfeiture of his beneficial interest in the shares).

[*ITEPA 2003, s 424(1)* (old)].

14.193 A person's interest was not to be treated as only conditional merely because:

(*a*)   the shares were unpaid or partly paid and as such liable to forfeiture for non-payment of calls (provided, of course, that there was no restriction on the holder's meeting such calls) [*ITEPA 2003, s 424(2)(a)* (old)]; or

(*b*)   the company's Articles of Association required a shareholder to offer his shares for sale or, if the shares were issued after 26 July

1999 transfer them, if he ceased to be an officer or employee of the company or, if the shares were issued after 26 July 1999, of one or more companies which were members of the same 51 per cent group [*ITEPA 2003, s 424(2)(b)* (old)]; or

(c)   in the case of a security, the security could be redeemed on payment of any amount [*ITEPA 2003, s 424(2)(d)* (old)]; or

(d)   the employee could be required to offer the shares for sale, or transfer them, if he ceased to be an officer or employee of the company or of one or more companies in the same 51 per cent group (i.e. over 50 per cent common control) as a result of misconduct. [*ITEPA 2003, s 424(2)(c)* (old), formerly *ICTA 1988, s 140C (3A)* inserted by *FA 1999, s 43* with retroactive effect]. In most cases it would have benefitted the employee for this change to have always had effect. However, if the value of the shares had fallen since issue, the employee was adversely affected as excluding the shares left the value at issue taxable at that time under normal Schedule E rules (*Hansard, 6 July 1999, col 867*).

14.194   The reference in 14.192 to 'circumstances arising' included the expiration of a period specified in (or determined under) the terms by which the holder was entitled to his interest, the death of the holder, the death of any other person and the exercise by any person of any power conferred on him by (or under) the terms on which the interest in the shares was held. [*ITEPA 2003, s 424(3)* (old)]. If the shares or security were issued between 17 March 1998 and 26 July 1999 and could remain only conditional for more than five years, the section also imposed an income tax charge on the value of the interest at the time of its acquisition. [*ICTA 1988, s 140A(2)*]. If the terms on which the employee acquired his interest were such that the interest had to either cease or cease to be only conditional within that five-year period, there was no charge under *ITEPA 2003, s 423* (old) on the acquisition of the employee's interest but there could, of course, still be a tax charge under *ITEPA 2003, s 479* (old) if the shares were acquired pursuant to an option (see 14.118) or *ITEPA 2003, s 193* if the shares were acquired at an undervalue (see 14.141).

14.195   *ITEPA 2003, s 427* (old) imposed an income tax charge for the year in which the shares ceased to be only conditional if at that time either the employee's beneficial interest in the shares continued (i.e. his interest was expanded to an unconditional one) or the employee sold or otherwise disposed of the interest that was granted to him (i.e. the 'employee's interest') or any other beneficial interest in the shares. [*ITEPA 2003, s 427(1)(3)* (old)]. The charge was, of course, on the difference between the open market value of the 'employee's interest' immediately after it ceased to be only conditional (or at the time of the sale or other disposal) over the aggregate of:

(a)   the consideration given for the acquisition of the employee's interest (see 14.200);

(*b*)   any amount taxed under Schedule E in respect of that acquisition; and

(*c*)   any amount taxed under Schedule E under *ITEPA 2003, ss 449, 453* (old) (see 14.158 and 14.166) (by reference to an event occurring before the shares ceased to be only conditional). [*ITEPA 2003, s 428* (old)].

14.196 If the employee died while his interest in the shares or securities was still only conditional, the tax charge was triggered at that time as if he had disposed of his interest immediately before his death, and the market value was calculated on the assumption that it was known that the employee would die immediately afterwards and disregarding any restriction that terminated on the death. [*ITEPA 2003, s 431* (old)].

14.197 For the purpose of this charge a person acquired shares or securities as a director or employee of a company both if he acquired them in pursuance of a right conferred on him (or an opportunity offered to him) by reason of his employment and if he acquired them (or acquired a right to acquire them) from some other person and that person himself acquired them by reason of his (i.e. the assignee's) office or employment. [*ITEPA 2003, s 423* (old)].

14.198 A right acquired after a person ceased to be a director or employee was nevertheless regarded as conferred by reference to his employment unless, had that right been offered or conferred in the last tax year in which the employment was held, it would not have fallen to be treated as received by reason of the employment. [*ITEPA 2003, s 423(2)* (old)]. For a right to be acquired or conferred by reason of an office or employment, the remuneration from that employment had to be taxable on a worldwide basis, i.e. under Case I of Schedule E. [*ITEPA 2003, s 425(1)* (old)].

14.199 If a person acquired shares or securities (or an interest in them) as a director or employee and as a result of any two or more transactions he ceased to be entitled to his interest and either he or a connected person (within *ICTA 1988, s 839*) became entitled to an interest in any shares or securities which was only conditional (or he or a connected person became entitled to any convertible shares—see 14.201), the interest in those new shares or securities was treated as having been acquired by reason of the office or employment. [*ITEPA 2003, s 423(3)–(5)* (old)]. The consideration given for the employee's interest obviously included any consideration given by the connected person in such a case. [*ITEPA 2003, s 429(2)(b)* (old)].

14.200 In calculating the tax charge on the interest ceasing to be only conditional, the consideration given for the acquisition of the interest included any value or consideration given for a right to acquire the shares or for anything by virtue of which the employee's interest in the shares ceased to be wholly conditional (e.g. if he made a payment to have the condition removed). [*ITEPA 2003, s 429(3)* (old)]. Consideration given partly for one thing and partly for another had to be apportioned on a just and reasonable basis. [*ITEPA 2003, s 429(4)* (old)]. The performance of any duties of or in connection with the employment in question was not consideration for this purpose. [*ITEPA 2003, s 429(5)* (old)]. Obviously, no amount could be counted as consideration more than once. [*ITEPA 2003, s 429(6)* (old)]. *ITEPA 2003, s 485*, (see 14.123 and 14.124), which dealt with consideration on assignments, etc., and on share exchanges, also applied for this purpose. [*ITEPA 2003, s 430* (old)]. So did *ITEPA 2003, s 487(1)*, which defines director and employee, with the modifications that references to a body corporate were limited to a company. References to the release of a right included agreeing to the restriction of its exercise and 'shares' included stock and any other interest of a member of a company. [*ITEPA 2003, s 430(6)* (old)].

Convertible shares

14.201 *ITEPA 2003, s 438* (old) applied where after 16 March 1998 a person acquired 'convertible shares' in a company as a director or employee of that or another company taxable on a worldwide basis, i.e. under Case I of Schedule E. [*ITEPA 2003, s 435(1)* (old)]. Subject to 14.204 below, these were any shares which either conferred on the holder an immediate or conditional entitlement to convert them into shares of a different class or were held on terms that authorised or required the grant of such an entitlement if certain circumstances (including the lapse of a period of time) arose (or did not arise). [*ITEPA 2003, s 435(2)* (old)].

14.202 It imposed an income tax charge at the time of conversion on the gain from the conversion. [*ITEPA 2003, s 438(1)* (old)]. This was the amount by which the market value of the new shares exceeded the sum of:

(*a*) the consideration given for the convertible shares (see 14.203);

(*b*) any consideration given for the conversion;

(*c*) any amount on which the employee was taxed under Schedule E in respect of his acquisition of the shares;

(*d*) any amount taxed as employment income, under *ITEPA 2003, ss 449, 555* (old) (see 14.158 and 14.166), by reference to an event occurring not later than the time of conversion; and

(*e*) if the convertible shares were acquired through a series of taxable conversions (i.e. conversions which were taxable under *section 439* or would have been so taxable had they given rise to a gain), the amount of any gain on each such conversion unless it was already included under (*c*).

[*ITEPA 2003, s 439* (old)].

14.203 The consideration for the shares included consideration given for the right to acquire the shares and, where the employee acquired the shares by an assignment within *ITEPA 2003, s 423(1)(c)* (old) (see 14.197), the consideration given by the assignor on his acquisition of the shares. [*ITEPA 2003, s 442(2)(3)* (old)]. If consideration was given partly in respect of one thing and partly for another, it had to be apportioned on a just and reasonable basis. [*ITEPA 2003, s 442(4)* (old)]. The consideration for the shares (or for the conversion) could not include the performance of duties of (or in connection with) the office or employment in question. [*ITEPA 2003, s 442(5)* (old)]. No amount could, of course, be taken into account more than once. [*ITEPA 2003, s 442(6)* (old)]. *ITEPA 2003, s 485* (old) (see 14.123 and 14.124), which dealt with consideration on assignment and on share exchanges, also applied for this purpose. [*ITEPA 2003, s 443* (old)].

14.204 There was an exemption from *ITEPA 2003, s 438* (old) where:

(*a*)   the shares of one class only (the original class) were converted into shares of one other class only (the new class);

(*b*)   the whole of the original class was converted into the new class; and

(*c*)   immediately before the conversion either:

    (i)   the majority of the shares of the original class were held otherwise than for the benefit of:

        (1)   directors or employees of the company;

        (2)   an associated company (within *ICTA 1988, s 416*); and

        (3)   directors or employees of an associated company; or

    (ii)   the company was 'employee-controlled' by virtue of holdings of shares of the original class.

[*ITEPA 2003, s 440* (old)].

A company was employee-controlled by virtue of holdings of shares of the original class for this purpose if the majority of the company's shares of that class (excluding any held by, or for the benefit of, an associated company) were held for the benefit of employees or directors of that company (or of a company controlled by it) and those directors or employees were together able as holders of those shares to control the company. [*ITEPA 2003, s 440(4)* (old)].

14.205 Tax was not charged under *ITEPA 2003, s 438* (old) if the interest in the new shares acquired on the conversion was an interest which was wholly conditional (within *section 442* (old) (see 14.191)). [*ITEPA 2003, s 441* (old)]. This was of course because an income tax charge was triggered under *section 422* when the condition was removed or the shares disposed of.

14.206 If the holder of convertible shares within *ITEPA 2003, s 438* (old) died and wholly or partly as a consequence of his death those shares were converted into shares of a different class either on his death or within the following twelve months, the conversion was deemed to have taken place immediately before the death so as to trigger the *section 438* (old) charge. [*ITEPA 2003, s 444* (old)].

14.207 References above to 'circumstances arising' included the expiration of a period specified in (or determined under) those terms, the death of the shareholder or of any other person and the exercise by any person of any power conferred on him by or under those terms. [*Section 140F(2)*]. The terms on which a person was entitled to an interest in shares included terms imposed by a contract or arrangement or in any other way. [*ITEPA 2003, s 446(1)* (old)]. The market value of any shares at any time was, of course, the amount that might reasonably be expected to be obtained from a sale in the open market at that time. [*ITEPA 2003, s 439(5)* (old)]. References to shares included an interest in shares. [*ITEPA 2003, s 435(1)* (old)]. The *ICTA 1988, s 840* meaning of 'control' applied. [*ITEPA 2003, s 719*]. Paragraphs 14.197–14.199 and the last part of paragraph 14.200 applied for the purpose of *ITEPA 2003, s 439* (old) as well as for *section 422* (old). In addition, the reference in paragraph 14.187 to shares being acquired as a director or employee included an acquisition in pursuance of a right or opportunity that arose from the fact that shares which a director or employee acquired (or was treated as acquiring under *section 423*) were convertible. [*ITEPA 2003, s 423(2)* (old)].

Information powers

14.208 A person who provided an individual with an interest in shares which was only conditional had to notify the Revenue in writing, within 30 days after the end of the tax year in which the relevant event occurred, of each of the following events:

(*a*)   the acquisition of that interest by the individual;

(*b*)   the interest ceasing to be only conditional;

(*c*)   a disposal of the interest if it triggered a *section 427* (old) charge; and

(*d*)   the death of the individual if it triggered a *section 427* (old) charge.

The employer (if different) also had the obligation to notify the Revenue of any of the above events. Where the employer was not the person who provided the individual with the interest in the shares, both apparently had to notify the Revenue; notification by one did not absolve the other from his obligation to do so. [*ITEPA 2003, s 432* (old)].

14.209 A person who provided an individual with convertible shares (and if different, the employer also) similarly had to notify the Revenue of their conversion (but not apparently of the issue of the shares). [*ITEPA 2003, s 445* (old)].

Capital Gains Tax

14.210 The effect of many of the above provisions is to treat as income part of the proceeds or value of shares, which is capital under general principles. Accordingly, relief against capital gains tax is needed to avoid double taxation. Where the income tax charge arises on an actual disposal, of either shares or rights, relief is given by *TCGA 1992, s 37(1)*, which excludes from the consideration for capital gains tax purposes the amount taxed as income.

14.211 Where the income tax charge arises on a notional disposal, relief is given by *TCGA 1992, ss 119A, 120*. This allows a capital gains tax deduction either on the disposal or on the first disposal of the shares or interest in shares after the trigger event for the amount on which tax was charged under:

(a) *ITEPA 2003, ss 447, 555* (old) (see 14.156 onwards) (including where the disposal is made by someone other than the employee) [*TCGA 1992, s 120(1)–(2)*];

(b) *ITEPA 2003, s 195(2)* (see 14.142) [*TCGA 1992, s 120(3)*];

(c) *ITEPA 2003, ss 476, 477* (old) (see 14.118) [*TCGA 1992, s 120(4)*];

(d) *ICTA 1988, s 138* (which applied between 6 April 1972 and 25 October 1997 and was replaced by the *Finance Act 1998* provisions) [*TCGA 1992, s 120(5)*];

(e) *ITEPA 2003, s 423* (old) (see 14.194) [*TCGA 1992, s 120(5A)*];

(f) *ITEPA 2003, s 439* (old) (see 14.202) [*TCGA 1992, s 120(5B)*];

(g) *ITEPA 2003, s 526* (see 16.12) [*TCGA 1992, s 120(6)*].

14.212 *TCGA 1992, s 119A* (inserted by *FA 2003, 22 Schedule 50*) treats 'the relevant amount' as part of the consideration for the acquisition of the securities on a disposal if it is the event giving rise to a relevant income tax charge or the first disposal after such an event. [*TCGA 1992, s 119A(1)(2)*]. The relevant amount for this purpose is of course the amount, or the aggregate of the amounts, treated as employment income by reason of events occurring no later than the disposal (and where there has been an earlier disposal of the employment-related securities, after that disposal – or the last such disposal. [*TCGA 1992, s 119A(4)*]. A relevant income tax charge is one resulting in an amount being treated as employment income under *ITEPA 2003*.

Section 426 (restricted securities) (see 14.22)
Section 438 (convertible securities) (see 14.50)
Section 446U (discharge of notional loan) (see 14.83)
Section 476 by virtue of *s 477(3)(a)* (acquisition pursuant to an option) (see 14.94)

[*TCGA 1992, s 119A(3)*]. Where the relevant amount arises under *section 476* it is to be increased by the aggregate of any amounts deducted under

ITEPA 2003, s 480(5)(a) or *(b)* (see 14.100(*d*) and (*e*)), *481* (see 14.102) or *482* (see 14.103). [*TCGA 1992, s 119A(5)*]. If securities cease to be employment-related securities by reason of *ITEPA 2003, s 421B(6)* (see 14.17(*b*) or *(7)* (see 14.17(*c*)) they are treated for the purpose of *section 119A* as continuing to be employment-related (so as to not trigger the section) until the next occasion on which they are disposed of. [*TCGA 1992, s 119A(6)*].

14.213 The capital gains tax legislation contains a general rule that where an asset is acquired or disposed of in consideration for, or in recognition of, the services or past services of the taxpayer or any other person in any office or employment, the transaction is deemed to be for a consideration equal to the market value of the asset. [*TCGA 1992, s 17*]. This is not appropriate where some of the special provisions outlined above apply. Accordingly, *TCGA 1992, s 149A* displaces this rule (for both parties) where the shares are acquired under a share option scheme. The effect is to calculate the tax by reference to the actual consideration. The section also makes clear that the value of the services themselves does not form part of the consideration. [*TCGA 1992, s 149A(3)*]. Similarly *TCGA 1992, s 149B* displaces the general rule where an individual acquires an interest in shares which are restricted securities within *ITEPA 2003, s 423*. Instead the acquisition cost is the consideration given for the interest as calculated under *ITEPA 2003, s 429* (old) (see 14.199). [*TCGA 1992, s 149B(2)*]. The general rule is also displaced by *ITEPA 2003, s 520*, formerly *ICTA 1988, s 185(3)* (see 16.11(*d*)) where shares are acquired under an approved share option scheme, and by *TCGA 1992, s 149C* inserted by *ITEPA 2003, 6 Schedule 212* (formerly *FA 1988, s 68(4)*) where shares are acquired under an employee priority share application within *ITEPA 2003, s 542* (see 14.151).

14.214 For capital gains tax purposes an option is a separate asset to the shares. [*TCGA 1992, s 144(1)*]. However, its exercise does not give rise to a disposal. Instead the acquisition of the option merges into that of the shares to become a single transaction taking place at the time of the acquisition of the shares, the option money (and any other allowable costs of acquiring the option) becoming part of the cost of the shares. [*TCGA 1992, s 144(2)*]. Any amount taxed under Schedule E at the time of disposal is excluded from the disposal proceeds of the shares. If an option is not exercised it is a wasting asset, wasting over the period during which it is capable of being exercised. This does not apply if the option is a quoted one, but that is rare in the context of employee incentives. [*TCGA 1992, s 146*]. Where an option is granted in consideration of services in an employment or office *TCGA 1992, s 17* would normally treat it as acquired at market value. However, unless the option was granted before 15 March 1993 this section is disapplied and only the actual price paid for the option is deductible. [*TCGA 1992, s 149A*]. It is not permissible to attribute a value to the services in calculating the actual consideration. [*TCGA 1992, s 149A(3)*].

14.215 The effect of *TCGA 1992, s 17* in relation to share options was considered by the Court of Appeal in *Mansworth v Jelley (2003 STC 53)*

14.218 The law was changed in relation to the exercise of an option after 9 April 2003 by *FA 2003, s 157* to restore the position to what most people had thought it to be before the decision in *Mansworth v Jelley*. This introduced a new *TCGA 1992, s 144ZA*. This provides that where the grant of an option and its exercise are treated as a single transaction under *TCGA 1992, s 144(2)* or *(3) TCGA 1992, s 17* does not apply for determining the consideration for the sale, or the cost to the person exercising the option, but does apply in accordance with *section 144(3)(a)* to determine the consideration for the option. Similarly, in the less common case of an put option it does not affect the consideration received on the sale but does apply to the grant of the option itself. Where *section 17* is disapplied the value of the consideration is of course the actual price paid for the shares. [*TCGA 1992, s 144ZA(4)*]. This is a logical approach. The market value of an option reflects the consideration that would be paid on its exercise, e.g. if the market value of an option to acquire shares for £5 in three years time is £1 that is the price that someone would be prepared to pay for the right to buy the shares at £5. If the actual cost of the option is 10p and at the time the option is exercised the shares are worth £8 it is logical to charge income tax on 90p and capital gains tax on £2 (£8 less 10p + 90p + £5). It is not logical to charge income tax on 90p, and allow the taxpayer a 90p loss!

14.219 Where a charge to tax on employment income arises on the grant or exercise of an option, special rules are needed to treat the taxed amount as a deduction in calculating the chargeable gain. *TCGA 1992, s 120* grants such relief. If an option obtained by virtue of an individual's employment is released in consideration of the grant of a fresh option after 28 November 1995 a form of roll-over relief applies, the new option merging in with the old and any expenditure on the acquisition of the new option becoming part of the cost of the old. [*TCGA 1992, s 237A*]. Prior to 28 November 1994 this only applied where the option was granted under an approved scheme and the reason for the exchange was a company takeover. [*TCGA 1992, s 238(4)* repealed by *FA 1996, s 112(2)*].

14.220 If the company obtains consideration for the grant of the option this is taxable as a capital gain (subject to the possibility of merging into a single transaction when the option is exercised). [*TCGA 1992, s 144*]. The grant of the option may well constitute a bargain made otherwise than at arm's length—and is in any event a disposal made partly in consideration of services in the employment—with the result that the market value of the option falls to be substituted as the consideration in calculating that gain. [*TCGA 1992, s 17(1)*]. In practice, the Revenue have not taken this point. However, *FA 1993, s 104* introduced a specific exemption from such a charge but in relation to approved schemes only. Accordingly, there seems a risk that the Revenue might as a result change their practice in respect of unapproved schemes.

Corporation Tax

14.221 There was generally no statutory right to a corporation tax deduction for payments to the trustees of employee share schemes prior to 1

January 2003. It had to be shown that the payment satisfied the normally wholly and exclusively test that applies to business expenses. In practice such payments are normally deductible following the decision of the Court of Appeal in *Heather v P & E Consulting Group Ltd (48 TC 293)* which held that annual contributions to a trust set up by the company to give its staff the opportunity to acquire shares in the company and to remove the possibility of the company coming under the control of outside shareholders was deductible. Later cases which mainly concern trusts where the intention was that the trustees should hold the shares not necessarily transfer them to individual employees are reviewed at 17.2. However no deduction could be claimed where no expense is actually incurred. In *Lowry v Consolidated African Selection Trust Ltd (23 TC 259)* certain employees of the company were entitled to be issued with ordinary shares in the company at par in consideration of their services. The House of Lords refused a deduction for the difference between the market value of the shares and their cost on the basis that no expense had been incurred by the company.

14.222 From 1 January 2003 a deduction can no longer be claimed under general principles for the cost of providing the shares. [*FA 2003, 23 Schedule 25(1)*]. Instead there is a statutory relief. This is in most cases far more generous than the old position as it allows a deduction for the market value of the shares at the time they are issued or otherwise acquired by the employee less the payments actually made by the employee to acquire the shares (or an option pursuant to which the shares were acquired). The government say that the new relief has been widely welcomed as a set of clear, well-written rules that work effectively to deliver what companies want; they give companies certainty against a background of uncertain accounting treatment (Hansard Standing Committee B, 12 June 2003, col 494). The new rules enable companies to dispense with the complex and costly trust structures that used to be needed to generate a tax deduction (*Hansard* SCB, 12 June 2003, col. 495).

14.223 The new rules give a corporation tax deduction where by reason of his (or someone else's) employment with the company a person acquires shares or obtains an option and acquires shares in exercise of that option. [*FA 2003, 23 Schedule 1(1)*]. Four conditions need to be met:

(1) The business for the purpose of which the award of shares or grant of the option is made must be carried on by the employing company and must be within the charge to corporation tax. [*FA 2003, 23 Schedule 3*].

(2) The shares must be fully paid, irredeemable ordinary shares and must be either of a class listed on a recognised stock exchange, shares in a company that is not under the control of another company or shares in a company that is under the control of a listed company which is not a close company (and would not be one if it were resident in the UK). [*FA 2003, 23 Schedule 4*].

(3) The shares must be shares in the employing company, or in a company which at the time of the award (or of the grant of the

417

option) is either its parent company, a company that is a member of a consortium that owns the employing company or its parent company or, if the employing company or its parent is a member of a consortium that owns another company (C), a company that is a member of the consortium (or the parent of a member) and is a member of the same commercial association of companies as C. In the case of an option the shares can also be shares in a qualifying successor company (see 14.224). [*FA 2003, 23 Schedule 6, 12*].

(4) The employee must:

    (*a*) in the case of an award of shares be subject to income tax in respect of the award under *ITEPA 2003* (or would be subject to such tax if at all material times he were resident and ordinarily resident in the UK and the duties of the employment were performed in the UK);

    (*b*) in the case of the grant of an option, was subject to income tax under *ITEPA 2003*, either in respect of the grant of the option or by virtue of *ITEPA 2003, ss 476* (either see old or new version) or *477* (see 14.94) in respect of the gain realised on the exercise of the option (or would be subject to an income tax charge or the exercise of the option but for a relevant exemption, or would be subject to such a charge (or covered by a relevant exemption) it at all material times he were resident and ordinarily resident in the UK and the duties of the employment by virtue of which the option was granted were performed in the UK); or

    (*c*) if the recipient acquires shares which are subject to forfeiture, is subject to income tax under *ITEPA 2003, s 427* (see 14.29) on the shares ceasing to be subject to forfeiture or on the recipient disposing of the shares or dying without the shares having ceased to be subject to forfeiture (or would be subject to such a charge if at all material times he were resident and ordinarily resident in the UK and the duties of the employment by reason of which the award was made or the option was granted were performed in the UK).

[*FA 2003, 23 Schedule 7, 14, 20*].

14.224 For the purpose of 3 above a qualifying successor company is one that acquires control of the company in which the option was granted and agrees with the option holder that he will release his right in consideration of the grant to him of a new option over shares in a qualifying company, i.e. one that would fall within 3 above if the acquiring company were the employing company. [*FA 2003, 23 Schedule 13(1)(2)(4)*]. Where there is such a take-over shares acquired in exercise of the new option are treated as having been acquired in exercise of the old one and any consideration given in respect of the grant or exercise of the new option is treated as if it had been given in respect of the old. [*FA 2003, 23 Schedule 13(2)*].

14.225 For the purpose of 14.223 *4(b)* a relevant exemption is one under *ITEPA 2003, ss 519, 520, 524* or *525* (exercise of option under approved SAYE scheme or approved CSOP scheme) or *530* (exercise of EMI option. [*FA 2003, 23 Schedule 14(2)*].

Where the shares acquired are subject to forfeiture head 14.223 *4(c)* needs to be satisfied in place of (a) or (b). [*FA 2003, 23 Schedule 20(1)*]. Shares are subject to forfeiture for this purpose if the terms on which the recipient is entitled to them (which includes terms imposed by any contract or arrangement or in any other way) provide that if certain circumstances arise (or do not arise) these will be a transfer, reversion or forfeiture as a result of which the recipient will cease to be entitled to any beneficial interest in the shares and any receipt in consideration will be less than what the market value of the shares at that time would have been if there were no provision for transfer, reversion or forfeiture. [*FA 2003, 23 Schedule 19(1)(2)(3)(4)(6)*]. Circumstances arising include the expiry of a period specified in (or determined under) the terms on which the recipient is entitled to the shares, the exercise by a person of a power conferred on him by or under those terms, and the death of any person. [*FA 2003, 23 Schedule 19(3)(a)*]. Shares are not subject to forfeiture merely because they are unpaid or partly paid and can be forfeited for unpaid calls (provided there is no restriction on the recipient meeting calls; because the Articles of Association (or equivalent document if it is a non-UK company) require the shares to be offered for sale or transferred if the employee 'ceases to hold specified employment'; or because the recipient can be required to offer the shares for sale (or transfer them) if the employee 'ceases to hold specified employment' as a result of misconduct). An employee ceases to hold specified employment if he ceases to be an employee of either the employing company, one or more group companies (51% subsidiaries) or any group company as specified by the terms on which he is entitled to the shares. [*FA 2003, 23 Schedule 19(4)(5)*]. It should be noted that whilst this definition is similar to that of restricted securities in *ITEPA 2003, s 423* (see 14.23) it is not identical.

14.226 The amount of the corporation tax relief is the difference between:

(*a*) the market value of the shares at the time of the award (or the exercise of the option or, in the case of shares subject to forfeiture, the time at which shares cease to be subject to forfeiture) or the time of the disposal or death where the shares are sold or the recipient dies without the shares having ceased to be subject to forfeiture; and

(*b*) the total amount or value of any consideration given by the recipient or any other person in respect of the shares (or in respect of the grant or exercise of the option or, in the case of shares subject to forfeiture in respect of the shares, the grant or exercise of the option (if applicable) or the shares ceasing to be subject to forfeiture).

[*FA 2003, 23 Schedule 8(1), 15(1), 21(2)(3)(a)*]. The consideration cannot include the performance of any duties of, or in connection with, the employee's employment with the employing company. In the case of an option (including in respect of shares subject to forfeiture) it also does not include employer's National Insurance paid by the employee by virtue of an agreement or election under *paragraphs 3A(2)* or *3B* of *Schedule 1* to the *Social Security Contributions and Benefits Act 1992* (or its Northern Irish equivalent). [*FA 2003, 23 Schedule 8(2), 15(2), 23(4)*].

14.227 In the case of shares subject to forfeiture the reference in (a) to the market value of the shares is that value immediately after they cease to be subject to forfeiture (or their (restricted) value at the time of the disposal or death if the relief is triggered without their ceasing to be subject to forfeiture). [*FA 2003, 27 Schedule 21(3)(b)*]. A just and reasonable apportionment must be made of any consideration given partly in respect of the shares (or grant and exercise of the option or, in the case of shares subject to forfeiture, the shares, the grant and exercise of the option or the shares ceasing to be subject to forfeiture) and partly in respect of other matters. [*FA 2003, 23 Schedule 8(3), 15*]. If the award was made partly for the purpose of a business within 14.223(1) above and partly for the purpose of a business in relation to which those requirements are not met the amount of the relief must be reduced to such extent as is just and reasonable. [*FA 2003, 23 Schedule 8(4), 15(4), 21(6)*].

14.228 The corporation tax deduction is given by treating the amount as an allowable business expense of the business for the purpose of which the award was made or option granted (or as a management expense in the case of an investment company or life insurance company). If the award was made (or option granted) for the purposes of more than one business within the charge to corporation tax the deduction is apportioned between them on a just and reasonable basis. [*FA 2003, 23 Schedule 9, 16*]. The deduction is made in the accounting period in which the recipient acquires the shares (i.e. when he acquires a beneficial interest in the shares, not, if different, the time they are transferred or conveyed to him). [*FA 2003, 23 Schedule 10, 17*]. In the case of shares subject to forfeiture it is made in the accounting period in which the shares cease to be subject to forfeiture or the recipient disposes of the shares or dies without them having ceased to be subject to forfeiture. [*FA 2003, 23 Schedule 22*].

14.229 If between the award of the shares (or the grant of the option) and the relief-triggering event (i.e. that mentioned in paragraph 14.226) there is a 'qualifying transfer' (or transfers) of the whole or substantially the whole of the business for the purposes of which the award or grant was made and, as a result of that transfer or transfers, the whole or substantially the whole of that business is carried on by a successor company at the time of the relief-triggering event the deduction is obviously given to the successor company. If there is more than one successor company the relief is not apportioned. The companies must jointly nominate one of their members to receive the entire relief. A transfer is a qualifying transfer only if the transferor and transferee companies are members of the same group (51% subsidiaries). [*FA 2003, 23 Schedule 23*].

14.230 If a deduction for a payment can be given under *ICTA 1988, 4AA, Schedule 2* (see 15.60), *3* (see 15.62) or *9* or *10* (see 15.68) in relation to a SIP such relief is given instead. [*FA 2003, 23 Schedule 24*].

14.231 Where a deduction is available under *Schedule 23* for any accounting period that is the only way of giving relief for the 'cost of providing the shares'. This is the case even if a deduction could otherwise have been claimed in a different accounting period or could have been claimed by some other company. The cost of providing the shares means expenses directly related to the provision of the shares including any amount paid or payable by the employing company in respect of the participation of the employee in an employee share scheme (i.e. any scheme or arrangement for enabling shares to be acquired by reason of employees' employment where the shares are acquired under such a scheme). It does not however include the expenses of setting up an employee share scheme, the costs of borrowing for the purposes of the scheme, or fees, commission, stamp duty and similar incidental expenses of acquiring the shares. [*FA 2003, 23 Schedule 25*].

14.232 For the purposes of *Schedule 23*:

(*a*) An employment includes an office and members of a company whose affairs are managed by the members themselves are treated as office-holders. [*FA 2003, 23 Schedule 26*].

(*b*) If an option to acquire shares obtained by reason of an employee's employment is exercised by the recipient after the employee's death the condition in para 14 (income tax position of the employee see 14.223(4)) is treated as met if it would be met were the employee still alive. If an option is exercised after the death of the recipient the Schedule applies as if the recipient were still alive and the acquisition of the shares were made by him. [*FA 2003, 23 Schedule 27*].

(*c*) Companies are members of the same group only if one is a 51% subsidiary of the other or both are 51% subsidiaries of a third company. A company is a parent company of another if that other is its 51% subsidiary. [*FA 2003, Schedule 28*].

(*d*) A company is a member of a consortium owning another company if it is one of five or fewer companies that between them beneficially own at least 75% of the other company's ordinary share capital and each of which owns at least 10% of that capital. [*FA 2003, 23 Schedule 29(1)*].

(*e*) A commercial association of companies mean a company together with such of its associated companies (within *ICTA 1988, s 416*) as carry on businesses that are of such a nature that the businesses of the company and the associated companies, taken together, may be reasonably considered to make up a single composite undertaking. [*FA 2003, 23 Schedule 29(2)*].

(*f*) The *ICTA 1988, s 840* definition of control applies. [*FA 2003, 23 Schedule 30*].

(*g*)   Market value has the same meaning as in *TCGA 1992, ss 272* and *273*. [*FA 2003, 23 Schedule 30*].

(*h*)   An option includes any right to acquire shares and shares includes an interest in shares and stock or an interest in stock. [*FA 2003, 23 Schedule 30*].

Chapter 15

Share Incentive Plans

Introduction

15.1   A new all-employee share incentive, 'The All Employee Share Ownership Plan' (AESOP) was introduced by the *Finance Act 2000*. Such plans have been renamed SIPs (Share Incentive Plans) in the *Income Tax (Earnings and Pensions) Act 2003*. The SIP is very attractive, not only because the benefits that can be obtained by employees are very generous but also because it is very flexible. Most companies will find that it enables them to devise a form of an incentive that is particularly suitable for their employees. However, like any all-employee share scheme, a SIP cannot be used to benefit selected employees only. For unlisted companies it also suffers from the usual problem that to obtain the full benefits of the scheme it needs to be shown that the issue price is not less than the market value of the shares at the date they are issued. This involves having to agree a value with the Revenue. Not only does this incur professional fees but in practice the company is generally anxious to get the scheme off the ground and is reluctant to enter into prolonged negotiations over the valuation. This creates pressure to accept the Inland Revenue's figure, or more likely to compromise at somewhere near the Revenue's figure, even though the company believes this to be excessive. Such a forced compromise could adversely affect the agreement of what the company believes to be more realistic valuations on subsequent transactions.

15.2   For this and other reasons most private companies are reluctant to introduce all-employee share schemes. However, a SIP is so attractive in other ways that it may be worthwhile to seek to overcome the problems in order to introduce such a scheme.

15.3   A SIP can provide the following:

(*a*)   free shares of up to £3,000 in value each tax year for each employee;

(*b*)   'partnership shares', which are paid for by the employee out of pre-tax income, at their current value, of up to £1,500 in each year;

(*c*)   'matching shares' of up to £3,000 in each year (these are free shares awarded to purchasers of partnership shares; an employee can give up to two matching shares for every partnership share); and

(*d*)   for up to £1,500 of dividends per employee to be invested in purchasing (at market value) dividend shares with no higher rate tax then being payable on the dividend.

15.4   Subject to a minimum holding period, the growth in value of all of the above types of shares is completely tax-free whilst the shares remain within the SIP. When they are taken out the employee starts with a capital gains tax base cost equal to the value of the shares at the time they leave the SIP. The issue of shares can if desired be tied to performance targets although the legislation is fairly prescriptive as to how this is done.

Conditions of establishment

15.5   An SIP must meeting the following conditions:

(*a*)   It must be established by a company and must provide either:

  (i)   for shares (free shares) to be appropriated to employees without payment; or

  (ii)   for shares ('partnership shares') to be acquired on behalf of employees out of sums deducted from their salaries. [*ITEPA 2003, 2 Schedule 2*].

(*b*)   It can also provide for shares ('matching shares') to be appropriated without payment in proportion to partnership shares. [*ITEPA 2003, 2 Schedule 3*].

(*c*)   The plan must be approved by the Revenue after it has been established. The application for approval must contain such particulars as the Revenue may require. [*ITEPA 2003, 2 Schedule 81*]. The Inland Revenue have published model plan rules, a model trust deed, specimen free share agreement and specimen partnership share agreement. These can be found on their website. If the Revenue refuse to approve a plan there is a right of appeal to the Special Commissioners, who can backdate the approval (but not before the application for approval. [*2 Schedule 82*].

(*d*)   The purpose of the plan must be to provide benefits to employees in the form of shares in a company which give them a continuing stake in that company. [*ITEPA 2003, 2 Schedule 7(1)*]. It must not contain features which are not essential (or reasonably incidental) to that purpose. [*2 Schedule 7(2)*].

(*e*)   The plan must provide that every employee who is eligible to be awarded shares under the plan and is taxable as a UK-resident taxpayer, i.e. under Case I of Schedule E must be invited to participate in the plan. [*ITEPA 2003, 2 Schedule 8(1)*]. It can, if so desired, allow eligible employees who are not UK-resident taxpayers to join also. [*2 Schedule 8(5), formerly 8 Schedule 8(3)*]. This requires that each time shares are issued under the scheme every eligible employee must be entitled to participate. [*2 Schedule 5*]. The meaning of eligible employees is considered at 15.6 below.

(*f*)   The plan must not contain any features which discourage any description of eligible employees from participating in it. [*ITEPA 2003, 2 Schedule 8(3)*].

where it was held that if the grant of an option fell within *section 17*, the acquisition of the shares in pursuance of the option also does so. This is because *TCGA 1992, s 144*, the special rules on options, provides that where an option is exercised the grant of the option and its exercise are to be treated as a single transaction. [*TCGA 1992, s 144(2)*]. Accordingly if one of those transactions falls within *section 17* both must do so. Chadwick LJ thought that the particular issue raised by the appeal was unlikely to be of widespread concern and said that the effect of *TCGA 1992, s 149A* may have the effect that *section 17(1)* can have no application on the grant of an option to an employee.

14.216 The Revenue thought otherwise. In a press release of 8 January 2003 they stated that the decision will generally increase the capital gains acquisition cost of the asset for people exercising options granted otherwise than by way of bargain at arm's length or by reason of employment. Most of the people affected would be employees who had sold shares that they acquired by exercising unapproved share options or Enterprise Management Incentive options. The base cost for such people would be the market value of the shares at the time the option was exercised plus the amount charged to income tax on the exercise (by virtue of *TCGA 1992, s 120*). Accordingly where an option was exercised and the shares immediately sold the overall result would be that the taxpayer would realise a CGT loss equal to the amount on which he was assessed to income tax. The other side of the coin however is that people who disposed of the shares on exercise of the option would have an unexpected CGT liability based not on the option price but on the value of the shares at the date the option was exercised.

14.217 The Revenue amplified their view in two further press releases of 17 March 2003 and 8 August 2003. The decision does not affect people who acquired shares through approved option schemes as they are exempt from tax on exercise of the option, except on the comparatively rare occasions where there was an income tax charge under *ITEPA 2003, s 526* (see 16.12). They consider that:

(*a*)   losses resulting from the *Mansworth v Jelley* decision for years up to 1995/96 can be brought forward and set against capital gains in the earliest 'open' year;

(*b*)   losses arising in 1996/97 cannot be utilised unless a claim to do so was made before 31 January 2003;

(*c*)   losses arising in 1997/98 can be utilised but only if a claim is made before 31 January 2004; and

(*d*)   it is too late to amend a return for 1996/97 to 2000/01 and an error or mistake claim is not competent as the assessment was made in accordance with the practice generally prevailing at the time; in effect this means that if the application of *Mansworth v Jelley* would have resulted in a smaller capital gain or results in a larger loss the excess cannot be reclaimed but if it turns a gain into a loss that loss (or increased loss) can be claimed (presumably under *TMA 1970, 1A Schedule*) within the normal time limits.

(*g*)   Every employee entitled to participate in an award of shares must do so on the same terms. [*ITEPA 2003, 2 Schedule 9(1)*]. This requirement is not infringed by the awarding of free shares by reference to an employee's remuneration, length of service or hours worked. [*2 Schedule 9(3)*]. However, if more than one of these criteria is used each factor must give rise to a separate entitlement and the total entitlement must be the sum of the separate entitlements. [*2 Schedule 9(4)*].

Example

X Ltd wishes to allocate 1,000 shares. It has eligible employees as follows:

Name	Salary	Weekly hours	Years of Service
Arthur	40,000	40	4
Barry	35,000	35	8
Charles	15,000	35	6
Doreen	45,000	40	10
Evelyn	20,000	35	10
Fanny	8,000	15	15
	163,000	200	53

It decides to issue 500 by reference to remuneration, 250 by reference to hours worked and 250 by reference to length of service. It must therefore offer Arthur $40/163 \times 500$ (123), $40/200 \times 250$ (50) and $4/53 \times 250$ (19) a total of 192 shares. It must offer Fanny $8/163 \times 500$ (24), $15/200 \times 250$ (19) and $15/53 \times 250$ (71) a total of 114 shares. It could not for example allocate 500 by reference to salary and 500 by reference to weekly hours multiplied by the years worked.

The company cannot award free shares by reference to any other factor. [*2 Schedule 9(2)*]. It can, however, make the number of shares awarded to an individual subject to performance targets (called 'performance allowances'). [*2 Schedule 9(5)*]. Such allowances are explained at 15.23.

(*h*)   No feature of the plan must have the effect of conferring benefits wholly or mainly on directors or employees receiving higher levels of remuneration (except of course to the extent that they do so because the shares are awarded by reference to salary). [*ITEPA 2003, 2 Schedule 10*]. If the company is a member of a group the plan must not confer benefits wholly or mainly on such directors or employees of the group as a whole either. [*2 Schedule 10(2)(3)*].

(*i*)   The shares must form part of the ordinary share capital of the scheme company, a company that controls it or a company which is (or controls) a member of a consortium which owns the company (or its parent company). [*ITEPA 2003, 2 Schedule 26*].

(*j*)   The shares must either be of a class listed on a recognised stock exchange, shares in a company which is controlled by a listed company which is not a close company (and if it is non-UK resident would not be close were it UK resident) or shares in a company which is not under the control of another company. [*ITEPA 2003, 2 Schedule 27*]. In other words, shares in a subsidiary company can be used only if the parent company is listed and non-close or the subsidiary is itself a listed company.

(*k*)   The shares must be fully paid up and (unless they are shares in a works co-operative, i.e. a registered industrial and provident society which meets specified conditions set out in *para 128*) not redeemable and not subject to terms which could make them redeemable at a future date. [*ITEPA 2003, 2 Schedule 28*].

(*l*)   The shares must not be subject to any restrictions other than that:

    (i)   they can be subject to a minimum holding period—it appears that these permit only a holding period under *para 36* (see 15.21), *61* (see 15.37) or *67* (see 15.41) and that there is no minimum holding period for partnership shares (see 15.35);

    (ii)   they can carry restrictions which affect all ordinary shares in the company;

    (iii)   they can have no, or limited, voting rights;

    (iv)   free or matching shares can be subject to forfeiture during a period of up to three years from the date of issue of the shares on the participant ceasing to be in relevant employment or the participant withdrawing the shares from the plan (or in the case of matching shares, on the participant withdrawing the matching partnership shares from the plan); but the shares must not be subject to forfeiture by reason of an event within *2 Schedule 32(2)* (the terms of which are identical to *section 498*) (see 15.50(*b*)), forfeiture must not be linked to the performance of any person or persons, and the same provision for forfeiture must apply in relation to all free or matching shares included in the same award under the plan;

    (v)   they can be subject to pre-emption rights requiring shares awarded to an employee under the plan (and which are held by the employee or a person to whom he is permitted to transfer the shares under the company's Articles of Association) to be offered for sale on the employee ceasing to be employed by his employer company or an associated company, provided that the pre-emption required is contained in the Articles of Association and applies to all employees of the company (or of the company and any company that it controls), requires the shares to be offered for sale at a specified consideration and also requires non-employee holders of the same class of shares who dispose of shares to do so on the same (or not better terms).

[*ITEPA 2003, 2 Schedule 30–33*, formerly *FA 2000, 8 Schedule 63–66*].

(*m*)   The shares must not be shares in a 'service company' (originally called an 'employer company') or in a company that controls such a company and is itself under the control of the people who make the subsidiary a service company. A 'service company' for this purpose means one whose business consists substantially in the provision of services of persons employed by it where the majority of such services are provided either to persons who control the company (including a partnership) or to an associated company. For this purpose a company is associated if both are under the control of the same person or persons (determined in accordance with *ICTA 1988, s 416 (2)–(6)*). If a partner (either alone or together with others) controls a company the partnership must also be treated as controlling it. [*ITEPA 2003, 2 Schedule 29*].

(*n*)   No conditions can be imposed on the employee's participation in an award of shares under the plan other than those specifically permitted by *Schedule 2*. [*ITEPA 2003, 2 Schedule 11*].

(*o*)   The arrangement for the plan must not make any provision for loans to be made to some or all of the employees of the company (or in the case of a group plan—see 15.8 below) of any participating company. Nor can those arrangements (which includes any scheme, agreement undertaking or understanding) or the operation of the plan be associated with any such provision. [*ITEPA 2003, 2 Schedule 12*].

Eligible employee

15.6   The plan must provide that an individual can participate in an award of shares only if:

(*a*)   in the case of free shares he is eligible to participate in it at the time the award is made, and

(*b*)   in the case of partnership or matching shares he is eligible to participate in the award at the time the partnership share money relating to it (or to the matched partnership shares) is deducted from his salary (or if there is an accumulation period (see 15.31)) at the time of the first deduction of partnership share money relating to it [*2 Schedule 14*].

15.7   The individual must be an employee of the company (or in the case of a group plan (see 15.9) of a participating company). [*2 Schedule 15*]. If the plan provides for a qualifying period he must at all times during that period have been an employee of a qualifying company, namely of the company itself or of some other company that at the time the individual was employed by it was an associated company of either the company or another company qualifying under *paragraph 15*. [*2 Schedule 17(2)*]. In the case of a group plan a qualifying company is:

(*a*)   a company that is a participating company at the end of the qualifying period; or (*b*)   a company that when the individual was employed by it was a participating company; or

(*c*)   a company that when the individual was employed by it was an associated company of one within (*a*) or (*b*) or of another company qualifying under *paragraph 15*.

[*2 Schedule 17(3)*].

Where the award of shares was made before 12 May 2001 the individual had to be an employee of either the company or of a participating company throughout the qualifying period. The change ensures that a person who has moved around within a group of companies is not thereby disqualified from participating. From 7 January 2003, where a reservist is called up for service under the *Reserve Forces Act 1996* the Revenue will by concession treat the employment with the Ministry of Defence as fulfilling these employment conditions. [*ESC A103*]. The Revenue have asked to be informed (Sahd.Ullah@ir.gsi.gov.uk) when this concession is used.

15.8   Such a qualifying period cannot be longer than 18 months before the date on which the award is made. In the case of partnership or matching shares it cannot be longer than 18 months before the deduction of the partnership share money or, if there is an accumulation period, longer than six months before the start of that period. [*2 Schedule 16(2)–(6)*]. As an accumulation period cannot be longer than 12 months before the issue of the shares this means that in no case can the qualifying period exceed 18 months before entitlement to the shares arise. The plan can authorise the company to specify different qualifying periods in respect of different awards of shares, but for each award the same qualifying period must apply to all employees. [*2 Schedule 16(7)(8)*].

15.9   An employee share ownership plan established by a company that controls other companies can extend to the employees of those other companies. [*2 Schedule 4*]. Such a plan is called a group plan and the companies to which it extends are known as participating companies. Where a group plan is used, the identity of the participating companies must not be such that the plan is likely to confer benefits wholly or mainly on directors of group companies or on employees of group companies who receive higher levels of remuneration. [*2 Schedule 10*].

15.10   A group plan can also extend to employees of a jointly owned company (and of a company controlled by such a company) if one of the 50% shareholders is a member of the group. A jointly owned company for this purpose is one 50 per cent of the issued share capital of which is owned by one person and 50 per cent by another and which is not controlled by any one person. A jointly owned company cannot participate in more than one plan. Nor from 2002/03 onwards can a company controlled by a jointly owned company (unless it was a member of the second plan prior to 24 July 2002). [*2 Schedule 91*].

15.11   The plan must exclude an individual from participation in an award of shares under the scheme if at the time (or at any time within the previous 12 months) he had a material interest in:

(*a*)   a close company whose shares can be awarded under the plan; or

(*b*)   a company which controls such a company or is a member of a consortium which owns such a company. [*2 Schedule 19*].

15.12   For this purpose a material interest is beneficial ownership of over 25 per cent of the ordinary share capital of the company. [*2 Schedule 20*]. The ability to control directly or through the medium of other companies or by any other indirect means, more than 25 per cent of the ordinary share capital is also treated as a material interest. [*2 Schedule 20*]. If the company is a close company (or would be one if the exclusions in *ICTA 1988, s 414(1)(a)* (non-resident companies) or *section 415* (certain quoted companies) did not apply) a person will also have a material interest in the company if he possesses or is entitled to acquire such rights as would in the event of a winding up or in any other circumstances give an entitlement to receive over 25 per cent of the assets then available for distribution among the participators. [*2 Schedule 20(1)(3)(4)*].

15.13   An individual is also treated as having a material interest if he and associates of his have such an interest or if an associate or associates of his has a material interest in the company. [*2 Schedule 19(2)*]. An associate for this purpose is:

(*a*)   any relative (spouse, parent or remoter ancestor, child or remoter issue, brother or sister) or partner of the individual;

(*b*)   the trustees of a settlement (within *ICTA 1988, s 660G(2)*) in relation to which the individual or any relative of his, living or dead, was the settlor; or

(*c*)   where the individual is interested in any shares or obligations of the company which are subject to any trust (or are held in the estate of a deceased person), the trustees (or personal representatives). [*2 Schedule 22*].

15.14   If the individual was previously a discretionary object of a trust, the trust owns (or has at any time in the past owned) shares or obligations of the company, and the individual ceased to be a beneficiary as the result of an irrevocable disclaimer or release, or of an irrevocable exercise by the trustees of a power to exclude him as a beneficiary, the individual is not regarded as having been interested in the shares or obligations during the 12 months prior to the award of shares, provided that both immediately after he ceased to be a beneficiary no associate of his was interested in the trust's shares or obligations and neither the individual or any associate of his received any benefit from the trust within the 12 months prior to the individual ceasing to be a beneficiary. [*2 Schedule 24*].

15.15   If the individual has an interest in shares or obligations of a company as a beneficiary of an employee benefit trust (within *ICTA 1988, Sch 8, para 7*—see 18.41), the trustees are not regarded as associates of his for the purpose of 15.13(b) if neither the individual nor he and associates of his (or any associate or associates of his) has at any time after 14 March 1989 been the beneficial owner of (or able to control) more than 25 per cent of the ordinary share capital of the company (either directly or through the medium of other companies or by any other indirect means).

[*2 Schedule 23*].

15.16   *ICTA 1988, Sch 8, para 7(9)–(12)*—see 18.42—which has been re-enacted as *ITEPA 2003, ss 549–554* apply in relation to the individual for this purpose. [*8 Schedule 21(4)*]. In testing whether an employee benefit trust can be ignored as an associate, another employee benefit trust which also holds shares in the company is treated as not being an associate of the first trust. [*8 Schedule 21(5)*]. In determining whether an individual has a material interest in a company he is treated as having a right to control shares if he has a right to acquire them (such as an option). [*2 Schedule 21(2)*]. This requires option shares to be brought into account even if the option is not immediately exercisable. If the option is over unissued shares which the company is contractually bound to issue on the exercise of the option the ordinary share capital of the company must be increased by the number of such shares in applying the 25 per cent test. [*2 Schedule 21(4)*]. Although irrational, it appears that only options held by the individual or by an associate are reflected in this adjustment. For example, suppose an individual owns 240 out of 1000 issued shares. 20 employees, including that individual have an option to acquire 15 new shares each. If all the options were exercised the individual would hold 255 out of 1300 shares which is under 25 per cent. However, it appears that only his option can be taken into account. He is therefore deemed to hold 255 out of 1015 shares which is over 25 per cent, so he must be excluded from participation in the employee share ownership plan.

15.17   In considering whether an individual has a material interest in a company, shares held by the trustees of either an approved profit sharing scheme (see 16.4) or another SIP which have not been appropriated to or acquired on behalf of an individual can also be ignored [*2 Schedule 21(6)*], i.e. a person is not interested in shares held generally by such an approved scheme merely because at a future date the trustees could decide to allocate some of them to him.

15.18   An employee cannot participate at the same time in two or more approved share schemes established by the same company. The plan must therefore provide that an individual is not to be awarded free shares under the plan in a tax year if in that year either:

(*a*)   shares have been (or are being) appropriated to him in accordance with an approved profit sharing scheme established by the company or a connected company (i.e. one which controls, or is controlled by, the company, one which is controlled by a third company which also controls the scheme company, or one which is a member of a consortium which owns the company or which is owned in part by the scheme company as a member of a consortium); or (*b*) he has (or is about to) participated in another *Schedule 2* approved SIP established by the company or a connected company—or would have done so but for his failure to meet a performance target. [*2 Schedule 18*].

(*c*) For plans established after 10 July 2003 the plan must also provide that if the employer participates in an award of shares in a tax year and he has already participated in an award under another SIP established by the same or a connected company *2 Schedule 35* (maximum award), *46* (maximum partnership share money deductions) and *64* (limit on amount reinvested) apply as if both (or all) of the plans were a single plan. [*2 Schedule 18A*].

The shares

15.19 Different rules apply to free shares, partnership shares and matching shares.

Free shares

15.20 If the plan provides for free shares it must provide that the initial market value of free shares awarded to a participant (the market value on the date of the award, but ignoring the existence of any restrictions or any risk of forfeiture if the shares are restricted shares) cannot exceed £3,000. Shares are restricted for this purpose if there is any contract, agreement, arrangement or condition that would bring them within *ITEPA 2003, s 423* (see 14.23) if they were employment-related securities. [*2 Schedule 35* as amended by *FA 2003, 22 Schedule 43*, formerly *8 Schedule 2A*]. Prior to 6 April 2003 such restrictions were ignored if the interest acquired was only conditional within the meaning of *ITEPA 2003, s 424* (old) (see 14.192). It is not clear whether or not a risk of forfeiture under *2 Schedule 32(1)(b)* or (*c*) (which permits a provision for forfeiture in certain circumstances in the event of the participant withdrawing free or matching shares from the plan or withdrawing the partnership shares that triggered the right to matching shares) needs to be ignored; that risk would probably not make the acquisition 'only conditional'. *Section 424* itself provides that a risk of forfeiture in the event of the employee ceasing to be an employee does not make the shares 'only conditional'. It is not clear if that risk can be ignored or must be taken into account in valuing the shares. It appears from the wording that it is the latter, but as it would substantially devalue the shares the intention is probably that that risk should be ignored.

15.21 The plan must require the company in respect of each award of free shares to specify a holding period during which a participant is contractually bound to permit his free shares to remain in the hands of the trustees and not to assign, charge or otherwise dispose of his beneficial interest in the shares. [*2 Schedule 36(1)*]. The holding period must be between three and five years, must begin on the date of the award and must be the same in respect of all shares in the same award (although different periods can apply to different awards). [*2 Schedule 36(2)(3)*]. The participant's obligation in relation to the holding period ceases if during that period he ceases to be an employee and they are subject to the provisions of *para 37* (see 15.22) *79* (see 15.77) and *90(5)* (see 15.86). [*2 Schedule 36(4)*].

15.22   During the holding period a participant can direct the trustees:

(*a*)   to accept a take-over bid that will result in the new holding being treated as the same as the old (i.e. as not giving rise to a CGT disposal by virtue of *TCGA 1992, ss 135* and *136*);

(*b*)   to accept an offer of a qualifying corporate bond for his free shares under a general offer which is made to holders of shares of the same class in the company and which is made in the first instance on a condition which if satisfied would give the offeror control of the company (within *ICTA 1988, s 416*);

(*c*)   to accept an offer of cash (with or without other assets) for the shares which is made under such a general offer;

(*d*)   to agree to a transaction affecting the shares pursuant to a compromise, arrangement or scheme affecting all of the ordinary shares of the company (or all of those of the same class as the free shares or all of the shares which are held by a class of shareholders identified otherwise than by reference to their employment or to their participation in an approved AESOP).

[*2 Schedule 37*].

15.23   If the plan provides for the issue of free shares (or the number to be awarded) being conditional on performance targets being met, the following conditions must apply:

(*a*)   the performance measure used must be based on business results or other objective criteria and must be fair and objective measures of the performance of the units to which they are to be applied [*2 Schedule 39(3)*];

(*b*)   the performance targets must be set for performance units comprising one or more individuals and an individual must not be a member of more than one performance unit in relation to a particular award [*2 Schedule 39(2)(4)*];

(*c*)   the performance allowance must be calculated by one of the two methods described below [*2 Schedule 34(1)*]; and

(*d*)   the plan must require the company (as soon as reasonably practicable):

(i)   to notify each employee participating in the award of the performance targets and measures which will be used to determine the number of free shares awarded to him, and

(ii)   to notify all qualifying employees (i.e. those eligible to participate in an award) in general terms of the performance measures to be used to determine the number or value of the free shares to be awarded to each employee participating in the award—but there is no need to tell employees in general any information which the company reasonably considers would prejudice commercial confidentiality. [*2 Schedule 40*].

Performance allowance—method 1

15.24

(*a*)   At least 20 per cent of the shares in the award must be awarded without reference to performance (and as if they were the only shares included in the award);

(*b*)   the remaining shares must be awarded by reference to performance (participation in these shares needs to be on the same terms under *2 Schedule 9*) (see 15.5(*g*)); and

(*c*)   the highest number of shares within (*b*) awarded to an individual must not be more than four times the highest number of shares within (*a*) awarded to an individual. [*2 Schedule 41*].

Presumably head (*c*) requires an individual award to be capped at the four times figure. As the performance targets have to be set in advance it would not be possible to adopt criteria which ensures that the four times figure will not be exceeded.

If free shares of more than one class are awarded the shares of each class must separately meet these rules.

Performance allowance—method 2

15.25

(*a*)   Some or all of the shares must be awarded by reference to performance; and

(*b*)   The awarding of the shares to qualifying employees who are members of a performance unit must be on the same terms within *2 Schedule 9* (see 15.5(*g*)), but the same terms need not apply to different performance units.

[*2 Schedule 42*].

15.26   *Para 42* is a peculiar provision. As a performance unit can be a single person it appears to permit different targets being set for each individual and for the bulk of the shares to go to senior executives, i.e. it could be used as a highly attractive executive share scheme by giving the executives fairly easy targets and attracting 95 per cent of the available shares to executives and giving the rest of the staff tougher targets to meet to get the remaining 5 per cent. Presumably it is hoped that the need to tell all employees what is going on under *para 40* would prevent this as it would result in a lot of very disgruntled employees.

Partnership shares

15.27   If the plan provides for partnership shares it must require each qualifying employee to enter into a partnership share agreement with the company under which the employee authorises the company to deduct money from his salary (called partnership share money) for the purchase of partnership shares, and the company undertakes to arrange for partnership shares to be awarded to the employee in accordance with the plan. [*2 Schedule 44*]. The agreement must specify what amounts (or what percentage of salary) are to be deducted and at what intervals—although the employee and the company can subsequently agree to vary both the amounts and the intervals. [*2 Schedule 45(3)*]. The deduction must not exceed either £1500 in any tax year (£125 in any month prior to 2003/04) or 10 per cent of the salary payment from which it is being deducted (or if the plan provides for an accumulation period—see 15.32—10 per cent of the aggregate of the salary payments over that period). [*2 Schedule 46* as amended by *FA 2003, 21 Schedule 7*]. Salary for this purpose is the amount subject to PAYE but excluding expenses and benefits in kind. [*2 Schedule 43(4)*]. This appears to be the amount net of pension contributions where these are deducted from salary. If these limits are exceeded the excess must be repaid to the employee as soon as practicable. [*2 Schedule 46(5)*]. Where the time at which the individual is required to be eligible to participate (in accordance with *ITEPA 2003, 2 Schedule 14*—see 15.6(*b*)) falls after 11 May 2001, 'salary' also includes any amount that would have been subject to tax as employment income (and less any expenses that would have been deductible) if the individual were within the scope of such tax. [*2 Schedule 43(4)(b)*]. Different limits can be set for each award of shares. [*2 Schedule 46(4)*]. The plan can provide that the deduction must not be less than £10 on any occasion (in any month prior to 2003/04) (or such lower figure as the company may decide). [*2 Schedule 47* as amended by *FA 2003, 21 Schedule 8*]. This appears to allow a deduction of £10 even if the employee's salary is less than £100.

15.28   A partnership share agreement must include a notice in a prescribed form containing prescribed information as to the possible effect of deductions on an employee's entitlement to social security benefits, statutory sick pay and statutory maternity pay. [*2 Schedule 48*]. The prescribed information is set out in the *Employee Share Ownership Plans (Partnership Shares—Notice of Effects on Benefits, Statutory Sick Pay and Statutory Maternity Pay) Regulations 2000 (SI 2000 No 2090)*.

15.29   The plan must provide that partnership share money deducted by the employer must be paid to the trustees as soon as practicable and held by them on the employee's behalf pending investment. It must require the trustees to keep such money in a bank (authorised under the *Banking Act 1987*) building society or relevant European institution (within *ICTA 1988, s 840A(2)*). If interest is earned on the monies the trustees must be required to account for it to the employee. [*2 Schedule 49*].

15.30   If the plan does not provide for an accumulation period the partnership share money must be applied by the trustees in acquiring shares on behalf of the employee on 'the acquisition date'. This is set by the trustees. It must be within 30 days of the last date on which the partnership share money was deducted. The number of shares to be awarded to each employee must be determined by reference to the market value of the shares on the acquisition date. If there is a surplus (e.g. because the money will not buy an exact number of shares) this must be repaid to the employee unless he agrees to it being carried forward and added to the amount of the next deduction. [*2 Schedule 50*].

15.31 Most companies will not want to issue new shares every month. Even if the trustees can buy shares in the market they may feel that the costs of doing this on a monthly basis are prohibitive. Accordingly, the plan can provide for accumulation periods. An accumulation period cannot exceed 12 months. [*2 Schedule 51(1)*]. If the plan provides for accumulation periods the partnership share agreement must specify when each such period begins and ends (the first obviously beginning not later than the date of the first deduction. [*2 Schedule 51(3)*]. The accumulation period in respect of each award must be the same for all participants. [*2 Schedule 51(4)*]. The plan can also provide that in the event of a share for share exchange in relation to the company during an accumulation period the employee can agree that the money accumulated can be used to buy shares in the acquiring company. [*2 Schedule 51(5)*].

15.32 Where the plan provides for an accumulation period it must provide for the partnership share money to be used by the trustees in acquiring shares on 'the acquisition date', which in this instance is 30 days after the end of the accumulation period. [*2 Schedule 52(2)(5)*]. The number of shares awarded to each employee must be based on the lower of the market value of the shares at the start of the accumulation period and that on the acquisition date. [*2 Schedule 52(3)*]. Any surplus must be repaid to the employee as soon as practicable after the acquisition or, if the employee agrees, carried forward to the next accumulation period. [*2 Schedule 52(6)*]. If the employee leaves before the end of the accumulation period the full amount deducted must be repaid to him. [*2 Schedule 52(7)*]. If an accumulation period comes to an end on the occurrence of a specified event the plan can provide that the partnership share money can be returned to the employee rather than used to purchase shares. [*2 Schedule 52(8)*]. It is not readily apparent what this is intended to cover.

15.33 The plan can, and usually will, allow the company to place a ceiling on the shares to be included in an award of partnership shares. [*2 Schedule 53(1)*]. For example, it could provide that no more shares are to be issued in a particular award than amounts to 2 per cent of the company. Without such a provision if the performance targets are significantly exceeded the company could find itself having to dilute existing shareholdings by a greater amount than was authorised by the shareholders. The partnership share agreement not surprisingly needs to contain an undertaking to notify the employees of any such restriction. [*2 Schedule 53(3)*]. Again, not surprisingly, the employees must be notified of the limit before any money is deducted from their salaries. [*2 Schedule 53(4)*]. If the ceiling is reached the entitlement of each individual included in the particular award of shares must be reduced proportionately. [*2 Schedule 53(5)*].

15.34   The employee must be entitled to tell the company to stop making deductions in pursuance of his partnership share agreement. He can also subsequently tell it to resume deductions—but may not make up the amounts that would have been deducted whilst the agreement was suspended. Where the plan provides for accumulation periods, it can if desired prevent the employee re-starting deductions more than once in any such period. If an employee asks for deductions to stop or to restart, the request must be actioned within 30 days (a restart requiring a deduction on the first pay day after the expiry of the 30 days). [*2 Schedule 54*].

15.35   The employee must have an entitlement to withdraw at any time from the partnership share agreement on giving 30 days notice in writing. In such an event any deductions held on his behalf must be repaid to him. [*2 Schedule 55*]. Any deductions held on behalf of an employee must also be repaid to the employee if approval of the plan is withdrawn or a plan termination notice (see 15.83) is received in respect of the plan. [*2 Schedule 56*]. In all cases the repayment must be made as soon as practicable after the trigger event. The employee must also be entitled to withdraw all or any of his partnership shares from the plan at any time. [*2 Schedule 57*]. If he does so within five years of acquiring the shares a tax charge will arise (see 15.47).

Matching shares

15.36   If the plan provides for matching shares it must provide for them:

(*a*)   to be of the same class and carry the same rights as the partnership shares to which they relate;

(*b*)   to be awarded on the same day as the partnership shares; and

(*c*)   to be awarded to all employees who participate in the award on exactly the same basis. [*2 Schedule 59*].

The partnership share agreements need to specify the ratio of matching shares to partnership shares for the time being offered by the company (which must not exceed two matching shares for each partnership share and must be applied by reference to the number of shares not the percentage holdings); the circumstances and manner in which the company can change the ratio; and that the company will inform the employee of any change in the ratio before partnership shares are awarded to him under the agreement. [*2 Schedule 60*].

15.37   The holding period that relates to free shares (see 15.21) must also apply to matching shares. [*2 Schedule 61*].

Reinvestment of dividends

15.38   The plan can either require or permit (at the company's option) any cash dividends in respect of plan shares held by the trustees on behalf of participants to be applied in acquiring further shares ('dividend shares'). [*2 Schedule 62*]. However, the total dividend reinvestment per employee is limited to £1,500 in any tax year. [*2 Schedule 64*]. If the employee is a participant in more than one SIP established by the company or an associated company, the £1,500 applies to the aggregate dividends from all of those SIPs. [*2 Schedule 64(2)(6)*]. The company can revoke its decision to require or permit the acquisition of dividend shares. [*2 Schedule 62(4)*]. Any dividends which are not required for reinvestment must be paid to the participant as soon as practicable. [*2 Schedule 64(3)*].

15.39   Dividend shares must be of the same class and carry the same rights as the shares on which the dividend is paid and must not be subject to any provision for forfeiture—even apparently in the event of the employee leaving the employment in circumstances that his main shares become subject to forfeiture. [*2 Schedule 65*].

15.40   In exercising their power in relation to the acquisition of dividend shares the trustees must treat participants fairly and equally. [*ITEPA 2003, 2 Schedule 66(1)*]. They must acquire the dividend shares on 'the acquisition date', which for this purpose is a date fixed by the trustees which must be within 30 days of the receipt of the dividend by the trustees. [*ITEPA 2003, 2 Schedule 66(2)(4)*]. The number of dividend shares must be determined by the market value of the shares on the acquisition date. [*ITEPA 2003, 2 Schedule 66(3)*]. If the dividend is insufficient to allow the acquisition of any shares (or there is a surplus after the acquisition of such shares) the excess dividend can be retained by the trustees (whether the participant likes it or not!) and carried forward to add to the next cash dividend. They must identify such cash separately to ensure that it is only used for this purpose. [*ITEPA 2003, 2 Schedule 68(1)–(3)*]. Any carried forward amount that is not invested in dividend shares within three years from the date the dividend was paid must be paid over to the recipient. If the employee leaves the employment before the amount is invested or a plan termination notice (see 15.83) is received the cash in hand must similarly be paid to the participant. [*ITEPA 2003, 2 Schedule 68(4)*]. Where cash is held from more than one dividend the cash from the earliest dividend is deemed to be invested first. [*ITEPA 2003, 2 Schedule 68(6)*].

15.41   The minimum holding period requirement that applies to free shares (see 15.21) also applies to dividend shares with the proviso that the holding period for dividend shares must be three years. [*ITEPA 2003, 2 Schedule 67*].

The tax position

15.42   In general no tax is payable in relation to free shares, partnership shares, matching shares, dividend shares or cash awaiting investment while the shares or cash remain in the hands of the trustees. If shares are taken out of the plan during the holding period their removal will trigger a tax charge though. The detailed rules are considered below. From 18 June

2004 these tax exemptions do not apply if the main purpose (or one of the main purposes) of the arrangements under which the shares are awarded or acquired is the avoidance of tax or NIC. [*ITEPA 2003, s 489(4) inserted by FA 2004, s 88(4)*].

Income Tax

15.43

(*a*)   The value of the shares at the time of an award or acquisition of shares under the plan is not treated as taxable income. [*ITEPA 2003, s 490*].

(*b*)   *ITEPA 2003, s 193* (deemed loan in case of shares acquired at an undervalue) (see 14.141) does not apply to plan shares up to 1 September 2003 but *ITEPA 2003, s 199* (see 14.153) which imposes an income tax charge where the shares are sold for a price in excess of their market value at the date of disposal does. [*ITEPA 2003, s 491 (repealed by FA 2003, 22 Schedule 26)*].

(*c*)   An income tax charge will arise on any capital sum received by a participant if it relates to dividend shares that were acquired within three years prior to the receipt of the capital sum, or if it relates to other plan shares that were acquired within the prior five years. [*ITEPA 2003, s 501*]. A 'capital receipt' for this purpose includes any amount of money's worth other than proceeds of disposal of the shares, new shares received on a take-over or an amount which constitutes income of the recipient (or would do but for *Schedule 2*). [*ITEPA 2003, s 502*]. If the participant asks the trustees to sell some of his shares in order to take up the rights on the remainder under a rights issue (to acquire shares in the same company only) those sale proceeds are not a capital receipt. [*ITEPA 2003, s 502(5)*]. Up to 1 September 2003 no income tax charge arose on a capital receipt by the personal representatives of a deceased participant. [*ITEPA 2003, s 501(6) (repealed by FA 2003, 22 Schedule 27)*].

(*d*)   *ITEPA 2003, s 427* (see 14.195) or *s 449* (see 14.156) do not apply where any provision for forfeiture within *para 32(1)* (see 15.5(l)(iv)) is varied or removed. [*ITEPA 2003, s 494*].

(*e*)   No charge to tax will arise under *ITEPA 2003, ss 449 or 450,* formerly *FA 1988, ss 78 or 79* (see 14.158 and 14.166) if the trigger event is the ending of the holding period in relation to plan shares. [*ITEPA 2003, s 495*].

(*f*)   Partnership share money deducted from an employee's salary is not taxable as employment income [*ITEPA 2003, s 492*], i.e. partnership shares are brought out of pre-tax income.

(*g*)   Nevertheless, the deduction of partnership money does not reduce the salary for the purpose of determining the amount of the employee's pensionable earnings under either a retirement benefit scheme (ie a company pension scheme) a retirement annuity or a personal pension. [*ITEPA 2003, s 492(2)*].

(*h*)   An income tax charge will arise on any amount paid over to the employee under *ITEPA 2003, s 2, Schedule 46(5)* (see 15.27), *50(5)(b)* (see 15.30), *52(6)(b)* (see 15.32), *52(7)* (see 15.32), *52(8)* (see 15.32), *55(3)* (see 15.35) or *56(1)* (see 15.35). The amount is taxable as income of the year in which the amount is paid over to the employee. [*ITEPA 2003, s 503*].

(*j*)   An income tax charge arises on the amount or value of any money or money's worth received by the participant in respect of the cancellation of his partnership share agreement. [*ITEPA 2003, s 504*].

(*k*)   The amount applied by the trustees in acquiring dividend shares is not treated as income of the participant for any tax purpose and the recipient has no entitlement to tax credit in respect of any such amount. [*ITEPA 2003, s 493*].

(*l*)   Similarly, no income tax charge (and no tax credit) arises on the amount of a dividend that is retained by the trustees under *2 Schedule 68(2)* (see 15.40) pending investment. [*ITEPA 2003, s 496*]. However, if any such amount is subsequently paid over to the participant under *2 Schedule 68(4)* (see 15.40) the participant is taxable on that amount under Schedule F (Case V of Sch D if it is a foreign dividend) for the tax year in which it is paid over to him and the tax credit is at the rate in force in that year not the year in which the dividend was received by the trustees. [*ICTA 1988, s 68B, ITEPA 2003, s 493(4)*].

(*m*)   Dividends or other distributions received by the trustees are not liable to tax in their hands under *ICTA 1988, s 686* (tax at the rate applicable to trusts) except to the extent that:

(i)   the shares to which they relate are not awarded to participants (treating earlier acquisitions as awarded first) within two years of their acquisition (five years if at the time of their acquisition none of the shares in the company in question are readily convertible assets (see 2.88) but if they subsequently become so the two year period again applies from the date of the change and ten years if a deduction is allowed under *8 Schedule 112A*); or

(ii)   if earlier, the shares are disposed of by the trustees (other than by being awarded to a participant. [*ICTA 1988, s 686B* inserted by *ITEPA 2003, s 722*].

Where the trustees acquire shares because they are forfeited by the participant the date of acquisition is the date of forfeiture. [*8 Schedule 88(6)*].

FA 2001, 13 Schedule 6 changed the wording slightly in relation to shares acquired after 11 May 2001 to give greater clarity.

(*n*)   *ICTA 1988, s 234A(4)* (information relating to distributions to be provided by nominee) does not apply in relation to any amount applied by the trustees in acquiring dividend shares on behalf of a participant. [*ITEPA 2003, s 493*]. However, it (and *s 234A(5)–(11)*) does apply to an amount chargeable to Sch F (or Case V of Sch D) under *2 Schedule 68*, (see 15.40), or *s 502* (see 15.43(*c*)). [*ITEPA*

2003, s 493, 2 Schedule 80(4)]. Section 234A(4)–(11) also applies in relation to the balance of any cash dividend paid over to the participant under *2 Schedule 64*, formerly *8 Schedule 54(3)*, (see 15.38). [*2 Schedule 80(4)*, formerly *8 Schedule 90*].

(*o*)   Incidental expenditure of the trustees or the employer in operating the plan (i.e. the running costs) does not give rise to any charge to income tax on employees. [*ITEPA 2003, s 499*].

Charge on shares ceasing to be subject to plan

Free or matching shares

15.44   If free or matching shares cease to be subject to the plan (eg. because they are removed by the participant, sold by the trustees at his direction, or the plan ceases to be approved) less than three years after the date they were awarded to the participant an income tax charge arises on the market value of the shares when they cease to be subject to the plan. [*ITEPA 2003, s 505(1)(2)*].

15.45   If they have been in the plan for at least three years but less than five, an income tax charge still arises but in this case it is on the lower of the market value at the date the shares were awarded to the participant or at the date when they ceased to be subject to the plan. [*ITEPA 2003, s 505(3)*]. If the charge is on the market value on the date of the award and a charge has previously arisen under *ITEPA 2003, s 501* (see 15.43(*c*)) in relation to a capital receipt from the shares, the tax due under *section 505(3)* is reduced by that already paid under *section 501*. [*ITEPA 2003, s 505(4)*]. It should be noted that this relief is given by reducing the tax not the income. The tax due is reduced by any tax paid under *section 446L* (see 14.72) where the shares have an artificially enhanced market value. [*ITEPA 2003, s 505(4A)* inserted by *FA 2004, s 88(5)*].

15.46   If the shares cease to be subject to the plan by virtue of the participant assigning, charging or otherwise disposing of his beneficial interest in the shares in breach of *2 Schedule 36(1)(b)* (see 15.21) the full market value of the shares at the date they cease to be subject to the plan is taxed irrespective of how long they have been held in the plan [*ITEPA 2003, s 507*]. As the tax charge is calculated on the value of the shares when they leave the plan no relief needs to be given for tax previously paid on capital receipts under *section 501*.

Partnership shares

15.47   If partnership shares cease to be subject to the plan less than three years from their acquisition date (see 15.30 and 15.32) the employee is again taxable as income on the market value of the shares when they cease to be subject to the plan. [*ITEPA 2003, s 506(1)(2)*]. If the shares have been held for at least three years but less than five the income tax charge is on the lower of the amount of partnership share money used to acquire the shares or the market value of the shares when they cease to be subject to the plan. [*ITEPA 2003, s 506(3)*]. If the tax charge is on the partnership share money and there has been a previous charge under *section 501* on a capital receipt the tax payable under *section 506(3)* is reduced by that previously paid under *section 501*. [*ITEPA 2003, s 506(4)*]. The tax due is reduced by any tax paid under *section 446L* (see 14.72) where the shares have an artificially enhanced market value. [*ITEPA 2003, s 506(4A)* inserted by *FA 2004, s 88(5)*].

15.48   As the partnership share money should be equal to the value of the shares at the time of acquisition it will be seen that for all practical purposes the charge on partnership shares is the same as that on free or matching shares. It is reasonable that no deduction should be allowed for the cost of the shares as the shares were purchased out of pre-tax income so by taxing the entire value the legislation both claws back the initial tax exemption and if the shares were in the plan for less than three years taxes the growth in value.

Dividend shares

15.49   If dividend shares cease to be subject to the plan within three years from the date they were acquired, the participant is taxable on the amount of the dividend used to acquire the shares, but in the tax year in which they cease to be subject to the plan. [*ICTA 1988, s 251C* inserted by *ITEPA 2003, s 722*]. The charge is not under Schedule E. It is under Schedule F (or if the company is a non-UK company Case V of Schedule D). Any tax credit to which the participant is entitled is calculated by reference to the tax credit fraction in force when the shares leave the plan, not that when the initial dividend was paid. [*ICTA 1988, s 251C(3)*]. At least that seems to be the intention. Any tax due under *s 493* (after deduction of any related tax credit) can be reduced by the tax previously paid under *para 79* on a prior capital distributions. [*ITEPA 2003, s 493(3)*].

Exceptions

15.50   No income tax charge arises on shares ceasing to be subject to the plan:

(*a*)   if the shares have been held in the plan for at least five years—three in the case of dividend shares. [*ITEPA 2003, ss 497, 505, 507*]; or

(*b*)   if the shares cease to be subject to the plan on the participant ceasing to be in relevant employment if this is:

   (i)   because of injury or disability,

   (ii)   on dismissal by reason of redundancy,

   (iii)   by reason of a transfer to which the *Transfer of Undertakings (Protection of Employment) Regulations 1981* apply,

   (iv)   by reason by a change of control or other circumstance which ends the associated company status of his employer company,

   (v)   by reason of his retirement on or after reaching the retirement age specified in the plan (which must be the same for men and women and must not be less than 50), or

   (vi)   on his death

   [*ITEPA 2003, s 498*], or

(c)   if the participant is not chargeable to tax as employment income in respect of the employment at the time of the award giving rise to the shares. [*ITEPA 2003, s 500*].

PAYE

15.51   Where a participant becomes chargeable to income tax as a result of shares ceasing to be subject to the plan, *ITEPA 2003, s 696* (see 2.88) (readily convertible assets) applies as if he were being provided with assessable income in the form of those shares at the time the shares cease to be subject to the plan and in respect of the relevant employment and *s 696* applies as if the taxable amount were the amount referred to in that provision. [*ITEPA 2003, s 509*].

15.52   Where an obligation to make a PAYE deduction arises on the shares ceasing to be subject to the plan (which will be the case if they are readily convertible assets) the trustee must pay over the necessary sum to the company unless the plan requires the employee to make such a payment to the company. [*ITEPA 2003, s 510*]. If the amount so paid to the employer exceeds the PAYE due, the excess is repayable to the employee. [*ITEPA 2003, s 511*]. *Section 710* (see 2.111) applies to the PAYE. Accordingly, if the amount of the PAYE is not paid by the employee to the employer within 90 days the taxable amount must be grossed up. If the trustees transfer the shares to the employee they clearly ought to insist on his paying over the money to them before transferring the shares to him. They also have power to sell some of the shares, or other shares they hold for the employee, to raise the funds to pay the PAYE (see 15.77).

15.53   If at the time the shares cease to be subject to the trust there is no employer company to which the PAYE Regulations apply, or the Revenue consider that it is impracticable for any such company to account for the PAYE and direct that the trustees should do so, the trustees must themselves deduct PAYE and account for it as if the participant were a former employee of the trustees. This will require them to deduct tax at the basic rate. [*ITEPA 2003, s 511*]. If a participant disposes of his beneficial interest in any of his plan shares to the trustees (and they are deemed by *TCGA 1992, 7D Schedule 6* (see 15.80) to have disposed of the shares) PAYE must be applied as if the consideration paid by the trustees to the participant had been an amount received by them as the proceeds of disposal of plan shares [*ITEPA 2003, s 512*]. The same provisions apply to the receipt by the trustee of money which constitutes (or forms part of) a capital receipt on which a participant is chargeable to income tax (see 15.43(*c*)). [*ITEPA 2003, s 514*].

Capital Gains Tax

15.54 The increase in value of the shares is not chargeable to capital gains tax on either the beneficiary or the trustees while the shares remain 'subject to the plan', ie until the earliest of the times at which either the shares are withdrawn from the plan, the employee ceases to be employed by the company without remaining or immediately becoming employed by an associated company, or the trustees dispose of the shares under 2 *Schedule 79* (see 15.79) to meet a PAYE obligation. [*TCGA 2002, 7D*]. Shares are withdrawn from the plan for this purpose if they are transferred to the employee (or another person) on the direction of the employee, the employee assigns, changes or otherwise disposes of his beneficial interest in the shares, or the shares are disposed of by the trustees on the direction of the participant with the trustees having an obligation to account for those proceeds to the participant or some other person.

15.55 It accordingly appears that if the employee wishes (and the trustees agree) he can leave the shares in the plan indefinitely and thus prolong the period of this capital gains tax exemption.

15.56 When the shares cease to be subject to the plan there is a deemed (tax free) disposal and reacquisition at the market value at that time. [*TCGA 1992, 7D Schedule 2* inserted by *ITEPA 2003, 6 Schedule 221*]. Notwithstanding, this, the beneficiary is (and must be) treated as becoming absolutely entitled to the shares as against the trustees at the initial date that the shares are awarded to him under the plan. [*TCGA 1992, 7D Schedule 3*]. This relieves the trustees of any risk of CGT from that date. So that plan shares do not distort the CGT identification rules, whilst they remain subject to the plan they are treated as being of a different class to other shares in the company held by the employee. [*TCGA 1992, 7D Schedule 4*]. If the trustees acquire shares from an *FA 1989* ESOT (see 17.58) such shares are also treated as a separate class from other unallocated shares held by the trustees while they have not been appointed to an employee. [*TCGA 1992, 7D Schedule 4*]. For 2002/03 onwards shares acquired by virtue of a payment for which a deduction was allowed under *ICTA 1988, 4AA Schedule 9* (see 15.68) which have not yet been awarded under the plan must be treated as of a different class from other shares held by the trustees which were not acquired out of that payment [*TCGA 1992, 7D Schedule 4(6)*].

15.57 The exemption of the trustees on gains accruing prior to the shares being awarded to employees is dependent on the shares having been awarded to employees (or acquired on their behalf as dividend shares) under the plan within a specified period. If none of the shares in the company are readily convertible assets this is five years from the date of their acquisition. If they are, it is two years (and if they become readily convertible during the trustees' period of ownership they must be awarded within two years of that time if that is earlier than the expiry of the five-year period). [*6 Schedule 221*]. In applying this test shares acquired by the trustees are deemed to be awarded to employees on a first in/first out basis. [*6 Schedule 221*]. For shares acquired by the trustees before 12 May 2001 the two-year period applied only if the shares acquired by the trustees were (or became) themselves readily convertible assets.

15.58 If shares allocated to an employee are subsequently forfeited they are treated as having been disposed of by the employee to the trustees (as a tax free disposal) and reacquired by the trustees at their then market value. [*7 Schedule 86*]. If the trustees acquire shares from an existing approved profit sharing scheme (see 17.31(*a*)) the disposal and acquisition is deemed to be at a no gain/no loss price and, for the purpose of determining whether they are taxable when they dispose of the shares, the plan trustees are treated as acquiring the shares when the profit sharing scheme trustees did so (i.e. to avoid tax they need to allocate the shares to employees within five or two years as appropriate of the profit sharing trustees having acquired them). [*7 Schedule 86*]. If a CGT charge does arise on the SIP trustees the date of the transfer from the profit sharing scheme must be used as the acquisition date for taper relief purposes though. [*7 Schedule 86*].

15.59 If on a rights issue the SIP trustees sell some of the rights in order to take up the others (see 15.70) the gain on that disposal is not taxable provided that the rights issue extends to all ordinary shares in the company. [*6 Schedule 221*]. This is an odd provision. It is clearly intended to stop rights being offered to the trustees only, but where a company has more than one class of ordinary shares a rights issue will often be confined only to the class which comprises the rights shares. The meaning of 'ordinary shares' is unclear. Although 'ordinary share capital' is defined 'ordinary shares' is not and there is no logical reason to assume that the two expressions have the same meaning.

Corporation Tax

15.60 The employer company (e.g. the subsidiary company that employs a participant not the parent company whose shares he is awarded) is allowed a deduction in calculating its trading profits for the market value of free or matching shares awarded to its employees. The amount deductible is the value at the time the shares are acquired by the trustees (not when they are awarded to the employee if that is a later date) but is allowed only in the accounting period in which they are awarded to employees. [*ICTA 1988, 4AA Schedule 2* inserted by *ITEPA 2003, 6 Schedule 109*]. That is the only way in which relief can be given in respect of the provision of the shares, e.g. if a deduction falls to be made under generally accepted accounting principles as the cost of providing an employee benefit, that deduction is specifically disallowed for tax purposes. In determining what shares are awarded to employees the shares held by the trustees are deemed to be awarded on a first in/first out basis. [*ICTA 1988, 4AA Schedule 2(6)*].

15.61 If the shares are awarded under a group plan the market value is the relevant proportion (that which the number of shares awarded to employees of the company concerned bears to the total number of shares in the award) of the total market value of all of the shares included in the award. [*ICTA 1988, 4AA Schedule 2(4)*]. In theory this is helpful in the case of unquoted shares, as the total award is likely to have a greater value per share than if the shares awarded to employees of a single company had to be looked at separately. In practice it may be unworkable. It appears to assume that all of the shares included in an award will have been acquired by the trustees on the same date, which need not necessarily be the case.

15.62   A corporation tax deduction is also allowed to the employer company in relation to partnership shares to the extent, if any, that the market value of those shares at the time that they were acquired by the trustees exceeds the partnership share monies (see 15.27) paid by the employees. Again, the deduction is given only in the accounting period in which the award is made. [*ICTA 1988, 4AA Schedule 3*].

15.63   Clearly, a corporation tax deduction cannot be given (unless it appears that it would have been due apart from these SIP rules) if at the time the shares are awarded to an employee he is not taxable on them as employment income (or would not be so taxable if his earnings were remitted), ie if the shares are awarded in breach of the SIP rules. [*ICTA 1988, 4AA Schedule 4*]. No deduction can be allowed if either the company or an associated company has already had a deduction for the same shares on providing them to the same or any other trust (even apparently to one which is not for the benefit of qualifying employees). A first in/first out basis applies to determine which shares are caught by this provision. [*ICTA 1988, 4AA Schedule 4(6)*].

15.64   No deduction is allowed for shares that are acquired on behalf of employees as dividend shares. [*ICTA 1988, 4AA Schedule 5*]. No deduction is allowed either for 'funny' shares that are liable to depreciate substantially in value for reasons that do not apply generally to shares in the company. [*ICTA 1988, 4AA Schedule 4(5)*]. This is obviously an anti-avoidance provision to prevent the rights of shares being rigged so that the company would obtain a far greater deduction than the benefit accruing to the employee. If plan shares are forfeited they are treated for corporation tax purposes as having been acquired by the trustees at that time for no consideration and no deduction is given to the company in respect of any subsequent award of those shares under the plan (as relief will already have been given when they were previously awarded). [*ICTA 1988, 4AA Schedule 6*].

15.65   A corporation tax deduction is allowed to the company which establishes the SIP for expenses incurred in doing so. [*ICTA 1988, 4AA Schedule 7*]. This deduction is lost (and no deduction can be claimed even if one would otherwise have been due under general tax law) if any shares are acquired by the trustees or rights are granted to employees before the Inland Revenue approve the plan. [*ICTA 1988, 4AA Schedule 7(2)*]. If the Revenue approve the SIP more than nine months after the end of the period of account in which an expense is incurred, relief is given at the time of approval not when the expense is incurred. [*ICTA 1988, 4AA Schedule 7(3)*]. It is unclear why a taxpayer should be penalised for Revenue delays.

15.66   It should particularly be noted that if in the case of a group plan the parent company recharges a proportion of the costs to the subsidiaries (as it would naturally do if it wants each subsidiary to have budgetary responsibility for its own employee costs) the subsidiary cannot obtain a deduction for the amount borne by it. It may well be that the parent cannot do so either as it is questionable whether it has incurred an expense which it has entered into on behalf of the subsidiary and which is not borne by the parent.

15.67   No specific right of deduction is given for any contribution by a company towards the expenses of the trustees in respect of operating the SIP (including interest on sums borrowed to acquire shares and any fees, commission, stamp duty and similar incidental costs attributable to the acquisition of shares, but excluding the purchase price of the shares themselves). However, it is specifically provided that such a deduction is not disallowed. [*ICTA 1988, 4AA Schedule 8*]. Accordingly, a deduction can be claimed for such a contribution if it satisfies the normal Schedule D wholly and exclusively test.

15.68   For contributions to a SIP after 6 April 2003 a deduction is specifically allowed where:

(*a*)   the payment is to enable the SIP to acquire shares in the paying company or a company which controls it;

(*b*)   the payment is applied by the trustees to acquire such shares;

(*c*)   the shares are not acquired from the company; and

(*d*)   at the end of the period of 12 months following the acquisition the trustees hold shares that constitute at least 10% of the ordinary share capital of the company and carry rights to not less than 10% of any profits available for distribution to shareholders and of any assets of the company available for distribution to shareholders in the event of a winding-up.

[*ICTA 1988, 4AA Schedule 9(1)*]. For the purpose of (d) above shares that have been appropriated to and acquired on behalf of an individual under the plan are treated as held by the trustees while they remain subject to the plan [*ICTA 1988, 4AA Schedule 9(3)*]. The deduction is claimable at the time that condition (d) is met, not at the time of the payment if earlier [*ICTA 1988, 4AA Schedule 9(1)*].

15.69   The Inland Revenue can by notice direct that the benefit of a deduction under *4AA Schedule 9A* should be withdrawn if either:

(*a*)   30% of the shares acquired by virtue of the payment in respect of which the deduction was made have not been awarded under the plan within five years of their acquisition; or

(*b*)   all of the shares acquired by virtue of that payment have not been awarded within ten years of their acquisition.

[*ICTA 1988, 4AA Schedule 10(1)*]. Where such a direction is made the withdrawal of the relief is made by treating the amount as a trading receipt for the period of account in which the direction is given [*ICTA 1988, 4AA Schedule 10(2)*]. If the requisite shares are subsequently awarded under the plan the sum again becomes deductible, in this case in the period of account in which the requisite condition is met [*ICTA 1988, 4AA Schedule 10(3)*]. If any of the qualifying shares are awarded to a person who is not taxable on them as employment income, part of the deduction is withdrawn by treating as a trading receipt for the period of account in which that award was made the proportion of the payment that the shares awarded to that taxpayer bears to the total number of shares acquired out of the payment [*ICTA 1988, 4AA Schedule 10(6)–(8)*]. Where shares are acquired on different days they are treated as awarded to employees on a first in first out basis [*ICTA 1988, 4AA Schedule 10(10)*].

15.70   If the employer company is an investment company relief is again given both for the value of free shares (and the excess value of partnership shares) and for expenses, but as a management expense. [*ICTA 1988, 4AA Schedule 13*].

15.71   If the approval of a SIP is withdrawn the Inland Revenue can direct that the cost of the shares (but not the expenses of setting up the scheme) should be disallowed. If they do so the company is treated as receiving a trading receipt (or Case VI income in the case of an investment company), at the time that the Revenue give notice of withdrawal of approval, equal to the deductions previously allowed to the company. [*ICTA 1988, 4AA Schedule 11*]. There is a right of appeal against such a direction. [*ITEPA 2003, 2 Schedule 85(1)(c)*—see 15.82]. The appeal is to the Special Commissioners and notice of appeal must be given within 30 days of notice of the decision being given to the company. [*2 Schedule 85(2)(3)*].

Stamp duty

15.72   There is no stamp duty or stamp duty reserve tax on a transfer after 11 May 2001 (i.e. where the relevant instrument is executed or the agreement to transfer the shares is made after that date) of partnership shares or dividend shares by the trustees of a SIP to an employee. [*FA 2001, s 95* inserted by *ITEPA 2003, 6 Schedule 257*]. The transfer of free shares and matching shares being for no consideration is exempt under general principles as a transfer from trustees to a beneficiary.

The trustees

15.73   The plan must provide for the establishment of a body of trustees resident in the UK to operate it. [*2 Schedule 71*]. Their functions must be regulated by a trust deed constituted under the law of some part of the UK and complying with the requirements of *Schedule 2*. [*2 Schedule 71(3)*]. The trust deed must not contain any terms that are neither essential nor reasonably incidental to complying with the requirements of *Schedule 2*.

[*2 Schedule 71(4)*]. From 6 April 2003 it can contain terms that define who is a professional trustee and who a non-professional one, can provide that the trustees include at least one person who is a professional trustee and at least two non-professional ones, can provide that at least half of the non-professional trustees are to be selected in accordance with a specified process of selection and can provide that trustees so selected are to be employees of the company (or of a participating company in the case of a group plan. [*2 Schedule 71(5)*]. From 10 July 2003 the trust deed must also require the trustees to maintain records of participants who have participated in one or more SIPs established by the company or a connected company. [*2 Schedule 71A inserted by FA 2003, 21 Schedule 6*].

15.74   The deed has to require the trustees to give notice to the employee of any award of shares to him as soon as practicable after that award. In the case of free or matching shares the notice must specify the number and description of the shares, their market value on the date they were awarded and the holding period applicable to them (which must be between three and five years—see 15.21 and 15.37). [*2 Schedule 75*]. It is unclear how the trustees are expected to know the market value of unquoted shares. In the case of partnership shares it needs to state the number and description of the shares, the amount of partnership share money applied in acquiring the shares, and their market value on the date of acquisition. [*2 Schedule 75(3)*].

15.75   The trustees must similarly give the employee notice of the acquisition of dividend shares on his behalf. This must specify the number and description of the shares, their market value on the date of acquisition, their holding period (which must be three years—see 15.41) and any uninvested amount of the dividend carried forward. If the shares are in a non-UK company the notice must also show the amount of any foreign tax deducted. [*2 Schedule 75(4)*].

15.76   The trust deed must also require the trustees to dispose of a participant's plan shares and to deal with any right conferred in respect of them as directed by or on behalf of the participant. [*2 Schedule 72(1)*]. The plan can authorise employees to give general directions to the trustees. [*2 Schedule 72(3)*]. Subject of course to the rights of the trustees to dispose of the shares to subscribe for a rights issue or pay PAYE, the deed must prohibit the trustees from disposing of free, matching or dividend shares—even to the employee—at any time during the holding period (other than where the employment terminates during that period. [*2 Schedule 73*]. It must also require the trustees to pay over to the participant any money or money's worth received in respect of the shares. [*2 Schedule 74*].

15.77   The trustees can be given power to borrow to acquire shares for the purpose of the plan and for such other purposes as may be specified in the trust deed. [*2 Schedule 76*]. They are entitled to dispose of some of the rights arising under a rights issue in order to take up the remainder, but only if the employee directs them to do so. [*2 Schedule 77*].

15.78   The trust deed must also provide that if there is a transfer of shares to the plan from an *FA 1989* ESOT which is a qualifying transfer under

FA 1989, s 69(3AA) (see 17.32(*a*)) those shares must not be awarded to anyone as partnership shares but must be awarded as free or matching shares at the next award in priority to any other shares. [*2 Schedule 78*].

Tax obligations

15.79   The deed must ensure that where a PAYE obligation is imposed on the trustees as a result of any of an employee's plan shares ceasing to be subject to the plan the trustees can raise the cash either by selling some of those shares (including to themselves), by selling other plan shares held on behalf of the employee, or by receiving an appropriate sum from the employee. [*2 Schedule 79*].

15.80   If at any time an employee disposes of a beneficial interest in plan shares, those shares are deemed to have been disposed of at that time by the trustees for an amount equal to the consideration for the disposal of the beneficial interest. If that disposal is not at arm's length the market value of the shares is adopted instead. If the employee becomes insolvent the operation of the insolvency rules is deemed to give rise to a disposal of his beneficial interest in the shares. [*TCGA 1992, 7D, Schedule 6*].

15.81   The trust deed must require the trustees to maintain such records as are needed for both themselves and the company to meet their PAYE obligations in relation to the plan and to be able to notify the employee of any amounts on which he becomes liable to tax by reason of the occurrence of any event (it presumably means only in relation to the plan) such as on a failure to acquire dividend shares within the relevant period. [*2 Schedule 80*, formerly *8 Schedule 75*].

Withdrawal of approval

15.82   The Revenue have power to withdraw approval of a SIP on the occurrence of any disqualifying event. Such withdrawal can be from the time of that event or such later time as they may specify. [*2 Schedule 83*]. There is a right of appeal by the company to the Special Commissioners. [*2 Schedule 85*]. Notice of appeal must be given within 30 days after notice of the Revenue's decision to withdraw approval is given to the company. [*2 Schedule 85(3)*]. There is a similar right of appeal against a refusal by the Revenue to approve an alteration to the plan. [*2 Schedule 85(1)(b)*].

15.83   The disqualifying events are:

(*a*)   Any contravention of *Schedule 2*, the plan rules or the trust deed.

(*b*)   Any alteration in a key feature of the plan or in the trust deed without Revenue approval. A key feature for this purpose is something relating to a provision that is necessary to meet the requirement of *Schedule 2*. The Revenue cannot withhold approval to a change unless it appears to them that if approval were then sought for the amended plan it would not be approved.

(c)   If the plan provides for performance allowances under method 2 (see 15.25), performance targets being set in respect of an award of shares that cannot reasonably be regarded as comparable (such targets are comparable only if they are comparable in terms of the likelihood of their being met by the performance units to which they apply).

(d)   Any alteration being made in the share capital of the scheme company (or the rights attaching to any of its shares) that materially affects the value of participants' plan shares.

(e)   Shares which have been awarded to participants receiving different treatment to the other shares of the same class. This applies in particular to differences in dividends, repayment, the restrictions attaching to the shares, or any offer of substituted or additional shares, securities or rights of any description in respect of the shares. It does not apply where the difference in treatment is a key feature of the plan or results from an employee's plan shares being subject to forfeiture. Nor does it apply if the only difference is that newly issued shares receive less favourable treatment to existing shares in relation to dividends payable for a period beginning before the date of their issue.

(f)   The trustees, the scheme company or any participating company (in the case of a group scheme) failing to furnish information in accordance with *para 93* (which enables the Revenue to seek such information as they reasonably require for the purpose of their functions under *Schedule 2*).

[*2 Schedule 84*].

15.84   The withdrawal of approval will not affect the operation of the plan in relation to shares that were awarded to participants in the plan before the time of such withdrawal (and at a time when the plan was approved. [*2 Schedule 83(3)*].

Termination of plan

15.85   The SIP can provide for the company to issue a plan termination notice. If it does it must also provide that where such a notice is issued a copy must be sent without delay to the Revenue, the trustees and each individual who either owns plan shares or has entered into a partnership share agreement. [*2 Schedule 89*].

15.86   If a company issues a plan termination notice no further shares can then be awarded under the plan and the trustees must remove all of the plan shares from the plan as soon as practicable at the end of the notice period (three months after the date on which the copy notices under *para 89* are issued—if these are sent on different dates it is probably three months after the last) or, if later, the first date on which they can be removed from the plan without triggering an income tax charge on the participant, i.e. three years after they were acquired in the case of dividend shares and five years after they were awarded in relation to other shares. [*2 Schedule 90*].

15.87 The trustees can remove the shares from the plan earlier if the participant consents, i.e. if he agrees to accept a tax charge, but only if that consent is given after he receives a copy of the plan termination notice. [*2 Schedule 90(5)(6)*]. They remove the shares from the plan either by transferring them to the employee (or to whoever else he may direct) or by selling them and accounting to the employee for the proceeds. [*2 Schedule 90(8)*]. If the employee has died the transfer or payment of the funds is obviously to be made to his personal representatives. [*2 Schedule 90(9)*]. The trustees must also of course pay the employee any uninvested partnership share money or dividends in accordance with *para 56* (see 15.35) and *68(2)* (see 15.40) and any other money held on the employee's behalf. [*2 Schedule 90(7)*]. Such money must be paid over on receipt of the plan termination notice, not at the end of the three-month notice period. For 2002/03 onwards if a deduction has been allowed under *ICTA 1988, 4AA Schedule 9* (see 15.68) and not withdrawn under *ICTA 1988, 4AA Schedule 10* and not all of the shares acquired by virtue of the payment have been awarded before the issue of the plan termination notice there must be treated as a trading receipt for the period of account in which the termination notice is given the proportion of the payment that the awarded shares bears to the total shares purchased from the payment. [*ICTA 1988, 4AA Schedule 12*].

15.88 It is unclear why a company should want to issue a plan termination notice. If it simply decides not to make any further awards under the plan it will die a natural death and the same results will accrue but without the statutory time pressure on the trustees. The termination notice procedure might be desirable if the company is sold or ceases trading and it is wished to stop ongoing duties for the trustees where, for example, a few employees have left the shares with the trustees for more than five years to obtain the capital gains tax benefits.

Company reconstructions

15.89 A company reconstruction is treated as not involving a disposal of shares comprised in the original holding but the new shares are treated as having been awarded or acquired to the employee when the original ones were awarded. [*2 Schedule 86*]. The new shares do not have to meet the tests in *paras 25–33* (see 15.5(*i*)–(*m*)) provided that the original ones did. [*2 Schedule 87(2)(c)*]. The income tax and capital gains tax rules apply in relation to the new shares as they would have applied to the old. [*2 Schedule 87(2)(d)*]. Any reference in the rules to an employee's plan shares become of course a reference to his new shares that replace or supplement the old. [*2 Schedule 87(6)*].

15.90 A company reconstruction for this purpose means a transaction which results in a new holding being equated with the original holding for

CGT purposes (i.e. one within *TCGA 1992 ss 132–137*) or which would have done so but for the fact that the new holding consists of or includes a qualifying corporate bond. [*2 Schedule 86*]. Such a transaction is excluded from being a company reconstruction if the new holding includes shares which are taxable as income on the recipient under *ICTA 1988, s 209(2)(c)* (redeemable shares issued otherwise than wholly for new consideration), *s 210(1)* (bonus issue following repayment of share capital) or *s 249* (stock dividends). [*2 Schedule 86(4)*]. It is not clear what happens where a transaction includes both such shares and other shares. *Para 86(2)* suggests that the transaction is not a company reconstruction at all but *para 86(3)* suggests that it is not one only in relation to those shares which attract the income tax charge. If, as part of a reconstruction the trustees receive cash, that cash is deemed to arise before the new holding comes into being. [*2 Schedule 87(5)*]. It is not immediately apparent what this deeming is intended to achieve.

Rights issues

15.91   Where the trustees acquire shares under a rights issue in respect of an employee's plan shares the rights shares are treated as identical to the original shares and as having been appropriated to (or acquired on behalf of) the employee in the same way and at the same time as the original shares. [*2 Schedule 88*].

15.92   This rule does not apply where either—

(*a*)   the funds used to acquire the rights shares were not raised by the trustees selling the rights in some of the shares in order to take up the remainder (e.g. where the employee put the trustees in funds to take up the rights issue), or

(*b*)   similar rights are not conferred in respect of all ordinary shares in the company (as indicated earlier it is not at all clear that 'ordinary shares'—which is not defined—is the same as 'ordinary share capital', which is). [*2 Schedule 88(4)(5)*]. In both of these cases the new shares will not be plan shares and they are excluded from *TCGA 1992, s 127–130*, i.e. they are not treated as forming a single asset with the original shares.

Chapter 16

Approved Share Option and Profit Sharing Schemes

Introduction

16.1 Although Chancellors of the Exchequer have often been suspicious of employee share incentives, seeing them as little more than a device to enable an employee to receive part of his remuneration in a capital form, attempts have been made in recent years to encourage employee share ownership provided that this is done in a politically acceptable way. There are currently five approved ways to enable employees to take shareholdings in the company for which they work:

(*a*)   Share Incentive Plans (SIP) (formerly called All Employee Share Option Plans (AESOP)). These are the most attractive ways to provide a tax incentive but can be used only where it is proposed that all of the employees of an enterprise should have the opportunity to acquire shares. SIPs are dealt with in Chapter 15 and are not considered further here.

(*b*)   Approved SAYE option schemes (formerly called savings-related share option schemes). Again such a scheme can be used only where it is proposed to include in the scheme all of the employees of an enterprise.

(*c*)   Approved CSOP (company share option plan) Schemes (formerly called executive share option schemes, or sometimes *FA 1984* share option schemes or discretionary share option schemes). Selected employees only can participate in a CSOP scheme.

(*d*)   Enterprise Management Incentives (EMI schemes). These are aimed at selected, generally senior, employees.

(*e*)   Employee share ownership trusts (ESOTs). An ESOT is a sort of halfway house. The concept is that it should acquire shares for later distribution to employees so the tax benefits are temporary whilst the shares are held in the trust. ESOTs are dealt with in Chapter 17 and not considered further here.

16.2 Under all such schemes, in return for accepting restrictions on the benefits that can be provided, the tax charges that would otherwise arise under the various provisions considered in Chapter 14 are disapplied.

16.3 Many of the conditions that must be met by the two types of approved share option schemes are identical, or virtually so. On consolidation of the income tax legislation in 1988 the draftsman collected these together in *Schedule 9* to the *Act*. This treatment seems sensible and is followed below, albeit that it was abandoned by the tax law rewrite team, the basic principles of the two types of scheme being considered before the qualifying conditions for both are examined.

16.4 There used to be a further type of plan, approved profit sharing schemes but the use of such schemes was discouraged following the introduction of SIPs in April 2001 and such schemes no longer confer tax benefits except to the extent that shares were appropriated to employees before 1 January 2003. Such schemes are dealt with at 16.36.

Share option schemes

16.5 There are two types of approved share option schemes: SAYE option schemes and CSOP schemes. From 28 July 2000 there are also Enterprise Management Incentive options which are considered at 16.72. Under a SAYE option scheme the employee enters into a Save As You Earn contract with a bank, building society or other approved financial institution. This commits him to save a regular monthly amount for at least three years. The maximum permissible monthly figure is £250. At the end of the contract (which can be for three or five years) he is credited with a tax-free bonus. If he leaves the funds to accumulate for a further two years he will be entitled to a second bonus. At the same time as he starts his SAYE scheme the employee is granted an option to subscribe for (or acquire) shares in the employer company. The option price must be satisfied out of the proceeds of the SAYE scheme. Accordingly, the amount he can acquire must be based on the estimated value of the scheme in five years' time (or seven years if he opts to tie up his savings for that longer period). From 30 April 1996 three-year savings schemes can also be used but the £250 per month limit still applies. The tax-free bonus is 2.75 times the monthly contribution for three-year contracts, 7.5 times for five-year ones and 13.5 times for seven-year contracts. With monthly payments of £250 this will produce £9,687 at the end of three years, £16,875 after five years or £24,375 after seven years. As the shares can be issued at 80 per cent of their market value at the time the option is granted (see 16.15(*j*)), this will allow an employee to acquire options over £30,468 worth of shares.

Employees eligible to join scheme

16.6 All full-time employees with at least five years' service must have a right to participate in the scheme. Accordingly, a SAYE option scheme cannot be targeted at specific employees.

16.7 Furthermore, the employee cannot normally exercise his option for at least three years. SAYE option schemes are aimed at enabling a broad spread of employees to acquire a share stake in their employer company. They are generally used by major listed companies who feel that providing an employee with a share stake will enable him to identify more closely with the company. They are not really suitable for unquoted companies where an employee will acquire a tiny, unmarketable holding which is unlikely to have any value. As a profit sharing scheme does not require the employee to do anything other than to continue in his employment, such a scheme is likely to be more acceptable to employees than a SAYE option scheme under which the employee has to save money out of his post-tax income, which in most cases he will 'repay' to the employer company to acquire the shares.

Executive share option schemes

16.8   A CSOP scheme is very different. The scheme can be targeted at executives only; indeed, it is possible to grant options to a single person.

16.9   Prior to 17 July 1995 such schemes were very attractive. However, the limit on the benefit that can be provided was substantially reduced from that date, although such schemes can still be attractive for junior and middle range executives and in other circumstances where it is not wished to motivate the entire workforce by the grant of share option. Most of the tax benefits are common to both types of schemes.

Tax benefits of approved schemes

16.10   If, in accordance with the provisions of an approved share option scheme, an individual obtains an option (or other right) to acquire shares in a company by reason of his employment as a director or employee (of that or any other company) tax is not to be charged, under any provision of the *Tax Acts*, in respect of the receipt of the option (subject to a minor exception considered at 16.12 below).

16.11   The tax position under approved option schemes is as follows:

SAYE option scheme:

(*a*)   No income tax liability arises on the grant of an option. This is now the normal rule in relation to options under *ITEPA 2003, s 475* (see 14.90). Prior to the appointed day under *FA 2003, 22 Schedule 3(2)* there was a specific statutory exemption. [*ITEPA 2003, s 518*]. *Section 518* was repealed by *FA 2003, 22 Schedule 29.*

(*b*)   No income tax liability arises on the exercise of the option provided that it is exercised in accordance with the terms of the scheme and unless the option was exercised before 18 June 2004, the avoidance of tax or NIC is not the main purpose (or one of the main purposes) of any arrangements under which the option was granted or is exercised: and either:

(i)   it is not exercised within three years of being granted; or

(ii)   although it is exercised in the first three years this is by virtue of *ITEPA 2003, 3 Schedule 34(5)* (which allows options to be exercised within six months after the termination of the employment where the ownership of a company or business is transferred) (see 16.16(d)) or 37 (which allows options to be exercised within six months of a takeover of the company) (see 16.20) [*ITEPA 2003, s 519* as amended by *FA 2004, s 88(6)*].

(c)   The general exemption from tax on the exercise of an option by personal representatives under *ITEPA 2003, s 477(2)* (see 14.94) applies to an SAYE option in the same way as any other option. Prior to 1 September 2003 there was a specific exemption, *ITEPA 2003, s 519(4)* but this was repealed by *FA 2003, 22 Schedule 30.*

(d)   Prior to 1 September 2003, provided that the option was exercised in accordance with the terms of the scheme and not within the first three years (unless the exemption at (b)(ii) applies, there was no income tax liability in relation to shares acquired under the option under *ITEPA 2003, ss 449* (removal of restrictions) (see 14.158) or *453* (dependent subsidiaries) (see 14.166). [*ITEPA 2003, s 520*]. *Section 520* was repealed by *FA 2003, 22 Schedule 31.*

CSOP schemes:

(a)   No liability to income tax arises on the grant of the option except where it was granted at a discount (see below). [*ITEPA 2003, s 475*]. Prior to 1 September 2003 this was a specific exemption, *ITEPA 2003, s 523. Section 523* was repealed by *FA 2003, 22 Schedule 32.*

(b)   No liability to income tax arises on the exercise of the option in accordance with the provisions of the scheme provided that, unless the option was exercised before 18 June 2004, the avoidance of tax or NIC is not the main purpose (or one of the main purposes) of any arrangements under which the option was granted or is exercised, and either:

(i)   it is not exercised within the first three years or more than ten years after it was granted; or

(ii)   from 9 April 2003 if the option was exercised within the first three years, this was in accordance with *4 Schedule 24* (see 16.18) and the individual exercising the option did so within six months of ceasing to be a full-time director or employee because of injury, liability, redundancy (within the *Employment Rights Act 1976*) or retirement after reaching a retirement age specified in the scheme;

up to 8 April 2003 it also had to be shown that the individual had not made an exempt exercise of another option within the prior three years (either under the scheme or under another approved CSOP scheme, but an exercise under another scheme on the same day is acceptable).

[*ITEPA 2003, s 524* and *FA 2004, s 88(7)*].

(*c*)   The general exemption from tax on the exercise of an option by personal representatives under *ITEPA 2003, s 477(2)* (see 14.94) applies to a CSOP option scheme in the same way as any other option. Prior to 1 September 2003 there was a specific exemption, *ITEPA 2003, s 524(4)*, but this was repealed by *FA 2003, 22 Schedule 33*.

(*d*)   Prior to 1 September 2003, provided that the option was exercised in accordance with the scheme and within (*b*) above no liability to income tax arose under *ITEPA 2003, ss 449* or *453* in relation to shares acquired under the option [*ITEPA 2003, s 525*]. *Section 525* was repealed by *FA 2003, 22 Schedule 33*.

16.12   For the purpose of (a) above an option is granted at a discount if at the time when it was granted the aggregate of any consideration given for the option under a CSOP scheme, plus the option price, is less than the market value of the same quantity of issued shares of the same class at the time the option is granted. This taxable amount is treated as employment income if it would not otherwise have been so—it is difficult to envisage circumstances in which it would not. [*ITEPA 2003, s 526*]. This is intended to cover small accidental undervalues. One of the conditions for approval of a CSOP scheme is that the option price must not be manifestly less than the value of the shares at the time the option is granted. Accordingly, if the difference is significant this would probably lead to the complete withdrawal of approval of the scheme.

Circumstances in which tax charge reduced

16.13   If a charge to tax arises under *section 526* on the grant of the option (see 16.12) and because, for example, one of the conditions in *Schedule 4* is breached, the tax exemptions for approved option schemes do not apply, the amount on which the participant is taxable under *section 479* (old) (see 14.112 above) will be reduced by the amount on which he was taxed under *section 526)*. If the individual is treated under *section 194* (see 14.141 above) as having acquired shares at an undervalue the amount of the notional beneficial loan will be reduced by the amount on which he was taxed under *section 526)*. [*ITEPA 2003, s 194(2), 479(2)* (old)]. From 1 September 2003 the relief is instead given under *section 480(4)* (see 14100(*c*)). [*ITEPA 2003, s 526(4)* as substituted by *FA 2003, 22 Schedule 35*].

16.14   To qualify for approval both types of option scheme must satisfy the conditions at 16.15 below. A savings-related option scheme must also satisfy the further conditions set out at 16.16 below, and an executive share option scheme those at 16.17 below.

Conditions for approval

16.15   This paragraph describes the conditions common to both types of scheme. *ITEPA 2003, 3 Schedule* deals with SAYE option schemes and *4 Schedule* deals with CSOP schemes.

Previously both were contained in *ICTA 1988, 9 Schedule.*

(*a*)   Scheme shares must form part of the ordinary share capital of either:

   (i)   the scheme organiser (formerly called the grantor) (i.e. the company that set up the scheme);

   (ii)   a company which controls the scheme organiser; or

   (iii)   a company which is (or controls a company that is) a member of a consortium that owns the scheme organiser or a company that controls it (prior to 27 July 1989, the consortium member also had to own at least 15 per cent of the share capital of the grantor company).

   [ITEPA 2003, 3 Schedule 18, 4 Schedule 16].

   'Ordinary share capital' means all the issued shares other than those entitled to a dividend at a fixed rate with no further right to share in the profits of the company. *[ITEPA 2003, 3 Schedule 49, ICTA 1988, s 832(1)].*

(*b*)   The shares must be either:

   (i)   of a class quoted on a recognised stock exchange;

   (ii)   shares in a company which is not controlled by another company; or

   (iii)   shares which, although unquoted, are in a company which is under the control of one whose shares are quoted and which is not a close company (and if it is an overseas company would not be close if it were UK resident).

   [ITEPA 2003, 3 Schedule 19, 4 Schedule 17].

   This prevents shares in a subsidiary company being scheme shares unless they are quoted shares or the grantor is a subsidiary of a listed company that is not a close company.

(*c*)   The shares must be fully paid. *[ITEPA 2003, 3 Schedule 20(a), 4 Schedule 18(a)].*

(*d*)   The shares must not be redeemable. *[ITEPA 2003, 3 Schedule 20(b), 4 Schedule 18(b)].*

(*e*)   The shares must not be subject to any restrictions, other than

   (i)   restrictions attaching to all the shares of the same class, or

   (ii)   a restriction imposed by the Articles of Association (or equivalent document in the case of an overseas company) requiring:

      (A)   all shares held by directors or employees of the company or of any other company of which it has control to be disposed of (or offered for sale) immediately the holder ceases to be a director or employee, and

      (B)   all shares acquired by non-directors or employees (or ex-directors or employees) in pursuance of rights or interests obtained by directors or employees to be disposed of (or offered for sale) on acquisition

and providing that any such disposal must be by way of sale for a consideration in money on terms specified in the Articles, and that the Articles also require any other person who disposes of shares of the same class to sell their shares on those same terms. [*ITEPA 2003, 3 Schedule 21(1)–(3), (7), 4 Schedule 19(1)–(3), (8)*].

Points to note are that it appears that the Articles need to contain both provisions (A) and (B) in (ii) above even if the scheme does not permit options to be exercised after a person ceases to be an employee; and that all holders of shares of the same class must be obliged to sell the shares under the formula (or at the price) fixed in the Articles if they sell under the pre-emption clause in the Articles. The intention is to ensure that an employee is not deprived of the value of his shares when he ceases his employment. It is felt that if other non-employee shareholders (including the major shareholders) are prepared to accept the same terms, such terms are likely to be fair. This is not necessarily the case as the formula in the Articles can be such as to produce a different value per share depending on the size of the holding. It should be stressed that the restrictions under head (ii) must be contained in the Articles. It is not sufficient to impose them under a shareholders' agreement. Restrictions under head (i) need not be contained in the Articles but can be imposed by some outside document.

Any contract, agreement, arrangement or condition by which the employee's freedom to dispose of his shares (or an interest in them, or of the sale proceeds) or to exercise any right conferred by them, or under which a disposal or exercise of rights could result in a disadvantage to the employee (or a connected person of his), must be regarded as a restriction attaching to the shares. [*ITEPA 2003, 3 Schedule 21(4), 4 Schedule 19(4)*]. This does not apply:

(I)   in relation to any terms of a loan covering how the loan is to be repaid or the security to be given for it if the scheme is a CSOP scheme; or

(II) to a restriction on disposal imposed by the Financial Services Authority's Model Code for Securities Transactions by Directors of Listed Companies (the 'yellow book') or by any agreement having the same purpose or effect.

(III) From 6 April 2003 only, to a discretion of the directors under the Articles of Association of the company to refuse to accept a transfer of shares if the directors have undertaken to the Revenue not to exercise it in such a way as to discriminate against persons participating in the scheme and have notified all those who are eligible to participate in the scheme of the existence of the undertaking.

[*ITEPA 2003, 3 Schedule 21(5)–(6), 4 Schedule 19(5)–(7)*].

(*f*)   Unless the grantor company has only one class of shares (or only one class of ordinary shares plus fixed rate preference shares) the majority of the issued shares of the same class as the scheme shares must either be:

(i)   employee-controlled shares, i.e. held by employees or directors (or ex-employees or directors) of the company (or of a company controlled by it) and who (by virtue of their holdings of such shares) are together able to control the company; or

(ii)   open market shares, i.e. held by persons other than:

(A)   directors or employees (or rather, persons who acquired their shares in pursuance of a right conferred on them or an opportunity afforded to them as a director or employee of the grantor or some other company and not in pursuance of an offer to the public);

(B)   trustees of people who acquired their beneficial interest in the shares as directors or employees (within (A) above); and

(C)   in the case of shares which are not of a class listed on a recognised stock exchange but which are in a company which is under the control of a listed company (as defined in b(iii) above), companies which control the grantor company or with which the grantor is associated.

[*ITEPA 2003, 3 Schedule 22, 4 Schedule 20*].

In other words, the company must either be under the control of directors and employees (including former directors and employees) and the scheme shares must be part of the class that gives control, or the class of shares used for the scheme (which does not need to control the company) must be held by a spread of shareholders the majority by value of whom are not, and have not at any time been, directors or employees (with the exception that an employee's shares can be regarded as held by non-employees if he acquired them in pursuance of an offer to the public). Some people contend that the people who set up a company acquire their initial shares not as persons who are to become directors or employees but rather as entrepreneurs. However, the Inland Revenue do not subscribe to this view (*Press Release 26 October 1987*). Accordingly, it would be rare for a company to meet the test in head (ii) unless it is a listed company. Unquoted companies will normally need to satisfy head (i). In approaching this test care needs to be taken. Where a company is formed by two 'partners' it is not uncommon to have two classes of shares, A shares and B shares, with separate but identical rights. It appears that such a structure will result in no class of shares controlling the company so that the test in head (i) could not be met.

(*g*) In the case of a SAYE option scheme it must specify what age is to be the specified age, i.e. the retirement age. This must be between 60 and 75 and must be the same for men and women. [*ITEPA 2003, 3 Schedule 31*]. There is no requirement for a CSOP scheme to specify a retirement age but from 10 July 2003 if it does so it must be the same for men and women and must not be less than 35. [*4 Schedule 35A* inserted by *FA 2003, 21 Schedule 15*].

(*h*) The only people eligible to participate in the scheme at a particular time must be employees or directors of the scheme organiser (or in the case of a group scheme a constituent company) – which can include part-time employees and can also include part-time directors in a SAYE option scheme but not in a CSOP scheme. [*ITEPA 2003, 3 Schedule 10, 4 Schedule 8*]. A CSOP scheme approved before 1 May 1995 had to exclude an employee who was not required under the terms of his employment to work for the company for at least 20 hours a week but this restriction was removed by *FA 1995, s 137(3)*. If such a scheme is altered to extend it to part-time employees that alteration will have effect from the date of that change. [*FA 1995, s 137(7)(8)*]. A full-time director is not defined. The Revenue have indicated that they consider it to mean a director who works for at least 25 hours a week on average. The meaning of 'full-time' is considered in more detail at 6.11. Although an ex-director or ex-employee cannot be granted options under the scheme this does not prevent such a person from exercising an option acquired whilst he was a director or employee. [*9 Schedule 27(1)*]. From 7 January 2003, where a reservist is called up for service under the *Reserve Forces Act 1996* the Revenue will by concession treat the employment with the Ministry of Defence as fulfilling these employment conditions. [*ESC A103*]. The Revenue have asked to be informed (Sahd.Ullah@ir.gsi.gov.uk) when this concession is used.

(*i*) No person with a material interest in a close company which is either the company whose shares may be acquired under the option, a company which has control of such a company or a company which is a member of a consortium which owns a company which in turn has control over such a company (or who had such an interest within the previous 12 months) can be eligible to participate in the scheme. [*ITEPA 2003, 3 Schedule 11(1), 4 Schedule 9(1)*]. An individual has a material interest in a close company for this purpose if he beneficially owns or has the ability to control more than 25% of the ordinary share capital of the company (either directly or through the medium of other companies or by any other indirect means) in the case of a SAYE option scheme or, after 10 July 2003, a CSOP scheme, or more than 10% in the case of an approved CSOP scheme prior to 11 July 2003. He also has a material interest if he owns or is entitled to acquire such rights as would in the event of a winding up of the company or in any other circumstances give an entitlement to receive more than 25% or 10% of the assets as the case may be that would then be available for distribution among the participators (as defined in *ICTA 1988, s 417(1)*). [*ITEPA 2003, 3*

Schedule 12, 4 Schedule 10 as amended by *FA 2003, 21 Schedule 16*, formerly *ICTA 1988, s 187(3)*].

An individual is treated as having a material interest if either he, he together with one or more of his associates (see below) or any such associates (with or without any other associates) does so. A non-UK company which would be close if it were resident in the UK and a quoted company which is not close only because at least 35% of the voting power is held by the public under *ICTA 1988, s 415* must be treated as close companies for this purpose. [*ITEPA 2003, 3 Schedule 11(2)(4), 4 Schedule 9(2)(4)*].

For the purpose of deciding whether a person has a material interest a right to acquires shares, however arising is regarded as a right to control them. If a person would be entitled to subscribe for new shares in the event of his exercise of a right the issued share capital must be treated as increased by that number of shares in applying the 25% of ordinary share capital test at a time prior to their issue. However the interests of the trustees of an approved SIP in any shares held by them in accordance with the plan but which have not been appropriated to, or acquired on behalf of, an individual, and any rights exercisable by the trustees as a result of that interest are ignored. [*ITEPA 2003, 3 Schedule 13, 4 Schedule 11*].

An associate of an individual for the purpose of the material interest test means:

(i) any relative (spouse, parent, child or remoter relation in the direct line, brother or sister) or partner of that individual;

(ii) the trustee or trustees of any settlement in relation to which that individual (or any relative of that individual, living or dead), is or was a settlor; and

(iii) where that individual is interested in any shares or obligations of the company concerned which are subject to any trust, or are part of the estate of a deceased person, the trustees or personal representatives.

[*ITEPA 2003, 3 Schedule 14, 4 Schedule 12*].

For the purpose of (*c*) the trustees of an employee benefit trust are not to be regarded as associates of the individual merely because of the individual being so interested if neither the individual, he and one or more associates (as defined above but excluding an employee benefit trust within this exception) or any associate or associates has at any time after 13 March 1989 been the beneficial owner of (or able, directly or through the medium of other companies or by any other indirect means, to control) more than 25% of the ordinary share capital of the company. Chapter 11 of Part 7 of *ITEPA 2003* which contains further rules about employee benefit trusts applies for this purpose. [*ITEPA 2003, 3 Schedule 15, 4 Schedule 13*]. These rules replicate those in *ICTA 1988, 8 Schedule 7* (see 18.41). Also for the purpose of (iii) if the individual was formerly a beneficiary of a discretionary trust which at any time held shares or obligations of the company concerned but ceased to be a beneficiary, either as a result of an irrevocable disclaimer or release executed by the beneficiary or the irrevocable exercise by the trustees of a power to exclude the beneficiary from the object of the trust, the individual is not regarded as having an interest in shares or obligations of the company held by the trust at any time during the previous 12 months, provided that immediately after he ceased to be a beneficiary no associate of his (as defined above) was interested in those shares or obligations and neither the beneficiary or any associate received any benefit under the trust in the 12 months period. [*ITEPA 2003, 3 Schedule 16, 4 Schedule 14*].

(*j*)   The price at which shares may be acquired on exercise of the option:

(i)   must be stated at the time when the option is granted; and

(ii)   must not be manifestly less than 80% of the market value of shares of the same class at that time in the case of a SAYE option scheme or less than 100% of the value in the case of a CSOP scheme.

The Revenue and the scheme organiser can agree in writing that the not manifestly less test is to be applied by reference to an earlier time or times stated in the agreement. This will enable a value to be agreed with the Revenue in advance of issuing the option. The scheme can (but need not) provide for the option price, the number of shares covered by the option or the description of shares covered by the option to be varied so far as necessary to take account of a variation in the company's share capital, but if it does so it must provide that no such variation is to be made without the prior approval of the Revenue. [*ITEPA 2003, 3 Schedule 28, 4 Schedule 22*].

(*k*)   Share options granted to a participant must not be assignable. [*ITEPA 2003, 3 Schedule 29, 4 Schedule 23*].

(*l*)   A SAYE option scheme must provide that if a participant dies before exercising his option, it can be exercised within 12 months after the date of death if he dies before the bonus date or within 12 months after the bonus date if he dies on or within 12 months after that date. A CSOP scheme does not have to allow an option to be exercised after the individual's death but if it chooses to do so must provide that it must be exercised within 12 months of the death. [*ITEPA 2003, 3 Schedule 32, 4 Schedule 25*].

16.16   Further conditions to be met by SAYE option schemes

(*a*)   The scheme must provide for the scheme shares to be paid for out of the proceeds (including interest and either including or excluding as the participant chooses any bonus, such choice to be made at the time that rights under the option scheme are obtained) of a certified contractual savings scheme which has been approved by the Revenue. [*ITEPA 2003, 3 Schedule 24, 26*].

(*b*)   The rights obtained under the scheme must not be capable of being exercised before the bonus date or more than six months after that date, i.e. the date on which repayments under the certified contractual savings scheme are due. [*ITEPA 2003, 3 Schedule 30*]. Where the proceeds of the scheme are regarded as including the maximum bonus (i.e. where the scheme will continue for at least seven years), the bonus date is the end of seven years. If they are not, it is the earliest date on which any bonus is payable under the scheme (which is the fifth anniversary of the scheme).

(*c*)   The scheme must provide that if an option-holder ceases to hold his office or employment (namely, the one under which he is eligible to participate in the scheme, together with any other office or employment in the grantor company or in any associated company over which the grantor has control [*9 Schedule 23*]) by reason of either:

   (i)   injury, disability, or redundancy within the meaning of the *Employment Rights Act 1996*, or

   (ii) retirement on reaching the age specified in (*f*) below or, for schemes approved before 26 July 1991, pensionable age (or any other age at which he is bound to retire under the terms of his contract of employment)

   the option must be exercised within six months of the employment ceasing (or it must then lapse). [*ITEPA 2003, 3 Schedule 34(2)*].

(*d*)   The scheme must provide that if an option-holder ceases to hold his office or employment for any other reason within three years of having been granted the option, it must lapse. [*ITEPA 2003, 3 Schedule 34(4)*].

   If the cessation is solely because the scheme organiser ceases to have control of the employer company, so that the employment ceases to be an eligible employment (for example, it is with a subsidiary of the grantor which is sold), or it is with a division of a company which is transferred to a person who is not an associated company of (or under the control of) the grantor, the scheme can allow the option to be exercised within six months of the participant ceasing to be an eligible employee. [*ITEPA 2003, 3 Schedule 34(5)*].

   The scheme can also permit an option-holder to exercise his option within six months of the bonus date (see (*b*) above) if at that time he is a director or employee of a company which, although not a participating company, is an associated company of the scheme organiser or a company over which the scheme organiser has control. [*ITEPA 2003, 3 Schedule 36*].

(*e*)   The scheme must provide that if an option-holder ceases to hold his office or employment for any reason (other than those in (*d*) above) more than three years after being granted the option it must either immediately lapse or the option-holder must exercise it, if at all, within six months of the employment ceasing. [*ITEPA 2003, 3 Schedule 34(3)*].

(*f*) The scheme must provide that if the option-holder's employment continues after he reaches a specified age between 60 and 75 which is selected by the employer but which must be the same for men and women or, for schemes approved before 25 July 1991, after he reaches pensionable age, he can nevertheless exercise the option within six months of reaching that age. [*ITEPA 2003, 3 Schedule 31, 33*].

(*g*) The scheme must provide for a person's contributions under the certified contractual savings scheme to be of such amount as to produce (as near as may be) the purchase money for the shares under the option scheme. [*ITEPA 2003, 3 Schedule 25(1)(2)*].

(*h*) The scheme must not permit the aggregate amount of a person's contributions under all contractual savings schemes linked to approved savings-related share option schemes (with the same or other employees) to exceed £250 per month and if it imposes a minimum on the amount of a person's contributions this must not exceed £10 per month. The Treasury have power to amend these figures. [*ITEPA 2003, 3 Schedule 25(3), (4)*].

(*i*) Every person who has been an employee (whether full or part-time) or full-time director of the grantor or other participating companies (other than one having a material interest in the company if it is close) for a qualifying period (which can be determined by the grantor but must not exceed five years) and who is taxable on his remuneration as a person who is resident and ordinarily resident in the UK, must be eligible to be granted options (and to exercise them) on similar terms. Part-time employees could be excluded from participating in schemes which were approved before 1 May 1995 but this was prohibited by *FA 1995, s 137(2)(7)*. All those who actually participate in the scheme must in fact do so on similar terms. [*ITEPA 2003, 3 Schedule 7(1)*]. It is permissible to determine the number of shares over which a person is to be granted options by reference to levels of remuneration, length of service or similar factors. [*ITEPA 2003, 3 Schedule 7(2)*].

(*j*) A person must not be eligible to participate in the scheme at any time (except as permitted by (*d*)–(*f*) above) unless at that time he is a director or employee of the grantor or another participating company. [*ITEPA 2003, 3 Schedule 10(1)*].

(*k*) There must be no features of the scheme (other than those required by any of the above conditions) which have the effect of discouraging any description of employees or former employees who fulfil the conditions in (*m*) above from actually participating in the scheme. [*3 Schedule 6*].

(*l*) If the grantor is a member of a group of companies, the scheme must not have the effect of conferring benefits wholly or mainly on directors of companies in the group or on those employees of companies in the group who are in receipt of the higher or highest levels of remuneration. [*3 Schedule 8*]. This would prevent, for example, the inclusion in the scheme only of companies with higher-paid employees or the exclusion as a participating company of a subsidiary with a large number of lower-paid employees. There is no definition of higher or highest levels of remuneration. This is presumably a question of fact to be determined by reference to each individual group of companies.

16.17   Further conditions to be met by CSOP schemes. The scheme must provide that the aggregate market value of the shares over which a participant has options under the scheme (and any other executive share option scheme established by the grantor or by any associated company of the grantor) at the time the option is granted must not exceed £30,000.

16.18   If desired a CSOP scheme can allow an individual to exercise his share options after ceasing to be a full-time director or employee. [*ITEPA 2003, 4 Schedule 24*]. There is no time limit for doing so but the exercise will not attract tax benefits unless it falls within 16.11(iii).

Exchange of options

16.19   Both a SAYE option scheme and a CSOP scheme can provide that if a company either:

(i)   obtains control of the grantor company as a result of making a general offer:

   (A)   to acquire the whole of the issued ordinary share capital of the company (and the offer is made on a condition that if satisfied would give the offeror control of the company); or

   (B)   to acquire all of the shares of the same class as the scheme shares; or

(ii)   obtains control of the grantor company in pursuance of a compromise or arrangement sanctioned by the courts under *section 425* of the *Companies Act 1985*; or

(iii)   becomes bound or entitled to acquire shares in the grantor company under *Companies Act 1985, ss 428–430*,

a participant may release his option under the scheme ('the old rights') in consideration of the grant to him of an option relating to shares in a different company (which can either be the acquiring company or a company which controls it or a consortium company within head (*a*)(iii) of 16.15 above) ('the new rights'). [*ITEPA 2003, 3 Schedule 38(1)(2), 39(2), 4 Schedule 26(1)(2), 27(2)*].

The new option must be equivalent to the old; in particular:

(I)   the new option shares must satisfy the conditions in heads (*c*)–(*f*) in 16.15 above;

(II) the new rights must be exercisable in the same manner as the old rights, and subject to the provisions of the scheme as it had effect immediately before the release of the old;

(III) the total market value immediately before the release of the old rights of the option shares must be equal to the total market value immediately after the grant of the new rights of the new option shares; and

(IV) the total amount payable to acquire the shares under the new option must be the same as was payable to acquire shares under the old.

[*ITEPA 2003, 3 Schedule 39(4), 4 Schedule 27(4)*].

The exchange of options must take place within six months from the time that the person making the offer obtains control of the company (and any condition subject to which the offer was made is satisfied). In the case of an arrangement under the *Companies Act 1985, s 425* it must take place within six months of the court approving the compromise or arrangement; and in the case of an acquisition under *Companies Act 1985, ss 428–430* within the period during which the company is bound or entitled to acquire the shares. [*ITEPA 2003, 3 Schedule 38(3), 4 Schedule 26(3)*].

The new option is regarded as having been granted at the time the corresponding old option was granted. [*ITEPA 2003, 3 Schedule 39(5)(6), 4 Schedule 27(5)(6)*].

16.20   In the case of an SAYE option scheme (but not a CSOP scheme) If it is wished, the scheme can provide that:

(i) if any person obtains control of the grantor company as a result of a general offer falling within head (*q*)(i) above, the options can be exercised within six months of the time that he does so (and any condition subject to which the offer was made is satisfied);

(ii) if the court sanctions an arrangement under *section 425* of the *Companies Act 1985* in connection with a scheme for the reconstruction of the grantor company or its amalgamation with any other company, the options can be exercised within six months of the court sanctioning the compromise;

(iii) if any person becomes bound or entitled under *Companies Act 1985, ss 428–430* to acquire shares in the grantor company, the options can be exercised at any time during the period that person remains bound or entitled to acquire shares; and

(iv) if the grantor company passes a resolution for voluntary winding up, the options can be exercised at any time within six months of the passing of the resolution.

[*ITEPA 2003, 3 Schedule 37*].

In the event of a takeover, the option-holder can be given a choice to exchange his option for a new option in the acquiring company (under the above provision), to exercise his option prematurely to enable him to accept the offer in relation to the shares, (see 16.16(*d*) above) or to do nothing and exercise the option when it would otherwise be exercisable (although in practice the terms of the takeover are likely to require the options to be cancelled if they are not immediately either exercised or exchanged). Although the exercise of the option, either in due course or prematurely, can be permitted by the scheme such an exercise will not normally attract the tax benefits expected from the use of an approved scheme as the shares will not usually qualify as eligible shares. An exchange of options will preserve the tax benefits.

16.21 Procedure for approval

The Revenue have to approve a SAYE option scheme or a CSOP scheme if the scheme organiser applies for approval and the scheme fulfils the necessary requirements. [*ITEPA 2003, 3 Schedule 40(1), 4 Schedule 28(1)*]. In practice, the Revenue scrutinise such schemes vigorously and will try to insist on amendments to meet their own internal requirements even if the document satisfies the statutory requirements. An application for approval must be made in writing and contain such particulars and be supported by such evidence as the Revenue may require. [*ITEPA 2003, 3 Schedule 40(2), 4 Schedule 28(2)*]. A scheme can be expressed to extend to all or any subsidiaries of the company setting up the scheme (or other companies of which it has control). [*ITEPA 2003, 3 Schedule 3, 4 Schedule 3*].

16.22 Each joint owner of a jointly owned company can include that company (and any company controlled by it) in its own group scheme. A jointly owned company for this purpose is one of which 50% of the issued share capital is owned by one person and 50% by another, or which is otherwise controlled by two persons taken together. Each joint owner is treated as controlling the jointly owned company (and any company controlled by it). A company cannot however be a constituent company in more than one group scheme. Nor can it be a constituent company in a particular group scheme if another company in the jointly owned group is a constituent company of another scheme. Accordingly once one of the companies in the jointly owned group becomes a member of the group scheme of one of joint owners, no other company in that group can join the group scheme of the other joint owner. [*ITEPA 2003, 3. Schedule 46, 4 Schedule 34* enacting *ESC B27*].

16.23 All the companies covered by a scheme are referred to as constituent (formerly participating) companies and such a scheme is called a group scheme.

Prohibited features

16.24 The Revenue are prohibited from approving a scheme if in their view it contains any features which are not essential to the purpose of providing for directors and employees rights to acquire shares, or which are not reasonably incidental to that purpose. [*ITEPA 2003, 3 Schedule 5, 4 Schedule 5*].

16.25   In *IRC v Burton Group plc [1990] STC 242* an option scheme incorporated tasks which the employee had to meet before he became entitled to acquire shares. The company wished to amend the scheme to ensure that it operated effectively as an incentive scheme by enabling it to vary such tasks after an option had been granted. The Revenue refused to approve the change. They contended that for an employee to 'have obtained a right to acquire shares' the machinery by which his entitlement to them could be identified must be known at the time the option is granted. They also claimed that the amendment was neither essential nor reasonably incidental to the purpose of providing share benefits. Both these claims were dismissed in the High Court. The new conditions did not affect the number of shares the employee could acquire and there was no objection to the requirement that he should meet subsequently imposed conditions. On the second point, the scheme has to be looked at as a whole. The changes were designed to ensure that the scheme worked more effectively. Accordingly, the Revenue would not refuse approval for the amendments.

16.26   Applications for approval should be sent to:

Employee Share Schemes Team, Room 76, New Wing, Somerset House, Strand, London WC2R 1LB. Tel: 0207 438 7438

Approval of draft proposal

16.27   In practice, it is normally wise to send a draft of a proposed scheme for approval. The Inland Revenue are likely to suggest (or sometimes demand) changes before they are willing to approve a document. Once the wording has been agreed the scheme can then be formally adopted by the company and formal approval sought from the Revenue. Approval is not granted retrospectively. Options issued prior to formal approval of the scheme cannot benefit from the favourable tax treatment that approval attracts.

Withdrawal of approval

16.28   The Revenue have power to withdraw approval if an alteration is made in a key feature of the scheme (one necessary to meet the requirements of this *Act*) without Revenue approval and the Revenue would not approve the change if it were a new scheme or the company refuses to provide information requested by the Revenue under *3 Schedule 45* or *4 Schedule 33* (see 16.34 below). Such withdrawal can be retrospective to the date that the conditions cease to be met or from any later date that the Revenue may choose. [*ITEPA 2003, 3 Schedule 42(1)(2), 4 Schedule 30*].

16.29   If approval of a SAYE option scheme (but not a CSOP scheme) is withdrawn, the tax benefits are preserved in relation to options granted before the withdrawal. [*ITEPA 2003, 3 Schedule 42(3)*].

16.30   The Revenue could withdraw approval of a profit sharing scheme (see 16.34 below) if at any time:

(*a*)   any participant was in breach of his obligations under *9 Schedule 2(2)(a)(c)(d)* (see 16.63(*l*));

(*b*)   any contravention of any of the relevant requirements in *Schedule 10*, the scheme itself, or the terms of the trust, took place;

(*c*)   any shares of a class of which shares had been appropriated to participants received different treatment in any respect from any other shares of that class, particularly in relation to:

    (i)   the dividend payable (which would seem to include one holder waiving his dividend);

    (ii)   repayments (as the shares cannot be redeemable shares this presumably meant repayment on a winding up);

    (iii)   the restrictions attaching to the shares; or

    (iv)   any offer of substituted or additional shares (or securities or rights of any description) in respect of the shares;

(*d*)   the Revenue ceasing to be satisfied that the scheme complied with *9 Schedule 2(3)* (see heads (*m*) and (*n*) at 16.63 above) or *9 Schedule 36* (see head (*j*) at 16.63 above); or

(*e*)   the trustees or the grantor (or another participating company) failing to furnish any information which they were required to furnish under *9 Schedule 6* (see 16.34) [*9 Schedule 3(2)*];

(*f*)   the trustees appropriating shares to a participant who has had free shares awarded to him at an earlier time in the same year of assessment under a SIP (see Chapter 15) established by the grantor company or a connected company (or would have done so but for his failure to meet a performance target (see 15.23);

(*g*)   the Revenue ceasing to be satisfied that the arrangements for the scheme prohibited loans to employees within *9 Schedule 2 (2A)* (see 16.62(*q*)). [*9 Schedule 3(2)*].

For the purpose of (*f*) above a connected company was one which controlled the grantor company; one which was controlled by the grantor company or by a company which also controlled the grantor company; or one which was a member of a consortium which either owned the grantor or of which the grantor was one of its part owners. [*9 Schedule 3(6)*].

16.31   The Revenue had discretion as to whether to withdraw approval with effect from the time of the trigger event or from a later date. They could not, however, withdraw approval merely because shares which have been newly issued receive a lesser dividend than shares issued earlier in respect of a period beginning before the date of their issue. [*9 Schedule 3(3)*].

Alterations to scheme

16.32   If the scheme is altered in any way after approval, the approval lapses from the date of the change unless the alteration is approved by the Revenue. [*ITEPA 2003, 3 Schedule 43, 4 Schedule 31*]. It is not clear if the Revenue have power to approve an alteration retrospectively. In any event, it is obviously wise to seek approval for an alteration before putting it into effect.

Right of appeal

16.33 The company has a right of appeal if the Revenue do not approve a scheme or an alteration to a scheme or withdraw approval (or in the case of a savings-related share option scheme, decide that a condition subject to which approval was given is satisfied). This appeal is to the Special Commissioners and must be made within 30 days of the company being informed of the Revenue's decision. [*ITEPA 2003, 3 Schedule 41, 44, 4 Schedule 29, 32*].

In *IRC v Eurocopy plc [1991] STC 707*, the court upheld the Revenue's refusal to allow the application to existing options of an alteration that reduced the period before which options could be exercised from nine to six years. The Revenue's stance was based on the fact that the rights attaching to the options prior to the alteration were not the same as the rights attaching to them after it. The Eurocopy decision was distinguished in *IRC v Reed International plc 67 TC 552*. Before the alteration an option-holder would have had to exercise his option within six months of the merger of Reed and Elsevier NV, albeit that such a merger had not been in contemplation when the option was granted. The alteration removed that as a trigger. The Court of Appeal felt that the removal of one out of ten or eleven events on the earliest of which an existing right would be exercisable could not realistically be described as the obtaining of a new and different right to acquire shares (as could the bringing forward of the exercise date in *Eurocopy*); it was simply a variation of an existing right.

Information

16.34 The Revenue can require any person to supply such information as the Revenue consider is necessary in connection with the approval (or continuing approval) of a scheme. They must allow him at least 3 months (30 days prior to 6 April 2003) to provide the information. The information they can request includes that necessary to determine whether to withdraw approval of a scheme, to determine the liability to tax of any participant in the scheme, and to monitor the administration of the scheme and any alteration to it. [*ITEPA 2003, 3 Schedule 45, 4 Schedule 33*].

Approved profit-sharing scheme (up to 1 January 2003)

16.35 It was possible to set up approved profit sharing schemes between 5 April 1999 and 31 December 2002. An approved profit sharing scheme was actually something of a misnomer as there is no requirement that the benefits should be related to profits. The company set up a trust to which it allocated money which the trustees used to subscribe for shares in the company (or to buy such shares on the open market). Immediately on acquisition of the shares, the trustees had to allocate them among participating employees, whilst retaining ownership of the shares.

Drawbacks of the schemes

16.36   Such schemes had a number of drawbacks. All full-time, UK resident employees with at least five years' service had to have a right to participate in the scheme and those who opted to participate had to do so on equal terms. Accordingly, it was not an appropriate vehicle to provide incentives to senior executives. All employees (other than any who opted to be excluded) had to be allotted shares each time a batch was acquired. The value of shares that could be allotted to any one individual in a year of assessment could not exceed £8,000, so the benefit that could be provided was limited.

16.37   The trustees normally had to retain the shares for at least three years, so the scheme really provided a future benefit rather than an immediate one. A disposal prior to the third anniversary trigger a tax charge, normally on 100 per cent of the value of the shares at the time of acquisition (see 16.43).

Tax benefits of the schemes

16.38   The tax benefits of such schemes derived from the fact that when the trustees of an approved profit sharing scheme appropriated to a participant in the scheme shares which had previously been acquired by the trustees (and as to which the qualifying conditions of *Schedule 9* were met):

(*a*)   the value of the shares at the time of appropriation was not treated as employment income of the individual (even though the beneficial interest in the shares passed to him) provided that such appropriation was made before 6 April 2002; and

(*b*)   the individual was not taxed under *FA 1988, ss 78, 79* (see 14.158 and 14.166 above) or by virtue of *ICTA 1988, s 162(1)–(5)* (see 14.141 above) in respect of the shares.

[*ICTA 1988, s 186(1)(2)*].

Capital receipt before release date

16.39   If either the trustees or the participant (i.e. the individual to whom shares were appropriated) became entitled before the release date (see 16.66 below) to receive any money or money's worth ('a capital receipt') in respect of any of a participant's shares, the participant was taxable on employment income for the year of assessment in which such entitlement arose on the 'appropriate percentage' of so much of the receipt as exceeded the 'appropriate allowance' for that year. [*ICTA 1988, s 186(3)*].

Meaning of 'appropriate allowance'

16.40 The appropriate allowance was £20 multiplied by one plus the number of years of assessment between the time of the appropriation of the shares and the start of the year of assessment in which the capital receipt arises. [*ICTA 1988, s 186(12)*]. It could not, however, exceed £60 (£100 prior to 1997/98). If the trustees or the participant became entitled to more than one capital receipt in any year of assessment (and before the release date) the appropriate allowance was set against them in the order in which they were received. [*ICTA 1988, s 186(12)*].

Items not regarded as capital receipts

16.41 Money or money's worth was not to be regarded as a capital receipt for this purpose to the extent that either:

(*a*)   it constituted income of the recipient for income tax purposes;

(*b*)   it consisted of the proceeds of a disposal falling with *ICTA 1988, s 186(4)* (see 16.43 below);

(*c*)   it consisted of new shares within *10 Schedule 5* (see 16.51 below) [*10 Schedule 4(1)(a)–(c)*];

(*d*)   it was the proceeds of disposal of some of the rights arising under a rights issue (provided that the disposal was pursuant to a direction given to the trustees by the participant or any other person in whom the participant's beneficial interest in the shares vested) [*10 Schedule 4(2)*]; or

(*e*)   the entitlement to the receipt arose after the death of the participant. [*10 Schedule 4(4)*].

16.42 If the amount of a capital receipt exceeded the locked-in value of the shares (see 16.43 below) immediately before the entitlement to the receipt arose, the charge under *section 186(3)* was limited to tax on the locked-in value. [*10 Schedule 4(3)*].

Disposal before release date

16.43 If the trustees disposed of any of a participant's shares at any time before the release date (or, if earlier, the date of the participant's death) the participant was taxable on employment income, for the year of assessment in which the disposal occurred, on the appropriate percentage of the locked-in value of the shares at the time of disposal. [*Section 186(4)*]. The locked-in value was normally the initial market value of the shares. If the participant had previously been taxed under *section 186(3)* in relation to a capital receipt from the shares, it was the initial market value less the amount of that receipt (or aggregate receipts). [*Section 186(5)*]. If the locked-in value exceeded the disposal proceeds of the shares the locked-in value had to be treated as being equal to the proceeds. [*Section 186(6)*]. The release date was the third anniversary of the date on which the shares were appropriated to the employee. [*Section 187(2)*]. The appropriate percentage was 100 per cent except where the employee has reached retirement age, been made redundant or left because of injury or disability, when it was 50 per cent. [*10 Schedule 3*].

16.44   If the disposal was made out of a holding of shares which were appropriated to the participant at different times, the shares were deemed to be disposed of in the order of acquisition (i.e. on a first in, first out basis) for the purpose of determining the initial market value, the locked-in value, and the appropriate percentage in relation to the shares. [*Section 186(8)*].

16.45   This assumption applied even if the different acquisitions and disposals were identifiable (by reference to numbered share certificates, for example) or the participant specified to the trustees that they were to dispose of shares appropriated to him at a particular time. [*Section 186(9)*].

Payment for rights

16.46   If at any time prior to the disposal a payment was made to the trustees to enable them to take up rights on a rights issue, the proceeds of disposal first had to be reduced by an amount equal to the proportion of that rights payment (or of the aggregate of all such payments if more than one) which the market value of the shares immediately before the disposal bore to the market value of all the participant's shares held by the trustees at that time. [*Section 186(7)*]. In other words, if the participant (or, indeed, anyone else) had previously made a payment to the trustees to enable them to take up a rights issue, that payment was, not unnaturally, deducted in arriving at the taxable amount.

16.47   However, a payment that was previously made to the trustees from, say, stockbrokers arising from a sale of rights, for example, where some of the rights were sold to provide funds to take up the rest, obviously could not be deducted from the disposal proceeds of the shares as it was not an extraneous sum but derived from those shares. [*Section 186(8)(a)*]. If there have been earlier share disposals any amount deducted from those proceeds clearly could not be deducted again. [*Section 186(8)(b)*].

Disposal of beneficial interest

16.48   If the participant's beneficial interest in any of his shares was disposed of, *section 186(4)* (see 16.43 above) applied as if the shares themselves had been disposed of by the trustees for the consideration that was received on the disposal of the beneficial interest. The vesting of the beneficial interest on the insolvency of the participant or by operation of law did not trigger this tax charge, however. [*Section 186(9)*].

16.49 If the disposal by the trustees was a transfer of shares (before the release date) to the participant himself, or the Board of Inland Revenue considered that the disposal was not at arm's length, or the disposal was a disposal of the beneficial interest only and took place within the period of retention, the income tax charge had to be calculated by reference to the market value of the shares at the time of the disposal, not the disposal proceeds. [*Section 186(10)*].

Additional rate tax

16.50 Provided that the trustees of an approved scheme appropriated qualifying shares in accordance with the scheme within 18 months from the date of their acquisition, the 34 per cent tax rate applicable to trusts that applies to discretionary and accumulation trusts [*section 686*] was not payable on dividends from the shares. Shares were deemed to be appropriated to participants on a first in, first out basis. [*Section 186(11)*].

Company reconstructions

16.51 If the participant's shares were disposed of on a reconstruction or amalgamation that qualified as a company reconstruction for capital gains tax purposes, any part of the new holding (i.e. the new shares received in exchange for (or in addition to) the old) which consisted of:

(*a*) redeemable shares or securities issued otherwise than wholly for new consideration (e.g. as a scrip issue);

(*b*) a scrip issue of shares where the company previously repaid any share capital since 6 April 1965; or

(*c*) share capital which was taxed as a stock dividend,

were not to be treated as forming part of the new holding. [*10 Schedule 5(1)(2)*]. In each of the above circumstances the value of the shares was already taxed as income under other provisions (under (*a*) or (*b*) it was a distribution and under (*c*) taxable under *section 249*). This provision accordingly prevented double taxation. By taking the shares out of the new holding their value became a capital receipt—but one that was excluded from tax under *10 Schedule 4* (see 16.41 above).

16.52 A company reconstruction was not treated as involving a disposal of the original holding, but the new shares received on the reconstruction had to be treated as having been appropriated to the participant at the time the old shares were appropriated. Provided that the conditions in *9 Schedule 10–12, 14* (see 16.15) were fulfilled with respect to the old shares, they were treated as also being fulfilled with respect to the new. [*10 Schedule 5(4)*].

Market value of shares after reconstruction

16.53 *Section 186(5)* (see 16.43 above) applied to the new holding as if the initial market value of the shares were equal to their locked-in value immediately after the reconstruction. This was arrived at as follows.

(*a*) Ascertain the aggregate amount of locked-in value (immediately before the reconstruction) of those shares comprised in the original holding which at the time had the same locked-in value.

(*b*) Distribute that amount among:

  (i) such of the original shares as are retained as part of the new holding; and

  (ii) the new shares received on the reconstruction,

in proportion to their market values immediately after the date of the reconstruction. [*10 Schedule 5(5)*]. *Section 186(5)(a)* then applied only to capital receipts after the date of the reconstruction.

Capital receipt on reconstruction

16.54 If, as part of the reconstruction, the trustees became entitled to a capital receipt (e.g. there was a cash payment to shareholders), that receipt was treated as having arisen before the new holding came into being and before the date on which the locked-in value of shares comprised in the original holding fell to be ascertained. [*10 Schedule 5(6)*]. In the context of a new holding, references in *10 Schedule 5* to shares included securities and rights of any description (e.g. warrants) which formed part of the new holding. [*10 Schedule 5(7)*].

16.55 The rules in paragraphs 16.51–16.54 also applied where qualifying corporate bonds were received on a reconstruction, provided that the trust deed had been altered to prohibit the trustees from disposing of the bonds in such circumstances in accordance with *9 Schedule 33(a)* (see 16.63(*f*)). [*10 Schedule 5A* and *FA 1994, s 101(4)–(13)*].

Value of shares exceeding relevant amount

16.56 If the total amount of the initial market value (see head (*b*) at 16.63 below) of all the shares appropriated to an individual in a year of assessment (whether under one or more approved schemes) exceeded the relevant amount:

(*a*) the appropriate percentage (see head (*l*) at 16.63 below) in relation to the excess shares (see 16.57 below) for the purpose of any charge to income tax by reason of the occurrence of an event relating to the shares was 100 per cent (and the event had to be treated as relating to shares which were not excess shares in priority to those that were) [*10 Schedule 6(4)*];

(*b*)   excess shares that had not been disposed of before the release date (or, if earlier, the death of the participant) had to be treated as disposed of by the trustees immediately before that date at their market value—so as to trigger on income tax charge on 100 per cent of that value [*10 Schedule 6(5)*]; and

(*c*)   the locked-in value of the excess shares at any time was their market value at that time. [*10 Schedule 6(6)*].

Meaning of 'excess shares'

16.57   For this purpose the 'excess shares' were the shares which caused the relevant amount to be exceeded and any further shares appropriated subsequently. [*10 Schedule 6(2)*]. If shares were appropriated to an individual at the same time under two or more schemes the excess shares were treated as coming rateably from both schemes. [*10 Schedule 6(3)*]. Where there had been a company reconstruction a new share received on the reconstruction had to be treated as an excess share if the original share from which it derived was an excess share. [*10 Schedule 6(7)*].

16.58   If the trustees appropriated shares to an individual at a time when he was ineligible to participate in the scheme those 'unauthorised shares' were taxed in the same way as described above in relation to excess shares. [*10 Schedule 6(1)(b)*].

PAYE deductions

16.59   If the trustees received a sum of money which constituted (or formed part of) either:

(*a*)   the proceeds of a disposal of shares falling within *section 186(4)* (see 16.43 above); or

(*b*)   a capital receipt (see 16.39 above),

in respect of which a participant was taxable on employment income by virtue of *section 186*, they had to pay that money not to the participant but to the employer company. If he was employed by more than one company, both of which were participants in the scheme, they had to pay it to such of the companies as the Revenue directed. The company had to deduct tax under PAYE and pay the balance to the participant. [*10 Schedule 7(1)(3)*]. If at the time the trustees received the money there was no company which both employed the individual and was a participant in the scheme, or if the Revenue considered it impractical to require the employer company to make a PAYE deduction and directed the trustees to do so, the trustees themselves had to deduct tax under PAYE when paying the money to the participant. For this purpose the participant was treated as if he were a former employee of the trustees, so the PAYE deduction was made at the basic rate. [*10 Schedule 7(4)*]. The Revenue were empowered to direct the trustees to pay the capital sum to any company that they specified (e.g. the participant's current employer) even though that company may have had nothing to do with the scheme, in which case that company had to apply PAYE when paying the amount over to the employee. However, such a direction required the consent of the trustees, all the employer company or companies that were participants in the scheme (if any), and the company on which the Revenue wished to impose the obligation to deduct PAYE. [*10 Schedule 7(5)*]. The *PAYE Regulations* obviously applied to the payment as if it were remuneration. [*10 Schedule 7(6)*].

16.60   If a participant disposed of his beneficial interest in his shares to the trustees, so that there was a deemed disposal by the trustees under *section 186(9)* (see 16.45 above) the amount had to be subjected to PAYE in the same way as on an actual disposal by the trustees. [*10 Schedule 7(2)*]. If the participant directed the trustees to transfer the shares to himself before the release date, and therefore had to make a payment to them of tax at the basic rate on the appropriate percentage of the locked-in value (see 16.43 above), that amount had to be accounted for by the trustee as if it were an amount deducted under PAYE in respect of the disposal proceeds of the shares. [*10 Schedule 7(7)*].

16.61   In determining the amount on which PAYE was payable the trustees could ignore the fact that some of the shares might be excess shares unless the Revenue otherwise directed. [*10 Schedule 7(8)*]. The trustees would not necessarily know that they were excess shares. This accordingly relieved them of the obligation to account for tax on a higher amount than, on the face of things, appeared due.

16.62   A profit sharing scheme had to satisfy the conditions for approval set out at 16.16(*a*)–(*f*) with the modifications that:

(*a*)   head (*d*) did not apply to a scheme set up by a workers' co-operative, A workers' co-operative was a registered industrial and provident society (within *section 486*) which is a co-operative society whose rules include provisions to ensure that its members are limited to either employees of the grantor company or its subsidiaries and trustees of its profit sharing scheme, and that all such persons can join the society (subject to qualifications by reference to age, length of service or other factors) [*section 187(10)*].

(*b*)   the permitted restrictions under head (*e*) could not be framed so as to require a person to dispose of his beneficial interest in shares before the release date if the ownership of the shares had not been transferred to him at that stage (*9 Schedule 12(4)*);

(*c*)   head (I) in (*e*) also applied to an approved profit sharing scheme; and

(*d*)   the tests in (*f*) were applied at the time the trustees acquired the shares, not the time the shares were appropriated to employees.

16.63   In addition a profit sharing scheme had to satisfy a number of further conditions.

(*a*)   The scheme had to provide for the establishment of a UK resident trust (the terms of which were embodied in a trust deed which complies with the conditions set out below), the trustees of which were required by the scheme to acquire shares in respect of which the conditions in 16.46 above were fulfilled out of moneys paid to them by the grantor (or another participating company), and who were under a duty to appropriate the shares acquired by them to eligible individuals who were participants in the scheme. [*9 Schedule 9(1), 30(1)*].

(b) The scheme had to provide that the market value (at the time of appropriation or such earlier date as the trustees may have agreed with the Revenue) of the shares appropriated to any one individual in a year of assessment (the initial market value) did not exceed 10 per cent of the employee's salary (i.e. such of the emoluments of his employment as were subject to PAYE) for the year of assessment (or, if higher, the previous year) subject to a maximum of £8,000 (where the salary exceeds £80,000) and a minimum of £3,000 (where it was less than £30,000). [*Section 187(2)(5), 9 Schedule 30(3)*]. Prior to 1991/92, the maximum and minimum were lower: £5,000 and £1,250 from 1983/84 to 1988/89 and £6,000 and £2,000 for 1989/90 and 1990/91.

(c) The trust deed had to provide that as soon as practicable after an appropriation of shares the trustees would tell the participant the number and description of the shares and the value used for the purpose of the appropriation. [*9 Schedule 31*].

(d) The trust deed had to prohibit the trustees from disposing of any shares (even to the participant) during the period of retention (see head (*l*) below) except as permitted by *10 Schedule 1(1)(a)–(c)*. [*9 Schedule 32(1)*].

(e) The deed had to prohibit the trustees from disposing of the shares between the end of the period of retention and the release date except

  (i) in accordance with a direction given by (or on behalf of) the participant or any other person in whom the beneficial interest in the participant's shares were vested, and

  (ii) by a transaction which did not involve a breach of the participant's obligations under head (*l*) below.

(f) The deed had to require the trustees to pay to the participant any money or money's worth received by them in relation to the shares, unless that amount consisted of new shares (see 16.51 above), or a payment prohibited by *10 Schedule 7* (see 16.59 above), or *10 Schedule 4(2)* (see 16.41 above). [*9 Schedule 33(a)*].

(g) The deed had to require the trustees to deal with rights arising under a scrip or rights issue in relation to the shares only in accordance with a direction given by the participant (or other beneficial owner of the participant's interest in the shares). [*9 Schedule 33(b)*].

(h) The deed had to impose an obligation on the trustees to maintain such records as were necessary to comply with their obligation to apply PAYE, and to inform the participant of such facts as were relevant to determine the amount of any income tax liability which arose under the scheme. [*9 Schedule 34*].

(*j*)   Every person who was an employer or full-time director of the grantor or of another participating company (other than one with a material interest in the company, if it is close) who was taxable on his remuneration as a person who was resident and ordinarily resident in the UK and had been a director or employee throughout a qualifying period (which was fixed by the company but could not exceed five years) had to be eligible to participate in the scheme on similar terms. [*9 Schedule 36(1)*]. Furthermore, those that did participate actually had to do so on similar terms. Schemes approved before 1 May 1995 could exclude part-time employees but this was prohibited by *FA 1995, s 137(4)(7)*.

[*9 Schedule 36(2)*].

(*k*)   An individual was not eligible to have shares appropriated to him at a particular time if either:

   (i)   he was not then a director or employee of the grantor or a participating company (unless he was one at some time during the preceding 18 months); or

   (ii)   shares had been appropriated to him in the same year of assessment under another approved scheme established by either:

      (A)   the grantor;

      (B)   a company which controlled the grantor, was controlled by the grantor, or was under common control with the grantor;

      (C)   a member of a consortium which owned the grantor; or

      (D)   a company which was owned by a consortium one of the members of which was the grantor.

[*9 Schedule 35*].

(*l*)   Every participant in the scheme had to be contractually bound with the grantor:

   (i)   to permit his shares to remain in the hands of the trustees throughout the period of retention;

   (ii)   not to assign, charge or otherwise dispose of his beneficial interest in his shares during the period of retention (if this undertaking was breached the participant was treated as if he were ineligible to participate in the scheme at the time of appropriation [*10 Schedule 1*];

   (iii)   to pay to the trustees (before the transfer) a sum equal to basic rate tax on the appropriate percentage of the then locked-in value of the shares if he directed the trustees to transfer the shares to him before the release date [*10 Schedule 1(2)*]; and

(iv)   not to direct the trustees to dispose of his shares before the release date (other than to himself) except by a sale for the best consideration in money that could reasonably be obtained at the time of sale (or in the case of redeemable shares in a workers' co-operative (see 16.72 below) by redemption).

[9 Schedule 2(2)].

Provided that the contractual arrangement with the grantor allowed it, these prohibitions did not prevent the participant from:

(A)   directing the trustees to accept an offer for his shares by way of a share exchange which is treated as a reorganisation of capital for capital gains tax purposes;

(B)   directing the trustees to agree to participate in a compromise, arrangement or scheme affecting all the ordinary share capital of either the company or the class of shares of which the scheme shares formed part (or affecting all of such shares as were held by a class of shareholders which is identified otherwise than by reference to their employment or their participation in an approved scheme);

(C)   directing the trustees to accept an offer of cash or of qualifying corporate bonds (within *TCGA 1992, s 117*) for the shares (with or without other assets) which formed part of a general offer made to the holders of shares of the class and which was made (in the first instance) on terms that, if satisfied, would leave the offerer controlling the company; or

(D)   agreeing after the end of the period of retention to sell the beneficial interest in the shares back to the trustees for the same consideration [*9 Schedule 2(2)(b)*] as would be required for a sale of the shares themselves. [*10 Schedule 1(1)*].

The 'period of retention' was the period of two years from the date the shares were appropriated to a participant. It however, terminated on the first occasion during that period when the participant either:

   (I)   ceased to be a director or employee of the grantor and/or all other participating companies by reason of either:

      (1)   injury or disability, or

      (2)   being dismissed by reason of redundancy (within the meaning of the *Employment Protection (Consolidation) Act 1978*); or

  (II)   reached pensionable age (under the *Social Security Contributions and Benefits Act 1992, s 122(1)*); or

 (III)   died; or

 (IV)   ceased to be employed (for any reason) by (or by a subsidiary of) the co-operative if the scheme shares were redeemable shares in a workers' co-operative. [*10 Schedule 2*].

The 'appropriate percentage' was

50% — if the trigger event occurred by the participant ceasing to be a director or employee by reason of injury, disability or redundancy (within (I)(2) above) or reaching the relevant age.

100% — in any other case.

[*10 Schedule 3*].

Where the trigger event occurred before 29 April 1996 the appropriate percentage depended on when that event occurred, namely

100% — if the triggering event occurs within four years of the date of appropriation.

75% — if the triggering event occurs in the fifth year following the appropriation.

50% — (instead of the above) if the trigger event occurs before the fifth anniversary by the participant ceasing to be a director or employee by reason of injury or disability or of redundancy (within (I)(2) above) or reaching the relevant age.

[*10 Schedule 3*].

For schemes approved after 25 July 1991, the relevant age in (II) above was the age specified in the scheme as retirement age for the purpose of *9 Schedule 8A* (see 16.15(*g*)). For schemes approved before that date it was pensionable age under the *Social Security Contributions and Benefits Act 1992, s 122(1)* and *Pensions Act 1995, 4 Sch*, i.e. 65 for men and 60 for women, unless the scheme defined the period of retention by reference to the age of 60 for both men and women. [*10 Schedule 3A* and *FA 1994, s 100(3)*].

(*m*)   The scheme could not contain features (other than those required by any of the above conditions) which had the effect of discouraging any description of employees or former employees who fulfilled the conditions in (*j*) above, from actually participating in the scheme. [*9 Schedule 2(3)(a)*].

(*n*)   If the grantor was a member of a group of companies (i.e. a company and other companies of which it had control), the scheme could not have the effect of conferring benefits wholly or mainly on directors of companies in the group or on those employees of companies in the group who were in receipt of the highest levels of remuneration. [*9 Schedule 2(3)(b), (4)*]. This prevented, for example, the inclusion in the scheme only of companies with higher-paid employees or the exclusion as a participating company of a subsidiary with a large number of lower-paid employees. There was no definition of higher or highest levels of remuneration. This was presumably a question of fact to be determined by reference to each individual group of companies.

(*o*)   If the shares were acquired by the trustees after 20 March 2000, they could not be shares in an 'employer company' or in a company that controlled such a company or was under the control of a person or persons who controlled an employer company. A company was an employer company if its business consisted substantially in the provision of the services of the persons employed by it and the majority of such services were provided to a person who controlled the company (or two or more persons who together controlled it) or to an associated company (i.e. one under the control of the same person or persons). For this purpose a person included a partnership. Where a partner (alone or with others) controlled a company the partnership had to be treated as also controlling it. Control was determined in accordance with *ICTA 1988, s 416(2) to (6)*. [*9 Schedule 11A* inserted by *FA 2000, s 52(3)*].

(*p*)   If the shares were acquired by the trustees after 20 March 2000, they could not be subject to any restrictions affecting the rights attaching to the shares which related to dividends or to assets on a winding up of the company unless those restrictions attached to all other ordinary shares in the same company. [*9 Schedule 12(1B)*].

Unfortunately 'ordinary shares' did not appear to be defined anywhere so it was anyone's guess what restrictions were allowed if the company's ordinary share capital consisted of more than one class.

(*q*)   From 21 March 2000 the arrangements for the scheme could not make any provision for loans to some or all of the employees of the grantor company or any participating company (or be in any way associated with any such provision) and the operation of the scheme could not be in any way associated with such loans. Arrangements for this purpose included any scheme, agreement or understanding, even if it was not legally enforceable [*9 Schedule 2(2A)*].

16.64   For capital gains tax purposes the employee was treated as owning the shares while they were held by the trustees. [*TCGA 1992, s 238(1)*].

16.65   Paragraphs 16.21–16.33 above, which deal with approval and give a right of appeal against the refusal or withdrawal of approval also applied to profit sharing schemes.

Definitions

16.66   There are a number of special definitions for the purpose of those provisions. Where the meanings are not obvious, these have generally been inserted in the text above where appropriate. It may be helpful to list the main expressions for which specific definitions are included together with the paragraphs above where the definition can be found.

appropriate percentage: (16.63(*l*))

associated company: two companies are associated companies at a given time if at that time or at any time within the previous year one has control of the other or both are under the control of the same person or persons. [*ITEPA 2003, 3 Schedule 47(1), 4 Schedule 35(1)*].

bonus date: (16.16(*b*))

capital receipt: (16.39)

certified contractual savings scheme: an approved SAYE scheme

connected person: the *section 839* definition applies [*ITEPA 2003, s 718*]

consortium: a company is a member of a consortium owning another company if it is one of a number of companies which between them beneficially own at least 75% of the other company's ordinary share capital and each of which beneficially owns at least 5% of that capital. [*ITEPA 2003, 3 Schedule 48(2), 4 Schedule 36(2)*].

control: the *ICTA 1988, s 416* definition of control applies from 6 April 2003. The section 840 definition applied previously. [*ITEPA 2003, 3 Schedule 47(2), 4 Schedule 35(2)*].

grantor: the company that established the scheme

initial market value: (16.63(*b*))

locked-in value: (16.43)

market value: as defined in *TCGA 1992, s 272* [*ITEPA 2003, 3 Schedule 48(1), 4 Schedule 36(1)*]

material interest: (16.15(i))

participant: an employee who participates in the scheme

pensionable age: as defined in *Social Security Contributions and Benefits Act 1992, s 122(1)* as amended by *Pensions Act 1995, 4 Schedule*

period of retention: (16.63(*l*))

release date: the third anniversary of the date on which shares are apportioned under a profit sharing scheme (previously the fifth anniversary)—the new date applies where the third anniversary is after 28 April 1996 and where it fell before that date the release date was 29 April 1996 if it had not occurred earlier. [*FA 1996, s 116*)]

relevant amount: the amount referred to in 16.63(*b*)

shares: includes stock

Capital gains tax

16.67 If a tax charge arises under *ITEPA 2003, s 526* (see 16.12) the taxable amount is treated as part of the cost of the shares for capital gains tax purposes. [*TCGA 1992, s 120(2)(6) 7D Schedule 12* inserted by *ITEPA 2003, 6 Schedule 221*]. This applies whether or not the option is exercised in accordance with the terms of the scheme and irrespective of whether or not the scheme is still approved at the time the option is exercised. The charge under *section 526* is, of course, one that would not have arisen but for the scheme being an approved scheme, so it is reasonable to expect relief to be given in such circumstances. Where an option under an approved share option scheme is granted after 15 March 1993 and *TCGA 1992, s 17(1)* would apply to require the company to calculate its capital gain on the grant of the option by reference to its market value, that provision is not to apply but the company is treated as granting the option only for the actual consideration received (if any). Furthermore, the value of the employee's services to the company is not to be treated as consideration for either a SAYE or CSOP option. [*TCGA 1992, s 149A, 7D Schedule 10, 13* inserted by *ITEPA 2003, 6 Schedule 221*]. This ensures that the company is not taxed on a notional capital gain if it grants the option at an undervalue—as would frequently be the case.

Corporation tax relief

16.68   A company is entitled to corporation tax relief for expenditure that it incurs:

(*a*)   on establishing a share option scheme which the Revenue approve (but only if no employee or director obtains rights under the scheme prior to such approval); or

(*b*)   prior to 5 April 2002 on establishing a profit sharing scheme which the Revenue approved (provided that the trustees acquired no shares before such approval was given).

[*ICTA 1988, s 84A(1)(2)*].

16.69   The deduction is given as a trading expense (or management expense if the company is an investment company). Relief is normally given in the period of account in which the expenditure is incurred but if the scheme is not approved within nine months after the end of that period it is instead given in the period in which the approval is given. [*ICTA 1988, s 84A(2)(3)*].

16.70   A corporation tax deduction was similarly given for any sum expended in making a payment to the trustees of an approved profit sharing scheme by either the grantor company or another participating company provided that either:

(*a*)   the sum in question was applied by the trustees within nine months after the end of the period of account in which it was paid to them (or such longer time as the Revenue may allow) in acquiring shares for appropriation to eligible employees or directors; or

(*b*)   the sum was necessary to meet the reasonable expenses of the trustees in administering the scheme.

[*ICTA 1988, s 85*].

16.71   No deduction can be claimed for such a payment made after 5 April 2002. [*FA 2000, s 50(3)*]. In the case of sums paid to the trustees between 21 March 2000 and 5 April 2002 relief was given for sums applied by the trustees in acquiring shares only if such shares were acquired before 6 April 2002. [*FA 2000, s 50(2)*]. Relief will continue to be given for sums applied by the trustees as administration expenses for three years following the date of the last appropriation (prior to 6 April 2002) of shares made to individuals under the scheme. [*FA 2000, s 50(4)*].

Enterprise Management Incentives

16.72   Enterprise Management Incentives (EMIs) aim to help 'young, growing businesses which often have insufficient cashflow to reward their employees, recruit and retain the people they need' (*IR Press Release 21 March 2000*). They are share options granted after 27 July 2000 'to reward key people who are prepared to take a risk and use their skills and talents in helping those companies achieve their potential'. EMIs allow a small unquoted trading company to issue employees with options up to £100,000 of shares each. The scheme is fairly complex.

16.73   Actually it seems doubtful whether they will often be attractive. An employee of a young and growing company would often be better off to acquire his shares immediately on joining the company unless it has by then already become very valuable. Whilst companies are often reluctant to allow executives to acquire shares before they have proved their worth, it is normally not that difficult to issue the shares with an obligation to sell them back for a nominal figure if the executive leaves the company within a specified period, and companies are increasingly willing to do this.

Purpose of granting the option

16.74   An EMI option is a qualifying option only if:

(*a*)   it is granted for commercial reasons in order to recruit or retain an employee of the company; and

(*b*)   it is not granted as part of a scheme or arrangement one of the main purposes of which is the avoidance of tax.

[*ITEPA 2003, 5 Schedule 4*].

16.75   Options granted before 12 May 2001 had to be granted to recruit or retain a key employee. This created major problems as there was no definition of a key employee. The government told Parliament, 'The "key employee"' is one who makes an essential contribution to the business of the company, which is best placed to decide who can make such a contribution. It would be unhelpful and restrictive to attempt a further definition in the Bill.' [*Hansard SC H 6 June 2000, col 509*]. The company may well have known why it granted an option. But knowing why and convincing the Revenue of that purpose are not necessarily the same thing. It was not much of an incentive to expect both employer and employee to guess whether the option might qualify and take the risk that the Revenue might challenge it.

16.76   There is still no guidance as to when an option is granted in order to recruit or retain a person rather than, for example, simply to incentivise him, and no indication as to whether there are circumstances in which an option might be regarded as having a purpose of avoiding tax by virtue of the knowledge that the gain will be taxed less heavily than salary.

16.77   One of the problems of the absence of an advance clearance procedure, namely the question of whether a company is carrying on a qualifying business, has been alleviated informally. From 5 April 2001 the company can submit written details of the company to the Small Company Enterprise Centre (TIDO, Ty Glas, Llanishen, Cardiff CF14 5ZG tel 029 2032 7400) before the EMI options are granted and the Revenue will give written confirmation if they believe, on the basis of the information provided to them, that the company qualifies.

Maximum entitlement

16.78   An employee must not hold unexercised qualifying options which were granted by reason of his employment with a single company (or group of companies) in respect of shares with a total value (at the date of the grant of the option) of more than £100,000. [*ITEPA 2003, 5 Schedule 5(1)*].

16.79   If the grant of an option causes that limit to be exceeded the excess is not a qualifying option. [*ITEPA 2003, 5 Schedule 5(3)*]. If an employee has been granted options up to the £100,000 limit and, for example, exercises or releases some he cannot be granted further qualifying options (by either the company or another member of the same group) within three years of the date of the last qualifying option, i.e. the one that brought the total up to £100,000. [*ITEPA 2003, 5 Schedule 6*].

16.80   If at the time an option is granted to an employee he holds unexercised options under an approved CSOP scheme (see 16.11 granted by reason of employment with the same company (or another member of its group) those executive share options must be brought into account in testing the £100,000 limit. [*ITEPA 2003, 5 Schedule 5(4)(5)*].

16.81   The value of shares under option is the market value at the time the option is granted of the maximum number of shares of the same class as those which may be acquired on its exercise. If the shares are restricted shares (prior to 1 September 2003 subject to restrictions or risk of forfeiture) the restrictions or risk must be ignored in valuing the shares. Shares are restricted shares if there is any contract, arrangement or condition that would bring them within *ITEPA 2003, s 423* (see 14.23). [*5 Schedule 5(8)* as amended by *FA 2003, 22 Schedule 45*]. Shares are subject to risk of forfeiture if the interest that may be acquired is 'only conditional' within *ITEPA 2003, s 424* (see 14.190). [*ITEPA 2003, 5 Schedule 5(6)(a)(7)(8)* as amended by *FA 2003, 22 Schedule 45*].

Maximum value of options

16.82   The total 'value' of shares in the company in respect of which qualifying options exist must not exceed £3 million. [*ITEPA 2003, 5 Schedule 7(1)*]. This test is applied at the time each option is granted. [*ITEPA 2003, 5 Schedule 7(2)*]. The value of shares for this purpose is the sum of the market values of shares of the same class as the option shares at the time each option was granted. Para 16.85 applies in ascertaining such values. [*ITEPA 2003, 5 Schedule 7(6)*]. If the grant of an option causes the limit to be exceeded it is only the excess that is non-qualifying. If two or more options are granted at the same time such an excess is divided amongst them in proportion to the value of the shares over which each option is granted. [*ITEPA 2003, 5 Schedule 7(3)–(5)*].

16.83   This overall limit did not apply for options granted before 12 May 2001. Instead the total number of employees who could be granted EMI options was limited to 15. [*14 Schedule 11* as originally enacted]. This gave an effective overall limit of £1.5 million.

Qualifying company

16.84   The company must satisfy the following conditions at the time the options are granted.

(*a*)   It must not be a 51 per cent subsidiary of another company (or otherwise under the control (within *ICTA 1988, s 840*) of another company, or of another company together with any other person connected with that company). Also no arrangements must exist (other than arrangements within para 40—see 16.122) by virtue of which the company could become a 51 per cent subsidiary or fall under such control. [*ITEPA 2003, 5 Schedule 9*].

(*b*)   If the company has subsidiaries they must all be qualifying subsidiaries, i.e.

  (i)   the company must possess at least 75 per cent of the issued share capital and 75 per cent of the voting power in the subsidiary;

  (ii)   in the event of a winding up of the subsidiary (or in any other circumstances) the company (or another of its subsidiaries) must be beneficially entitled to at least 75 per cent of the assets which would then be available for distribution to the shareholders of the subsidiaries;

  (iii)   the company (or another of its subsidiaries) must be beneficially entitled to at least 75 per cent of any profits of the subsidiary which are available for distribution to its shareholders;

  (iv)   no other person (other than another subsidiary of the company) must have control (within *ICTA 1988, s 460 (s 840* prior to 5 April 2003)) of the subsidiary; and

  (v)   there must be no arrangements in existence by virtue of which any of the above conditions could cease to be met.

[ITEPA 2003, 5 Schedule 10, 11].

(c)   The value of the company's gross assets must not exceed £30 million (£15 million prior to 1 January 2002—amended by EMI (Gross Asset Requirement) Order 2001—SI 2001 No 3799). If the company has subsidiaries the consolidated value of the group assets (the aggregate value of the gross assets of the group disregarding any that consist in rights against, shares in or securities of another group company) must not exceed £15 million. *[ITEPA 2003, 5 Schedule 12]*.

(d)   The company must exist wholly for the purpose of carrying on one or more qualifying trades, disregarding any incidental purposes (see below), or of preparing to do so. In the case of a parent company the business activities of the group as a whole must not consist wholly or to a substantial extent in the carrying on of non-qualifying activities (see below) and at least one group company must satisfy the above qualifying purpose and qualifying trade test. *[ITEPA 2003, 5 Schedule 13, 14]*.

16.85   For the purpose of (b) above a subsidiary will not be treated as ceasing to be a qualifying one at a time when it (or another company) is being wound up if the subsidiary would have qualified but for the winding up and the winding up is for commercial purposes and not part of a scheme or arrangement one of the main purposes of which is the avoidance of tax. *[ITEPA 2003, 5 Schedule 11(5)(7)*, formerly *14 Schedule 15(3)]*. Similarly it will not cease to be a qualifying subsidiary if arrangements are in existence for the disposal of the group's entire interest in the subsidiary provided that the disposal will be for commercial purposes and not part of a tax avoidance scheme. *[ITEPA 2003, 5 Schedule 11(6)(7)]*.

16.86   For the purpose of determining under head (d) whether a company exists wholly for the purpose of carrying on one or more qualifying trades the holding or management of property used in its trade can be ignored. In the case of a group so can the holding of shares in (or lending money to) other group companies, holding or managing property used for the purposes of a qualifying trade by a group company, and incidental activities of a company that meets the trading requirements applicable to a single company. *[ITEPA 2003, 5 Schedule 13(2), 14(3)]*. The reference in head (d) to non-qualifying activities means excluded activities (see 16.95) other than the letting of ships or the receiving of royalties or licence fees and any activities carried on otherwise than in the course of a trade. *[ITEPA 2003, 5 Schedule 14]*. Incidental activities means activities carried on in pursuance of incidental purposes, and incidental purposes means purposes having no significant effect (other than in relation to incidental matters) on the extent of the company's activities. *[ITEPA 2003, 5 Schedule 13, 14]*.

Meaning of qualifying trade

16.87   To be a qualifying trade it must:

(a)   be carried on wholly or mainly in the UK;

(*b*)   be conducted on a commercial basis and with a view to the realisation of profits; and

(*c*)   not consist wholly or to a substantial part in the carrying on of excluded activities.

[*ITEPA 2003, 5 Schedule 15(1)*].

The Revenue say that whether a trade is carried on wholly or mainly in the UK will depend on the relevant facts and circumstances. A company will satisfy the test if over half of the trading activities taken as a whole is carried on in the UK (*SP3/00*).

16.88   Research and development from which it is intended that a qualifying trade will be derived (or will benefit) is treated as carrying on a qualifying trade provided that the intended trade will be carried on by the company carrying out the research and development or by another group company. [*ITEPA 2003, 5 Schedule 15(2)(4)*]. Curiously if A Ltd is carrying out research and development with the intention that a new subsidiary, B Ltd will carry on the trade, that research and development will not qualify unless A Ltd is already a member of a group. Preparing to carry out research and development cannot however be regarded as the carrying on of a qualifying trade. [*ITEPA 2003, 5 Schedule 15(3)*].

Excluded Activities

16.89   The activities which are prohibited (unless they are insubstantial) are:

(*a*)   dealing in land, commodities or futures or in shares, securities or other financial instruments;

(*b*)   dealing in goods otherwise than in the course of an ordinary trade of wholesale or retail distribution (see 16.90);

(*c*)   banking, insurance, money lending, debt factoring, HP financing or other financial activities;

(*d*)   leasing (including letting ships on charter or other assets on hire (see 16.91);

(*e*)   receiving royalties or licence fees (see 16.93);

(*f*)   providing legal or accountancy services;

(*g*)   property development (see 16.94);

(*h*)   farming or market gardening;

(*i*)   holding, managing or occupying woodlands, any other forestry activity or timber production;

(*j*)   operating or managing hotels or comparable establishments (i.e. a guest house, hostel or other establishment the main purpose of maintaining which is the provision of facilities for overnight accommodation (with or without catering) or managing property used as a hotel or comparable establishment, where the company has an estate or interest in (or is in occupation of) the hotel, etc in question [*ITEPA 2003, 5 Schedule 21*];

(*k*)   operating or managing nursing homes (i.e. establishments that exist wholly or mainly to provide nursing care for persons suffering from sickness, injury or infirmity or for women who are pregnant or have given birth to children) or residential care homes (i.e. establishments that exist for the provision of residential accommodation, together with board and personal care, for persons in need of such care by reason of old age, mental or physical disability, past or present dependence on drugs or alcohol, any past illness or past or present mental disorder), or managing property used as a nursing home or residential care home, where the company has an estate or interest in (or is in occupation of) the home in question [*ITEPA 2003, 5 Schedule 22*];

(*l*)   providing services or facilities by a business carried on by another person if that business consists to a significant extent of excluded activities (within (*a*) to (*k*)) and the same person has a controlling interest in both the company and that other business [*ITEPA 2003, 5 Schedule 23*].

[*ITEPA 2003, 5 Schedule 16*].

16.90   A trade of retail distribution is one in which the goods are offered for sale and sold to members of the general public for their use or consumption. A trade of wholesale distribution is one where the goods are sold to an intermediary for resale (including after processing) to members of the general public. [*ITEPA 2003, 5 Schedule 17(2)(3)*, formerly *FA 2000, 14 Schedule 20(1)(2)*]. A trade is likely to be an ordinary trade if the goods are bought by the trader in quantities larger than those in which he sells them, the goods are bought and sold in different markets and the trader employs staff and incurs expenses in the trade in addition to the costs of the goods and any remuneration paid to a person connected with the trader (if it is a company). [*ITEPA 2003, 5 Schedule 17(5)(6)*]. Factors that suggest that a trade is not an ordinary one are if there are purchases or sales from or to connected persons, purchases are matched with onward sales, the goods are held for longer than is normal for goods of that kind, the trade is carried on somewhere not commonly used for wholesale or retail trade, and the trader does not take physical possession of the goods. [*ITEPA 2003, 5 Schedule 17(5)(7)*]. A trade cannot be an ordinary trade if it consists to a substantial extent in dealing in goods of a kind which are collected or held as an investment if a substantial proportion of those goods are held for a longer period than a vendor seeking to dispose of them at their market value would keep them. [*ITEPA 2003, 5 Schedule 17(4)*].

16.91   A trade of leasing ships (but not oil rigs or pleasure craft) can be a qualifying one if:

(*a*)   every ship it lets on charter is beneficially owned by the company;

(*b*)   every ship beneficially owned by the company (including any not let on charter) is registered in the UK;

(*c*)   the company is solely responsible for arranging the marketing of the services of its ships (this probably prevents it using an agent);

(*d*)   in relation to every letting of a ship on charter by the company:

    (i)   the letting is for twelve months or less (and no provision is made for extending it beyond twelve months other than at the option of the charterer);

    (ii)   during the period of the letting there is no provision in force for the grant of a new letting which would extend beyond that twelve-month period (other than at the option of the charterer);

    (iii)   the letting is to an unconnected person and under a bargain made at arm's length (unless the letting is between a company and its qualifying subsidiary or between two qualifying subsidiaries of the trader); and

    (iv)   under the terms of the charter the company is responsible for taking the management decisions in relation to the ship (other than those generally regarded in the trade as matters of husbandry) and for defraying substantially all expenses in connection with the ship throughout the charter period other than those directly attributable to particular voyages (and no arrangements exist by virtue of which someone other than the company could be appointed to be responsible for such matters).

[*ITEPA 2003, 5 Schedule 18*].

16.92   If any of these requirements are not met but non-qualifying lettings (together with any other excluded activities carried on by the company) do not amount to a substantial part of the trade it can be treated as a qualifying trade. [*ITEPA 2003, 5 Schedule 24*].

16.93   A company that receives royalties or licence fees can nevertheless be treated as carrying on a qualifying trade if the royalties and licence fees (or all except a part that is not substantial in terms of value) are attributable to the exploitation of relevant intangible assets. [*ITEPA 2003, 5 Schedule 19*]. A relevant intangible asset is one the whole or greater part (in terms of value) of which has been created by the company carrying on the trade (or by a company which at all times during which it created the asset was the parent or a fellow qualifying subsidiary of that company). [*ITEPA 2003, 5 Schedule 19*]. If the asset is intellectual property (which is defined, restrictively, as any patent, trade-mark, registered design, copyright, design right, performer's right, plant breeder's right or any corresponding or similar right under the laws of another country) the creation of the asset means its creation in circumstances in which the right to exploit it vests in the company (whether alone or jointly with others). Thus, for example, if A is commissioned by B to write a book in return for a royalty so that the entire copyright vests in B the royalty does not derive from a relevant intangible asset of A.

16.94   Property development means the development of land by a company which has an interest in the land (or did so at any time) with the sole or main object of realising a gains from the disposal of an interest in the land when it is developed. [*ITEPA 2003, 5 Schedule 20(2)*]. For this purpose an interest in land is any estate, interest or right in or over land (including any right affecting the use or disposition of land), and any right to obtain such an estate, interest or right from another which is conditional on the other's ability to grant it. [*ITEPA 2003, 5 Schedule 20(3)*]. An option to acquire land does not appear to fall within this definition but probably would do so on exercise. The interest of a creditor (other than for a rentcharge) whose debt is secured on land is not an interest in land. [*ITEPA 2003, 5 Schedule 20(4)*].

16.95   For the purpose of 16.89(*l*) a person has a controlling interest in a business carried on by a company if either:

(*a*)   he controls the company (applying *ICTA 1988, s 416(2)–(6)*),

(*b*)   the company is a close company and he (or an associate of his) is a director and beneficially owns over 30 per cent of the ordinary share capital of the company (or is able directly or indirectly to control over 30 per cent), or

(*c*)   not less than half of the business could (in accordance with *ICTA 1988, s 344(2)*) be regarded as belonging to him for the purpose of *ICTA 1988, s 343* (disallowance of losses following a change in ownership of a company). [*ITEPA 2003, 5 Schedule 23(4)*].

A person has a controlling interest in an unincorporated business if he is entitled to at least half of the assets used for the business or half of the income arising from the business. [*ITEPA 2003, 5 Schedule 23(5)*]. In applying these tests there must be attributed to a person any rights or powers of any associate of his (within *ICTA 1988, s 417(3)(4)*) but excluding a brother or sister. [*ITEPA 2003, 5 Schedule 23*].

Eligible Employees

16.96   An employee is eligible to participate in EMIs only if:

(*a*)   he is an employee of the relevant company (the one over which he will be granted the option) or a qualifying subsidiary (see 16.84(*b*)) of it [*ITEPA 2003, 5 Schedule 25*];

(*b*)   the time that he is required to spend on the business of the relevant company (or of its group if it is a parent company) is either:

   (i)   at least 25 hours a week, or

   (ii)   if less, 75 per cent of his working time,

(including any time that he would have been required to spend but for injury, ill-health or disability, pregnancy, childbirth, maternity or paternity leave or parental leave, reasonable holiday entitlement, and garden leave). Interestingly time counts towards this test both if the income from it is taxed as employment income and if it is taxed as self-employment income under Case I or II of Schedule D. [*ITEPA 2003, 5 Schedule 26, 27*]. This is called the 'commitment of working time'

(c) He does not have a material interest—broadly over 30 per cent—in the company (or if it is a parent company in any group company. [*ITEPA 2003, 5 Schedule 26–28*].

From 7 January 2003, where a reservist is called up for service under the *Reserve Forces Act 1996* the Revenue will by concession treat the employment with the Ministry of Defence as fulfilling these employment conditions. [*ESC A103*]. The Revenue have asked to be informed (Sahd.Ullah@ir.gsi.gov.uk) when this concession is used.

16.97 For the purpose of (c) above an individual has a material interest in a company if he (or he together with one or more associates, or one or more associates alone) is either:

(a) the beneficial owner of more than 30 per cent of the ordinary share capital of the company (or able to control, directly or indirectly more than 30 per cent), or

(b) if the company is a close company, he possesses (or is entitled to acquire) such rights as would in the event of a winding up of the company or in any other circumstances give an entitlement to receive more than 30 per cent of the assets that would then be available for distribution among the participators (as defined in *ICTA 1988, s 417(1)*). [*ITEPA 2003, 5 Schedule 29*].

16.98 In applying these tests the option shares themselves are ignored until the option is exercised. [*ITEPA 2003, 5 Schedule 30(3)*]. A person with 29 per cent of the shares could therefore be granted an option that would bring him well above 30 per cent but once he exercises it could not be granted a new qualifying option. A company is treated as a close company if it would be close but for being non-UK resident or because it is a listed company and 35 per cent of the shares are held by members of the public. [*ITEPA 2003, 5 Schedule 29(4)*]. A right to acquire shares (other than under the EMI or other approved schemes) must be treated as a right to control them. [*ITEPA 2003, 5 Schedule 30(2)*]. If the right is to acquire unissued shares, the issued share capital must be increased by the option shares (but not it appears by option shares held by other people) in applying the 30 per cent test. [*ITEPA 2003, 5 Schedule 30(4)(5)*]. The interest of the trustees under a SIP (see Chapter 15), and any rights exercisable by those trustees by virtue of any such interest, are ignored to the extent that the shares have not been appropriated to, or acquired on behalf of, the individual concerned. [*ITEPA 2003, 5 Schedule 30(7)*].

16.99 In applying *paragraph 26–28* (see 16.96) 'associate' in relation to an individual means:

(a) any relative (spouse, parent or remoter forebear and child or remoter issue, but not a brother or sister) or partner of that individual;

(*b*)   the trustees or trustees of any settlement in relation to which that individual or any of the above relatives of his (living or dead) was a settlor;

(*c*)   if the individual is interested in any shares or obligations of the company which are subject to a trust (or are part of a deceased estate) the trustees or personal representatives.

[*ITEPA 2003, 5 Schedule 31*].

16.100 However, the trustees of an employee benefit trust (within *ICTA 1988, 8 Schedule 7*—see 18.41) are not regarded as associates by reason only of the individual being interested as a beneficiary of that trust if the individual (or the individual together with associates of his—other than the trustees of another employee benefit trust—or associates of his on their own) has at any time since 13 March 1989 been the beneficial owner (or able to control directly or indirectly) over 30 per cent of the ordinary share capital of the company. [*ITEPA 2003, 5 Schedule 32*].

16.101 In applying *paragraph 31* (see 16.100) the trustees of a discretionary settlement of which the individual was formerly a beneficiary are not treated as his associates if at some time within the following 12 months he ceases to be a beneficiary by an irrevocable release or disclaimer of his interest or by the irrevocable exercise by the trustees of a power to exclude him, and

(*a*)   immediately after he ceased to be a beneficiary no associate of his was interested in the shares held by the trust; and

(*b*)   neither the individual nor any associate of his received any benefit from the trust in the 12 months ending with his ceasing to be a beneficiary. [*ITEPA 2003, 5 Schedule 33*]

Terms of options, etc

16.102   The option itself has to satisfy the following conditions:

(*a*)   it must be over shares that are fully paid up, irredeemable (and not becoming redeemable at a future date) and forming part of the ordinary share capital of the relevant company [*ITEPA 2003, 5 Schedule 35*];

(*b*)   the option must be capable of being exercised within 10 years from the date of its grant—or if its exercise is subject to conditions they must be capable of being fulfilled within that 10-year period [*ITEPA 2003, 5 Schedule 36*];

(*c*)   the option must take the form of a written agreement and this must state:

(i)   the date on which the option is granted;

(ii)   that it is granted under the provisions of *Schedule 5*,

(iii) the number (or maximum number) of shares that may be acquired;

(iv) the price payable by the employee to acquire them (or the method by which that price is to be determined);

(v) when and how the option may be granted;

(vi) details of any conditions, such as performance conditions, affecting the terms or extent of the employee's entitlement;

(vii) details of any restrictions attaching to the shares;

(viii) whether the shares are subject to risk of forfeiture (ie if the interest that may be acquired is restricted within *ITEPA 2003, s 426*—see 14.22).

[*ITEPA 2003, 5 Schedule 37*].

(*d*) the terms on which the option is granted must prohibit the employee from transferring any of his rights under it [*14 Schedule 41(a)*]; and

(*e*) if the terms permit the option to be exercised after the employee's death they must require this to be done within 12 months after the death. [*ITEPA 2003, 5 Schedule 38*].

Notification to the Revenue

16.103 EMI options do not have to be approved in advance by the Revenue. Indeed there is no procedure for the Revenue to do so. However for the option to be a qualifying option it must be notified to the Revenue within 92 days of the grant of the option (30 days for options granted before 12 May 2001). [*ITEPA 2003, 5 Schedule 44*]. The Revenue do not have power to extend this 92-day period. Failure to notify timeously will negate the EMI tax benefits.

16.104 The notice must:

(*a*) be given by the employer (not the relevant company if different);

(*b*) be in such form as the Revenue may require;

(*c*) contain (or be accompanied by) such information as the Revenue may require for the purpose of checking that the conditions of *Schedule 15* are met;

(*d*) contain a declaration by a director or the secretary of the employer company that in his opinion the requirements of *Schedule 14* are met and that the information provided is, to the best of his knowledge and belief, correct and complete; and

(*e*) contain a declaration by the employee that he meets the commitment of working time (see 16.102).

[*ITEPA 2003, 5 Schedule 44*].

16.105 The Revenue can amend the notice (by notice to the employer) within 9 months of receiving it to correct obvious errors or omissions. The employer can override that correction by giving notice to the Revenue rejecting it within three months from the date it is issued. [*ITEPA 2003, 5 Schedule 45*].

16.106 The Revenue are entitled to enquire into the notice at any time within 12 months after the end of the 92 day notification period (30 days for options granted before 12 May 2001). They do so by giving notice to the employer company. If they intend to enquire into the employee's commitment of working time they must instead give the notice to the employee. The twelve-month limit does not apply if the Revenue discover that any of the information provided in, or in connection with, the notice was false or misleading in a material particular. In the absence of such a discovery they cannot enquire more than once into the same notice. [*ITEPA 2003, 5 Schedule 46*].

16.107 When the Revenue complete their enquiry they must inform the employer company and tell it whether or not in their opinion the conditions for the option to qualify as an EMI option are met. If they agree that they are they must also notify the employee of that fact. On completion of an enquiry into the commitment of working time they must notify both employer and employee. At any time after an enquiry has been opened the employer (or if it related to the commitment to working time the employee) can apply to the General or Special Commissioners for a direction that the Revenue should give a closure notice within a specified period. [*ITEPA 2003, 5 Schedule 47, 48*].

16.108 If the Revenue do not give an enquiry notice the EMI conditions are taken to be met. If they do, their decision following their enquiry is conclusive as to whether or not they are met—subject, if they decide that they are, to any later discovery. [*ITEPA 2003, 5 Schedule 49*].

16.109 If the Revenue decide that the EMI conditions are not met, or that the notice under *paragraph 2* was not properly given, the employer company can appeal against that decision within 30 days of the issue of the closure notice under *paragraph 5*. If the decision is that the commitment of working time is not met the employee can similarly appeal. The appeal goes to the General Commissioners unless the company (or the employee) elects for it to be heard by the Special Commissioners. [*ITEPA 2003, 5 Schedule 50*].

16.110 Those familiar with self-assessment will recognise this procedure. There is however one notable difference. There is no protection against discovery for documents sent with the notice. This is an odd procedure for an 'incentive'. It leaves the employee in a state of uncertainty as to whether the Revenue may at a later date make a discovery and deny him the tax benefits that he anticipated from his EMI option.

Income tax position

16.111   Income tax is not charged on the grant of an EMI option, provided that it is exercised within 10 years of the grant (or of the grant of the original option if it is a replacement option. [*ITEPA 2003, ss 528* (repealed by *FA 2003, 22 Schedule 36* from 1 September 2003), *529*]. This is not giving much away as that is the normal rule that applies to any option (see 14.90).

16.112   Income tax is not charged on the exercise of the option either provided that the option price is not less than the market value of the shares at the time the option was granted (or if it is a replacement option, the time the original one was granted). [*ITEPA 2003, s 530*]. If the option price is less than the original market value of the shares an income tax charge arises at the time the option is exercised but this is limited to the excess of the 'chargeable market value' over the aggregate of the consideration for the grant of the option and the option price paid for the shares. The chargeable market value for this purpose is the lower of the market value of the shares at the time the option was granted (or if it is a replacement option—see 16.118—at the time the original option was granted) and their market value at the time the option is exercised. [*ITEPA 2003, s 531*]. In other words the employee is taxed on the lower of the discount or the profit he can realise by immediately selling the shares. If the price paid exceeds the then value of the shares there is obviously no tax charge. [*ITEPA 2003, s 530*, formerly *FA 2000, 14*]. If the shares are subject to restrictions, such as a requirement to sell them if the employee leaves the employment, it will normally be sensible to make an election under *ITEPA 2003, s 431* (see 14.42A). Where an option was exercised before 13 May 2001 the charge was limited to the difference between the option price and the market value of the shares when the option was granted or, if lower, the difference between the option price and the market value of the shares at the time the option was exercised. [*14 Schedule 45* as originally enacted]. The original legislation omitted to give relief for any consideration paid for the option. If the option price is nil the tax charge is on the difference between the chargeable market value and any consideration given for the grant of the option (and no charge arises if that consideration exceeds the value of the shares). [*ITEPA 2003, s 531*]. For options exercised before 13 May 2001 it was on the lower of the value of the shares at the time the option was exercised and the value at the time it was granted.

Disqualifying Events

16.113   If a disqualifying event occurs before the option is exercised and it is not then exercised within 40 days of that event the amount which is taxable on exercise of the option is increased by the amount, if any, by which the market value of the shares when the option is exercised exceeds their market value immediately before the disqualifying event (called 'the post-event gain') less the amount of any consideration given for the grant of the option. [*ITEPA 2003, s 532*]. If the option was granted at below the then market value of the shares the taxable amount is the difference between the chargeable market value under *Section 531* (see 16.112) (broadly, the market value of comparable shares at the time the option was granted) plus the post-event gain and the aggregate of the option price (if any) plus any consideration given for the grant of the option. [*ITEPA 2003, s 532*]. This is of course the aggregate of the undervalue on the grant of the option and the growth in the value of the shares subsequent to the disqualifying event. For options exercised before 13 May 2001 no relief was given for any consideration paid for the grant of the option.

Example

Joan was granted an EMI option on 12 December 2001 to acquire £50,000 worth of shares for £50,000 at any time within the next 10 years. She exercised the option on 10 April 2007 when the shares were worth £600,000. A disqualifying event occurred in June 2005 when the shares were worth £400,000.

Joan is taxable on the exercise of the option on

(*a*) the lower of—

   (i)   the option price £50,000 less the 2001 value of

   the shares   £50,000   =   NIL

   (ii) the option price £50,000 less the 2007 value of

   the shares   £600,000   =   £550,000

   the lower is   NIL

plus

(*b*) the excess of the 2007 value £600,000 over the 2005

   value £400,000   £200,000

                                                 £200,000

In other words the increase in value since the disqualifying event is taxed under Schedule E in addition to any tax charge arising by reference to the grant of the option at an undervalue.

16.114 The following are disqualifying events.

(*a*) The relevant company becoming a 51 per cent subsidiary of another company (or coming under the control of another company, or of another company and any person connected with it, without becoming a subsidiary). If a replacement option is granted (see 16.118) and at some time during the six-month period referred to in 16.118(*b*) (and before the surrender of the old option) such a loss of independence occurs in relation to the old option that will not be a disqualifying event. That is commonsense. A loss of independence is bound to occur as a result of the take-over and the qualifying conditions for the replacement option to be treated as such are as stringent as those that apply on the grant of the original option;

(*b*) The relevant company ceasing to meet the trading activities requirement (see 16.87);

(*c*) The employee ceasing to be eligible either by ceasing his employment with the company (or group) or by failing to meet the commitment of working time (see 16.96). A disqualifying event also occurs if that commitment is not satisfied in any tax year. [*ITEPA 2003, s 535(2)(4)*]. This must be tested on a monthly basis, i.e. at the end of each calendar month the 25 hours per week and 75 per cent of time tests are applied on a cumulative basis from the beginning of the tax year. If these tests are not met in any month the disqualifying event is deemed to have incurred at the end of the previous month (and if they are not met in April it is deemed to have occurred at the end of the previous tax year). The tests are applied from the beginning of the tax year in which the option is granted. If they are not met at a month end prior to the grant the option is disqualified *ab initio*. If the employment begins during the year (or ceases during a month) the test period obviously starts when the employment starts (or ends when it ceases) [*ITEPA 2003, s 535(2)(6)*];

(*d*) The terms of the option being varied if the effect of the variation is either to increase the market value of the shares that are subject to the option or to prevent the option satisfying the requirement of *Schedule 15*;

(*e*) An alteration to the share capital of the relevant company if it:

　(i) affects the value of the shares subject to the option (or but for the occurrence of some other event would do so);

　(ii) consists of (or includes) the creation, variation or removal of a right relating to any shares in the company (including rights conferred by any contract or arrangement or in any other way), the imposition of a restriction relating to any shares (or which is imposed by any contract, etc.) or the variation or removal of a restriction to which any shares are subject; and

　has the effect either

　　1. that the requirements of *Schedule 15* would no longer be met in relation to the option, or

　　2. unless the alteration is made for commercial reasons or its main purpose (or one of its main purposes) was not to increase the market value of option shares, of increasing the value of the shares that are subject to the option.

　[*ITEPA 2003, s 537*].

Prior to 12 May 2001 an alteration was a disqualifying event if it was made without the approval of the Revenue. There was a right of appeal against a refusal of approval. [*14 Schedule 49* as originally enacted].

(*f*)   A conversion of any of the shares to which the option relates into shares of a different class, unless:

   (i)   the conversion is a conversion of one class only ('the original class') into shares of one other class only ('the new class'),

   (ii)   all of the shares of the original class are converted into shares of the new class, and

   (iii)   immediately before the conversion either –

      (A)   the majority of the shares of the original class were not held by (or for the benefit of) an associated company or directors or employees of the company or of an associated company, or

      (B)   the company was employee-controlled (within *ITEPA 2003, s 421H*—see 14.48) by virtue of holdings of shares of the original class.

   [*ITEPA 2003, s 538*].

(*g*)   The grant to the employee of an option under a CSOP scheme (see 16.11) in relation to the same company or any other company in the same group if immediately after it is granted the employee holds unexercised employee options (i.e. under the EMI scheme, a different EMI scheme relating to employment with the same group, or under the CSOP scheme) in respect of shares with a total initial value of over £100,000. [*ITEPA 2003, s 539*].

(*h*)   If when the option was granted the relevant company was a qualifying company by reason only of preparing to carry on a qualifying trade, its ceasing such preparations or it (or if it is a parent company it or another group company) not commencing that trade within two years of the grant of the option [*ITEPA 2003, s 534(3)–(5)*].

[*ITEPA 2003, ss 534–537*].

16.115   No charge will arise under *ITEPA 2003, s 194* (see 14.141) on the grant of a qualifying EMI option, but any other income tax charges under ITEPA 2003:

ss 422–470 (see 14.22 onwards) in relation to the shares; or under *ss 471–484* (see 14.89 onwards) apply in the normal way. [*ITEPA 2003, s 541* as amended by *FA 2003, 22 Schedule 40,41*]. Similarly income tax charges applied in the normal way under the earlier legislation, namely

(*a*)   in relation to a sale at an overvalue under *ITEPA 2003, s 199* (see 14.153);

(*b*)   under *ITEPA 2003, s 476* (old) in respect of the release of rights conferred by a qualifying option (see 14.122);

(*c*)   under *ITEPA 2003, ss 449, 453 or 457*, formerly *FA 2000*, in respect of post acquisition benefits in relation to shares acquired by the exercise of a qualifying option (see 14.156, 14.166 and 14.179);

(*d*) under *ITEPA 2003, s 427* (old) on an interest in shares ceasing to be only conditional (see 14.195) or *s 438* on convertible shares (see 14.202) in relation to shares acquired under a qualifying option—but in calculating the charge under *sections 437* or *438* a deduction can be made equal to the EMI relief given (i.e. the difference between the taxable amount (if any) on exercise of the EMI option and the amount that would have been taxable had it been taxable under *ITEPA 2003, s 479* (old) (see 14.118), namely the market value of the shares at the time of the exercise of the option.

[*ITEPA 2003, ss 540, 541*].

Capital Gains Tax relief

16.116 On a disposal of shares acquired under an EMI option taper relief is calculated as if the shares had been acquired when the original option was granted. [*TCGA 1992, 7D Schedule 15* inserted by *ITEPA 2003, 6 Schedule 221*]. This also of course applies to replacement shares on a company reorganisation within *TCGA 1992, s 127* provided that they meet the conditions of *5 Schedule 35* (see 16.102(*a*)). [*TCGA 1992, 7D Schedule 14(3)*]. If a disqualifying event (see 16.113) occurs in relation to a qualifying option this treatment applies only if the option is exercised within 40 days of that event. If it is not, taper relief runs only from the time the shares are actually acquired. [*TCGA 1992, 7D Schedule 14(4)*].

16.117 If there is a rights issue in respect of shares acquired under an EMI option the rights shares are not treated as a single holding with the option shares. [*TCGA 1992, 7D Schedule 16*]. Accordingly the date of acquisition for taper relief purposes of the rights shares is the date of the rights issue; it does not relate back to the grant of the option.

Company re-organisations

16.118 If there is a take-over of the relevant company and

(*a*) the holder of a qualifying option by agreement with the acquiring company releases his rights under that option ('the old option') in consideration of the grant to him of equivalent rights ('the new option') over shares in the acquiring company, and

(*b*) the new option is granted within six months of the take-over (or if the acquirer becomes bound or entitled to acquire the shares under a court order within the time specified in that order), and

(*c*) the new option meets the specified conditions (see 16.102)

the new option is treated as a 'replacement option' and is treated as if it had been granted on the date the old option was granted (and references in *Schedule 5* to a qualifying option include a replacement option). [*ITEPA 2003, 5 Schedule 39, 40, 42*].

16.119 The conditions that the new option must meet to qualify as a replacement option are

(*a*) it must be granted to the holder of the old option by reason of his employment with the acquiring company, or if that company is a parent company another group company—so a replacement option cannot be granted to a person who leaves his employment as a result of the take-over,

(*b*) at the time of the release of the old option the requirements of *paragraph 4* (purpose of granting the option) (see 16.74) and *paragraph 7* (£3-million overall limit) (see 16.82) are met in relation to the new option,

(*c*) at that time, the independence requirement (see 16.84(*a*)) and the trading activities requirement (see 16.84(*d*)) are met in relation to the acquiring company,

(*d*) at that time the individual to whom the new option is granted is an eligible employee (see 16.96) in relation to the acquiring company,

(*e*) at that time the requirements as to the terms of the option, etc. (see 16.102) are met in relation to the new option,

(*f*) immediately before the release of the old option the total market value of the shares subject to that option is equal to the total market value, immediately after the grant) of the shares to which the new option relates, and

(*g*) the total amount payable by the employee to acquire the shares in pursuance of the new option is the same as that payable under the old.

[*ITEPA 2003, 5 Schedule 43*].

16.120 In effect the old option can be replaced by the new with effect from the initial date only if the employee would have been able to acquire an EMI option over shares in the acquiring company had the old option not been granted.

16.121 A take-over (or 'company reorganisation' as the legislation terms it) will trigger these replacement option rules only where a company ('the acquiring company') either

(*a*) obtains control of the relevant company (i.e. the one to which the option relates) either as a result of making a general offer to acquire all of the issued ordinary share capital and which is made on a condition which, if satisfied, will give the acquiring company control of the relevant company, or as a result of making a general offer to acquire all of the shares of the same class as those to which the option relates, or

(*b*) obtains control of the relevant company in pursuance of a compromise or arrangement sanctioned by the court under *Companies Act 1985, s 425*, or

(*c*) becomes bound or entitled under *Companies Act 1985, ss 428–430* to acquire shares of the same class as those subject to the option, or (*d*) obtains all the shares of a company whose shares are subject to an EMI option as a result of a qualifying exchange of shares (which is where a new holding company with virtually identical shareholdings is put over the top of the existing company by means of a share exchange).

[*ITEPA 2003, 5 Schedule 39*].

16.122 For the purpose of (*d*) above a qualifying exchange of shares is where a company acquires all of the shares in another ('the old company'), and

(*a*) the consideration for the old shares consists wholly of the issue of shares in the acquiring company,

(*b*) the new shares are issued in consideration of old shares only, at a time when there are no issued shares in the acquiring company other than subscriber shares and new shares previously issued in consideration of old shares,

(*c*) the consideration for new shares of each description consists wholly of old shares of the corresponding description (i.e. on the assumption that they were shares in the same company they would be of the same class and carry the same rights),

(*d*) the new shares of each description are issued to the holders of old shares of the corresponding description in proportion to their holdings, and

(*e*) the exchange of shares does not constitute a disposal by virtue of *TCGA 1992, s 127*.

[*ITEPA 2003, 5 Schedule 40*].

Information powers

16.123 The Revenue have power by notice to require any person to provide them within such time as they may direct (which must not be less than three months) with such information as they think necessary for the performance of their functions under *Schedule 15* that the person has or can reasonably obtain. [*ITEPA 2003, 5 Schedule 51*].

16.124 The company whose shares are subject to EMI options must make an annual return for each tax year in which such options are unexercised containing such information as the Revenue may require. This must be submitted within 92 days after the end of the year. [*ITEPA 2003, 5 Schedule 44*].

Market value of shares

16.125 Subject to *5 Schedule 5(7)* (see 16.81) the market value of shares has the same meaning as for capital gains tax purposes under *TCGA 1992,* *ss 272* and *273*. [*ITEPA 2003, 5 Schedule 55*]. Where the market value on any date falls to be determined the Revenue and the employer company can agree that it should be determined by reference to a different date or dates, or to an average of the value on a number of dates. [*ITEPA 2003, 5 Schedule 56*]. This will enable a value to be agreed in advance of the grant of the option subject to the option being granted within an agreed time of the date of the agreement.

16.126 If the Revenue and the employer company cannot agree on the value of shares the employer company can require the valuation to be referred to the General Commissioners (or if it so elects the Special Commissioners). If it does not do so the Revenue can determine the value. The employer company then has a right of appeal to the Commissioners against that determination. [*ITEPA 2003, 5 Schedule 57*].

Other matters

16.127 The Treasury have power to amend *paragraphs 17–26* (the trading activities requirement) (see 16.84(*d*)) and to substitute different sums for the £100,000 limit in *paragraph 5* (see 16.78) or the £15m gross asset figure in *paragraph 16* (see 16.84(*c*)). [*ITEPA 2003, 5 Schedule 54*].

For the purpose of *ITEPA 2003, 5 Schedule 44–59* (but not for the rest of the *Schedule*) a person is not taken to have failed to do something required to be done within a limited time if

(*a*)   he had a reasonable excuse for not doing it within that time; and

(*b*)   if the excuse ceased, he did without unreasonable delay after it did so.

[*ITEPA 2003, 5 Schedule 53*].

Chapter 17

FA 1989 Employee Share Ownership Trusts

Introduction

17.1   The *Finance Act 1989* introduced a new form of employee incentive; the employee share ownership trust or ESOT (renamed QUEST – qualifying share trusts – immediately prior to their abolition). Although the legislation is both voluminous and complex the ESOT is not really a new arrival. Employee share trusts have been around for many years. The Chancellor of the day, however, felt that some employers were deterred from using them because of uncertainties as to the tax treatment. Whether a complex statutory code is likely to encourage the use of such trusts is open to question. The 1989 legislation has not been included in the *ITEPA 2003* as it is aimed at giving tax relief to the employer rather than specific tax benefits to the employee. This tax relief was withdrawn in relation to contributions after 31 December 2002. [*FA 2003, s 142*].

17.2   Reference below to ESOTs are to statutory ESOTs except where the context suggests otherwise. In practice, most employee trusts do not qualify as ESOTs. They rely for their efficiency on general law. An ESOT is a species of employee trust set up to acquire shares in the employing company. However, many of the tax benefits of an ESOT are available to any employee trust. A contribution by a company to a trust set up for the benefit of its employees is normally wholly and exclusively incurred for the benefit of the company's trade and thus an allowable corporation tax deduction. In *Heather v P-E Consulting Group Ltd 48 TC 293* the Court of Appeal held that annual contributions to such a trust were allowable. This was followed in *Jeffs v Ringtons Ltd 58 TC 680* and *E Bott Ltd v Price 59 TC 437*. In the latter case the payments were not a specific annual amount and lasted for only three years, so it is likely that regularity is unimportant and a single payment would be deductible. Although a deduction was denied in *Rutter v Charles Sharpe & Co Ltd 53 TC 163* the facts in that case were peculiar. Only the dividends were to be distributed to staff, with the capital being returnable to the company after 80 years. In these circumstances it is not surprising that the contributions were regarded as capital as they would ultimately result in an enduring asset for the company. It did not seem to do so.

17.3   The contributions will not normally have a revenue nature as far as the trustees are concerned provided that the arrangements do not create 'annual payments' in the tax sense. Assuming that the trust is a discretionary one, the income will be taxable on the trustees at the 35 per cent rate applicable to trusts in the normal way but is not assessable on the employees as no part belongs to any individual employee. A distribution from the trust to an employee is income at the time of the distribution—even if at that stage the employment has ceased. The employee cannot claim credit against the tax on such a distribution for the tax already paid by the trustees. However, by concession the Revenue will make a tax repayment to the trustees (*ESC A68*). The repayment for a year of assessment is the lesser of the tax offset that would have been due under *ICTA 1988, s 687(2)* or tax at the rate applicable to trusts on the distributions to employees during the year. As this is a concession, no repayment supplement will be given. The trustees must have completed tax returns each year and produce evidence of the tax that they have suffered if they want to claim the benefit of this concession. If the employee trust is non-UK resident *ESC A68* does not apply but *ESC B18* gives broadly the same effect. This taxes the employee on the grossed up amount of the distribution but gives him credit for the underlying tax (*Taxline, November 1994, Item 139*).

17.4   A non-statutory ESOT is far more flexible than a statutory one. It does not have to include all employees—although if it only covers a few it may be difficult to show that the contributions are wholly for the purpose of the company's trade, particularly if those few are already shareholders. There is no difficulty in the directors being the trustees. The beneficiaries can include former employees. There is flexibility on when shares are acquired and an ability to invest other than shares in the employee company. The main disadvantage is that the capital gains tax roll over relief considered at 17.54 onwards did not apply to the transfer of shares to a non-statutory ESOT.

17.5   A major problem with a non-statutory ESOT is the period in which contributions by the company attract a corporation tax deduction. Urgent Issues Task Forces abstract No 13 (UITF 13) states that for accounting purposes cash and shares held by the trustees should be treated as assets of the employer until the rights in the shares is transferred to employees. This means that contributions by the company to the ESOT will not be recognised as an expense until the time of such transfer, which may be several years distant. The Revenue view is that UITF 13 needs to be followed in calculating profits for tax purposes. They do not consider that this principle of timing is affected by the fact that UITF 13 'strays' from the legal form of transactions, i.e. it ignores the fact that the ESOT is a legal entity distinct from the employer (*Revenue Tax Bulletin 27, Feb 1997*). With a statutory ESOT on the other hand the law probably allows a deduction at the time the contribution is paid—although it is possible that *FA 1989, s 67(2)(a)* addresses deductibility only, not the timing of the deduction. This is indeed the approach taken by the Revenue who appear to be challenging all payments into employee benefit trusts. Paragraph 8 of UITF13 states, 'The Task Force reached a consensus that the principles of FRS5 require the sponsoring company of an ESOP trust to recognise certain assets and liabilities of the trust as its own whenever it had de facto control of the shares held by the ESOP and bears their benefit or risks. This will generally be the case when the trust is established in order to hold shares for an employee remuneration scheme and may do so in other circumstances'. If the references to 'shares' is replaced by 'assets' the logic of this approach seems compelling. It is nevertheless likely that the Revenue approach will be challenged in the courts at some stage. Until that is done most employee trusts have little or no tax benefit. The main issue is whether accountants can alter the tax effect of a transaction by treating assets belonging to A as if they belonged to B. Tax law follows accountancy principles only to the extent that these are not over-ridden by law. It probably makes no difference if the trustees of the employee trust are all non-directors as paragraph 2(*d*) of UITF 13 points out that 'most ESOP trusts (particularly those established as a means of remunerating employees) are specifically designed so as to serve the purposes of the sponsoring company, and to ensure that there will be minimal risk of any conflict arising between the duties of the trustees and the interest of the company. Where this is so, the sponsoring company has de facto control'. It probably also does not matter that UITF 13 is expressed not to apply to small companies as the Revenue view (which is believed to reflect that of the Accounting Standards Board) is that where small companies are exempted from following the details of a standard they are still expected to comply with its spirit.

17.6   Particular care is needed where the trust will buy shares from a controlling shareholder. In *Mawsley Machinery Ltd v Robinson [1998] STC (SCD) 236* Mr Kimbell, the controlling shareholder, did not wish his employees and fellow directors, who could not afford to buy his shares, to lose control of the company on his death. The company accordingly set up a discretionary trust for the benefit of employees with the intention that it should buy Mr Kimbell's shares on his retirement. It was held that although the trust was for the benefit of employees it was also a convenience for Mr Kimbell so the company's contributions to it could not be said to have been incurred wholly and exclusively for the purposes of the its trade. It is not clear to what extent UITF 13 applies where an employee trust is not set up to hold shares in the employer company but holds other assets. In principle this should make no difference.

17.7   The Revenue took a different point in *Macdonald v Dextra Accessories Ltd and others (2004 STC 339)*, namely the application of *FA 1989, s 43*. This prohibits a deduction in respect of emoluments or potential emoluments (amounts reserved in the accounts of an employer or held by an intermediary with a view to their becoming relevant emoluments) from an office or employment if the emoluments are not paid within nine months after the end of the accounting year. The

Revenue contended that payments into an employee benefit trust were potential emoluments and as such no deduction was due until the potential emoluments became actual emoluments and were paid. the company contended that, as the trustees of the employee benefit trust had powers entitling them to deal with the funds other than by making payments of emoluments to the beneficiaries, the contributions were not paid to the trustees 'with a view to their becoming potential emoluments'. In fact the trustees had allocated the funds to sub-trusts for each director and made loans from the sub-trust to the director. The Commissioners and Neuberger J agreed that the payments were not potential emoluments but the Court of Appeal disagreed. The words 'with a view to' coupled with 'potential' indicate a future event that may or may not occur. This test is to be applied not by reference to the intention of the trustees but by looking at the terms on which the funds are held by the trustees. The phrase is accordingly apt to embrace the whole range of possibilities open to the trustees under the trust deed, one of which was the payment of emoluments. The Court did, however, stress that 'it is not possible to lay down any hard and fast rule applicable to all cases, as to how the expression "with a view to" is intended to apply to any given set of facts. Each case will turn on its own facts'. It is interesting to note that the Revenue do not seem to have argued at any stage that the company's accounting treatment is not in accordance with UITF 13. It may be that they felt that they could not show that the company had de facto control over the trustees. If so that would seem to call into question much of what the Revenue say in their *Tax Bulletin* article.

Provisions applying generally to employee trusts

17.8   If a close company or an individual transfers assets to an employee trust and the exemption under *IHTA 1984, s 13* or *s 28* applies *TCGA 1992, s 17* (see 19.32) does not apply. Instead, the actual consideration paid is adopted for capital gains tax purposes. If the disposal is by way of gift or sale at less than the transferor's CGT base cost it is treated as taking place at a no gain/no loss price and the trustees inherit the transferor's CGT history. [*TCGA 1992, s 239(1)(2)*]. Such a disposal by a close company will not trigger a charge on the shareholders under *TCGA 1992, s 125* if the actual disposal proceeds is at least equal to the company's base cost of the shares. [*TCGA 1992, s 239(3)*].

17.9   The above no gain/no loss rule applies to a disposal by a non-close company in certain circumstances. The disposal must not be an arm's length sale to the trustees and the trusts must not only satisfy *IHTA 1984, s 86(1)* but the persons for whose benefit the trust permit the property to be applied must include all or most of the directors or employees of the company (or if preferred the company and its subsidiaries). This is subject to the proviso that it must not permit the trust property to be applied for a participator in the company (or in any other company that has transferred assets to the trust), a person who has been such a participator at any time in the previous 10 years or a connected person of such a person. A participator owning less than 5 per cent of any class of share (or the issued share capital as a whole) and who would be entitled to less than 5 per cent of the assets on a winding up need not be excluded. The fact that income can be distributed to a participator is also ignored as is the possibility of the trustees appropriating shares to such a person under an approved profit sharing scheme (see Chapter 16). [*TCGA 1992, s 239(4)–(7)*].

17.10   There are also inheritance tax reliefs on the transfer of assets to an employee trust. The settled property must be held on trusts which, either indefinitely or until the end of a period (which can be defined by reference to a fixed date or in some other way), do not permit any of that property to be applied otherwise than for the benefit of:

(*a*)   persons of a class defined by reference to employment in a particular trade, or profession (or employment by, or office with, a body carrying on a trade profession or undertaking), or

(*b*)   persons of a class defined by reference to marriage or relationship to (or dependence on) persons of such a class.

[*IHTA 1984, s 86(1)*].

It is acceptable to also include a power to apply the property for charitable purposes. Where the class is defined by reference to employment with a particular body the class must either comprise all or most of the employees and directors of that body or the trust must hold its property for the purpose of an approved profit sharing scheme within Chapter 16 above. [*IHTA 1984, s 86(2)(3)*].

17.11   A transfer of property by a close company to such an employee trust is not a transfer of value if the beneficiaries include all or most of the directors and employees of that company—or if preferred of the company and any one or more of its subsidiaries. [*IHTA 1984, s 13(1)*]. The exemption is lost if the trust permits any of the property to be applied at any time (including after the trust ceases to qualify as an employee trust) for the benefit of a participator in the company (other than one owning less than 5 per cent), a participator in another close company that made a transfer to the same trust which was exempt under *section 13*, a person who was a participator in the company or such company at any time within the previous ten years, or a connected person of one of the above. A power to pay income to a participator will not lose the relief though. Nor will the relief be lost if the trust is an approved profit sharing scheme within Chapter 16. [*IHTA 1984, s 13*].

17.12   A transfer of shares or securities by an individual to an employee trust (within *IHTA 1984, s 86(1)*) is also exempt provided that the potential beneficiaries include all or most of the directors and employees of the company (subject to the exclusion for participators described at 17.10). At the date of the transfer (or at some time within the following 12 months) the trustees must hold over half of the ordinary shares in the company and have powers of voting on all questions affecting the company as a whole which, if exercised, would yield a majority of the votes capable of being exercised (and there must be no power under which these conditions could cease to be exercised without the consent of the trustees). If the company has shares or securities of a class which confers powers of voting only on the question of a winding up and/or questions primarily affecting shares or securities of that class those shares can be ignored in applying the control test. [*IHTA 1984, s 28*]. This relief is intended to allow a shareholder to transfer a controlling interest in the company to an employee trust. A similar exemption from the tax charge on property ceasing to be held on discretionary trust applies where a trust owning shares or securities of a company becomes an employee trust within *IHTA 1984, s 86(1)*. The above conditions again apply. [*IHTA 1984, s 75*].

17.13   Where property is held in an employee trust (within *IHTA 1984, s 86(1)*) all the property in treated as comprised in a single settlement (even if it was settled by different settlors at different times) and an interest in possession is less than 5 per cent of the assets will not trigger IHT charges. [*IHTA 1984, s 86(4)*]. If assets are transferred from one employee trust to another they are treated for IHT purposes as remaining in the first trust. This also applies to an indirect transfer provided the gap during which the assets are not comprised in an employee trust does not exceed one month. [*IHTA 1984, s 86(5)*]. If the trust ceases to qualify as an employee trust an IHT charge arises on the whole of the settled property at a special rate, dependent on how long the property has been in the trust. This reaches a maximum of 30 per cent where the property has been in the trust for 50 years or more. [*IHTA 1984, s 72(2)(a), (5)*]. This special charge also arises on a distribution by the trust to a person who has directly or indirectly provided property to it (unless it did not exceed £1,000 in any one year) or if the beneficiary is an employee of a close company to a participator owning 5 per cent or more of the company, or to a person who bought his interest in the settlement or to a connected person of such people. [*IHTA 1984, s 72(2)(b), (3)*]. It also applies if the trustees make any other disposition which reduces the value of the settled property. [*IHTA 1984, s 72(2)(c)*]. There is an exemption for the appropriation of shares under an approved profit sharing scheme. [*IHTA 1984, s 72(4)*].

Restriction on deductions

17.14   Where a person (the employer) makes an 'employee benefit contribution' to an employee benefit trust after 26 November 2002 and a deduction would otherwise be allowed for that contribution in computing his taxable profits the deduction is allowable only to the extent that:

(*a*)   during the accounting period in question, or within nine months after it, qualifying benefits are provided (or qualifying expenses paid) out of the contributions; or

(*b*)   where the making of the contributions is itself the provision of qualifying benefits, the contributions are made during the accounting period or within nine months thereafter. [*FA 2003, 24 Schedule 1*].

17.15   For this purpose a person makes an employee benefit contribution if he pays money or transfers assets to another person (the third party) and that other person is entitled or required, under the terms of an employee benefit scheme, to hold or use the money or assets for (or in connection with) the provisions of benefits to employees (or office holders) of the employer [*FA 2003, 24 Schedule 1(2)*]. An employee benefit scheme (EBS) means 'a trust, scheme or other arrangement for the benefit of persons who are, or include, employees of the employer'. [*FA 2003, 24 Schedule 9(1)*].

17.16   Qualifying benefits are provided where there is a payment of money or transfer of assets (other than by way of loan) that either:

(*a*)   gives rise to both an income tax charge (either on the recipient or someone else) under *ITEPA 2003*, and to an NIC charge;

(*b*)   would have given rise to such charges if the duties of the employment in respect of which the payment was made were performed in the UK and the person in respect of whose employment it was made fulfilled the conditions of residence to attract NIC (i.e. the only reason that an income tax and NIC charge do not arise is because the employee is resident or ordinarily resident outside the UK); or

(*c*)   is made in connection with the termination of the recipient's employment with the employer.

[*FA 2003, 24 Schedule 2*]. Where the qualifying benefit takes the form of the payment of money it is treated as provided at the time that the money is treated as received under *ITEPA 2003, s 18* (see 2.46) [*FA 2003, 24 Schedule 2(5)*].

17.17   Qualifying expenses include any expenses of the third party (other than the provision of benefits to employees of the employer) in operating the employee benefit scheme in question but cannot include expenses that, if they had been incurred by the employer, would not be deductible by the employer for tax purposes (in any accounting period). [*FA 2003, 24 Schedule 3*].

17.18   If the provision of a qualifying benefit takes the form of a transfer of an asset to the employee the amount provided is the aggregate of the amount (if any) expended on the asset by the third party and, if the asset was transferred to the third party by the employer, the amount that would have been deductible by the employer on making the transfer if *Schedule 24* had not been enacted. [*FA 2003, 24 Schedule 3*].

17.19   When the deduction is restricted by *Schedule 24* the relief is not lost. The deduction can be claimed in a subsequent period (or periods) in which qualifying benefits (but curiously not qualifying expenses) are paid. [*FA 2003, 24 Schedule 1(4)*]. Qualifying benefits provided (or qualifying expenses paid) by the third party after the recipient of an employee benefit contribution are deemed to be provided or paid out of that contribution up to the amount of the contribution (as reduced by the amount of any benefits or expenses previously paid or provided in the accounting period or within nine months thereafter). [*FA 2003, 24 Schedule 4*]. This appears to deny relief completely to the extent that the third party makes a payment in anticipation of receiving the employee benefit contribution before he receives it.

17.20   If the employer's tax computations are submitted before the end of the nine months period a deduction can be claimed only for qualifying benefits or expenses paid before the computations are submitted, and relief for later payments within the nine months period is claimed by amending the computations. [*FA 2003, 24 Schedule 6*]. Obviously if it is believed that subsequent payments will be made it is likely to make more sense in most cases to delay submitting the computations until the nine months period has expired.

17.21   The restriction does not apply to a payment or transfer which constitutes:

(*a*)   the consideration for goods or services provided in the course of a trade or profession;

(*b*)   contributions under an approved retirement benefit scheme;

(*c*)   contributions under an approved personal pension scheme;

(*d*)   contributions under an accident benefit scheme (i.e. an employee benefit scheme under which benefits can be provided only by reason of a person's disablement or death caused by an accident occurring during his services as an employee of the employer). [*FA 2003, 24 Schedule 9(1)*];

(*e*)   contributions to a SIP;

(*f*)   contributions (prior to 31 December 2002) to a FA 1989 qualifying ESOT; and

(*g*)   a payment which attracts corporation tax relief under *FA 2003, Schedule 23* (see 14.222)

or to one which was made before 1 January 2003 in respect of a person acquiring or having a right to acquire qualifying shares (within the *Schedule 23* meaning), either in the same period or subsequently, by reason of his or another's employment with the company. [*FA 2003, 24 Schedule 8, 11(4)*].

17.22   *Schedule 24* is an anti-avoidance provision. It effectively both nullifies for the future the decision in *Dextra Accessories* (see 17.7) and overrides the accounting treatment permitted by UK GAAP. It should particularly be noted that if the employee benefit scheme makes a payment that is neither a qualifying benefit nor a qualifying expense no deduction will ever be obtained by the employer for that part of the contributions even if the employer would have obtained a deduction had he made the payment direct. Accordingly such a scheme should not in future make charitable donations or payments that do not relate to an identifiable employee and so do not attract an income tax charge as earnings of anyone.

The statutory relief

17.23   The legislation grants a tax deduction for a contribution by a UK resident company to a qualifying ESOT at a time when the company (or a company under its control within *section 840*) has employees who are eligible to benefit under the ESOT—provided that before the end of the 'expenditure period' the contribution is expended by the trustee for a 'qualifying purpose' and a claim for relief is made before the end of the 'claim period'. [*FA 1989, s 67(1)–(3)*]. As indicated earlier this statutory tax relief ceased to apply from 31 December 2002 – or in some cases a little later, it is withdrawn for payments during accounting periods beginning after that date. [*FA 2003, s 142*]. That does not mean that contributions to an ESOT can no longer qualify for relief. It means that an employer needs to rely on general tax law to obtain a deduction. Because of the provisions outlined in paras 17.14 onwards, which delay relief for the employer until the benefits are actually paid, the effect of general tax law will in most cases be to defer the relief.

17.24   The contribution is treated as a deduction in computing the company's trading profit, or as management expenses if it is an investment company. [*FA 1989, s 67(2)*]. If it is neither, no tax relief is due. It appears that the contribution cannot be in kind, but must be in money as it is stated in *FA 1989, s 67(1)(a)* that the *section* applies where the company 'expends a sum in making a payment by way of contribution'. The conditions that must be satisfied to constitute a qualifying ESOT are considered at 17.50 below.

17.25   Corporation tax relief is similarly given on expenditure by a company after 31 March 1991 on establishing a *FA 1989* qualifying ESOP. Such expenditure is treated as a trading expense (or a management expense if the company is an investment company). Relief is normally given in the period of account in which the expenditure is incurred but if the trust is not established within nine months after the end of that period of account it is instead given in the period in which the trust is established. [*ICTA 1988, s 85A*].

17.26   An ESOT must be set up by a company (called the founding company) for the benefit of its employees and employees of members of its group. A non-UK resident company cannot set up a qualifying ESOT. Nor can it obtain a deduction for a payment to an ESOT under these special provisions even if it is liable to corporation tax because it is carrying on a trade in the UK. Most people consider that the 1989 legislation was unnecessary as payments to an employee share trust qualify for tax relief under general principles, as being wholly and exclusively for the purpose of the company's trade and not for a capital purpose. The legislation does not displace the pre-existing law so a non-UK company might well be able to obtain a deduction under general principles. However, the existence of a statutory code seems likely to encourage Inspectors to resist granting a deduction under general principles. A qualifying ESOT will not be able to rely on general principles where the legislation is unfavourable.

It will obviously be bound by the specific legislative provisions. In practice few companies have used statutory ESOTs because these are very restrictive. Anyone considering using one ought first to consider whether its objective might be better met by a SIP (see Chapter 15).

17.27 A number of expressions used in 17.23 above call for explanation. The 'expenditure period' is the nine months following the end of the period of account in which the contribution is charged as an expense. [*FA 1989, s 67(5)*]. As the trustees have from the date they receive the contribution to the end of the expenditure period to expend the money this allows them a period of between nine and 21 months (longer if the period of account exceeds a year) depending on when in the period of account the contribution is made. If the money is not spent in this period, or is spent other than for a qualifying purpose, the company cannot deduct the contribution (or so much of it as has not been spent).

Qualifying purposes

17.28 There are five 'qualifying purposes' on which the ESOT can expend its funds:

(*a*)   the acquisition of shares in the founding company;

(*b*)   the repayment of sums borrowed;

(*c*)   the payment of interest on sums borrowed;

(*d*)   the payment of any sum to a beneficiary (i.e. a qualifying employee); and

(*e*)   the meeting of expenses.

[*FA 1989, s 67(4)*].

Deemed order in which receipts spent

17.29 If it is necessary to determine what funds are spent (for example, because the ESOT receives contributions from more than one company and does not spend them all, or spends some for a non-qualifying purpose) contributions must be regarded as having been spent in the order in which they are received by the trustees. [*FA 1989, s 67(7)*]. *Section 67* does not say whether other income, such as bank deposit interest, for instance, is to be treated as spent in the same way in priority to contributions from participating employers or after them, but *FA 1989, 5 Sch 6* requires the rules of the ESOT to provide that all receipts must be treated as spent in the order that they are received.

Time limit on claim

17.30 The relief must be claimed within the 'claim period', i.e. within two years after the end of the period in which the contribution is charged as an expense by the company.

17.31   Although an ESOT can only purchase shares in the founding company, it is possible for it to hold debentures or similar securities of the company if it receives these on a share exchange or company re-organisation, or as a result of a scrip or rights issue. Accordingly, the *Act* uses the expression 'securities' rather than shares, and defines this as meaning shares and debentures. [*FA 1989, s 69(12)*]. References below to securities have the same meaning.

Charges to tax

17.32   Although the company obtains a deduction, a charge to tax can be made on the trustees in certain circumstances to withdraw this relief. This charge is intended to claw back the tax relief given to the company if the funds are used for a non-qualifying purpose. If the trustees do not pay it the tax can be collected from the company. The 'chargeable events' that trigger a tax charge are as follows.

(*a*)   A transfer of securities by the trustees, unless it is a qualifying transfer. [*FA 1989, s 69(1)(a)*]. Subject to (*b*) below, a transfer to a beneficiary of the ESOT is a qualifying transfer and does not attract tax. [*FA 1989, s 69(2)*]. So is a transfer to the trustees of an approved profit sharing scheme provided that it is made for a consideration which is not less than the price the shares might reasonably be expected to fetch on a sale in the open market. [*FA 1989, s 69(3)*]. It would probably be a breach of trust for the trustees of the profit sharing scheme to pay more than the market price, so in practice such a transfer would have to take place at market value. This will, for example, allow a listed company to fund an ESOT to buy in shares on the open market which can be passed on in due course to the company's profit sharing scheme, although if the profit sharing scheme has the necessary funds there is no reason why it should not itself buy shares in the open market. A disposal after 1 January 1992 in exchange for shares is also a qualifying transfer provided that it qualifies for roll-over relief under *TCGA 1992, s 135*. [*F(No 2)A 1992, s 36*]. A transfer is also a qualifying transfer if it is a transfer of relevant shares made to the trustees of a SIP (see Chapter 15) provided that any consideration received does not exceed the market value of the shares. [*FA 1989, s 69(3AA)* inserted by *FA 2000, s 55(3)*]. Where the trustees dispose of part of a holding of shares after 27 November 2002 (20 March 2000 before 1 January 2002) (whether or not by way of a qualify-ing transfer) the 'relevant shares' in the holding must be treated as disposed of before other shares. [*FA 1989, s 69(3AB)*]. Relevant shares for this purpose means shares held by the trustees at midnight on 26 November 2002 or shares purchased by them out of money held in a bank or building society account at that time (treating all payments (for anything) by the trustees after that time as coming first out of such money. [*FA 1989, s 69 (3AC)(3AD)* as amended by *FA 2003, s 142(2)*].

(*b*) A transfer of shares (or debentures) by the trustees to a beneficiary of the ESOT if the transfer is not made on qualifying terms. [*FA 1989, s 69(1)(b)*]. A transfer is made on qualifying terms only if

    (i) all the shares transferred at the same time are transferred on similar terms (except where they are transferred under an approved savings-related share option scheme),

    (ii) shares have been offered to everyone who is a beneficiary of the ESOT (other than those who are beneficiaries only by virtue of an approved savings-related share option scheme) at the time the transfer is made, and

    (iii) shares are transferred to all such beneficiaries who have accepted the offer.

[*FA 1989, s 69(4)*].

It will be seen that this prevents an ESOT transferring shares to selected employees only, without triggering a tax charge—or rather without triggering the charge to claw back the company's tax relief, as the trustees will have a capital gains tax charge even where the transfer to beneficiaries is on qualifying terms, except where the concession discussed at 17.46 below applies. For the purposes of condition (i) it is permissible to allocate shares according to levels of remuneration, length of service or similar factors. [*FA 1989, s 69(6)*]. In the case of a large company it will be very difficult to meet condition (ii) if it is interpreted literally, as it does not allow for the possibility of people becoming eligible beneficiaries between the date a decision to pass shares to beneficiaries is made and the date that the transfer actually takes place.

A transfer from an ESOT established after 28 April 1996 is also made on qualifying terms if it is made to a person exercising an option under an approved savings-related share option scheme established by the company which established the ESOT (or a company controlled by it), the option is exercised in accordance with that scheme, and the consideration for the transfer is payable to the trustees. [*FA 1989, s 4(4ZA)*]. This allows the trustees to grant options for an employee to buy his shares from the ESOT rather than the employing company, so giving greater flexibility. Such options will not be granted under the company's savings-related share option scheme itself. Membership of that scheme is merely a test of eligibility. However, the legislation requires the ESOT to grant options in accordance with the requirement of *ICTA 1988, 9 Schedule*, i.e. to mirror what would be required under an approved scheme (see 17.50(*ga*)).

(*c*) The retention of shares or debentures by the trustees for more than 20 years (seven years where the trust was established before 3 May 1994). [*FA 1989, s 69(1)(c)* and *4A* inserted by *FA 1994, 13 Sch 6*].

For this purpose shares or debentures are treated as disposed of by the trustees in the order that they acquire them. [*FA 1989, s 69(7)*]. The expiration of seven years from the time of acquisition of the shares will trigger the tax charge. The concept is to discourage the use of an ESOT to hold shares for long periods, perhaps so as to have a block of shares held in friendly hands.

(*d*)   The expenditure of any sum by the trustees other than for a qualifying purpose. [*FA 1989, s 69(1)(d)*]. The qualifying purposes are the same as those specified in 17.28 above. [*FA 1989, ss 67(4), 69(5)*]. In applying the above rules the trustees of the ESOT acquire shares or debentures when they become entitled to them, with the exceptions that:

(i)   if they are new shares or debentures obtained on a share exchange [*TCGA 1992, s 135(1)*] or a reorganisation [*TCGA 1992, s 126*] which constitutes a company reorganisation for capital gains tax purposes they are treated as having been acquired at the time the original securities were acquired [*FA 1989, s 69(9)*]; and

(ii)   if the trustees agree to take a transfer of shares or debentures they are treated as having become entitled to them at the date of the agreement, not the later date of transfer. [*FA 1989, s 69(10)*].

Similarly they transfer shares to another person when that other person becomes entitled to them (or if earlier, when they agree to make the transfer), and retain shares if they remain entitled to them. [*FA 1989, s 69(8)(11)*].

(*e*)   If after 27 July 2000 the trustees make a qualifying transfer within *s 69(3AA)* (see (*a*) above) for a consideration and they do not expend the entire consideration for one or more qualifying purposes within nine months after the end of the period of account (of the grantor company) in which the qualifying transfer took place. [*FA 1989, s 69(1) (e) and 69(5A) inserted by FA 2000, s 55*].

Meaning of chargeable amount

17.33   Where the chargeable event is one of those described in heads (*a*)–(*c*) at 17.32 above, and the transaction constitutes a disposal of the shares by the trustees for capital gains tax purposes, the amount on which this special tax charge is assessed, the 'chargeable amount', is the sums allowable under *TCGA 1992, s 38(1)(a)(b)*, i.e. the cost of the shares (including acquisition costs) plus any enhancement expenditure. If the chargeable event is not a disposal for capital gains tax purposes the chargeable amount is the sum that would have been allowable under *section 38(1)(a)(b)* had it constituted such a disposal. [*FA 1989, s 70(1)(2)*]. FA 1989, s 72 (see 17.44 below) can impose an overriding limit on the chargeable amount. [*FA 1989, s 72(2)(c)*].

17.34   If the chargeable event is the expenditure of money for a non-qualifying purpose (i.e. within head (*d*) at 17.32 above) the chargeable amount is the sum so spent. [*FA 1989, s 70(3)*].

17.35   If the chargeable event is the failure to invest money received from a *FA 2000* qualifying ESOP (i.e. within head (*e*) at 17.32 above) the chargeable amount is the part of that consideration not used for a qualifying purpose within nine months after the end of the period of account. [*FA 1989, s 70(4)* inserted by *FA 2000, s 55(6)*].

17.36   The tax charge is imposed by treating the trustees as receiving on the occurrence of a chargeable event annual profits or gains taxable under Case VI of Schedule D for the year of assessment in which the event occurs equal to the chargeable amount. [*FA 1989, s 68(1)(2)*]. Tax is chargeable at the rate applicable to trusts, thus giving, on current rates, a charge at 34 per cent. [*FA 1989, s 68(2)(c)*].

Late payment of tax

17.37   If any part of the tax is not paid by the trustees within six months from the date on which assessment becomes final and conclusive, a notice of liability to tax can be served on the founding company, or on any other company that has paid a sum to the trustees and obtained a tax deduction for it, and the unpaid tax (together with any accrued interest and interest accruing after the service of the notice of liability) then becomes payable by that company instead of by the trustees. [*FA 1989, s 68(3)(4)(6)(7)*]. If the company does not pay the full amount due within three months from the date of service of the notice of liability the amount outstanding again becomes recoverable from the trustees although the Revenue still have a continuing right to recover it instead from the company. [*FA 1989, s 68(5)*].

Potential future liability to tax

17.38   It should be noted that once a company has obtained a deduction for a contribution to an ESOT, however small that contribution may be, it is thereafter potentially liable for all tax payable by the trustees at any time in the future even though that tax may arise in relation to funds deriving from some other company and may far exceed the contributions that the unfortunate company made to the ESOT. Anyone purchasing a company that has contributed to an ESOT needs to be aware of this risk. As it is an open-ended and unquantifiable commitment an indemnity from the vendor against such tax may not be a sufficient protection. It may be that the purchaser should consider requiring the ESOT trust to be wound up as that seems to be the only way to limit the risk.

Borrowing by the ESOT

Further chargeable events

17.39   If a chargeable event (within 17.32 above) (called 'the initial chargeable event') occurs in relation to an ESOT at a time when any amount borrowed by the trustees is outstanding, and it is one to which *FA 1989, s 72(2)(b)* (see 17.35 below) applies (i.e. the chargeable amount was restricted), a further chargeable event is deemed to occur at the end of the year of assessment in which any part of the borrowing is repaid. [*FA 1989, s 71(1)–(3)*]. The chargeable amount on that further chargeable event is the amount of the loan repayments in the year of assessment. [*FA 1989, s 71(5)*]. The tax consequences are the same as for an actual chargeable event, i.e. there is a Case VI charge at 34 per cent. [*FA 1989, s 71(4)*].

17.40   Although, on the face of it, this creates a double charge—once when the chargeable event occurs and again when the loan is repaid—this is not in fact the case as *FA 1989, s 72* (which is considered at 17.44 below) puts a limit on the total sums that can be treated as chargeable amounts. The intention of *FA 1989, s 71* is to ensure that a tax charge cannot be avoided by the ESOT borrowing funds, using them to make non-qualifying transfers, etc., and then receiving contributions from the employer company to repay the borrowing. It effectively treats the chargeable event as occurring when the borrowing is repaid only if a charge cannot be made when the actual non-qualifying transfer or payment takes place.

Chargeable amount on further chargeable event

17.41   If *FA 1989, s 72(2)(b)* had effect at the time of the initial chargeable event the chargeable amount on the deemed further chargeable event is the smaller of:

(*a*)   the aggregate of the loan repayments made in the year of assessment; and

(*b*)   the result of the formula A minus B minus C, where

A = the sum which would be the chargeable amount for the initial chargeable event apart from *section 72(2)*,

B = the chargeable amount for the initial chargeable event (i.e. applying *section 72(2)*), and

C = an amount equal to the aggregate of the chargeable amounts for any prior chargeable events, i.e. any loan repayments in earlier years of assessment but subsequent to the initial chargeable event.

[*FA 1989, s 71(6)–(8)*].

Later chargeable events

17.42   If, after the occurrence of a further chargeable event (within 17.39 above), a second chargeable event occurs in circumstances within *FA 1989, s 71(1)* (so that there is potentially a second 'further chargeable event') at a time when the borrowing at head (*b*) of 17.41 above is still outstanding, that borrowing (i.e. that was outstanding at the time of the first event) is ignored to determine whether a deemed further chargeable event can arise in relation to that second event. In other words, only any additional borrowing since the time of the first chargeable event will generate a charge under *section 71*. [*FA 1989, s 71(9)*].

17.43 In ascertaining what borrowings are repaid, amounts borrowed earlier (even, apparently, if from a different lender) must be treated as repaid before later borrowings. [*FA 1989, s 71(10)*].

Limit on chargeable amounts

17.44 Where a chargeable event within *FA 1989, s 69* (see 17.32 above) or a deemed further chargeable event within *FA 1989, s 71* (see 17.39 above) occurs:

(*a*) the amount which would otherwise be the chargeable amount must be aggregated with the chargeable amounts for all prior chargeable events; and

(*b*) if such aggregate amount exceeds 'the deductible amount' the chargeable amount on that event must be reduced by that excess.

[*FA 1989, s 72(1)(2)*].

For the purpose of head (*b*) above, the deductible amount is the total of all sums received by the trustees before the occurrence of the event in question which either:

(i) has qualified for a deduction under *FA 1989, s 67(2)* (see 17.24 above) by the company that paid it; or

(ii) would qualify for a deduction if a claim for a relief were made immediately before the occurrence of that event.

[*FA 1989, s 72(3)(4)*].

17.45 The purpose of *FA 1989, s 72* is to limit the total amounts that can be taxable on the trustees to the sums which have qualified for a deduction by the company or companies that have made contributions to the ESOT. This test is looked at over the entire life of the ESOT.

Tax position of the ESOT

17.46 The legislation does not confer any tax exemption on the ESOT itself. The trustees will be liable to income tax on their investment income, such as dividends from the shares or bank deposit interest, in the normal way. The trustees will also be liable to capital gains tax when they transfer shares to beneficiaries, or if they make any non-qualifying transfers of shares. By concession the Revenue do not charge the trustees to capital gains tax on a transfer of assets to a beneficiary for no consideration if the employee is liable to income tax on the full market value of the assets transferred (*IR Press Release 5 December 1990*).

This concession applies even if the employee trust is not a qualifying ESOT, provided that it qualifies as a trust for the benefit of employees for inheritance tax purposes under *IHTA 1984, s 86* (see 17.12) (or would do but for *section 86(3)*) and that the employee does not own more than 5 per cent of the company (within *IHTA 1984, s 28(4)–(6)*).

17.47 A company that contributes funds to the ESOT is not liable for the tax on such liabilities of the trustees. It can only be called upon to pay the tax arising in relation to chargeable events.

17.48 Curiously, the payment of tax does not seem to be a qualifying purpose. The reason is probably because there is no need to pay such tax out of funds provided by the company as the existence of the tax liability predicates the trustees themselves having generated either income or capital gains out of which the tax can be met. Unfortunately, *FA 1989, 5 Sch 9* states that the trust deed must require all sums received by the trustees (not merely contributions from the company) to be expended only for qualifying purposes. It may be that the draftsman considered that tax can qualify as an expense of the trustees.

Tax position of the beneficiary

17.49 The legislation does not confer any tax exemption on the beneficiary. The value of shares he receives from the ESOT will constitute emoluments in the normal way. This is why the Government envisages that an ESOT might be combined with an approved profit sharing scheme. If the beneficiary receives shares under the profit sharing scheme, the company should obtain a corporation tax deduction for such payments in any event, so, if a company has an approved profit sharing scheme, it is difficult to see why it should want an ESOT as well. If the company's profits fluctuate, a combination of the two types of scheme will enable funds to be set aside in good years in excess of the profit sharing scheme limits so that the ESOT can 'warehouse' shares which can be appropriated to beneficiaries of the profit sharing scheme in years when the company is less able to make payments to that scheme.

Qualifying conditions

17.50 A trust will be a qualifying ESOT at the time it is established if it satisfies the following conditions. [*FA 1989, 5 Sch 1*]. If a trust established before 4 May 1994 is a qualifying ESOT at the time it is established it will continue to be an ESOT throughout its life, but will not be a qualifying ESOT during any period that condition (*d*) below is not met. [*FA 1989, 5 Sch 12, 13*]. Similarly, one established after 3 May 1994 will continue to be an ESOT throughout its life other than for any period during which all of the conditions about trustees are not met. [*FA 1989, 5 Sch 12A*]. The distinction seems to be that once a trust is an ESOT it must comply with all the regulations governing ESOTs, but a company can obtain a corporation tax deduction for a contribution to an

ESOT only if it is a qualifying ESOT at the time the contribution is made.

(*a*)   It must be established under a trust deed. [*FA 1989, 5 Sch 2(1)*]. It is not possible to have an oral ESOT even though under general law it is possible to have an oral trust.

(*b*)   It must be established by a company (the founding company) which at the time is resident in the UK and is not under the control of another company [*FA 1989, 5 Sch 2(2)*], i.e. an ESOT cannot be set up by a subsidiary; it must be established by the holding company of a group. An ESOT cannot be established for the employees of a UK branch of an overseas company or even for those of a UK subsidiary of such a company. In the light of the substantial amount of investment by overseas companies in the UK in recent years this seems a somewhat strange restriction as it prevents large numbers of employees from being able to participate.

(*c*)   The trust deed must provide for the establishment of a body of trustees, must appoint the initial trustees, and must contain rules for the retirement and removal of trustees and the appointment or replacement of additional trustees. [*FA 1989, 5 Sch 3(1)(2)*]. If the trustee is to be a trust company the deed must provide that only such a company can be the trustee. [*FA 1989, 5 Sch 3C*].

(*d*)   The trust deed must provide either that:

  (i)   there must be at least three trustees all of whom must be UK residents; or

  (ii)   the trustee must be a company controlled by the founding company;

and in the case of individual trustees that either (*e*) or (*f*) below must apply.

(*e*)   In the case of individual trustees either:

  (i)   the trustees must include one person who is a trust corporation, a solicitor, or a member of such other professional body as the Revenue may allow (which is likely to include all the main UK accountancy bodies);

  (ii)   most of the trustees must be persons who are not, and never have been, directors of the founding company or any other UK resident company that at the time is controlled by the founding company;

  (iii)   most of the trustees must be employees of the founding company (or of another UK resident company controlled by the founding company) who do not have a material interest in any of such companies and have never had such an interest; and

  (iv)   the trustees within (iii) above must have been selected (before being appointed) by a majority of the employees falling within the founding company's group (i.e. that company and all UK resident companies controlled by it at that time) at the time of the selection, or by persons elected to represent those employees.

[*FA 1989, 5 Sch 3(3)(4)*]; or

(*f*)   (i)   the trustees must include at least one professional trustee and two non-professional ones;

     (ii)   at least half of the non-professional trustees must have been selected (by a majority of votes, or by elected representatives of the employees) by all of the employees of the founding company's group other than any having a material interest in the company; and

     (iii)   such trustees must be employees of the founding company (or of another group member) who do not have a material interest in the company. [*FA 1989, 5 Sch 3B(4)(7)(8)* inserted by *FA 1994, 13 Sch 3*].

Trusts established before 3 May 1994 had to comply with head (*e*)(i). Even after that date a trust company can be used only if the board of directors satisfies the test at (*f*)(i) above with the substitution of a reference to the directors for the trustees. [*5 Schedule 3C*].

For the purpose of (*f*)(i) a professional trustee means a trust corporation, a solicitor, or a member of any other professional body that the Revenue may designate, who has been selected by (and only by) the non-professional trustees (trustees designate in the case of the initial appointment), and who is not a director or employee of the founding company. [*5 Schedule 3B(5)(6)*].

For the purpose of (*e*)(iii) and (*f*)(iii) above, a person has a material interest in a company if he (with his associates), or any one or more associates of his:

(A)   is the beneficial owner of, or able to control (directly or indirectly) more than 5 per cent of the ordinary share capital of the company; or

(B)   possesses, or is entitled to acquire, such rights as would in the event of a winding up or in any other circumstances give an entitlement to receive more than 5 per cent of the assets which would then be available for distribution among the participators.

[*FA 1989, 5 Sch 16(1)*].

The definition of control in *section 840* and that of participator in *section 417* apply. [*FA 1989, 5 Sch 16(2)*]. An associate of a person means:

(I)   any relative (i.e. spouse, parent or remoter forebear, child or remoter issue, or brother or sister) of that person;

(II)   a partner of that person;

(III)   the trustees of any settlement in relation to which the person is a settlor (or any relative of his, living or dead, is or was a settlor);

(IV) where the person is interested in any shares or obligations of the company which are subject to any trust (or are part of the estate of a deceased person),

    (1) the trustees of the settlement (or the personal representatives of the deceased), and

    (2) if that person is a company, any other company that is interested in those shares or obligations.

[*ICTA 1988, s 417(3)(4), FA 1989, 5 Sch 16(2)(a)*].

Head (IV) does not apply if the trust is an employee benefit trust (within *ICTA 1988, 8 Schedule 7* see 18.41 below) unless at some time after 26 July 1989 the person in question (either on his own or with associates), or an associate or associates of his, has been the beneficial owner of, or able directly or indirectly to control, more than 5 per cent of the ordinary share capital of the company. *8 Schedule 7(9)–(12)* (see 18.41–18.44 below) applies for the purpose of this provision. [*FA 1989, 5 Sch 16(3)–(6)*].

It should be noted that the majority of the trustees must be elected by the employees or their representatives, e.g. their trade union. The idea is that the employees, not the directors or senior executives, should control the votes attaching to the shares from time to time held by the ESOT. One of the trustees must be a trust corporation or a professional person. The Revenue will require him to ensure that the trust operates properly and any aggrieved employees will probably look to him for recompense as the employee trustees (the majority) might not be expected to have the necessary expertise. This does not appear to be an enviable role for a professional person to accept!

(g) The trust deed must provide that a person is a beneficiary at a particular time (the relevant time) if:

    (i) at that time he is an employee or director of a company which falls within the founding company's group;

    (ii) at each given time in (i.e. throughout) a qualifying period he was an employee or director of a company falling within the founding company's group; and

    (iii) in the case of a director at that given time he worked at the rate of at least 20 hours a week (ignoring holidays and sickness).

[*FA 1989, 5 Sch 4(2)*].

A qualifying period for this purpose is a period of up to five years which is specified in the trust deed and which ends at the relevant time. [*FA 1989, 5 Sch 4(5)*]. In other words, the founding company can choose what qualifying period of service is needed before a person can be a beneficiary, but this cannot be more than five years. A company falls within the founding company's group at a particular time if it is UK resident at that time and either it is the founding company or it is controlled by the founding company (within *section 840*). [*FA 1989, 5 Sch 4(9)*]. It should be noted that for the purpose of (ii) the company needs to meet these tests throughout the qualifying period. For example, if the company selects a qualifying period of five years, an employee of a company purchased by the founding company within the five years prior to the relevant time cannot be a beneficiary at the relevant time—even though he may have worked for his employer company for over five years.

(*ga*)   The deed can allow a person to be a beneficiary at a given time if at that time he is eligible to participate in an approved savings-related share option scheme established by a company within the founding company's group. The deed must provide that the trustees of the ESOT must conform with the *ICTA 1988, 9 Schedule* requirements in relation to such a beneficiary.

[*FA 1989, 5 Sch 4(2A)(2B)*].

(*h*)   The deed can allow a person to be a beneficiary at a particular time (the relevant time) if:

(i)   he was an employee or director of a company in the founding company's group throughout a qualifying period, and

(ii)   he ceased to be such an employee or director, or the company left the group, less than 18 months before the relevant time.

[*FA 1989, 5 Sch 4(3)*].

A qualifying period in this case means a period equal in length to that adopted under head (*g*), above, but which ends when the person ceased to be an employer or the company left the group. [*FA 1989, 5 Sch 4(3)*].

In other words it is permissible (but, unlike with existing employees, not mandatory) to include ex-employees who ceased to be employed by the group within the previous 18 months provided that they qualified as beneficiaries at the date the employment ceased or the employing company left the group. The deed can also allow a charity to be a beneficiary but only as a long-stop, i.e. if there are no qualifying employees or directors in existence and the ESOT is in consequence being wound up. [*FA 1989, 5 Sch 4(4)*]. Subject to this the deed must not permit any person not falling within heads (*g*) or (*h*) to be a beneficiary. [*FA 1989, 5 Sch 4(7)*]. It should be particularly noted that a statutory ESOT must include all employees as beneficiaries including part-time employees (but not part-time directors) with more than five years' service. It can if it wishes include those with shorter service, and can include pensioners and other ex-employees but only for the first 18 months after their employment ceases. A non-statutory employee trust can include all pensioners and can pick and choose which employees to include.

(*j*)   The deed must provide (other than by virtue of an approved savings-related share option scheme) that a person cannot be a beneficiary at a particular time (the relevant time) if either at that time or at any time within the previous twelve months he had a material interest in the founding company. [*FA 1989, 5 Sch 4(8)*]. The meaning of material interest is considered in head (*f*) above.

(*k*) The functions of the trustees must be so expressed in the trust deed that it is apparent that their general functions are:

   (i)   to receive sums from the founding company (and other sums— by way of loan or otherwise);

   (ii) to acquire securities, i.e. shares and debentures;

   (iii) to transfer securities or money (or both) to beneficiaries;

   (iv) to grant rights to acquire shares to persons who are beneficiaries;

   (v)   to sell securities to the trustees of approved profit sharing schemes at open market value; and

   (vi) pending transfer, to retain securities and to manage them (whether by exercising voting right or otherwise).

[*FA 1989, 5 Sch 5*].

(*l*) The deed must require all sums received by the trustees:

   (i)   to be expended within nine months from the day the sum is received (except where it is received from the founding company or a company under its control, when it must be expended within nine months from the end of the period of account in which the sum is charged as an expense);

   (ii) to be expended only for qualifying purposes (as listed in 17.28 above);

   (iii) whilst retained by the trustees, to be kept as cash or kept in an account with a bank or building society.

[*FA 1989, 5 Sch 6(1)–(3)*].

It must also provide that, in ascertaining whether a particular sum has been expended, sums received earlier by the trustees must be treated as expended before those received by them later. [*FA 1989, 5 Sch 6(4)*].

(*m*) The deed must provide that where the trustees pay sums to different beneficiaries at the same time all the sums must be paid on similar terms (but the fact that terms vary according to levels of remuneration of beneficiaries, the length of their service, or similar factors does not mean that the terms are not similar). [*FA 1989, 5 Sch 6(5)(6)*].

(*n*) The trust deed must provide that the only securities that can be acquired by the trustees are shares in the founding company, which:

   (i)   form part of the ordinary share capital;

   (ii) are fully paid up;

(iii) are not redeemable; and

(iv) are not subject to restrictions—other than restrictions attaching to all shares of the same class or a restriction which:

(A) is imposed by the founding company's Articles of Association;

(B) requires all shares held by directors or employees of the founding company (or of any other company which it controls) to be disposed of on ceasing to be so held; and

(C) requires all shares acquired by other people in pursuance of rights or interests obtained by such directors or employees to be disposed of on acquisition.

[*FA 1989, 5 Sch 7(1)(2)*].

A restriction within (iv) above must require that any disposal under it must be by way of sale for a consideration in money on terms specified in the Articles, and the Articles must provide that any person disposing of shares of the same class (whether or not a director or employee) must be required to sell them on the same terms. [*FA 1989, 5 Sch 7(3)*].

The deed can, if desired, provide that the trustees can acquire other securities if they are issued to the trustees on a share exchange or company reorganisation which does not constitute a disposal for capital gains tax purposes. [*FA 1989, 5 Sch 8*]. Clearly the deed ought to contain such a power.

(*o*) The deed must provide that shares in the founding company cannot be acquired by the trustees at a price in excess of their open market value. [*FA 1989, 5 Sch 7(4)*].

(*p*) The deed must provide that shares in the founding company must not be acquired by the trustees at a time when that company is under the control (within *section 840*) [*FA 1989, 5 Sch 15*] of another company. [*FA 1989, 5 Sch 7(5)*].

(*q*) The trust must provide that:

(i) where the trustees transfer shares (or other securities) to a beneficiary they must do so on qualifying terms; and

(ii) the trustees must transfer all securities within 20 years from the date they acquire them (seven years if the trust was created before 3 May 1994). [*FA 1989, 5 Sch 7(1)*].

For the purpose of (i), a transfer is made on qualifying terms only if:

(A) all the securities transferred at the same time (other than by virtue of an approved savings-related share option scheme) are transferred on similar terms (however, they may vary according to levels of remuneration, length of service or similar factors);

(B)   securities have been offered to all persons who are beneficiaries (other than solely by virtue of an approved savings related share option scheme) when the transfer is made; and

(C)   securities are transferred to all those beneficiaries who have accepted the offer.

[*FA 1989, 5 Sch 9(1)–(3)*].

A transfer is also made on qualifying terms if it is made to a person exercising an option granted under an approved savings-related share option scheme established by the founding company (or a company controlled by it), the option is being exercised in accordance with the provisions of that scheme and the consideration for the transfer is payable to the trustees. [*ICTA 1988, 5 Sch 9 (2ZA)*].

The deed must also specify that in determining whether particular securities have been transferred in accordance with the rules, securities must be treated as transferred in the order in which they were acquired. [*FA 1989, 5 Sch 9(4)*].

(*r*)   The trust deed must not contain features which are not essential (or reasonably incidental) to the purpose of acquiring sums and securities, granting share options to persons who are eligible to participate in approved savings-related share option schemes, transferring shares to such persons, transferring sums and securities to employees and directors, and transferring securities to the trustees of approved profit sharing schemes. [*FA 1989, 5 Sch 10*].

(*s*)   The deed must provide that the trustees acquire securities when they become entitled to them, transfer securities to another person when that person becomes entitled to them, and retain securities if they remain entitled to them. [*FA 1989, 5 Sch 11(1)*]. If it permits trustees to acquire on a share exchange, etc., securities other than qualifying shares in the founding company (see head (*n*) above) the deed must provide that such securities must be treated as acquired when the trustees become entitled to the original shares for which they were exchanged or in respect of which they were issued. [*FA 1989, 5 Sch 11(2)*]. The deed must also state that if the trustees agree to take (or to make) a transfer of securities, the acquisition (or disposal) takes place when the agreement is made, not when the transfer takes place. [*FA 1989, 5 Sch 11(3)*].

Information

17.51   An Inspector of Taxes can require the trustees of an ESOT (whether a qualifying one or not) to make a return if they have at any time received (from anyone) a contribution that has qualified for a corporation tax deduction by the payer. [*FA 1989, s 73(1)*]. The request for a return must specify the information that it is to contain. This must only be information that the Inspector needs for the purposes of *FA 1989, ss 68–72* but may include information about:

(*a*)   sums received by the trustees, including borrowings (and the persons from whom the sums were received);

(*b*)   expenditure incurred by the trustees (including the purpose of the expenditure and the recipient);

(*c*)   assets acquired by the trustees (including the person from whom they were acquired and the consideration given by the trustees); and

(*d*)   transfers of assets made by the trustees (including to whom they were transferred and the consideration, if any, furnished by them).

[*FA 1989, s 73(2)–(7)*].

17.52   When a company is granted a corporation tax deduction for a contribution to an ESOT, the Inspector of Taxes must send the trustees a certificate stating:

(*a*)   that a deduction has been allowed; and

(*b*)   the amount of the deduction.

[*FA 1989, s 73(8)*].

17.53   It is somewhat unusual for the Revenue to be required to provide information to taxpayers. However, the trustees need this information to determine whether the limit on the size of a chargeable amount applies (see 17.34 above).

17.54   Failure by the trustees to make a return when required to do so renders them liable to a penalty of up to £300, plus a further £60 a day after it has been declared by the court or Commissioners before whom proceedings for the penalty have commenced. [*TMA 1970, ss 73(9), 98*].

Transfer of shares to ESOTs

17.55   If a person transferred shares to an ESOT between 21 March 1990 and 6 April 2001 he could claim a form of capital gains tax roll-over relief provided that the following conditions were met. [*TCGA 1992, s 227 and FA 2000, s 54*].

(*a*)   The ESOT must have been established by a trading company or the holding company of a trading group and it must have been a qualifying ESOT (see 17.50 above) at the time of the transfer. [*TCGA 1992, s 227(2)*].

(*b*)   The shares must have been shares in the founding company satisfying the condition in head (*n*) at 17.50 above. [*TCGA 1992, s 227(3)*].

(*c*)   At some time in the twelve months following the disposal the ESOT must have been beneficially entitled to at least 10 per cent of the ordinary share capital of the founding company (and of profits available for distribution to equity holders, and of assets on a winding up). [*TCGA 1992, ss 227(4), 228(2)*].

(*d*) The disposal must not have been by way of gift (as relief would already be available under *TCGA 1992, s 165*), and within six months after the date of transfer (or the date that (*c*) above is first satisfied) the proceeds must have been reinvested in chargeable assets (i.e. anything within the scope of capital gains tax other than shares or debentures of the founding company or another company in its group, EIS (formerly BES) shares, or a dwelling which is the vendor's principal private residence (or an option over such a residence)). [*TCGA 1992, ss 227(5), 228(3)*].

(*e*) Between the date of the acquisition of the new asset and the date the 10 per cent limit at (*c*) above was first reached, neither the vendor nor a person connected with him could have been entitled to acquire any of the shares being transferred (except under pre-emption rights or rights applying under the Articles to all share-holders). [*TCGA 1992, ss 227(6), 228(4)*].

(*f*) No chargeable event (see 17.30 above) must have occurred in the year of assessment (accounting period for a company) in which the shares were transferred, that in which the new asset was bought, or an intervening year. [*TCGA 1992, s 227(6)*].

(*g*) The transferor had to be resident or ordinarily resident in the UK at the time he acquired the new assets. [*TCGA 1992, s 228(b)*].

17.56 The relief had to be claimed within two years from the acquisition of the new asset (not the end of the year of assessment in which it took place). The disposal was treated as being at a no gain, no loss price and the acquisition price of the new assets as being reduced by the excess of the actual consideration over that sum. [*TCGA 1992, s 229*]. Partial relief was given if part only of the proceeds are reinvested.

17.57 If a chargeable event (see 17.30 above) occurs in the ESOT during the lifetime of the transferor (or its existence if it was a trust) and at that time the transferor still owns the new asset (or a replacement asset on the acquisition of which the gain was again deferred) tax becomes payable by the transferor on the gain that was deferred. [*TCGA 1992, ss 232–234*]. The transferor, of course, has no control over the actions of the ESOT trustees, who cannot include directors (see the condition in head (*e*) at 17.50 above). There is accordingly always the risk that his relief may be withdrawn by an event over which he has no control.

17.58 Where a person has claimed this roll-over relief the Inspector of Taxes can require the ESOT to provide him with whatever information he may specify that he needs for the purpose of these provisions. [*TCGA 1992, s 235*].

Transfers to Share Incentive Plans (see Chapter 15)

17.59   *FA 2000, section 48* and *9 Schedule* introduced a new *Schedule 7C* to the *TCGA 1992* which grants a form of roll-over relief where shares are transferred to a SIP.

17.60   It applies as where:

(*a*)   An individual or trust (i.e. a person other than a company, which will of course include an unapproved ESOT) (called 'the claimant') makes a disposal of shares to the SIP. [*7C Schedule 2(1)*].

(*b*)   Those shares can qualify as eligible shares under *ITEPA 2003, s 2 Schedules 25–33* (see 15.5)(*j*)) but as if the parts of *paragraph 27* which apply only to listed shares were omitted i.e. they can be awarded as plan shares to participants in the SIP. [*7C Schedule 2(2)*].

(*c*)   At any time in the 12 months following the date of that disposal the SIP holds for the benefit of plan beneficiaries shares in the company that constitute at least 10 per cent of its ordinary share capital (within *ICTA 1988, s 832(1)*) and carry rights to at least 10 per cent of any profits available for distribution to shareholders and of any assets available for distribution to shareholders in the event of a winding up. [*7C Schedule 2(3), 4(2)*].

(*d*)   At all times in the period from the date of the disposal to the trustees to the date that the claimant acquires his new assets (or, if later, to the date that the 10 per cent test in (*c*) above is fulfilled) there are no unauthorised arrangements under which the claimant (or a connected person) could be entitled to acquire (directly or indirectly) from the SIP trustees any shares or any interest or right deriving from shares. [*7C Schedule 2(5), 4(A)*]. All arrangements are unauthorised for this purpose unless they only allow shares to be appropriated to or acquired on behalf of an individual under the plan. [*7C Schedule 4(5)*].

(*e*)   The claimant obtains consideration for the disposal, i.e. he sells the shares to the SIP rather than gifts them. [*7C Schedule 3(1)*].

(*f*)   At some time during the six months from the date of the disposal or, if later, the six months from the time that the SIP meets the 10 per cent ownership test at (*c*) the entire consideration for the disposal is applied in acquiring assets, or an interest in assets, which:

(ii)   are chargeable assets of the claimant; and

(iii)   are not shares in (or debentures of) the scheme company or another company in the same group as the scheme company.

[*7C Schedule 3(1), 4(3)*].

17.61   If all of the above conditions are met the claimant can claim (within two years from the date of acquisition of the replacement assets) to be treated as if he had sold the shares for a price that gives neither a gain nor a loss and as if the consideration for the replacement assets were reduced by the excess of the actual consideration over the no gain/no loss price. [*7C Schedule 5(1)*].

17.62   If conditions (*a*) to (*e*) above are met but the whole of the consideration is not reinvested in acquiring the replacement assets, partial relief is given if the amount not reinvested is less than the gain accruing on the disposal. [*7C Schedule 3(2)*]. In such a case the claim will be to reduce the gain accruing on the disposal to the amount not invested and to reduce the acquisition cost of the replacement assets by the same amount. [*7C Schedule 5(2)*].

17.63   The replacement assets are treated as meeting condition (*f*) if an unconditional contract for their acquisition is entered into during the six-month period. [*7C Schedule 3(1)*]. It should particularly be noted that, if the SIP does not satisfy the 10 per cent test at the date of the disposal, an acquisition of replacement assets before it meets that test will not qualify for the rollover relief. The acquisition must be delayed until after the 10 per cent test is satisfied. The rollover relief of course only affects the claimant; the deeming does not flow through to the other party to the transaction. [*7C Schedule 5(3)*]. Any provision of the *TCGA 1992* which fixes the consideration deemed to be given on a disposal or acquisition is applied before the rollover relief. [*7C Schedule 5(4)*].

17.64   Rollover relief cannot be claimed if the replacement asset is land or a dwelling house (or part of a dwelling house) and at any time in the period from its acquisition to the time that relief is given under *7C Schedule* the house qualifies for CGT exemption as being the principal private residence of the claimant or his spouse. [*7C Schedule 6(1)(2)*]. It is not clear if this limitation applies where the shares are disposed of by an employee trust. It probably does. The doubt is because the legislation refers to the new asset being within *TCGA 1992, s 222(1)*. A gain by a trust on a residence occupied by a beneficiary falls within *section 225*. However, as that applies *ss 222–224* the courts will probably hold that the restriction applies.

17.65   Where this exclusion does not apply on the acquisition of land or of a dwelling house (or interest in a dwelling house) but after the rollover relief claim has been allowed it becomes the principal private residence of the claimant or his spouse, it must be treated as never having been eligible for rollover relief but the resultant gain (or additional gains) in relation to the disposal to the SIP is deemed to arise at the time that the property first qualifies for the principal private residence exemption, not at the time of the sale to the SIP. [*7C Schedule 6(3)(4)*].

17.66   If the replacement asset was an option to acquire a dwelling house or land and after that option is exercised the dwelling house or land becomes the principal private residence of the claimant or his spouse the above restrictions again apply. [*7C Schedule 6(5)–(8)*]. The restrictions also apply if the dwelling house or land qualifies as the principal private residence of a person entitled to occupy it under the terms of a settlement. [*7C Schedule 6(9)*].

17.67   A similar restriction applies if the replacement asset is shares on which enterprise investment scheme (EIS) income tax relief is claimed (this carries with it exemption from capital gains tax on a disposal of the shares). [*7C Schedule 7*]. Again, rollover relief is not given at all if the EIS relief claim has been made before the rollover relief claim. [*7C Schedule 7(2)*]. If the EIS relief claim is made subsequently the rollover relief claim must be adjusted, but in this case the capital gain is deemed to arise at the time of the actual disposal to the ESOP, not when the EIS claim is made. [*7C Schedule 7(4)*].

17.68   Rollover relief cannot be claimed if at the time of the acquisition of the replacement asset the taxpayer is neither resident nor ordinarily resident in the UK unless he would be chargeable to CGT on a gain on the replacement asset because it is used in connection with a trade carried on in the UK through a branch or agency. Nor can it be claimed if the claimant will not be liable to CGT in respect of the replacement asset under the terms of a double taxation agreement. [*7C Schedule 8*].

Chapter 18

Profit-related Pay

Introduction

18.1   The profit-related pay scheme ceased on 31 December 1999. It was introduced in order to encourage employees to take an interest in the profitability of the business unit for which they work. The concept was that if employees were prepared to link part of their remuneration to profitability, the Government was prepared to exempt that profit-related element from tax (but not from national insurance) up to a qualifying limit. Whilst take up was initially slow, the scheme benefits were improved and a growing number of employers adopted profit-related pay (PRP) schemes. At its peak there were 14,000 schemes covering 3.7 million employees in total, albeit that the benefits that could be provided were limited and PRP could not be closely targeted to people whose efforts could particularly influence profitability, but had to be provided for everyone in the employment unit concerned. PRP was apparently intended only as a temporary measure. It was phased out over the period from 1 January 1988 to 31 December 1999. It was certainly much abused in the late 1990s.

The relief

18.2   Profit-related pay paid to an employee by reference to a profit period and in accordance with a registered scheme was exempt from income tax up to 31 December 1999, but only so far as it did not exceed the lower of two limits. [*Section 171(1)(2)*]. These were:

(a)   20 per cent of the aggregate of:

(i)   the employee's pay (excluding PRP) paid to him in the profit period (or in so much of the period as he was eligible to receive PRP); plus

(ii)   the PRP paid to him by reference to that period;

and

(b)   £2,000 (£3,000 prior to 1 April 1989 and £4,000 prior to 1 December 1997) (reduced proportionally if the profit period was less than twelve months or if the employee was not eligible to receive PRP) throughout the profit period. [*Section 171(3)(4)*]. This ceiling was reduced to £1,000 for profit periods beginning during the year to 31 December 1999, when PRP ceased. [*FA 1997, s 61(1)(2)*].

Prior to 1 April 1991, only half of such pay was exempt. [*FA 1991, s 37*].

18.3   The reason that head (*a*) looked at PRP *for* the profit period and other emoluments *paid in* that period was that it was administratively complicated to apply the limit by reference to PRP paid in the period. It also somewhat destroyed the incentive effect if the reward for one year's hard work were restricted by reference to the previous year's performance.

Meaning of 'employment'

18.4   Employment for PRP purposes was defined as an office or employment the emoluments from which fell to be assessed under Schedule E. [*Section 169(1)*]. A PRP scheme could accordingly—in theory at least—include employees assessed under Case II or III of Schedule E, not merely those assessable under Case I (although in practice it would be unusual for a Case III employment to be taxed under PAYE). 'Pay' (except in the expression profit-related pay itself) meant emoluments paid under deduction of PAYE less any expenses or benefits included therein which were taxable only under the special rules relating to directors and higher-paid employees (see 6.39 above). [*Section 169(1)*]. It should particularly be noted that the emoluments must actually have been paid under PAYE; it was not sufficient for there to have been a liability to apply PAYE if this was not in fact done. Apparently the Revenue considered that a service company for a partnership could not normally have a PRP scheme unless the partnership had at least eight partners (*Taxline, September 1994, Item 111*). Neither the logic or the statutory basis for this view is readily apparent.

Meaning of 'profit periods'

18.5   PRP was calculated in relation to 'profit periods', i.e. an accounting period by reference to which any PRP was calculated. In practice, this normally coincided with the company's corporation tax accounting period, but there was no requirement for it to do so. A profit period is normally a twelve-month period.

18.6   Although the PRP was calculated by reference to a particular profit period, it was taxed in the year of assessment during which it was paid. [*Section 170*]. This is, in any event, now the normal rule for Schedule E.

Payments not exempted from tax

18.7   The exemption of PRP from tax did not apply if either:

(*a*)   the PRP was paid to an employee in respect of an employment during a time when he had a second employment in respect of which he had received PRP which was exempt from tax, i.e. a person could not earn PRP under two separate schemes at the same time [*section 172(1)*];

(*b*)   employer's national insurance contributions were not payable in relation to the PRP (because the employer did not have a place of business in the UK, for instance) unless the only reason that no such contributions were payable was that the employee's earnings were below the contribution limit [*section 172(2)(3)*];

(*c*)   the payment was made to a person who was not eligible to receive PRP.

Registration

18.8   The bulk of the legislation was concerned with registration. This does not appear to have been accidental. It emphasised that, in return for the PRP benefits, an employer had to accept rigid controls over his PRP scheme.

18.9   An application for registration had to be in such form as the Revenue prescribed; contain a declaration by the applicant that the scheme complied with the requirements of *Schedule 8* (see 18.34 below); specify the profit period or periods to which the scheme related, and be supported by such information as the Revenue required. [*Section 175(1)*].

18.10   Up to 28 July 1998 if minimum wage legislation (i.e. *Trade Union Reform and Employment Rights Act 1993, s 35*, the *Agricultural Wages Act 1948* or their Scottish or Northern Irish equivalents) applied to any of the employees covered by the PRP scheme, the application for registration also had to contain an undertaking that the employee would be paid the statutory minimum wage without taking account of PRP. In other words, the PRP had to be in addition to the statutory minimum wage. [*Section 175(1)(c), (4)*]. A scheme could not be registered if it related only to profit periods beginning after 31 December 1999. Registration of other schemes ceased on 31 December 2000. [*FA 1997, s 61(3)*].

Accountant's report

18.11   The application for registration had to be accompanied by a report by an independent accountant (in a form prescribed by the Revenue) that, in his opinion, the scheme complied with *Schedule 8* and that the books and records maintained, or proposed, by the applicant were adequate for the purpose of enabling the statutory annual return (see 18.45 below) to be prepared. [*Section 175(2)*].

Persons eligible to apply for registration

18.12   The employer of the people that it was intended to include in the PRP scheme was the only person eligible to apply for registration. It was not possible for a PRP scheme to cover employees of more than one person unless all those employees were members of the same group of companies (i.e. a parent and its 51 per cent subsidiaries). If it was wished to register such a group scheme, the application for registration needed to be made by the parent company of the group. [*Section 173*].

Exclusion of Crown employees

18.13   A PRP scheme could not be set up to cover employees of the Crown, a body under the control of the Crown, a local authority or a body under the control of one or more local authorities or of the Crown and Local authorities. [*Section 174(1)(2)*]. For this purpose a person (or persons) has control over a body if (and only if) either:

(*a*)   where the affairs of the body are managed by its members, he has power to appoint more than half of the members;

(*b*)   where the body has a share capital, he holds more than half of the issued share capital;

(*c*)   where the members of the body vote in general meeting, he has the power to exercise more than half of the votes exercisable in a general meeting; or

(*d*)   the articles of association or other rules regulating the body give him the power to secure that the affairs of the body are conducted in accordance with his wishes.

[*Section 174(3)*].

18.14   For the above purpose a person must be taken to possess all rights and powers exercisable by a person that he has appointed to an office by virtue of which those rights are exercisable, or by a body that he controls. [*Section 174(4)*].

Time of application

18.15   If an application for registration of a PRP scheme was made at least three months before the beginning of the first profit period to which it related, the Revenue had a statutory obligation to register it before the beginning of that profit period (assuming that they were satisfied it met the statutory requirements). [*Section 176(1)*]. If it was made less than three months before it was to take effect they endeavoured to register it in time. If the scheme was not registered before the start of the first profit period the application was regarded as having been refused. [*Section 176(6)*].

Refusal of applications

18.16   If, on receipt of an application for registration, the Revenue were not satisfied that it complied with the statutory requirements they could either refuse the application, or notify the applicant that they required him to amend the application, or provide them with such further information as they might specify. [*Section 176(2)*]. If such a notice was complied with and the Revenue were then satisfied that the scheme was eligible for registration they had to register the scheme before the start of the first profit period if the application was made more than three months in advance. [*Section 176(3)*]. If it was not, they had to register it before the start of the profit period if they were satisfied in time, but if they had not dealt with the application by then it lapsed and had to be treated as refused. If in the light of the further information the Revenue were still not satisfied that the scheme was eligible they had to refuse to register it. [*Section 176(4)*]. They did not have power to ask for additional information. [*Section 176(5)*].

18.17   After registering a PRP scheme the Revenue had to notify the applicant that they had done so. [*Section 176(7)*]. If they refused the application they also had to notify him. [*Section 176(8)*].

Cancellation of registration

18.18   If at any time after its registration it appeared to the Revenue that either:

(*a*)   the scheme had not been administered in accordance with its terms (or would not be so administered) in relation to a profit period;

(*b*)   the circumstances relating to the scheme had become such during a profit period that they would refuse a fresh application to register it; or

(*c*)   the undertaking given under *section 175(1)(c)* (to meet minimum wage requirements) had not been complied with in relation to employment at any time during a profit period,

they could cancel the registration. [*Section 178(1)*]. Such cancellation was retrospective to the beginning of that profit period. If the PRP scheme used method B (see head (*j*) of 18.36 below) to calculate the distributable pool of profits the Revenue could also cancel the registration with effect from the start of a profit period if losses were incurred in that profit period or in the preceding twelve months. [*Section 178(1)(c)*]. In such circumstances the calculation would show no PRP payable.

Non-compliance with statutory requirements

18.19   If it appeared to the Revenue after a scheme had been registered that, at the time of registration, the scheme did not in fact comply with the requirements of *8 Schedule* or the application did not meet the statutory requirements (see 18.10–18.14 above), they could also cancel the registration—but in this case from the start of the first profit period to which the scheme related, so that it would never have had any effect. [*Section 178(2)*].

Failure to submit annual return

18.20   The Revenue could also cancel the registration, retrospectively to the start of the profit period, if the employer did not submit the annual return within the time allowed (see 18.45 below). [*Section 178(3)*].

Alteration of scheme

18.21   If, after it had been registered, the terms of a PRP scheme were altered, the Revenue could also cancel the registration, with effect from the start of the profit period during which the alteration took effect (or the start of any later profit period) unless the alteration was made in accordance with *section 177B* (see 18.31 below). [*Section 178(3)(a)*, inserted by *FA 1989, 4 Sch 4(3)*]. They were not prevented from cancelling a registration if an alteration was registered in accordance with *section 177B* but it was subsequently discovered that the application for registration of the alteration did not comply with *section 177B(4)* or the declaration required by *section 177B(4)(c)* was false. [*Section 178(3B)*].

Request by employer

18.22   The employer could apply for the registration to be cancelled. In the event of such a request the Revenue had to cancel it from the beginning of the profit period specified by the employer. [*Section 178(4)*]. If the scheme employer died and his personal representatives applied to cancel the registration from the date of the death the Revenue had to comply with that request provided that it was made within a month from the date of the grant of probate or letters of administration. [*Section 178(5A)*].

Notification of changes to a scheme

18.23   The employer was required to notify the Revenue without delay if he became aware of anything that was a ground for cancellation of the scheme's registration. [*Section 181(3)*]. Curiously, there does not appear to have been a penalty for omitting to do so. If in accordance with *section 181(3)* the employer gave notice of a change in the employment unit, or in other circumstances relating to the scheme, and requested the Revenue to cancel the registration with effect from the date of the change, they had to do so, provided that the notice of the change was given within one month of its taking place and the Revenue were satisfied that the change has not been deliberately brought about with a view to registering a new scheme. [*Section 178(5)*].

18.24 It should be noted that, except in the circumstances set out in 18.22 above, or following the death of an employer who was an individual, both of which required notification within a one-month time limit, the Revenue could not cancel a registration during the course of a profit period.

Date of deregistration

18.25 The date of deregistration was very important to the employer. If a registration was cancelled with effect from an earlier time, and payments of PRP had already been made as a result of which less tax had been deducted under PAYE than would have been due if the PRP scheme had not been in place, the shortfall in PAYE deductions needed to be made good to the Revenue by the employer (or, if he had died, by his personal representatives). [*Section 179*]. If the scheme employer was not resident in the UK the Revenue had power to recover the underpaid tax from the person who made the PRP payment. [*ICTA 1988, s 179(4)*]. There was no power for the employer to recover such tax from the employees concerned. Accordingly, this tax could represent a substantial penalty on the employer for failure to comply with the requirements of the PRP legislation. The Revenue had to notify the employer when a scheme's registration was cancelled, for whatever reason. [*Section 178(6)*].

Alterations to a scheme

18.26 Once a PRP scheme had been registered alterations could not normally be made to its terms. If changes were required it was necessary to apply for deregistration and register a fresh scheme. There were three exceptions.

Sale of business

18.27 First, if the business was sold (so that the scheme employer was no longer eligible to register the scheme but some other person became eligible to do so) but there was otherwise no material change in the employment unit or in the circumstances relating to the scheme, the scheme employer and his successor could jointly apply for the scheme to be amended by substituting the successor for the previous scheme employer. Such an application had to be made within one month of the date of the change of employer. [*Section 177(3)*]. The Revenue had to agree to such an application if they were satisfied that the necessary conditions were met. [*Section 177(5)*].

Applications made by successor employer

18.28 It was not necessarily in the interests of the successor to join in making such an application, because if the Revenue accepted it, the successor was treated as having been the scheme employer throughout. [*Section 177(4)*]. He was accordingly liable for any tax payable if the Revenue subsequently withdrew registration retrospectively because of a breach of the rules by his predecessor.

18.29 *Section 177* was of fairly limited application. Apart from the sale of a business (as opposed to a company) the only other circumstance in which it was likely to apply was on the transfer of a business from one company in a group to another where no group scheme existed. The transferor company would cease to be the eligible employer but would be succeeded by the transferee company. The *section* could not normally apply on the sale of a subsidiary which was part of a group scheme as such a sale would give rise to a material change in the employment unit (as employees of companies remaining in the group would cease to be members of it). Equally, the sale of a major subsidiary could give rise to a major change in the employment unit thus bringing to an end the PRP scheme for the retained businesses.

Death of employer

18.30 The second circumstance was where the scheme employer was an individual and he died. His personal representatives could apply to amend the scheme by substituting themselves as the scheme employer. [*ICTA 1988, s 177A(1)(2)*]. Such an application had to be made within one month from the date of the grant of probate or letters of administration. [*Section 177A(3)*]. The Revenue had to agree to such an application if, apart from the death of the employer, there would have been no grounds for cancelling the registration of the scheme. [*Section 177A(2)*].

Minor alterations

18.31 Thirdly, certain minor alterations could be made by the employer and approval sought for registration of the alteration. [*ICTA 1988, s 177B(3) inserted by FA 1989, 4 Sch 3*]. An application to register an alteration had to:

(*a*) be in such form as the Revenue might prescribe;

(*b*) be made within one month of the date the alteration was made;

(*c*) contain a declaration that the alteration was within one of the permitted categories and that the scheme as amended complied with the requirements of *Schedule 8*; and

(*d*) be accompanied by a report by an independent accountant (in a form prescribed by the Revenue) that, in his opinion, the declaration at (*c*) was correct. [*Section 177B(4)*].

18.32 The categories of alteration that could be made are alterations that:

(*a*)   relate to a term which is not relevant to the question of whether the scheme complies with the requirements of *Schedule 8*;

(*b*)   relate to a term identifying any person (other than the scheme employer) who pays the emolument of employees to whom the scheme relates;

(*c*)   consist of the addition of a term making provision for an abbreviated profit period of the kind referred to in *8 Schedule 10(3)* (see 18.36(*h*) below);

(*d*)   amend the provisions by reference to which the employees covered by the scheme may be identified, but this can be done only for profit periods beginning after the date of the alteration;

(*e*)   relate to a provision of a kind referred to in *8 Schedule 13(4)(5), 14(3)–(5)* (see head (*h*) of 18.36 below) and have effect only for profit periods beginning after the date of the alteration;

(*f*)   amend the provisions regarding date of payment to employees, but do so only for profit periods beginning after the date of the alteration;

(*g*)   are necessary to bring the scheme into compliance with the requirements of *Schedule 8* (if it is discovered that it did not do so at the time of registration), provided that any such alteration is made retrospectively to take effect for all profit periods to which the scheme relates, it is made within two years of the start of the first profit period, and it does not invalidate (in whole or in part) any payment of profit-related pay already made under the scheme; or

(*h*)   enable an existing scheme to adopt the 1995 changes in respect of exceptional items (see (*n*) (viii) in 18.36). [*FA 1995, s 136(10)*].

[*Section 177B(8)*].

18.33   If an alteration complied with the above requirement, the Revenue had to register it. [*Section 177B(6)*]. If they were not satisfied they could refuse to register it. [*Section 177B(7)*]. In such a case it was virtually inevitable that they would cancel the registration of the scheme entirely. Although the making of an alteration to the scheme was expressly stated not of itself to invalidate the scheme [*section 177B(1)*] it is hard to conceive the Revenue leaving the scheme in place if they did not accept that the alteration itself met the requirements of *section 177B*. [*Section 177B(5)*].

Conditions for registration

18.34   The legislation closely defined the form that a PRP scheme could take and laid down a large number of specific matters that had to be included in the scheme. These conditions are contained in *Schedule 8*. The terms of the scheme had to be set out in writing. [*8 Schedule 1*]. The Revenue published model rules (in an unnumbered Booklet called *PRP—*

Setting up a scheme) to seek to encourage the use of PRP schemes. These are very user-friendly. A scheme could not be registered unless a declaration (which must be reported on by an independent accountant) was made that these conditions were fulfilled. The registration of a scheme could not be regarded as an indication that the Revenue accepted that the conditions had been complied with. In the tight time limit allowed, their review of an application could not be more than cursory and was intended to do no more than weed out those schemes which were clearly unacceptable.

Dangers of non-compliance

18.35   As indicated above, the real penalty for not complying with the conditions was not that registration would be refused but rather that when the non-compliance came to light the registration was likely to be cancelled retrospectively, thus creating a tax bill for the employer in relation to PAYE that was not deducted because he had assumed the scheme to be effective.

18.36   The conditions that had to be met are as follows.

(*a*)   The terms of the scheme must be set out in writing. [*8 Schedule 1*].

(*b*)   The scheme must identify the scheme employer (i.e. the person who registered the scheme). [*8 Schedule 2*].

(*c*)   If the scheme employer does not pay the emoluments of all of the employees to whom the scheme relates it must identify each of the persons who pays emoluments (e.g. a subsidiary company, a payroll service). [*8 Schedule 3*].

(*d*)   The scheme must identify the undertaking (or part of an undertaking) to which it relates. That undertaking must be carried on with a view to profit. If the scheme relates to part of an undertaking it must be described sufficiently (otherwise than by name only) to distinguish it from other parts of the undertaking. [*8 Schedule 4*].

(*e*)   The scheme must contain provisions by reference to which the employees to whom it relates can be identified. [*8 Schedule 5*].

(*f*)   It must contain provisions to ensure that no payments are made under it if the employees to whom the scheme relates form less than 80 per cent of all the employees in the employment unit (excluding people within heads (*g*) below) at the beginning of the profit period. [*8 Schedule 6*]. The 80 per cent also need not include those who have not been employed for a minimum period specified in the scheme—which must not exceed three years. [*8 Schedule 8*]. A scheme registered before 1 May 1995 could also exclude part-time employees, i.e. those who are not required under the terms of their employment to work in the employment unit for 20 hours or more a week, but such workers must be included in new schemes. [*FA 1995, s 137(1)*].

(*g*)   It must contain provisions to ensure that no payments are made under the scheme to any person who has a material interest in the company. Material interest for this purpose is defined at 18.37 below. [*8 Schedule 7(1)*].

(*h*)   The scheme must identify the profit periods (i.e. the accounting period or periods by reference to which any PRP is to be calculated). [*8 Schedule 9*]. A profit period must normally be twelve months. [*8 Schedule 10(1)*]. If the scheme is a replacement scheme it cannot provide for more than two profit periods but the first may be less than twelve months. [*8 Schedule 10(2)*]. This enables the scheme to run for the broken period and then a full year to give time for it to be superseded by a completely new scheme. In other words, a replacement scheme is seen as a temporary stop-gap. A scheme is a replacement scheme only if:

  (i)   it succeeds another scheme (or two or more other schemes) the registration of which was cancelled under *section 178(1)(a)* (see 18.18 above) on the ground of a change in the employment unit or in the circumstances relating to the scheme;

  (ii)   that change occurred within three months before the start of the first profit period of the new scheme (this presumably means the replacement scheme) and the Revenue are satisfied that it was not brought about with a view to the registration of the new scheme or in circumstances within *section 177(1)* (see 18.27 above), which would enable the old scheme to continue with a new scheme employer; and

  (iii) at least half of the employees covered by the new scheme were covered by the old scheme (or schemes) at the time of the change.

[*8 Schedule 10(4)*].

A replacement scheme must provide that the distributable pool for a profit period is equal to a specified percentage of the profit of that period. [*8 Schedule 15*]. This effectively means it must use Method A (see head (*j*) below).

The scheme can also provide for a profit period to be abbreviated if its registration is cancelled other than with effect from the start of a profit period. In such an event it can exclude the operation of *8 Schedule 13(4)(5), 14(3)(b)(4)(5)* (which are cut-offs to the profit to be taken into account: see head (*j*) below). [*8 Schedule 10(3)*].

(*j*)   The scheme must specify how the aggregate sum that may be paid to employees in respect of a profit period (the distributable pool) is to be determined. [*8 Schedule 11*]. Except where the scheme is a replacement scheme (within head (*h*) above) there are only two ways this can be calculated, namely Method A [*ICTA 1988, 8 Sch 13(1A)*] and Method B. [*8 Schedule 12*].

Method A

Under this method the distributable pool is a percentage of the profits of the employment unit in the profit period. [*8 Schedule 13(1)*]. This must be a fixed percentage specified in the scheme. The same percentage must apply for each profit period covered by the scheme. [*ICTA 1988, 8 Sch 13(1)(a)*]. The Revenue initially allowed a scheme to include a formula the application of which would produce the percentage figure. However, since 3 August 1992 they have not been prepared to accept such a method unless the formula uses only factors available when the scheme is written, i.e. so that the actual percentage can be ascertained before the scheme starts (*SP 7/92*).

The scheme may, if desired, disregard any excess of the profits over 160 per cent (or such greater percentage as the scheme may specify) of:

(i)   in the first profit period, the profits of a base year specified in the scheme; and

(ii) in subsequent profit periods, the profits for the previous period. [*8 Schedule 13(4)*].

In other words, there can be a cut-off if the profits of the profit period exceed those of the previous year by more than the specified percentage. The scheme can also provide that there will be no distributable pool if the profits in the profit period are below a figure specified in the scheme (or ascertainable by reference to the scheme), although that figure must not exceed the profits for a base year specified in the scheme. [*8 Schedule 13(5)*]. Thus, it may provide that there will be no distributable pool if the profits of the profit period are less than those of the base year (or less than a lower target than the profits of the base period). For the purpose of both these optional cut-offs the base year must be a period of twelve months ending within two years before the first profit period under the scheme. [*8 Schedule 13(6)*]. The scheme may provide that these cut-offs apply from the first profit period or from a specified later one. [*8 Schedule 13(7)*].

Example

Inn Centive Limited introduced a PRP scheme, the first profit period of which began on 1 August 1997. The scheme provides that employees will receive 15 per cent of the profits of the company up to 200 per cent of the profits of the base year, but will receive nothing if profits are not at least 80 per cent of those of the base year. The scheme provides that the base year is the year to 31 July 1996. Inn Centive Ltd made £200,000 profit during the year to 31 July 1996 and £620,000 during the year to 31 July 1998.

The distributable pool for the profit period to 31 July 1998 is:

	£
Profit	620,000
But limited to 200% of £200,000	400,000

This exceeds 80 per cent of £200,000 so the minimum profit level does not apply.

Distributable pool 15% of £400,000 = 60,000

From 1 December 1993 schemes adopting such an upper limit must provide that it will be increased if the taxable pay of employees in the part of the business covered by the scheme in the profit period is lower than it was in the previous one (or the base year). In such circumstances the upper limit must be increased by the percentage of the previous year's profit represented by the reduction in salaries. [8 *Schedule 13A(4)–(6)* inserted by *FA 1994, s 98(2)*].

Example

Recession Ltd has a PRP scheme for the year to 31 March 1998 with an upper limit of 180 per cent of the profits of its year to 31 March 1997, its base year. In the year to 31 March 1997 it paid its employees £150,000. It laid off a large number of staff in June 1997 as a result of which its salary bill for the year to 31 March was only £90,000. The profits of the year to 31 March 1997 were £70,000.

The upper limit is:

$$\frac{\text{decrease in taxable pay}}{\text{1997 profits}} = \frac{60,000}{70,000} = 86\%$$

Basic upper limit	180%
	226%

In other words, the limit will not apply unless the 31 March 1997 profits exceed 266% of £70,000 = £186,200.

The idea is to discourage salary sacrifice arrangements under which the basic pay of employees is reduced, thus increasing profits above the PRP limit—so that a PRP formula can be used to produce a figure which will merely replace the taxable pay given up. Unfortunately, the wording adopted will also, as in the above example, trigger the provision where the salary bill reduces for other reasons.

From 1 December 1993 the rules must require PRP and related employer's national insurance contributions to be treated in the same way in calculating the profits for the current and the previous year (or base year) to arrive at both upper and lower limits. [8 *Schedule 13A(1)* inserted by *FA 1994, s 98(2)*]. The Revenue's guidance note of December 1993 actually says that the PRP must be deducted in both years, but the *Act* seems to permit it instead to be added back in both.

Method B

Under this method the distributable pool is a percentage of the distributable pool for the previous profit period (or in the case of the first profit period a percentage of a notional pool of an amount specified in the scheme [*8 Schedule 14(1)*]). In other words, it is based on the increase in the profit of the profit period over those for the previous period. The percentage must be either:

(i)   the profits of the profit period as a percentage of the profits of the previous twelve months; or

(ii) such percentage reduced (if more than 100) or increased (if less than 100) by a specified fraction of the difference between it and 100. Such a fraction must be specified in the scheme and must not be more than one-half. The same fraction must apply if profits are reduced or increased.

[*8 Schedule 14(3)*].

Where a notional pool is used its amount must be known before the profit period starts. It is normally simply a figure chosen by the employer. Since 3 August 1992 it has not been possible to adopt a formula to arrive at the notional pool unless it is such that the figure it produces can be calculated when the scheme starts (*SP 7/92*).

As with Method A, the scheme can disregard profits which exceed 160 per cent (or such greater percentage as the scheme may specify) of the profits of the preceding twelve months and can provide that there will be no distributable pool if the profits of the profit period are less than a figure ascertainable by reference to the scheme, but that figure must not exceed the profits of the twelve months immediately preceding the first profit period. [*8 Schedule 14(4)(5)*]. As the profits of the twelve months preceding the first profit period will not be known when the scheme is submitted for registration, it is safest to calculate this minimum by reference to a formula. If a figure is taken and the profits turn out to be less than that figure, the scheme would be invalidated.

Where this minimum cut-off applies, the cut-off is ignored in calculating the distributable pool for the next profit period, i.e. the actual profits must be used; they cannot be assumed to be nil. [*8 Schedule 14(6)*].

The cut-offs and the percentage adjustment at (ii) above need not apply for the first profit period but can take effect from a later period determined in accordance with the scheme. [*8 Schedule 14(8)*].

Example

P. R. Pay Ltd has had a PRP scheme since 1 January 1996. The notional distributable pool was £50,000. Profits which exceed

180 per cent of those of the previous twelve months are disregarded. There is no distributable pool if profits are less than 70 per cent of those of the previous twelve months. The profits are as follows:

Year to 31 December 1995	£350,000
Year to 31 December 1996	£400,000
Year to 31 December 1997	£250,000
Year to 31 December 1998	£520,000

For the profit period to 31 December 1996 the distributable pool is:

$$\frac{400,000}{350,000} \times 100 = 114.29\% \text{ of £50,000} \qquad \text{£57,145}$$

For the profit period to 31 December 1997 the distributable pool is nil as £250,000 is less than 70% of £400,000.

There is however a notional pool for the purpose of the following year's calculation, namely:

$$\frac{250,000}{400,000} \times 100 = 62.5\% \text{ of £57,145} \qquad \text{£35,776}$$

For the profit period to 31 December 1998 the distributable pool is as follows:

180% of profits to 31 December 1997 = £450,000 (being less than £520,000).

Distributable pool

$$\frac{450,000}{250,000} \times 100 = 180\% \text{ of £35,776} \qquad \text{£64,397}$$

The special provisions applying from 1 December 1993 noted under Method A above in relation to the upper and lower limits also apply to Method B. [*8 Schedule 14A* inserted by *FA 1994, s 98(3)*].

(k) The scheme must provide that the whole of the distributable pool is to be paid to employees in the employment unit. [*8 Schedule 16*].

(l) The scheme must state when payments will be made to employees. [*8 Schedule 17*]. There is nothing to prevent payments being made weekly or monthly during the profit period. However, if this is done care needs to be exercised. If, when the distributable pool is calculated after the end of the profit period, it is found to be less than the payments made, the employer will have to pay over to the Revenue the PAYE that was not deducted in respect of the difference.

(m) The scheme must provide that employees will participate in it on similar terms. However, the payments to employees may vary according to the levels of their remuneration, length of service and similar factors. [*8 Schedule 18*]. It is up to the employer whether or not he treats maternity pay as pay for PRP purposes (*Taxline, January 1995, Item 18*).

(*n*)   The scheme must require the preparation of a profit and loss account for each profit period of the employment unit (and any other period for which profits need to be ascertained for PRP purposes). [*8 Schedule 19(1)*]. The profit and loss account must give a true and fair view of the profit or loss. [*8 Schedule 19(2)*]. No deduction may be made in arriving at such profits for remuneration of persons excluded from the PRP scheme (under head (*g*) above) as having a material interest in the company. [*8 Schedule 19(4)*]. For this purpose remuneration includes fees and percentages, expenses allowances chargeable to income tax, pension contributions and the estimated value of benefits in kind. [*8 Schedule 19(4A)*]. The profit and loss account need not include, if the company so decides, all or any of:

(i)   interest receivable and similar income;

(ii)   interest payable and similar charges;

(iii)   goodwill;

(iv)   tax on ordinary activities (but penalties must be deducted);

(v)   research and development costs;

(vi)   PRP under the scheme (or under another scheme to which paragraph 21 applies (see head (o) below);

(vii)   employer's national insurance contributions in respect of the PRP;

(viii) any exceptional items which, in accordance with accounting practices, are regarded as standard should be shown separately on the face of the profit and loss account, being:

(A)   profits or losses on the sale or termination of an operation;

(B)   costs of a fundamental reorganisation or restructuring having a material effect on the nature and focus of the employment unit's operation;

(C)   profits or losses on the disposal of fixed assets; and

(D)   the effect on tax of any of the items in (A) to (C).

[*8 Schedule 19(5)(6)*].

Subject to the above adjustments, the profit and loss account must comply (with any necessary modifications) with *Schedule 4* to the *Companies Act 1985*. [*8 Schedule 19(3)*]. Unless it would not produce a true and fair view, in preparing the profit and loss account no changes in accounting policies from those used in earlier periods can be made if their effect (either singly or taken together) would alter the profit or loss of more than 5 per cent. [*8 Schedule 20*]. Head (viii) did not apply in relation to accounts for a period beginning before 1 May 1995 and does not apply to a scheme in existence at that date unless the scheme is altered by 1 November 1995 to permit its adoption. The prohibition in *para 20* against changes which alter the profit by more than 5 per cent does not apply to such a change, but if the distributable pool is determined by reference to the increase in profits over those of the previous year (which it will do under Method B) the earlier year's profits must be recalculated on the new basis to arrive at the distributable pool. [*8 Schedule 19(6A)* and *FA 1995, s 136(1)–(11)*]. Prior to 1 May 1995 extraordinary income, extraordinary charges, extraordinary profits and losses and tax on extraordinary profits and losses could all be excluded. The Treasury have power by statutory instrument to amend the above list. In the period 22 June 1993 to 1 November 1995 the Revenue are prepared by concession to allow an existing scheme to follow either the old or the new rules. The change results from the replacement of SSAP 6 by FRS 3 which results in a different meaning of extraordinary items needing to be adopted for *Companies Act* purposes. Any such amendment will have effect for periods beginning from the date the order comes into force and will not apply to an existing scheme unless it is altered in accordance with the rules set out above. [*8 Schedule 19A* inserted by *FA 1995, s 136(12)*].

(*o*) If the employment unit is part only of an undertaking and the scheme provides that the profit or loss of the unit are to be taken to be equivalent to those of the whole undertaking (which must be identified in the scheme), references above to the profit or loss of the employment unit must be read as referring to that of the undertaking of which it forms part. [*ICTA 1988, 8 Sch 21*]. Such a scheme is called a special scheme. Where this applies, the scheme must contain provisions to ensure that no payments are made under the scheme by reference to a profit period unless at the beginning of that period:

(i) there is at least one other registered scheme which relates to employees employed in the same undertaking (and that scheme does not itself relate to part of the undertaking with the profits being calculated by reference to the whole undertaking, and is not one under which the distributable pool is nil); and

(ii) the number of employees to whom the scheme (for the part of the undertaking) relates does not exceed 33 per cent of the employees to whom that other scheme (or schemes in aggregate) relate. [*8 Schedule 22(1)(2)*]. Where there are several PRP schemes an employee is not to be counted twice in applying the 33 per cent test.

[*8 Schedule 22(3)*].

In other words, a scheme can be set up for part of an undertaking that is not itself a profit centre but the PRP must then be based on the profit of the larger undertaking of which it forms a part, and there must already be an existing scheme for other employees of the undertaking which is much more substantial than the one proposed. The concept is to prevent manipulation of the profits—if the same profit and loss account needs to be used to calculate PRP for a much larger scheme it is unlikely that the figures will be artificial.

From 1 December 1993 the scheme must also provide that its fixed percentage under Method A, or notional or distributable pool under Method B, does not exceed a permitted percentage (for Method A) or permitted limit (for Method B), namely

$$\frac{\text{PRP of employees in other scheme or schemes in the relevant year}}{\text{Pay of such employees in relevant year}} \times \begin{array}{l}\text{pay of} \\ \text{employees in} \\ \text{special scheme} \\ \text{in relevant} \\ \text{year}\end{array} = \text{permitted limit}$$

$$\frac{\text{permitted limit}}{\text{profits of relevant year}} = \text{permitted percentage}$$

The relevant year is the period of twelve months identified in the scheme and ending within two years preceding the profit period. [8 *Schedule 23, 24* inserted by *FA 1994, s 99*].

This provision prevents the creation of a nominal scheme for the bulk of employees paying out only small amounts so as to enable a special scheme to be set up for selected employees offering far better benefits. It effectively requires the same level of PRP to be paid under both schemes. It should be noted that it also prevents a special scheme being set up until the other scheme has been in existence for at least a year because PRP needs to have been paid in that other scheme in the relevant year.

Meaning of 'material interest'

18.37   A person had a 'material interest' in a company for the purpose of head (*g*) at 18.36 above, if he (on his own or with his associates), or one or more associates of his:

(*a*)   was the beneficial owner of, or able (directly or indirectly) to control, more than 25 per cent of the ordinary share capital of the company; or (*b*)   if it was a close company, possessed (or was entitled to acquire) such rights as would, in the event of a winding up or in any other circumstance, give an entitlement to receive more than 25 per cent of the assets which would then be available for distribution among the participators (as defined in *section 417(1)*). [*ICTA 1988, 8 Sch 7(2)*].

18.38   The definition of control in *section 840* applied, and that definition also applied to an unincorporated association such as a partnership. [*8 Schedule 7(3)*].

Meaning of 'associate'

18.39   The normal definition of associate was modified. The following were associates of a person:

(*a*)   any relative (i.e. spouse, parent or remoter forebear, child or remoter issue, or brother or sister) or any partner of that person;

(*b*)   the trustees of a settlement in relation to which that person is (or any relative of his, living or dead is, or was) a settlor; and

(*c*)   where the person is interested in any shares or obligations of the company which are held by a trust (or the estate of a deceased person):

(i)   the trustees (or personal representatives); and

(ii)   if the person is a company, any other company interested in those shares or obligations.

[*Section 417(3)(4), 8 Schedule 7(3)*].

18.40   However, if an employee of a company had an interest in shares or obligations of the company as a beneficiary of an 'employee benefit trust' the trustees were not to be regarded as associates of his under (*c*) above by reason only of that interest, unless, at any time on or after 14 March 1989 either:

(*a*)   the employee (either or his own or with his associates); or

(*b*)   any associate of his (with or without other associates of the employee),

had been the beneficial owner of (or able to control, directly or indirectly) more than 25 per cent of the ordinary share capital of the company. For the purpose of (*a*) and (*b*) above the reference to associates in relation to an employee did not include the trustees of an employee benefit trust (see 18.41 below) by reason only that the employee had an interest in shares or obligations held by the trust. [*ICTA 1988, 8 Sch 7(4)(8)(12)*].

Meaning of 'employee benefit trust'

18.41   A trust was an employee benefit trust if:

(*a*)   all or most of the employees were eligible to benefit under it; and (*b*)   none of the property subject to it had been disposed of (by sale, loan or otherwise) after 13 March 1989 except either:

  (i)   in the ordinary course of management of the trust;

  (ii)   by applying it for the benefit of:

    (A)   individual employees or former employees of the company;

    (B)   spouses, former spouses, widows or widowers of employees or former employees of the company;

    (C)   relatives (which for this purpose only, means a parent or remoter forebear, child or remoter issue, brother, sister, uncle, aunt, nephew or niece), or spouses of relatives, of persons within (A) or (B) above; or

    (D)   dependants of individual employees or former employees of the company;

  (iii)   by applying it for charitable purposes; or

  (iv)   by transferring it to the trustees of an approved profit sharing scheme (see 16.4 above), of another employee benefit trust, or of a qualifying ESOT (see 17.13 above).

[*8 Schedule 7(5)–(7)*].

18.42   If after 13 March 1989:

(*a*)   an employee of a company or an associate of his (which expression does not for this purpose automatically include the trustees of an employee benefit trust) received a payment (the relevant payment) from an employee benefit trust; and

(*b*)   at any time during the three years prior to the day the relevant payment is received, the property in the trust included any part of the ordinary share capital of the company,

the employee (or associate) had to be treated, for the purpose of determining whether he was the beneficial owner of more than 25 per cent of the ordinary share capital under 18.40 above, as if he were the beneficial owner of the 'appropriate percentage' of the ordinary share capital of the company on the day when the relevant payment was received.

[*8 Schedule 7(9)*].

The appropriate percentage for this purpose is that given by the formula:

$$\frac{A}{B} \times 100$$

where

A = the smaller of:

(i) the aggregate of the relevant payment and any earlier payments received by the employee or associates of his in the previous twelve months, and

(ii) the aggregate of the distributions made to the trust by the company in respect of its ordinary share capital during the three years ending on the date the relevant payment is received.

B = the aggregate of:

(i) any distributions made by the company in respect of its ordinary share capital during the twelve months prior to the receipt of the relevant payment;

(ii) any distributions so made during the twelve months prior to that (i.e. the year prior to the period in (i)); and

(iii) any distributions so made during the twelve months prior to the period in (ii),

divided by the number of the periods mentioned in paragraphs (i) to (iii) in which distributions were so made.

If the company made no distributions to the trustees in the three years prior to the receipt of the relevant payment the appropriate percentage was nil. An example may be helpful.

Example

On 10 July 2001 John received £5,000 from an employee benefit trust which owns 40,000 ordinary shares in John's employer, Complexity Limited. Complexity had previously paid the following dividends to the trust.

	£
14 August 1998	18,000
8 July 1999	14,000
26 February 2001	12,000
20 April 2001	3,000

The trust had previously made a payment of £800 to John's son on 13 January 2001 to meet school fees.

John must be treated as having an interest in:

$$\frac{A}{B} \times 100\% \text{ of the 40,000 shares}$$

A = the smaller of:

		£
(i)	£5,000 (paid to John) + £800 (paid to John's son)	= 5,800
(ii)	the distributions in the three years to 10 July 2001	= 47,000

B = the aggregate of: £

   (i)   distributions in year to 10 July 2001   15,000

  (ii)   distributions in year to 10 July 2000   —

  (iii) distributions in year to 10 July 1999   32,000

                                              47,000

As there were distributions in only two of those years
   this figure is divided by 2   = 23,500

The calculation is accordingly $\dfrac{5,800}{23,500} \times 100 = 24.68\%$ of £40,000.

John is treated as having an interest in 9,872 of the shares held by the trust.

18.43   If these shares, together with those held by John and his associates exceed 25 per cent of the ordinary share capital of Complexity Limited, the exemption in *8 Schedule 7(4)* (see 18.40 above) will not apply. Accordingly, the whole 40,000 shares held by the trust will be treated as held by John (although this will be a somewhat pointless exercise as the 25 per cent already held constitutes a material interest).

18.44   If an employee (or associate) was treated under *8 Schedule 7(9)* (see head (*b*) of 18.42 above) as the beneficial owner of part of the ordinary share capital of the company, and during the twelve months prior to receiving the relevant payment he (or an associate) also received another payment from a different employee benefit trust which also held shares in the company, *8 Schedule 7(9)* has effect in its application to the second (or other) trust as if the relevant payment had been received from that other trust (or each of the other trusts if more than one). It could thus increase the number of shares held by each of the trusts in which the employee is deemed to have an interest. [*8 Schedule 7(11)*].

Administration

18.45   Within ten months of the end of every profit period (seven months if the employment unit was an undertaking or part of an undertaking of a public company (within *section 1(3)* of the *Companies Act 1985*, i.e. a plc)) the scheme employer had to make an annual return to the Revenue. This had to be in such form and contain such information as the Revenue prescribed. It had to be accompanied by a report by an independent accountant in such form and containing such information as the Revenue prescribed stating that in his opinion the terms of the scheme had been complied with in respect of the profit period. [*Section 180(1)(2)(4)*]. If a three-month extension for filing accounts was granted under *section 244(3)* of the *Companies Act 1985* substituted by the *Companies Act 1989, s 11* the time limit for the annual return was similarly extended provided the Revenue was notified of this fact within the ten- or seven-month period. [*Section 180(3)*]. If the scheme employer had died the annual return had to be made by his personal representatives. [*Section 180(5)*].

18.46   A person could carry out the functions of independent accountant under a PRP scheme only if:

(*a*)   he is qualified for appointment as auditor;

(*b*)   he is not an employer of any employees to whom the scheme relates;

(*c*)   he is not a partner, or an employee (or partner of an employee), of a person having employees to whom the scheme relates or of a company which is the subsidiary, holding company or fellow subsidiary of such an employer; and

(*d*)   he is not an employee of a person within (*c*) above.

[*Section 184*].

Information

18.47   The Revenue could require any person to give them such information as they may specify which:

(*a*)   that person either has or can reasonably be required to obtain; and

(*b*)   the Revenue consider that they need to perform their functions under the PRP provisions.

18.48   In particular they could require information:

(*a*)   to enable them to determine whether the registration should be cancelled;

(*b*)   to enable them to determine the liability to tax of an employee or ex-employee covered by a registered PRP scheme or someone who has paid emoluments to such a person;

(*c*)   about the administration of a PRP scheme; and

(*d*)   about any change of persons paying emoluments to employees covered by a PRP scheme.

[*Section 181(1)–(3)*].

18.49   They had to allow the person at least 30 days to provide such information.

18.50   The scheme employer had to notify the Revenue without delay if he became aware of anything that was (or might be) a ground for cancellation of the scheme's registration. [*Section 181(3)*].

18.51   A scheme employer could appeal to the Special Commissioners against:

(*a*)   a refusal of an application for registration of a PRP scheme;

(*b*)   a refusal of an application under *section 177* to amend the scheme on a change of scheme employer;

(*c*)   a refusal of an application under *section 177B(3)* to register an alteration; and

(*d*)   a cancellation of registration.

[*Section 182(1)*].

18.52   The personal representatives of a deceased employer could appeal to the Special Commissioners against a refusal to transfer the scheme registration to them under *section 177A*. [*Section 182(1A)*].

18.53   Notice of appeal had to be given to the Revenue within 30 days of the date on which notification of the Revenue's decision was given. [*Section 182(2)*].

18.54   For PRP purposes the members of a partnership which was a scheme employer were treated as a single continuing body of persons irrespective of partnership changes. [*Section 183*].

Transitional anti-avoidance provision

18.55   A number of employers with PRP schemes sought to extend the PRP benefits by a further year by manipulating the start dates of their profit periods. For example, if a profit period ended on 31 December 1997 the employee would start a new scheme starting on 30 December 1997, which would thus avoid the reduced limits for an extra 364 days. Whether such avoidance justifies a three-page anti-avoidance provision seems doubtful. The government indicated that the tax at stake was almost £6 million, but that would require everyone with a PRP scheme to adopt such a device, which is an unlikely scenario.

18.56   The provision applied where the profit period for a PRP scheme (the relevant period) ends before 31 December 2000, the employee was eligible to receive PRP from a related scheme for an earlier profit period which began before the first day of the relevant period, and the relevant anniversary of that other scheme ended in a later calendar year than that in which the relevant period began. [*FA 1998, 11 Sch 1(1)(2)*]. For example, suppose an employer operated a PRP scheme to 31 December 1997. He starts a new scheme from 1 January 1998 and another from 1 January 1999. The provision will not apply, as the second scheme does not start before the anniversary of the first. Suppose, however, the employer starts a new scheme from 1 April 1998. The provision will apply, as the old scheme anniversary of 1 January 1999 falls into a later calendar year than 1998 when the new scheme starts.

18.57   The *Schedule* provided a special limit arrived at by apportioning the limit that would have applied to the previous scheme. At the employer's option this could either be based on the actual anniversary date of the previous scheme or on the calendar year. [*FA 1998, 11 Sch 1(4)(2)*].

Example

Fred is a member of a PRP scheme for the calendar year 1998. A new scheme is set up from 1 March 1998. The old scheme would have had an anniversary date of 1 January 1999.

Accordingly the limit under the new scheme for its profit period to 28 February 1999 is:

	£
Limit for the period to 31.12.1988	
$^{10}\!/_{12} \times £2,000$	1,667
Limit for the two months to 28.2.1999	
$^{2}\!/_{12} \times £1,000$	167
	1,834

There is accordingly no benefit to Fred in joining the new scheme. The effective limit is the same as under the old.

18.58   As a person cannot earn PRP from two schemes at the same time, Fred in the example would have to cease to be a member of the first scheme. The legislation provided for the limit to be further reduced to take account of any overlap period when the employee would have been eligible to benefit from either scheme. [*FA 1998, 11 Sch 2(2)(b)*].

Example

Fred in the above example does not join the new PRP scheme until 1 June 1998. The limit would be further reduced by £250 to £1,584 as Fred is expected to benefit from the old scheme, not the new, for the first three months of the profit period.

18.59   The change does not affect payments to the employee before 17 March 1998. A related scheme is one for which the scheme employer is the same person or a connected person (within *ICTA 1988, s 879*). [*FA 1998, 11 Sch 3*].

Chapter 19

Miscellaneous

Workers supplied by agencies

19.1   If an individual:

(*a*)   personally provides (or is under an obligation personally to provide) services to another person ('the client');

(*b*)   is supplied to the client by or through a third party ('the agency');

(*c*)   provides (or is under an obligation to provide) his services under the terms of a contract between the individual and the agency; and

(*d*)   is subject to (or to the right of) supervision, direction or control as to the manner in which he renders such services–

those services must be treated as if they were the duties of an employment held by the individual. Accordingly, the remuneration arising under (or in consequence of) the contract is emoluments of that deemed employment and will be taxable as employment income. [*ITEPA 2003, s 44*].

19.2   This does not apply if the remuneration is already taxable as employment income under some other provision. [*ITEPA 2003, s 44(1)(d)*]. Accordingly, it would not apply where the individual is an employee of the intermediary. However, from 6 April 2001 other anti-avoidance rules (see 19.33) have been introduced to deal with that situation. An agency includes an unincorporated body, such as a trade union, of which the individual is a member. [*ITEPA 2003, s 46(1)(b)*]. All remuneration which the client pays or provides by reason of the individual supplying the services has to be treated as receivable in consequence of the contract between the individual and the agency. [*ITEPA 2003, s 44(2)(b)*]. For the purpose of the *section* remuneration includes every form of payment and all perquisites, benefits and profits whatsoever, other than anything that would not have been taxable under Schedule E, if the individual had held a real employment. [*ITEPA 2003, s 47(3)*].

19.3   *ITEPA 2003, s 44* applies even if the individual performs the services in question as a partner in a firm or a member of an unincorporated body. In such circumstances, as the income is treated as earnings of the individual from his deemed employment, it ceases to be taxable income of the partnership or body. [*ITEPA 2003, s 46(1)(a), (2)*].

19.4   If an individual enters into arrangements with another person with a view to the rendering of personal services by that individual, and the effect of such an arrangement is that remuneration for those services is taxable on that other person under *ITEPA 2003, s 44*, all remuneration receivable under (or in consequence of) the arrangement must be treated as emoluments of a deemed employment held by the individual. [*ITEPA 2003, s 45*]. This prevents the interposition of someone else with a lower tax rate. It is not clear if this provision can apply if the other person is a limited company or, indeed, if by interposing a limited company the services can be taken out of *ITEPA 2003, s 44* entirely. The probability is that they can although that is unlikely to help unduly as the IR 35 legislation (see 19.33) will then apply to the company.

19.5   *ITEPA 2003, s 44* does not apply to the following.

(*a*)   Services as an actor, singer, musician or other entertainer or as a fashion, photographic or artist's model. Such people traditionally obtain work through agencies but such work is normally one-off assignments which are not analogous to a continuous employment.

(*b*)   Services rendered wholly in the individual's own home—or at other premises which are neither under the control or management of the client, nor premises at which the worker is required, by reason of the nature of the service, to render them. This is because where the work is not done on the client's premises the element of control that would be normal between employer and employee is generally lacking.

[*ITEPA 2003, s 47(2)*].

19.6   Prior to 6 April 1998 the section did not apply to building industry sub-contractors within *ICTA 1988, s 560* This exemption was withdrawn by *FA 1998, s 55* in relation to payments (whenever made) for services rendered after 5 April 1998. The *ITEPA 2003, s 44* charge takes priority over the sub-contractors deduction scheme, i.e. in relation to work obtained through an agency the worker is treated as an employee, not as self-employed. Because of this change the worker was treated as having ceased his trade at 5 April 1998 and, if he also generated non-agency income, as having started a new trade restricted to such income from 6 April 1998. [*FA 1998, s 56(1)(2)*]. Losses of the old trade could be carried forward to the new and the Revenue option to adjust the assessments for 1995/96 and 1996/97 where a trade ceased in 1997/98 was disapplied. [*FA 1998, s 56(3)–(5)*]. In some cases, such as where the agency income was a small part of the individual's earnings, this could be unfair. The taxpayer could accordingly elect to treat his trade as continuing throughout, with the post 5 April 1998 agency income (and related expenses) being simply excluded from his accounts. [*FA 1998, s 56(6)*]. Such an election had to be included in a timeously filed tax return, which probably meant that it had to be made by 31 January 1999, although as the Inland Revenue did not publicise that time limit it is possible that it could be made in the individual's 1998/99 return. [*FA 1998, s 56(7)*].

19.7   *ITEPA 2003, section 44* is, of course, an anti-avoidance provision aimed at thwarting the non-operation of PAYE where the employer/employee relationship is broken by interposing the agency. Many workers, having been paid fees by the client, omitted to declare such fees to the Inland Revenue with a substantial resultant loss in tax. However, it does not merely impose a PAYE liability. It changes the assessable nature of the income for all tax purposes.

19.8   A particular problem arises with travelling expenses. Although the *Act* does not provide that the deemed employment is with either the agency or the client, there is an inference that it is with whoever pays the individual, which will normally be the agency. Unfortunately, the Revenue consider that the place where this deemed employment is carried on is not the office of the agency; it is the premises of whichever client the individual may from time to time be working for, the cost of travel from the individual's home (or the agency's office) to the client's premises is not travel in the course of the duties of the deemed employment. It is an expense incurred to put the individual into a position to carry out the duties. It is accordingly not an expense wholly, exclusively and necessarily incurred in the course of the employment. Many types of activity where workers are supplied through an agency require skills that are in short supply, so the clients serviced by an individual frequently cover a wide geographical area and extensive travel can be required. The cost of such travel is generally reimbursed to the individual in addition to his fee. An unwelcome side-effect of deeming the engagements to be in the course of an employment is to tax the employee on such reimbursed travel costs. These would normally have constituted business expenses had the individual actually been an employee of the agency. Furthermore, they consider that the premises of the client will normally be the place at which the duties are performed and say that this will typically be a permanent workplace (Employment Status Manual ESM 2016) (see 5.17). This is questionable. It is clearly based on the premise that each assignment is a separate employment. It is arguable that if there is a deemed employment with the agency the workplace for that deemed employment is wherever the agency sends the worker from time to time. A client's premises seem to fit more comfortably within the definition of a temporary workplace (see 5.17) than a permanent one. The Revenue do accept that if the worker is 'genuinely required to work temporarily away from the normal base at the client's premises' travel to and from that second place of work will be allowable, but they warn their staff that that would be exceptional. They also accept (albeit pragmatically) that if an agency sends a worker to two or more clients in the course of a single day travel between the two is allowable provided that the clients were all obtained through the same agency and the worker starts and finishes the day at his or her own home (ESM 2017).

The payroll deduction scheme

19.9   The payroll deduction scheme allows an employee tax relief at source for regular charitable payments that he requests his employer to deduct from his salary. There was a limit of £1,200 p.a. up to 1999/00 but this was abolished by *FA 2000, s 38(5)(b)*. The deductions must be made in accordance with an approved scheme. This involves the employer entering an arrangement with an 'agency charity'. The agency charity—which has to be approved by the Inland Revenue for the purpose—receives the weekly or monthly contributions from the employer, deducts a handling fee and pays the money over to the charity or charities that the employee has selected. [*ITEPA 2003, ss 713–715*].

19.10 The scheme is voluntary. Employees cannot force an employer to start up a scheme and if he opts not to do so they cannot obtain tax relief for direct charitable payments (other than under a charitable deed of covenant or the special rules for gift aid donations). If an employer sets up a scheme he cannot require employees to participate in it or require any particular level of contribution. The agency charity may impose a minimum contribution level, however. The employee must have complete freedom as to which charity or charities he wishes to assist (although the agency charity can set a minimum donation to any one charity). Accordingly, a scheme cannot be set up to benefit a particular charity only. From 6 April 2000 payroll giving donations can also be made to the national heritage bodies set out in *ICTA 1988, s 507.* [*ITEPA 2003, s 714(2)*].

19.11 The deduction must be made from emoluments taxable under PAYE. Accordingly, anyone who is taxable under PAYE can participate even if he is not an employee, e.g. if he is a pensioner.

19.12 The regulations with which the employer must comply, and the obligations placed on him, are very onerous. They are not considered in detail here. Consequently, it is not surprising that, although the legislation has been in force since 1987/88, in the first ten years only around 9,000 such schemes had been introduced and the Revenue had stopped publicising the number of schemes.

19.13 In an effort to revitalise the payroll giving scheme, *FA 2000, s 38(1)–(4)* as amended by *FA 2003, s 146* gives a 10 per cent supplement on payroll giving donations deducted during 2000/01 to 2003/04. The supplement is paid by the agency charity to the recipient charity and reclaimed by the agency charity from the Revenue. There is a fair amount of bureaucracy surrounding this procedure.

Ministers of religion

19.14 Special reliefs apply to clergymen and ministers of religion (of whatever religious denomination), holding a full-time office as a clergyman or minister. They apply where a charity or ecclesiastical corporation has an interest in any premises and (in right of the charity's interest) the clergyman has a residence in these premises from which to perform his duties. [*ITEPA 2003, s 290(4)*].

19.15   The following items in relation to the property do not constitute emoluments:

(*a*)   the making good to the clergyman of statutory amounts payable in connection with the premises or statutory deductions falling to be made in connection with them (except insofar as any such amount is referable to part of the premiseś which the clergyman lets out);

(*b*)   the payment on his behalf of any such statutory amount; and

(*c*)   unless he is in director's or higher-paid employment, any expenses incurred in connection with the provision in the premises of living accommodation for him including heating, lighting, cleaning and gardening expenses (*ESC A61*) (and which are incurred in consequence of his holding his office).

[*ITEPA 2003, s 290(1)(2)*].

19.16   The following deductions can be made from a clergyman's emoluments.

(*a*)   Any payment or expenses incurred by him wholly, exclusively and necessarily in the performance of his duties (this is a relaxation of the general expenses rule which also requires the taxpayer to be necessarily obliged to incur the expense);

(*b*)   if the minister pays rent in respect of a dwelling house any part of which is used mainly and substantially for the purposes of his duties 25 per cent of that rent or, if less, the part that on a just and reasonable apportionment is attributable to that part of the house; and

(*c*)   if an interest in the premises belongs to a charity or ecclesiastical corporation, 25 per cent of the expenses borne by the minister on the maintenance, repair, insurance or management of premises in which he has a residence from which to perform his duties. (Any such expenses deductible under (*a*) must obviously be deducted first.)

[*ITEPA 2003, s 351*].

From 2002/03 onwards no deduction can be claimed in respect of qualifying travelling expenses in relation to a vehicle (other than a company vehicle) if mileage allowance payments (see 7.79) are made or mileage allowance relief (see 7.81) is available in respect of the clergyman's use of the vehicle.

[*ITEPA 2003, s 359*].

19.17   Where the clergyman is in beneficial occupation of his residence the 'business' element of the running costs is deducted from his salary before calculating the 10 per cent limitation on the benefit on such expenses (see 8.31). The Revenue did not allow such a deduction prior to 1991/92. The relief under *ITEPA 2003, s 351(1)* (19.16(*a*) above) is, however, calculated on the full amount of the expenses ignoring such limitation. Up to 1991/92 the business element was taken to be 25 per cent—as provided in *section 332(3)(c)*. However, for 1992/93 onwards the Revenue will not necessarily accept this as the right figure but might adopt a different amount (*Taxation, 22 October 1992, page 95*). It is not clear on what basis, as the *Act* specifies 25 per cent, not up to 25 per cent, other than in relation to rent.

Relief for loan interest

19.18   In certain circumstances a director or employer (both higher and lower-paid) can obtain tax relief for interest paid on a loan to acquire shares in (or make a loan to) the company for which he works. This applies where the employer is either a close company or a co-operative or employee-controlled company. A number of conditions must be met both initially and throughout the period up to the time of each interest payment.

19.19   In the case of a close company these are that:

(*a*)   the company must be a trading company or a specified category of investment company;

(*b*)   the individual must own part of the ordinary share capital of the company;

(*c*)   he must either have worked for the greater part of his time in the actual management or conduct of the company or of an associated company or must have a material interest in the company (broadly, own over 5 per cent of the ordinary share capital);

(*d*)   he must not have recovered any capital from the company (other than capital which has already triggered a restriction of the relief); and

(*e*)   if the company is an investment company and the individual does not meet the first test in (*c*), i.e. he qualifies only under the material interest test, the company must not own a property that is occupied as a residence by the individual.

[*ICTA 1988, s 360(2)(3)*].

The Revenue interpret actual management or conduct for the purpose of (*c*) above as requiring the individual to be involved in the overall running and policy-making of the company as a whole, not merely having responsibility for one particular area. They also consider that the individual must either be a director or have significant managerial or technical responsibilities (*Tax Bulletin, Issue 9*).

19.20   The loan must have been borrowed to defray the cost of acquiring part of the ordinary share capital of the company (broadly, any shares other than fixed rate preference shares), or lending money to the company which is used wholly and exclusively for its business (or that of an associated company) or replacing an earlier loan that satisfied one of these tests or replaced another that satisfied them. [*ICTA 1988, s 360(1)*]. Shares acquired after 13 March 1989 that attracted Business Expansion

Scheme relief or Enterprise Investment Scheme relief cannot also attract loan interest relief. [*ICTA 1988, s 360(3A)*].

19.21 For the purpose of (*c*) in paragraph 19.19 an individual has a material interest in a company if he is the beneficial owner of over 5 per cent of the ordinary share capital of the company; or is able to control, directly or through other companies, over 5 per cent or possesses or is entitled to acquire such rights as in the event of a winding up of the company or in any other circumstance would give him a right to over 5 per cent of the assets available for distribution to participators (broadly, shareholders). [*ICTA 1988, s 360A(1)*]. For this purpose the individual is deemed to own shares held by any associate (or to be able to exercise rights of an associate). An associate means for this purpose:

(*a*) the individual's spouse; parent or remoter issue; child or remoter issue; brother or sister; or partner (in the commercial sense, not in the sense of a live-in companion);

(*b*) the trustees of a settlement of which the individual or any of his above relatives (or deceased relatives) is or was the settlor; and

(*c*) if the individual is interested in any shares or obligations of the company which are subject to a trust (other than an approved profit sharing scheme—within Chapter 16—unless the loan was made before 6 April 1987 or an employee benefit trust—see 18.41—unless the loan was made before 27 July 1989 or at some time after that date the 5 per cent test had been met), or are part of the estate of a deceased person, the trustees or personal representatives.

[*ICTA 1988, s 360A(2)–(7)*].

19.22 In the case of a co-operative the loan must have been either to acquire a share or shares in the co-operative or to lend to it money which was used wholly and exclusively for the purpose of its business (or a subsidiary's business) or to replace a previous qualifying loan. The conditions that need to be met throughout the entire period up to each loan interest payment date are:

(*a*) the body continues to be a co-operative;

(*b*) the individual has worked for the greater part of his time as an employee of the co-operative (or of a subsidiary); and

(*c*) he must not have recovered any capital from the company (other than capital which has already triggered a restriction).

[*ICTA 1988, s 361(1)(2)*].

A co-operative for this purpose means a common ownership enterprise or a co-operative enterprise within the *Industrial Common Ownership Act 1976, s 2*.

19.23 In the case of an employee-controlled company the loan must have been to acquire part of the ordinary share capital or to replace a previous loan. [*ICTA 1988, s 361(3)*]. There is no relief for a borrowing to lend to such a company. An employee-controlled company is one where over 50 per cent of both the issued ordinary share capital and the voting power is beneficially owned by full-time employees (including directors)—but for this purpose where an individual owns over 10 per cent of the ordinary shares or voting power the excess over 10 per cent is deemed not to be held by employees. [*ICTA 1988, s 361(5)(6)*]. A person works full-time if he works for the greater part of his time as an employee or director of the company or a 51 per cent subsidiary. [*ICTA 1988, s 361(8)*]. This definition appears to include part-timers provided that working for the company is their only occupation. The shares must have been acquired either before the company became employee-controlled or within twelve months after that time, and the company must be employee-controlled for at least nine months of the tax year in which the interest payment is made (unless it first became employee-controlled during that year). [*ICTA 1988, s 361(4)(b)(c)*]. In addition, and throughout the entire period up to each interest payment date:

(*a*) the company must have been unquoted, UK resident (and not dual resident) and a trading company or the holding company of a trading group (a group, the business of whose members, taken together, consists wholly or mainly of carrying on one or more trades);

(*b*) the individual must have been a full-time employee of the company—this condition is deemed to be met if he ceased to be such an employee within the previous twelve months and satisfied the condition up to the date of such cessation; and

(*c*) the individual must not have recovered any capital from the company, other than capital that has already triggered a reduction in the relief [*ICTA 1988, s 361(4)(a)(d)(e)*].

19.24 It should be noted that a full-time employee will not qualify under the close company test unless he is employed in a managerial or technical capacity, but all employees are eligible for the co-operative or employee-controlled company test.

19.25 For the purpose of all three tests an individual is regarded as recovering capital from the company if either:

(*a*) he receives any consideration for the sale, exchange or assignment of any of his shares, or any of his shares are redeemed by the company;

(*b*) the company repays a loan or advance from him; or

(*c*) he receives consideration for assigning a debt to him by the company.

[*ICTA 1988, s 363(2)*].

19.26 Where this happens if he does not use the amount so received to reduce the loan he is treated as if he had done so—so that thereafter the interest applicable to the amount deemed to have been repaid will not attract tax relief. If the transaction giving rise to the capital repayment was not a bargain at arm's length, the amount of capital deemed repaid is the market value of the consideration. [*ICTA 1988, s 363(1)(2)*]. Obviously, if there is a subsequent replacement loan the restriction carries through to the new loan. [*ICTA 1988, s 363(4)*].

19.27 It was held in *Lord v Tustain* [*1993*] *STC 755* that if a company is set up with the intention that it should acquire a trade but at the time of the subscription for the shares it had not yet done so, it is nevertheless a company which exists 'for the purpose of' carrying on a trade.

Diplomats, etc.

19.28 Diplomatic Agents, i.e. heads of missions or members of diplomatic staff of foreign states, are exempt from UK tax on their UK earnings under the *Diplomatic Privileges Act 1964*. This exempts a diplomatic agent 'from all dues and taxes, personal or real, national, regional or municipal' (with some exceptions that do not affect earnings). [*Schedule 1, Article 34*]. *Article 33* provides a similar exemption from national insurance. *Article 37(2)* extends this exemption to members of the administrative and technical staff of the diplomatic mission and *Article 37(3)(4)* exempts from tax, and national insurance earnings of members of the service staff of the mission and of private servants of members of the mission provided that they are neither UK nationals nor permanently resident in the UK. This exemption is extended by *ICTA 1988, s 320* to an Agent General for any state or province of a country within *Schedule 3* to the *British Nationality Act 1981*, the Republic of Ireland, or any self-governing colony and to an employee who is either:

(*a*) a member of the personal staff of an Agent-General;

(*b*) an official agent for any of the countries mentioned in *Schedule 3* to the *British Nationality Act 1981* or the Republic of Ireland (of any state or province of such a country); or

(*c*) an official agent for a self-governing colony.

The exemption for such staff applies only if the High Commissioner of the country, or Agent-General for the state, province or self-governing colony in question certifies that the employee is ordinarily resident outside the UK and is resident here solely for the purpose of the performance of his diplomatic duties. [*ICTA 1988, s 320*]. It will not therefore normally apply to staff recruited in the UK.

19.29 There is a similar exemption for foreign consuls. The income from a person's employment as a consul or an official agent in the UK for any foreign state is exempt from UK tax, and also ignored for the purpose of calculating UK tax on other income. A consul for this purpose is a person recognised by Her Majesty as being a consul-general, consul, vice-consul or consular agent. An official agent is a person who is not a consul, but is employed on the staff of any consulate, official department or agency of a foreign state—other than a department or agency that carries on a trade, business or undertaking carried on for the purposes of profit. [*ITEPA 2003, ss 300, 301*]. It has been held that for a country to be a foreign state for the purpose of *section 300* it does not have to be one recognised by the UK (*R v IRC ex parte Caglar* [*1995*] *STC 741*).

19.30 The income from a person's employment in the UK as a consular employee of a foreign state (to which the section applies) is similarly exempt from income tax (but not excluded to calculate the tax rate on other income) unless the employee is a British citizen, a British Dependent Territories citizen, a British national (overseas) or a British overseas citizen and is not a citizen of the foreign state concerned. [*ITEPA 2003, s 302*]. A consular employee includes any person employed for the purposes of the official business of a consular office at any consulate, consular establishment, or any other premises used for such purposes. [*ITEPA 2003, s 302(4)*]. Subsistence allowances paid by the European Commission to experts seconded to the Commission by their employers are also exempt from tax (see 5.78).

19.31 There is also an exemption for the UK earnings of personnel of the armed forces of designated foreign countries, namely, Belgium, Canada, Denmark, Germany, France, Greece, Italy, Luxembourg, the Netherlands, Norway, Portugal, Turkey and the USA; and for persons attached to a designated NATO allied headquarters, namely, the Channel Committee, Channel Command, Eastern Atlantic Area Command, Supreme Headquarters Allied Powers and Allied Command Atlantic Headquarters. [*ITEPA 2003, s 303*, formerly *ICTA 1988, s 323* and *Visiting Forces and Allied Headquarters (Income Tax and Death Duties) (Designation) Order SI 1961 No 580* and *SI 1964 No 924*]. The salary must be paid by the foreign government and the employee must not be a British citizen, British Dependent Territories citizen or British National (Overseas) or British Overseas citizen (except to the extent that the NATO treaty requires the earnings of such people to be exempted). The exemption extends to civilian employees of a visiting force. A period while a person is a member of a visiting force or allied headquarters is ignored in considering his residence or domicile position (but not so as to deny him personal allowances).

Capital Gains Tax

19.32 For capital gains tax purposes where a person acquires or disposes of an asset wholly or partly in connection with:

(*a*) his or another's loss of office or employment or diminution of emoluments; or

(*b*) in consideration for (or recognition of) his or another's services (or past services) in any office or employment

the asset is deemed to be acquired or disposed of for a consideration equal to its market value. [*TCGA 1992, s 17(1)(b)*]. This does not apply to the acquisition of an asset if there is no corresponding disposal of it and no consideration in money or money's worth is given. If there is such consideration the deemed cost cannot exceed that amount [*TCGA 1992, s 17(2)*]. Nor does it apply:

(i)   in respect of certain priority share allocations to employees [*FA 1988, s 68(4)*—see 14.151];

(ii) in relation to employee share options [*TCGA 1992, s 149A*—see 14.213]; or

(iii) on a disposal by a close company or an individual to an employee trust [*TCGA 1992, s 239(2)*—see 17.7].

Provision of services through an intermediary

19.33   From 2000/01 a taxpayer who operates through a personal services company (or other intermediary) and would have been an employee of the intermediary's client had he worked direct for it will be taxed under Schedule E on a notional amount to the extent that such notional amount falls short of his deemed earnings. This was described by the government as an anti-avoidance provision in its well-known *IR35 1999 Budget Day Press Release*, although many people would question whether choosing a particular method of structuring a transaction over a different method and accepting the normal tax consequences of that structure can properly be described as avoidance. The real reason for the provision appears to be that the government, having introduced legislation to make it more attractive to receive dividends than remuneration, became concerned that people were 'avoiding' National Insurance by opting to pay those lower tax rates on dividends.

19.34   The tax charge arises where:

(*a*) an individual ('the worker') personally performs services for another person ('the client') (or is under an obligation personally to perform such services);

(*b*) the services are provided under a contract directly between the client and the worker but under arrangements involving a third party ('the intermediary'); and

(*c*) the circumstances (including the terms on which the services are provided, having regard to the terms of the contracts under the arrangements) are such that if the services were provided under a contract directly between the client and the worker, the worker would be regarded for income tax purposes as an employee of the client.

[*ITEPA 2003, s 49(1)*].

19.35   A typical example is the one-man company which loans out its sole employee. The company contracts with a client to provide services which are then personally performed by its sole employee. The provision applies if that employee would have been an employee of the client had the company not existed. The normal tests of employment set out at 4.12 onwards apply. Accordingly, if the individual is providing a service rather than his labour the provision will not apply. The Revenue have said that where a contract requires workers to work where the client requests, for an agreed number of hours per week, at an agreed rate of pay and to keep a timesheet checked by the client, be subject to the directives of the client and not subcontract the work to any one else, and the engagement is for a month or more, they consider that the legislation will apply unless the worker can demonstrate a recent history of work including engagements which have the characteristics of self-employment (*IR Press Release 7 February 2000*).

19.36   In *R (on the application of Professional Contractors Group Ltd) v IRC [2001] EWHC Admin 236 [2001] STC 629)* the judge emphasised that it is not correct to look simply at the contract between the client and the intermediary because what has to be ascertained is what the contractual relationship between the client and the worker would have been if they had contracted direct. 'It appears to me clear that the Revenue must bear in mind that under IR35 they are not considering an actual contract between the service company and the client, but imagining or constructing a notional contract which does not in fact exist. In those circumstances, of course the terms of the contract between the agency and the client as a result of which the service contractor will be present at the site are important, as would be the terms of any contract between the service contractor and the agency. But, particularly given the fact that, at any rate at present, a contract on standard terms may or may not be imposed by an agency, or may be applicable not by reference to a particular assignment, but on an ongoing basis and may actually bear no relationship to the (non-contractual) interface between the client and the service contractor, such document can only form a part, albeit obviously an important part, of the picture'. The Professional Contractors Group decision was appealed to the Court of Appeal (*[2001] EWCA Civ 1945)* (*[2002] STC 165)* but the issues under appeal were not *Schedule E* ones.

19.37   The first case to be litigated under these provisions, or rather their National Insurance equivalent, was *Battersby v Campbell ([2001] STC (SCD) 189) (SpC 287)*. This was an appeal by a taxpayer in person who seems to have mainly argued that he took the risks of self-employment and had not sought to avoid tax. It is unsurprising in those circumstances that the Commissioner accepted the Revenue's view that had the taxpayer been employed under a contract with the client it would have been a contract of service. The second was *F S Consulting Ltd v McCaul ([2002] STC (SCD) 138) (SpC 305)*. This was another National Insurance case. The taxpayer challenged the interpretation of the regulation rather than addressing the deemed relationship between the worker and the client, so again the Commissioner considered that relationship based only on the Revenue's arguments. In *Synaptic v Young (2003 STC 543)* the case was fully argued before the General Commissioners, who held that, on balance, if there had been a contract it would have been a contract of employment. On appeal Hart J felt that the identification and characterisation of the arrangements is a matter of fact for the fact-finding tribunal. The fact that the tribunal is then asked to hypothesise a contract comprising those arrangements directly between the worker and the client does not by itself convert the question from being a question of mixed fact and law into a pure question of law. Accordingly the court can interfere only if it concludes that the decision reached by the Commissioners is an impossible one on the facts found by them, or that they have misdirected themselves. He felt there was evidence on which they had been entitled to conclude that the notional contract was a contract of employment.

19.38   The taxpayer also won in *Lime-IT Ltd v Justin (2003 STC (SCD) 15 Sp C 542)* but in that case the Commissioners pointed out that no evidence had been called from the client and warned that 'In future cases on this legislation (and its income tax equivalent) the Special Commissioners will wish to explore at a preliminary hearing whether it is possible to obtain evidence from the client'. In *Tilbury Consulting Ltd v Gittins (2004, STC (SCD) 1, Sp C 379)* the Revenue duly sought, and were given, a witness summons for someone from the client to attend the hearing of the appeal to give oral evidence, albeit that he had already written twice to the Revenue in response to letters they had sent to the client. The taxpayers won despite such evidence, although the facts were a little unusual. Ford Motor Co had contracted with a company called Compuware Ltd to set up, service and staff a particular IT contract. Tilbury Consulting Ltd was engaged by Compuware to provide services to it by making available Mr Tilbury's services. Accordingly, Mr Tilbury was not answerable to Ford; he was answerable to Compuware. Similarly, Ford dealt with Compuware. It was of no concern of Ford what particular individuals Compuware used in the contract. In these circumstances a notional contract between Ford and Mr Tilbury would not have been a contract of employment. Ford did not exercise control over the performance of Mr Tilbury's services and was happy to accept a substitute if Compuware wanted to send along someone else. This may point to a lacuna in the legislation or, more likely, an error of judgement by the Revenue. Mr Tilbury might well have been an employee under a notional contract between himself and Compuware but the Revenue did not seek to apply the provisions by reference to such a contract.

19.39   The taxpayer was less successful in *Usetech Ltd v Young (2004 STC(SCD) 213, Sp C 404)*, another National Insurance case. In that case two employees of the client gave evidence that whilst Mr Hood (the worker) had some flexibility over the hours he worked he was expected to agree them with the client. Mr Hood worked as a member of a team and was expected to accept the work allocated to him at weekly meetings. They also made clear that although the contract allowed for substitution they would not have accepted a substitute without interview and would not have done so at all if Mr Hood was available. The Commissioners stressed in particular that 'there must be mutuality of obligations, but that does not imply that the "employer" is required to provide work … the requirement of mutuality may be satisfied by the obligation, on the one hand to work and, on the other, to remunerate'. The client also gave evidence in *Future Online Ltd v Faulds (2004 STC (SCD) 213, Sp C 406)* where the Revenue again won. The judge commenting 'it seems to me … that the mutual obligations that actually existed between Mr Roberts and E D S were above the irreducible minimum'.

19.40   The Revenue have said that if, as part of an employer compliance review, they feel they need to check information about working practices with the client to check that the service company has reached a correct view on the application of IR35 they will ask the worker's permission. If the worker is unhappy for the Revenue to speak to the client the Revenue are willing 'to explore a mutually acceptable other way for the contact to be made'. But, if a mutually acceptable way cannot be agreed the Revenue will approach the client direct 'for information on the details of the day to day working arrangements' where they think this necessary (Press Release 7.1.2004). It is of course up to the client what information he is willing to volunteer to the Revenue, although at the end of the day *TMA 1970, s 20(3)* enables them to require the client to provide information.

19.41   For services performed before 10 April 2003, in 19.34(*a*) above the services had to be performed for the purposes of a business carried on by the other person. A business is defined as a trade, profession, vocation or a Schedule A business. [*ITEPA 2003, s 61(1)*, formerly *FA 2000, 12 Schedule 21(1)*]. However, any activity carried on by a government, a public or local authority, a body corporate, unincorporated body or partnership is deemed to be a business for this purpose. [*ITEPA 2003, s 49(2)*, formerly *FA 2000, 12 Schedule 1(2)*]. This effectively means that the only excluded clients were likely to be where the client is a private individual (or is a charity set up by deed of trust rather than as a company limited by guarantee). This limitation (and *section 49(2)*) was removed by *FA 2003, s 136(2)*. The government apparently envisaged hordes of nannies and other domestic staff forming companies to seek to avoid tax, albeit that the level of earnings of such people is generally such that the cost of operating the company would be likely to cancel out any tax saving. The change is not limited to domestic staff. It could potentially apply to anyone who provides services to private householders, such as builders, gardeners, personal secretaries and even financial managers, although it is unlikely to do so in most cases as such people are usually genuinely self-employed.

19.42   The intermediary is treated as making a deemed salary payment to the worker if in any tax year the worker (or an associate of the worker) either:

(*a*)   receives from the intermediary (directly or indirectly) a payment or other benefit that is not taxable under Schedule E, or (*b*) has rights which in any circumstances would entitle him to receive from the intermediary (directly or indirectly) any such payment or other benefit.

[*ITEPA 2003, s 50(1)*].

19.43 The deemed salary is not related to the payment or benefit received; it is 95 per cent of the income from relevant engagements after deducting expenses and capital allowances that would be allowable under the rules relating to employment income, pension contributions, salary and benefits already paid to the worker and the related employer's NI and the NI generated by the notional salary itself. It is calculated as follows:

(*a*) ascertain the total of all payments and benefits received by the intermediary in the tax year in respect of relevant engagements (i.e. engagements within 19.34 above which do not fall within any of the exceptions set out in 19.51 below);

(*b*) reduce that figure by 5 per cent;

(*c*) add any payments or other benefits (calculated as for employment income purposes, i.e. under chapters 6–9) received direct by the worker in respect of relevant engagements;

(*d*) deduct expenses met in that year by the intermediary that would have been deductible from the emoluments of the employment if the worker had been employed by the client (see Chapter 5)—for 2002/03 onwards also include expenses met by the worker and reimbursed by the intermediary and, where the intermediary is a partnership of which the worker is a partner, expenses met by the worker on behalf of the partnership;

(*e*) deduct any capital allowances on expenditure incurred by the intermediary that could have been deducted by the worker if he had been employed by the client and had incurred the expenditure;

(*f*) deduct any pension contributions made by the intermediary to an approved pension scheme, either a company pension scheme or personal pension in respect of the worker (but excluding of course any excess contributions later repaid);

(*g*) deduct any employee's national insurance paid by the intermediary for the tax year in respect of the worker;

(*h*) deduct the amount of any payments or other benefits received in the tax year by the worker from the intermediary which are taxable as earnings from employment;

(*i*) the resultant figure is the notional salary plus related employer's National Insurance, so the notional salary is the figure remaining after deducting the employer's National Insurance element.

[*ITEPA 2003, s 54*].

19.44   If the intermediary provides a car or other vehicle for the worker and he would have been entitled to mileage allowance relief (see 7.70) in respect of the use of the vehicle had he been an employee of the client, and the vehicle had not been a company vehicle (see 7.72), the amount of such mileage allowance relief is treated as an expense deductible at (*d*) above [(*ITEPA 2003, s 54(4)*]. If the intermediary is a partnership of which the worker is a partner and he provides a vehicle for the purpose of the partnership business it is treated as provided by the intermediary to the worker so as to trigger the right to this relief [*ITEPA 2003, s 54(5)(b)*]. If the worker receives exempt mileage allowance payments or passenger payments (see 7.68 and 7.74) from the intermediary those are treated as taxable (and thus as deductible at (*h*) above) for the purpose of calculating the deemed salary payment [*ITEPA 2003, s 54(7)*]. As the payments will have been treated as income at step (*a*) this adjustment effectively excludes them from the calculation.

19.45   The government have confirmed that 'a worker who is continuously employed by his service company, and undertakes contracts for clients of the service company in different places, can claim the costs of travelling to and from those clients' premises. That is because a client's premises can be treated as a temporary place of work, provided that the worker does not expect to work there for more than 40 per cent of the time in a period exceeding 24 months. The legislation will allow this more generous treatment to continue, even where there is the same employee relationship'. The minister pointed out that this is a more generous treatment than if a person had a series of short employments with different clients in different parts of the country. *Hansard SC H 6 July 2000 Column 465.*

19.46

Example

Jim is a computer programmer. He is a single parent with two children and cannot do a full-time job as he needs to collect his children from school. He has a concept for a new internet product. Jim is trying to devote as much time as he can to the product which is being developed by his company, Internet Wizard Ltd. In order to support his family Jim advertises his services as a computer consultant. Jim has also registered with an agency. During 2002/03 the agency found him a three-month contract servicing the computers of Alpha Ltd, a two-month contract as a member of a development team for Beta plc and a contract to develop a stock control system for Gamma plc which took Jim three months. All these contracts were entered into by Internet Wizard Ltd. The accounts of Internet Wizard Ltd for the year to 5 April 2003 contains the information set out below.

At the end of the assignment Alpha Ltd gave Jim a laptop which had cost them £3,000 and had a then value of £1,800.

		£
Income:	computer consultant – home computer	9,000
	business computer	11,000
	Alpha Ltd	12,000
	Beta plc	9,000
	Gamma plc	10,000
		51,000
Expenses:	Salary for Jim	5,000
	N.I. on salary	1,600
	Pension contribution	1,000
	Agency commission—15%	3,600
	Motor expenses	12,000
	Computer disks etc	3,000
	Stationery	1,000
	Training courses to keep up to date	2,500
	Administrative costs of company	3,000
		32,700
Net profit before depreciation (which Internet		
Wizard Ltd. needs to buy more equipment)		18,300

The capital allowances on Jim's company car (which was first registered before 1.1.1998) for the year to 5 April 2003 amount to £2,000. The car was used 10 per cent of the time on travelling in the course of the Alpha Ltd. contract, 8 per cent for the Beta contract, and 12 per cent for the Gamma contract, and 40 per cent on consultancy work. The other 30 per cent was private use. The capital allowances on the company's computer equipment were £6,000. Jim did not use the computers on the Alpha and Beta contracts as those companies will not permit outside disks to be input into their systems. 40 per cent of the computer usage was private. The cost to the company of the computers was £40,000 and the cost of the car was £26,000.

It seems likely that the work done for Alpha Ltd and Beta plc are relevant engagements. The consultancy work on business computers and the work done for Gamma plc are unlikely to be relevant engagements as in those cases Internet Wizard Ltd is selling services of troubleshooting and system creation respectively, not Jim's labour. On this basis the notional salary is as follows:

	Alpha Ltd	Beta Ltd	Total
Income from relevant engagements	12,000	9,000	21,000
Less 5%	(600)	(450)	(1,050)
	11,400	8,550	19,950
Value of gift from Alpha Ltd.	1,800	–	1,800
	13,200	8,550	21,750

			Alpha Ltd	Beta Ltd	Total
Less	Jim's salary	5,000			
	Benefits:				
	Use of computers	2,400			
	Use of car				
	22% of 26,000	5,720			
	Petrol	2,850			
		15,970	(9,692)	(6,278)	(15,970)
National Insurance			(996)	(604)	(1,600)
Pension Contributions			(622)	(378)	(1,000)
Motor Expenses			(1,200)	(960)	(2,160)
Capital Allowances on car			(200)	(160)	(360)
Taxable amount			490	170	660
Of which NI $\frac{11.8}{111.8} \times 660$			52	18	70
Notional Salary			438	152	590

Notes

1 It appears that the whole of Jim's earnings from Internet Wizard Ltd and the related National Insurance can be deducted even though only 41 per cent of the company's income is from relevant engagements

2 The engagements have been considered separately above for clarity. However, the notional salary from all relevant engagements is calculated globally. Accordingly a loss in one will reduce the notional salary payment in relation to the others.

3 The Class 1A NIC-free band has been ignored for simplicity.

19.47 Where tax is deducted under the building industry sub-contractors scheme the income from the relevant engagements is of course the gross receipt before such deductions. [*ITEPA 2003, s 54(2)*, formerly *FA 2000, 12 Schedule 8*]. Many people would see this as double taxation. The Revenue do not. They say that the sub-contractors deductions is a payment on account of the company's corporation tax liability and the PAYE and NI on the notional salary relates to the worker's tax liability. Whilst in theory that is right, in most cases the notional salary will eliminate the corporation tax liability so the single amount of income has to bear two tax deductions albeit that the sub-contractor's deductions will fall to be repaid in due course. To avoid this from 6 April 2002 sub-contractor deductions suffered by a company can be set against its PAYE liabilities [*ICTA 1988, s 599* inserted by *FA 2002, s 40*].

19.48   Where an amount received by the intermediary either relates to the services of more than one worker or relates partly to the services of the worker and partly to other matters any necessary apportionment is to be made on a just and reasonable basis. [*ITEPA 2003, s 54(8)*]. This should enable VAT to be excluded from the calculation. It is not clear whether it will allow materials to be excluded where a single price is charged to cover both labour and materials.

19.49   In calculating the notional payment a 'payment or other benefit' includes anything that if received by an employee for performing the duties of his employment would be taxed as an emolument of that employment. [*ITEPA 2003, s 55(2)*]. The amount of a non-cash benefit is the greater of the amount that would be taxable under *ITEPA 2003, ss 6, 62* (the charging provision on earnings) if the benefit were an emolument (normally the resale value of the benefit) or the cash equivalent of the benefit under *ITEPA 2003, ss 19* or *398* (see 10.61). [*ITEPA 2003, s 55(3)(4)*]. A payment or cash benefit is treated as received when a payment is made of or on account of it. (Where a payment on account is received it is probably only that receipt not the full 'payment' that is deemed to be received at that time). A non-cash benefit is deemed to be received when it is used or enjoyed. [*ITEPA 2003, s 55(5)*]. Where a benefit is enjoyed over a period it is presumably deemed to be received on a day by day basis.

19.50   The provisions apply where the service is performed or to be performed after 5 April 2000. Payments in respect of such services received before that date must be treated as received in 2000/01. [*FA 2000, 12 Schedule 22*]. Subject to that, the calculations are all on a cash basis, i.e. it is the cash received during a tax year, not fees earned in relation to services performed during that year. Similarly, only salary actually paid during a tax year can be deducted in arriving at the notional salary payment.

Exceptions

19.51   There are a number of exceptions to the personal service company rules.

(*a*)   As indicated at 19.43 the provision does not apply to the extent that the income of the company does not derive from relevant engagements.

(*b*)   If the intermediary is a company, the provision applies only if *both*

    (i)   the intermediary is not an associated company of the client by reason of both of them being under the control of the worker (or of the worker and another person); and

    (ii)   either;

        (A)   the worker has a material interest in the intermediary (see below) or

      (B)   all payments or benefits received or receivable by the worker come directly from the intermediary and can reasonably be taken to represent remuneration for services provided by the worker to the client.

[*ITEPA 2003, s 51*].

(*c*)   If the intermediary is a partnership, the provisions apply only if either:

     (i)   the worker, alone or with one or more relatives (spouse, parent or remoter forebear, child or remoter issue or brother or sister) is entitled to 60 per cent or more of the profits of the partnership; or

    (ii)   most of the profits of the partnership derive from the provisions of services under relevant engagements to a single client or to a single client together with associates (see 19.54) of that client; or

   (iii)   under the profit-sharing arrangements the income of any of the partners is based on the amount of income generated by that partner by the provision of services under relevant engagements.

[*ITEPA 2003, s 52(2)*].

(*d*)   If the intermediary is a partnership and the worker is not a partner, or it is an individual, the provisions apply only if the payment or benefit is received or receivable by the worker directly from the intermediary and can reasonably be taken to represent remuneration for services provided by the worker to the client. [*ITEPA 2003, s 52(3)*].

(*e*)   The provision does not apply to payments subject to deduction of tax under *ICTA 1988, s 555* (payments to non-resident entertainers or sportsmen). [*ITEPA 2003, s 48(2)(b)*]. It does apply to payments subject to deduction of tax under *ITEPA 2003, s 44* (workers supplied by agencies—see 19.1) [*ITEPA 2003, s 48(2)(a)*] or under *ICTA 1988, ss 559–567* (sub-contractors in the construction industry), although it does not affect the operation of those provisions.

19.52   For the purpose of 19.51(*b*) a worker has a material interest in a company if either:

(*a*)   he himself has a material interest in the company (either alone or with one or more associates); or

(*b*)   an associate (see 19.54) (or associates) of his has a material interest in the company (even though the worker himself has no interest in it).

[*ITEPA 2003, s 51(3)*].

19.53 A material interest for this purpose means either:

(*a*) beneficial ownership of more than 5 per cent of the ordinary share capital of the company (or the ability to control, directly or indirectly—such as through the medium of other companies—more than 5 per cent); or

(*b*) possession of (or entitlement to acquire) rights entitling the holder to receive more than 5 per cent of any distributions that may be made by the company; or

(*c*) if the company is a close company, possession of (or entitlement to acquire) rights that in the event of a winding up or in any other circumstances would entitle the holder to receive more than 5 per cent of the assets that would then be available for distribution among the participators (as defined in *ICTA 1988, s 417(1)*).

[*ITEPA 2003, s 51(4)*].

19.54 For the purpose of *ITEPA 2003, ss 48–61*, the *ICTA 1988, s 417(3)(4)* definition of an associate applies in relation to an individual (see 17.50(*f*)). [*ITEPA 2003, s 60(1)*]. However, where the individual has an interest in shares or obligations of the company as a member of an employee benefit trust within *ITEPA 2003, ss 550, 551* which reflect that in *ICTA 1988, 8 Schedule 7* (see 18.41) the trustees are not regarded as associates of his by reason only of that interest unless the individual (either on his own or within one or more associates – excluding the trustees of an employee benefit trust merely because the individual has an interest in the trust) or associates of the individual have at any time since 13 March 1989 been the beneficial owner of or able to control (directly, through the medium of other companies or by any other indirect means) more than 5 per cent of the ordinary share capital of the company. [*ITEPA 2003, s 60(2)–(6)*].

19.55 It is doubtful if this exception includes shares allocated to the employee under a SIP (see Chapter 15) as the participant appears to be the beneficial owner of (or at least has the ability to control) such shares.

19.56 In the case of a company an associate means a person connected with the company within *ICTA 1988, s 839* [*ITEPA 2003, ss 60(1)(b), 718*]. In the case of a partnership associate means an associate of any member of the partnership. [*ITEPA 2003, s 60(1)(c)*].

19.57 It should be noted that 19.51(*b*) excludes from the IR 35 rules a loan-out where the intermediary is an associated company of the client. This will ensure that intra-group charges in respect of staff, particularly where there is a central payroll function, are not accidentally caught. It might logically also let out the situation where the intermediary is the service company of a partnership. Unfortunately it does not appear to do so. The use of the expression 'associated company' rather than associate and the definition in *ICTA 1988, s 416* imply that both intermediary and client must be companies. Of course in most cases it will not matter as an employee of a partnership service company is unlikely to have a shareholding in it, let alone own over 5 per cent. Care may, however, be needed where the spouse of a partner is an employee of the service company.

19.58   The let out for partnerships in 19.51(*c*) appears to leave significant scope for avoidance. Whether this will occur probably depends on clients. Currently, most clients seem reluctant to engage a partnership, preferring to engage someone via a company, but the possibility of behavioural changes should not be ruled out.

19.59   The obvious situation is if two friends enter into partnership sharing profits equally and each works for one customer. This will be exempt as it satisfies all three sub-heads of 19.51(*c*). Some people think this an unlikely scenario. Will someone willingly take on the risks of joint and several liability inherent in a partnership and are they prepared to share profits equally? In practice, the answer to both questions is likely to be 'Yes'. Most people do not realise the risks of entering into a partnership and the variation between earnings of two friends in the same line of business will not generally be significant. There is nothing to stop the profit-sharing ratio being changed in subsequent years if incomes diverge significantly, provided that the entitlement of any one individual never reaches 60 per cent and no attempt is made to tie the profit-sharing to the income generated by each partner.

19.60   The restrictions relate to the profit-sharing arrangements. There is nothing to prevent drawings being tied to the income generated by each partner if profits are shared equally. There is probably also nothing to stop this being supplemented with an agreement that the tax of both partners will be paid by the partnership and in the event of a dissolution of the partnership, the assets at the time of the dissolution will be shared equally irrespective of the balances on partners' capital accounts.

19.61   There also seems nothing to prevent a partnership between two friends and their respective spouses with profits being shared equally up to twice the amount of income generated by the lowest earning of the two workers and the spouse of the other being entitled to the balance of the profits (which will be the excess income generated by the higher earning worker). The 60 per cent figure will not be breached; there will be at least two clients of the partnership, and the income of no partner is based on the profits generated by that partner. Although head (*a*) looks at the worker and his relatives, head (*c*) does not do so. Nor does *ITEPA 2003, s 61(3)(b)* seem to apply, which provides that a payment provided to a member of an individual's family is treated as provided to the worker, as this is looking at payments whereas head (*c*) is looking at profit-sharing arrangements.

Timing of Notional Payments

19.62 The notional payment is normally deemed to be made at the end of the tax year concerned (i.e. on 5 April). [*ITEPA 2003, s 50(3)*]. However, if one of the following events occurs during the tax year that will trigger a notional payment at the time of that event.

(*a*) If the worker is employed by the intermediary, his ceasing to be so employed.

(*b*) If the worker is a member of the intermediary company, his ceasing to be a member, e.g. by disposing of all of his shares, even if the disposal is to a trust of which he is the principal beneficiary. A disposal of shares will often not signify a cessation of the worker's association with the company, so the logic of its triggering an interim notional payment is not readily apparent.

(*c*) If the worker holds an office with the intermediary company, his ceasing to hold that office. Take care if the worker agrees to be company secretary temporarily to fill a casual vacancy, perhaps for a few days only, as when he hands over the reins to a permanent incumbent this will trigger a tax charge.

(*d*) If the intermediary is a partnership, its dissolution.

(*e*) If the intermediary is a partnership its ceasing to trade. (Curiously, if the intermediary is a company a cessation of the trade will not trigger the notional payment).

(*f*) If the intermediary is a partnership, a partner ceasing to act as such —apparently even if the worker is not a partner or, if he is, is not the partner ceasing to act. It is not clear what is meant by ceasing to act as a partner. For example, if a general partner becomes a limited partner does he cease to act as a partner as he becomes prohibited from taking part in the management of the partnership business?

(*g*) For 2002/03 onwards, the company ceasing to trade.

[*ITEPA 2003, s 57*].

19.63 It is not clear how the notional salary payment is calculated on the occurrence of one of the above events. Logically it ought to be based on the income from relevant engagements from the previous 6 April up to the date of the trigger event, with a further notional salary payment being calculated (where relevant) from that time up to the following 5 April. However, *ITEPA 2003, s 57(5)* states, 'The fact that the deemed payment of earnings is treated as made before the end of the tax year does not affect what receipts and other matters are taken into account in calculating its amount'. This seems to imply that only a single notional payment is calculated at the end of the year and that the entire payment is deemed to be made at the time of the trigger event. As interest on PAYE runs only from 5 April after the end of the tax year it may not matter unduly for income tax purposes but would have an affect on employees' National Insurance as the 'pay period' would appear to end at the date of the trigger event.

Relief for distributions

19.64 If the intermediary is a company and it makes a distribution either during the same tax year or in a year subsequent to that in which a notional payment is deemed to be made the intermediary (not the worker) can make a claim for relief. It is an odd claim. It's the worker that is doubly taxed not the intermediary. It is not for any particular relief. It is for such relief as appears to the Revenue to be appropriate in order to avoid a double charge to tax. [*ITEPA 2003, s 58(5)*]. The claim must be made within five years after the 31 January following the tax year in which the distribution is made. [*ITEPA 2003, s 58(2)(b)*]. This was not specifically stated in the previous legislation but was implied as it is the normal rules for claims under *TMA 1970, s 43*.

19.65 If the Revenue are satisfied that some sort of relief is appropriate (i.e. it is for the company to convince them that some relief should be given) they must give this by treating the amount of the distribution as reduced, not the amount of the deemed employment income payment. [*ITEPA 2003, s 58(3)(4)*]. They must exercise the power so as to secure that, as far as practicable, relief is given against relevant distributions of the same tax year before those of other years, against relevant distributions received by the worker before those received by another person, and against relevant distributions of earlier years before those of later years. [*ITEPA 2003, s 58(5)*]. Where a distribution is reduced the related tax credit is obviously correspondingly reduced. [*ITEPA 2003, s 58(6)*].

19.66 Where Parliament gives a wide discretion to the Revenue such as here there is no effective right of appeal against their decision. The taxpayer can apply for judicial review but not only is this costly but he has to show (probably without the Revenue having to explain the reason for their decision) that the decision was unreasonable in the sense that nobody acting judicially could have arrived at it on the facts or that it was made maliciously. It is accordingly likely to be virtually impossible to challenge a refusal to give relief.

19.67 Although at one stage there was doubt whether the Revenue would grant relief where the dividend is received by a third party they have confirmed that relief can be given against any distributions.

19.68 A distribution is a dividend or certain other payments to shareholders or, in the case of a close company, expenses incurred in providing benefits to shareholders [*ICTA 1988, ss 209–211, 418, 832; ITEPA 2003,*

1 Schedule]. A loan is not a distribution so relief could not be given against tax due under *ICTA 1988, s 419* (loans to participators).

19.69   Worse, a payment of salary is not a distribution. This creates a major problem where the profits of the intermediary are distributed as bonuses subsequent to 5 April – perhaps at or shortly after the end of the intermediary's accounting period, which is what very often happens with personal service companies. The bonus cannot be deducted in calculating the notional payment as it is not a payment received by the worker in the relevant year (which is all that *step 7* of *paragraph 7* will allow to be deducted). It can be deducted in calculating the notional salary payment for the following year, but apart from the fact that there will be double taxation in the year of payment this is likely to lead to anomalies as if in a particular year no notional payment arises excess actual salary payments cannot be taken into account in calculating the notional payment of a different year. Accordingly, once a notional payment has arisen it may be that the only safe way to avoid double taxation is to stop paying remuneration and pay only dividends to the worker in future years!

Corporation Tax or Income Tax deduction

19.70   Corporation tax or income tax relief is given for the amount of the notional payment and related employer's national insurance by allowing it as a deduction in calculating the profits of the intermediary's business. [*FA 2000, 12 Schedule 17(1)*]. The deduction must be taken into account for the period of account in which the notional salary payment is made. [*FA 2000, 12 Schedule 17(2)*]. No deduction can be claimed under any other provision in respect of the notional payment. [*FA 2000, 12 Schedule 17(3)*]. It should be noted that the notional salary payment does not have to satisfy the normal 'wholly and exclusively' test.

19.71   This provision creates a mismatch.

Example

Personal Services Ltd prepares its accounts to 31 March. These show the following profits.

Year to 31 3 2001*	£50,000
Year to 31 3 2002	70,000
Year to 31 3 2003	80,000

*no income arising before 6.4.2000.

It is deemed to make the following notional salary payments

5.4.2001	£40,000
5.4.2002	60,000
5.4.2003	70,000

The corporation tax position (ignoring National Insurance) will be as follows

Year to 31 March	*2001*	*2002*	*2003*
Profits	£50,000	£70,000	£80,000
Less notional salary paid In the accounting period	nil	40,000	60,000
Chargeable to corporation tax	£50,000	£30,000	£20,000

Over the three years the company has received £200,000, of which the employee has been taxed on £170,000. One would therefore expect the company to have a corporation tax liability on £30,000 not on the £100,000 that in fact applies.

19.72 The Revenue appear unsympathetic to this problem. They point out that if the company calculates the notional salary every month (before the end of the month of course) and actually pays it as real salary the notional salary calculation at the end of the year will produce a nil figure. Most people will not find the suggestion of having to do monthly calculations particularly helpful. If the company has a 31 March year end consideration might be given to calculating the notional salary immediately before the year end and making an actual salary payment of an equivalent amount. A more practical solution might be to change the company's accounting date to 5 April so that the notional payment date falls in the accounting period.

19.73 The notional payment can create a trading loss for a company, which can of course be dealt with like any other trading loss.

Example

Suppose that in the Example in 19.71 the profit for the year to 31 March 2004 is £30,000. The corporation tax position for that year (ignoring National Insurance) will be:

	£
Profit	30,000
Notional salary payment 5.4.2003	(70,000)
Loss	(40,000)

£20,000 of this loss can be carried back and set against the £20,000 profits for the year to 31 March 2003 and the balance can be carried forward. It might be worth considering a cessation so that the full £40,000 can be carried back under a terminal loss relief claim.

19.74 In contrast, if the intermediary is a partnership the notional salary payment cannot create a loss. The deduction is limited to the amount that reduces the profits of the partnership for the tax year to nil. Worse, if the expenses of the partnership in connection with the relevant engagement exceed the sum of:

(*a*)   the amount deductible at 19.43(*d*) above in calculating the notional salary; and (*b*) '5 per cent of the amount taken into account in Step One of the calculation in paragraph 7' (this is probably intended to be 5 per cent of the gross income not 5 per cent of the 95 per cent of the gross income which is the figure at Step One),

the excess expenses must be left out of account in calculating the profits of the business. [*FA 2000, 12 Schedule 18*].

19.75 The reason for this is probably that if a loss could be created by deducting the notional payment a partner who was deemed to receive that notional payment would claim to set the loss against the notional payments. It operates very unfairly if there is a mismatch between profit share and notional payment, or if the worker to whom the notional payment relates is not a partner at all. This can be illustrated by comparing the position between a corporate and partnership intermediary.

Example

An intermediary has the following profile for the year to 5 April 2003.

	£	£
Income (wholly from relevant engagements)		100,000
Business expenses relating to relevant engagements		
Within Schedule E rules	8,000	
Not within Schedule E rules	20,000	
Other business expenses	10,000	38,000
		62,000
The notional salary payment is:		
95% of income	95,000	
Less Schedule E expenses	8,000	
	87,000	
Less employer's National Insurance on		
notional salary payment at 12.2%	9,460	
Notional salary payment	77,540	

If the intermediary is a company its corporation tax position will be

Profit as adjusted for tax purposes	62,000
Less notional salary and N.I.	87,000
Adjusted loss available for carry back or forward	(25,000)

If the intermediary is a partnership of which the worker is not a partner the position will be

Profit as adjusted for tax purposes		62,000
Add back expenses	38,000	
Less allowable under Schedule E	(8,000)	
5% of 100,000	(5,000)	25,000
		37,000
Less notional payment (restricted)		37,000
		NIL

Application of employment income rules

19.76   The government of course want to collect real tax and real National Insurance in respect of the notional payment. To achieve this rules in relation to the taxation of employment income, and in particular the PAYE provisions, apply as if the worker were employed by the intermediary and the relevant engagements were undertaken by the worker in the course of that employment. [*ITEPA 2003, s 56(2)*]. The notional payment is also treated as an emolument of the employment to determine whether the worker is higher paid for benefit-in-kind purposes (see 6.4) and for the purpose of *ITEPA 2003, ss 336* and *337* (see 5.2) (and from 2002/03 mileage allowance relief (see 7.70)). [*ITEPA 2003, s 56(3)*]. Where the intermediary is a partnership or unincorporated association the deemed salary payment is of course treated as received by the worker in his personal capacity and not as income of the partnership or association. [*ITEPA 2003, s 56(6)*].

19.77   The notional salary payment is treated as relevant earnings of the worker for the purpose of *ICTA 1988, s 644* (relevant earnings for personal pension purposes). [*ITEPA 2003, s 56(8)*]. It is unclear why it is not also statutorily treated as relevant earnings for the purposes of *section 623* (retirement annuities) or indeed for the purposes of *section 592* and *593* (occupational pension schemes). The Revenue have always indicated that it would do so. On the face of it the deeming requirement under *ITEPA 2003, s 56(1)* would automatically make it earnings for those purposes, but it should have automatically made it earnings under *section 644* as well.

19.78   The worker is not chargeable to tax in respect of a notional salary payment if (or to the extent that) the payment would not be taxable as employment income on an actual payment by the client of emolument from an actual employment with him by reason of any combination of:

(*a*)   the worker being resident, ordinarily resident, or domiciled outside the UK,

(*b*)   the client being resident or ordinarily resident outside the UK, or

(*c*)   the services in question being provided outside the UK. [*ITEPA 2003, s 56(5)*].

19.79   This is an interesting provision. It is not possible to remit a notional amount to the UK. Accordingly, if the worker is non-UK domiciled, the client is non-UK resident and the services are performed outside the UK no tax charge will arise in respect of that relevant engagement even if the duties of the worker's real employment with the intermediary are partly carried on in the UK (e.g. for other clients). Furthermore, the subsection does not prevent the notional salary payment arising; it merely excludes it from tax. Accordingly, the intermediary will still be entitled to claim a deduction for the payment.

19.80   If the worker is resident in the UK, and the services in question are provided in the UK the intermediary is treated as having a place of business in the UK, whether or not it in fact does so. [*ITEPA 2003, s 56(7)*]. This will allow the Revenue to require the intermediary to apply PAYE, although how they will enforce this obligation is another matter if the intermediary is non-UK resident and does not in fact have a place of business in the UK. The Revenue consider that this provision supplements rather than replaces their power to require the client to apply PAYE under *ITEPA 2000, s 689* (see 2.59). A third condition, that the client or employer (which probably meant the intermediary) carried on business in the UK, also applied for services performed before 10 April 2003 but this was repealed by *FA 2003, s 136(3)* consequent on the broadening of the provision to cover services supplied to private individuals.

Transitional Provisions

19.81   If an individual or partnership was carrying on a business at 5 April 2000 and was treated as making one or more notional salary payments during 2000/01 he (or it) could elect to treat the business as having been permanently discontinued at 5 April 2000 and a new business as having commenced at 6 April 2000. [*FA 2000, 12 Schedule 23(1)(2)*]. This deeming does not effect the carry forward of losses under *ICTA 1988, s 385*. [*FA 2000, 12 Schedule 23(3)*].

19.82   Such an election enabled the self-assessment transitional overlap relief to be crystallised whilst there were profits available to offset it. The effect of the personal services provisions will often be to eliminate or severely reduce future profits for the partnership or individual. This relief is particularly necessary in the context that the deduction for the notional salary payment cannot create in a loss.

19.83   The election had to be made on a return filed timeously. [*12 Schedule 23(4)–(6)*]. If the return is filed late the ability to claim the election is lost. This probably means that the election needed to be made in the 2000 return, the due date for which was 31 January 2001.

Other Matters

19.84   If the arrangement for an engagement involves more than one relevant intermediary, ie one which is within the scope of the personal service provisions, *Sections 48–61* must be applied separately to each of them. [*ITEPA 2003, s 59(6)*]. However, where a payment or other benefit passes from one of those intermediaries to the other (or another) in relation to the same engagement the amount of income brought into the calculation must be reduced to such extent as is necessary to avoid double-counting. [*ITEPA 2003, s 59(4)(5)*]. The legislation does not indicate which intermediary is to make the adjustment. Nor does it require either to notify the other of any adjustment to ensure that both do not claim the relief. It probably does not matter unduly as all of the relevant intermediaries in relation to an engagement are made jointly and severally liable for the tax attributable to it (other than one which receives no payment or benefit in relation to that or any other relevant engagement). [*ITEPA 2003, s 59(2)(3)*].

19.85 For the purpose of *Schedule 12* a man and a woman living together as husband and wife are treated as if they were married to each other. [*ITEPA 2003, s 61(4)*]. Anything done by (or in relation to) an associate of an intermediary is treated as done by the intermediary. [*ITEPA 2003, s 61(3)(a)*]. A payment or other benefit provided to a member of an individual's family or household is treated as provided to that individual. [*ITEPA 2003, s 61(3)(b)*]. References to payments or benefits received or receivable from a partnership obviously include those to which a person is or may be entitled in his capacity as a partner. [*ITEPA 2003, s 61(2)*].

Chapter 20

National Insurance

20.1   Although not, in theory at least, a tax, the taxation of income from employment is incomplete without a brief consideration of national insurance. Although this is a social security contribution, the rates can be high. Indeed, in many cases the national insurance contributions generated by a person's earnings will exceed the income tax thereon.

20.2   Since 6 April 1999 National Insurance has been administered by the Inland Revenue's National Insurance Contributions Office (NICO). Prior to that date it was administered by the Contributions Agency although much of it was collected by the Revenue on behalf of the Contributions Agency. The main reason for moving responsibility to the Inland Revenue was to make it easier to align the rules for income tax and National Insurance. The then government formed the view that industry wanted such an alignment. Actually what industry wanted was to be able to use the same base for payroll deductions, which requires an alignment of National Insurance with PAYE, not with income tax. While PAYE is dealt with on a cumulative basis and National Insurance on a non-cumulative one even alignment with PAYE would probably not achieve a great deal.

20.3   References continues to be made below to the Contributions Agency to make clear that the practices referred to pre-date the formation of NICO. It is too early to assess to what extent such practices are likely to continue under NICO.

Gross pay

20.4   National insurance contributions are based on an employee's 'gross pay'. This is not necessarily the same thing as earnings for income tax purposes. In particular where an employer incurs an expense to provide a benefit for an employee, or relieves the employee of a pecuniary liability, such as where he settles the bill for an expense incurred by the employer, the cost is normally regarded as pay for National Insurance purposes, whereas for income tax it would normally give rise to a benefit in kind on the employer. *Section 4* of the *Social Security Contributions and Benefits Act 1992* specifically treats as earnings for national insurance purposes statutory sick pay, statutory maternity pay, sickness benefit, gains on the exercise of share options taxed under *ITEPA 2003, ss 479* or *480* (old) (see 14.120) and *473* (new) (see 14.91) and sums received after 10 July 1997 for restrictive covenants, taxed under *ITEPA 2003, ss 225* or *226* (see 11.75).

20.5   The Contributions Agency took a far harder line than the Inland Revenue on business expenses incurred by employees although NICO seem to be mellowing a little. Recent editions of *CWG2 Employer's Further Guide to PAYE and NICs*, are far less prescriptive than in the past as to what evidence is acceptable to substantiate that an expense is a business expense. After listing the evidence it would ideally like for different types of expense it adds. 'This is not a complete list and any evidence will be considered'. On the other hand there are some items, such as a payment to an employee on his birthday or marriage, and ex gratia payments, which the Contributions Agency do not consider should be included in gross pay but which the Inland Revenue generally consider to be part of emoluments. The Contributions Agency relaxed their view a little in early 1995. When they accepted that payments made to cover business expenses incurred by an employee are not gross pay. They still insist that the employer must have evidence to identify the business expenses actually incurred and to demonstrate the amount, and that the expense was incurred as part of the employee's work, but accept that a log is not the only acceptable way to identify business telephone calls or business car mileage. They also accept that expenses covered by an Inland Revenue dispensation do not attract an NIC liability. (*Taxline, January–April 1995*). Hopefully, a benefit of the Contributions Agency moving to the Inland Revenue will in time be a move towards the Inland Revenue approach.

20.6   It is understood that the Contributions Agency sometimes contend that where a termination agreement is signed in advance of cessation of the employment, that is a variation of the employment agreement so that the receipt of compensation attracts national insurance (*Taxline, July 1998*). In most cases that is probably incorrect. Agreement of compensation for breach of contract is not a variation of the contract and the receipt of an ex gratia payment is often unconnected with the employment. It is of course generally convenient to everyone to seek compensation for breach of the employment agreement while the employee is still at work if at all possible and it would be unfortunate if the tax system discourages people from common-sense procedures. Most of the exclusions from earnings for tax purposes, such as payment of qualifying travelling expenses, mileage allowance payments and passenger payments, are also excluded from earnings for NIC purposes. In recent years exemptions from income tax have been mirrored by NIC exemptions, but some old exemptions may not have yet been brought into line.

20.7   Where an employee is taxable under *ITEPA 2003, ss 473* or *479* (old) on a gain on the exercise of an unapproved share option (see 14.89 and 14.118) the employee and employer can jointly elect that the employee should be liable for all or part of the employer's National Insurance on the share option (visit **www.inlandrevenue.gov.uk/nic/forms.htm**). The Revenue have to approve in advance both the form of the election and the arrangements made for ensuring that the employee will in fact pay the National Insurance (*Social Security Contributions and Benefits Act 1992, s 38 inserted by Child Support, Pensions and Social Security Act 2000,*

s 78). They have published a model form of election. It is obviously sensible, although not essential, to use this. The effect of the election is to completely relieve the employer of the liability. Where such an election is made
the employer's National Insurance liability can be deducted from the gain
taxable under *section 478* (but it does not reduce the employee's own
National Insurance liability (if any) on the gain (*ITEPA 2003, s 481*).

20.8   Where the option was granted between 6 April 1999 and
19 April 2000 and it had not been exercised by 8 November 2000 the
company could as an alternative elect to pay 12.2 per cent of the deemed
gain that would have arisen had the option been exercised on that date.
The election to do so had to be made by 10 August 2001 and the
National Insurance had to be paid by that date. No employee's National
Insurance is payable where the company adopted this route. [*Social
Security Contributions (Share Options) Act 2001*]. The procedure for
making the election is contained in the *Social Security (Share Options)
Regulations 2001 (SI 2001 No 1817)*.

20.9   This provision was introduced because many 'dot-com' companies were worried that the gain on exercise of share options is unquantifiable until the option is exercised and might be so large that it could force
the employer into insolvency. Whether many employers will actually ask
employees to take on part of their tax liability is questionable. However,
there seems no reason why the employee should not be asked to enter
into the election at the time the option is granted. If it is explained that it
means that he has to pay the current value of the shares plus 8.68 per
cent of the growth in value to acquire the shares (1 per cent additional
primary percentage plus 12.8 per cent of 60 per cent after the tax relief
(see 20.7) of 40 per cent assuming the option is exercised after 2002/03)
this is likely to still appear very attractive to the employee.

20.10   The Contributions Agency have said that they believe that most
payments into FURBS (see 10.57) are earnings for national insurance
purposes. As the Contributions Agency guideline did not make this clear
where a FURBS takes the form of a discretionary trust they only sought
to enforce this liability in such cases from 6 April 1998 (*Press Release 17
November 1997*). The Revenue have been reconsidering its position following the decision in *Tullet & Tokyo Forex International Ltd and others
v the Secretary of State for Social Security (2000 EWHC Admin 350)*
where the High Court held that payments by the employer of short-dated
gilts to a life assurance policy held by the employee was not earnings
'paid to or for the benefit of' the employee; what was paid for the benefit
of the employee was what the employee received namely the enhancement in the value of the life assurance policy which was a payment in
kind that fell to be disregarded under the *Social Security (Contributions)
Regulations 2001, 3 Sch Part 2(1)*. The Revenue do not accept that this
reasoning applies to a payment into a FURBS; although the reasons they
give for not doing so seem to be that they think the *Tullett v Tokyo*
decision was wrong as it relied too much on *Schedule E* case law and the

definition of earnings for NIC purposes is wider than for income tax. As the Revenue are bound by the *Tullett & Tokyo* decision this probably means that anyone who does not follow the Revenue's view is at risk of being taken at least to the Court of Appeal. *Section 3(2A) of the Social Security and Benefits Act 1992* inserted by *section 48 of the Social Security Act 1998* enables regulations to be made to apportion a payment for the benefit of two or more employees so that this can be done. The regulations do not seem to have yet been made. The *Press Release* indicated that they would come into force by April 1999.

Benefits in kind

20.11   Prior to 6 April 2000, benefits in kind did not, in general, attract national insurance. [*Social Security (Contributions) Regulations 1979, Regulation 19(1)(d) (SI 1979 No 591)*]. There were, however, a growing list of exceptions where the benefit was regarded as pay. All benefits in kind are liable to National Insurance from 6 April 2000, unfortunately in a somewhat odd manner. The items that were treated as pay prior to 6 April 2000 are still treated as pay. This means that they attract both employers' and employees' contributions by reference to the week (or month or other pay period) in which they are paid. Other benefits attract only employers' contributions and these are not collected weekly or monthly through the PAYE system. Instead, they are NICable under Class 1A (see 20.19) which is collected in a single payment after the end of the tax year. The benefits that are taxed as pay are:

(*a*)   The conferment of any interest in any of the following assets.

  (i) Shares and stock of any company (including a non-UK one).

  (ii) Debentures, bonds, certificates of deposit and other instruments creating or acknowledging indebtedness.

  (iii) Loan stock, bonds and other instruments creating or acknowledging indebtedness issued by or on behalf of a government, local authority or public authority.

  (iv) Warrants or other instruments entitling the holder to subscribe for assets within (*a*)(i)–(iii).

  (v) Unit trusts and interests in other collective investment schemes including OEICs.

  (vi) Options to acquire or dispose of:

   (A)   an asset within (*a*)(i);

   (B)   UK or foreign currency;

   (C)   gold, silver, palladium or platinum.

  (vii) A contract for the sale of a commodity or any other property under which delivery is to be made at a future date at a fixed price,

(viii) Any contract whose purpose is to generate a profit or loss by reference to fluctuations in the price of any property or an index or similar factor.

(ix) Any alcoholic liquor in respect of which no duty has been paid under *Alcoholic Liquor Duties Act 1979, s 1.*

(x) Any gemstone such as diamond, emerald, ruby, sapphire, amethyst, jade, opal or topaz and organic gemstones such as amber or pearl, whether cut or uncut and whether or not having an industrial use.

(xi) Certificates or other instruments which confer:

(A)   property rights in respect of any asset within (*a*)(i)–(iv) above, and after 24 August 1994 (ix) and (x);

(B)   a right to acquire, dispose, underwrite or convert an asset where such right would be exercisable by a person who owned the asset direct;

(C)   a contractual right to acquire any such asset.

(xii) Any voucher capable of being exchanged for such an asset falling into one of the above paragraphs.

(xiii) Any voucher stamp or similar document which is capable of being exchanged (either singly or together with other vouchers or documents) for an asset falling within (i) to (ix) or (xi) above.

Some of these items were brought into the national insurance net to counter payment of bonuses in the form of gilts, debentures and similar debt instruments, futures, options or certificates of deposit, National Savings Certificates or Premium Bonds. Payments in equities and units in authorised unit trusts were added in November 1991. Gold bars and vouchers were added from 1 December 1993 and fine wines in bond and similar liquor, and diamonds and other gemstones from 24 August 1994, and finally the general sweep-up head (xii) was added from 6 April 1995.

(*b*)   The conferment of an interest in any long-term (life insurance, etc.) insurance contract.

(*c*)   Company cars—see 20.19.

(*d*)   From 9 April 1998, any amount on which an employed earner is taxable under *ITEPA 2003, ss 417–446* (see Chapter 14) in respect of the acquisition of shares or an interest in shares. The taxable amount is the same as for income tax purposes. Broadly speaking, the same exemptions apply.

(*e*)   From 1 October 1998, a readily convertible asset (as defined from income tax—see 2.88) is one, readily convertible under *ITEPA 2003, s 701* (see 2.92) or a voucher capable of being exchanged for such an asset. Prior to that date, only assets for which trading arrangements existed were subject to national insurance. [*3 Schedule 2* and *Parts III & IV* Social Security (Contributions) Regulations 2001 (*2001 No 1004*)].

Other payments in kind, or by way of the provision of services, board and lodgings or other facilities are exempt from NIC. It was held in *Tullet & Tokyo Forex International Ltd and others v the Secretary of State for Social Security* (*2000 EWHC Admin 350*) (see 20.10) that payments that enhanced the value of an insurance policy already held by an employee did not fall within (*b*) above.

20.12 There are a number of specific exemptions from national insurance including the transfer to an employee of ordinary shares in the company for which he works (or its parent, etc.) and options over such shares provided that for transactions after 5 December 1996 either the shares are issued under an approved scheme or they are non-tradeable shares; reimbursement of travel and lodging expenses incurred as the result of the disruption to public transport by industrial action; reimbursement of taxi or car hire costs where an employee works beyond 9pm at the request of his employer on exceptional occasions (not more than 60 times a year); reimbursement of overseas travel expenses where these are deductible for income tax under *ITEPA 2003, ss 341, 342, 370* and *371* (see 13.36–13.49) and most benefits that are exempted from income tax. [*3 Schedule Parts I & II Social Security (Contributions) Regulations 2001 (SI 2001 No 1004)*].

20.13 There is also an exemption for 'gratuities and offerings' where either the payment is not made directly or indirectly by the employer (and does not represent sums previously paid to the employer) or the employer does not allocate the payment, directly or indirectly to the earner (*Social Security (Contributions) Regulations 2001, 3 Schedule Part X (5)*). This was in issue in *Channel 5 TV Group Ltd v Morehead (2003 STC (SCD) 327* SpC *369*). One of the shareholders of Channel 5 sold its shares at a substantial profit. It decided to give some of its profits to the staff of Channel 5. It paid $4.9 million to a firm of solicitors who made out cheques to the individual staff members. The solicitors deducted tax but not National Insurance on the basis that the payments were gratuities not provided or allocated by Channel 5. The Revenue contended that the word 'gratuity' meant 'tip'. The Special Commissioners held that it is not so limited. A gratuity is 'a voluntary payment given in return for services rendered where the amount of the payment depended on the donor and where there was no obligation on the part of the donor to make the payment'. Channel 5 did not make or allocate the payments. The US company allocated the payments, albeit on the recommendation of the chief executive of Channel 5 acting in a personal capacity after consulting his fellow executive directors. That did not mean that they have been acting for Channel 5 though. Nor did the assistance given to the solicitors by Channel 5's payroll department amount to allocating the payments. Accordingly no National Insurance was payable.

Earnings periods

20.14   Unlike PAYE, national insurance is not calculated on a cumulative basis. It is based on the employee's pay in an earnings period. This is the period for which earnings are normally paid if they are paid on a regular basis. In other words, if a person is paid weekly, the earnings period is a week, if he is paid monthly it is a month. Company directors have a special earnings period, namely the fiscal year. Accordingly, their national insurance is effectively calculated on a cumulative basis. From 6 April 1999 national insurance can be applied to directors during the year as if this special rule did not apply, provided that any necessary adjustment is made at the end of the year. This will enable the national insurance deductions to be spread, whereas the special rule bunches the entire deductions into the early part of the year. Once the earnings period has been identified national insurance is calculated on the aggregate of all payments of gross pay made in the period.

Contributions

20.15   National insurance is payable by both the employer and the employee. The weekly employer's contribution for 2004/05 (called the secondary contribution) is as follows.

Gross pay per week	
first £91	nil
excess over £91	12.8% (of the excess only)

The employee's contribution for 2003/04 (called the primary contribution) is:

Gross pay per week	
First £91	nil
Next £91–£610	11%
excess over £610	1%

The maximum weekly contribution is £57.09 (11% of £(610–91)) on the first £610 of earnings plus 1% of the excess.

The limits (called respectively the lower and upper earnings limit) for 2003/04 were £89 and £595 per week.

20.16   It is possible to contract out of the earnings related portion of the State pension scheme provided that there is a pension scheme in place that promises greater benefits than the State scheme. Where this is done, both employer and employee pay a reduced rate on up to £610 per week earnings. For 2004/05 the rate is 9.4 per cent for employees. For employers it is 9.3 per cent if the pension scheme provides salary related benefits (i.e. a pension of a fixed proportion of benefits) and 11.8 per cent if the scheme is a money purchase one (i.e. the pension is the annuity that the scheme contributes on behalf of the employee). For older employees a rebate applies where a money purchase scheme is in place.

Maximum contributions

20.17 The maximum weekly contribution by an employee for 2004/05 is £57.09 plus 1 per cent of the excess earnings over £610. There is no limit on the employer's contribution. The contributions are collected by being deducted by the employer from the employee's pay. The contributions are collected by the Inland Revenue, the employer paying them over monthly along with his PAYE tax deductions.

Employees excluded

20.18 No national insurance is payable (by either employer or employee) if the employee is under 16 at the time the earnings are paid to him. The employee's contributions are not payable where the employee is over the State retirement age (65 for men and 60 for women) but the employer's contribution is still payable in respect of such people. A married woman who was married before 6 April 1977 and has remained in employment (not necessarily the same employment) since that date, may be entitled to pay contributions at a reduced rate. This does not affect the amount of the employer's contribution, however.

Class 1A contributions

20.19 The employer, but not the employee, also has to pay a Class 1A contribution in relation to:

(*a*) employees to whom he provides company cars, and

(*b*) from 1 April 2000 those benefits in kind not treated as pay (see 20.11) and not specifically excluded from National Insurance (see 20.20).

[*Social Security Contributions and Benefits Act 1992, s 10*].

The Class 1A contribution is at the same rate as the employer's Class 1 contribution (10 per cent for 1998/99; 12.2 per cent for 1999/00 and 2000/01, 11.9 per cent for 2001/02, 11.8 per cent for 2002/03 and 12.8 per cent for 2003/04 and 2004/05) but is payable annually in arrears. The Class 1A contribution in relation to cars is payable on the car use and car fuel benefits assessable for income tax purposes (see 7.8 and 7.46 above). As for income tax, the car use element (but not the fuel figure) was reduced up to 2001/02 where a car was used for 18,000 or more business miles in a year of assessment (see 7.39). The Contributions Agency did not expect employers to keep detailed records of the employee's business miles but it was nevertheless be up to the employer to show that the highest contribution level, that for under 2,500 miles, did not apply in such year. In many cases this would be obvious from the nature of the employee's job (*ICAEW TR 843 14 August 1991*).

20.20   The Class 1A charge on benefits in kind does not apply to:

(*a*)   certain amounts which are excluded from earnings under the *Social Security (Contributions) Regulations 2001, (2001 No 1004)* as awarded, namely:

    (i)   meal vouchers of 15p per working day; (*s 40(2)* and *3 Schedule Pt V para 6A*)

    (ii)   a gratuity from someone other than the employer (e.g. a tip by a passenger to an employed taxi driver); (*s 40(2)* and *3 Schedule Pt X para 5*)

    (iii)   a payment to a minister of religion which does not form part of his stipend or salary (e.g. Christmas donations by parishioners); (*s 40(2)* and *3 Schedule Pt X para 13*)

    (iv)   a payment by way of ordinary share capital of the employer (or certain connected companies) if the shares are not readily convertible assets or ones received under an approved profit sharing scheme; (*s 40(2)* and *3 Schedule Pt IX para 2*)

    (v)   (*a*)   an option under an approved share option scheme where the shares and the options are both not readily convertible assets; (*s 40(2)* and *3 Schedule Pt IX para 3, 3A*)

        (*b*)   a payment deducted from earnings under a partnership share agreement (see 15.27); (*s 40(2)* and *3 Schedule Pt IX para 6*)

        (*c*)   free shares awarded under a SIP (see 15.20); (*s 40(2)* and *3 Schedule Pt IX para 7*)

        (*d*)   an EMI option which is capable of being exercised more than ten years after the grant; (*s 40(2)* and *3 Schedule Pt IX para 4*)

    (vi)   the benefit of a priority application of shares which is not treated as an emolument by *FA 1988, s 68(1)* (see 14.151); (*s 40(2)* and *3 Schedule Pt IX para 5*)

    (vii)   a payment of travel expenses that is excluded from tax under *ITEPA 2003, ss 341, 342* and *370–375* (formerly *ICTA 1988, s 193* or *194*) (see 13.27–13.37); (*s 40(2)* and *3 Schedule Pt VIII para 4*)

    (viii)   a cost of overseas living allowance paid to a member of the Commonwealth War Graves Commission or the British Council; (*s 40(2)* and *3 Schedule Pt VIII para 13*)

    (ix)   travel expenses of a person not domiciled in the UK which are taxable under *ITEPA 2003, s 373*, formerly *ICTA 1988, s 195(7)*; (*s 40(2)* and *3 Schedule Pt VIII para 5*)

(x) a payment of a benefit under an unapproved pension scheme attributable to contributions before 6 April 1998 or which derives from contributions which were assessed on the employee; (*s 40(2)* and *3 Schedule Pt VI para 4, 5*)

(xi) a contribution to a pension scheme which is awaiting Revenue approval; (*s 40(2)* and *3 Schedule Pt VI para 6*)

(xii) a payment to a French, Irish or Danish pension scheme which is exempted from tax under the relevant double tax agreements; (*s 40(2)* and *3 Schedule Pt VI para 7*)

(xiii) a subscription etc exempt from tax under *ITEPA 2003, s 343* (formerly *ICTA 1988, s 201*) (see 5.82); (*s 40(2)* and *3 Schedule Pt X para 11*)

(xiv) the VAT on any supply of goods or services by the employer to the employee where the remuneration includes a sum for that supply; (*s 40(2)* and *3 Schedule Pt X para 9*)

(xv) a payment made by an issuer of charge cards, cheque guarantee cards, credit cards or debit cards as a reward to an individual who assists in identifying or recovering lost or stolen cards in the course of his or her employment (other than employment by the issuer); (*s 40(2)* and *3 Schedule Pt X para 15*)

(*b*) payments of qualifying travelling expenses or other expenses incurred in carrying out the employment, (*reg 40(3)*)

(*c*) a payment in respect of removal expenses not within 9.53 where the change of residence occurred before 6 April 1998, (*reg 40(4)*)

(*d*) a payment in connection with all or part of the costs and expenses of child care (but not school fees) for a child under 17 for whom the employee has parental responsibilities, (*reg 40(5)*)

(*e*) a payment in kind of coal made to a miner, (*reg 40(2)* and *3 Schedule Pt X para 14*)

(*f*) benefits under an approved pension scheme, (*reg 40(6)*)

(*g*) an amount exempted from income tax under the following extra-statutory concessions: (*reg 40(7)*)

A11	residence in the UK-year of commencement or cessation
A22	long service awards
A37	directors fees received by partnerships
A56	accommodation in Scotland
A57	suggestion schemes
A58	travelling and subsistence when public transport is disrupted
A59	home to work travel of severely disabled employees
A65	transfers to and from the mainland of workers on offshore oil and gas installations
A66	employees' late night journeys from work to home
A70	small gifts to employees by third parties and staff Christmas parties

A72   Pension schemes and accident insurance policies
A74   meals provided by employers
A85   transfers of assets by employers and directors to employees and others
A91   living accommodation provided by reason of employment
A97   jobmatch programme

(Reg 40 and *3 Schedule, Social Security (Contribution) Regulations 2001 (SI 2001 No 1004)).*

20.21   For the purpose of (*d*) above 'childcare' includes:

(*a*)   care provided by a child minder or day carer under *Part X* and *Schedule 9, Children's Act 1989* (child minding and day care for young children),

(*b*)   where the child is 8 or over, care provided by a child minder,

(*c*)   where the child is under 8, care provided by a child minder but only if it does not exceed in total two hours in any day,

(*d*)   care provided by a relative (within *Children Act 1989, s 71(13)*) or a nanny (within *s 105(1)* of that *Act*),

(*e*)   care provided during out-of school hours and school holidays,

(*f*)   full-time and part-time care.

(Reg 40(8)).

20.22   A third party who provides a benefit for the employee of someone else can agree with the Revenue to account for Class 1A National Insurance on that benefit (*Social Security Contributions and Benefits Act 1992, s 10ZA*, inserted by *Child Support, Pensions and Social Security Act 2000, s 76*). If the third party has entered into an arrangement with the Revenue to pay the employee's tax liability, that tax payment does not itself attract Class 1A contributions (*section 10ZA(2)*).

PAYE Settlement Agreements (Class 1B Contributions)

20.23   *Section 53* of the *Social Security Act 1998* introduced a new Class 1B National Insurance contribution. This is payable by employers only. It applies from 1997/98 onwards. The rate is 12.8 per cent (10 per cent for 1997/98 and 1998/99, 12.2 per cent for 1999/00 and 2000/01, 11.9 per cent for 2001/02 and 11.8 per cent for 2002/03) (the same as the employer's Class 1 contributions). It is payable on the aggregate of:

(*a*)   the amount of emoluments included in a PAYE Settlement Agreement (see 6.87) which relates to items which would otherwise be subject to NIC if they had not been included in the PSA; and

(*b*)   the income tax due on the PSA.

Head (*a*) is obviously reasonable. Head (*b*) has given rise to a great deal of adverse comment. The tax on a PSA is a liability of the employer; it is not employees' liabilities which are being settled by the employer. Accordingly, this element is contrary to the basic principle that National Insurance is payable only on emoluments of employees.

Occupational pension schemes

20.24 If an employer has an occupational pension scheme that provides certain levels of benefit, he can contract his employees out of the earnings related element of the State pension scheme. The occupational pension scheme needs to provide benefits at least equivalent to those under the State scheme. In return the contributions of both employer and employee are reduced and in addition there was an extra rebate for the three years 1999/00 to 2001/02 reducing further, the employer's contributions by three percentage points (but only on the first £575 per week of earnings – £535 to 2000/01) and the employee's by 1.6 percentage points. If the pension scheme is a money purchase scheme the rebate for the employer was only 0.6 per cent.

Multiple employments

20.25 Where a person has more than one job, national insurance is calculated separately for each of them in most cases, even if they are with associated employers. If it is clear that the employee's earnings from one of the employments will exceed £610 a week (or £31,720 per annum) NICO can authorise the other employer not to deduct employee's contributions, (or only to deduct 1 per cent) although the employer's contribution will obviously still have to be paid. In other cases, if the total contributions by an employee exceed £3,025.77 (53 × £(610   91) × 11 per cent) plus 1 per cent of the excess over £610, the excess will be refunded direct to the employee by the Contributions Agency after the end of the fiscal year.

Overseas employers

20.26 If an overseas employer does not have a place of business in the UK, employer's contributions are not payable in respect of UK-based employees. A UK office is not necessarily a place of business for this purpose if management is not exercised from it. An employee who has come from the European Economic Area, or from Austria, Australia, Barbados, Bermuda, Canada, Cyprus, Finland, Guernsey, Iceland, Israel, Jamaica, Japan, Jersey, Korea, Malta, Mauritius, New Zealand, Norway, Philippines, Sweden, Switzerland, Turkey, the USA or Yugoslavia (including Bosnia, Croatia and Slovenia) and who continues to pay social security in his own country can claim exemption from national insurance. Where a person who previously worked in another country is sent to the UK by his overseas employer (i.e. he is recruited overseas) national insurance is not payable for the first twelve months that he is in the UK, provided that the overseas employer has a place of business outside the UK (whether or not he also has one in the UK).

20.27   If an employee who is ordinarily resident in the UK works overseas and his employer has a place of business in the UK, his overseas earnings remain within the scope of national insurance. If he is working overseas for more than twelve months, liability for national insurance ceases after 52 weeks.

Meaning of 'employee'

20.28   The meaning of an employee for national insurance purposes is the same as for income tax (see Chapter 4). If a person's status is established with the Inland Revenue this will be accepted by NICO (in theory at least) and vice versa. In practice the Contributions Agency seemed to refuse to accept that a person's status has been 'established' unless there had been a very thorough Inland Revenue investigation. The *Social Security (Categorization of Earner) Regulations 1978 (SI 1978 No 1689)* deem certain categories of people to be employees for national insurance purposes even if they can show that they are actually self-employed. The categories concerned are office cleaners, ministers of religion, lecturers and teachers and a husband or wife working for their spouse.

20.29   An anomaly existed for a long time in relation to actors and musicians, where the Contributions Agency regarded all performers as employees and insisted on the theatre, promoter, TV company, etc. deducting national insurance even though the Inland Revenue accepted that many such persons were self-employed. This caused a great deal of resentment, particularly as the logic for this approach was never clear. In a parliamentary reply the Minister answered that the Agency had taken legal advice to the effect that this approach was not sustainable and that under the existing law entertainers should generally be regarded as self-employed. The *Social Security (Categorization of Earner) Regulations 1978 (SI 1978 No 1689)* were therefore amended to make entertainers employees for national insurance purposes from 17 July 1998 except where 'the remuneration (disregarding benefits in kind) does not consist wholly or partly of salary' or after 6 April 2003 does not include any payment by way of salary with 'salary' being defined as payments made for services rendered under a contract for services, computed by reference to the amount of time for which work has been performed and, where there is more than one payment, payable at a specific period or interval. [*Social Security (Categorisation of Earners) Amendment Regulations 2003 (SI 2003 No 736)*]. The Minister's intention was to 'require the majority of performers to be treated as employees for national insurance purposes'. It is beneficial to many performers to be treated as employees so as to have a right to unemployment benefit when they are 'resting'. The reason for the 2003 amendment is that the original wording was largely ineffective. Many entertainers receive, as part of the remuneration package, pre-purchase payments as compensation for the loss of future repeat fees and rights or royalties which far exceed the salary element. Very few actors are therefore paid wholly or mainly by salary. Where between 17 July 1998 and 5 April 2003 a person whose remuneration did not consist wholly or mainly of salary was incorrectly categorised as an employed earner he can claim a refund of contributions paid in error. If he does so he must give credit for any social security benefit claimed on the basis of the contributions. Alternatively he can choose not to claim a refund and let the contributions count towards Additional Pensions entitlement. The Revenue say that Class 1 NICs still do not apply to session musicians and session singers engaged through Musicians Union approved contractors (*Tax Bulletin 65*, June 2003).

20.30   The result of the confusion caused by the various changes to the regulations is that some entertainers may have paid Class 1 NIC incorrectly between 17 July 1998 and 5 April 2003. Such people have a choice of leaving the position as it is or claiming a refund. Anyone claiming a refund will, however, have to refund any benefits they claimed by reference to the NIC in question, and the refund will obviously be reduced by the Class 2 and Class 4 contributions that should have been paid. Anyone who did not claim benefits in relation to that period ought to consider claiming a refund.

IR 35

20.31   The IR 35 rules considered at 19.33 apply also for NIC by virtue of the *Social Security Contributions (Intermediaries) Regulations 2000 (SI 2000 No. 727)* as amended by the *Social Security Contributions (Intermediaries) (Amendment) Regulations 2003 (SI 2003 No 2079)*.

Drawings by directors

20.32   In many family companies, directors are not paid a regular salary but take money from the company during the year which is posted to a current account pending a decision when the accounts are prepared how much is to be voted as salary, or as dividend or whether the overdrawn balance on the current account is to be left outstanding as loan. The Contributions Agency considered that such drawings constitute 'earnings' at the time of each individual payment unless the current account is in credit at the time. Their view is based on *Regulation 22(2)* of the *Social Security (Contributions) Regulations 2001 (SI 2001 No 1004)*. This provides that 'any payment made by a company to or for the benefit of any of its directors' is to constitute earnings if it would not otherwise do so and the payment is made on account of, or by way of an advance on, a sum which would be earnings.

20.33   This view seems of doubtful validity. When a drawing is made it is not drawn on account of remuneration. It is not normally drawn on account of anything! It is simply a payment which will fall to be reimbursed to the company if it is not at a later date offset by an entitlement coming into existence at a future time to a payment from the company. It is understood that this was confirmed by an unpublished appeal decision given by the Minister in 1990. Unfortunately, the Contributions Agency (and presumably now NICO) considered that such decisions have no precedential value and that they were therefore entitled to ignore them (other than in respect of the specific case), on the basis that they are far more likely than a Government Minister to know what the Government intends its legislation to do! (*ICAEW Guidance Note Tax 21/92*).

Dividends

20.34   The Contributions Agency also considered that where a company pays a dividend to a director or employee and the dividend turns out to be unlawful, e.g. because the company does not have sufficient distributable reserves or because it has not been properly declared, it constitutes earnings for NIC purposes (letter of 7 December 1993 reproduced in *ICAEW Tax 5/94*). This also seems of very doubtful validity. If a dividend is declared it cannot change its nature if it transpires that it should not have been paid. Nor is it clear how a payment in respect of shares can be earnings if the shareholder happens to be an employee but something different if it is not. Furthermore, company law enables the company to call for repayment, which is inconsistent with the amount being earnings—or indeed income at all. As in the same letter the Contributions Agency indicate that a trust cannot exist without a document, which is clearly wrong, and that in the absence of a specific power in the trust deed trustees have no legal right to waive a dividend however much they believe this to be in the interests of the beneficiaries, which is almost certainly wrong, there must at least be a question mark over the quality of the legal input, if any, into the letter.

Income from property

20.35   The Contributions Agency considered that where a property owner collects the rents, furnishes and maintains the property and carries out repairs, or contracts for them to be carried out, he is gainfully employed as a self-employed earner and therefore liable to Class 2 national insurance contributions. This is presumably on the basis that his property investments constitute a business. NICO can draw a degree of support for this view from VAT Tribunal decisions. It is probably a question of fact and degree. In *American Leaf Binding Co Sdn Bhd v Director-General of Inland Revenue ([1978] STC 561)*, a Privy Council case, Lord Diplock said, albeit obiter, 'In the case of a private individual it may well be that the mere receipt of rents from property that he owns raises no presumption that he is carrying on a business'. This is worth quoting to NICO if they contend that national insurance is due unless the provision of services is effectively a full-time job *(Taxline, April 1998)*. It may well be that NICO are less enthusiastic about pursuing such a claim. In *Rashid v Garcia* (2003 STC (SCD) 36) Mr Rashid who received income from letting properties sought to pay Class 2 contributions but the Revenue decided that he was not entitled to do so. The Special Commissioners felt that whether property rental was a business in any particular case was a matter of degree. Whilst Mr Rashid clearly had responsibilities when things went wrong he did nothing more than what a landlord normally did. They were accordingly not satisfied that there was sufficient activity to constitute a business; it was an investment which by its nature required some activity to maintain it.

Statutory Sick Pay

20.36   One of the benefits provided under the national insurance scheme is statutory sick pay (SSP). However, SSP is not payable in the first three qualifying days in such a period (called a PIW or period of incapacity for work). A qualifying day means a day on which the employee is required to be available for work, so weekends and public holidays will not be qualifying days for most employees. If there was a previous period of sickness within the previous 56 days (even if the employee was then working for a different employer) the two periods are linked together to form a single PIW, so that statutory sick pay will be payable for all of the qualifying days in the second period.

20.37   An employee is not entitled to SSP for more than 28 weeks in a tax year. SSP paid by a previous employer needs to be taken into account for this purpose.

20.38   The current weekly rates of SSP are £NIL if the employee's average earnings are below £79 per week and £66.15 if they are above. SSP is payable for each qualifying day (at one-seventh of the weekly rate).

20.39   The Statutory Sick Pay Small Employer's Relief Scheme was abolished from 6 April 1995 and replaced by the Percentage Threshold Scheme (PTS). Unless the employer qualifies under the new scheme he cannot recover any SSP paid to his employees. Under the PTS the employer must calculate his ratio of SSP paid to Class 1 contributions. If the SSP exceeds 13 per cent of the contributions liability in that month the employer can recover the excess from the monthly payment to the Collector of Taxes (see booklet E14 (2003) 'What to do if your employee is sick').

20.40   A pregnant employee is entitled to statutory maternity pay (SMP) for a period of up to 26 weeks off work, starting between the eleventh and sixth week before the expected confinement. For 2004/05 she is entitled to 90 per cent of her normal weekly pay for the first six weeks (provided she has worked for the same employer for at least six months) and to the lower of £102.80 or 90 per cent of normal weekly pay per week for the other 20. The SMP is paid by the employer who can recover 92 per cent of the SMP if he does not qualify for Small Employers' Relief. If the employer does qualify for the Small Employers' Relief he can recover 100

per cent of SMP and an additional 4.5 per cent of the gross SMP (6.5 per
cent up to 1998/99 and 5 per cent up to 2001/02) as compensation for the
NIC paid on the SMP (see E15 (2003) 'Pay and Time off work for
Parents'). A small employer is one whose NI contributory payments (i.e.
both employers and employees Class 1 contributions) do not exceed
£40,000 (£20,000 up to 2001/02).

20.41   For 2003/04 onwards there is also a right to statutory adoption pay
(SAP) and statutory paternity pay (SPP). Statutory adoption pay is payable
for 26 weeks. Only one of an adopting couple is entitled to SAP but they can
choose which is to claim it. The other is entitled to statutory paternity pay.
The partner of a woman entitled to SMP (whether or not the biological father)
is also entitled to SPP. SPP is payable only for two weeks. The rate of both
SAP and SPP is the lower of £100 or 90% of the employee's average weekly
earnings (see booklet E16(2003) Pay and Time off work for adoptive
parents).

Tax Credits

20.42   From 6 April 2000 to 5 April 2003 employers were also required
to pay Working Families Tax Credits (WFTC) and Disabled Person's Tax
Credit (DPTC). From 6 April 2003 employers are instead required to pay
working tax credits (WTC), which is a government funded earnings top-up
payable to some low-paid staff. WTC replaced WFTC and DPTC.
Although called 'tax credits' both WTC and its predecessors are nothing
to do with tax. They are social security benefits. They have been called
tax credits because the government want people to view them as an addition to earnings which is generated by the existence of the person's
employment. The government regard these tax credits as 'central to
demonstrating the rewards of work and making work pay for families on
low income' (*Hansard 6 March 2000, col 522*). These provide a minimum family income for the low paid. The employer is not required to
calculate the payments due. He is notified by the Revenue both of those
individuals for whom he is required to make a payment and the amount
to be paid. Payments of WTC are of course recoverable in full from the
Inland Revenue by reduction in the form of the employer's monthly
PAYE contributions. If the WTC payments are likely to exceed the
monthly PAYE debt, there is provision for the Inland Revenue to put the
employer in funds to make the payment. The detailed rules are set out in
the *Tax Credits (Payments by Employers) Regulations 1999 (SI 1999 No
3219)*. An employer who does not operate a PAYE scheme or only
operates a simplified PAYE scheme for domestic staff is not required to
pay these tax credits (*Hansard 6 March 2000, col 522*).

20.43   From 6 April 2000 employers are also required to deduct student
loan repayments from salary payments. Such loans are made to university
students towards the cost of their courses. This obligation is not a tax but
needs to be borne in mind as it will involve administration responsibilities
and penalties can be incurred if these are not carried out properly.

Chapter 21

VAT

Motor vehicles

21.1   There is a deemed supply on which VAT is accountable to Customs and Excise where fuel that was supplied to a taxable person in the course of his business is provided to an individual by reason of his employment or office for use in his own vehicle or in a vehicle allocated to him (i.e. a company car which is not a pool car—the definition [*VATA 1994, s 56(9)*] is the same as the income tax one). [*VATA 1994, s 56(1)(a)*]. The VAT is calculated on a scale charge. [*VATA 1994, s 57*]. Up to 5 April 1998 this mirrored the amount of the income tax scale fuel charge (see 7.46 above), the main difference being that the income tax charge applied only to company cars whereas the VAT charge applies to all cars for which fuel supplied by the employer is used for private motoring.

21.2   From 5 April 1998 the figures are different. This is because the derogation that the UK has from the EC rules only permits it to increase the charge in line with inflation, whereas the income tax increases are now deliberately in excess of inflation. The VAT scale figures for 2003/04 (applying where the return period starts after 5 April 2003) are:

	Quarterly rate		Annual rate	
Engine size	*Petrol*	*Diesel*	*Petrol*	*Diesel*
	£	£	£	£
Under 1400cc	232	216	930	865
1401–2000cc	293	216	1,175	865
Over 2000cc	432	273	1,730	1,095

21.3   The charge does not apply if the employee pays an amount at least equal to the cost of the fuel to the employer. [*VATA 1994, s 56(2)*]. If fuel is provided for a car used by a third party by reason of the individual's employment, such as to a member of his family, the scale figure will apply to that car also. [*VATA 1994, s 56(3)(d)*]. Any fuel provided by an employer for private use in a company car is automatically deemed to be provided by reason of the individual's employment. [*VATA 1994, s 56(3)(e)*]. Where the scale charge applies, the whole of the input tax is of course treated as being for the purpose of the employer's business; it is not necessary to disallow the private element as being for non-business use. [*VATA 1994, s 56(5)*]. The fuel is treated as supplied to the employee at the time it is put into the car's fuel tank.

[*VATA 1994, s 56(6)*]. If the employee changes his car during a VAT accounting period (normally a three-month period), only one scale charge applies for that accounting period. [*VATA 1994, s 56(8)*]. If the two cars fall into different bands, the appropriate figure for each is apportioned on a daily basis to arrive at a scale figure for that accounting period. [*VATA 1994, s 57(5)(6)*].

21.4   If an employer charges an employee for the use of a car, including under a salary sacrifice arrangement, the charge is treated as outside the scope of tax provided that the input VAT on the acquisition of the car was wholly or partly blocked. [*Business Brief 10/95*]. Salary sacrifice arrangements are, in any event, statutorily outside the scope of VAT where the right to private use of a car is given in lieu of the salary (except to the extent of any actual cash payment). [*VAT (Treatment of Transactions) Order 1992 (SI 1992 No 630)*]. Where an employee pays the employer an amount so that he can be provided with a more expensive car than would otherwise be the case, Customs regard the payment as consideration for a supply. [*Business Brief 9/92*].

Entertaining

21.5   An employer cannot deduct input tax on goods or services used for the purposes of business entertainment. [*VAT (Input Tax) Order 1992 (SI 1992 No 3222), Article 5(1)*]. If he makes an onward supply of such items he need charge VAT only on the excess of the consideration, if any, over his own cost. [*Article 5(2)*]. Business entertainment includes hospitality of any kind, but does not include the provision of entertainment for employees or directors (or other persons engaged in the management of the employer) unless that provision is incidental to its provision for others. [*Article 5(3)*]. Customs interpret this restrictively. For example, if a company throws a party for staff at which the staff are entitled to bring a guest either free or at a small charge, Customs accept that the cost of entertaining the employee is not business entertaining but contend that input tax attributable to the cost of entertaining his guest is disallowable as business entertaining.

21.6   Following the VAT Tribunal decision in *Ernst & Young v Customs and Excise Comrs* [*1997*] *V&DR 183 (VAT Decision 15/00)*, Customs accept that where a business provides entertainment to its employees in order to maintain and improve staff relations, it does so wholly for business purposes. However, if the expenditure 'has no discernible business purpose and no connection with the business activity' they will seek to disallow the input tax.

21.7   Where a company arranged a lunch to mark the opening of new premises which was attended by 25 senior employees and 130 actual or potential customers, the staff entertaining was held to be incidental to the provision of entertaining for customers so that the input tax was not deductible (*Wilsons Transport Ltd 1983 (VAT Decision 1468)*). A similar decision was reached in *Elizabethan Banquets (1985) (VAT Decision 1795)*, where employees attended banquets to maintain the expected atmosphere for paying customers. In contrast, where a promoter of rock concerts provided free beer at the concerts for both customers and staff the whole of the input tax was allowed, that for customers because they had paid for the beer in the ticket price so that it was not business entertaining and that for staff as staff entertaining *(D Lumby (1995) VAT Decision 12972)*.

21.8   In the case of *Julius Fillibeck Sohne GmbH & Co KG v Finanzamt Neustadt (Case C-258/95) [1998] STC 513*, the European Court of Justice held that free transport for employees from home to work is in principle a supply of services within *Article 6(2)* of the *Sixth Directive*, so that output tax falls to be accounted for on the value of that supply. The company was a building company which transported workers from their homes to building sites in company vehicles. The employees made no payment for the transport. The ECJ indicated that in certain circumstances the needs of the business might necessitate the provision of transport, e.g. if there was no alternative public transport, in which case the personal benefit accruing to the employees would be of secondary importance compared to the needs of the business. The fact that only the employer was able to provide suitable transport or that the workplace was liable to change could be indications of such circumstances. So could the fact that a building firm has special characteristics and that the transport was provided under a collective agreement. In practice, Customs do not normally seek output tax in relation to transport in company vehicles, but are coming under some pressure from the European Commission to do so in the light of this case.

21.9   It should be noted that the exemption does not apply to volunteers or the self-employed. However, there is an Extra-Statutory Concession *(para 2.10* of *Customs Notice 48)* in relation to sports clubs. Customs allow the deduction of input tax necessarily incurred on the provision of meals and accommodation for team members selected to represent their country or county and to committee members of the club even though such persons are not employees. This concession does not extend to alcoholic drinks or tobacco.

Other benefits

21.10   If an employer provides, free of charge to his employees, food or beverages in the course of catering (e.g. in a staff canteen) or accommodation in a hotel, inn, boarding house or similar establishment, the consideration for that supply is deemed to be nil—but as it is a supply in the course of the employer's business this will entitle him to recover the related input tax. If the supply is for a consideration consisting wholly or partly of money, the supply is deemed to be for a consideration equal to that money (any other consideration being ignored). [*VATA 1994, 6 Sch 10*].

21.11 Customs accept that the provision of goods (such as overalls or tools) to employees for the purpose of their employment is not a supply if no charge is made. [*para 2.4* of *Notice 700*]. There is accordingly no input tax restriction and no requirement to account for any notional output tax. A gift of a free meal to an employee is similarly not a supply. [*para 3.10* of *Notice 700*].

21.12 In contrast, if an employee is allowed to use a business asset for his personal use, such as use at weekends or for holidays, that is a supply on which VAT needs to be accounted. If such use is permanent and there is no consideration, e.g. the employer gives the employee a redundant computer, the value of such supply is the amount that would have to be paid by the employer to purchase an identical item (including age and condition) at the time of the supply. If an identical item cannot be purchased, it is the cost of a similar item. If there is no similar item, it is the cost of making the item at the time of the supply. [*VATA 1994, 4 Sch 5, 6 Sch 6*].

21.13 If the private use is temporary, e.g. the provision of a computer for as long as the employee continues with the company, the supply is a supply of services. The consideration is the full cost to the employer of providing the service. [*VATA 1994, 4 Sch 5, 6 Sch 7*]. Customs say that this is the amount of depreciation on the goods, plus any other standard-rated costs related to the goods, multiplied by the proportion that the private use bears to total use. [*para 3.13* of *Notice 700*].

21.14 If an employer provides domestic accommodation free of charge to an employee, any VAT incurred is deductible as input tax. [*para 4.8* of *Notice 700*]. However, input tax is not deductible on the provision of accommodation for a director, except to the extent that the accommodation is used for business purposes. There is neverthless a deemed taxable supply under *VATA 1994, 4 Sch 5*.

21.15 If an employee receives a prize, e.g. for exceeding sales targets or selling more than anyone else in a month, Customs accept that that is not a supply for a consideration so no notional output tax needs to be accounted for. If the reward extends to a non-employee, such as the employee's spouse, the input tax on the non-employee element is, however, blocked as business entertainment. [*para 6* of *Notice 700/7/94, Business Promotion Schemes*].

21.16 If a person gives goods to someone else's employees, e.g. free goods to a customer's staff for selling that person's goods, VAT is due on a deemed supply unless the value of the goods is less than £50 or they form part of a series of gifts to the same person. [*VATA 1994, 4 Sch 5, SI 2001 No 735*].

Index

Abode
usual place of, 12.32, 12.33
Accommodation
agricultural workers, free board and
lodging, 8.15
benefits in relation to
additional charge for valuable
property, 8.1, 8.18–8.29
annual value, 8.5
anti-avoidance, 8.2
basic charge, 8.1, 8.3–8.17
basis of assessment, 2.51, 8.3
directors, 8.11–8.13
family or household of employee,
8.14
generally, 6.15, 6.42, 8.1
higher-paid employees, 8.1
more than one employee sharing,
8.29
more than one property provided,
8.28
net earnings, 8.31, 8.32, 8.33,
8.34
occasions of charge, 8.1
rent payable, where, 8.3, 8.4
rental value, 8.3, 8.4
representative occupation, 8.1,
8.6–8.10
running costs, 8.30–8.40
Schedule E, 8.2
board and lodgings, 8.8, 8.15
cleaning costs, 8.30–8.32
community charge, 8.40
council tax, 8.39, 8.40
decoration, costs of, 8.30–8.32
employee reimbursing part of cost,
8.27
employer providing, 21.10,
21.14
furniture etc, provision, 8.30
heating, 8.30–8.32, 8.37
lease or sub-lease, employee paying
premium for, 8.27
lighting, 8.30–8.32
ministers of religion, provided for,
8.3, 8.9, 8.16, 8.17,
19.14–19.17
National Insurance contributions,
20.22
necessary for proper performance of
duties, 8.6–8.10
overnight, travelling expenses,
5.40–5.42

overnight, where public transport
disrupted, 9.118
overseas employment, 13.38
repairs and maintenance, 8.30–8.32,
8.38
running costs, 8.30–8.40
Scotland, in, 20.20
security of employee threatened,
provision where, 8.6
sports club providing, 21.9
telephone expenses, 8.37
Accounts basis. *See* BASIS OF
ASSESSMENT
Actor
employed or self-employed,
determination, 4.25, 4.61–4.66,
20.29, 20.30
tax treatment, 19.5
**Additional voluntary contribution
(AVC)**
generally, 10.18
Adoption pay
statutory, 2.38
statutory, National Insurance
contributions, 20.41
Agency charity
payroll deduction scheme,
19.9–19.13
Agency worker
employee of intermediary, 19.2
excluded trades and professions,
19.5
meaning, 19.1
Pay As You Earn, 2.117, 19.7
remuneration, meaning, 19.2
services rendered wholly in
individual's own home, 19.5
tax treatment, 2.117, 19.1–19.8
travelling expenses, 19.8
unincorporated body as agency,
19.2
Agent
commission paid to, 5.93
Agricultural worker
accommodation provided for, 8.9
board and lodging provided for,
8.15
Aircraft
worker on
tax treatment, 2.23, 2.24
travel concessions, 6.50
Airline pilot
travelling expenses, 5.33

611